Fintech Applications in Islamic Finance:

AI, Machine Learning, and Blockchain Techniques

Mohammad Irfan
Business School, NSB Academy, Bangalore, India

Seifedine Kadry
Noroff University College, Norway

Muhammad Sharif
Department of CS, COMSATS University Islamabad, Wah Cantt, Pakistan

Habib Ullah Khan
Qatar University, Qatar

IGI Global
PUBLISHER of TIMELY KNOWLEDGE

A volume in the Advances in Finance, Accounting, and Economics (AFAE) Book Series

Published in the United States of America by
IGI Global
Business Science Reference (an imprint of IGI Global)
701 E. Chocolate Avenue
Hershey PA, USA 17033
Tel: 717-533-8845
Fax: 717-533-8661
E-mail: cust@igi-global.com
Web site: http://www.igi-global.com

Library of Congress Cataloging-in-Publication Data

Names: Irfan, Mohammad, 1986- editor. | Kadry, Seifedine, 1977- editor. | Sharif, Muhammad, 1967- editor. | Khan, Habib Ullah, 1976- editor.
Title: Fintech applications in Islamic finance : AI, machine learning, and blockchain techniques / edited by Mohammad Irfan, Seifedine Kadry, Muhammad Sharif, Habib Ullah Khan.
Description: Hershey, PA : Business Science Reference, [2024] | Includes bibliographical references and index. | Summary: "This book identifies the process of AI and machine learning in the Islamic finance industry and strengthens the building blocks of AI and machine learning"-- Provided by publisher.
Identifiers: LCCN 2023049083 (print) | LCCN 2023049084 (ebook) | ISBN 9798369310380 (hardcover) | ISBN 9798369310397 (ebook)
Subjects: LCSH: Finance--Islamic countries--Technological innovations. | Finance--Religious aspects--Islam. | Financial institutions--Islamic countries.
Classification: LCC HG187.4 .F57 2024 (print) | LCC HG187.4 (ebook) | DDC 332.0917/697--dc23/eng/20231109
LC record available at https://lccn.loc.gov/2023049083
LC ebook record available at https://lccn.loc.gov/2023049084

This book is published in the IGI Global book series Advances in Finance, Accounting, and Economics (AFAE) (ISSN: 2327-5677; eISSN: 2327-5685)

British Cataloguing in Publication Data
A Cataloguing in Publication record for this book is available from the British Library.

For electronic access to this publication, please contact: eresources@igi-global.com.

Advances in Finance, Accounting, and Economics (AFAE) Book Series

Ahmed Driouchi
Al Akhawayn University, Morocco

ISSN:2327-5677
EISSN:2327-5685

Mission

In our changing economic and business environment, it is important to consider the financial changes occurring internationally as well as within individual organizations and business environments. Understanding these changes as well as the factors that influence them is crucial in preparing for our financial future and ensuring economic sustainability and growth.

The **Advances in Finance, Accounting, and Economics (AFAE)** book series aims to publish comprehensive and informative titles in all areas of economics and economic theory, finance, and accounting to assist in advancing the available knowledge and providing for further research development in these dynamic fields.

Coverage

- Economic Theory
- Economics of Innovation and Knowledge
- Ethics in Accounting and Finance
- Corporate Finance
- Economics of Intellectual Property Rights
- International Trade
- Labor Economics
- Accounting information systems
- Macroeconomics
- Economic Indices and Quantitative Economic Methods

IGI Global is currently accepting manuscripts for publication within this series. To submit a proposal for a volume in this series, please contact our Acquisition Editors at Acquisitions@igi-global.com or visit: http://www.igi-global.com/publish/.

The Advances in Finance, Accounting, and Economics (AFAE) Book Series (ISSN 2327-5677) is published by IGI Global, 701 E. Chocolate Avenue, Hershey, PA 17033-1240, USA, www.igi-global.com. This series is composed of titles available for purchase individually; each title is edited to be contextually exclusive from any other title within the series. For pricing and ordering information please visit http://www.igi-global.com/book-series/advances-finance-accounting-economics/73685. Postmaster: Send all address changes to above address.

Titles in this Series

For a list of additional titles in this series, please visit: www.igi-global.com/book-series

Sustainable Investments in Green Finance
Sanjay Taneja (Graphic Era University (Deemed), India) Pawan Kumar (Chandigarh University, India) Simon Grima (Department of Insurance, Faculty of Economics Management and Accountancy, University of Malta, Malta & Faculty of Business, Management and Economics, University of Latvia, Latvia) Ercan Ozen (Usak University, Turkey) and Kiran Sood (Chitkara Business School, Chitkara University, India)
Business Science Reference • copyright 2024 • 373pp • H/C (ISBN: 9798369313886) • US $275.00 (our price)

Empowering Women Through Microfinance in Developing Countries
Yahaya Alhassan (University of Sunderland in London, UK) and Uzoechi Nwagbara (University of Sunderland in London, UK)
Business Science Reference • copyright 2023 • 281pp • H/C (ISBN: 9781668489796) • US $240.00 (our price)

Management, Technology, and Economic Growth in Smart and Sustainable Cities
Jorge A. Ruiz-Vanoye (Universidad Politécnica de Pachuca, Mexico)
Business Science Reference • copyright 2023 • 341pp • H/C (ISBN: 9798369303733) • US $240.00 (our price)

Enhancing Sustainability Through Non-Financial Reporting
Albertina Monteiro (ISCAP, CEOS, Polytechnic of Porto, Portugal) Ana Pinto Borges (ISAG - European Business School, Portugal & CICET-FCVC, Portugal & COMEGI, Portugal) and Elvira Vieira (ISAG - European Business School, Portugal & CICET-FCVC, Portugal & Polytechnic Institute of Viana do Castelo, Portugal & UNIAG, Portugal)
Business Science Reference • copyright 2023 • 313pp • H/C (ISBN: 9781668490761) • US $225.00 (our price)

The Importance of Entrepreneurship in Fostering Economic Progress
Mohammed El Amine Abdelli (University of Brest, France) Naima Bentouir (Ain Temouchent University, Algeria) and Esra Sipahi Döngül (Aksaray University, Turkey)
Business Science Reference • copyright 2023 • 205pp • H/C (ISBN: 9781668471272) • US $240.00 (our price)

Circular Economy Implementation for Sustainability in the Built Environment
Nicoleta Cobîrzan (Technical University of Cluj-Napoca, Romania) Radu Muntean (Transilvania University of Braşov, Romania) and Raluca-Andreea Felseghi (Technical University of Cluj-Napoca, Romania)
Business Science Reference • copyright 2023 • 330pp • H/C (ISBN: 9781668482384) • US $250.00 (our price)

Optimizing Energy Efficiency During a Global Energy Crisis
Meltem Okur Dinçsoy (Trakya University, Turkey) and Hamit Can (Trakya University, Turkey)
Business Science Reference • copyright 2023 • 408pp • H/C (ISBN: 9798369304006) • US $240.00 (our price)

IGI Global
PUBLISHER of TIMELY KNOWLEDGE

701 East Chocolate Avenue, Hershey, PA 17033, USA
Tel: 717-533-8845 x100 • Fax: 717-533-8661
E-Mail: cust@igi-global.com • www.igi-global.com

Table of Contents

Detailed Table of Contents

This chapter explores the transformative impact of artificial intelligence (AI) and machine learning (ML) technologies on the Islamic Capital Market (ICM). As the global financial landscape evolves, the ICM is no exception, facing challenges and opportunities alike. AI and ML have emerged as pivotal tools for enhancing efficiency, mitigating risks, and fostering innovation within Islamic finance. The chapter begins by providing a comprehensive overview of the Islamic financial principles and the unique features of the ICM. It then delves into the key areas where AI and ML are being applied, including Shariah-compliant investment screening, risk management, asset allocation, trading strategies, and customer services. The study scrutinizes the implications of these technologies on financial inclusion, ethical finance, and regulatory compliance in the ICM.

In core, Islamic finance and the sustainable development goals (SDGs) initiated by the United Nations have the same goal to educate and create good livelihood for the human life. For this chapter, the researchers collected few research articles in Scopus Database towards the intersection of Islamic finance and SDGs. The authors have selected few Islamic finance and Sustainable Developmental Goals articles as an inclusion criteria along with the year of publication from 2015 to October 2023. They selected papers that focused on Islamic finance as an inclusion criterion and excluded papers that from 1990 to 2015. They retrieved 32 papers and book chapters published from 2015 to 2022 from the Scopus database. By using Vos viewer, the researchers analyzed the keyword from the article, year wise prediction, and authors' contribution for Islamic finance for Sustainable Development Goals. The researchers used the data to predict the future growth of Islamic finance the researcher found that there is a wide gap for Islamic finance supports the SDGs.

This study investigates the impact of Islamic Shariah compliance on customer satisfaction, focusing on the mediating effect of service quality within the context of Islamic banking services. Data obtained randomly from 124 Islamic bank customers in Indonesia were analyzed using multiple linear regression in SPSS. The results demonstrate that various factors, including attitude, subjective norms, and behavioral control, significantly influence the propensity of Islamic bank customers to adopt financial technology services offered by Islamic banks. It is important to note that this study is primarily centered on fintech-enabled Islamic banking services. This study underscores the need for Islamic Financial Institutions to enhance the success of fintech services and to promote these offerings to customers. Furthermore, it encourages Islamic financial institutions to harness technological advancements that streamline customer banking transactions. This study provides Islamic banks with valuable insights into the optimization of technology-driven financial services.

Thematic finance a study of financial investment approach on specific trends in society or economy with broader concept related to social, environmental, or economic changes that can include clean energy, technology innovation, healthcare advancements, or demographic shifts. It considers factors like asset class and geographical region. It covers investment details of companies or industry that are related to a specific trend. The area of Islamic finance with a thematic approach in India is growing, due to increase demand for ethical and Shariah-compliant investment option, the country's significant infrastructure needs, and the potential for socially responsible and sustainable investing. However, overcoming regulatory hurdles and increasing awareness remain essential for the growth of Islamic finance, including thematic finance, in the Indian financial landscape.

The cohabitation of Financial Technology (FinTech) and Islamic Finance have far-reaching implications for the global financial market. This bibliographic review surveys pivotal research papers that elucidate diverse aspects of this amalgamation, encapsulating ethical considerations, regulatory complexities, technological vulnerabilities, and the ramifications of digital assets. Furthermore, it scrutinizes FinTech's role in advancing sustainability objectives, navigates the intricacies of peer-to-peer lending, and scrutinizes the manifold viewpoints regarding the digital metamorphosis of Islamic finance. Collectively, these scholarly works furnish a holistic comprehension of the evolving rapport between Islamic finance and FinTech, proffering invaluable insights for the future evolution of Islamic financial technology, all while upholding the tenets of Sharia principles.

Virtual technological development has revolutionized banking, financial, and capital market transactions in the world. A majority of transactions are taking place through online banking, net banking, or Unified Payments Interface (UPI) transactions, with few other portals giving the ease and comfort to do transaction in one's comfort zone without going to banks or withdrawing money in offline modes to be paid. The rapid evolution of online and UPI transactions has transformed the way transactions are conducted, shifting a significant portion of commerce to the digital realm. In this context, the efficiency of legal frameworks for secure transactions is of paramount importance to ensure trust, reduce risks, and foster economic growth without sabotaging the customers transactions security concerns. The transactions taking place in past in offline mode and presently in online mode had delves into the nexus between secure transactions and electronic transactions, exploring the impact of emerging technologies such as blockchain, UPI, and net banking that have posed challenges.

Islamic Finance is one of the legitimate fields of investment these days. A mechanism which adopts ethical practices and sustainable growth altogether is what Islamic Finance is. The last several years have seen a notable rise in the Islamic finance sector due to growing consumer interest in ethical banking and financial services. Experts in this field claim that as the market grows, the industry is making an effort to incorporate ESG factors into future planning and projections. In an attempt to create a more equitable and sustainable future, non-financial principles known as environmental, social, and governance, or ESG, are being progressively integrated into financial operations.

Increasing users of Sharia financial products can provide a stimulus for economic growth contribution in Indonesia. Considering that fact, this study aims to monitoring Islamic Finance activities on Economic Growth in the long and short term. Granger causality and VECM tests are appropriate analytical tools to determine the purpose study. The data from this research was taken from Indonesia financial service authority and Indonesia central bureau of statistics from 2009Q1 to 2023Q1. The results obtained show that the Islamic capital market influences economic growth, because investment can develop countries

Nothing could have prepared any of us for the recent outbreak of COVID 19. It has impacted individuals, communities, economies, and countries around the world. It has acted as a catalyst for growth because its impact has gone beyond a physical, financial, and economic level. The purpose of this study was to discuss the impact of strategic partnerships on driving innovation, accelerating digital transformation across financial services in the Kingdom of Bahrain, and economic growth. The Central Bank of Bahrain (CBB) Digital Lab, a collaborative effort, between the CBB and several strategic Partners of FinHub973 including the Bahrain Economic Development Board, Bank ABC, Benefit, BisB, ila Bank, and the National Bank of Bahrain, enables local and global FinTechs to connect seamlessly to explore, test, and prototype new and innovative solutions on a centralized digital sandbox. These new solutions are commonly referred to as fintech. Collaborative partnerships are essential to catalyse innovation in finance, for the benefit of the industry, economy, and society at large.

This chapter examines the transformative power of blockchain technology and smart contracts in the financial industry. It explores the advantages of blockchain, such as enhanced security, transparency, and traceability, along with the automation capabilities offered by smart contracts. The research investigates their potential impact on traditional financial systems, focusing on areas like cross-border payments, trade finance, supply chain finance, and asset tokenization. It discusses the benefits of increased efficiency and cost reduction that can be achieved through blockchain implementation. The study also addresses the challenges associated with scalability, energy consumption, privacy, and smart contract vulnerabilities. Regulatory considerations and the importance of collaboration between industry stakeholders, regulators, and policymakers are emphasized. The chapter concludes by highlighting the transformative role of blockchain and smart contracts in creating a more inclusive, secure, and efficient future for finance.

In recent years, there has been a noticeable surge in the popularity of Islamic financing. The utilization of Fin-Tech tools assumes significance for investors adhering to Islamic principles in order to effectively navigate investing choices. The utilization of these technologies enables the generation of more precise price forecasts for investors. This will facilitate investors adhering to Islamic principles in making more precise investing choices. This study utilized a dataset consisting of 3453 daily observations of the MSCI ACWI Islamic Index. The acquired data was subjected to processing utilizing various machine learning algorithms, including LSTM, CNN, GRU, RF, and XGBoost. Subsequently, an evaluation was conducted to ascertain the predictive performance of each method and establish the superior approach. Based on the results, it was found that the GRU approach exhibited the highest level of prediction performance.

Preface

"Islamic Finance is Finance with the remembrance of God" -: Amanah Advisors

Islamic finance refers to the financial management and activities by following the Islamic Laws (Shariah) and principles and rules. Islamic laws are guiding the people in avoiding receipt and payment of interest and restricting the financial activities which are harmful to the society. It is very significant to have a proper knowledge of shariah to manage and engage in the financial activities adhering shariah. Fintech applications are the inevitable part of finance, hence the study and discussion on fintech applications in islamic finance is most relevant. The book will give you proper insight on how the islamic finance work in fintech applications for financial analysis, financial management, financial inclusion, financial services, financial risk and management etc.

Artificial intelligence has a significant role in financial analysis, and financial decisions, as the book discusses the importance of role of AI in Islamic finance especially in the area of analysis and risk management. And the book covers the machine learning and block chain technologies. Fintech applications are having major role in efficient and effective utilization of financial resources. The book focuses to analyses the role of fintech application to signifies the adherence of the Islamic laws.

In detail the book covers the discussion on machine learning in islamic capital market, awareness of islamic finance and interest free banking system, block chain in islamic finance, AI and ethical finance, Robo advisers in shariah compliant to mitigate the risk in islamic investment, and use of ML/AI in prediction of islamic stock market.

The current book offers an insight of the numerous fintech applications in islamic finance. This book, which was written in an approachable manner, will be helpful to policymakers, students, instructors, and other participants in the education system. We hope the present volume will result in some meaningful contribution and lead to more debate and discussion to throw further insights.

We would like to acknowledge the support we got from our contributors, reviewers, publisher and well-wishers.

We hope you enjoy reading the book and we wish you success.

Mohammad Irfan
Business School, NSB Academy, Bangalore, India

Seifedine Kadry
Noroff University College, Norway

Muhammad Sharif
Department of CS, COMSATS University Islamabad, Wah Cantt, Pakistan

Habib Ullah Khan
Qatar University, Qatar

Chapter 1
Fintech and Islamic Banking: A Systematic View and Future Research Agenda

P. Sheela
https://orcid.org/0000-0003-3689-1530
GITAM University, India

K. Kusuma
GITAM University, India

Rashmi Ranjan Panigrahi
https://orcid.org/0000-0002-2199-293X
GITAM University, India

Zakir Hossen Shaikh
https://orcid.org/0000-0003-4733-4166
Kingdom University, Bahrain

ABSTRACT

In an era of unprecedented technological advancement, the convergence of financial technology (Fintech) and Islamic finance has emerged as a dynamic and transformative force in the global financial landscape. Fintech, characterized by innovations such as blockchain, artificial intelligence, mobile payments, and peer-to-peer lending, has redefined traditional financial services, offering unprecedented efficiency, accessibility, and convenience, The convergence of Fintech and Islamic finance promises to enhance financial services' efficiency and inclusivity and facilitate Sharia-compliant offerings' expansion to a broader audience. This amalgamation could address long-standing challenges in Islamic finance, such as accessibility, transparency, and product diversity. The primary objective of this research is to comprehensively investigate the convergence of Fintech and Islamic finance, aiming to uncover the implications, challenges, opportunities, and potential outcomes of their integration.

DOI: 10.4018/979-8-3693-1038-0.ch001

1. INTRODUCTION

In an era of unprecedented technological advancement, the convergence of financial technology (Fintech) and Islamic finance (IF) has emerged as a dynamic and transformative force in the global financial landscape, El Basri, M., & Mirakhor, A. (2019). Fintech, characterized by innovations such as blockchain (Panigrahi *et al.*, 2023), artificial intelligence, mobile payments, and peer-to-peer lending, has redefined traditional financial services, offering unprecedented efficiency, accessibility, and convenience, Hassan, M. K., et al. (2020). Concurrently, IF, grounded in principles that promote ethical and Sharia-compliant financial practices, has witnessed substantial growth and international recognition over the past few decades, Zaman, M., & Khairudin, N. H. (2021). The amalgamation of Fintech and IF is reshaping how financial services are delivered, challenging conventional norms, and expanding the frontiers of Sharia-compliant solutions, Khan, T. (2020). In today's rapidly evolving economic landscape, Fintech and IF is a compelling nexus that holds significant relevance for the global financial industry and the Islamic financial ecosystem, Abdul Razak, D., & Noordin, B. A. (2020). Fintech, fuelled by technological innovation, has revolutionized traditional financial services worldwide, reshaping how individuals and businesses access, manage, and transact with their financial resources, Akhtar, S. A., & Akhtar, M. F. (2020) Concurrently, IF, with its foundation in ethical and Sharia-compliant principles, has garnered increasing attention as an alternative financial model that aligns with the values of many individuals and institutions, El-Galfy, A. S. (2021).

The convergence of Fintech and IF promises to enhance financial services' efficiency and inclusivity and facilitate Sharia-compliant offerings' expansion to a broader audience, Chapra, M. U. (2019). This amalgamation could address long-standing challenges in IF, such as accessibility, transparency, and product diversity, Hasan, M., & Dridi, J. (2019). Examine the mechanisms and strategies employed to ensure that Fintech solutions are ethically and Sharia-compliant, addressing the compatibility of technological advancements with Islamic financial principles. Investigate the evolving regulatory landscape surrounding Fintech and IF integration, highlighting the problems and opportunities for both sectors under regulatory scrutiny. Analyse the potential for growth in the Fintech-based IF services market, examining how these solutions can tap into new segments and enhance customer engagement.

A set of focused research questions has been developed to address the overarching objective of advancing knowledge in the rapidly evolving intersection of Fintech and IF. These research questions aim to provide clarity and structure to the systematic review, enabling a comprehensive examination of the current state of the field and its implications. These questions will guide the systematic literature selection and in-depth bibliometric analysis, facilitating the synthesis of critical findings and the presentation of the most recent advances in Fintech and IF. By addressing these research questions, this study seeks to contribute to informed decision-making among stakeholders, inspire further research endeavors, and elevate the standards of transparency and rigor in research practices, ultimately fostering a deeper understanding of this dynamic and transformative domain within the global financial industry.

RQ 1: How do emerging Fintech innovations impact the growth and sustainability of IF?
RQ 2: What are the top contributions of Prominent Researchers towards Fintech and IF?
RQ 3: To what extent do the top-rated research journals explore the potential combined effect between IF and emerging technologies through research journals and prominent Institutions?
RQ 4: What prominent themes and research directions could strengthen fintech adaptions into IF in emerging countries?

Structuring the research with the above four specific questions allows for a targeted exploration of essential aspects, enabling a comprehensive and in-depth analysis. This approach ensures that the research objective is achieved by systematically investigating and addressing every facet of the convergence between Fintech and IF. In doing so, it contributes to a thorough understanding of this dynamic and transformative phenomenon within the global financial landscape of IF.

The present study will be the roadmap for future research by highlighting critical areas of inquiry where in-depth investigations can further contribute to knowledge, practice, and policy development in this evolving domain. This systematic review is designed to comprehensively analyse the multifaceted convergence between Fintech and IF, uncovering its numerous opportunities, challenges, and potential impacts within the global financial ecosystem.

The study seeks to explore the relevance and implications of this collaboration by examining the potential benefits, regulatory considerations, and challenges associated with integrating these two domains, all while maintaining a steadfast adherence to the principles of IF. Additionally, the research has identified crucial research gaps in this intersection, emphasizing the need for further investigations into leveraging Fintech for enhancing IF, addressing regulatory and compliance issues, promoting financial inclusion, and assessing the ethical and social implications, ultimately paving the way for a deeper understanding of this emerging field's potential to reshape the financial landscape globally. These gaps underscore the opportunities for future research to propel knowledge and practice forward in the evolving realm of Fintech and IF.

The rest of the paper is arranged as follows. Section 2 reviews the previous research on Fintech and Islamic Banking. Section 3 discusses the methodology used in the empirical analysis and data collection process. Section 4 presents the findings and its discussion (Includes answers to the research question and research direction). Section 5 contains the conclusion.

2. RELATED LITERATURE

2.1 Definition of FinTech

A consensus has yet to be reached on the precise definition of Fintech and its underlying essence. In broad conceptual terms, FinTech represents a novel category of financial services delivered through technology to a wide-ranging user base (Schueffel, 2016). Fintech, short for "financial technology," refers to the innovative use of digital and software technology to design and deliver financial services more efficiently and effectively (Shaikh, Sarea and Irfan, 2022). McKinsey & Company. (2016). Fintech is the convergence of Information Technology and Finance to provide cost-effective financial services that offer a smooth and user-friendly experience (Rabbani et al., 2020).

The scope of fintech is broad and dynamic, driven by ongoing technological advancements and changing consumer preferences. Fintech companies and traditional financial institutions continually innovate to provide more convenient, efficient, and accessible financial services to individuals and businesses worldwide. According to the following authors, fintech deals with Digital Payments and Transfers, Gomber, P. et al. (2017). Online Banking and Neo banks. Leimeister, J. M. et al. (2009). Digital Lending and Crowdfunding, Belleflamme, P. et al. (2014). Robo-Advisors and Wealth Management, Chen, Z., et al. (2020). Insurtech, Silva, T. F., & Santos, R. (2017). Regtech (Regulatory Technology), Tabachnick,

D. (2019). Blockchain and Cryptocurrency, Gipp, B (2019). AI and Data Analytics, Loonam, J., & McDermott, J. (2019). Cybersecurity and Fraud Prevention, Zhang, Y., & Xiao, X. (2020).

The scope of fintech continues to expand as technological innovations evolve, and consumer preferences change. Fintech is crucial in reshaping the financial industry by improving accessibility, efficiency, and user experience across various financial services. Irfan, M.. et al. (2023), discussed role of financial applications in the financial sectors.

IF denotes a financial system and a suite of financial offerings and solutions that align with the principles of Islamic law, commonly referred to as Shariah, under the umbrella of Islamic Financial Services suggested by Board. (2005). These principles govern economic and financial transactions in ways compliant with Islamic ethics and morals. Key principles of IF include the prohibition of interest (usury or "riba"), avoidance of excessive uncertainty (Gharar) and gambling (Maysir), and adherence to ethical and social responsibility in financial dealings. Islamic Research and Training Institute. (2015).

2.2 Evaluation of FinTech and Islamic Financing

The Influence of AI on banking Sectors in the Age of Industry 5.0 becomes a vital tool, driving developments that will influence the financial landscape going forward. Irfan.M. et al. (2023)". The evaluation of fintech in the context of Islamic financing is an essential area of research and practice. It involves assessing the impact of technology innovations on the IF industry, considering compliance with Shariah principles and the broader implications for financial inclusion, ethical considerations, and efficiency. Mansoor, A. (2019). Evaluating fintech in Islamic financing requires a multidimensional approach considering financial and ethical aspects. Ensuring that fintech innovations align with Islamic principles while promoting financial inclusion and economic development is essential, Alqahtani F. et al. (2020).

3. METHODS USED

In this study, we employ a SLR approach to address the query on the emergence of Islamic Fintech as a new frontier in finance and its potential to revolutionize financial services while adhering to Sharia principles Khan, T. (2020). The PRISMA "(Preferred Reporting Items for Systematic Reviews and Meta-Analyses)" protocol ensures the study's repeatability Page, M.J. et al. (2021). The review is organized into three phases, following methodology recommended by Yigitcanlar T. et al. (2019) and Regona M. et al.(2022). The three phases encompass (a) the initial planning phase involving the formulation of research objectives, questions, and search criteria; (b) the execution of the review; and (c) the final stage dedicated to reporting and dissemination.

Creating the core dataset involved designing a protocol in advance to outline the analysis method and inclusion criteria. We performed a search based on only Scopus as it was recognized as the largest database worldwide (Delafenestre, 2019; Al-Khoury *et al.*, 2022; Umar *et al.*, 2022), targeting papers from 32 "FinTech" and "IF" journals listed in the Australian Business Deans Council (ABDC) quality list, and featuring the term "review" in their titles, abstracts, and/or keywords. The search was conducted on 01st September 2023, without imposing any restrictions on publication dates. Notably, the search term "systematic" was not employed to ensure the inclusion of reviews that did not explicitly mention the term.

Figure 1. PRISMA step-1 identification: The PRISMA flow diagram of selection process

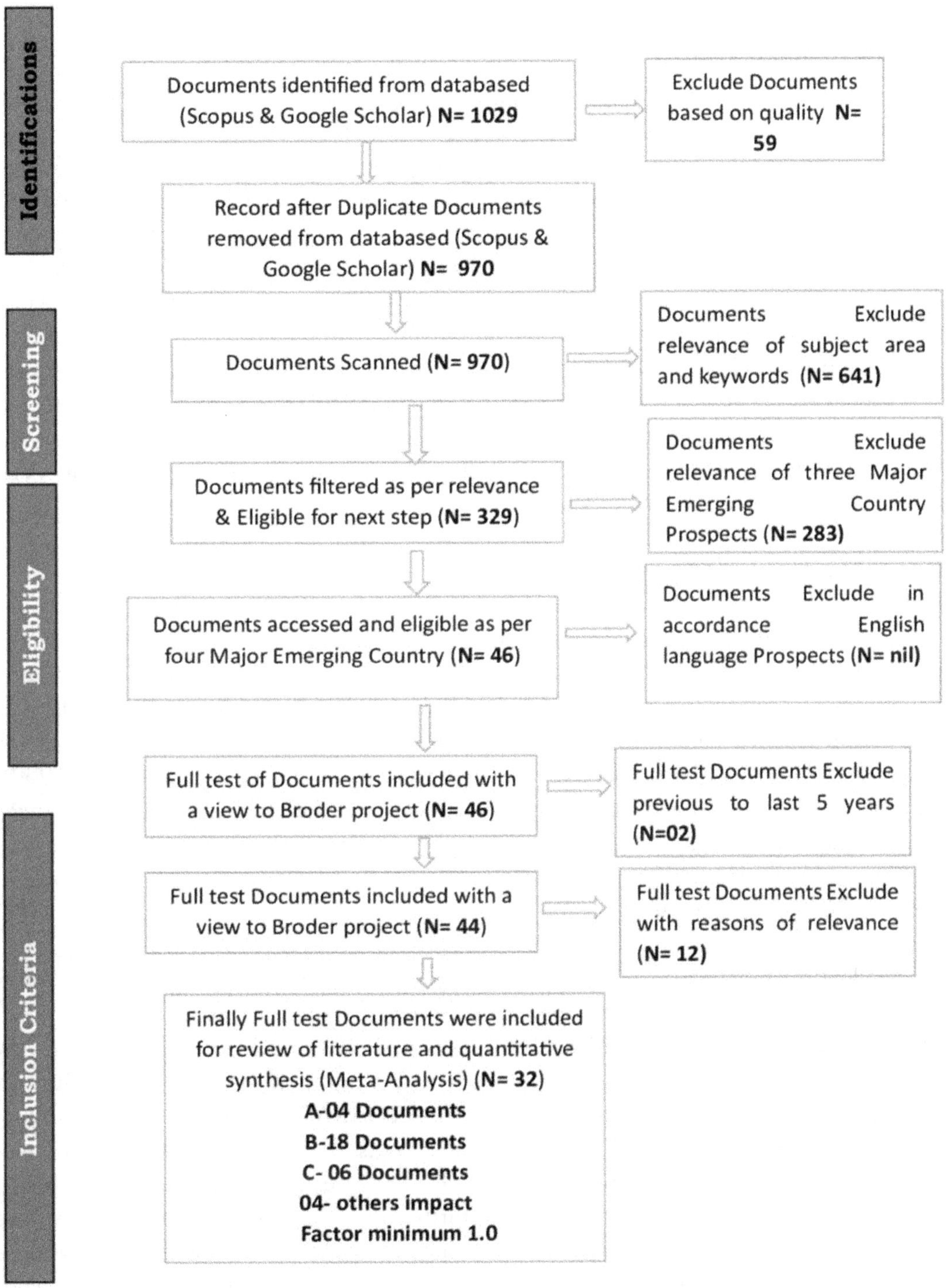

Source: Authors

The review study employed the Scopus database for document collection, as this database host the most significant number of indexed journals relevant to the subject under investigation, Martín-Martín et al. (2018).

The research established a review strategy at the outset by defining "inclusion and exclusion criteria" in the initial phase. To gather relevant materials, the study defined the keywords "FinTech" and "IF," considering both singular and plural forms, and utilized these terms to construct the search query. During this stage, specific inclusion criteria were established, encompassing the requirement for complete articles accessible online, composed in the English language, and directly pertinent to the study. Subsequently, exclusion criteria were outlined, as outlined in Figure 1.

Duplicate papers, conference papers, reports, books, chapters, materials that do not directly address the convergence of Fintech and IF. unpublished materials, preprints, or materials lacking peer review, and materials in languages not relevant to our research, did not find a place in the inclusion criteria.

In the present times, PRISMA, a widely recognized framework from (Liberati, 2009; Pahlevan-Sharif et al., 2019; Pahlevan Sharif et al., 2019) for conducting systematic reviews and meta-analyses, emphasizes a structured and transparent approach to ensure the quality and reliability of research outcomes. This process entails several crucial steps, including identification, screening, establishment of eligibility criteria, and determination of inclusion criteria (Refer Figure 1).

3.1 PRISMA Step-1 Identification

The initial step in the PRISMA methodology is identification. During this phase, researchers conduct thorough searches across worldwide databases and sources to pinpoint all relevant studies related to the research question. This exhaustive search strategy minimizes the risk of bias by reducing the likelihood of omitting pertinent studies that could impact the overall findings. Based on these recommendations of (Liberati, 2009; Pahlevan-Sharif et al., 2019; Pahlevan Sharif et al., 2019), present study identified Scopus was the platform for present study as recommended by earlier studies (H. K. Baker et al., 2021; M. A. Khan et al., 2021).

3.2 PRISMA Step-2 Screening

Following the identification phase, the screening process involves evaluating the identified studies based on their titles, abstracts, and keywords. In this stage, studies that are evidently irrelevant are excluded, thus refining the list of potential candidates for inclusion. This screening process often involves the participation of multiple reviewers to enhance objectivity and minimize potential errors. Study applied search criteria based on title, abstract and keywords i.e. "TITLE-ABS-KEY [(inventor*) AND (supply AND chain*) AND (literature*)]" and found 1029 documents related to our study from Scopus database. Out of which duplicate and irrelevant manuscripts found was 59 documents, which subsequently removed and filtered document reached to 970 nos. further scanning done on the basis of subject wise like "business management and social science and economics only" as well as keyword wise i.e. "fintech" and "Islamic Finance" and (limit-to (exactkeyword, "fintech") or limit-to (exactkeyword, "if") or limit-to (exactkeyword, "fintech") or limit-to (exactkeyword, "finance") or limit-to (exactkeyword, "financial technology") or limit-to (exactkeyword, "islamic banks") or limit-to (exactkeyword, "financial services") or limit-to (exactkeyword, "islamic fintech") or limit-to (exactkeyword, "islamic banking") or limit-to (exactkeyword, "islamic bank") or limit-to (exactkeyword, "islamic social finance") or limit-to (exactkeyword, "ifs") or limit-to (exactkeyword, "islamic fintech") or limit-to (exactkeyword, "islamic") or limit-to (exactkeyword, "financial markets") or limit-to (exactkeyword, "shari'ah")) and (limit-to (subjarea, "econ") or limit-to (subjarea, "busi") or limit-to (subjarea, "soci"))– documents not matching to subject area as well as above keywords are 641 documents, which is excluded, final 329 documents are stepping to next step.

3.3 PRISMA Step-3 Eligibility Criteria

Once the screening phase is concluded, researchers establish precise eligibility criteria that studies must fulfil to be considered for inclusion. These criteria frequently encompass study design, population characteristics, intervention/exposure, outcomes of interest, and other pertinent variables. The establishment of these criteria ensures that selected studies closely align with the research objectives, thereby enhancing the relevance and validity of the systematic review. In this stage documents eligible document received from previous step are 329. In this step further documents excludes as per the study objectives focusing only on top three emerging countries (India, China, Brazil) i.e. (LIMIT-TO (AFFILCOUNTRY, "India") OR LIMIT-TO (AFFILCOUNTRY, "China") OR LIMIT-TO (AFFILCOUNTRY, "Brazil")) AND (LIMIT-TO (LANGUAGE, "English")) which counts as 283 documents which was excluded as per criteria. Along with to provide more strength to the quality exclusions criteria also applied to language as "English only", which further reducing nil (zero) documents. Finally, this steps 46 documents send for inclusion and move to last step of PRISMA methods.

3.4 PRISMA Step-4 Inclusion Criteria

The inclusion criteria serve as the definitive set of conditions that studies must meet to be incorporated into the systematic review or meta-analysis. These criteria are tailored according to the research question and the specific objectives of the review. Studies that fulfil these criteria proceed to the subsequent phases of data extraction and analysis, contributing to the eventual synthesis of results. Out of 46 filtered documents received from eligibility stage, this stage applied further filtration criteria i.e. last five years publications trends consider for greater visibility of research trend i.e. (limit-to (pubyear, 2019) or limit-to (pubyear, 2020) or limit-to (pubyear, 2021) or limit-to (pubyear, 2022) or limit-to (pubyear, 2023)), which also leads to exclusion of 02 documents and on the basis of relevance 12 documents are excluded. finally, documents included for present study with full paper accessed as 32 manuscripts. one important points observed that this prisma analysis helps to brings qualitative manuscripts for this research which included 12.5% of abdc-a category manuscripts (04 no's of documents), 56% of abdc-b category of manuscripts (18 no's of documents) and 19% of abdc- c categories of manuscripts (06 no's of documents) rest four documents (12.5% of 32 documents) are minimum impact factors at least 1.0. these steps ensure a comprehensive, transparent, and unbiased review process, thereby enhancing the quality and reliability of research findings. adhering to prisma guidelines not only facilitates research reproducibility but also advances evidence-based practices across various disciplines, aiding decision-making and progress in the academic and professional arenas.

4. RESEARCH PERFORMANCES ANALYSIS

4.1 Research Performances and Scientific Output

Ridho Kismawadi. et., al (2023), studied importance stems from the fact that it fills a gap in the literature about AI technology integration in Islamic banking. Analysing the possible benefits and difficulties of using AI in the sector. Financial Technology (FinTech) has emerged as a disruptive force in the global financial sector, reshaping how financial services are delivered, consumed, and regulated. Concurrently, IF, grounded in Sharia principles, has become a viable alternative to conventional finance. The Fintech and Islamic Banking scientific research shift plots the total articles annually and is as published. Figure 1 This figure provides an overview of the research landscape related to FinTech and IF, highlighting key themes, trends, and the significance of this evolving field. The present study focuses on the last five years of publications (2019 to 2023*). Starting from the most prominent year 2019 with (2 articles), 2020 with (8 articles), 2021 with (6 articles), 2022 with (15 articles) and 2023 -1st September 2023 (23 articles). The convergence of FinTech and IF represents a dynamic intersection that has garnered substantial attention from researchers and practitioners alike. A total of forty six articles from 2019 to 2023 were published in the area of fintech and IF.

4.1.1 Top Rated Research Articles on Fintech and Islamic Banking

Table 1 showcases in detail the top-rated research articles published between the year 2019 to 2023. Hassan M.K. et al. (2020) is the best, most significant, and most relevant article in the Scopus database (78), followed by Syed M.H. et al.(2020) research article with a citation of (64). The next best research article is by Rabbani M.R et al. (2020) with a citation of (56). Another significant article (2021) was by Rabbani M.R et al., citing (54). Rabbani M.R. et al. authored the most recent and relevant article in (2022) with a citation of (54), Zou, Z., Liu, X., Wang, M., & Yang, X. (2023). With citation of (05), Sampat, B., Mogaji, E., & Nguyen, N. P. (2023) with citation (04) and Al-Shari, H. A., & Lokhande, M. A. (2023) and Jena, J. R., Biswal, S. K., Shrivastava, A. K., & Panigrahi, R. R. (2023) with citation (02). The appropriate cited topic by (Hassan M.K. et al.) was Challenges for IF and banking in the COVID era and the role of Fintech. This paper explores the critical challenges faced by Islamic financial institutions in the post-COVID era and the evolving role of Financial Technology (Fintech) in addressing these challenges.

Syed M.H. et al. (2020), in their research paper titled "An artificial intelligence and NLP based Islamic FinTech model combining zakat and Qard-Al-Hasan for countering the adverse impact of COVID-19 on SMEs and individuals", this paper presents an innovative FinTech model leveraging Artificial Intelligence (AI) and Natural Language Processing (NLP) techniques. The model aims to address the adverse economic effects of the pandemic by combining two fundamental Islamic financial instruments: Zakat and Qard-Al-Hasan.

The most recent research paper was authored by Khan M.S. et al. (2022) titled "Determinants of Behavioural Intentions to Use Islamic Financial Technology: An Empirical Assessment', presents an empirical assessment that contributes to the growing body of knowledge on Islamic FinTech adoption by identifying and analysing the determinants of behavioural intentions. It offers practical insights for stakeholders in the IF and technology sectors, facilitating the development and promotion of Sharia-compliant financial solutions in the digital age. Likewise, Usman H et al. (2022) "Integrating Trust,

Table 1. Top rated research articles on Fintech and Islamic banking

Top Rated Research Articles on Fintech and IF			
Authors	**Title of the research paper**	**Year**	**Total Citation**
Hassan M.K.; Rabbani M.R.; Mohd. Ali M.A.	Challenges for the IF and banking in post COVID era and the role of Fintech	2020	78
Syed M.H.; khan S.; Rabbani M.R.; Thalassinos Y.E.	An artificial intelligence and NLP based Islamic FinTech model combining zakat and Qard-Al-Hasan for countering the adverse impact of COVID 19 on SMEs and individuals	2020	64
Rabbani M.R.; khan S.; Thalassinos E.I.	FinTech, blockchain and IF: An extensive literature review	2020	56
Rabbani M.R.; Bashar A.;Nnawaz N.; Karim S.; Ali M.A.M.; Rahiman H.U.; Alam M.S.	Exploring the role of Islamic fintech in combating the aftershocks of covid-19: The open social innovation of the Islamic financial system	2021	54
Shaikh I.M.; Qureshi M.A.; Noordin K.; Shaikh J.M.; Khan A.; Sahbaz M.S.	Acceptance of Islamic financial technology (FinTech) banking services by Malaysian users: an extension of technology acceptance model	2020	48
Alam N.; Gupta I.; Zameni A.	Fintech and IF: Digitalization, development and disruption	2019	45
Usman H.; Mulia D.; Chairy C.; Widowati N.	Integrating trust, religiosity and image into technology acceptance model: the case of the Islamic philanthropy in Indonesia	2022	35
Rabbani M.R.; Ali M.A.M.;Rahiman H.U.; Atif M.;Zulfikar Z.;Naseem Y.	The response of Islamic financial service to the covid-19 pandemic: The open social innovation of the financial system	2021	35
Hudaefi F.A.	How does Islamic fintech promote the SDGs? Qualitative evidence from Indonesia	2020	34
Ali M.; Raza S.A.; khamis B.; Puah C.H.; Amin H.	How perceived risk, benefit and trust determine user Fintech adoption: a new dimension for IF	2021	34
Darmansyah; Fianto B.A.; Hendratmi A.; Aziz P.F.	Factors determining behavioural intentions to use Islamic financial technology: Three competing models	2020	33
Mohamed H.; Ali H.	Blockchain, fintech, and IF: Building the future in the new Islamic digital economy	2018	32
Nasir A.; Shaukat k.; khan k.I.; Hameed I.A.; Alam T.M.; Luo S.	What is Core and What Future Holds for Blockchain Technologies and Cryptocurrencies: A Bibliometric Analysis	2021	31
Rabbani M.R.; Abdulla Y.; Bashar A.; khan S.; Moh'd Ali M.A.	Embracing of Fintech in IF in the post COVID era	2020	30
khan M.S.; Rabbani M.R.; Hawaldar I.T.; Bashar A.	Determinants of Behavioral Intentions to Use Islamic Financial Technology: An Empirical Assessment	2022	28
Baber H.	FinTech, Crowdfunding and Customer Retention in Islamic Banks	2020	28
Meera A.K.M. (2018)	Crypto Currencies from Islamic Perspectives: The Case of Bitcoin	2018	27
Buallay A.; Cummings R.; Hamdan A.	Intellectual capital efficiency and bank's performance: A comparative study after the global financial crisis	2019	24
Baber H. (2020a)	Financial inclusion and FinTech: A comparative study of countries following IF and conventional finance	2020	21
Atif M.; Hassan M.K.; Rabbani M.R.; khan S. (2021)	Islamic FinTech: The digital transformation bringing sustainability to IF	2021	21

Religiosity, and Image into Technology Acceptance Model: The Case of Islamic Philanthropy in Indonesia." acknowledges the growing significance of technology in facilitating and enhancing philanthropic activities in the Islamic world. In the Indonesian context, where philanthropy is central to culture and religious practices, understanding the dynamics of technology adoption is paramount.

Some other substantial articles focus on Fintech and IF Alam N. et al. (2019). "Fintech and IF: Digitalization, development and disruption'. Hudaefi F.A. (2020) "How does Islamic fintech promote the SDGs? Qualitative evidence from Indonesia". Rabbani M.R.(2021)" The response of Islamic financial service to the COVID-19 pandemic: The open social innovation of the financial system.". Hudaefi F.A. (2020) "How does Islamic fintech promote the SDGs? Qualitative evidence from Indonesia". Ali M. (2020) ". How perceived risk, benefit and trust determine user Fintech adoption: a new dimension for IF". Darmansyah; et al. (2020)" Factors determining behavioural intentions to use Islamic financial technology: Three competing models". Mohamed H.; Ali H. (2018) "Blockchain, fintech, and IF: Building the future in the new Islamic digital economy.", etc.

4.1.2 Top Research From Top Four Emerging Countries on Fintech and IF

The top research papers authored by individuals from four emerging countries presumably top authors like Hassan M.K., Rabbani M.R., and Mohd. Ali M.A, Baber H. and Syed M.H., Khan S., and Rabbani M.R. concerning the intersection of Fintech and IF.

Pal, T., Irfan, M., Kassim, S.B., How do Machine Learning (ML) techniques benefit the insurance industry? An exploratory study, (2023), examined astounding success and previously unheard-of accuracy, artificial intelligence and machine learning have grown in significance within the finance industry. Whereas topmost author stressed on the challenges faced by IF and banking in the aftermath of the COVID-19 pandemic. It is likely to explore the role that Fintech can play in overcoming these challenges and reshaping the IF sector.2nd top author Baber H.'s research appears to focus on financial inclusion and how Fintech is contributing to it in both IF and conventional finance systems. The comparative aspect likely provides insights into how Fintech is impacting financial inclusion differently in these two domains. 3rd top author's research paper, likely a literature review, explores the extensive relationship between Fintech, blockchain technology, and IF. It may discuss the potential applications, challenges, and opportunities that arise from the integration of Fintech and blockchain within the context of IF. As per Table 2 rest top cited authors are Syed M.H. et al., with a citation of (56). Furthermore, the work of Rabbani M.R., Bashar A., Nawaz N., Karim S., Ali M.A.M., Rahiman H.U., and Alam M.S., garnering 54 citations, showcases a collaborative effort that has gained notable attention, potentially delving into pertinent challenges and advancements in the field. Lastly, in 2020, Shaikh I.M., Qureshi M.A., Noordin K., Shaikh J.M., Khan A., and Shahbaz M.S. made a noteworthy contribution with their research titled "Acceptance of Islamic Financial Technology (FinTech) Banking Services by Malaysian Users: An Extension of Technology Acceptance Model," amassing a total of 48 citations. This study likely delves into the acceptance and adoption of FinTech-based banking services within the IF context in Malaysia, extending the Technology Acceptance Model to shed light on the factors influencing users' attitudes and behaviours towards incorporating technology in Islamic financial transactions.

Table 2. Top prominent researchers on Fintech and IF

Authors	Total Documents	Total Citations
Hassan M.K.; Rabbani M.R.; Mohd. Ali M.A.	1	78
Baber H.	5	76
Syed M.H.; Khan S.; Rabbani M.R.; Thalassinos Y.E.	1	64
Rabbani M.R.; Khan S.; Thalassinos E.	1	56
Rabbani M.R.; Bashar A.; Nawaz N.; Karim S.; Ali M.A.M.; Rahiman H.U.; AlamM.S.	1	54
Shaikh I.M.; Qureshi M.A.; Noordin K.; Shaikh J.M.; Khan A.; Shahbaz M.S.	1	48
Alam N.; Gupta l.; Zameni A	1	45
Rabbani M.R.; Ali M.A.M.;Rahiman H.U.; Atif M.; Zulfikar Z.; Naseem Y.	1	35
Usman H.; Mulia D.; Chairy C.; Widowati N.	1	35
Ali M.; Raza S.A.; Khamis B.; Puah C.H.; Amin H.	1	34
Hudaefi F.A.	1	34
Mohamed H.; Ali H.	2	34
Darmansyah; Fianto B.A.; Hendratmi A.;Aaziz P.F.	1	33
Nasir A.; Shaukat K.; Khan K.I.; Hameed I .A.; Alam T.M.; Luo S.	1	31
Rabbani M.R.; Abdulla Y.; Bashar A.; Khan S.; Moh'd Ali M.A.	1	30
Khan M.S.; Rabbani M.R.; Hawaldar I.T.;Bbashar A.	1	28
Meera A.KMm.	1	27
Buallay A.; Cummings R.; Hamdan A.	1	24
Atif M.; Hassan M.K.; Rabbani M.R.; Khan S.	1	21

4.1.3 Prominent Journals of Fintech and Islamic Financing.

As per the information available in table -3 on top-rated journals in the field of Fintech and IF, showcasing their influence and relevance in academic research. The “International Journal of Economics and Business Administration” emerges as a leading journal, with 8 documents and an impressive total citation count of 222, underscoring its high impact and recognition within the academic community. “Foresight” and “Journal of Islamic Marketing” also stand out, with 4 documents and 3 documents respectively, accompanied by significant citation counts of 95 and 74, reflecting their substantial contributions to the discourse in Fintech and IF. Additionally, the “International Journal of Islamic and Middle Eastern Finance and Management” contributes significantly with 7 documents and 66 citations, further establishing its importance as a prominent journal in this field.

Moreover, specialized publications like “Blockchain, Fintech, and IF: Building The Future in The New Islamic Digital Economy” and “Fintech in IF: Theory and Practice” are notable for their focused content, offering 2 documents each with citation counts of 34 and 33 respectively. These journals delve into the future of IF in the digital age, providing valuable insights and perspectives. Overall, these top-rated journals serve as critical platforms for disseminating research and advancing knowledge in the burgeoning intersection of Fintech and IF.

Table 3. Top rated journals on Fintech and IF

Source	Total documents	Total citations
International Journal of Economics and Business Administration	8	222
Foresight	7	184
Journal of Islamic Marketing	5	74
International Journal of Islamic and Middle Eastern Finance and Management	7	66
Blockchain, FinTech, and IF: Building The Future in The New Islamic Digital Economy	2	34
Fintech in IF: Theory and Practice	12	33
IEEE Access	2	31
Journal of Islamic Accounting and Business Research	9	29
Heliyon	3	28
Journal of Islamic Monetary Economics and Finance	7	27
Islamic Quarterly	2	16
Technological Forecasting and Social Change	2	16

4.1.4 Top University/Institution Researching on Fintech and IF

The overview of the prominent universities and institutions that have made significant contributions to research at the intersection of Fintech and IF are presented in table 4. The University College of Bahrain in Bahrain emerges as a leading institution, contributing 5 documents and accumulating a notable total citation count of 154. This suggests the substantial impact and recognition of their research endeavours in this domain. Similarly, Kingdom University, also located in Bahrain, has made a significant mark with 4 documents and a commendable citation count of 133, reaffirming the active engagement and influence of academic research in Fintech and IF within the region.

Table 4. Top university/institution researching on Fintech and IF

Institutions	Total documents	Total citations
University College of Bahrain, Bahrain	5	154
kingdom University, Bahrain	4	133
University of New Orleans, United States	10	92
IMS Unison University, Dehradun, India	3	86
University of Bahrain, Sakhir, Bahrain	13	18
Stellar Consulting Group, Singapore	3	4
Ahlia University, Bahrain	3	3
International Shari'ah Research Academy for IF (ISRA), Kuala Lumpur, Malaysia	3	3

5. DISCUSSION

Study discussion based on proposed research questions and performances analysis. As per the four research questions raised in the introduction section authors address three research questions in this section.

RQ 1: How do emerging Fintech innovations impact the growth and sustainability of IF?

The primary focus of this study was to identify the emerging Fintech innovations that have an influence on the growth and long-term sustainability of Islamic Finance (IF). Scholars worldwide have focused on Fintech and IF articles that have gathered over 25 citations.

"Table 1: Top rated articles on Fintech and IF, Hassan M.K. et al. (2020)" received the highest number (78) of citations for their paper titled "Challenges for IF and Banking in the COVID Era and the Role of Fintech.". This top-rated article explores how the transformative technological innovation known as Fintech can be harnessed to tackle these challenges. This article is the top-rated article in the line of fintech and IF. The proposed comprehensive Islamic FinTech Model by Syed M.H et al. (2020), has the second highest citation (64). Their research paper titled "An artificial intelligence and NLP based Islamic FinTech model combining Zakat and Qard-Al-Hasan for countering the adverse impact of COVID-19 on SMEs and individuals." integrates Artificial Intelligence and NLP and incorporates both Zakat (Islamic tax) and Qard-Al-Hasan (benevolent loan), has the potential to mitigate the negative repercussions of COVID-19 on individuals and small and medium-sized enterprises (SMEs) within the economy. Mustafa Raza Rabbani. Et al. (2020), with the third highest citation (56), titled "FinTech, blockchain, and IF: An extensive literature review." identified and emphasized the prospects and obstacles Islamic financial institutions can discover from conventional FinTech organizations worldwide. Rabbani M.R. et al. (2021), with the fourth highest citation (54), titled "Exploring the Role of Islamic fintech in Combating the Aftershocks of covid-19: The Open Social Innovation of the Islamic financial system." Examined the role played by the Islamic financial system in the post-COVID-19 recovery and emphasized as to how Fintech can be harnessed to address the economic challenges stemming from the COVID-19 pandemic. Shaikh I.M. et al. (2020), the fifth highest cited article (48) titled "Acceptance of Islamic Financial Technology (FinTech) Banking Services by Malaysian Users: An extension of Technology Acceptance Model." This paper seeks to investigate the factors that impact the willingness of bank users in Malaysia to adopt Islamic financial technology (FinTech) services, expanding upon the Technology Acceptance Model (TAM).

RQ 2: "What are the top contributions made by prominent Researchers towards Fintech and IF?

This research was an attempt to explore the top contributions made by researchers towards Fintech and IF. Table 2: Top Prominent Researchers on Fintech and IF clearly describes the top researchers who have contributed their findings, which adds more insight to the knowledge base of fintech and IF. Hassan M.K. et al., with the highest citation of (78). This paper presented a critical analysis of IF and sustainable financial system. Baber H. (2020), titled "Financial Inclusion and FinTech: A Comparative Study of Countries Following Islamic and Conventional Finance." Is the second prominent researcher with a citation of (76). The outcome of this paper provides valuable insights into the strengths and weaknesses of each system, shedding light on potential areas for improvement. Syed M.H. et al. titled "An artificial intelligence and NLP based Islamic FinTech model combining zakat and Qard-Al-Hasan for countering the adverse impact of COVID-19 on SMEs and individuals." Is the third prominent authors with a citation of (64). The study's results indicate that IF possesses significant potential to combat various situations, including pandemics, effectively. Combining Zakat and Qard-Al-Hasan can be a potent strategy for mitigating the adverse impacts of COVID-19. Rabbani M.R.et al. titled "FinTech, blockchain, and IF: An extensive literature review." Are the following prominent authors with a citation of (54). This study's unique contribution lies in exploring FinTech technologies, such as cryptocurrency and blockchain, from a Sharia-compliant perspective.

RQ 3: How extensively do top research journals and institutions explore the synergy between IF and emerging technologies like AI and big data analytics?

This study was an attempt to analyse the prominent research journals and institutions contributing extensively towards Fintech and IF focusing on emerging technologies like AI and Big Data Analytics. Top journals such as International Journal of Economics and Business Administration, Foresight, Journal of Islamic Marketing, International Journal of Islamic and Middle Eastern Finance and Management, etc have emerged as top journals as displayed in table 3. Research articles form these journals have well revealed the ways and means through which Fintech and IF have been speedily evolving sector hovering for substantial growth in the coming years. The combination of new technologies such as blockchain, AI, and machine learning is projected to translate the way that financial services are served and utilized in the IF industry.

6. FUTURE RESEARCH AGENDA AND PROPOSED THEMES

In the subsequent paragraphs, we delve into potential research trajectories stemming from the summaries and insights gleaned through our preceding analyses. The aim is to provide a forward-looking perspective on the study of Fintech and IF, particularly focusing on emerging countries. As we address the last research question RQ4: "What prominent themes and research directions could strengthen fintech adaptions into IF in emerging countries".? our intent is to illuminate promising areas where further investigation can significantly enrich the discourse. By doing so, we aspire to contribute to the advancement of research in both Fintech and IF, offering insights that could potentially guide scholars and practitioners in these evolving domains.

6.1 Theme 1: Blockchain and Financial Technology (FinTech)

The intersection of blockchain, fintech, and IF is a promising area of research and innovation, El-Qorchi, M. (2018). As a result, Researchers are actively exploring how blockchain technology can enhance financial services' efficiency, transparency, and compliance while aligning with Islamic principles, Al-Twaijry A., et al. (2020). Blockchain and Fintech can be integrated into Islamic banking systems to ensure compliance with Shariah principles, El-Qorchi, M. (2018). Works like (Yusof et al., 2019) analyse the emergence of Islamic crowdfunding platforms that utilize blockchain technology to facilitate Shariah-compliant crowdfunding. Bashir et al. (2020) discussed the development of digital wallets and payment solutions that cater to IF customers. Emerging research in the intersection of Blockchain and Financial Technology (Fintech) in the context of Islamic Financing reveals a growing body of work exploring the potential of blockchain technology to enhance financial services while adhering to Islamic principles (Rashid et al. (2019. Hassan and Ali, (2021). Ali et al. (2018). Han Blockchain 19).

6.2 Theme 2: Cryptocurrency and Financial Technology

Research at the intersection of cryptocurrency, fintech, and IF is rapidly evolving as these fields continue to develop and intersect. Razak & Aziz, (2020) discuss the concept of Shariah-compliant cryptocurrencies and evaluate the compliance of existing cryptocurrencies like Bitcoin with IF principles. The connection of cryptocurrency, fintech, and IF is an exciting and evolving field, with research exploring the compatibility of blockchain technology and cryptocurrencies with Shariah principles, the impact of fintech platforms on IF, regulatory challenges, and real-world case studies (Tariq and Malik, (2021). Fahmi and Rosly (2020). Algharaballi & Elamir, (2019). Iqbal and Ahmad, (2019). Mansoor et al. (2020)). As these areas continue to develop, addressing compliance, ethics, and financial inclusion will remain essential for their successful integration into the IF industry (Zakariya et al., (2021). Elamir and Algharaballi, (2020)).

6.3 Theme 3: Environmental, Social, and Governance (ESG) in Fintech

Emerging research in Environmental, Social, and Governance (ESG) in Fintech is gaining significance as financial technology companies increasingly integrate ESG principles into their products and services Bassen & Mählmann,(2019). Combining ESG principles into fintech is an emerging and dynamic area of research and innovation. Researchers are exploring ESG data integration, the development of ESG-linked financial products, regulatory challenges, and the ethical and social dimensions of ESG in fintech (Scholtens and Tiba, (2021). Gampfer and Hock, (2020)). Bhattacharya et al. (2020) analyses the development of ESG scoring models used in fintech platforms to assess the sustainability performance of companies. (Du et al., 2020) discuss the regulatory challenges of establishing uniform ESG reporting standards and the implications for fintech firms. (Simpson et al., 2021) analyse how fintech innovations can promote financial inclusion, particularly in ESG-related initiatives. (Lai et al., 2019) investigate the emergence of fintech platforms dedicated to impact investing and philanthropy. As ESG considerations continue to gain importance in the financial industry, addressing these aspects will be essential for fintech firms seeking to align with sustainable and responsible finance (Meng et al., (2020). Sarkis et al. (2021). Wong et al., (2020))

6.4 Theme 4: Islamic Bank and Fintech

Promising research on integrating Islamic banking and fintech is growing as Islamic financial institutions seek to harness technology to provide more efficient and Shariah-compliant financial services (Elamir et al., 2021). Yusof et al. (2019) analyse the development of Islamic crowdfunding platforms that utilize fintech to facilitate Shariah-compliant crowdfunding. Ali et al., 2018) discuss the development of ethical frameworks for fintech companies operating in IF and the ethical dimensions of blockchain technology. (Hassan et al., 2021) explore how fintech tools can be used for risk assessment and mitigation in Islamic banking. (Saiti et al., 2020) discuss the integration of fintech and insurtech in Islamic insurance (Takaful) and its implications for risk management.

The conjunction of Islamic banking and fintech represents a dynamic and promising field of research and innovation; in this connection, researchers are exploring various aspects, from regulatory challenges to ethical considerations, as well as the potential for fintech to improve customer experience, enhance risk management, and promote financial inclusion in Islamic banking. As fintech continues to shape the IF industry, addressing these aspects will be essential for its successful integration (Ali et al., (2018). Hassan et al. (2021). Haneef et al. (2020).

7. CONTRIBUTION OF THE STUDY, CONCLUSION, AND LIMITATIONS

This research explores the transformative potential of Fintech in the financial industry. Traditional financial services were often seen as expensive and inefficient, but Fintech has evolved to better address the diverse needs of stakeholders. The study delves into various research papers and studies examining the application of Fintech in Islamic Finance (IF) within the financial services sector, offering valuable insights for both scholars and practitioners.

Furthermore, future research could analytically assess the impact of Fintech on Islamic banking, non-banking, insurance, and other IF-related services. Fintech is still in its developmental phase, with ongoing testing in various business environments. Like any emerging technology, it brings both opportunities and inherent risks to Islamic business, trade, and society.The study concludes that existing research on Fintech and Islamic Financial services, primarily conducted by reputable research organizations and prominent scholars, tends to be experimental, with a focus on qualitative or quantitative analyses of the Fintech adoption process, benefits, and potential challenges.

The study has some notable limitations. It relied on data from the Scopus core collection, potentially limiting its scope. Additionally, the research had geographical and thematic constraints, which may have restricted the comprehensiveness, generalizability, and representativeness of the findings. To address these limitations and gain a more comprehensive understanding of the Fintech and IF landscape, further research is warranted.

REFERENCES

Abdul Razak, D., & Noordin, B. A. (2020). Fintech and IF: A Perfect Symbiosis. *ISRA International Journal of IF*, *12*(1), 83–98.

Abdullah, N. (2021). AML/KYC Compliance in Islamic Fintech: A Blockchain-Based Approach. *Journal of Financial Crime*, *28*(2).

Abdulrazzaq, A. (2019). Developing an AI-Based Personalized Investment Recommender System in Islamic Banking. *International Journal of Financial Research, 10*(2).

Akhtar, M. F., & Ali, F. (2021). Exploring the Nexus between Fintech and IF: Challenges and Opportunities. *Journal of Financial Regulation and Compliance*, *29*(3), 489–508.

Akhtar, N. (2020). A review of the applications of artificial intelligence in IF. *Journal of Islamic Marketing*, *11*(6).

Akhtar, S. A., & Akhtar, M. F. (2020). Fintech and IF: A Synergy to Foster Financial Inclusion. *ISRA International Journal of IF*, *12*(1), 35–47.

Al-Shari, H. A., & Lokhande, M. A. (2023). The relationship between the risks of adopting FinTech in banks and their impact on the performance. *Cogent Business & Management*, *10*(1), 2174242. doi:10.1080/23311975.2023.2174242

Al-Twaijry, A. A. (2020). Smart Contracts in IF: A Use Case of Musharakah Mutanaqisah Smart Contracts. *Journal of King Abdulaziz University: Islamic Economics*, *33*(1).

Algharaballi, W., & Elamir, E. A. H. (2019). Digital Islamic Banks: A Framework for Ensuring Compliance with Shariah Principles. *Journal of Islamic Marketing*, *10*(1).

Ali, H. (2018). Ethical Considerations in the Blockchain Ecosystem: A Case of IF. *IEEE Access : Practical Innovations, Open Solutions*.

Ali, M. (2021). Artificial Intelligence for Ethical Finance in Islamic Banking: Issues and Challenges. *Sustainability*, *13*(8).

Alqahtani, F., Mayes, D. G., & Brown, K. (2020). Fintech in Islamic banking and finance: A review and research agenda. *Research in International Business and Finance*, *54*, 101281.

Alvi, U. H., & Butt, S. A. (2020). Digital Transformation in Islamic Banking and Finance: A Comprehensive Review. *Journal of Islamic Marketing*, *11*(2), 517–530.

Ammar, A. (2021). RegTech Adoption in IF: An Empirical Investigation. *Journal of Financial Services Marketing*.

Arif, A. I. M. (2019). Social Responsibility Practices of Islamic Fintech Companies: A Comparative Analysis. *Journal of Islamic Marketing*, *10*(4).

Arif, M., & Majid, M. S. A. (2021). Machine Learning for Sukuk Selection: An Empirical Analysis. *Pacific-Basin Finance Journal*.

Bashir, N. (2020). Design and Development of Shariah-Compliant Digital Wallet: A Proposed Framework. *Journal of Islamic Marketing*, *11*(2).

Bassen, A., & Mählmann, T. (2019). The impact of ESG information on market performance: Evidence from the European real estate market. *Sustainability*, *11*(18).

Belleflamme, P., Lambert, T., & Schwienbacher, A. (2014). Crowdfunding: Tapping the right crowd. *Journal of Business Venturing*, *29*(5), 585–609. doi:10.1016/j.jbusvent.2013.07.003

Bhattacharya, U. (2020). Assessing sustainability reporting from the perspective of financial analysts. *European Accounting Review*, *29*(1).

Bhatti, I. (2020). Microfinance in the Era of Islamic Fintech: An Exploratory Study. *Journal of Islamic Marketing*.

Cakir, M., & Raei, R. (2021). Fintech in IF: A Catalyst for Inclusion and Innovation. IMF Working Paper, WP/21/78.

Chapra, M. U. (2019). IF and the Global Economy. *Islamic Economic Studies*, *27*(1), 1–18.

Chen, Z., Da, Z., & Zhao, H. (2020). The fintech advantage: Robo-advisors and their potential impact on individual investors. *Journal of Financial Services Research*, *57*(2), 149–176.

Du, X. (2020). Evaluating the financial market effects of the global ESG disclosure standards: A multi-country study. *Journal of Corporate Finance*, •••, 62.

El Basri, M., & Mirakhor, A. (2019). Fintech and IF: A Convergence towards Financial Inclusion. *Islamic Economic Studies*, *27*(1), 51–70.

El-Galfy, A. S. (2021). Fintech and the Transformation of IF. In Handbook of Blockchain, Digital Finance, and Inclusion (pp. 363-374). Springer.

El-Qorchi, M. (2018). *IF and Blockchain: The Potential of Distributed Ledger Technology*. (IMF Working Paper). IMF.

Elamir, E. A. H. (2019). Artificial Intelligence and Credit Risk Assessment: A Case of Islamic Banks in the UAE. *Journal of Enterprise Information Management*.

Elamir, E. A. H. (2021). Digital Islamic Banks: A Framework for Ensuring Compliance with Shariah Principles. *Journal of Islamic Marketing*, *10*(1).

Elamir, E. A. H., & Algharaballi, W. (2020). Financial Inclusion and Fintech Adoption in Muslim-Majority Countries. *Journal of Islamic Marketing*, *11*(3).

Elzarka, A. (2020). Blockchain-Based Sukuk: A Comprehensive Case Study. *Journal of Corporate Finance*.

Elzarka, A. (2021). Tokenization of Sukuk on Blockchain: A Comprehensive Case Study. *Journal of Islamic Marketing*.

Fahmi, I., & Rosly, S. A. (2020). The Impact of Fintech on Islamic Crowdfunding in Malaysia: A Conceptual Framework. *Journal of Islamic Marketing*, *11*(1).

Gampfer, S., & Hock, S. (2020). Machine learning for ESG investment. *Frontiers in Artificial Intelligence*, 3.

Gomber, P., Koch, J. A., & Siering, M. (2017). Digital finance and fintech: Current research and future research directions. *Journal of Business Economics*, *87*(5), 537–580. doi:10.100711573-017-0852-x

Guidotti, R. (2018). A Survey of Methods for Explaining Black Box Models. *ACM Computing Surveys*.

Hafiz, M. R. (2020). Smart Contracts in IF: Concept and Operational Framework. *International Journal of Islamic and Middle Eastern Finance and Management*, *13*(3).

Haneef, M. A. (2019). Blockchain Technology, Fintech, and Islamic Social Finance: Building Ethical Finance for Unbanked and Underprivileged Communities. *Frontiers in Blockchain, 2*.

Haneef, M. A. (2020). Ethical Considerations in Islamic Fintech: Issues and Challenges. *Journal of Islamic Marketing*, *11*(6).

Haneef, M. A. (2020). Financial Inclusion and Fintech Adoption in Muslim-Majority Countries. *Journal of Islamic Marketing*, *11*(3).

Haneef, M. A. (2021). Artificial Intelligence in Islamic Microfinance for Financial Inclusion: A Conceptual Framework. *Frontiers in Artificial Intelligence*.

Hasan, M., & Dridi, J. (2019). *IF: Opportunities, Challenges, and Policy Options*. IMF Staff Discussion Note, SDN/19/08.

Hassan, M. K., Aliyu, S. U. R., & Chiappetta Jabbour, C. J. (2020). Fintech and IF: A Review and Research Agenda. *Journal of Islamic Accounting and Business Research*, *11*(6), 1135–1156.

Hassan, M. K., & Mahlknecht, M. (2019). IF: Debt versus Equity-based Financing in the Light of Basel III. *Pacific-Basin Finance Journal*, *53*, 482–498.

Hassan, R. (2019). Exploring the Role of AI Transparency in Shariah Compliance. *Pacific-Basin Finance Journal*.

Hassan, R. (2021). Role of FinTech in Islamic Banks' Risk Assessment and Mitigation: A Conceptual Model. *Journal of Financial Crime*, *28*(4).

Hassan, R., & Ali, M. (2021). Enhancing AML/KYC Compliance in IF Using Blockchain Technology. *Journal of Money Laundering Control*, *24*(3).

Hassan, R., & Rashid, B. (2020). An Empirical Analysis of Anti-Money Laundering (AML) Risk Assessment using Machine Learning Techniques in Islamic Banking. *Journal of Financial Crime*.

Hassan, R., & Safi, S. (2020). The Role of Mobile Banking in Financial Inclusion: A Study in Islamic Countries. *Journal of Islamic Marketing*.

Iqbal, M., & Abbas, S. (2020). Shariah-Compliant Cryptocurrencies: An Analysis of Digital Currencies under Islamic Law. *Journal of Islamic Marketing*.

Iqbal, M., & Ahmad, A. (2019). Regulation of Cryptocurrencies and Fintech in IF. *Journal of Financial Regulation and Compliance*, *27*(1).

Iqbal, Z., & Mirakhor, A. (2020). Fintech and IF: A New Era of Convergence. In Handbook of Blockchain, Digital Finance, and Inclusion (pp. 347-361). Springer.

Irfan, M., Elhoseny, M., Kassim, S., & Metawa, N. (2023). *Advanced Machine Learning Algorithms for Complex Financial Applications*. doi:10.4018/978-1-6684-4483-2

Irfan, M., Elmogy, M., Majid, M.S.A., & El-Sappagh, S. (2023). *The impact of AI innovation on financial sectors in the era of industry 5.0*. Research Gate.

Islamic Research and Training Institute. (2015). *Principles of IF*. IRTI. https://www.irti.org/English/Research/Documents/ISF1.pdf

Jena, J. R., Biswal, S. K., Shrivastava, A. K., & Panigrahi, R. R. (2023). A bibliographic overview of financial engineering in the emerging financial market. *International Journal of System Assurance Engineering and Management*, 1-18.

Kamilaris, A., et al. (2021). RegTech and SupTech: A survey of enabling technologies for regulatory and supervisory challenges. *Frontiers in Blockchain, 4.*

Kari, F. (2020). FinTech Innovation in IF: A Conceptual Framework and Research Agenda. *Pacific-Basin Finance Journal*, 61.

Karim, A., & Tarazi, A. (2020). Fintech in Islamic Microfinance: A Review. *IF Development Report, IFDI 2020.*

Kempf, A. (2019). Does financial education impact financial knowledge and financial behavior, and if so, when? *Journal of Banking & Finance*, 98.

Khalid, S., & Abbas, S. (2019). Regulatory Challenges and Opportunities in Islamic Fintech. *Journal of Financial Regulation and Compliance*, *27*(4).

Khan, T. (2020). Fintech meets IF: The Digital Transformation of Islamic Financial Services. *ISRA International Journal of IF*, *12*(1), 1–16.

Lai, K., et al. (2019). Social impact investing with blockchain: A systematic review. *Frontiers in Blockchain, 2.*

Leimeister, J. M., Huber, M., Bretschneider, U., & Krcmar, H. (2009). Leveraging crowdsourcing: Activation-supporting components for IT-based ideas competition. *Journal of Management Information Systems*, *26*(1), 197–224. doi:10.2753/MIS0742-1222260108

Lewis, M. K., & Algaoud, L. M. (2019). Fintech, Financial Inclusion, and IF. In Fintech, IF and Financial Inclusion (pp. 3-24). Springer.

Loonam, J., & McDermott, J. (2019). AI and financial services: Understanding the rise of chatbots, robo-advisors and beyond. *Business Horizons*, *62*(6), 645–657.

Mansoor, A., Hassan, M. K., & Rehman, M. A. (2019). Fintech and IF: A Review and Research Agenda. *Pacific-Basin Finance Journal*, *55*, 306–324.

Mansoor, S., & Ahmed, Z. U. (2021). Responsible Artificial Intelligence in IF: A Framework. *Pacific-Basin Finance Journal.*

Martín-Martín, A., Orduna-Malea, E., Thelwall, M., & Delgado López-Cózar, E. (2018). Google Scholar, Web of Science, and Scopus: A Systematic Comparison of Citations in 252 Subject Categories. [CrossRef]. *Journal of Informetrics*, *12*(4), 1160–1177. doi:10.1016/j.joi.2018.09.002

McKinsey & Company. (2016). *The Fintech Sector in Germany: An Analysis of the Status Quo and the Opportunities for German FinTech Companies*. McKinsey. https://www.mckinsey.com/~/media/mckinsey/industries/financial%20services/our%20insights/the%20fintech%20sector%20in%20germany%20opportunities%20and%20challenges/the-fintech-sector-in-germany-opportunities-and-challenges-vf.ashx

Meng, L. (2020). Blockchain applications in global supply chains. In Sustainable Supply Chain Management (pp. 71-84). MDPI.

Mettler, T. (2020). Detecting Fraud in Islamic Banks Using Machine Learning: A Systematic Review. *Journal of Financial Services Marketing*, *25*(3).

Moher, D., Stewart, L., & Shekelle, P. (2016). Implementing PRISMA-P: Recommendations for prospective authors. *Systematic Reviews*, *5*(1), 1–6. doi:10.118613643-016-0191-y PMID:26822481

Mohieldin, M. (2020). *Fintech and IF: Technology and Ecosystem Evolution*. World Bank Group.

Mohieldin, M., & Metwally, M. (2019). The Role of Fintech in Enhancing Financial Inclusion in the Arab World. *Islamic Economic Studies*, *27*(1), 189–204.

Page, M. J., McKenzie, J. E., Bossuyt, P. M., Boutron, I., Hoffmann, T. C., Mulrow, C. D., Shamseer, L., Tetzlaff, J. M., Akl, E. A., & Brennan, S. E. (2021). The PRISMA 2020 Statement: An Updated Guideline for Reporting Systematic Reviews. [CrossRef]. *BMJ (Clinical Research Ed.)*, *88*, 105906. PMID:33782057

Pal, T., Irfan, M., Kassim, S.B. (2023). *How do Machine Learning (ML) techniques benefit the insurance industry? An exploratory study*. OUCI.

Panigrahi, R.R. (2023). Review of Machine Learning Techniques in the Supply Chain Management of Indian Industry. *Advanced Machine Learning Algorithms for Complex Financial Applications*. IGI Global. . doi:10.4018/978-1-6684-4483-2.ch013

Rabbani, M. R. (2022). IF and Cryptocurrency: A Systematic Review. In *FinTech in Islamic Financial Institutions* (pp. 279–306). Springer International Publishing. doi:10.1007/978-3-031-14941-2_14

Rahman, M. (2021). Islamic Fintech and Financial Inclusion: A Conceptual Discussion. *Frontiers in Blockchain, 4*.

Rammal, H. G., & Zurbruegg, R. (2020). Fintech and IF: A Review and Research Agenda. *Pacific-Basin Finance Journal*, *66*, 101488.

Rashid, S. (2019). Blockchain Technology Adoption in IF: Regulatory Challenges and the Way Forward. [IJEAT]. *International Journal of Engineering and Advanced Technology*, *9*(2).

Razak, D. A. (2019). Enhancing Regulatory Compliance in IF through Blockchain Technology. *Journal of Financial Regulation and Compliance*, *27*(4).

Razak, D. A., & Aziz, M. R. A. (2020). Bitcoin and IF: What are the Opportunities and Challenges? *Journal of Islamic Accounting and Business Research*, *11*(5).

Regona, M., Yigitcanlar, T., Xia, B., & Li, R. Y. M. (2022). Opportunities and Adoption Challenges of AI in the Construction Industry: A PRISMA Review. *Journal of Open Innovation*, *8*(1), 45. doi:10.3390/joitmc8010045

Ridho Kismawadi, E., Irfan, M., Shah, S.M.A.R. (2023). Artificial intelligence's role in the future of industry. *The Impact of AI Innovation on Financial Sectors in the Era of Industry, 5.0,* 184-207

Saiti, B. (2018). Blockchain and Islamic Banking: A Comprehensive Literature Review. *Journal of King Abdulaziz University: Islamic Economics*, *31*(2).

Saiti, B. (2020). InsurTech Innovations in Islamic Insurance: A Review and Potential Research Directions. *Journal of Financial Services Marketing*, *25*(3).

Sampat, B., Mogaji, E., & Nguyen, N. P. (2023). The dark side of FinTech in financial services: A qualitative enquiry into FinTech developers' perspective. *International Journal of Bank Marketing*. doi:10.1108/IJBM-07-2022-0328

Sandhu, H. S., & Ramayah, T. (2019). Fintech in IF: A Comprehensive Literature Review and Research Agenda. *Journal of Islamic Marketing*, *11*(2), 494–516.

Sarkis, J. (2021). A systematic review of blockchain applications in supply chains, transportation, and logistics. *Sustainability*, *13*(6).

Scholtens, B., & Tiba, S. (2021). Green fintech's: The new insurgents in sustainable and responsible finance. *Sustainability*, *13*(8).

Schueffel, P. (2016). Taming the beast: A scientific definition of fintech. *Journal of Innovation Management*, *4*(4), 32–54. doi:10.24840/2183-0606_004.004_0004

Shah, S. Z. A., & Safi, S. (2020). Blockchain-Based Waqf Management: A Case Study. *Journal of Islamic Marketing*.

Shahzad, A., & Rahman, Z. (2021). Fintech and Islamic Banking: A Framework for Financial Inclusion. *Thunderbird International Business Review*, *63*(2), 175–188.

Shaikh, Z. H., Sarea, A., & Irfan, M. (2022). Islamic Banking Strategies in the World of Fintech: Success Story of Bahrain. In *Artificial Intelligence for Sustainable Finance and Sustainable Technology. ICGER 2021. Lecture Notes in Networks and Systems* (pp. 97–104). Springer. doi:10.1007/978-3-030-93464-4_10

Silva, T. F., & Santos, R. (2017). Insurtech: Overview and future prospects. *The Geneva Papers on Risk and Insurance. Issues and Practice*, *42*(4), 647–667.

Simpson, L. (2021). Fintech for financial inclusion: A study of government-supported savings groups in Papua New Guinea. *Frontiers in Blockchain, 4*.

Sulaiman, S. (2020). Ethical and Social Responsibility of Islamic Fintech Companies: A Comparative Analysis. *Journal of Islamic Marketing*, *11*(6).

Tabachnick, D. (2019). Regtech for fintech: A framework for regulatory and supervisory responses. *Georgetown Journal of International Law*, *50*(2), 451–504.

Takaful, M. A. (2019). Blockchain-Based Takaful: An Empirical Study on Its Feasibility. *Journal of Islamic Marketing*, *10*(4).

Tarazi, A., & Fechtali, O. (2020). Fintech and IF: A New Dawn for Financial Inclusion? *The World Bank Research Observer*, *36*(1), 29–54.

Tarazi, A., & Trinugroho, I. W. (2021). Fintech in Islamic Banking: A Review and Future Research Directions. *Research in International Business and Finance*, *58*, 101391.

Tariq, U., & Malik, I. H. (2021). Development of Shariah-Compliant Cryptocurrency: Challenges and Prospects. *Journal of Islamic Marketing*.

Wilson, R. (2020). The Global IF Ecosystem: Mapping the Territory. *ISRA International Journal of IF*, *12*(1), 17–34.

Wilson, R., & El-Desouky, A. (2019). Fintech, IF, and Financial Inclusion. In Routledge Handbook of Social and Sustainable Finance (pp. 433-447). Routledge.

Wong, R. Y. (2020). An ethical framework for blockchain-enabled sustainable supply chains. *Frontiers in Blockchain, 3.*

Yigitcanlar, T., Kamruzzaman, M., Foth, M., Sabatini-Marques, J., da Costa, E., & Ioppolo, G. (2019). Can Cities Become Smart without Being Sustainable? A Systematic Review of the Literature. *Sustainable Cities and Society*, *45*, 348–365. doi:10.1016/j.scs.2018.11.033

Youssef, T., & Allam, M. (2020). AI Chatbots in IF: Adoption Barriers and Ethical Considerations. *Journal of Islamic Marketing.*

Yusof, N. M. (2019). Crowdfunding for Islamic Social Finance: A Blockchain-Based Framework. *International Journal of Islamic and Middle Eastern Finance and Management*, *12*(4).

Yusuf, M., & Rahman, M. (2019). Emerging Trends of Islamic Fintech Startups in the Middle East. *Journal of Islamic Marketing.*

Zakariya, H. (2021). Sukuk Tokenization on Blockchain: A New Era of IF. *Journal of Islamic Marketing.*

Zaman, M., & Khairudin, N. H. (2021). Fintech and IF: A Review. *Journal of IF, 10*(Special Issue), 086-097.

Zavvar Sabegh, M., & Tarofder, A. K. (2022). Fintech Innovations in IF: A Systematic Literature Review. *Journal of IF and Business Research*, *11*(1), 18–34.

Zhang, Y., & Xiao, X. (2020). Machine learning and financial market anomalies. *Journal of Accounting and Economics*, *69*(1), 101295.

Zhu, Y., & Tarazi, A. (2021). Fintech and IF: A Comprehensive Review and Future Research Agenda. *Pacific-Basin Finance Journal*, *66*, 101477.

Zou, Z., Liu, X., Wang, M., & Yang, X. (2023). Insight into digital finance and fintech: A bibliometric and content analysis. *Technology in Society*, *73*, 102221. doi:10.1016/j.techsoc.2023.102221

Zulkhibri, M. (2020). Fintech and IF: The Convergence of Two Worlds. *ISRA International Journal of IF*, *12*(1), 75–82.

Chapter 2
Fusion of AI and Ethical Finance:
Changing the Outlook of Financial Companies and Society

Neelam Yadav
https://orcid.org/0009-0007-1505-7965
Central University of Haryana, India

Divya
Central University of Haryana, India

Ashish Mathur
Central University of Haryana, India

Jyoti Thanvi
University of Birmingham, UK

ABSTRACT

Artificial intelligence (AI) and ethical finance constitute a dynamic and developing field with major consequences for both the financial sector and society at large. AI is in financial decision-making processes, including fraud detection, portfolio optimization, and investment analysis. AI's growing use in evaluating ESG standards and locating opportunities for ethical investment is changing the standards of ethical finance. The fusion of ethical finance and AI represents an exciting frontier with the potential to drive more responsible and sustainable financial practices. The current study aims to explore the practical AI application for ethical financing implementations. The study will systematically review publicly available research manuscripts and reports and challenges faced by companies while exercising. This study will emphasis on the need for proactive ethical involvement in the development and application of AI in the financial industry.

DOI: 10.4018/979-8-3693-1038-0.ch002

1. INTRODUCTION

The financial environment could undergo significant changes due to the revolutionary power of artificial intelligence (AI). Most industries have gone digital due to the introduction of new technology and the widespread use of artificial intelligence methods to improve everyday activities and even forecast and anticipate changes (Meg, 2019). Thanks to the new concept of digital finance, or e-finance, investors and stakeholders may now predict the best time to complete their transactions, the financial industry has also profited from this shift. Because the information processed in e-finance is financial in nature and requires a very small margin of error to prevent economic crises and occasionally individual or corporate bankruptcy, this field of study is both active and sensitive (Najem, et.al,2022). India is poised to drive the world AI economy, with the market for AI expected to reach $7.8 billion by 2025 in the country, according to the India Brand Equity Foundation.(Abrahim, 2023). Even though the concept of "machine ethics" was proposed around 2006, AI ethics is still in the infancy stage (Keng Siau, Weiyu Wang, 2020). Ethics in AI, or ethics in general, lacks the means to support its own existence. It goes without saying that upholding ethical standards may result in consequences for misconduct, such as harm to one's reputation or exclusion from some professional associations. Overall though, these systems are not very strong and do not present a serious risk. Researchers, policymakers, consultants, managers, and activists must address this fundamental ethical shortcoming. But it's also the reason that a lot of AI organisations and businesses find ethics to be so interesting. Efforts to build a really enforceable legal framework are consistently resisted when businesses or research institutes adopt morally driven "self-commitments," constantly integrate ethical issues into their public relations activity, or set their own ethical guidelines (Hagendorff, 2020).

1.1 AI in Finance

In the world of finance, artificial intelligence (AI) has become a disruptive force that is drastically altering the landscape of the sector. A number of financial activities now use AI technologies, such as machine learning and data analytics, which have improved efficiency and facilitated data-driven decision-making. Professionals in the finance sector are becoming more and more interested in "alternative data," which comes from sources other than typical firm fundamentals, security prices, and macroeconomic indicators. Voice recordings, news articles, social media posts, and satellite photos fall within this category. These incredibly huge data sources now have a big impact on trading decisions. (Goodell, et. al, 2020) AI's predictive abilities, which can spot possible market swings and vulnerabilities, support risk management are the areas being impacted by AI. Financial fraud is considerably decreased by real-time transaction data scanning provided by AI-powered fraud detection systems. AI is also essential to customer service since it enables chatbots and virtual assistants to be deployed, giving customers individualised and responsive assistance. AI's increased data sources and variables are beneficial to credit scoring algorithms, which produce more accurate and equitable creditworthiness ratings. AI also helps with regulatory compliance by automating the examination of large datasets to make sure financial regulations are followed. It is undeniable that artificial intelligence (AI) has transformed the financial sector, presenting chances for more productivity and creativity while also bringing up serious issues with data security, privacy, bias, and ethical use that need to be taken into consideration as the sector continues to change. The technological advancement in the field of finance has increased giving it a new identity as FinTech (Chen et.al. 2021).

1.2 Ethical Finance

Aligning financial practises with values and principles that prioritise responsible and good impacts on society and the environment is primary goal for promoting ethical and sustainable economic development. Incorporation of environmental, social, and governance (ESG) factors into financial strategy of the company for taking investment decisions is known as ethical finance, also often known as sustainable finance or socially responsible finance. Researchers have recently become interested in what motivates organisations to act morally and responsibly. It is believed that both internal and external forces could operate as motivators for managers to perform honourably. According to Vormedal and Ruud (2006), the rise in sustainability reporting may be clarified by mentioning a variety of social, political, regulatory, ethical, and market-based factors. Because For instance, there is rising evidence of commercial forces behind ethical, social, and environmental investment funds, which has led to an increase in stockbrokers' need for sustainability disclosures and analysts (Slater & Gilbert, 2004; Holden Meehan, 1999). Ethical finance has given rise to a debate in the past year, about amalgamation of the increased investors' interests toward the responsibility and the social performance of firms in society. The directions of the research have been primarily concerned with the utility function of the ethical investor generically understood (Cowton,1999)A wide range of tactics are included in ethical finance, such as impact investing, screening ethical investments, and supporting companies and initiatives that follow strict environmental and ethical guidelines. This strategy yields financial gains while promoting accountability, openness, and a dedication to moral principles. It is a reaction to the growing demand for ethical investing options as well as to the need for a more sustainable and ethical financial system that can deal with urgent global issues including environmental degradation, social injustice, and climate change (Darush, et. al, 2015).

The financial system greatly affects our cultures and economies, the idea of ethical finance arose as management of prudent resources. The outlook of economic activities, investment and money has greatly changed due to ethical finance, as terms like socially responsible finance or sustainable finance are being used widely. This encourages financial institutions to do more than just the objective of profit and consider moral, environmental, and social implications as well of financial decisions they take.

An experience of great shift in the fundamental ways in which we approach our financial institutions ethical finance has bought. A balance between environmental, social and moral principles and the financial goals has been encouraged.

As the end of an era approaches, a pool of opportunities by the financial sector's use of AI has opened and investors, consumers, and financial institutions navigate the complex change of world of money management. But this progress has moral and ethical ramifications as well, which are equally important and should be carefully considered. With a strong emphasis on ethics and sustainability, this introduction provides a starting point for examining the significant implications of this merger and how it can transform the way that financial institutions and society at large view the world. We will travel across the domains of innovation and responsibility in this dynamic context in an effort to comprehend how ethical finance and artificial intelligence (AI) may coexist to promote good change and build a more transparent and equitable financial environment. The general deployment of AI-based systems in organisations and this autonomy in decision-making raise ethical questions about the different environmental aspects in which an organisation functions (Brendel et.al, 2021)

The fusion of ethical finance and Artificial Intelligence (AI) is indeed an exciting and transformative frontier in the financial industry. It has the potential to revolutionize the way financial practices are conducted, making them not only more efficient but also more responsible and sustainable. This convergence holds promise for creating a financial ecosystem where profitability goes hand in hand with ethical considerations and sustainability, leading to positive outcomes for individuals, society, and the environment.

1.3 ESG and AI

Sentiment analysis algorithms hold a significant portion of the artificial intelligence potential in ESG investment. These techniques enable computers to perform a task that code could not accomplish as well: analyzing the tone of a conversation. Programs designed to analyze sentiment may be trained to read a specific kind of communication and compare word usage to an existing reference set in order to determine the tone of the exchange. A program trained to read the transcripts of a business's quarterly earnings calls, for instance, could detect the tenor of the CEO's speech, employ natural language processing to quickly pinpoint the sections of the conversation where the CEO discusses ESG-related subjects, and then deduce from the words used how dedicated the business seems to be to mitigating environmental risk (Svetlana, 2022). Artificial intelligence (AI) uses numerical techniques to address a variety of prediction, optimisation, and classification/clustering issues. In order to solve the environmental, social, and governance (ESG) issues related to sustainable company development, artificial intelligence (AI) technologies have recently been developed. While a lot of articles talk about the promise of AI, very few concentrate on real-world applications in all three ESG categories, and even fewer point out the potential ethical and social concerns that AI may raise (Burnaev, 2023).

1.4 AI in Ethical Finance

AI practises included both technical and non-technical approaches and covered a wide range of AI life cycle stages. This shows that companies are conscious of the ethical AI frameworks and principles that are currently in place, as well as the importance of ethical AI (Seppälä, 2021). Businesses will benefit greatly from AI, but there is also a great deal of responsibility involved. Because of its direct effect on people's life, several concerns about AI ethics, data governance, trust, and legality have been raised. In fact, according to Accenture's 2022 Tech Vision research, only 35% of global customers have faith in the way that businesses are implementing AI. Furthermore, 77% of respondents believe businesses should be held responsible for misusing AI.

The introduction of AI in ethical finance has changed the outlook of finance and the way the society and financial institutions take it into consideration. The following are the positive points of this mix of technology and moral:

- **Ethical Screening and Portfolio Management**:

Algorithms powered by AI can automatically verify that investments adhere to moral principles and ethical standards. This lessens the possibility of human bias while also allowing investors to create portfolios that represent their choices for sustainability and ethics. AI can also assist with real-time portfolio rebalancing and ongoing monitoring to make sure it stays in line with evolving environmental and ethical standards.

- **Risk Mitigation and Compliance**

Compliance with sustainability standards and stringent adherence to laws are common requirements of ethical finance. AI can help keep an eye on these regulations, assisting investors and financial institutions in avoiding reputational and legal hazards. AI-powered solutions have the ability to recognise possible ethical transgressions and notify the appropriate parties in advance so that problems can be resolved before they get worse.

- **Personalized and Responsible Financial Services**

AI can be used to tailor financial services to individuals according to their sustainability and ethical inclinations. This includes encouraging responsible consumption, providing investment solutions that reflect company principles, and even assisting clients in lowering their carbon footprint. As a result, the clientele is happier and more involved, believing that their financial institution understands their ethical issues.

- **Transparency and Accountability**

The foundation of ethical finance is accountability and transparency. Financial institutions may reliably track and report on their sustainability and ethical initiatives with the use of AI. It can offer real-time statistics to stakeholders, showcasing the organization's dedication to responsible finance.

- **Tackling Green washing**

A major ethical finance concern is green washing, which is the dishonest marketing of a company's goods or services as environmentally benign when they are not. Artificial intelligence (AI) can be used to examine and validate businesses' sustainability statements, lowering the possibility of green washing and guaranteeing that investments are actually in line with moral and sustainable goals.

- **Unlocking Innovation and Efficiency**:

AI can spur innovation in ethical finance by making it possible to create new, profitable, and ethically sound financial services and products. By drawing in more investors and promoting further developments in sustainable practises, these technologies may help the ethical finance industry expand.

2. NEED OF THE STUDY

A thorough investigation of this revolutionary subject is necessary for a number of reasons, including the great potential for ethical finance and AI to alter the financial sector and advance ethical and sustainable financial practises.

Cultural shifts in attitudes and technical breakthroughs in industry, it is critical to comprehend how AI can be used to align financial practises with these changing values, as ethical issues and sustainability become central to global conversation.

Research on the intersection of ethical finance and artificial intelligence can shed light on how technology can be used to accomplish social and environmental issues.

Ethical finance is not just a matter of ethics; it has significant economic implications. Investors are increasingly considering ESG factors in their decision-making.

Financial decision-making, ethical issues such algorithmic bias, data privacy, and transparency surface are issues that needs to be addressed to make sure that the combination of AI and ethical finance complies with ethical standards.

3. OBJECTIVE OF THE STUDY

The objective of the study is to examine how AI is currently being adopted in ethical finance space. To particularly know how much of it is being used in financial decision-making processes that prioritise environmental, social, and governance (ESG) factors. To determine how AI integration will be in line with socially responsible banking and ESG standards. To know the obstacles that business must overcome in order to use artificial intelligence (AI) in ethical finance.

4. LITERATURE REVIEW

Rabbani states that Artificial Intelligence (AI) is being used in every aspect of society and industry. It is also one of the subjects that has been studied the most recently. These days, banks and other financial organisations are required by AI and machine learning to gather vast volumes of client data; nonetheless, it is unclear how all of this data will be used. This research makes an effort to pinpoint the moral dilemmas surrounding the use of artificial intelligence and provides solutions based on Shariah law (Rabbani et. al, 2022). Though it seems that everyone agrees that AI should be "ethical," there is disagreement on what "ethical AI" actually is and what ethical standards, best practises, and technical requirements are necessary to make it a reality (Jobin et. al., 2019).A rapidly developing field of study, artificial intelligence (AI) uses numerical techniques to address a variety of prediction, optimisation, and classification/ clustering issues. In order to solve the environmental, social, and governance (ESG) issues related to sustainable company development, artificial intelligence (AI) technologies have recently been developed. While a lot of articles talk about the potential of AI, very few concentrate on real-world applications in all three ESG areas, and even fewer point out the possible ESG risks that AI may present.(Burnaev et. al,2023). We have seen a broad adoption of artificial intelligence (AI)-based algorithms over the past ten years. The development of AI raises a number of ethical questions. The characteristics of AI use that include responsibility, non-maleficence, transparency, fairness, and privacy have drawn attention from the growing discipline of AI ethics.(Svetlova,2022). Since the question of whether AI serves people or humanity serves AI, autonomy is the first requirement for ethical investing. Fundamentally, AI inquires as to whether information and algorithms empower or weaken a person individually: Does technology lead to a rise in self-determination? Because of this, AI humanism differs from ESG investing and advocates for a new, distinct model for moral engagement in AI-intensive enterprises: evaluation that begins with unique persons rather than groups or demographic segments and their goals. Individual principles of privacy and dignity are inherently consistent as KPIs, while both Environmental Social Governance and AI Human Impact are nonfinancial investment methods, their economic operations differ. In the larger industrial sector, ESG standards are appropriate for traditional businesses. (Brusseau,2023). Artificial intelligence (AI) is going to open up new technical possibilities that will upend the banking sector. Numerous opportunities and benefits will result from the changes for the industry, its clients, and society at large. Examples of the benefits include increased efficiency and cost savings, improved customer service offerings, and more consistent adherence to compliance rules. We discuss the ethical ramifications of AI in finance in this chapter. The application of AI in the financial sector brings up a number of general concerns in addition to ethical and legal accountability concerns. Individualised service offerings, data collecting ownership and security, the loss of many employment in the financial sector, and the systemic concerns associated with AI consolidation are additional ethical issues that need to be discussed in public debate.(Max et.al,2021). In the financial services sector, artificial intelligence has found many uses. Fair and ethical AI is becoming a goal for the entire industry as the quantity and importance of applications grow. Many ethical rules, norms, and methods have been put out in recent years. But creating moral AI solutions presents significant obstacles for model development companies. (Kurshan et.al, 2021). The importance of recognising these macroeconomic issues and their connections, with a focus on the financial industry due to its substantial investment in IT projects. As artificial intelligence continues to advance, regulatory frameworks must also change and adapt in order to properly identify and mitigate macroeconomic impacts. Ensuring responsible and ethical AI deployments will depend on the ongoing pursuit of a complete and nuanced approach to AI ethics and enforcement in an ever-evolving technological context. (Huang, et.al, 2021). AI systems have the potential to optimise resources, lessen administrative workloads, enhance human decision-making, and solve complicated problems. When AI systems are used improperly, they can result in widespread prejudice, intrusions of privacy, and a decline in democratic values. Nonetheless, federal procurement law continues to be a risky reformist agenda blind spot.(Rubensetin, 2021). The financial services sector is one that is now undergoing significant change and has drawn a lot of attention. In fact, machine learning "promises to shake up large swathes of finance," according to a recent Economist article. Financial supervisors who are worried about the behaviour and/or prudent functioning of financial organisations may also be affected by the changes brought about by AI, and ML in particular. Supervisors must, at the very least, consider the opportunities AI presents for improved safety and compliance, as well as the ways AI may be exploited to subvert the objectives of current regulations. (Wall, 2018). In India, artificial intelligence is only a continuation of computer science, not a novel concept. However, AL/ML has emerged as the most practical method across all industries. It is difficult to work without artificial intelligence, just as the insurance industry cannot function without AI and machine learning. Numerous data entry issues are quickly resolved by the automated processes, which also speed up the underwriting and simplify the claim process. The most recent developments in artificial intelligence offer an automated procedure that accurately and quickly solves any problem at a low cost. (Tripti Pal, et. al, 2023). AI technology integration into Islamic banking offers important opportunities as well as challenges that must be overcome. These challenges include following Islamic law, moral considerations, risk reduction, and the potential for decision-making bias. (Kismawad et.al, 2023). The banking and finance industry is facing previously unheard-of issues as a result of the integration of artificial intelligence (AI) and machine learning (ML) in the quickly changing financial landscape. Financial institutions must make complex decisions about investments, macroeconomic analysis, and credit evaluation as Industry 5.0 develops. To handle this complexity, sophisticated technology are needed. Moreover, effective data processing and analysis are necessary due to the steadily increasing volume of financial activities. In light of these urgent problems, researchers, academics, and business professionals are looking for thorough understandings of how AI and ML might support resilience, guarantee sustainable development, and implement human-centered practises in the financial sector. (Irfan, 2023). The way financial services are provided and used in the modern world has been profoundly impacted by developments in artificial intelligence and machine learning. The field of finance is seeing an increase in the complexity of key financial decisions like credit evaluation, macroeconomic analysis, and investment decision making. In the realm of finance, artificial intelligence and machine learning have grown in significance due to their remarkable success and previously unheard-of accuracy. (Irfan, et. al, 2023). Ahmed examined the moral issues surrounding artificial intelligence's application in banking. Numerous ethical problems, such as inaccurate credit rating, misinformation spreading, miss-selling, and unauthorized banking transactions, have been found through the use of AI(Ahmed,2022). Society and humanity is already impacting due to AI applications. A large number of jobs can be replaced by the autonomous vehicles, and this can totally transform the transportation and industries that are associated with it. For example, short-haul flights and hospitality services along highways will be impacted if driverless cars enable passengers to sleep and work during the journey. AI-recruiters are known to exhibit human biases because the training data inherits the same return on capital and return on labor is posed to create social unrest and upheavals. The future of work and future of humanity will be affected by AI and plans need to be formulated and put in place. Building AI ethically and having ethical AI are urgent and critical. Unfortunately, building ethical AI is an enormously complex and challenging task.(Keng Siau, Weiyu Wang, 2020). The ethical behaviour of AI will be determined by its industrial and practical applications. Practical issues pose a significant barrier to fairness metrics and ethical AI research, despite their abundance. attaining moral systems in practical applications. Industrial systems have many difficulties, such as competing financial motivations and organisational difficulties, among others and the absence of regulatory frameworks. Addressing such issues is of crucial role in raising the likelihood of moral AI systems that advance society at large (chen et.al.,2021).

5. CONCLUSION

The fusion of AI and ethical finance is becoming a transformative era for both financial institutions and society as a whole. This dynamic and evolving field holds the promise of reshaping financial decision-making processes, with profound implications for the industry's sustainability and ethical commitment. AI's increasing integration into financial operations, encompassing fraud detection, portfolio optimization, investment analysis, and risk management, has been instrumental in enhancing efficiency, accuracy, and risk mitigation. On the other side, ethical finance, rooted in principles of environmental, social, and governance (ESG) standards and socially responsible banking, has been revolutionized by AI's ability to evaluate these standards and pinpoint opportunities for ethical investments.

The present study has provided an extensive investigation into the pragmatic implementations of artificial intelligence in the field of ethical finance. It has shed light on the existing conditions and obstacles encountered by financial institutions in their efforts to leverage the combined influence of these two formidable entities. By conducting a methodical examination of publicly accessible research articles and reports, the investigation has unveiled the complex terrain where ethical finance and artificial intelligence intersect. This convergence is a social and moral imperative as well as a frontier in technology.

It is the necessity of proactive ethical participation in the development and implementation of AI inside the financial industry. To guarantee that the combination of AI and ethical finance promotes ethical and sustainable financial practises, it is crucial to strike a balance between technology and ethics. The demand for financial firms to incorporate social responsibility and ethical issues into their AI-driven initiatives must be heard. In addition to creating more ethical investment options, this equilibrium will boost confidence among investors and the general public.

Ethical finance being a very broad term in itself the integration of AI with ethical finance had made it more applicable and accurate while overcoming the challenge it used to face. Technology is helpful in every field of work, and keeping an eye on the ethical practices followed by the companies is itself a huge task. AI has eased this task many folded. Commitment to openness, responsibility, and the larger welfare of society should be maintained by financial institutions they integrate ethical finance and artificial intelligence into their operations. Combining these two fields could enhance financial decision-making while also advancing the more general objectives of social responsibility and environmental sustainability. The financial industry holds a responsibility this convergence and sculpt the financial landscape of the future into one that is ethically and technologically progressive. By doing this, financial institutions may set the example for more ethical and sustainable financial practises, which will ultimately improve society's perception of both financial institutions and individuals.

6. FURTHER SCOPE OF STUDY

The finance sector will unavoidably undergo change when AI technologies are integrated with ethical finance. With this combination of functioning, the current marketplaces and corporate models will experience significant changes. The industry would undergo a major transformation as a result of new inventions and technical developments. This is just start of a new era where the technology will also help with the moral and ethical policing, this study cannot totally tell about the effect of this integration as it is at the initial stage. But it can further be elaborated and studied as to assess the effects of implementing AI in ethical finance, by quantitative evaluation. This could involve evaluating how integrating AI affects risk mitigation, investment performance, and compliance with ESG guidelines. Examine viewpoints of stakeholders on the application of AI in ethical finance from a range of stakeholders, including investors, financial institutions, regulatory agencies, and the general public. Further, methods for evaluating how ethical investments powered by AI will affect societal and environmental aspects like lowering carbon emissions, promoting social justice, and strengthening corporate governance.

7. LIMITATION

The study's effectiveness in systematically reviewing research manuscripts and reports is dependent on the availability and quality of the data sources. Limited or biased data may impact the comprehensiveness and validity of the findings. Findings from this study may be specific to the sample of research manuscripts and reports reviewed and may not be entirely generalizable to all companies or regions, given the diversity of AI applications and ethical finance practices. The challenges faced by companies when blending AI and ethical finance may vary significantly by industry. This study might not capture the nuances specific to different sectors within the financial industry.

REFERENCE

Anshari, M., Almunawar, M. N., Masri, M., & Hrdy, M. (2021). Financial technology with ai-enabled and ethical challenges. *Society*, *58*(3), 189–195. doi:10.100712115-021-00592-w

Brendel, A. B., Mirbabaie, M., Lembcke, T. B., & Hofeditz, L. (2021). Ethical management of artificial intelligence. *Sustainability (Basel)*, *13*(4), 1974. doi:10.3390u13041974

Brusseau, J. (2023). AI human impact: Toward a model for ethical investing in AI-intensive companies. *Journal of Sustainable Finance & Investment*, *13*(2), 1030–1057. doi:10.1080/20430795.2021.1874212

Chen, J., Storchan, V., & Kurshan, E. (2021). Beyond fairness metrics: Roadblocks and challenges for ethical ai in practice. *arXiv preprint arXiv:2108.06217.*

Chen, T. H., & Chang, R. C. (2021). Using machine learning to evaluate the influence of FinTech patents: The case of Taiwan's financial industry. *Journal of Computational and Applied Mathematics*, *390*, 113215. doi:10.1016/j.cam.2020.113215

Cowton, C. (1999). Accounting and financial ethics: From margin to mainstream? *Business Ethics (Oxford, England)*, *8*(2), 99–107. doi:10.1111/1467-8608.00134

Darus, F., Mad, S., & Nejati, M. (2015). Ethical and social responsibility of financial institutions: Influence of internal and external pressure. *Procedia Economics and Finance*, *28*, 183–189. doi:10.1016/S2212-5671(15)01099-0

Eitel-Porter, R. (2021). Beyond the promise: Implementing ethical AI. *AI and Ethics*, *1*(1), 73–80. doi:10.100743681-020-00011-6

Floridi, L., Cowls, J., Beltrametti, M., Chatila, R., Chazerand, P., Dignum, V., & Vayena, E. (2021). An ethical framework for a good AI society: Opportunities, risks, principles, and recommendations. *Ethics, governance, and policies in artificial intelligence*, 19-39.

Floridi, L., Cowls, J., Beltrametti, M., Chatila, R., Chazerand, P., Dignum, V., & Vayena, E. (2021). An ethical framework for a good AI society: Opportunities, risks, principles, and recommendations. *Ethics, governance, and policies in artificial intelligence*, 19-39.

Gardner, A., Smith, A. L., Steventon, A., Coughlan, E., & Oldfield, M. (2022). Ethical funding for trustworthy AI: Proposals to address the responsibilities of funders to ensure that projects adhere to trustworthy AI practice. *AI and Ethics*, *2*(2), 1–15. doi:10.100743681-021-00069-w PMID:34790951

Goodell, J. W., Kumar, S., Lim, W. M., & Pattnaik, D. (2021). Artificial intelligence and machine learning in finance: Identifying foundations, themes, and research clusters from bibliometric analysis. *Journal of Behavioral and Experimental Finance*, *32*, 100577. doi:10.1016/j.jbef.2021.100577

Hagendorff, T. (2020). The ethics of AI ethics: An evaluation of guidelines. *Minds and Machines*, *30*(1), 99–120. doi:10.100711023-020-09517-8

Huang, J. Y., Gupta, A., & Youn, M. (2021). Survey of EU ethical guidelines for commercial AI: Case studies in financial services. *AI and Ethics*, *1*(4), 569–577. doi:10.100743681-021-00048-1

Irfan, M., Elhoseny, M., Kassim, S., & Metawa, N. (2023). *Advanced Machine Learning Algorithms for Complex Financial Applications*. https://www.scopus.com/inward/record.uri?eid=2-s2.0-85147390132&doi=10.4018%2f978-1-6684-4483-2&partnerID=40&md5=, doi:10.4018/978-1-6684-4483-2

Irfan, M., Elmogy, M., Majid, M. S. A., & El-Sappagh, S. (2023). The impact of AI innovation on financial sectors in the era of industry 5.0. *The Impact of AI Innovation on Financial Sectors in the Era of Industry 5.0,* (pp. 1-320). Research Gate. 10.4018/9798369300824

Jobin, A., Ienca, M., & Vayena, E. (2019). The global landscape of AI ethics guidelines. *Nature Machine Intelligence*, *1*(9), 389–399. doi:10.103842256-019-0088-2

Max, R., Kriebitz, A., & Von Websky, C. (2021). Ethical considerations about the implications of artificial intelligence in finance. *Handbook on Ethics in Finance*, 577-592. Research Gate.

Najem, R., Amr, M. F., Bahnasse, A., & Talea, M. (2022). Artificial Intelligence for Digital Finance (Vol. 203). Axes and Techniques,Procedia Computer Science., https://www.sciencedirect.com/science/article/pii/S1877050922006974, , ISSN 1877-0509. doi:10.1016/j.procs.2022.07.092

Pal, T., Irfan, M., & Kassim, S. B. (2023). How do Machine Learning (ML) techniques benefit the insurance industry? An exploratory study. *The Impact of AI Innovation on Financial Sectors in the Era of Industry 5.0*, (pp. 108-130). IGI Global. doi:10.4018/979-8-3693-0082-4.ch007

Rabbani, M. R., Sarea, A., Khan, S., & Abdullah, Y. (2022). Ethical concerns in artificial intelligence (AI): The role of RegTech and Islamic finance. In *Artificial Intelligence for Sustainable Finance and Sustainable Technology: Proceedings of ICGER,* (pp. 381-390). Springer International Publishing

Ridho Kismawadi, E., Irfan, M., & Shah, S. M. A. R. (2023). Revolutionizing Islamic finance: Artificial intelligence's role in the future of industry. *The Impact of AI Innovation on Financial Sectors in the Era of Industry 5.0*, (pp. 184-207). IGI Global. https://www.scopus.com/inward/record.uri?eid=2-s2.0-85173027737&doi=10.4018%2f979-8-3693-0082-4.ch011&partnerID=40&, 10.4018/979-8-3693-0082-4.ch011

Seppälä, A., Birkstedt, T., & Mäntymäki, M. (2021, December). From ethical AI principles to governed AI. In *Proceedings of the 42nd International Conference on Information Systems (ICIS2021)*. Research Gate.

Siau, K., & Wang, W. (2020). Artificial intelligence (AI) ethics: Ethics of AI and ethical AI. [JDM]. *Journal of Database Management*, *31*(2), 74–87. doi:10.4018/JDM.2020040105

S&P Global. (2020). *How can AI help ESG investing?* S&P Global. https://www.spglobal.com/en/research-insights/articles/how-can-ai-help-esg-investing

Svetlova, E. (2022). AI ethics and systemic risks in finance. *AI and Ethics*, *2*(4), 713–725. doi:10.100743681-021-00129-1 PMID:35043105

Wall, L. D. (2018). Some financial regulatory implications of artificial intelligence. *Journal of Economics and Business*, *100*, 55–63. doi:10.1016/j.jeconbus.2018.05.003

Chapter 3
Fintech Innovations:
Risk Mitigation Strategies in Islamic Finance

Early Ridho Kismawadi
https://orcid.org/0000-0002-9420-5212
IAIN Langsa, Indonesia

Mohammad Irfan
https://orcid.org/0000-0002-4956-1170
Business School, NSB Academy, India

Uun Dwi Al Muddatstsir
MAN Insan Cendekia, Indonesia

Fatima Muhammad Abdulkarim
Federal University Dutse, Nigeria

ABSTRACT

The purpose of this research is to examine risk mitigation strategies in Islamic finance, specifically fintech, in depth. The research methodology for this conceptual chapter consists of an exhaustive examination of the existing literature, academic papers, industry reports, and case studies that pertain to fintech innovation and risk mitigation strategies in Islamic Finance. By means of synthesising and analysing pre-existing information, this chapter endeavours to furnish an all-encompassing comprehension of the subject matter. This study is anticipated to make a valuable contribution to the growth of an Islamic finance industry characterised by safety, stability, innovation, and adherence to Islamic principles.

DOI: 10.4018/979-8-3693-1038-0.ch003

1. INTRODUCTION

The Islamic financial system has experienced substantial growth in recent decades as a result of the increasing need for financial products and services that adhere to Shariah principles. (Beik & Nursyamsiah, 2021; Young, 2018). However, as in the conventional financial industry, risk remains a crucial component of the Islamic financial system's success and stability. The difficulty of mitigating risk is exacerbated by the complexity of the structure of Islamic financial products and transactions involving sharia principles. In this regard, innovations in financial technology (fintech) offer the potential to address these issues(Alexander & Karametaxas, 2021; Anshari et al., 2021; Truby et al., 2022). Fintech, which includes technologies such as artificial intelligence, blockchain, big data analytics, and digital financial services, can enhance the Islamic financial system's efficiency, transparency, and dependability.

In the context of Islamic finance, a sharia-based financial system has emerged as a more moral and religiously-compliant alternative. However, Islamic finance also confronts significant risks that threaten the system's stability and viability. Risks such as market risk, credit risk, operational risk, and Islamic compliance risk must be effectively managed. In recent years, innovations in financial technology, such as fintech, have garnered worldwide attention. Fintech provides a variety of technological solutions that can reduce risk and boost efficiency in the financial sector. Fintech has the potential to be a powerful risk mitigation instrument within the context of Islamic finance.

Consequently, research on risk mitigation strategies in Islamic finance enabled by fintech innovation has become crucial(Rahadian & Thamrin, 2023). This study seeks to examine fintech-based risk mitigation strategies applicable to the Islamic financial system. In addition, the study seeks to identify the benefits and challenges associated with the application of AI, Machine Learning, and Blockchain in mitigating Islamic finance risks, and to offer practical guidance for practitioners and policymakers in the Islamic fintech industry. This research is anticipated to contribute to the sustainable and stable growth of the Islamic fintech industry by enhancing the understanding of how AI, Machine Learning, and Blockchain can be employed to mitigate risks in Islamic fintech systems.

The purpose of this study is to examine in-depth risk mitigation strategies in Islamic finance, particularly in fintech. We will identify viable strategies, assess the associated benefits and challenges, and provide practitioners and policymakers in the Islamic fintech industry with practical guidance. Thus, it is anticipated that this research will contribute significantly to the development of a secure, stable, and innovative Islamic fintech system. Our research seeks to increase understanding of the use of AI, Machine Learning, and Blockchain for risk mitigation in Islamic finance, particularly fintech, by providing a comprehensive background.

It is anticipated that the findings of this study will provide valuable insights for the Islamic finance industry and encourage the adoption of suitable risk management strategies. Models of artificial intelligence must be developed in accordance with sharia principles. Although the application of artificial intelligence and big data analytics is promising for mitigating Islamic finance risks, the incorporation of Islamic aspects into algorithms is still insufficient. Therefore, additional research is required to develop AI models that take sharia requirements into account more thoroughly. AI technology and big data analytics can help identify patterns and risk trends in general, but more research is required to identify specific risk patterns within the context of Islamic fintech. This includes the risks of sharia compliance, contracts that violate sharia principles, and the reputational risk associated with sharia compliance. The development of Islamic finance-relevant and -appropriate fintechs will be aided by research that focuses on identifying typical risk patterns in Islamic finance.

In Islamic fintech, there is a dearth of research focusing on the comprehensive implementation of AI, Machine Learning, and Blockchain. AI, Machine Learning, and Blockchain are recognised as promising risk mitigation technologies, but require additional research. By bridging this research divide, it is anticipated that your research will make a significant contribution to understanding and addressing the challenges of using AI, Machine Learning, and Blockchain for risk mitigation in Islamic-compliant fintech innovations.

2. ARTIFICIAL INTELLIGENCE IN RISK MITIGATION

The goal of the computer science discipline of Artificial Intelligence (AI) is to develop systems capable of simulating human intelligence. (Barredo Arrieta et al., 2020; Goodfellow et al., 2020; Miller, 2019; Q. Yang et al., 2019). In artificial intelligence, algorithms and computational techniques are used to enable computers to perform tasks that normally require human intellect, such as speech recognition, natural language comprehension, decision making, and learning(Ridho Kismawadi et al., 2023). AI incorporates a variety of techniques, including machine learning, natural language processing, artificial neural networks, and fuzzy logic, for processing information, identifying patterns, and making intelligent decisions. AI's primary objective is to create systems that can think, learn, and adapt autonomously to a variety of situations, as well as effectively and efficiently address problems.

Figure 1. Artificial intelligence (AI) market size worldwide in 2021 with a forecast until 2030(in million U.S. dollars)
(Next Move Strategy Consulting Graph by Statista)

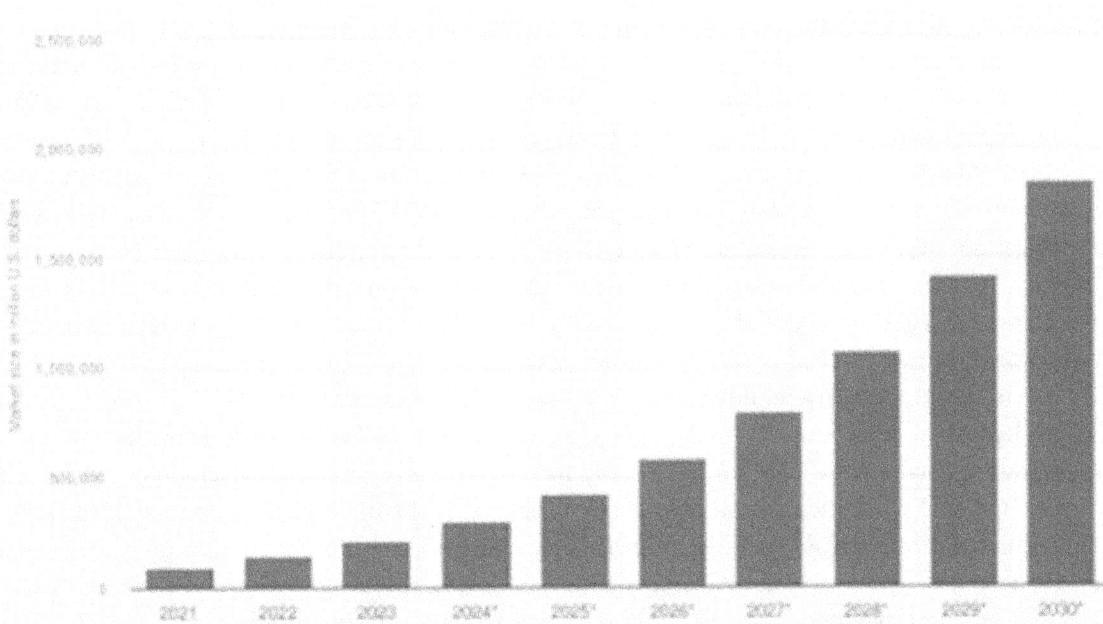

Next Move Strategy Consulting predicts a robust expansion in the artificial intelligence (AI) business over the next decade. The current value of approximately 100 billion U.S. dollars is projected to increase by a factor of twenty by 2030, reaching roughly two trillion U.S. dollars. The AI market encompasses a wide range of industries. Various business sectors, including supply chains, marketing, product development, research, analysis, and others, will use artificial intelligence into their operations. Chatbots, AI-powered picture generation, and mobile applications are prominent advancements that will enhance the field of AI in the upcoming years.

In the financial industry, artificial intelligence (AI) technology plays a crucial role in identifying, analysing, and mitigating risks. In this context, artificial intelligence techniques such as machine learning and predictive analytics can be used to process data and generate useful information for financial institutions. Initially, AI aids in risk identification by analyzing historical data with machine learning. Algorithms based on artificial intelligence can uncover concealed patterns in risk data, such as factors that contribute to credit risk. Moreover, AI is able to conduct a more in-depth risk analysis using machine learning techniques. Complex data can be processed to reveal complex relationships between risk variables, such as using predictive analytics to forecast market risk or policy shifts.

AI plays a crucial role in the creation of more accurate and efficient risk models (Mallikarjuna & Rao, 2019; Seo & Lee, 2021; X. Zhang & Mahadevan, 2019). Using machine learning, financial institutions can create risk models based on exhaustive and representative data. These models can combine historical data, real-time market data, and other risk factors to generate more accurate risk forecasts, such as credit risk models that can evaluate borrower eligibility and default risk more accurately. Using machine learning and predictive analytics, AI can also assist with portfolio management. By analysing market data and asset performance in real-time, AI algorithms can provide superior investment recommendations. AI plays a role in market surveillance and provides early warning signals for dangers that must be anticipated.

By analyzing data, recognizing patterns, and providing valuable insights, artificial intelligence becomes a potent instrument for mitigating financial risk, enabling financial institutions to make more informed decisions, mitigate risk, and optimize portfolio performance(Fallahi et al., 2022; Raffinetti, 2023). The deployment of AI to mitigate financial risks provides financial institutions with additional benefits. First, AI can increase operational efficiency by automating processes that previously required a significant amount of time and labor. For instance, AI can automate routine tasks such as credit analysis and portfolio monitoring, allowing employees to focus on tasks requiring strategic decision-making. Additionally, AI can reduce the impact of human bias on decision making. Using objective machine learning algorithms, decisions can be made based on the analysis of factual data, unaffected by personal preferences or opinions.

On fintech platforms, artificial intelligence (AI) technology can be used to predict Islamic financial risk. Using historical data, market trends, and economic factors, AI algorithms can identify potential threats to Islamic finance. In addition, AI is able to provide early warnings of emergent risks, allowing Islamic financial institutions to take proactive measures. AI can be used to analyze historical data related to financial transactions conducted on fintech platforms within the context of Islamic fintech. AI can, for instance, analyze historical information regarding the usage patterns of Islamic financial products and services, payment patterns, and other user behavior. Using algorithms for machine learning, AI can identify patterns and relationships concealed within this historical data. AI can, for instance, identify lending risk patterns that can impact loan repayment on Islamic fintech platforms. AI is capable of analyzing market trends and economic factors pertinent to Islamic finance, in addition to historical data. Algorithms powered by artificial intelligence can monitor and process market and economic data in real-time in order to obtain more accurate information about market conditions and factors that can impact Islamic finance. AI can analyze, for instance, changes in interest rates, fluctuations in exchange rates, or policy shifts that affect investment or financing in Islamic fintech.

In Islamic fintech, AI's ability to provide early warnings is equally as essential as its ability to predict risks. Algorithms based on artificial intelligence can be programmed to monitor market data in real-time and detect fluctuations or turmoil that may signal potential risk. For instance, if there is a significant change in the value of a currency that affects transactions in Islamic fintech, AI can provide financial institutions or platform users with an early warning to take appropriate action(Boto Ferreira et al., 2021; Lahmiri & Bekiros, 2019; Ogbeibu et al., 2022; Pnevmatikakis et al., 2021). By employing artificial intelligence technology, Islamic fintechs can benefit from improved risk forecasting. AI aids in identifying potential hazards by analyzing historical data, market trends, and economic factors. In addition, AI enables financial institutions or consumers of Islamic fintech to take proactive action by providing early warning of emerging risks. This contributes to the enhancement of risk management and financial stability within the context of Islamic fintech.

AI can be used to enhance Islamic fintech's supervision and monitoring of sharia compliance. Using AI algorithms, transactions and financial activities conducted on fintech platforms can be analyzed and any violations of sharia law automatically identified. AI can detect, for instance, transactions that contravene the principle prohibiting usury (interest) or the principle of fairness and fairness in risk sharing.

The primary benefit of AI in Islamic financial risk prediction is its ability to process and accurately analyze large and complex quantities of data. AI can extract insights from both structured and unstructured data, such as transaction data, user behavior data, financial reports, market news, and other data sources. By integrating these multiple data sources, AI is able to generate more thorough and comprehensive risk predictions(de Manuel et al., 2023; Y. Zhang et al., 2021; Zheng et al., 2023). In Islamic fintech, AI can also integrate predictive analytics and machine learning techniques to create more accurate and effective risk models. AI is able to predict potential future risks by utilizing predictive analytics techniques and machine learning algorithms that can identify patterns and relationships between various risk factors. For instance, AI can utilize historical data on asset price movement trends within Islamic financial markets to forecast price fluctuations and potential market risks.

In order to provide early warning of hazards, AI can monitor market data and factors affecting Islamic finance in real time. For instance, AI can incorporate data from multiple sources, such as market news, economic reports, and financial indicators, and notify financial institutions or Islamic fintech users of significant changes that may affect financial risk.

With the application of artificial intelligence technology to the prediction of Islamic financial risk, financial institutions and consumers of Islamic fintech are able to manage risk more quickly and effectively(Hu & Chen, 2022; Zhong & Wang, 2022). AI can assist in enhancing Islamic compliance, identifying potential risks, and providing early warning of emergent threats. In the context of fintech, AI technology can be a potent instrument for maintaining the stability and sustainability of Islamic finance.

3. METHODOLOGY

A comprehensive review of extant literature, academic papers, industry reports, and case studies pertaining to Fintech Innovations and Risk Mitigation Strategies in Islamic Finance comprised the research methodology for this conceptual paper. Through the process of synthesis and analysis of the existing information, the objective of this paper is to furnish a comprehensive comprehension of the subject. Furthermore, real-world illustrations and case studies will be incorporated where relevant to elucidate the concepts of Fintech Innovations and Risk Mitigation Strategies in Islamic Finance. It is essential to note that primary data collection was not conducted for this paper; rather, it is an expansion of prior research and knowledge in the field. Subsequently, we shall examine a multitude of facets pertaining to Fintech Innovations and Risk Mitigation Strategies within the context of Islamic Finance.

4. MACHINE LEARNING IN FINANCIAL RISK ANALYSIS

Machine learning is a subfield of artificial intelligence that enables a computer or system to enhance its own performance based on its own experience and data(Pal et al., 2023). Machine learning utilizes algorithms to analyze data, recognize patterns, and make predictions or decisions without being explicitly programmed(Al Janabi, 2022; Du & Elston, 2022; Fieberg et al., 2023; Gao, 2022; Mahmood et al., 2022; Moon & Kim, 2023). During the learning process, machine learning algorithms discover the relationship between data input and desired output, enabling them to generalize and make accurate predictions on previously unseen data. Several machine learning techniques, such as supervised learning, unsupervised learning, and reinforcement learning, can be applied to domains such as pattern recognition, natural language processing, and data analysis.

Figure 2. Leading machine learning operations/platform startups worldwide in 2023, by funding raised (in million U.S. dollars)
(NFX Graph by Statista)

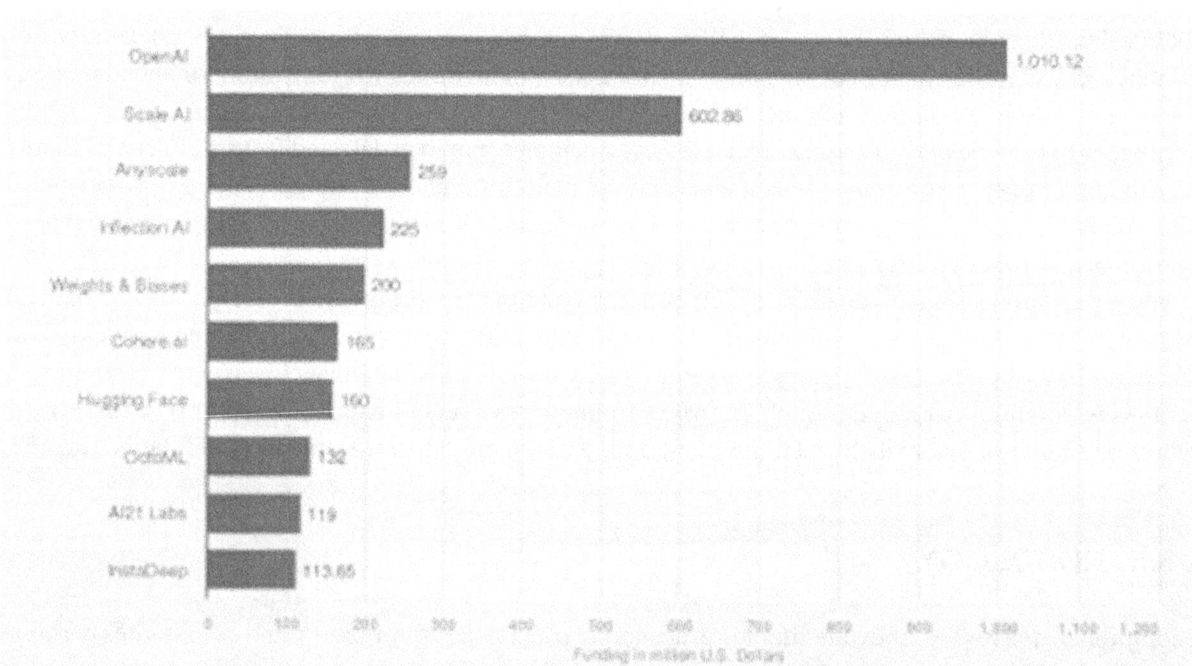

In 2022, Open AI, the organisation that produced the viral hits Dall-E and ChatGPT, received the most funding for machine learning operations and platforms. The total value of the funding secured for the company in 2015 surpassed one billion U.S. dollars. In contrast, the following business in the identical industry was valued at slightly more than $600 million. Nonetheless, each of the ten most heavily funded MLOps ventures had received more than $100 million in funding.

Islamic fintech, machine learning algorithms can be used to identify risk patterns, forecast future risk trends, and generate improved risk mitigation recommendations. Algorithms capable of learning from historical data and recognizing complex patterns can provide Islamic financial institutions with valuable risk management insights(Abuzov, 2023; Bian et al., 2023; Cheng, 2023; Lestari et al., 2023; Varma et al., 2022). In the case of credit risk mitigation on Islamic fintech platforms, for instance, machine learning algorithms can analyze loan-related historical data, such as borrower profiles, financial information, and previous transaction data. From this information, machine learning algorithms can identify default-related risk patterns. An algorithm may determine, for instance, that debtors with poor credit histories or inconsistent repayment patterns have a greater risk of default. Thus, machine learning algorithms can assist in identifying debtors with a high credit risk potential.

Machine learning algorithms are capable of predicting future risk trends by integrating historical data with external factors affecting Islamic finance(Irfan, Elhoseny, et al., 2023). By monitoring the most recent market and economic data, for instance, machine learning algorithms can identify patterns of asset price fluctuations, interest rate changes, and regulatory changes that affect financial risk. With this analysis, machine learning algorithms can anticipate risk trends and provide insight into potential future risk changes.

Next, based on the performed risk analysis, machine learning algorithms can generate more effective risk mitigation suggestions(Giri et al., 2021; Iqbal, 2022). For instance, in credit risk mitigation, machine learning algorithms can recommend more precise profit-sharing ratios, risk-appropriate funding limits, and efficient risk monitoring strategies. These recommendations are founded on a comprehensive analysis of data and risk patterns uncovered by machine learning algorithms.

Various Islamic fintech industries contain case studies demonstrating the successful implementation of machine learning in mitigating financial risk(Albastaki, 2020; Rabbani et al., 2023; Raza Rabbani et al., 2022). For instance, an Islamic finance platform could employ machine learning algorithms to analyze transactional and user profile data from the past. The algorithm can recognize risk patterns indicative of fraud or dubious activity. As a result, the platform can take prompt action to mitigate potential threats, such as barring suspicious accounts or enhancing identity verification procedures. In addition, there are case studies demonstrating the use of machine learning in Islamic fintech to mitigate investment risks(Al Janabi, 2022; Cheng, 2023; Lestari et al., 2023; Varma et al., 2022). A fintech company that offers an investment platform can analyze market data and asset performance with machine learning algorithms. The algorithm can foresee market risk trends and make asset allocation recommendations to reduce risk and increase profit potential.

This type of case study demonstrates how the implementation of machine learning algorithms in Islamic fintech has assisted financial institutions in identifying risk patterns, predicting future risk trends, and developing more effective risk mitigation recommendations. With ever-evolving machine learning techniques and more precise analytical capabilities, machine learning algorithms can become potent instruments for managing financial risk in the Islamic fintech industry more efficiently and effectively.

There are numerous advantages to implementing machine learning to mitigate financial hazards in Islamic fintech. One of machine learning's primary advantages is its capacity to improve the precision of risk predictions. Complex patterns can be learned by machine learning algorithms and big data can be utilized to generate more accurate risk predictions than traditional methods. With more accurate modelling, financial institutions can more precisely identify risks and take the necessary measures to mitigate them.

For instance, an Islamic fintech platform that provides Islamic financing could employ machine learning to analyze historical data and identify risk patterns in particular financing products. Using historical data such as borrower profiles, financial information, and other factors, machine learning algorithms can detect patterns of concealed default. Using this pattern, machine learning algorithms can construct predictive models that can identify prospective borrowers with a high default risk. Consequently, the platform can make more informed decisions regarding the approval or denial of financing applications based on the identified risks.

Moreover, machine learning can provide early warnings for emergent risks. Real-time machine learning algorithms can monitor Islamic finance-relevant market data, industry trends, and economic factors. Algorithms based on machine learning can alert financial institutions or consumers of Islamic fintech to significant changes that could affect financial risk. For instance, if there is a change in regulatory policy that has an impact on Islamic financial products, machine learning algorithms can alert financial institutions so they can make the necessary adjustments and take preventative action.

The use of machine learning to mitigate financial risk can also be advantageous for portfolio management. Algorithms that utilize machine learning can analyze market data and asset performance in real-time to improve investment recommendations. For instance, machine learning algorithms can provide information about trends and correlations between various assets, enabling financial institutions to diversify their portfolios more effectively and reduce risks.

In studies involving Islamic fintech platforms, the application of machine learning has proved effective in enhancing financial risk management. A platform for Islamic financing, for instance, utilizes machine learning algorithms to analyze historical data and external factors such as market developments, regulatory changes, and industry-related news. By utilizing this analysis, the platform is able to more precisely identify risks and provide borrowers with improved risk mitigation recommendations. The effect is an increase in the quality of disbursed financing and a decrease in the risk of default. Through such case studies, it is evident that the implementation of machine learning algorithms in Islamic fintech has yielded tangible benefits in terms of identifying risk patterns, predicting future risk trends, and providing more effective recommendations for risk mitigation. By continually enhancing machine learning techniques and leveraging technological advancements, the potential for machine learning in Islamic fintech to mitigate financial risks is growing.

5. BLOCKCHAIN FOR RISK MITIGATION

Blockchain is a technology that employs a distributed network to transparently and securely record and verify transactions(J. Chen et al., 2023; Ivanchenkova et al., 2023; Kazancoglu et al., 2023; Kolisnyk et al., 2023). These transactions are arranged in blocks that are cryptographically linked, producing an immutable chain of transactions. Every transaction in the blockchain is recorded and accessible to all participants, creating a high level of transparency.

Blockchain is a technology that can be used to enhance the transparency, security, and dependability of financial transactions in Islamic fintech. Blockchain is a distributed network that transparently and securely verifies and records every transaction. In the context of Islamic finance, blockchain technology can reduce the risk of fraud, counterfeiting, and noncompliance with Islamic law. Transparency is one of the primary advantages of blockchain in Islamic fintech(Dong et al., 2023; Dua et al., 2023; Malhotra et al., 2022; Sharma et al., 2022; Vannucci et al., 2021). Every transaction in a blockchain is recorded in blocks that are cryptographically linked, and the transaction data is accessible to all parties. This enables users of Islamic fintech to easily monitor and verify each transaction without the need for a third-party intermediary. In Islamic finance, for instance, blockchain can be used to record every financing and payment transaction so that stakeholders can transparently monitor the flow of funds and ensure sharia compliance.

Security is another significant benefit of blockchain. Each transaction recorded in the blockchain is secured by robust cryptography, making it difficult to alter or falsify. In addition, blockchain employs a consensus mechanism for validating and approving legitimate transactions among its participants. This implies that all transactions recorded in the blockchain have been subjected to a rigorous validation procedure, thereby enhancing confidence and reducing the risk of deception or data manipulation. In the settlement of asset purchasing and selling transactions in Islamic fintech, for instance, blockchain can be used to digitally record asset ownership and guarantee that transactions are conducted securely and in accordance with sharia principles.

The implementation of blockchain technology in Islamic financial institutions can also aid in risk management. For instance, in microfinance or the financing of small- and medium-sized enterprises (SMEs), blockchain can be used to document and verify pertinent data such as borrower profiles, financial information, and credit history. By employing blockchain technology, financial institutions can reduce fraud risk, optimize risk management processes, and offer more efficient financing to sharia-compliant SMBs.

Moreover, blockchain technology can be implemented in Islamic payment and remittance systems. In this context, blockchain technology can record every payment transaction and assure shariah compliance for disbursements. For instance, Islamic fintech platforms can use blockchain to provide low-cost, transparent, and intermediary-free money transmission services directly between senders and receivers. This can help reduce the risk of fraud in the Islamic finance industry and expedite the payment process.

By implementing blockchain in Islamic fintech, financial institutions can reduce the risk of fraud, counterfeiting, and Islamic noncompliance by leveraging the technology's transparency, security, and dependability. By providing verifiable and transparently verifiable records, blockchain provides a solid foundation for Islamic financial institutions and fintech users to establish trust and preserve the integrity of the Islamic financial system.

6. ISLAMIC FINTECH INNOVATION

Islamic fintech innovation plays a crucial role in the development of a financial system that adheres to sharia principles. Islamic fintech combines sharia principles with contemporary technology to provide financial solutions that are more inclusive, efficient, and consistent with religious values. In this context, AI, machine learning, and blockchain technologies play a crucial role in spurring innovation and strengthening the Islamic financial system(Irfan, Elmogy, et al., 2023). First, AI (Artificial Intelligence) and machine learning have the potential to improve Islamic fintech's efficacy, precision, and decision-making(Burger & Weinmann, 2022; Jena, 2022; Mohd Haridan et al., 2023; Thompson & Rust, 2023).

Figure 3. Number of fintech users worldwide from 2017 to 2027, by segment (in billions)
(Statista Digital Market Insights Graph by Statista)

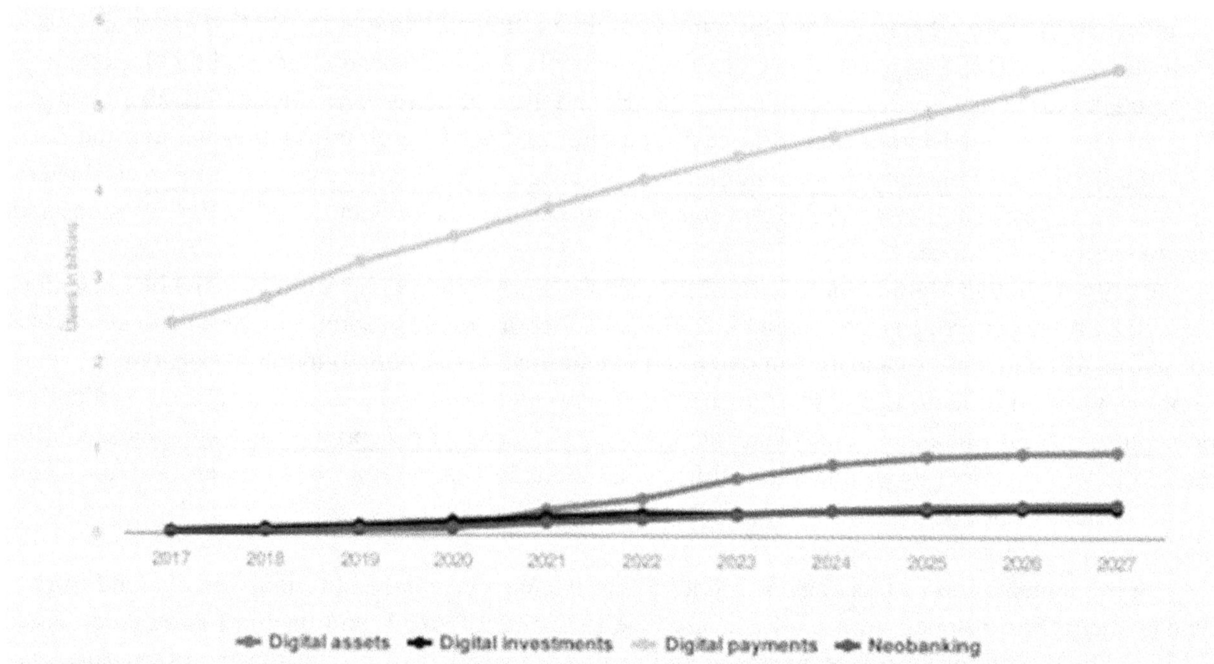

AI and machine learning can analyze historical data, market trends, and economic factors in the context of risk mitigation to identify potential threats to Islamic finance. Algorithms that utilize machine learning can identify complex risk patterns and predict future risk trends. This enables Islamic financial institutions to take proactive measures for risk management, such as a more accurate determination of interest rates, risk-appropriate credit limits, and effective risk monitoring strategies.

Global fintech user growth is anticipated to accelerate annually across all industry segments between 2023 and 2027. Global fintech users were estimated to number 5.62 billion as of 2023, with the digital payments sector comprising the greatest proportion of users (4.4 billion). It is anticipated that by 2027, the quantity of fintech users will surpass seven billion. Additional details and methodology explanations are available in the Digital Market Insights report by Statista.

AI and machine learning can be utilized in various aspects of Islamic fintech, including credit risk analysis, transaction monitoring, portfolio management, Islamic pattern recognition, and natural language processing for user interaction. By analyzing credit patterns, for instance, Islamic financing platforms can use machine learning to identify consumers with a high risk of default. The use of AI and machine learning improves the efficacy and precision of delivering Islamic financial services and reduces the risks associated with sharia compliance. Second, blockchain plays an important function in Islamic financial technology. Blockchain's transparent, secure, and decentralized character can increase the transparency, security, and dependability of Islamic finance transactions. Blockchain enables transparent recording of verified transactions, thereby facilitating the tracking and verification of every transaction by all parties involved. In addition, blockchain protects transactions from the risk of forgery or manipulation due to the irreversibility of every recorded transaction. Blockchain can be used to document and verify sharia compliance in financial transactions such as financing, investment, and fund transfers. Islamic peer-to-peer financing platforms are an example of a blockchain implementation in Islamic commerce. Using blockchain, the platform captures every financial transaction in a transparent and secure manner, ensuring sharia compliance and reducing the risk of fraud. In addition to enhancing efficiency, eliminating intermediaries, and accelerating transaction settlement, the use of blockchain technology in Islamic financial institutions can also boost productivity, eliminate middlemen, and expedite transaction settlement.

Integration of AI, machine learning, and blockchain serves an essential role in advancing Islamic fintech innovation. AI and machine learning aid in risk analysis, decision-making, and Islamic pattern recognition, while blockchain enhances financial transaction transparency, security, and dependability. Islamic fintech can provide better financial services, mitigate risks more effectively, and enhance sharia compliance in the Islamic finance industry by harnessing the power of this technology.

The significance of Islamic fintech innovation and its relationship to AI, machine learning, and blockchain, integrating these technologies offers several additional benefits. First, the incorporation of AI, machine learning, and blockchain can increase Islamic financial services' inclusivity. This technology enables Islamic fintech to reach more individuals and communities that were previously inaccessible to conventional financial institutions. For instance, Islamic financing platforms based on AI and machine learning can provide access to financing for small and medium-sized businesses (SMEs) that are frequently overlooked by conventional financial institutions(Alvarado Quito & Campodónico Durango, 2023; C. Chen et al., 2023; Hoque, 2023; Nugraha et al., 2022; Thomas, 2023; Tian et al., 2023; Y. Zhang et al., 2023). Those who do not have access to the traditional financial system can also benefit from the use of blockchain when it comes to transferring funds internationally.

Second, the integration of these technologies can enhance data security and privacy in Islamic financial technology. The secure and encrypted storage of transaction data in blockchain reduces the risk of identity theft and data breaches. In the meantime, AI and machine learning can be utilized to identify suspicious activity or security concerns in financial transactions and prevent cyberattacks. Thus, this technology can provide greater security and privacy protection for Islamic fintech users against potential threats. Thirdly, the combination of AI, machine learning, and blockchain can enhance the operational efficiency of Islamic financial institutions. Using AI and machine learning, internal processes such as identity verification, credit analysis, and risk management can be automated. Thus, financial institutions are able to reduce operational expenses, accelerate transaction settlement, and enhance service quality. All verified transaction information is recorded in a single distributed block chain, which reduces the time and cost associated with verifying and reconciling transactions between parties.

Fourth, the incorporation of this technology can enhance sharia compliance in Islamic financial technology. Islamic principles can be incorporated into the used algorithms, models, and contracts when utilizing AI, machine learning, and blockchain. For instance, machine learning algorithms can be programmed to analyze and update products and services to ensure Shariah compliance. Smart contracts can be programmed in a blockchain to ensure that all transactions and agreements made within it comply with Islamic law. The incorporation of artificial intelligence, machine learning, and blockchain in Islamic fintech not only provides innovation in financial services, but also enhances inclusivity, security, operational efficiency, and sharia compliance. Islamic fintech can bring significant benefits to society, financial institutions, and sustainable economic development by harnessing the power of this technology.

7. THE URGENCY OF ISLAMIC FINTECH INNOVATION

Due to the growing awareness of sharia-based finance and Islamic values, the global demand for Islamic financial products and services continues to rise. Individuals and businesses are more likely to seek out financial options that adhere to sharia principles, such as the prohibition of riba (interest) and investments that adhere to halal capital principles.

7.1 Meet Consumer Needs

Faced with this demand, Islamic fintech innovation is becoming indispensable. Islamic fintech integrates sharia principles with modern technology to provide consumers with financial solutions that meet their ever-growing complexity (Hendershott et al., 2021; Lee & Kim, 2022; J. Li et al., 2020; Osei-Assibey Bonsu et al., 2023). AI, machine learning, and blockchain technologies are becoming essential pillars of Islamic fintech innovation.

Initially, AI and machine learning can be utilized to create more innovative Islamic financial products and services. Through data analysis and pattern recognition, AI algorithms can assist in identifying customer requirements and preferences, allowing financial institutions to design products that are more personalized and suited to the customer's needs. For instance, an Islamic fintech platform could employ AI to analyze user behavior and provide investment suggestions that correspond to their profile and financial objectives.

AI can be utilized in customer service. AI-powered chatbots can provide immediate and accurate responses to consumer inquiries regarding Islamic financial products and services(Castillo et al., 2021; S. Chen et al., 2023; Fotheringham & Wiles, 2023; L. Wang et al., 2023; X. Wang et al., 2022; Xu et al., 2020). This enhances the user experience and the efficiency with which required information is provided. Second, blockchain technology can provide Islamic financial services with efficient and sharia-compliant solutions. Blockchain technology can increase the transparency and dependability of financial transactions. For instance, in Islamic peer-to-peer financing, blockchain can be used to decentralize the recording and verification of transactions. The immutability of blockchain-stored transaction data guarantees the integrity and legality of transactions in accordance with sharia principles. Additionally, blockchain technology can be utilized to facilitate international transactions in Islamic finance. By utilizing smart contracts on the blockchain, financial institutions can streamline the process of making international payments that are quick, secure, and compliant with Shariah law. For instance, an Islamic financial institution utilizes blockchain for fund transfers between countries with substantial Muslim populations, thereby reducing transaction costs and ensuring sharia compliance. By adopting technologies such as artificial intelligence, machine learning, and blockchain, Islamic financial institutions can provide their clients with more innovative and efficient solutions. This includes the creation of more personalized products and services, improved customer service via chatbots, transparent and sharia-compliant transactions via blockchain, and increased operational efficiency. Overall, Islamic fintech innovation with this technology can meet the increasing complexity of consumer demands and expectations for Islamic financial products and services.

7.2 Increase Efficiency

Islamic fintech has great potential for enhancing the efficacy of financial service delivery and lowering the operational expenses of conventional financial institutions. Islamic fintech innovation can accomplish this by employing technologies such as AI, machine learning, and blockchain(Günaydın et al., 2022; C. Li et al., 2023; Mishra et al., 2022). First, AI and machine learning technologies can be employed to automate the internal processes of Islamic financial institutions. Using facial recognition or voice recognition algorithms, for instance, the process of verifying a customer's identity can be automated. This decreases the time and expense required for manual verification and increases the efficiency of establishing an account or registering a financial product.

IBM has observed a substantial improvement in the operational effectiveness of supply chains for organizations that are implementing artificial intelligence (AI). Companies who implemented artificial intelligence (AI) experienced enhanced efficiency and decreased structural costs. AI and machine learning can be utilized to conduct more efficient data analysis. By utilizing data analysis techniques and pattern recognition, financial institutions are able to identify customer behavior patterns, conduct credit risk analysis, and provide more precise decision-making recommendations. For instance, an Islamic fintech platform can use machine learning to predict the risk of customer default using historical data and pertinent variables. Second, blockchain technology can eliminate the need for intermediaries in financial transactions, thereby reducing the operational expenses of conventional financial institutions. In the conventional financial system, a third entity, such as a bank or other financial institution, is frequently required to facilitate transactions and validate their legitimacy. Using blockchain, parties can conduct transactions directly without the need for middlemen.

Figure 4. Business benefits of supply chains transformation with artificial intelligence (AI) worldwide in 2022
(IBM Graph by Statista)

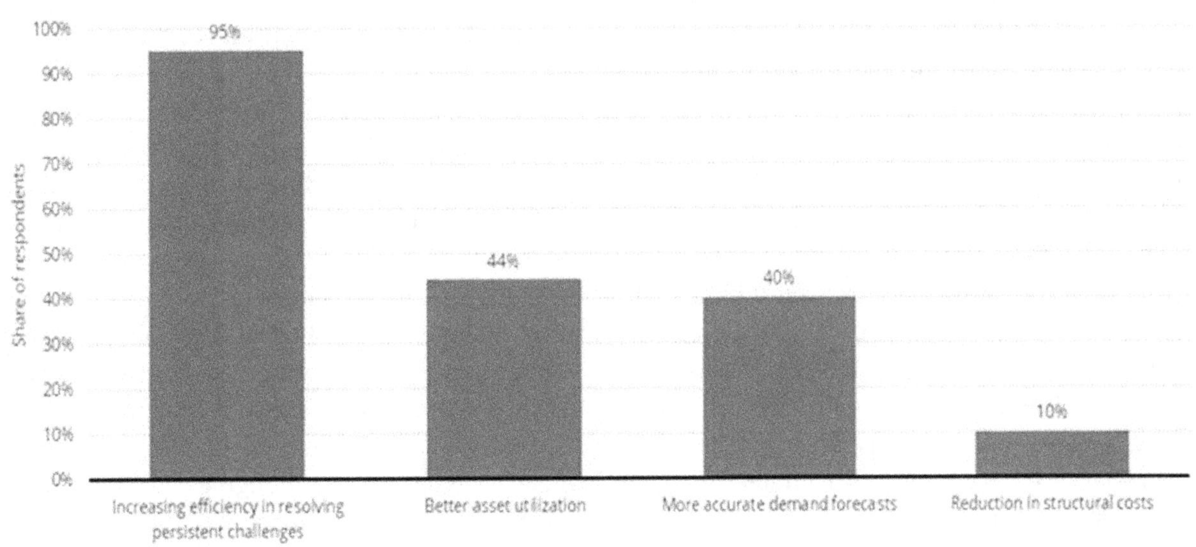

In peer-to-peer financing, for instance, Islamic fintech platforms utilize blockchain to document and verify transactions between lenders and borrowers. These transactions are recorded in interconnected segments, and it is impossible to alter any of them. By utilizing blockchain technology, platforms can eliminate intermediaries such as banks and other financial institutions, thereby reducing operational expenses and accelerating transaction settlement. Moreover, blockchain enhances the security of transactions. Since blockchain transactions are recorded in a decentralized manner, transaction data cannot be modified. This increases clients' and parties' confidence in financial transactions and reduces the risk of fraud or theft.

By incorporating AI, machine learning, and blockchain technologies, Islamic fintech innovations can provide the public with financial services that are faster, cheaper, and more accessible. This will enhance financial inclusion, particularly for those who lacked access to the conventional financial system previously. In addition, by reducing operational expenses, Islamic financial institutions are able to provide products and services at more competitive prices, thereby enhancing their efficiency and competitiveness in financial markets.

7.3 Increased Transparency and Trust

Using blockchain technology, Islamic fintech has the potential to increase the transparency of financial transactions. In the form of a decentralized block chain, blockchain technology records and verifies transactions(Benedetti et al., 2020; Bhatia et al., 2023; Khanna & Haldar, 2023; Kumar et al., 2022; Merkaš et al., 2020). This is exceptional in establishing high levels of transparency and creating an auditable audit trace.

Every financial transaction in blockchain is recorded in blocks that are chronologically connected. Each block contains transaction information that is transparent and immutable. This means that every entity involved in the transaction, whether a customer, financial institution, investor, or regulator, can access and verify all transaction details. Islamic peer-to-peer financing transactions are an example of a blockchain implementation in Islamic fintech. Blockchain is used by Islamic fintech platforms to document every financing transaction between lenders and borrowers. Every transaction is recorded in verifiable, transparent blocks. Clearly documented transaction information includes the financing amount, term, and sharia requirements. This transparency inspires customer confidence that financing practices adhere to pertinent sharia principles.

With increased transparency, the risk of fraud, forgery, and non-compliance with sharia law can be drastically reduced. All financial transactions can be monitored and audited more easily, thereby reducing the likelihood of violations or unlawful activities. Stakeholders, including customers, investors, and regulators, can have greater faith in the compliance and integrity of Islamic financial institutions' business operations.

Blockchain-based Islamic fintech with a high level of transparency contributes to an increase in industry confidence. Trust is crucial to the development of Islamic financial technology. With greater transparency, investors are more likely to trust Islamic fintech products and services and invest in them. Similarly, customers will feel more at ease using blockchain-based financial services because they can plainly observe how their transactions are handled and securely stored. The use of blockchain technology in Islamic fintech increases the transparency of financial transactions and strengthens the industry's foundation of trust. Reduce the risk of fraud, forgery, and sharia noncompliance with an immutable audit trail. This increases the confidence of consumers, investors, and regulators in Islamic financial institutions and provides a stronger foundation for the development and sustainability of Islamic fintech.

7.4 Fulfillment of Market Needs

Using technologies such as AI, machine learning, and blockchain, Islamic fintech innovation provides solutions that are relevant and in line with the market's evolving requirements. Islamic financial institutions can remain competitive and pertinent in a dynamic marketplace by utilizing the technology to create more personalized products and services and improve the customer experience(Bonetti et al., 2023; Jan et al., 2023; Rahman et al., 2023; Söderlund, 2023; X. Yang, 2023). The first illustration is the use of AI-powered Islamic chatbots in customer service. Sharia chatbots are virtual assistants capable of interacting with customers to provide information, answer queries, and offer assistance regarding Islamic financial products and services. As a result of AI technology, chatbots are able to comprehend human language and identify individual preferences, enabling them to provide more personalized and pertinent services. For instance, Islamic chatbots can provide investment recommendations based on customers' financial profiles and objectives, provide explanations about products that are compliant with Islamic requirements, and provide personalized financial solutions. The use of machine learning to recognize customer behavior and preferences is another illustration. Islamic financial institutions can analyze historical client data such as transaction history, product preferences, and spending behavior by utilizing machine learning technology.

By learning patterns and trends from this data, machine learning algorithms can more precisely determine customer preferences and needs. For instance, machine learning can identify a customer's lifestyle or investment interests based on their transactional patterns. With this information, financial institutions can create products and services that are more tailored to individual requirements, such as home financing that accommodates customer preferences and investment products that adhere to Islamic principles.

Utilizing AI and machine learning in Islamic fintech has the advantage of being able to continuously learn and adapt to market changes. In a dynamic and diverse market, financial institutions must be able to adapt to new trends and requirements. By leveraging AI and machine learning technologies, Islamic financial institutions are able to rapidly identify trends, analyze data, and develop suitable products and services. This assists financial institutions in remaining competitive and pertinent in the ever-changing fintech market. Islamic fintech innovations utilizing AI, machine learning, and blockchain offer advantages in providing better customer experiences, product development tailored to preferences, and adjustments to shifting market trends in order to provide solutions that are relevant and individualized. By implementing these technologies, Islamic financial institutions can satisfy consumer expectations, enhance service quality, and maintain their relevance in the fintech industry.

7.5 Improve Financial Literacy

There is tremendous potential for Islamic fintech to contribute to economic growth and broader financial inclusion. Islamic fintech can have a positive effect on the SME sector, financial inclusion, and sustainable investment by expanding access to financial services that comply with sharia principles (Esmaeilpour Moghadam & Karami, 2023; Fersi et al., 2023; Mapanje et al., 2023; Mehrotra, 2023; Michael et al., 2022). The first instance is the impact of Islamic fintech on the SME (Small and Medium-Sized Enterprises) sector. SMEs are a crucial pillar of the economy, but their access to capital and financial services is frequently constrained. Islamic fintech can provide solutions by making Islamic financing more accessible to small and medium-sized enterprises. For instance, Islamic fintech platforms can offer sharia-based microfinancing with a straightforward application procedure and more flexible requirements. This aids the development of SME enterprises, increases productivity, and contributes to the expansion of the economy as a whole.

Islamic fintech promotes investments consistent with sharia principles. There are individuals and businesses in the conventional financial system who wish to invest in accordance with sharia principles but are unable to do so due to limited access and knowledge. By offering appropriate Islamic investment instruments, Islamic fintech can provide an adequate investment platform. For instance, Islamic fintech platforms can offer investments in sukuk instruments and other sharia-compliant investment products. This enables individuals and businesses to confidently invest in accordance with their values, thereby increasing sustainable investment in the economy.

Islamic fintech plays a crucial role in economic expansion and broader financial inclusion. By increasing access to sharia-compliant financial services, Islamic fintech strengthens the SME sector, increases financial inclusion for previously underserved individuals, and promotes sharia-compliant investments. This impact can lead to inclusive and sustainable economic growth, as well as wider social and economic benefits for society.

The adoption of AI and machine learning by Islamic fintech has the potential to provide a more interactive and educational approach to financial literacy and Islamic education. Using an inventive digital platform, users can gain access to Sharia-compliant financial information, educational resources, and planning tools.

The first illustration is the use of AI technology to provide pertinent and individualized financial information. Through data analysis and pattern recognition, AI algorithms can provide customers with customized recommendations and suggestions. For instance, Islamic fintech platforms utilize AI to analyze customer expenditure and fund usage patterns. Based on this data, AI can provide pertinent information about financial management, advice on savings or investments that comply with sharia requirements, and product recommendations that match customer profiles.

Machine learning technology can be utilized to provide interactive Islamic and financial education. Machine learning can identify individual learning preferences, comprehension abilities, and educational need through data analysis and pattern recognition. Based on this data, Islamic finance platforms can provide educational content that is tailored to the preferences and levels of comprehension of their customers. For instance, the platform may provide interactive learning modules on Islamic principles, Islamic financial products, or Islamic-compliant financial planning. This strategy enhances consumers' financial literacy and understanding of sharia in a more effective and personalized manner.

8. CONCLUSION AND RECOMMENDATIONS

Innovations in Islamic fintech that incorporate AI, machine learning, and blockchain offer substantial benefits to the Islamic finance industry. This technology enables Islamic financial institutions to improve the efficiency of their financial services, reduce risk, increase transparency, and provide consumers with more individualized solutions. Islamic fintech contributes to the expansion of financial access, the improvement of financial inclusion, and the promotion of inclusive and sustainable economic growth. As a recommendation, Islamic financial institutions should expedite their adoption of fintech by integrating

AI, machine learning, and blockchain into their operations. Collaboration between Islamic financial institutions, regulators, and fintech industry actors is required to develop an appropriate and technologically responsive regulatory framework. To increase public comprehension of Islamic financial products and services, financial literacy and education must be enhanced. In order to accelerate the development of Islamic fintech technology and innovation, collaboration between Islamic financial institutions, fintech startups, and educational institutions must be strengthened. Islamic financial institutions must continue to conduct research and development pertaining to the use of AI, machine learning, and blockchain technologies to ensure they remain at the vanguard of innovation and are able to meet the increasing challenges in the fintech industry.

REFERENCES

Abuzov, A. (2023). The role of technological innovations in institutional regulation of the financial capital market. *E3S Web of Conferences, 376*. doi:10.1051/e3sconf/202337605047

Al Janabi, M. A. M. (2022). Optimization algorithms and investment portfolio analytics with machine learning techniques under time-varying liquidity constraints. *Journal of Modelling in Management, 17*(3), 864–895. doi:10.1108/JM2-10-2020-0259

Albastaki, Y. A. (2020). When technology meets finance: A review approach to fintech. In Innovative Strategies for Implementing FinTech in Banking (pp. 1–21). IGI Global. doi:10.4018/978-1-7998-3257-7.ch001

Alexander, K., & Karametaxas, X. (2021). Digital transformation and financial inclusion. In Routledge Handbook of Financial Technology and Law (pp. 273–290). Routledge. doi:10.4324/9780429325670-15

Alvarado Quito, K., & Campodónico Durango, G. (2023). ANALYSIS OF FINTECH AND THEIR CONTRIBUTION TO THE DEVELOPMENT OF SMES IN GUAYAQUIL-ECUADOR. *Universidad y Sociedad, 15*(2), 475–483. https://www.scopus.com/inward/record.uri?eid=2-s2.0-85160102411&partnerID=40&md5=006d093931084e38c1dcc5e1e87eae66

Anshari, M., Almunawar, M. N., Masri, M., & Hrdy, M. (2021). Financial Technology with AI-Enabled and Ethical Challenges. *Society, 58*(3), 189–195. doi:10.100712115-021-00592-w

Barredo Arrieta, A., Díaz-Rodríguez, N., Del Ser, J., Bennetot, A., Tabik, S., Barbado, A., Garcia, S., Gil-Lopez, S., Molina, D., Benjamins, R., Chatila, R., & Herrera, F. (2020). Explainable Artificial Intelligence (XAI): Concepts, taxonomies, opportunities and challenges toward responsible AI. *Information Fusion, 58*, 82–115. doi:10.1016/j.inffus.2019.12.012

Beik, I. S., & Nursyamsiah, T. (2021). SWOT ANALYSIS ON RESEARCH METHODOLOGIES AND TECHNIQUES ADOPTED IN ISLAMIC ECONOMICS AND FINANCE. In Teaching and Research Methods for Islamic Economics and Finance (pp. 29–41). Taylor & Francis. doi:10.4324/9781003252764-5

Benedetti, H., Nikbakht, E., Sarkar, S., & Spieler, A. C. (2020). Blockchain and corporate fraud. *Journal of Financial Crime, 28*(3), 702–721. doi:10.1108/JFC-09-2020-0187

Bhatia, M. S., Chaudhuri, A., Kayikci, Y., & Treiblmaier, H. (2023). Implementation of blockchain-enabled supply chain finance solutions in the agricultural commodity supply chain: A transaction cost economics perspective. *Production Planning and Control*, 1–15. doi:10.1080/09537287.2023.2180685

Bian, W., Wang, S., & Xie, X. (2023). How valuable is FinTech adoption for traditional banks? *European Financial Management*, eufm.12424. doi:10.1111/eufm.12424

Bonetti, F., Montecchi, M., Plangger, K., & Schau, H. J. (2023). Practice co-evolution: Collaboratively embedding artificial intelligence in retail practices. *Journal of the Academy of Marketing Science*, *51*(4), 867–888. doi:10.100711747-022-00896-1 PMID:36035334

Boto Ferreira, M., Costa Pinto, D., Maurer Herter, M., Soro, J., Vanneschi, L., Castelli, M., & Peres, F. (2021). Using artificial intelligence to overcome over-indebtedness and fight poverty. *Journal of Business Research*, *131*, 411–425. doi:10.1016/j.jbusres.2020.10.035 PMID:33100428

Burger, C., & Weinmann, J. (2022). Blockchain Platforms in Energy Markets—A Critical Assessment. *Journal of Risk and Financial Management*, *15*(11), 516. doi:10.3390/jrfm15110516

Castillo, D., Canhoto, A. I., & Said, E. (2021). The dark side of AI-powered service interactions: Exploring the process of co-destruction from the customer perspective. *Service Industries Journal*, *41*(13–14), 900–925. doi:10.1080/02642069.2020.1787993

Chen, C., Xiao, B., Wang, J., & Ye, H. (2023). The effects of fintech development on financing constraints of small and medium-sized enterprises—Evidence from China. *MDE. Managerial and Decision Economics*, *44*(7), 4161–4172. doi:10.1002/mde.3920

Chen, J., Tong, Q. Q., Verma, H., Sharma, A., Dahbura, A., & Liew, J. K.-S. (2023). The Complexity of Blockchain Risks Simplified and Displayed: Introduction of the Johns Hopkins Blockchain Risk Map. *Journal of Financial Data Science*, *5*(1), 96–109. doi:10.3905/jfds.2022.1.117

Chen, S., Li, X., Liu, K., & Wang, X. (2023). Chatbot or human? The impact of online customer service on consumers' purchase intentions. *Psychology and Marketing*, *40*(11), 2186–2200. doi:10.1002/mar.21862

Cheng, A. (2023). Evaluating Fintech industry's risks: A preliminary analysis based on CRISP-DM framework. *Finance Research Letters*, *55*, 103966. doi:10.1016/j.frl.2023.103966

de Manuel, A., Delgado, J., Parra Jounou, I., Ausín, T., Casacuberta, D., Cruz, M., Guersenzvaig, A., Moyano, C., Rodríguez-Arias, D., Rueda, J., & Puyol, A. (2023). Ethical assessments and mitigation strategies for biases in AI-systems used during the COVID-19 pandemic. *Big Data & Society*, *10*(1), 20539517231179199. doi:10.1177/20539517231179199

Dong, L., Jiang, P., & Xu, F. (2023). Impact of Traceability Technology Adoption in Food Supply Chain Networks. *Management Science*, *69*(3), 1518–1535. doi:10.1287/mnsc.2022.4440

Du, G., & Elston, F. (2022). Financial risk assessment to improve the accuracy of financial prediction in the internet financial industry using data analytics models. *Operations Management Research : Advancing Practice Through Research*, *15*(3–4), 925–940. doi:10.100712063-022-00293-5

Dua, S., Sharma, M. G., Mishra, V., & Kulkarni, S. D. (2023). Modelling perceived risk in blockchain enabled supply chain utilizing fuzzy-AHP. *Journal of Global Operations and Strategic Sourcing*, *16*(1), 161–177. doi:10.1108/JGOSS-06-2021-0046

Esmaeilpour Moghadam, H., & Karami, A. (2023). Financial inclusion through FinTech and women's financial empowerment. *International Journal of Social Economics*, *50*(8), 1038–1059. Advance online publication. doi:10.1108/IJSE-04-2022-0246

Fallahi, S., Mellquist, A.-C., Mogren, O., Listo Zec, E., Algurén, P., & Hallquist, L. (2022). Financing solutions for circular business models: Exploring the role of business ecosystems and artificial intelligence. *Business Strategy and the Environment*. doi:10.1002/bse.3297

Fersi, M., Boujelbéne, M., & Arous, F. (2023). Microfinance's digital transformation for sustainable inclusion. *European Journal of Management and Business Economics*. doi:10.1108/EJMBE-10-2022-0332

Fieberg, C., Metko, D., Poddig, T., & Loy, T. (2023). Machine learning techniques for cross-sectional equity returns' prediction. *OR-Spektrum*, *45*(1), 289–323. doi:10.100700291-022-00693-w

Fotheringham, D., & Wiles, M. A. (2023). The effect of implementing chatbot customer service on stock returns: An event study analysis. *Journal of the Academy of Marketing Science*, *51*(4), 802–822. doi:10.100711747-022-00841-2

Gao, B. (2022). The Use of Machine Learning Combined with Data Mining Technology in Financial Risk Prevention. *Computational Economics*, *59*(4), 1385–1405. doi:10.100710614-021-10101-0

Giri, P. K., De, S. S., Dehuri, S., & Cho, S.-B. (2021). Biogeography based optimization for mining rules to assess credit risk. *International Journal of Intelligent Systems in Accounting Finance & Management*, *28*(1), 35–51. doi:10.1002/isaf.1486

Goodfellow, I., Pouget-Abadie, J., Mirza, M., Xu, B., Warde-Farley, D., Ozair, S., Courville, A., & Bengio, Y. (2020). Generative adversarial networks. *Communications of the ACM*, *63*(11), 139–144. doi:10.1145/3422622

Günaydın, Y., Correia, A., & Kozak, M. (2022). Comparing efficiency in all-inclusive and bed and breakfast hotel businesses: A multi-period data envelopment analysis in Turkey. *European Journal of Management and Business Economics*, *31*(4), 439–452. doi:10.1108/EJMBE-11-2021-0308

Hendershott, T., Zhang, X., Leon Zhao, J., & Zheng, Z. (2021). Fintech as a game changer: Overview of research frontiers. *Information Systems Research*, *32*(1), 1–17. doi:10.1287/isre.2021.0997

Hoque, A. (2023). Fintech's game-changing opportunities for SMEs: A study on selected SMEs in Bangladesh. *Asian Economic and Financial Review*, *13*(5), 308–319. doi:10.55493/5002.v13i5.4780

Hu, W., & Chen, Y. (2022). Application of Artificial Intelligence in Financial Risk Management. In Lecture Notes in Computer Science (including subseries Lecture Notes in Artificial Intelligence and Lecture Notes in Bioinformatics): Vol. 13338 LNCS (pp. 180–188). Springer. doi:10.1007/978-3-031-06794-5_15

Iqbal, M. (2022). Machine learning applications in e-commerce. In *The Future of E-Commerce* (pp. 65–89). SCOPUS. https://www.scopus.com/inward/record.uri?eid=2-s2.0-85144997084&partnerID=40&md5=475f705c5259c1a7c9ab9a72756ebb8d

Irfan, M., Elhoseny, M., Kassim, S., & Metawa, N. (2023). Advanced Machine Learning Algorithms for Complex Financial Applications. In Advanced Machine Learning Algorithms for Complex Financial Applications. IGI Global. doi:10.4018/978-1-6684-4483-2

Irfan, M., Elmogy, M., Majid, M. S. A., & El-Sappagh, S. (2023). The impact of AI innovation on financial sectors in the era of industry 5.0. In The Impact of AI Innovation on Financial Sectors in the Era of Industry 5.0. https://doi.org/ doi:10.4018/9798369300824

Ivanchenkova, L., Shevtsiv, L., Beisenova, L., Shakharova, A., & Berdiyorov, T. (2023). Analysis of the Risks of Using the Blockchain Technology in the Accounting and Audit of a Fuel and Energy Complex Enterprise. *International Journal of Energy Economics and Policy*, *13*(2), 316–321. doi:10.32479/ijeep.14047

Jan, I. U., Ji, S., & Kim, C. (2023). What (de) motivates customers to use AI-powered conversational agents for shopping? The extended behavioral reasoning perspective. *Journal of Retailing and Consumer Services*, *75*, 103440. doi:10.1016/j.jretconser.2023.103440

Jena, R. K. (2022). Examining the Factors Affecting the Adoption of Blockchain Technology in the Banking Sector: An Extended UTAUT Model. *International Journal of Financial Studies*, *10*(4), 90. doi:10.3390/ijfs10040090

Kazancoglu, Y., Ozbiltekin-Pala, M., Sezer, M. D., Luthra, S., & Kumar, A. (2023). Resilient reverse logistics with blockchain technology in sustainable food supply chain management during COVID-19. *Business Strategy and the Environment*, *32*(4), 2327–2340. doi:10.1002/bse.3251

Khanna, P., & Haldar, A. (2023). Will adoption of blockchain technology be challenging: Evidence from Indian banking industry. *Qualitative Research in Financial Markets*, *15*(2), 361–384. doi:10.1108/QRFM-01-2022-0003

Kolisnyk, O., Hurina, N., Druzhynska, N., Holovchak, H., & Fomina, T. (2023). INNOVATIVE TECHNOLOGIES IN ACCOUNTING AND AUDITING: THE USE OF BLOCKCHAIN TECHNOLOGY. *Financial and Credit Activity: Problems of Theory and Practice*, *3*(50), 24–41. doi:10.55643/fcaptp.3.50.2023.4082

Kumar, A. S., Katta Lakshmi Narayan Setty, V., & Ravi, G. (2022). How blockchain enables financial transactions in the banking sector. *International Journal of Business and Globalisation*, *31*(1), 1–6. doi:10.1504/IJBG.2022.124545

Lahmiri, S., & Bekiros, S. (2019). Can machine learning approaches predict corporate bankruptcy? Evidence from a qualitative experimental design. *Quantitative Finance*, *19*(9), 1569–1577. doi:10.1080/14697688.2019.1588468

Lee, S.-M., & Kim, H.-K. (2022). The Effect of System and User Characteristics on Intention to Use: An Empirical Study of Face Recognition Payment. *Journal of System and Management Sciences*, *12*(3), 318–344. 10.33168/JSMS.2022.0316

Lestari, N. I., Hussain, W., Merigo, J. M., & Bekhit, M. (2023). A Survey of Trendy Financial Sector Applications of Machine and Deep Learning. In Lecture Notes of the Institute for Computer Sciences, Social-Informatics and Telecommunications Engineering, LNICST: Vol. 467 LNICST (pp. 619–633). doi:10.1007/978-3-031-23944-1_68

Li, C., Xu, Y., Zheng, H., Wang, Z., Han, H., & Zeng, L. (2023). Artificial intelligence, resource reallocation, and corporate innovation efficiency: Evidence from China's listed companies. *Resources Policy*, *81*, 103324. doi:10.1016/j.resourpol.2023.103324

Li, J., Liu, Z., & Zhou, J. (2020). How to become the chosen one in the artificial intelligence market: The evidence from China. *International Journal of Technology Management*, *84*(1–2), 8–24. doi:10.1504/IJTM.2020.112122

Mahmood, F., Shahzad, U., Nazakat, A. L. I., Ahmed, Z., Rjoub, H., & Wong, W.-K. (2022). THE NEXUS between CASH CONVERSION CYCLE, WORKING CAPITAL FINANCE, and FIRM PERFORMANCE: EVIDENCE from NOVEL MACHINE LEARNING APPROACHES. *Annals of Financial Economics*, *17*(2), 2250014. doi:10.1142/S2010495222500142

Malhotra, A., O'Neill, H., & Stowell, P. (2022). Thinking strategically about blockchain adoption and risk mitigation. *Business Horizons*, *65*(2), 159–171. doi:10.1016/j.bushor.2021.02.033

Mallikarjuna, M., & Rao, R. P. (2019). Evaluation of forecasting methods from selected stock market returns. *Financial Innovation*, *5*(1), 40. doi:10.118640854-019-0157-x

Mapanje, O., Karuaihe, S., Machethe, C., & Amis, M. (2023). Financing Sustainable Agriculture in Sub-Saharan Africa: A Review of the Role of Financial Technologies. *Sustainability (Basel)*, *15*(5), 4587. doi:10.3390u15054587

Mehrotra, A. (2023). FinTech driven financial inclusion – the hype and the reality of missed targets. *International Journal of Public Sector Performance Management*, *11*(2), 165–176. doi:10.1504/IJPSPM.2023.129690

Merkaš, Z., Perkov, D., & Bonin, V. (2020). The significance of blockchain technology in digital transformation of logistics and transportation. *International Journal of E-Services and Mobile Applications*, *12*(1), 1–20. doi:10.4018/IJESMA.2020010101

Michael, B., Koroleska, N., Tai, A., & Wong, D. W. H. (2022). A critical look at using financial technology policy to promote the sustainable development goals. *Sustainable Development (Bradford)*, *30*(6), 1911–1920. doi:10.1002d.2358

Miller, T. (2019). Explanation in artificial intelligence: Insights from the social sciences. *Artificial Intelligence*, *267*, 1–38. doi:10.1016/j.artint.2018.07.007

Mishra, S., Ewing, M. T., & Cooper, H. B. (2022). Artificial intelligence focus and firm performance. *Journal of the Academy of Marketing Science*, *50*(6), 1176–1197. doi:10.100711747-022-00876-5

Mohd Haridan, N., Sheikh Hassan, A. F., Mohammed Shah, S., & Mustafa, H. (2023). Financial innovation in Islamic banks: Evidence on the interaction between Shariah board and FinTech. *Journal of Islamic Accounting and Business Research*, *14*(6), 911–930. doi:10.1108/JIABR-11-2022-0305

Moon, K.-S., & Kim, H. (2023). EFFICIENT ASSET ALLOCATION BASED ON PREDICTION WITH ADAPTIVE DATA SELECTION. *Economic Computation and Economic Cybernetics Studies and Research, 57*(1), 57–72. doi:10.24818/18423264/57.1.23.04

Nugraha, D. P., Setiawan, B., Nathan, R. J., & Fekete-Farkas, M. (2022). Fintech Adoption Drivers for Innovation for SMEs in Indonesia. *Journal of Open Innovation, 8*(4), 208. doi:10.3390/joitmc8040208

Ogbeibu, S., Chiappetta Jabbour, C. J., Burgess, J., Gaskin, J., & Renwick, D. W. S. (2022). Green talent management and turnover intention: The roles of leader STARA competence and digital task interdependence. *Journal of Intellectual Capital, 23*(1), 27–55. doi:10.1108/JIC-01-2021-0016

Osei-Assibey Bonsu, M., Wang, Y., & Guo, Y. (2023). Does fintech lead to better accounting practices? Empirical evidence. *Accounting Research Journal, 36*(2–3), 129–147. doi:10.1108/ARJ-07-2022-0178

Pal, T., Irfan, M., & Kassim, S. B. (2023). How do Machine Learning (ML) techniques benefit the insurance industry? an exploratory study. In The Impact of AI Innovation on Financial Sectors in the Era of Industry 5.0 (pp. 108–130). doi:10.4018/979-8-3693-0082-4.ch007

Pnevmatikakis, A., Kanavos, S., Matikas, G., Kostopoulou, K., Cesario, A., & Kyriazakos, S. (2021). Risk assessment for personalized health insurance based on real-world data. *Risks, 9*(3), 1–15. doi:10.3390/risks9030046

Rabbani, M. R., Khan, S., & Atif, M. (2023). Machine learning-based P2P lending Islamic Fintech model for small and medium enterprises in Bahrain. *International Journal of Business Innovation and Research, 30*(4), 565–579. doi:10.1504/IJBIR.2023.130079

Raffinetti, E. (2023). A Rank Graduation Accuracy measure to mitigate Artificial Intelligence risks. *Quality & Quantity, 57*(S2), 131–150. doi:10.100711135-023-01613-y

Rahadian, A., & Thamrin, H. (2023). Analysis of Factors Affecting MSME in Using Fintech Lending as Alternative Financing: Technology Acceptance Model Approach. *Brazilian Business Review, 20*(3), 301–322. doi:10.15728/bbr.2023.20.3.4.en

Rahman, M. S., Bag, S., Hossain, M. A., Abdel Fattah, F. A. M., Gani, M. O., & Rana, N. P. (2023). The new wave of AI-powered luxury brands online shopping experience: The role of digital multisensory cues and customers' engagement. *Journal of Retailing and Consumer Services, 72*, 103273. doi:10.1016/j.jretconser.2023.103273

Raza Rabbani, M., Hassan, M. K., Khan, S., & Muneeza, A. (2022). A Fintech-Based Zakat Model Using Artificial Intelligence. In *FinTech in Islamic Financial Institutions* (pp. 49–63). Scope, Challenges, and Implications in Islamic Finance. doi:10.1007/978-3-031-14941-2_3

Ridho Kismawadi, E., Irfan, M., & Shah, S. M. A. R. (2023). Revolutionizing islamic finance: Artificial intelligence's role in the future of industry. In The Impact of AI Innovation on Financial Sectors in the Era of Industry 5.0 (pp. 184–207). IGI Global. doi:10.4018/979-8-3693-0082-4.ch011

Seo, K. H., & Lee, J. H. (2021). The emergence of service robots at restaurants: Integrating trust, perceived risk, and satisfaction. *Sustainability (Basel), 13*(8), 4431. doi:10.3390u13084431

Sharma, A., Kumar, D., & Arora, N. (2022). Supply chain risk factor assessment of Indian pharmaceutical industry for performance improvement. *International Journal of Productivity and Performance Management*. Advance online publication. doi:10.1108/IJPPM-01-2022-0035

Söderlund, M. (2023). What is it like to be idle versus busy for a service machine? *Psychology and Marketing*, *40*(6), 1237–1248. doi:10.1002/mar.21806

Thomas, N. M. (2023). Modeling key enablers influencing FinTechs offering SME credit services: A multi-stakeholder perspective. *Electronic Markets*, *33*(1), 18. doi:10.100712525-023-00627-6 PMID:37220555

Thompson, B. S., & Rust, S. (2023). Blocking blockchain: Examining the social, cultural, and institutional factors causing innovation resistance to digital technology in seafood supply chains. *Technology in Society*, *73*, 102235. doi:10.1016/j.techsoc.2023.102235

Tian, H., Siddik, A. B., Pertheban, T. R., & Rahman, M. N. (2023). Does fintech innovation and green transformational leadership improve green innovation and corporate environmental performance? A hybrid SEM–ANN approach. *Journal of Innovation and Knowledge*, *8*(3), 100396. doi:10.1016/j.jik.2023.100396

Truby, J., Dahdal, A., & Ibrahim, I. A. (2022). Sandboxes in the desert: Is a cross-border 'gulf box' feasible? *Law, Innovation and Technology*, *14*(2), 447–473. doi:10.1080/17579961.2022.2113674

Vannucci, E., Pagano, A. J., & Romagnoli, F. (2021). *Climate change management: a resilience strategy for flood risk using Blockchain tools*. Decisions in Economics and Finance., doi:10.100710203-020-00315-6

Varma, P., Nijjer, S., Sood, K., Grima, S., & Rupeika-Apoga, R. (2022). Thematic Analysis of Financial Technology (Fintech) Influence on the Banking Industry. *Risks*, *10*(10), 186. doi:10.3390/risks10100186

Wang, L., Huang, N., Hong, Y., Liu, L., Guo, X., & Chen, G. (2023). Voice-based AI in call center customer service: A natural field experiment. *Production and Operations Management*, *32*(4), 1002–1018. doi:10.1111/poms.13953

Wang, X., Lin, X., & Shao, B. (2022). How does artificial intelligence create business agility? Evidence from chatbots. *International Journal of Information Management*, *66*, 102535. doi:10.1016/j.ijinfomgt.2022.102535

Xu, Y., Shieh, C.-H., van Esch, P., & Ling, I.-L. (2020). AI customer service: Task complexity, problem-solving ability, and usage intention. *Australasian Marketing Journal*, *28*(4), 189–199. doi:10.1016/j.ausmj.2020.03.005

Yang, Q., Liu, Y., Chen, T., & Tong, Y. (2019). Federated machine learning: Concept and applications. *ACM Transactions on Intelligent Systems and Technology*, *10*(2), 1–19. doi:10.1145/3298981

Yang, X. (2023). The effects of AI service quality and AI function-customer ability fit on customer's overall co-creation experience. *Industrial Management & Data Systems*, *123*(6), 1717–1735. doi:10.1108/IMDS-08-2022-0500

Young, K. E. (2018). Prioritizing renewable energy in a time of fiscal austerity. In The Economics of Renewable Energy in the Gulf (pp. 77–99). Routledge. doi:10.4324/9780429434976-5

Zhang, X., & Mahadevan, S. (2019). Ensemble machine learning models for aviation incident risk prediction. *Decision Support Systems*, *116*, 48–63. doi:10.1016/j.dss.2018.10.009

Zhang, Y., Ramanathan, L., & Maheswari, M. (2021). A hybrid approach for risk analysis in e-business integrating big data analytics and artificial intelligence. *Annals of Operations Research*. doi:10.100710479-021-04412-6

Zhang, Y., Xing, C., & Guo, X. (2023). The Shielding Effect of Access to Finance on Small and Medium-Sized Enterprises during the COVID-19 Crisis: Comparing Fintech and Traditional Finance. *Emerging Markets Finance & Trade*, *59*(8), 2383–2397. doi:10.1080/1540496X.2022.2072201

Zheng, G., Kong, L., & Brintrup, A. (2023). Federated machine learning for privacy preserving, collective supply chain risk prediction. *International Journal of Production Research*, *61*(23), 8115–8132. doi:10.1080/00207543.2022.2164628

Zhong, J., & Wang, Z. (2022). Artificial intelligence techniques for financial distress prediction. *AIMS Mathematics*, *7*(12), 20891–20908. doi:10.3934/math.20221145

Chapter 4
Blockchain Technology and Islamic Finance: A Decade of Growth Trends

K. Kusuma
GITAM University, India

P. Sheela
https://orcid.org/0000-0003-3689-1530
GITAM University, India

Rashmi Ranjan Panigrahi
https://orcid.org/0000-0002-2199-293X
GITAM University, India

Zakir Hossen Shaikh
https://orcid.org/0000-0003-4733-4166
Kingdom University, Bahrain

ABSTRACT

Financial technology (FinTech) has emerged as the application of innovative and disruptive technologies to provide financial services, gaining significant prominence in the late 2010s. The genesis of FinTech can be traced back to the global financial crisis of 2008, which necessitated a re-evaluation of traditional financial systems. Islamic financial systems emerged as a resilient response to this crisis, offering alternative solutions. This chapter embarks on a comprehensive review of academic research in the domain of Islamic financial technology, with a particular focus on the integration of blockchain management. Forecasts indicate that global cumulative investments in FinTech are poised to surpass $1.5 trillion over the next 3-5 years. Concurrently, the conventional banking and finance industry faces a notable dearth of innovation, presenting formidable challenges to banks and financial institutions worldwide. This study aims to address this innovation gap by investigating the potential of blockchain technology to revolutionize Islamic finance.

DOI: 10.4018/979-8-3693-1038-0.ch004

1. INTRODUCTION

In the heartlands of finance, a digital revolution marries ancient principles with cutting-edge technology, shaping a new era of economic transactions. The confluence of Blockchain Technology and Islamic Finance gives scope to potent collaboration, promising unprecedented growth and reshaping the financial landscape, Al-Tamimi, A. M., & Yasin, N. M. (2020). As the world rapidly adopts blockchain solutions, a pivotal question arises: how has this powerful tool impacted Islamic finance over the last decade? Ali, M. M. S., & Haneef, M. A. (2018). The intersection of Blockchain technology and Islamic finance is a compelling and relevant research topic, encompassing the fusion of modern technological advancements with traditional financial principles rooted in Islamic ethics. Blockchain technology offers transparency and immutability in financial transactions, aligning with the Islamic finance principle of transparency and fair dealing. The decentralized and distributed ledger system ensures trust among participants, promoting ethical practices within the Islamic financial framework, Hamid, S., & Omar, S. S. (2019). Through smart contracts and automated processes, Blockchain enhances operational efficiency. It reduces transaction costs, a crucial factor in Islamic finance, which encourages efficiency and discourages excessive fees and unnecessary complexity in financial transactions, Hassan, M. K., & Abubakar, B. (2018). Blockchain facilitates the tokenization of assets, including Sukuk (Islamic bonds), enabling fractional ownership and increased liquidity. This aligns with the Islamic finance concept of asset-backed securities and risk-sharing agreements, Yahaya, N. Z., & Alias, N. (2020). This study is an attempt to provide a comprehensive exploration of the intersection between blockchain technology and Islamic finance over the past decade. There is a need for comprehensive and standardized integration frameworks and guidelines for effectively incorporating blockchain into existing Islamic finance practices, Lacity, M., & Hirschheim, R. (2018). This research outlines the gaps and difficulties that must be addressed to successfully merge Blockchain and Islamic Finance. There is Limited research focused on developing precise and uniform regulatory frameworks that align both with Islamic finance guidelines and blockchain technology requirements. More research should address blockchain's sustainability implications in Islamic finance, considering energy consumption and environmental impact concerns. Likewise, there is a need for comprehensive and standardized integration frameworks and guidelines for effectively incorporating blockchain into existing Islamic finance practices, Zohar, A. (2015). Intensive research questions have been developed to address the primary objective of advancing knowledge in the rapidly evolving connection of blockchain technology and Islamic finance. These research questions aim to provide transparency and structure to the systematic review, assisting a comprehensive examination of the current state of the field and its implications. These questions were developed after a systematic literature review and in-depth analysis. The research was to answer the following research questions. The unique contribution of the study was addressed through the following questions.

RQ1: What are the essential theoretical and practical contributions of prominent research articles on blockchain Technology and Islamic finance, and how have these findings influenced the industry?

RQ2: "How has the integration of blockchain technology in Islamic finance evolved, and what are the prominent trends and challenges highlighted in research articles?"

RQ3: "What specific applications of blockchain technology within Islamic finance have been extensively researched, and what are the implications of these applications on the financial ecosystem?"

Following the impulse of de-colonization in the 1960s, Islamic finance emerged in the 1970s in Southeast Asia and parts of Arabia, David A. Suratga (1984). Islamic Finance development was not the 'comeback of any historical institutional arrangement but the advancement of a new phenomenon linking traditional Islamic teachings and modern commercial arrangements, Haider Ala Hamoudi (2007). Major financial markets are realizing solid indications that Islamic finance has already been mainstreamed within the global financial system and that it has the potential to help address the challenges of ending extreme poverty and boosting shared prosperity.

Organizing the research with the above status and supporting the three specific questions allows for a targeted assessment of essential aspects, enabling a thorough analysis. This methodology ensures that the research objective is achieved by systematically investigating and addressing every facet of the coming together between blockchain technology and Islamic finance. In doing so, it contributes to a systematic understanding of this energetic and transformative phenomenon that is taking place in the global financial landscape of Islamic finance. Ridho Kismawadi, E., Irfan, M., Shah, S.M.A.R., Revolutionizing Islamic finance: Artificial intelligence's role in the future of industry, (2023), studied importance stems from the fact that it fills a gap in the literature about AI technology integration in Islamic banking. Analysed the possible benefits and difficulties of using AI in the sector.

The rest of the paper is arranged as follows. Section 2 presents a systematic literature review on Blockchain Technology and Islamic Banking. Section 3 presents the Novelty of the study.

Section 4 discusses the methodology used in the empirical analysis and data collection process. Section 5 lays down the findings and analysis. Section 6 emphasizes the discussion (Includes answers to the research question and research direction). Section 7 contains the conclusion, future Scope, and limitations.

2. JOURNEY OF BLOCKCHAIN TECHNOLOGY

Blockchain technology is a decentralised and distributed ledger system that records transactions across a network of computers, Nakamoto, S. (2008). The transactions are grouped into blocks, each containing a set of records. These blocks are cryptographically linked, forming a chain. Once a block is added to the chain, it becomes immutable and cannot be altered, ensuring the integrity and security of the recorded data, Tapscott, D., & Tapscott, A. (2016). Satoshi Nakamoto introduced blockchain through the Bitcoin white paper, outlining the principles of a decentralized digital currency and the structure of the blockchain. Iansiti, M., & Lakhani, K. R. (2017), research delves into scalability, energy consumption, regulatory frameworks, and interoperability challenges. It also discusses potential solutions and the evolving landscape of blockchain technology. Irfan, M., Elhoseny, M., Kassim, S., Metawa, N., Advanced Machine Learning Algorithms for Complex Financial Applications, (2023), pp. 1-292 discussed with reference to complex financial applications like financial risk management in big data environments, Advanced Machine Learning Algorithms for Complex Financial Applications offers cutting edge research on the roles of artificial intelligence and machine learning algorithms in the financial sectors.

According to, Cocco, L., & Marchesi, M. (2016). Blockchain's decentralized, immutable ledger ensures data integrity and significantly reduces the risk of fraudulent activities within the financial sector. Blockchain streamlines process, reduces intermediaries, and accelerates transaction settlement, leading to substantial cost savings for financial institutions (Tapscott, D., & Tapscott, A. (2016). Catalini, C., & Gans, J. S. (2016)). Blockchain facilitates near-instantaneous settlement of financial transactions, improving liquidity and reducing counterparty risk, Cocco, L., Marchesi, M., & Setzu, A. (2017). Blockchain's transparency enhances trust by allowing all stakeholders to access and verify transactions and contracts, enhancing overall accountability, Catalini, C., & Gans, J. S. (2016). The primary compelling attribute of blockchain technology is its inherent resistance to data tampering and its ability to facilitate traceable transactions, Mustafa Raza Rabbani., et al. (2020).

Malik, S., et al. (2019) present a conceptual framework for ensuring Shariah compliance in implementing blockchain technology within the Islamic finance domain. Saeed, Z., & Al-Busaidi, A. (2018). explored the compatibility of intelligent contracts, an essential feature of blockchain technology, with Islamic finance principles. Azzi, M., & Alobaidy, M. (2018). Discussed the potential application of blockchain in enhancing transparency and efficiency in managing Waqf, an essential institution in Islamic finance. Wani, S. M., & Noordin, M. F. (2020). addressed the regulatory and compliance considerations associated with implementing blockchain technology in the Islamic finance sector. The Influence of AI Innovation on Financial Sectors in the Age of Industry 5.0 becomes a vital tool, driving developments that will influence the financial landscape going forward. "Irfan, M., Elmogy, M., Majid, M.S.A., El-Sappagh, S. 2023".

The intersection of blockchain technology and Islamic finance presents both opportunities and challenges. Blockchain technology offers an immutable and transparent ledger, aligning with the principles of transparency and trust emphasized in Islamic finance (Khan, M., Salah, K., Alazab, M., & Hitchens, M., 2018). Blockchain enables the creation of Shari'ah-compliant smart contracts, facilitating automated, trust less agreements and transactions for Islamic financial products (Turetsky, M., 2017). By automating processes and reducing the need for intermediaries, blockchain can enhance efficiency and result in cost savings, aligning with the efficiency objectives of Islamic finance (Idrees, M., & Mahmood, A. N., 2019). Blockchain can provide access to financial services for the unbanked or underbanked populations, aligning with Islamic finance's goal of financial inclusion (Idrees, M., & Mahmood, A. N., 2019).

The compliance of blockchain with Shari'ah principles and the development of a suitable legal framework that aligns with Islamic finance requirements remain significant challenges (Hakim, D., & Meressa, A., 2019). The limited understanding and expertise in blockchain technology and Islamic finance challenge its successful integration (Hakim, D., & Meressa, A., 2019). Addressing security and privacy concerns associated with blockchain, especially in financial transactions governed by Islamic finance, is crucial for widespread adoption (Hakim, D., & Meressa, A., 2019). The scalability issues and technical limitations of blockchain pose challenges for its effective implementation in large-scale Islamic financial systems (Idrees, M., & Mahmood, A. N., 2019).

Blockchain technology can streamline processes, reduce paperwork, and increase transparency in Islamic financial transactions (El Tiby, M., 2016). The decentralized nature of blockchain can enhance trust by providing a tamper-proof and verifiable record of transactions, aligning with the principles of Islamic finance (Malik, S., Kamal, M., & Qureshi, K., 2019). Blockchain can aid in extending financial services to the unbanked and underbanked populations, contributing to financial inclusion in line with Islamic finance goals (Ali, H. F., 2021). Blockchain enables the creation of innovative and Shari'ah-compliant financial products, expanding the offerings in the Islamic finance market (Iqbal, S., Asad, S., & Ayub, U., 2018).

Adhering to Shari'ah principles is paramount, and navigating how blockchain aligns with these principles and ensuring compliance is a significant challenge (Wani, S. M., & Noordin, M. F., 2020). Developing a robust legal and regulatory framework that aligns with blockchain technology and Islamic finance is crucial for overcoming hurdles (Iqbal, S., Asad, S., & Ayub, U., 2018). Integrating blockchain with legacy systems and infrastructure in Islamic financial institutions poses a technological challenge (Malik, S., Kamal, M., & Qureshi, K., 2019).

El Tiby, M., & Hassouna, A. (2017. Explored the integration of blockchain technology with Islamic finance, providing a conceptual framework to leverage the benefits of both domains. Akram, W., & Aboukhamseen, S. M. (2021). Presented a framework for Sukuk issuance using blockchain technology, demonstrating its potential application in Islamic finance. Al-Turjman, F. M., & Elbarrawy, A. M. (2018). Discussed the challenges and solutions for ensuring Shariah compliance in integrating blockchain technology, providing valuable insights into this crucial aspect. Pal, T., Irfan, M., Kassim, S.B., How do Machine Learning (ML) techniques benefit the insurance industry? An exploratory study, (2023), examined astounding success and previously unheard-of accuracy, artificial intelligence and machine learning have grown in significance within the finance industry.

The above literature review provides an overview of the fundamental concepts of blockchain, including its structure, decentralization, consensus mechanisms, immutability, security, and programmability through intelligent contracts. It forms the basis for a deeper understanding of blockchain technology, its application in Islamic finance, and its diverse applications in various domains of Islamic Finance.

3. STUDY METHODOLOGY

Blockchain Technology (BT) in Islamic finance research has experienced substantial growth in the last ten years. Emerging research domains often involve inductive methodologies like grounded theory and case studies. Blockchain Technology (BT) has indeed brought about significant innovation and novelty to the domain of Islamic finance in the areas like Transparency, Smart Contracts for Sharia Compliance, Efficient Payment Systems, Facilitating Zakat and Charity Distribution and Cross-Border Investments and Capital Flow. However, research brings novel practices that not only bring technological advancement but also align with Islamic financial principles' ethical and compliance requirements. It opens up new possibilities for financial inclusion, transparency, and efficiency in the Islamic finance industry. The integration of deductive approaches in Islamic research focused on Blockchain Technology is at its nascent stage.

Scopus is our primary repository due to its extensive compilation of financial scholarly articles, offering a comprehensive collection (Goodell et al., 2021). Our research efforts utilize a wide array of search terms, as demonstrated by the existing body of research (Alamad et al., 2021; Arnold et al., 2021). The approach for gathering the final datasets for 540 studies. Scopus and Google Scholar are a comprehensive and information-rich research databases, particularly for quantitative studies in the academic realm (Baas et al., 2020; Kumar et al., 2023; Kumar et al., 2022). The Scopus and Google Scholar database has recently seen extensive usage compared to the WOS and PubMed databases due to its advanced features and expansive coverage. According to recommendations from previous studies (Baas et al., 2020; Kumar et al., 2022), the current research employs the Scopus database to analyse and focus on the Blockchain Technology and Islamic Finance theme. The present study adopts PRISMA methods to conduct a literature review as recommended by (Harahap, Risfandy and Futri, 2023) refer figure 1. PRISMA (Preferred Reporting Items for Systematic Reviews and Meta-Analyses) is a widely recognised and recommended method for conducting systematic literature reviews (Baas et al., 2020; Kumar et al., 2023; Kumar et al., 2022). Steps adopted in PRISMA methods focusing on.

Figure 1. PRISMA flow diagram of selection process

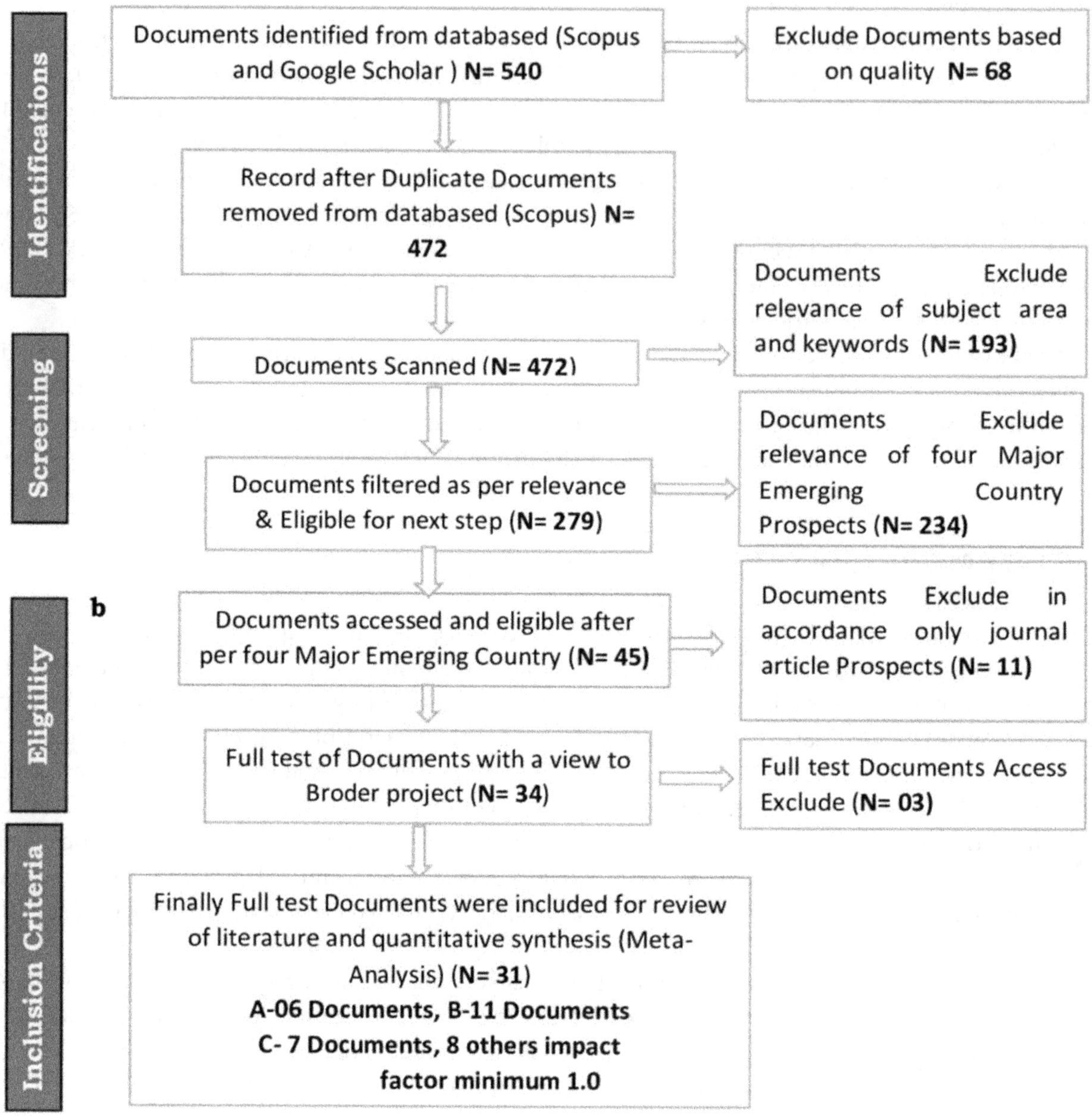

Source: Authors

PRISMA Step 1: Identification involves a comprehensive search to locate all relevant studies pertaining to the research question. This stage aims to minimize bias and ensure no important studies are overlooked. Following recommendations from Liberati (2009), Pahlevan-Sharif et al. (2019), and Pahlevan Sharif et al. (2019), the present study chose to utilize Scopus and google scholar as the primary platform for conducting this rigorous search. This decision was supported by earlier studies such as those by H. K. Baker et al. (2021) and M. A. Khan et al. (2021).

PRISMA Step 2: Screening involves a rigorous evaluation of the identified studies based on their titles, abstracts, and keywords. This process aims to exclude studies that are clearly irrelevant to the research objectives, thus refining the list of potential candidates for inclusion in the systematic literature review. To ensure accuracy and minimize errors, screening criteria, involving titles, abstracts, and keywords, are fundamental steps in the literature review process to identify relevant studies. Here's an interpretation of the provided screening information:

Initial Document Identification: Total Documents Identified (N=540): This refers to the total number of documents initially retrieved from the selected databases, Scopus and Google Scholar.

Exclusion Based on Quality: Documents Excluded Based on Quality (N=68): These are documents that were excluded from further consideration due to quality concerns. Quality assessment could involve factors like credibility of the source, methodology, or other relevant aspects that determine the robustness of the study.

Duplicate Document Removal: Remaining Documents after Duplicate Removal (N=472): After removing duplicate documents, the total number of unique documents remaining for further screening and analysis is 472.

Exclusion Based on Relevance of Subject Area and Keywords: Documents Excluded Based on Relevance (N=193): These are documents that were excluded during the screening process based on relevance to the subject area and keywords. If a document did not align with the research topic or did not contain the specified keywords, it was excluded at this stage.

PRISMA Step-3 Eligibility Criteria: The eligibility criteria for selecting documents related to Blockchain Technology (BT) in Islamic finance, along with exclusion terms, can be summarized as follows:

Documents filtered for relevance and eligibility (N=279): These documents passed the initial filtering process and met the criteria for relevance and eligibility, making them suitable for further consideration in the study.

Exclusion based on relevance to major emerging countries (N=234): These documents were excluded as they were not relevant to the major emerging countries (Brazil, Russia, India, China) in the context of Blockchain Technology (BT) in Islamic finance. Out of 279 documents 234 documents other than selected four countries are removed. For next documents accessible and eligible documents after major emerging countries 45 nos. These documents were both accessible and met the eligibility criteria specific to the major emerging countries (Brazil, Russia, India, China) concerning Blockchain Technology (BT) in Islamic finance.

Exclusion of other documents except journal articles (N=11): These documents were excluded as they did not fall under the category of journal articles, aligning with the specific inclusion criteria focusing on journal articles. Article filtered as per the exclusion criteria of "journal" only. 11 documents found to be irrelevant papers and these are based on conferences paper, book and other documents, it is excluded and next steps documents are available are 34.

Exclusion of Documents Based on full access (N=3): These documents were excluded based on specific relevance-related reasons, as determined by the criteria set for the study. Based on the above exclusion criteria of eligibility stage provide 31 final documents. Next and last step of PRISMA methods is inclusion criteria.

PRISMA Step-4 Inclusion Criteria: The inclusion criteria for selecting documents related to Blockchain Technology (BT) in Islamic finance can be interpreted as follows:

Documents Included for Review and Meta-Analysis (N=31): These are the documents that met the criteria for a full review of literature and potential inclusion in a quantitative synthesis, specifically a meta-analysis.

Quality Assessment Using ABDC Categories:

A Category Articles (N=6): These documents are categorized as 'A' based on ABDC (Australian Business Deans Council) category, indicating high quality and impact within the academic field.

B Category 11 Articles are identified under the 'B' category according to ABDC, denoting good quality and impact in the academic domain.

C Category 7 Articles are categorized as 'C' by ABDC, implying a satisfactory level of quality and impact within academia.

Scopus and Web of Science (WOS) Articles (N=8): These are additional selected papers sourced from Scopus and Web of Science, implying they meet certain criteria, although not categorized by ABDC. The selected 08 papers had a minimum impact factor of 1.0, indicating a level of significance and influence within their respective academic domains.

These inclusion criteria were employed to filter and select documents aligning with the research focus on Blockchain Technology (BT) in Islamic finance, considering factors such as relevance, publication frequency, document type, major emerging countries, and the broader project scope. The inclusion of documents for meta-analysis and the quality assessment through ABDC categories demonstrate a rigorous selection process to ensure the quality and relevance of the chosen literature for the study.

4. REVIEW RESULTS AND PERFORMANCES ANALYSIS

4.1 Growth Trend of Blockchain Technology and Islamic Finance

The convergence of Blockchain Technology and Islamic Finance represents a significant and evolving intersection within the financial industry. As the number of publications in this field has shown a remarkable growth trend over the past decade, the following interpretations can be made:

Early Interest (2013-2014): The initial years marked the inception of research interest in the intersection of Blockchain Technology and Islamic Finance. Although the number of publications was relatively low during this period, it laid the foundation for subsequent exploration and development in this field. Researchers likely began to recognize the potential compatibility between blockchain principles and Islamic finance principles, paving the way for future inquiries.

Gradual Expansion (2015-2018): The years from 2015 to 2018 witnessed a gradual but consistent increase in research output. This phase can be attributed to a growing awareness of the synergies between Blockchain Technology and Islamic Finance. Researchers and professionals started delving deeper into the compatibility of blockchain's features, such as transparency and decentralized ledgers, with the ethical and risk-sharing aspects of Islamic finance. This period represents a critical phase of theoretical exploration and experimentation.

Significant Acceleration (2019-2022): The most substantial growth occurred between 2019 and 2022, with the number of publications more than doubling each year. This acceleration is indicative of the broader recognition of the potential benefits and opportunities presented by integrating

Figure 2. Decade of growth trend on blockchain technology and Islamic Finance research (2013-2023)

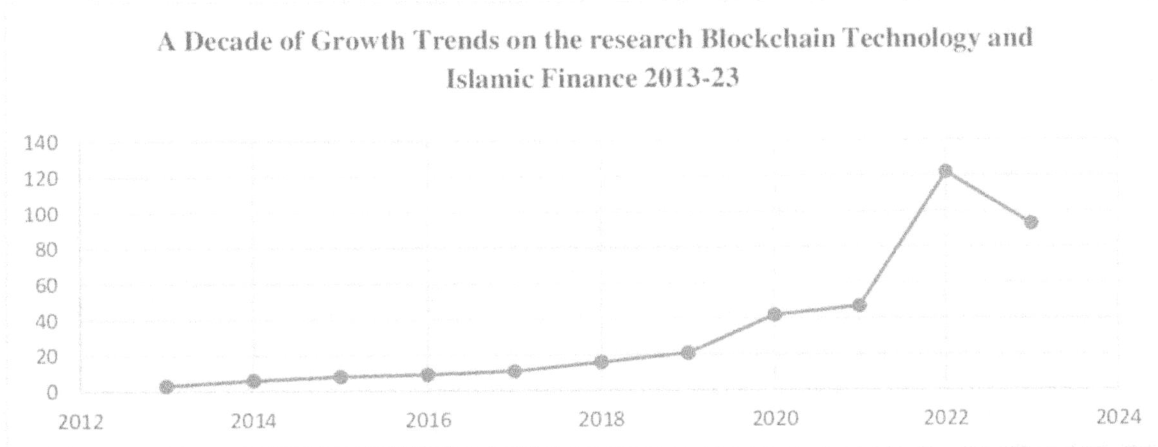

Sources: Authors

blockchain technology into the Islamic finance framework. During these years, groundbreaking studies, innovative use cases, and practical applications likely gained prominence. This period may have marked the transition from theoretical exploration to real-world implementations, attracting significant attention from both academia and industry.

Peak in 2022: The year 2022 stands out as the pinnacle of interest and research activity, with 122 publications. This peak might be attributed to major breakthroughs, increased investment in research, or regulatory developments that spotlighted the convergence of blockchain and Islamic finance. It's also plausible that 2022 marked a turning point, with a surge in pilot projects and tangible applications in this field, fuelling further curiosity and exploration.

Rising trend in 2023: The slight decrease in publications in 2023 may be interpreted as a phase of consolidation and refinement. It's common for emerging research areas to experience fluctuations as researchers review and consolidate existing work. This phase might also involve aligning research outcomes with practical applications and adapting to any evolving regulatory or market conditions.

The potential alignment of Fintech innovations with the principles of Islamic finance, such as transparency, ethical business standards, and risk-sharing, highlights the opportunity for Islamic finance to leverage these technological advancements effectively. Blockchain technology, with its public bookkeeping features, can enhance transparency and ethical standards, aligning with the principles of Islamic finance. Furthermore, the risk-sharing mechanisms inherent in fintech can align well with Shariah requirements, allowing for better risk management and investment structures.

The growth trend in publications on the intersection of Blockchain Technology and Islamic Finance indicates a thriving and dynamic research area with substantial potential for innovation and practical application. The convergence of blockchain technology and Islamic finance is not only academically promising but also holds significant real-world implications for the finance industry, particularly in terms of aligning with Islamic ethical and risk-sharing principles

4.2. Achievements in research and scientific output

4.2.1. Prominent Research Articles and Contributors on Blockchain Technology and Islamic Finance

The global financial crisis was marked when individuals lost faith in the conventional financial system and sought alternatives to offer greater confidence regarding their investments. The severity of the financial crisis in 2008 paved the way for the emergence of Islamic financial systems to recover from the crisis (Hussain, 2010). Further, Blockchain technology has garnered substantial attention and has captured global interest from diverse stakeholders. Since then, several prominent research papers have contributed significantly to blockchain technology and its intersection with Islamic finance. The following research papers have made substantial contributions, such as Blockchain for Business Management: Applications, challenges, and Potentials (Pal A.; Tiwari C.J.); Blockchain in Banking and Finance: A Bibliometric Review (Haldar et al.) The role of skills in Islamic financial innovation: Evidence from Bahrain and Malaysia (Poon et al.) Whether Cryptocurrency is a threat or a revolution? An analysis from an ESG perspective (Rabbani M.R. et al.) emerged as the most prominent contributors covering the diversified areas in blockchain and Islamic finance. Table 1 gives a detailed list of all the prominent research papers.

Table 2: Provides the details of Prominent researchers in the intersection of blockchain technology and Islamic finance who have made significant contributions to understanding how blockchain can align with the principles of Islamic finance, ensuring compliance with Sharia law. Line with blockchain technology and Islamic Finance, the research paper "Past, present, and future of sustainable finance: insights from big data analytics through machine learning of scholarly Research". Authored by Kumar S.; Sharma D.; Rao S.; Lim W.M.; Mangla S.K. (2022) emerged as the moist impressive and prominent author, accompanied by 82 citations, followed by a research paper "Islamic Finance and Cryptocurrency: A Systematic Review", Authored by Hassan M.K.; Rabbani M.R.; Mohd. Ali M.A. (2020) drew a citation of 78, next by Mosteanu N.R.; Faccia A. (2020) paper titled "Digital systems and new challenges of financial management – fintech, XBRL, blockchain, and cryptocurrencies", drew a citation of 77. Fourth prominent researcher Rabbani M.R., Khan S.; Thalassinos E.I. (2020), their paper on "FinTech, blockchain, and Islamic finance: An extensive literature review" drew a citation of 58. Fifth in order was Rabbani M.R., Bashar A.; Nawaz N., Karim S., Ali M.A.M., Rahiman H.U., Alam M.S. (2021), their paper titled "What Do We Know about Crowdfunding and P2P Lending Research? A Bibliometric Review and Meta-Analysis", had a citation of 54. The other prominent authors such as Secinaro S., Calandra D. (2021), Jha N., Prashar D., Khalaf O.I., Alotaibi Y.; Alsufyani A.; Alghamdi S. (2021), Ul Hassan M.; Rehmani M.H.; Chen J. (2020) etc had a citation between 52 to 45 range.

Several reputable journals publish research at the intersection of blockchain technology and Islamic finance. These journals provide a platform for scholars and researchers to share their insights and findings in these evolving fields. **Table 3** provides the most accessible journal on Blockchain and Islamic finance. Sustainability (Switzerland) has the highest citation of 91, with six renowned articles published. The second reputed journal is the Journal of Open Innovation: Technology, Market, and Complexity, which has 73 citations and has published three articles in line with blockchain and Islamic Finance, followed by Heliyon and Risks, which has published three articles and has a citation of 47. The fourth reputed journal is Qualitative Research in Financial Markets, which published six articles with a citation of 45. The fifth reputed journal publishing articles in Blockchain Technology and Islamic Finance is the Journal of Risk and Financial Management, with citations of 37 and four articles. The other reputed

Table 1. Performances analysis on blockchain technology and Islamic finance

Performances Analysis on Blockchain Technology and Islamic Finance		
Authors	**Title of the Article**	**Total citations**
Pal A.; Tiwari C.J.; Haldar N.	Blockchain for business management: Applications, challenges and potentials	1
Patel R.; Migliavacca M.; Oriani M.E.	Blockchain in banking and finance: A bibliometric review	1
Poon J.; Chow Y.W.; Ewers M.; Ramli R.	The role of skills in Islamic financial innovation: Evidence from Bahrain and Malaysia	1
Rabbani MR.; Alshaikh A.; Jreisat A.; Bashar A.; Moh'D Ali M.A.	Whether Cryptocurrency is a threat or a revolution? An analysis from ESG perspective	1
Rabbani M.R.; Bashar A.; Nawaz N.; Karim S.; Ali M.A.M.; Rahiman H.U.; Alam M.S.	Exploring the role of islamic fintech in combating the aftershocks of covid-19: The open social innovation of the islamic financial system	1
Rabbani M.R.; Khan S.; Thalassinos E.I.	FinTech, blockchain and Islamic finance: An extensive literature review	1
Rehman M.U.; Asghar N.; Kang S.H.	Do Islamic indices provide diversification to bitcoin? A time-varying copulas and value at risk application	1
Sabah N.; Sagheer A.; Dawood O.	Survey: (Blockchain-Based Solution for COVID-19 and Smart Contract Healthcare Certification)	1
Secinaro S.; Calandra D.	Halal food: Structured literature review and research agenda	1
Shin E.J.; Kang H.-G.; Bae K.	A study on the sustainable development of NPOs with blockchain technology	1
Siswantoro D.; Handika R.; Mita A.F.	The requirements of cryptocurrency for money, an Islamic view	1
Truby J.; Brown R.D.; Dahdal A.; Ibrahim I.	Blockchain, climate damage, and death: Policy interventions to reduce the carbon emissions, mortality, and net-zero implications of non-fungible tokens and Bitcoin	1
Ul hassan M.; Rehmani M.H.; Chen J.	Differential privacy in blockchain technology: A futuristic approach	1
Wang Z.; Li M.; Lu J.; Cheng X.	Business Innovation based on artificial intelligence and Blockchain technology	1
Yousaf I.; Yarovaya L.	Spillovers between the Islamic gold-backed cryptocurrencies and equity markets during the COVID-19: A sectorial analysis	1

journal in the area of Blockchain Technology and Islamic finance is the Journal of Islamic Marketing, Research in International Business and Finance, Journal of Islamic Accounting and Business Research, Technology in Society, Impact of Financial Technology (fintech) on Islamic Finance and Financial Stability, and International Journal of Islamic and Middle Eastern Finance and Management, having a citation between 35 to 6.

Research in blockchain technology and Islamic finance is a dynamic and interdisciplinary area that draws contributions from various countries globally. While specific rankings can vary based on research trends and academic institutions' activities, several countries are notable for publishing research papers

Table 2. Prominent researchers emerged in blockchain technology and Islamic finance

Authors	Title of the Article	Total citations
Kumar S.; Sharma D.; Rao S.; Lim W.M.; Mangla S.K. (2022)	Past, present, and future of sustainable finance: insights from big data analytics through machine learning of scholarly research	82
Hassan M.K.; Rabbani M.R.; Mohd. Ali M.A. (2020)	Islamic Finance and Cryptocurrency: A Systematic Review	78
Mosteanu N.R.; Faccia A. (2020)	Digital systems and new challenges of financial management – fintech, XBRL, blockchain and cryptocurrencies	77
Rabbani M.R.; Khan S.; Thalassinos E.I. (2020)	FinTech, blockchain and Islamic finance: An extensive literature review	58
Rabbani M.R.; Bashar A.; Nawaz N.; Karim S.; Ali M.A.M.; Rahiman H.U.; Alam M.S. (2021)	What Do We Know about Crowdfunding and P2P Lending Research? A Bibliometric Review and Meta-Analysis	54
Secinaro S.; Calandra D. (2021)	Halal food: structured literature review and research agenda	52
Jha N.; Prashar D.; Khalaf O.I.; Alotaibi Y.; Alsufyani A.; Alghamdi S. (2021)	Blockchain based crop insurance: a decentralized insurance system for modernization of indian farmers	49
Ul Hassan M.; Rehmani M.H.; Chen J. (2020)	Differential privacy in blockchain technology: A futuristic approach	49
Truby J.; Brown R.D.; Dahdal A.; Ibrahim I. (2022)	Blockchain, climate damage, and death: Policy interventions to reduce the carbon emissions, mortality, and net-zero implications of non-fungible tokens and Bitcoin	46
Alam N.; Gupta l.; Zameni A. (2019)	Fintech and Islamic finance: Digitalization, development and disruption	45
Liu Q.; Guan Q.; Yang X.; Zhu H.; Green G.; Yin S. (2019)	Education-Industry Cooperative System Based on Blockchain	45
Mehdiabadi A.; Tabatabeinasab M.; Spulbar C.; Yazdi A.K.; Birau R. (2020)	Are we ready for the challenge of banks 4.0? designing a roadmap for banking systems in industry 4.0	45

Table 3. Leading journals in the aera of blockchain technology and Islamic finance

Leading Journals in the Aera of Blockchain Technology and Islamic Finance		
Source	**Total documents**	**Total citations**
Sustainability (Switzerland)	6	91
Journal of Open Innovation: Technology, Market, and Complexity	3	73
Heliyon	3	47
Risks	3	47
Qualitative Research in Financial Markets	6	45
Journal of Risk and Financial Management	4	37
Journal of Islamic Marketing	3	35
Research in International Business and Finance	3	25
Journal of Islamic Accounting and Business Research	10	19
Technology in Society	4	18
Impact of Financial Technology (fintech) on Islamic Finance and Financial Stability	4	10
International Journal of Islamic and Middle Eastern Finance and Management	3	6

Table 4. Top countries publishing blockchain technology and Islamic finance research papers

Country	Total documents	Total citations
Malaysia	101	546
India	35	367
Bahrain	31	341
United Kingdom	25	235
Australia	10	229
United States	29	177
Pakistan	22	120
Oman	5	115
China	11	110
Qatar	15	101
United Arab Emirates	21	86
Saudi Arabia	18	84
Indonesia	32	76
South Korea	9	72
Egypt	8	61
Turkey	11	56

at the intersection of these domains. **Table 4** gives a detailed description of the top countries publishing research papers in the said area; Malaysia tops the list of countries publishing research papers on Blockchain Technology and Islamic Finance with the highest citations of 556 out of 101 research papers. The second top country is India, with 367 citations from thirty-five articles. The third top country is Bahrain, with 341 citations from thirty-one research papers. The United Kingdom stands as the fourth top country with a citation of 235 from 25 research papers, followed by Australia at the fifth position with a citation of 229 from 10 research papers. The order is followed by the United States, Pakistan, Oman, China, Qatar, United Arab Emirates, Saudi Arabia, Indonesia, South Korea, Egypt, and Turkey, all having citations between 177 and 56.

All the mentioned countries below have shown noteworthy involvement in researching and advancing blockchain technology's integration within the Islamic finance framework. However, it is essential to note that research is a global endeavour, and contributions and advancements can come from various countries worldwide. Researchers and scholars collaborate and contribute across borders to drive innovation and understanding in this evolving interdisciplinary field.

Table 5 provides an insight into Prominent research organizations engaged in blockchain technology and Islamic finance research, which play a crucial role in advancing understanding and applications at the intersection of these domains. School of Management, IMS Unison University, Dehradun, India, tops the list of organizations engaged in blockchain Technology and Islamic Finance research with the highest citations of 123 from seven articles. The second top organization engaged in research focusing on blockchain technology and Islamic finance was the Department of Economics and Finance, University of New Orleans, New Orleans, la, United States, with a citation of 97 from fourteen articles. Followed in the third position is the Faculty of Business and Management, University Sultan Zainal Abidin, Kuala

Table 5. Prominent research organization engaged in blockchain technology and Islamic finance research

Prominent Research Organization Engaged in Blockchain Technology and Islamic Finance Research		
Organization	**Total Documents**	**Total Citations**
School of Management, IMS Unison University, Dehradun, 248009, India	7	123
Department of Economics and Finance, University of New Orleans, New Orleans, 70148, la, United States	14	97
Faculty of Business and Management, University Sultan Zainal Abidin, Kuala Terengganu, Malaysia	3	25
International Centre for Education in Islamic Finance, Kuala Lumpur, Malaysia	4	17
College of Administrative Sciences, Seiyun University, Seiyun, Yemen	3	6
Department of Economics and Finance, College of Business Administration, University of Bahrain, Sakhir, Bahrain	5	6
Department of Economics and Finance, College of Business Administration, University of Bahrain, Zallaq, Bahrain	7	6
Islamic Business School, University Utara Malaysia, Sintok, Malaysia	5	6

Terengganu, Malaysia, with a citation of 25 from three articles. The fourth position in the order is the College of Administrative Sciences, Seiyun University, Seiyun, Yemen, with a citation of 17 from four articles. The fifth in the order is the Department of Economics and Finance, College of Business Administration, University of Bahrain, Sakhir, Bahrain, with a citation of 6 from five articles. Department of Economics and Finance, College of Business Administration, University of Bahrain, Zallaq, Bahrain and Islamic Business School, University Utara Malaysia, Sintok, Malaysia stands in the sixth position in the order with a citation of 6.

5. DISCUSSION

Present studies discussion are based on the research questions raised in the introduction section. Authors are tried to address the research question the previous chapter performances analysis of literature review.

RQ1: What are the essential theoretical and practical contributions of prominent blockchain Technology and Islamic finance research articles, and how have these findings influenced the industry?

5.1 Theoretical Contribution of the Research

The theoretical contributions of research on blockchain technology and Islamic finance are multifaceted and hold immense potential for reshaping the financial landscape in a Sharia-compliant manner. Blockchain's core features of immutability and transparency align well with Sharia principles. The decentralized and transparent nature of blockchain can facilitate real-time monitoring and auditing of financial transactions, ensuring compliance with Islamic finance principles, such as avoiding riba (usury) and maintaining transparency in financial dealings, Elkamhi, R., Ghandar, A., & Waring, A. (2017). Smart contracts can be designed to adhere to Sharia law, automating and enforcing Sharia-compliant financial agreements, ensuring fairness, transparency, and compliance with Islamic finance principles,

Lee, S. M., & Lee, S. (2018). Blockchain-enabled asset-backed tokenization can facilitate the creation of Sharia-compliant digital assets, promoting fractional ownership and efficient trading while adhering to principles of shared risk and ownership in Islamic finance, Li, X., Jiang, P, et al. (2017). Blockchain can enhance the efficiency and transparency of zakat distribution, ensuring accurate collection, tracking, and distribution of funds, promoting transparency, and maximizing the impact of philanthropic activities in line with Islamic teachings, Idrees, S., & Gani, A. (2018). Blockchain's capabilities can streamline cross-border transactions in Islamic finance, ensuring compliance with Islamic finance requirements, such as avoiding delays that could lead to riba, Yli-Huumo, J., et al. (2016)

These theoretical contributions underscore the potential of blockchain technology to revolutionize Islamic finance, providing innovative solutions that comply with Sharia principles while enhancing transparency, security, and efficiency within the financial ecosystem.

5.2 Practical Contribution of the Research

Research on blockchain technology and Islamic finance drives practical contributions shaping the development and implementation of innovative solutions within the financial ecosystem while adhering to Sharia principles. Research explores the creation and use of ICCs, adhering to Sharia principles. These digital currencies are designed to ensure compliance with Islamic finance rules, providing a practical solution for digital transactions while aligning with Sharia guidelines, Zohar, A., & Leloup, L. (2015). Blockchain facilitates the issuance and management of Sukuk, Islamic financial instruments. Smart contracts and tokenization on the blockchain streamline the Sukuk issuance process, enhancing transparency, security, and efficiency in compliance with Sharia principles, Hussein, R., Deng, H., & Luthra, S. (2018). Blockchain enables the creation of decentralized platforms for collecting and distributing zakat, ensuring transparency and efficiency in allocating funds to eligible recipients addressing socioeconomic challenges, Dhillon, G., & Madi, A. (2019). Blockchain facilitates secure and transparent trade finance transactions, including Murabahah (cost-plus financing). Smart contracts and blockchain enable real-time tracking of transactions, reducing fraud and ensuring Sharia compliance, Al-Turjman, F. M., & Bibi, I. (2019). Blockchain is utilized to trace and authenticate the halal status of products within the supply chain, ensuring compliance with halal requirements. This enhances consumer trust and confidence in halal products, Khan, Z., Anwar, Z., & Soomro, K. A. (2020).

These practical contributions highlight how blockchain technology is applied to address specific challenges within Islamic finance, offering solutions that enhance transparency, efficiency, and compliance with Sharia principles. As the field continues to evolve, these tical applications are expected to grow and transform the landscape of Islamic finance.

RQ2: "How has the integration of blockchain technology in Islamic finance evolved, and what are the prominent trends and challenges highlighted in research articles?"

The integration of blockchain technology in Islamic finance has evolved significantly over the years. Initially, there was a focus on understanding the compatibility of blockchain with Islamic finance principles. This evolved into exploring specific use cases, such as Islamic-compliant. Early research examined the fundamental features of blockchain technology and its potential alignment with Islamic finance principles, focusing on decentralization, immutability, and transparency. Cryptocurrencies, smart contracts for Sharia-compliant agreements, and tokenization of assets for Sukuk issuance, Elkamhi, R.,

Ghandar, A., & Waring, A. (2017). Recent research has focused on leveraging blockchain for Sukuk issuance, allowing for fractional ownership and efficient trading, thereby transforming the traditional Islamic bond market, Amin, H., & Hanifa, A. (2018). One of the primary challenges is the lack of clear regulatory frameworks governing blockchain integration within Islamic finance (Rabbani *et al.*, 2022). Regulatory ambiguity poses hurdles to broader adoption and implementation, Hasan, M. M., Hossain, M. S., & Zikria, Y. B. (2018). Scalability issues and performance constraints of blockchain networks hinder their widespread adoption in high-volume transactions required by the financial industry, Ouda, H., & Salah, K. (2018).

By examining the evolution, trends, and challenges in integrating blockchain technology within Islamic finance, this research provides insights into the current state of the field and identifies ares for further exploration and development.

RQ3: "What specific applications of blockchain technology within Islamic finance have been extensively researched, and what are the implications of these applications?

Several specific applications of blockchain technology within Islamic finance have been extensively researched, showcasing the potential for enhancing various aspects of the financial ecosystem while adhering to Sharia principles. Leveraging blockchain for Sukuk (Islamic bonds) issuance and asset tokenization to enable fractional ownership and streamline the trading of Sukuk securities, Amin, H., & Hanifa, A. (2018). Implementing blockchain for secure and transparent trade finance transactions, including Murabahah (cost-plus financing) transactions in Islamic finance, Al-Turjman, F. M., & Bibi, I. (2019). Using blockchain to trace and authenticate the halal status of products within the halal food supply chain, Khan, Z., Anwar, Z., & Soomro, K. A. (2020). Employing blockchain for secure and immutable identity verification processes while ensuring compliance with Islamic finance requirements, Alsalman, R., Salah, K., & Jayaraman, R. (2020). These applications illustrate the potential of AI based blockchain technology (Panigrahi *et al.*, 2023) to revolutionize in different files of manufacturing and services sectors and specifically in emerging country prospects focusing on Islamic finance (Shaikh *et al.*, 2021), offering solutions that enhance transparency, efficiency, and adherence to Sharia principles.

6. CONCLUSION, FUTURE SCOPE, AND LIMITATIONS

This study reviews the various factors, such as Blockchain Technology, Fintech, and Cryptocurrencies in Islamic Finance. Any innovation is appreciated in Islamic Finance as long as it does not disturb the Quran's and Sunnah's basic teachings. The likelihood for blockchain technology in Islamic finance is bright in the Islamic world and among the Muslim users of financial services as it grants and facilitates opportunities for more innovation and can provide financial services at affordable cost. Integrations of Blockchain technology with Islamic finance can undoubtedly gain faith among Muslim and non-Muslim communities predominantly because of its transparency.

Research in the future on blockchain technology and Islamic finance can build on this body of work on developing a rich and evolving landscape that offers numerous opportunities for further research. Here are some potential areas of future research to expand and deepen the understanding of this exciting interdisciplinary field:

Explore and develop advanced innovative contract frameworks and consensus mechanisms that ensure higher compliance with Sharia principles, such as interest-free transactions, avoidance of uncertainty (gharar), and adherence to ethical investment guidelines.

Investigate how blockchain can facilitate financial inclusion within the Islamic finance sector, particularly in underbanked regions. Study the role of blockchain in providing secure and portable digital identities for unbanked populations, aligning with Islamic finance principles of equitable financial access.

Investigate the use of blockchain to create transparent and ethical supply chain finance solutions for Islamic finance. Explore how blockchain can track and verify the halal status of products, ensuring compliance with Islamic principles throughout the supply chain.

Study the regulatory challenges and opportunities related to cross-border transactions in Islamic finance facilitated by blockchain technology. Propose frameworks for regulatory harmonization to facilitate international Islamic financial transactions while ensuring compliance with different regulatory environments.

Explore how blockchain can enhance transparency, efficiency, and risk management in the Takaful industry. Investigate the potential for smart contracts and decentralized platforms to automate Takaful contracts and claims processing while adhering to Sharia-compliant principles.

Investigate the creation of regulatory frameworks that guide blockchain integration in Islamic finance. Explore how auditable smart contracts and blockchain-based compliance mechanisms can enhance regulatory oversight and accountability.

Propose and evaluate educational initiatives to raise awareness and understanding of blockchain technology among stakeholders in Islamic finance. Develop training programs and workshops to facilitate the adoption of blockchain solutions in compliance with Sharia principles.

Study the usability and user experience of blockchain-based applications designed for Islamic finance users. Evaluate user adoption factors and propose design enhancements to ensure seamless, user-friendly interfaces. By focusing on these areas, researchers can contribute to advancing the integration of blockchain technology in Islamic finance, fostering innovation, and ensuring the alignment of financial systems with ethical and Sharia-compliant principles.

Limitations researchers might have encountered when studying blockchain technology and Islamic finance between 2018 and 2023. It is important to note that new developments, research, and advancements may have occurred beyond. Blockchain technology is rapidly evolving, with new consensus mechanisms, platforms, and tools emerging frequently. Keeping up with these changes and understanding their implications for Islamic finance can be challenging, potentially leading to outdated information. Despite the theoretical advancements, empirical research and real-world case studies demonstrating blockchain's practical implementation and impact in Islamic finance may be limited. This could restrict the depth of insights into its actual effectiveness.

REFERENCES

Akram, W., & Aboukhamseen, S. M. (2021). A Framework for Sukuk Issuance Using Blockchain. In: *2021 IEEE International Conference on Blockchain*. IEEE.

Al-Tamimi, A. M., & Yasin, N. M. (2020). An Analysis of Islamic Banking in the Age of Blockchain Technology: A Theoretical Framework. *Journal of Theoretical and Applied Information Technology, 98*(1), 108–118.

Al-Turjman, F. M., & Bibi, I. (2019). Blockchain for trade finance in the context of Islamic finance. In *Blockchain for Sustainable Business Models* (pp. 73–87). Springer.

Al-Turjman, F. M., & Elbarrawy, A. M. (2018). Enabling blockchain technology in industry 4.0: A survey, challenges, and future trends. *IEEE Access : Practical Innovations, Open Solutions, 6*, 32110–32127.

Ali, H. F. (2021). Islamic Finance and Decentralized Finance (DeFi): A Conceptual Overview and Potential Synergies. *International Journal of Islamic and Middle Eastern Finance and Management, 14*(5), 639–655.

Ali, M. M. S., & Haneef, M. A. (2018). Blockchain in Islamic Finance: Smart Sukuk as a Case Study. In 2018 *7th International Conference on Computer and Communication Engineering (ICCCE)* (pp. 197-201). IEEE.

Ali, M. M. S., & Haneef, M. A. (2019). Blockchain for Islamic Finance: Current Pitfalls and Future Directions. In *2019 8th International Conference on Computer and Communication Engineering (ICCCE)* (pp. 74-79). IEEE.

Alsalman, R., Salah, K., & Jayaraman, R. (2020). Secure and transparent user authentication system for Islamic finance based on blockchain. *IEEE Transactions on Industrial Informatics, 16*(9), 5769–5776.

Amin, H., & Hanifa, A. (2018). A blockchain-based model for Sukuk securities: A study of feasibility and viability. *Journal of Corporate Real Estate, 20*(3), 160–180.

Azzi, M., & Alobaidy, M. (2018). Blockchain and Waqf: An Opportunity for Transparency and Efficiency. In: *IEEE/ACS 15th International Conference on Computer Systems and Applications (AICCSA)*. IEEE.

Beck, T., Demirgüç-Kunt, A., & Merrouche, O. (2013). Islamic vs. conventional banking: Business model, efficiency, and stability. *Journal of Banking & Finance, 37*(2), 433–447. doi:10.1016/j.jbankfin.2012.09.016

Catalini, C., & Gans, J. S. (2016). Some Simple Economics of the Blockchain. *NBER Working Paper No. 22952.*

Cocco, L., & Marchesi, M. (2016). Modelling and Simulation of the Economics of Mining in the Bitcoin Market. *PLoS One, 11*(10), e0164603. doi:10.1371/journal.pone.0164603 PMID:27768691

Cocco, L., Marchesi, M., & Setzu, A. (2017). Payment Systems: A Blockchain Approach. *Journal of Economic Behavior & Organization, 141*, 233–246.

Dhillon, G., & Madi, A. (2019). Zakat distribution and the potential role of blockchain. In *Financial Cryptography and Data Security* (pp. 416–428). Springer.

El Tiby, M. (2016). Innovation in Islamic Finance: A Framework for Shari'ah Compliance. *Journal of Islamic Accounting and Business Research, 7*(1), 36–50.

El Tiby, M., & Hassouna, A. (2017). Integrating blockchain technology with Islamic finance: A framework. In: *2017 International Conference on Islamic Applications in Computer Science and Technologies (IMAN)*. IEEE.

Elkamhi, R., Ghandar, A., & Waring, A. (2017). Blockchain technology: Principles and applications. In Handbook of Blockchain, Digital Finance, and Inclusion, 1 (pp. 29-41). Academic Press.

Hakim, D., & Meressa, A. (2019). The Potential of Blockchain Technology in Islamic Finance. In: *2019 International Conference on Information Management and Technology (ICIMTech)*. IEEE.

Hamid, S., & Omar, S. S. (2019). Blockchain Technology in Islamic Finance: A Comprehensive Review. *International Journal of Engineering & Technology, 8*(1.8), 234-238.

Hamoudi, H. A. (2007). You Say You Want a Revolution: Interpretive Communities and the Origins of Islamic Finance, 48 [Hereinafter Hamoudi]. *Virginia Journal of International Law*, 249.

Harahap, B., Risfandy, T., & Futri, I. N. (2023). Islamic Law, Islamic Finance, and Sustainable Development Goals: A Systematic Literature Review. *Sustainability (Basel), 15*(8), 6626. doi:10.3390u15086626

Hasan, M. M., Hossain, M. S., & Zikria, Y. B. (2018). Legal and regulatory challenges of blockchain technology in Islamic finance. In *2018 IEEE International Conference on Engineering, Technology and Innovation (ICE/ITMC)* (pp. 1-6). IEEE.

Hasan, Z. (2019). Islamic finance: An ethical alternative to conventional finance. *Journal of Business Ethics, 157*(4), 995–1017.

Hassan, M. K., & Abubakar, B. (2018). Islamic Finance and Blockchain Technology: A New Opportunity. In Handbook of Blockchain, Digital Finance, and Inclusion, 1(pp. 115-130). Academic Press.

Hussain, I., & Sultan, S. (2010). Analysis of Procrastination among University Students. *Procedia: Social and Behavioral Sciences, 5*, 1897–1904. doi:10.1016/j.sbspro.2010.07.385

Hussein, R., Deng, H., & Luthra, S. (2018). Blockchain technology applications in Islamic finance: A comprehensive review. *Journal of King Saud University. Computer and Information Sciences.*

Iansiti, M., & Lakhani, K. R. (2017). The Truth About Blockchain. *Harvard Business Review, 95*(1), 118–127.

Idrees, M., & Mahmood, A. N. (2019). A Survey on the Application of Blockchain Technology in Islamic Finance. In: *2019 IEEE International Conference on Blockchain (Blockchain)*. IEEE.

Idrees, S., & Gani, A. (2018). A survey of blockchain technologies for open innovation. *Journal of Network and Computer Applications, 107*, 62–84.

Iqbal, S., Asad, S., & Ayub, U. (2018). Blockchain Technology for Supply Chain Financing in Islamic Banking and Finance. In: *International Conference on Frontiers of Information Technology (FIT)*. IEEE.

Irfan, M., Elhoseny, M., Kassim, S., & Metawa, N. (2023). *Advanced Machine Learning Algorithms for Complex Financial Applications*. doi:10.4018/978-1-6684-4483-2

Irfan, M., Elmogy, M., Majid, M.S.A., & El-Sappagh, S. (2023*). The impact of AI innovation on financial sectors in the era of industry 5.0*. Research Gate.

Khan, M., Salah, K., Alazab, M., & Hitchens, M. (2018). Blockchain and Internet of Things: A Survey. *IEEE Access : Practical Innovations, Open Solutions*, *6*, 32979–33001. doi:10.1109/ACCESS.2018.2842685

Khan, Z., Anwar, Z., & Soomro, K. A. (2020). Blockchain for halal food traceability: A comprehensive review. *Journal of Cleaner Production*, *256*, 120626.

Lacity, M., & Hirschheim, R. (2018). The Blockchain Folk Theorem. *MIS Quarterly Executive*, *17*(3), 139–153.

Lee, S. M., & Lee, S. (2018). Smart contract-based Islamic crowdfunding: A comprehensive analysis. *Sustainability*, *10*(9), 3034.

Li, X., Jiang, P., Chen, T., Luo, X., & Wen, Q. (2017). A survey on the security of blockchain systems. *Future Generation Computer Systems*, *82*, 1–14.

Malik, S., Kamal, M., & Qureshi, K. (2019). Towards Shari'ah Compliance in Blockchain Technology: A Comprehensive Analysis and Future Perspective. In: *Proceedings of the 2nd International Conference on Blockchain Computing and Applications*. Research Gate.

Mougayar, W. (2016). *The Business Blockchain: Promise, Practice, and Application of the Next Internet Technology*. John Wiley & Sons.

Nakamoto, S. (2008). *Bitcoin: A Peer-to-Peer Electronic Cash System*. Bitcoin. https://bitcoin.org/bitcoin.pdf

Narayanan, A., Bonneau, J., Felten, E., Miller, A., & Goldfeder, S. (2016). *Bitcoin and Cryptocurrency Technologies: A Comprehensive Introduction*. Princeton University Press.

O'Dair, M., & Hobson, A. (2019). The Politics and Performativities of Blockchain Communities: A Cross Case Analysis. *Journal of Information Technology*, *34*(2), 162–177.

Ouda, H., & Salah, K. (2018). Scalability challenges in blockchain systems: A comprehensive review. *IEEE Access : Practical Innovations, Open Solutions*, *6*, 55108–55133.

Pal, T., Irfan, M., & Kassim, S.B. (2023). *How do Machine Learning (ML) techniques benefit the insurance industry? An exploratory study*. OUCI.

Panigrahi, R.R. (2023). Review of Machine Learning Techniques in the Supply Chain Management of Indian Industry. *Advanced Machine Learning Algorithms for Complex Financial Applications*. IGI Global. . doi:10.4018/978-1-6684-4483-2.ch013

Rabbani., M., Khan, S., & Thalassinos, E. (2020). FinTech, Blockchain, and Islamic Finance: An Extensive Literature Review. *International Journal of Economics and Business Administration*, *VIII*(2), 65–86.

Rabbani, M. R. (2022). Islamic Finance and Cryptocurrency: A Systematic Review. In *FinTech in Islamic Financial Institutions* (pp. 279–306). Springer International Publishing. doi:10.1007/978-3-031-14941-2_14

Ridho Kismawadi, E., Irfan, M., Shah, S.M.A.R. (2023). Revolutionizing Islamic finance: Artificial intelligence's role in the future of industry. The *Impact of AI Innovation on Financial Sectors in the Era of Industry 5.0*, (pp. 184-207). IGI Global.

Saeed, Z., & Al-Busaidi, A. (2018). An Islamic Perspective on Smart Contracts: An Overview and Comparative Analysis. In: *15th International Conference on Smart Cities: Improving Quality of Life Using ICT & IoT*. Springer.

Shaikh, Z. H., Sarea, A., & Irfan, M. (2021, September). Islamic banking strategies in the world of Fintech: success story of Bahrain. In *The International Conference On Global Economic Revolutions* (pp. 97-104). Cham: Springer International Publishing.

Suratgar, D. A. (1984). Forward: The Impact of Islamic Banking on World Financial and Commercial Relations, 16 [Hereinafter Suratgar]. *Law and Policy in International Business*, 1089.

Tapscott, D., & Tapscott, A. (2016). *Blockchain Revolution: How the Technology Behind Bitcoin Is Changing Money, Business, and the World*. Penguin.

Turetsky, M. (2017). Smart Contracts in Islamic Finance. In: *2017 19th International Conference on Advanced Communication Technology (ICACT)*. Research Gate.

Wani, S. M., & Noordin, M. F. (2020). Blockchain technology in Islamic finance: Regulatory and compliance issues. In: *International Conference on Applied Internet and Information Technologies*. Research Gate.

Yahaya, N. Z., & Alias, N. (2020). The Potential of Blockchain Technology in Islamic Finance: A Review. *International Journal of Advanced Science and Technology*, *29*(7), 3091–3103.

Yli-Huumo, J., Ko, D., Choi, S., Park, S., & Smolander, K. (2016). Where is current research on blockchain technology? A systematic review. *PLoS One*, *11*(10), e0163477. doi:10.1371/journal.pone.0163477 PMID:27695049

Zohar, A. (2015). Bitcoin: Under the Hood. *Communications of the ACM*, *58*(9), 104–113. doi:10.1145/2701411

Zohar, A., & Leloup, L. (2015). Bitcoin, Islamic finance, and the compliance of non-interest banking and finance. In *Business Transformation through Blockchain* (Vol. 1, pp. 287–298). Springer.

Chapter 5
Assessing Public Awareness of Islamic Finance and Interest-Free Banking in India

Asif Hasan
Karnavati University, India

Swati Gupta
Karnavati University, India

Mohammad Irfan
https://orcid.org/0000-0002-4956-1170
Business School, NSB Academy, India

Rui Manuel Dias
https://orcid.org/0000-0002-6138-3098
Instituto Politécnico de Setúbal, Portugal

ABSTRACT

This study investigates the awareness of Islamic finance and interest-free banking in India. It delves into the unique characteristics of Islamic banks that operate under Sharia'h, the Islamic law. This study aims to clarify how well the general public understands these concepts in a financial environment where conventional banking dominates. By identifying areas that may need further attention and education, the study can contribute to fostering financial inclusivity and ethical financial practices in India.

1. INTRODUCTION

The financial world is undergoing a rapid transformation, witnessing the emergence of alternative systems that challenge traditional banking and finance. In this dynamic landscape, Islamic finance, guided by the principles of Shariah (Islamic law), has garnered global attention, transcending its origins in predominantly Muslim nations. Islamic finance, which encompasses interest-free banking, is underpinned

DOI: 10.4018/979-8-3693-1038-0.ch005

by a framework that prioritizes ethical market practices, social justice, and equitable wealth distribution. The growth and influence of Islamic finance in the 21st century have piqued the interest of both practitioners and academics.

Islamic finance distinguishes itself by its explicit prohibition of interest payments and its emphasis on profit-and-loss sharing mechanisms. This unique approach has made it an appealing alternative to conventional financial systems, with its appeal extending well beyond Muslim-majority countries, resonating with diverse populations around the world. This surge in interest underscores the potential of Islamic finance to serve as a reform agenda for conventional financial systems, with a focus on fostering financial inclusivity and justice.

As of 2021, the Islamic finance industry boasts an impressive global value of approximately USD 4 trillion, marking a substantial annual growth rate of 17%, an increase from the 14% growth observed in 2020. The industry is represented in numerous countries through a network of fully Shariah-compliant financial institutions and financial windows, totalling 1,389 entities globally. Nevertheless, certain regions remain relatively untouched by this financial paradigm. For instance, Algeria, as indicated by a recent IFSB Report, 2019, has not shown significant interest in adopting an Islamic finance system, highlighting the varied regional responses to this global financial phenomenon.

This chapter sets out to investigate the level of awareness among customers in India regarding Islamic finance, with a specific focus on interest-free banking. It seeks to address fundamental questions: What is the extent of public awareness regarding the terminologies, rules, and principles of Islamic finance? How familiar are customers with the diverse range of Islamic finance products and services offered by banks in India?

This study is motivated by the pressing need to bridge existing knowledge gaps within the field of Islamic finance, particularly within the context of India. By exploring the levels of awareness and perception among customers, this research aims to provide valuable insights and recommendations for improving awareness and understanding of Islamic finance principles and their associated benefits.

Furthermore, the chapter discusses the broader potential of Islamic banking and finance in India, a nation with a significant Muslim population of approximately 172 million, constituting 14.2% of the country's total demographic composition [Census 2011]. This chapter argues that Islamic banking has the potential to contribute to economic stability, promote socio-economic justice, and foster an investment-oriented society, unburdened by debt. While rooted in Islamic principles, interest-free banking is positioned to benefit all members of society, irrespective of religious affiliation. This chapter underscores the readiness of Indian society to embrace Islamic banking, provided they perceive equitable benefits and security compared to conventional systems.

In conclusion, this chapter paints a comprehensive picture of the evolving landscape of Islamic finance, its global reach, and its potential significance in various regional contexts. Through examining awareness and readiness, this research aims to contribute to a better understanding of Islamic finance and its opportunities in India and beyond.

2. PERFORMANCE OF ISLAMIC FINANCE GLOBALLY[1]

The Islamic finance industry, with its various sectors, experienced notable growth in 2021. Islamic banking, the largest sector accounting for 70% of the industry's assets, saw a substantial increase in net income, primarily due to eased provisions for credit losses. The growth in this sector was propelled by three main factors: government support for sectors affected by the pandemic, operational efficiency improvements like branchless banking and FinTech partnerships, and a sustained high demand for Islamic banking services (Irfan et al 2023a). Remarkably, the most significant growth occurred in non-core Islamic finance markets, indicating the emergence of new markets and the stabilization of the industry in more mature jurisdictions. Notable countries with substantial growth in Islamic banking included Tajikistan, Burkina Faso, and Ethiopia.

The sukuk sector, the second largest by assets, expanded by 14% in 2021, reaching a total of $713 billion in sukuk outstanding. New issuances also rose by 9%, totaling a record $202.1 billion. Long-term sukuk with tenors of five years or more saw an increase, reflecting a shift towards longer-term investment post-pandemic. Sovereigns and quasi-sovereigns continued to dominate new issuances, particularly in the realm of ESG (Environmental, Social, and Governance) sukuk, which reached a new high of $5.3 billion in 2021. Saudi Arabia, Indonesia, and Malaysia emerged as leaders in this segment, driven by the mainstreaming of ESG investments and strong demand from the Gulf Cooperation Council (GCC) for funding green and sustainability transition projects.

The Islamic funds sector, the third largest in the industry, experienced exceptional growth of 34%, with assets under management (AuM) reaching $238 billion in 2021. Despite its impressive growth, this sector is concentrated in a few countries, with Iran, Saudi Arabia, and Malaysia accounting for 81% of total global Islamic funds. Key asset classes in this sector included money market and equity, with the emergence of exchange-traded funds (ETFs) in various countries. The development of ESG funds marked a significant milestone in the Islamic finance landscape, with Malaysia's Employee Provident Fund (EPF) committing to a fully ESG-compliant portfolio by 2030 and a climate-neutral portfolio by 2050.

Other Islamic financial institutions (OIFIs), encompassing various entities like FinTech companies, investment firms, and leasing and microfinance firms, grew by 5%, with $169 billion in assets. Notable growth was observed in countries like Kazakhstan, Egypt, and the Maldives. The FinTech segment, in particular, gained substantial attention, with Saudi Arabia planning to significantly increase the number of FinTech firms by 2025.

Takaful, the smallest sector in Islamic finance, managed $73 billion in 2021, showing strong growth of 17%. This sector is undergoing consolidation in the Gulf Cooperation Council (GCC) countries, aiming to streamline operations and reduce costs. Moreover, significant regulatory changes in Southeast Asia are expected to enhance governance in Indonesia and Malaysia, potentially welcoming new entrants in the Philippines.

In summary, the Islamic finance industry experienced robust growth across its sectors in 2021. Islamic banking, sukuk, Islamic funds, OIFIs, and Takaful all demonstrated positive trends, underpinned by diverse factors and reflecting the industry's resilience and adaptability to changing global economic conditions.

3. LITERATURE REVIEW RELATED TO AWARENESS ABOUT ISLAMIC BANKING

The basic rule of Islamic finance is the prevention of interest from the banking and sharing of profit and loss (Khattak & Rehman, 2010). Awareness about Islamic finance positively influence the customers to adopt Islamic finance (Al Balushi, Locke & Boulanouar, 2019). In their study, Hamid and Nordin (2001) examined the extent to which banking customers possess knowledge regarding Islamic banking. Their findings indicate that a significant proportion of respondents lack the ability to distinguish between the offerings of Islamic and conventional banks. However, it is worth noting that a majority of customers demonstrated sufficient awareness of the services provided by Malaysian Islamic banks. Lateh, Ismail & Ariffin (2009) concluded that banking customers have very less awareness about the products and services offered by Islamic banks. Cheteni (2014) conducted a study to investigate the level of customer awareness regarding Islamic banking products and services. The findings of the study indicated that gender, age, race, and qualification exhibited statistical significance in their impact on customers' level of awareness. In their study, Rammal and Zurbruegg (2007) conducted an analysis on the level of awareness among Muslim Australians regarding Islamic banking. The findings revealed that a majority of Muslim banking customers expressed interest in acquiring Islamic banking products. However, it was observed that these individuals lacked accurate knowledge about the operational mechanisms of such products. Additionally, the research identified a general lack of awareness among respondents regarding the fundamental rules and principles governing Islamic banking.

Ahmad & Bashir (2014) examined the awareness level of customers about products and services offered by Islamic Banks. The researcher concluded that there is less awareness among customers related to Islamic banking terminology, products and services. Soumik Majumdar's (2008) study delved into the potential of Islamic Banking in India, Majumdar identified several compelling reasons for introducing Islamic Banking in India, including its potential to foster inclusive economic growth, exert control over inflation, and enhance financial inclusion for the Muslim population. Moreover, it holds the promise of attracting substantial investments, particularly Arab petro dollars, which could have a transformative impact on the Indian stock markets. Islam et al (2017) has reveal that respondents have very limited awareness about the products and services offered by Islamic finance. Naveed and Kashif. (2010) has concluded that customer's awareness regarding products of Islamic banking is good in terms of general products like current account and time deposit account but majority of the customers are unaware about the products like Murabaha and Ijara. The study also concluded that majority of the customers are satisfied with the services of Islamic bank. Majority of the Muslim banking customers in India want to adopt Islamic banking services if they get proper information and offered better customer experience (Islam & Rahman 2017). Khafafa and Shafii (2013) examined the awareness of banking customers about the product of Islamic banking provided through banks Islamic window and the researcher has concluded that customers are having awareness about the products Murabahah but very less number of customers having information about Ijarah financing. Islamic finance can stimulate product innovation in banking industry and it can be helpful in foster financial inclusion (Kavita and Krishan 2011; Irfan et al 2023b).

4. ISLAMIC FINANCIAL INSTRUMENTS

Islamic financial institutions have made significant advancements in the creation of diverse products and services, aiming to enhance customer satisfaction and offer alternatives that adhere to sharia principles (Ridho et al 2023). This paper provides a concise overview of the range of products and services offered by Islamic financial institutions.

Mudarabah, alternatively known as trustee finance or qirad, is a financial arrangement characterized by a collaborative partnership between a capital provider and an entrepreneur. According to Rahman (2018), Mudarabah is deemed as a viable alternative for diverse investment categories, including general or specific investments, project funding, bridge financing, working capital and small and medium financing, interbank investment, structured products, investment deposits, and other associated objectives. The Islamic bank generates its profits by establishing a predetermined ratio with investment account holders, and subsequently allocates these profits in a proportionate manner. On the contrary, in the case of financial losses, the responsibility for such losses is borne by the fund provider, unless there is substantiated evidence of misconduct, negligence, or non-compliance with the stipulated conditions by the Islamic bank. Mudarabah presents a viable alternative for diverse investment categories, encompassing general and specific investment, project funding, bridge financing, working capital and small and medium financing, interbank investment, structured products, and investment deposits, among other possibilities.

Musharakah, also known as Partnership Financing, is a financial concept that pertains to a collaborative endeavor wherein all participating partners collectively assume responsibility for both the profits and losses incurred within the joint venture (Usmani, 1999; Usmani, 2002). The allocation of profits among partners is determined by the predetermined ratios, while the distribution of losses is proportionate to each partner's capital share (Iqbal & Mirakhor 2011).

Murabaha, also known as bay' mu'ajjal, is a financial transaction characterized by the sale of goods at a predetermined profit margin. The sale contract involves the Islamic financial services provider selling assets that they already possess to a client. The selling price is determined by adding the original price and a pre-agreed profit (IFSB, 2019). According to Iqbal and Mirakhor (2011), the payment is to be resolved within a predetermined period, either through periodic payments or a single payment. During this time, the seller assumes full responsibility for any potential loss or damage to the products until they are successfully delivered to the buyer.

Bai Salam refers to a contractual agreement in which the buyer makes an upfront payment for products that will be delivered at a later date, also known as buyer's credit. It is not a requirement for the products to be immediately available at the time of signing the Bai Salam contract. However, the specific details regarding the quality, quantity, as well as the precise date and location of delivery, must be clearly and accurately specified within the contract (Visser, 2009).

Istisna'a refers to a contractual agreement wherein a manufacturer or contractor is obligated to produce and deliver specific products or premises at a predetermined price and date. This arrangement allows for the payment of the price to be deferred until the completion of the contract or may be made in installments, as per the mutually agreed terms between the parties involved (Iqbal & Mirakhor, 2011).

Ijarah, also known as leasing, refers to a contractual agreement wherein the provider of funds purchases and leases assets to a customer, with the option of selling the asset to the lessee upon the termination of the lease (Visser, 2009). The possibility exists for the inclusion of a unilateral binding promise from one of the contracting parties, as suggested by the International Financial Services Board (IFSB, 20194).

Takaful, also known as Islamic insurance, is a financial framework wherein the risk is collectively borne by all participants, thereby eliminating the presence of uncertainty and speculative elements within the contractual agreement (Kettell, 2010; Pal et al 2023)). In essence, a cooperative system is established whereby a collective of individuals mutually consent to distribute a particular risk, such as the destruction of a building due to fire, by pooling a predetermined amount from each participant. Consequently, any incurred losses are covered using the accumulated funds (Iqbal & Mirakhor, 2011).

The term "Quard Hassan" is commonly employed to denote interest-free loans that are provided with benevolent intentions (Gait & Worthington, 2008). This product is specifically designed to cater to individuals with limited financial resources, including farmers, small business owners, and economically disadvantaged consumers. Additionally, it has been suggested that it can serve alternative purposes (Visser, 2009).

The success or failure of Islamic financial institutions is contingent upon the significance of customer satisfaction. In their study, Anouze, Alamro, and Awwad (2019) conducted an analysis to identify the key factors that drive customer satisfaction within the Islamic banking sector. The researchers found that four primary drivers emerged as significant contributors to customer satisfaction: adherence to Sharia' principles, handling of customer complaints, pricing strategies, and convenience of banking services.

However, it is insufficient to merely consider the quality of products provided by Islamic financial institutions. In order to bolster their reputation and foster customer loyalty, it is imperative for businesses to adopt effective customer service practices and develop a comprehensive understanding of Shariah principles (Rahim & Mohamed, 2015). Visser (2009) asserts that the application of Islamic finance (IF) can yield several potential positive outcomes. These include a decreased risk of insolvency, safeguarding against financial crises, heightened participation in the official financial system, and a significant reduction in speculative activities. Nevertheless, it is important to acknowledge that Islamic finance, despite its merits, does have certain adverse consequences, as highlighted by Visser (2009) from the perspective of non-Muslim observers. These include:

(1) potential risks for depositors;
(2) increased costs;
(3) challenges related to principal-agent dynamics and their impact on economic growth;
(4) insufficient funding for small and medium-sized enterprises (SMEs);
(5) limited availability of consumer credit;
(6) potential drawbacks in insurance practices;
(7) reduced opportunities for diversification and hedging, and their implications for economic growth.

5. RESEARCH GAP AND OBJECTIVES OF THE STUDY

In the research paper, there are evident research gaps that need attention. First, while the study seeks to gauge the awareness and understanding of Islamic banking among both Muslim and non-Muslim respondents, it does not delve into the underlying factors that contribute to this awareness or its absence, creating an information void. Second, the study focuses on comprehending the various modes of finance within the interest-free banking system but neglects to explore the drivers and motivations behind individuals' preferences or aversions to these modes, leaving an essential aspect unexamined. Lastly, as the research delves into the myriad of products and services offered by interest-free banking institutions, it overlooks the investigation of barriers that might deter potential customers from utilizing these services or the specific factors that draw individuals towards these products. Hence, following objectives are addressed in the paper:

1. To assess the prior knowledge of respondents (Muslims & Non-Muslims) about Islamic Banking.
2. To study the mode of finance in Interest Free Banking.
3. To know the different product of Interest Free Banking.

6. RESEARCH METHODOLOGY

In conducting this research, a mixed-method approach is employed, drawing upon both primary and secondary sources of data to provide a comprehensive perspective on the topic under investigation.

The primary source of data is collected through the administration of structured questionnaires to a diverse range of respondents, including individuals from private and government sectors, businessmen, housewives, students, scholars, and retirees. This inclusive approach encompasses both Muslim and non-Muslim communities, specifically those who maintain bank accounts. The data collection efforts are concentrated in the geographic regions of Hyderabad and Secunderabad in Andhra Pradesh, India, ensuring a localized yet diverse dataset.

Complementing the primary data, secondary sources are harnessed to provide additional context and background information. These secondary sources encompass a wide range of materials, including books, journals, magazines, newspapers, and pertinent content sourced from the websites of various banking organizations. This comprehensive secondary data aids in enriching the study by providing a broader understanding of the subject matter.

The sample design is structured to ensure representativeness and comparability. Stratified Random Sampling is the chosen method for sample selection, allowing for a balanced and unbiased representation of participants.

The study's sample is distinctly categorized into two groups: Muslims with bank accounts and Non-Muslims with bank accounts. This stratification facilitates a comparative analysis, offering deeper insights into the research objectives and enabling a critical examination of the differences and commonalities between these two groups. By adopting a mixed-method approach and employing a stratified sampling technique, this research endeavours to provide a robust and insightful exploration of the subject matter.

7. ANALYSIS PART

The respondents were divided into Muslim and Non-Muslim based who are using Public and Private sector banking services.

The above table shows majority of Muslim respondents 65 percent know about Islamic Banking and 35 percent did not have knowledge about Islamic Banking while among Non-Muslim respondents 43.5 percent have knowledge about Islamic Banking and 56.5 percent did not have any knowledge about Islamic Banking. Collectively from both the community 54.25 percent of respondents know about Islamic Banking while 45.75 percent of respondents did not have knowledge about Islamic Banking.

Table 1. Respondents knowledge about Islamic banking

S.No	Particulars	Muslims		Non-Muslims		Total Percentage
		No. of respondents	Percentage	No. of respondents	Percentage	
1	Yes	130	65	87	43.5	54.25
2	No	70	35	113	56.5	45.75
Total		200	100	200	100	100

Table 2. Respondents gender on the basis of awareness about Islamic banking

S.No	Gender	Aware of Islamic Banking		Not Aware of Islamic Banking	
		No. of respondents	Percentage	No. of respondents	Percentage
1	Male	137	63.1	108	59
2	Female	80	36.9	75	41
Total		217	100	183	100

Table 3. Respondents qualification on the basis of awareness about Islamic banking

S.No	Qualification	Aware of Islamic Banking		Not Aware of Islamic Banking	
		No. of respondents	Percentage	No. of respondents	Percentage
1	Illiterate	12	5.5	08	4.4
2	Up to secondary education	27	12.4	14	7.7
3	Intermediate	21	9.7	20	10.9
4	Graduate	88	40.6	61	33.3
5	Post graduate & above	69	31.8	80	43.7
Total		217	100	183	100

Table 4. Respondents occupation on the basis of awareness about Islamic banking

S.No	Occupation	Aware of Islamic Banking		Not Aware of Islamic Banking	
		No. of respondents	Percentage	No. of respondents	Percentage
1	Student	25	11.5	56	30.5
2	Housewife	38	17.5	42	23
3	Businessman	43	19.8	17	9.3
4	Private employee	75	34.6	40	21.9
5	Government employee	30	13.8	26	14.2
6	Retired person	06	2.8	02	1.1
Total		217	100	183	100

The above table reveals that there are 63.1 percent male and 36.9 percent female who are aware of Islamic Banking, among respondents who do not know about Islamic Banking 59 percent male and 41 percent belongs to female.

The above table shows that among respondents who are aware of Islamic Banking 40.6 percent are graduate, 31.8 percent are belongs to post graduate and above, 12.4 percent are qualified upto secondary level, 9.7 percent are intermediate and 5.5 percent are illiterate while among respondents who are not aware of Islamic Banking 43.7 percent are post graduate and above, 33.3 percent are graduate, 10.9 percent are intermediate, 7.7 percent are qualified upto secondary education and 4.4 percent of respondents are illiterate.

Table 5. Source of information of Islamic banking

S.No	Particulars	Muslims		Non-Muslims		Total Percentage
		No. of respondents	Percentage	No. of respondents	Percentage	
1	Relative & friends	48	36.93	27	31.04	34.56
2	Internet	52	40	32	36.79	38.71
3	Newspaper	09	6.92	19	21.83	12.90
4	Other source	21	16.15	09	10.34	13.83
Total		130	100	87	100	100

Table 6. Respondents opinion on need to provide information about Islamic banking

S.No	Particulars	Muslims		Non-Muslims		Total Percentage
		No. of respondents	Percentage	No. of respondents	Percentage	
1	Strongly agree	94	72.31	31	35.64	57.60
2	Agree	31	23.85	20	22.99	23.50
3	Neither agree nor disagree	05	03.84	13	14.94	8.30
4	Disagree	00	00	13	14.94	5.99
5	Strongly disagree	00	00	10	11.49	4.61
Total		130	100	87	100	100

It is reveals from the above table that among the respondents who are aware of Islamic Banking 34.6 percent private employee followed by 19.8 percent are businessmen, 17.5 percent housewife, 13.8 percent government employee, 11.5 percent student and 2.8 percent retired person while among the respondents who did not have the knowledge of Islamic Banking 30.5 percent are students followed by23 percent housewives, 21.9 percent private employee, 14.2 percent government employee, 9.3 percent businessmen and 1.1 percent retired person.

The above table shows among Muslim respondents 40 percent get information about IB through 'internet', 36.93 get information by 'relative & friends' and 6.92 percent get information through 'newspaper' while 36.79 percent of Non-Muslim respondents get information about IB through 'internet', 31.04 percent by 'relative & friends' and 21.83 percent by 'newspaper'. Collectively from the community 38.71 percent of respondents get information about Islamic Banking through 'internet'.

The above table reveals 72.31 percent of Muslim respondents are 'strongly agree' to provide information about Islamic Banking and 23.85 percent are 'agree' among Non-Muslim respondents 35.64 percent are 'strongly agree' that there is need to provide information about IB 22.99 percent are 'agree' 14.94 percent are 'neither agree nor disagree' and same percent of respondents are 'disagree' while 11.49 percent of respondents are 'strongly disagree'. Collectively more than 80 percent of respondents are agree to provide information about IB.

8. MANAGERIAL IMPLICATION OF THE STUDY

The managerial implications of this study are manifold and carry substantial significance for banking institutions, particularly those contemplating the introduction of Islamic Banking in India.

First and foremost, the findings emphasize the need for financial institutions to tailor their products and services to the diverse education levels and preferences of potential customers. With a substantial portion of respondents having varied educational backgrounds, it is imperative that banks develop and promote banking solutions that are accessible and comprehensible to a wide range of customers. This could involve creating user-friendly mobile banking apps, simplified account structures, and comprehensive customer education initiatives.

The study underscores the importance of a strong online presence for banking institutions. With a significant portion of respondents, both Muslim and non-Muslim, turning to the internet for information on Islamic Banking, it is essential for banks to enhance their online visibility. This can be achieved by maintaining informative websites, providing online customer support, and leveraging social media platforms to engage with potential customers. Furthermore, internet-based educational campaigns can be an effective means of spreading awareness and knowledge about Islamic Banking.

The study's findings also indicate that there is a strong demand for information about Islamic Banking. This presents an opportunity for banking institutions to launch targeted marketing and educational campaigns to promote their Islamic Banking products and services. By emphasizing the principles and benefits of Islamic Banking, banks can attract and retain a larger customer base.

Overall, the managerial implications suggest that financial institutions in India should consider the diverse demographics and digital preferences of potential customers when planning the introduction and promotion of Islamic Banking. By addressing these factors, banks can effectively tap into the growing interest in Islamic Banking and foster financial inclusion in the sector.

9. LIMITATION OF THE STUDY

One limitation of this study is that it focuses on a specific geographic region, namely Hyderabad and Secunderabad in Andhra Pradesh. Therefore, the findings may not be fully representative of the entire Indian population. To gain a comprehensive understanding of the country's banking landscape, similar studies should be conducted in different regions.

10. FUTURE SCOPE OF THE STUDY

The study underscores the need for greater awareness about Islamic Banking in India. As the country continues to grow economically and diversify its banking sector, there is a promising future for Islamic Banking. Financial institutions should capitalize on the current interest in this banking system, especially among both Muslim and non-Muslim respondents who expressed a willingness to learn more. Future research can explore the effectiveness of educational campaigns and awareness programs aimed at introducing more people to the principles and benefits of Islamic Banking.

11. CONCLUSION

This study offers valuable insights into the awareness and knowledge levels regarding Islamic Banking among both Muslim and non-Muslim communities in India. The findings are instrumental in understanding the potential for introducing and promoting Islamic Banking in the country.

The study reveals that a significant proportion of Muslim respondents (65%) are aware of Islamic Banking, signifying a certain level of familiarity with this financial system. However, it is noteworthy that a substantial percentage of non-Muslim respondents (43.5%) also exhibit awareness, indicating that Islamic Banking transcends religious boundaries and piques the interest of a diverse audience.

The breakdown of awareness based on gender, education, and occupation provides essential information for financial institutions. For instance, the finding that a significant number of educated individuals, particularly graduates and postgraduates, are aware of Islamic Banking suggests that this target group may be more inclined to adopt these services. The data also highlights the role of the internet in disseminating information about Islamic Banking, emphasizing the importance of maintaining a robust online presence for banking institutions.

Furthermore, the study underscores the overwhelming support for the provision of information about Islamic Banking, with more than 96% of Muslim respondents and over 58% of non-Muslim respondents favoring such initiatives. This presents an opportunity for financial institutions to embark on educational and marketing campaigns aimed at raising awareness and disseminating knowledge about Islamic Banking.

From a managerial perspective, the implications of this study call for a customer-centric approach in product design and promotion. Tailoring banking solutions to cater to individuals with varying educational backgrounds is crucial, as is strengthening the online presence to accommodate the preferences of those who seek information through the internet. The study also highlights the significance of proactive measures to spread awareness and knowledge, suggesting that banks should prioritize the development of informative resources and marketing campaigns to foster a deeper understanding of Islamic Banking.

In the context of India's diverse demographic landscape and its substantial Muslim population, the findings present a compelling case for the introduction and promotion of Islamic Banking. As the interest in ethical and Sharia-compliant financial systems continues to grow globally, India stands at a pivotal juncture to harness the potential of Islamic Banking, ensuring financial inclusion and the broader accessibility of ethical financial services for all.

REFERENCES

Ahmad, A., & Bashir, R. (2014). An investigation of customer's awareness level and customer's service utilization decision in Islamic banking. *Pakistan Economic and Social Review*, *52*(1), 59–74.

Ahmad, A. U. F. (2001). *Problems of Islamic Banking in Bangladesh*. Islamic Economics Research Bureau, Dhaka, Bangladesh.

Ahmed, A, Rehman, K., & Saif, I. (2023). Islamic Banking Experience of Pakistan: comparison between Islamic and Conventional Banks. *International Journal of Business and Management, 5*(2), 137-143.

Ahsanul, H. (2010). Islamic Banking in Malaysia: A study of attitudinal difference of Malaysian customers. *European Journal of Economics Finance and Administrative Sciences*, *18*(1), 7–18.

Al Balushi, Y., Locke, S., & Boulanouar, Z. (2019). Determinants of the decision to adopt Islamic finance: Evidence from Oman. *ISRA International Journal of Islamic Finance*, *11*(1), 6–26. doi:10.1108/IJIF-02-2018-0020

Cheteni, P. (2014). Awareness of Islamic Banking Products and Services among Consumers in South Africa. *Mediterranean Journal of Social Sciences*, *5*(9), 96–103.

Hamid, A., & Nordin, N. (2001). A study on Islamic banking education and strategy for the new millennium Malaysian experience. *International Journal of Islamic Financial Services*, *2*(4), 3–11.

Iqbal, M., & Molyneux, P. (2005). *Thirty years of Islamic Banking:History,Performance and Prospects*. PalgraveMacmiltan. doi:10.1007/978-0-230-50322-9

Irfan, M., Elhoseny, M., Kassim, S., & Metawa, N. (2023a). *Advanced Machine Learning Algorithms for Complex Financial Applications.* IGI Global. . doi:10.4018/978-1-6684-4483-2

Irfan, M., Elmogy, M., Majid, M. S. A., & El-Sappagh, S. (2023b). The impact of AI innovation on financial sectors in the era of industry 5.0. The Impact of AI Innovation on Financial Sectors in the Era of Industry 5.0, (pp. 1-320). Research Gate. 10.4018/9798369300824

Islam, J. U., & Rahman, Z. (2017). Awareness and willingness towards Islamic banking among Muslims: An Indian perspective. *International Journal of Islamic and Middle Eastern Finance and Management*, *10*(1), 92–101. doi:10.1108/IMEFM-01-2016-0017

Karimi, A. (2005). Bank ka Sood Halal Hai-Subhat Azala, (3rd ed). Al-Halal Educational Society, Katihar.

Kavita, C., & Krishan, R. (2011). Challenges and opportunities of Islamic Banking in India. *Asian Journal of Research in Social Sciences and Humanities*, *1*(3), 34–40.

Khafafa, A. J., & Shafii, Z. (2013). Customer satisfaction and islamic banking awareness in the islamic banking window system in Libya. *Middle East Journal of Scientific Research.*

Khattak, N., & Rehman, K. (2010). Customer satisfaction and awareness of Islamic banking system in Pakistan. *African Journal of Business Management*, *4*(5), 662–671.

Lateh, N., Ismail, S., & Ariffin, N. M. (2009). Customers' Perceptions on the Objectives, Characteristics and Selection Criteria of Islamic Bank in Thailand. *Gadjah Mada International Journal of Business*, *11*(2), 167–189. doi:10.22146/gamaijb.5525

Majumadar, N. (2002). *Financial Sector Reforms & India's Economic Development.* Academic Foundation.

Naveed, A. K. (2010). Customer satisfaction and awareness of Islamic banking system in Pakistan. *African Journal of Business Management*, *4*(5), 662–671.

Pal, T., Irfan, M., & Kassim, S.B. (2023). How do Machine Learning (ML) techniques benefit the insurance industry? An exploratory study. *The Impact of AI Innovation on Financial Sectors in the Era of Industry 5.0,* (pp. 108-130). IGI Global. doi:10.4018/979-8-3693-0082-4.ch007

Rammal, H. G., & Zurbruegg, R. (2007). Awareness of Islamic banking products among Muslims: The case of Australia. *Journal of Financial Services Marketing*, *12*(1), 65–74. doi:10.1057/palgrave.fsm.4760060

Ridho Kismawadi, E., Irfan, M., & Shah, S.M.A.R. (2023). Revolutionizing Islamic finance: Artificial intelligence's role in the future of industry. The Impact of AI Innovation on Financial Sectors in the Era of Industry 5.0. IGI Global. doi:10.4018/979-8-3693-0082-4.ch011

Soumik, M. (2008). *Islamic Banking in India-What is the future potential.* Crisil Young Thought Leader.

Umer, C. (2009). The Global Financial Crisis: Can Islamic Finance Help. *International financial crisis from an Islamic perspective*. Islamic Economic Research Centre.

ENDNOTE

1 https://www.refinitiv.com/en/resources/special-report/islamic-finance-development-report-2022

Chapter 6
Harnessing the Power of Artificial Intelligence and Machine Learning in the Islamic Capital Market: A Comprehensive Analysis

Tripti Pal
RATM, India

Mohammad Irfan
https://orcid.org/0000-0002-4956-1170
Business School, NSB Academy, Bangalore, India

Syed Ahmad Chan Bukhari
St. John's University, USA

Salina Bt. Kassim
IIUM Gombak, Malaysia

ABSTRACT

This chapter explores the transformative impact of artificial intelligence (AI) and machine learning (ML) technologies on the Islamic Capital Market (ICM). As the global financial landscape evolves, the ICM is no exception, facing challenges and opportunities alike. AI and ML have emerged as pivotal tools for enhancing efficiency, mitigating risks, and fostering innovation within Islamic finance. The chapter begins by providing a comprehensive overview of the Islamic financial principles and the unique features of the ICM. It then delves into the key areas where AI and ML are being applied, including Shariah-compliant investment screening, risk management, asset allocation, trading strategies, and customer services. The study scrutinizes the implications of these technologies on financial inclusion, ethical finance, and regulatory compliance in the ICM.

DOI: 10.4018/979-8-3693-1038-0.ch006

INTRODUCTION

The Islamic capital market is a specialized financial system designed to operate in accordance with Islamic principles and Sharia law. It provides a framework for raising capital and making investments while ensuring compliance with ethical and religious guidelines (Bacha & Mirakhor, 2019).

Islamic capital market (ICM) transactions are conducted in manners that do not contradict Muslim conscience or Islam's religion (Hassan & Mahlknecht, n.d.). Here, Islamic rule is asserted so that the market is devoid of practices prohibited by Islam, such as usury (riba), gambling (maisir), and ambiguity (gharar).

The ICM is a component of Malaysia's total capital market. It contributes significantly to the country's economic progress. The ICM operates as a parallel market to the conventional capital market and complements the Islamic banking system in widening and deepening Malaysia's Islamic financial markets (Antonio & Hafidhoh, 2013). Malaysia's ICM remains a tempting location for all stakeholders to this day.

The SC's initial objective in establishing a specialized Islamic Capital Market Department (ICMD) was to offer critical infrastructure support. The ICMD's mandate is to conduct out development and research activities, such as developing and facilitating a long-term plan to enhance the ICM in Malaysia.

Malaysia has also pushed for the introduction of a two-tier Shariah governance framework for the ICM. In May 1996, the Securities Commission Act was amended to include a provision allowing the Shariah Advisory Council (SAC) to issue judgements.

Here's a detailed overview of the Islamic capital market:

1. Sharia Compliance:
   - (a) **Prohibition of Riba (Interest):** One of the fundamental principles of Islamic finance is the prohibition of riba, which refers to any form of interest or usury (Derigs & Marzban, 2008). In the Islamic capital market, interest-based transactions are strictly avoided.
   - (b) **Avoidance of Gharar (Uncertainty:** Transactions that involve excessive uncertainty or ambiguity (gharar) are not allowed. Contracts must be clear and transparent.
   - (c) **Ethical screening:** Investments in sectors deemed haram (forbidden) in Islam, such as alcohol, gambling, pork, and tobacco, are prohibited.
2. Islamic Financial Instruments:
   - (a) **Mudarabah**: A partnership where one party provides the capital (rabb-ul-mal) and the other party provides labor and expertise (mudarib) (Cox, 2005). Profits are shared according to a pre-agreed ratio, while losses are borne by the capital provider.
   - (b) **Musharakah:** A joint venture partnership where both parties contribute capital and share profits and losses based on the ratio of their contributions.
   - (c) **Ijara:** A leasing arrangement where one party leases an asset to another party for a specified period and rent. At the end of the lease period, ownership may be transferred or not, depending on the terms.
   - (d) **Sukuk:** Islamic bonds that represent ownership in an underlying asset, project, or venture. Sukuk generate returns through profit-sharing or rental income.
   - (e) **Wakala:** An agency agreement where one party acts as an agent to manage the assets of another party in exchange for a fee.

3. Ethical Screening (Sharia-Compliant Screening):
    - Sharia-compliant screening is conducted to ensure that investments align with Islamic principles (ISRA, 2011)
    - Businesses involved in alcohol, gambling, pork, tobacco, and other haram activities are excluded from Islamic investment portfolios.
4. Risk-Sharing:
    - Islamic finance encourages risk-sharing between investors and entrepreneurs. Profits and losses are shared based on agreed-upon ratios.
    - This risk-sharing aspect fosters a sense of partnership and fairness.
5. Takaful:
    - Takaful is Islamic insurance, where participants pool their contributions to provide coverage against specified risks.
    - Takaful operates on principles of mutual assistance and solidarity, with a Takaful operator managing the funds and distributing claims based on Sharia guidelines.
6. Regulatory Framework:
    - Many countries with significant Muslim populations have established regulatory bodies and frameworks to oversee Islamic capital markets.
    - These regulatory bodies ensure compliance with Sharia principles and provide a legal and regulatory framework for the industry (Ali, 2008)
7. Islamic Investment Funds:
    - Islamic investment funds pool funds from investors and invest in Sharia-compliant assets and instruments.
    - Types of funds include equity funds, real estate funds, and sukuk funds, providing investors with diversified options.
8. Global Presence:
    - Islamic finance has expanded beyond Muslim-majority countries and is now a global industry.
    - International financial centers like London, Dubai, and Kuala Lumpur have emerged as hubs for Islamic finance.
9. Innovation:
    - The Islamic capital market continues to evolve, with financial institutions and scholars working on innovative products and structures to meet the evolving needs of investors while remaining Sharia-compliant.

The Islamic capital market serves as a vital component of Islamic finance, offering ethical investment and financing opportunities for individuals and businesses adhering to Islamic principles. Its principles of risk-sharing, asset backing, and ethical screening make it distinct from conventional finance.

KEY APPLICATIONS OF AI AND ML IN THE ISLAMIC CAPITAL MARKET

Artificial Intelligence (AI) and Machine Learning (ML) have the potential to revolutionize various aspects of the Islamic capital market, just as they do in conventional financial markets. Here are some key applications of AI and ML in the Islamic capital market:

1. **Risk Assessment and Management:** AI and ML can be used to assess and manage risks associated with Islamic financial instruments and portfolios. These technologies can analyze historical data, market trends, and other relevant information to identify potential risks and recommend risk mitigation strategies.
2. **Portfolio Management:** AI and ML algorithms can help Islamic fund managers in constructing and managing Sharia-compliant investment portfolios (##NO_NAME##, 2017). These algorithms can optimize asset allocation, balance risk and return, and adapt to changing market conditions.
3. **Trading and Execution:** AI-powered trading systems can execute trades efficiently and at optimal prices, taking into account Islamic principles such as avoiding riba (usury) and excessive uncertainty (gharar). These systems can also detect and respond to market anomalies in real-time.
4. **Market Analysis:** AI can analyze vast amounts of market data to identify investment opportunities that adhere to Islamic principles (DinarStandard, 2018). Sentiment analysis and predictive modeling can provide valuable insights into market sentiment and trends.
5. **Customer Service and Chatbots:** AI-driven chatbots can assist customers in navigating Islamic financial products, answering questions, and providing support. These virtual assistants can help improve customer service and reduce response times.
6. **Compliance and Screening:** ML algorithms can automate the screening of financial instruments to ensure they comply with Islamic principles. They can detect any non-compliance and provide recommendations for Sharia-compliant alternatives.
7. **Fraud Detection:** AI can be employed to detect fraudulent activities in the Islamic capital market. Advanced analytics can identify suspicious transactions and patterns that may indicate fraudulent behavior.
8. **Predictive Modeling**: ML models can forecast market movements and asset prices, helping investors make informed decisions (DinarStandard, 2018). These models can be particularly useful in Islamic capital markets, where adherence to Sharia principles can impact investment strategies.
9. **Regulatory Compliance:** AI can assist financial institutions in ensuring compliance with Islamic finance regulations. It can automate the monitoring of transactions and reporting, reducing the risk of non-compliance.
10. **Customer Profiling and Personalization:** AI can analyze customer data to create personalized investment strategies that align with individual preferences and risk tolerance while adhering to Islamic principles (Alam et al., 2019).
11. **Economic Research:** AI and ML can enhance economic research in the Islamic finance sector by analyzing economic data, trends, and factors affecting the market, helping policymakers and analysts make informed decisions.
12. **Block Chain and Smart Contracts**: Combining AI with blockchain technology can facilitate the creation of smart contracts that automatically enforce Sharia-compliant financial agreements and transactions (Alam et al., 2019).

It's important to note that while AI and ML can offer significant advantages in the Islamic capital market, they must be implemented in a manner that aligns with Sharia principles and ethics. Moreover, regulatory bodies and Islamic scholars may need to provide guidance on the use of these technologies to ensure they comply with Islamic finance principles.

CONTRACTS RELATING TO ICM

Contracts related to the Islamic capital market play a crucial role in ensuring compliance with Islamic finance principles, which are based on Shariah law. These contracts are designed to facilitate financial transactions while adhering to Islamic ethical and legal guidelines. Here, I'll provide an overview of some of the key contracts used in the Islamic capital market:

1. Mudarabah (Profit-and-Loss Sharing):
    - Mudarabah is a partnership contract where one party provides the capital (the Rab ul Mal), while the other party (the Mudarib) provides expertise and management
    - Profits are shared based on a predetermined ratio, while losses are borne by the capital provider (Giancaspro, 2017)
    - Commonly used in investment funds and Islamic banking for profit-sharing arrangements.
2. Musharakah (Joint Venture):
    - Musharakah involves a joint venture between two or more parties where all partners contribute capital and expertise.
    - Profits are shared based on the agreed-upon ratio, and losses are shared in proportion to the capital contribution.
    - Often used for project financing and equity-based investments (Idelberger et al., 2016)
3. Ijara (Lease):
    - Ijara is a leasing contract where one party (the lessor) leases an asset to another party (the lessee) for a specified period.
    - The lessee pays rent, and at the end of the lease term, the asset may be sold or transferred.
    - Commonly used in Islamic finance for real estate and equipment financing.
4. Sukuk (Islamic Bonds):
    - Sukuk are certificates that represent ownership in an underlying asset or a project. They provide a way for investors to earn a return without violating Islamic prohibitions on interest (Riba).
    - Sukuk structures can vary, including Ijara, Musharakah, and Wakala, among others, and are often used for raising capital in the Islamic capital market (Idelberger et al., 2016)
5. Wakala (Agency):
    - Wakala is an agency contract where one party (the principal) authorizes another party (the agent) to act on their behalf for a fee.
    - Commonly used in the management of investment funds, where the agent manages the assets on behalf of the investors (Idelberger et al., 2016).
6. Tawarruq (Monetization):
    - Tawarruq involves a buyer purchasing a commodity from a seller on a deferred payment basis.
    - The buyer then sells the commodity in the open market to obtain cash.
    - It is used for short-term liquidity management while adhering to Islamic finance principles.
7. Wadiah (Safekeeping):
    - Wadiah is a safekeeping and custody contract where a party (the custodian or depository) holds assets on behalf of another party (the owner) without any obligation to pay a return.
    - It is used for the safekeeping of assets, such as stocks and commodities.

8. Hawala (Transfer of Debt):
    - Hawala is an informal, person-to-person money transfer system widely used in the Islamic world.
    - It involves transferring a debt obligation from one party to another, often used for cross-border remittances.

It's important to note that these contracts are designed to comply with Shariah law, which prohibits the payment or receipt of interest (Riba) and prohibits investments in certain industries like gambling, alcohol, and pork. Additionally, contracts in Islamic finance often involve a Shariah board or advisor to ensure that they are in compliance with Islamic principles (Idelberger et al., 2016). The use of these contracts varies depending on the specific needs and structures of Islamic financial institutions and investors in the Islamic capital market.

PLAYERS IN THE ISLAMIC CAPITAL MARKET

The Islamic capital market consists of various participants who comply with Islamic finance principles and regulations. These participants include:

1. **Islamic Banks:** These are financial institutions that offer Sharia-compliant banking and financial services. They play a crucial role in the Islamic capital market by providing a range of Islamic financial products and services, including Islamic bonds (Sukuk), Islamic mutual funds, and Islamic financing (Tabash & Dhankar, 2018).
2. **Takaful (Islamic Insurance) Companies:** Takaful companies offer insurance products that comply with Islamic principles. They invest their funds in the Islamic capital market, including Islamic equities and Sukuk (Tabash & Dhankar, 2018).
3. **Investment Banks:** Islamic investment banks facilitate the issuance of Islamic financial instruments, such as Sukuk. They also provide advisory services to corporations and governments seeking to raise funds in a Sharia-compliant manner (Tabash & Dhankar, 2018).
4. **Asset Management Companies:** These firms manage Islamic investment funds, including mutual funds and exchange-traded funds (ETFs), which invest in Sharia-compliant assets.
5. **Regulatory Authorities:** Government and regulatory bodies play a significant role in overseeing and regulating the Islamic capital market to ensure that it adheres to Islamic finance principles and remains in compliance with legal and regulatory standards (Schmelzer, 2019).
6. **Islamic Scholars (Ulema):** Islamic finance and capital markets rely on the guidance and expertise of Islamic scholars who provide religious oversight to ensure that financial transactions and instruments comply with Islamic law (Sharia) (Schmelzer, 2019). They issue fatwas (legal opinions) on the permissibility of financial activities.
7. **Investors:** Individuals, institutions, and sovereign wealth funds that invest in Sharia-compliant financial instruments, such as Sukuk, Islamic equities, and other Islamic investment products.
8. **Corporations and Governments:** Entities seeking to raise funds in compliance with Islamic finance principles issue Sukuk and other Islamic financial instruments to attract investors in the Islamic capital market.

9. **Auditors and Rating Agencies:** Audit firms and rating agencies specializing in Islamic finance assess the compliance of financial institutions, instruments, and transactions with Islamic principles, providing transparency and confidence to investors (DinarStandard, 2018).
10. **Legal Firms:** Legal experts specializing in Islamic finance help structure financial transactions and ensure they adhere to Sharia-compliant principles and local regulatory requirements.
11. **Market Intermediaries:** Brokers and other intermediaries facilitate trading and transactions in the Islamic capital market.
12. **Educational Institutions**: Universities and training centers offer courses and programs in Islamic finance and capital markets, producing professionals with expertise in this field.
13. **Technology Providers**: Companies providing technology solutions for Islamic finance, such as Islamic banking software, trading platforms, and financial technology (fintech) services tailored to Sharia-compliant finance (Hussain, 2015).

These players collectively contribute to the functioning and growth of the Islamic capital market, which seeks to provide financial services and investment opportunities in line with Islamic principles and values.

BENEFITS OF ISLAMIC CAPITAL MARKET

The Islamic capital market plays a significant role in Islamic finance and provides several benefits to both individuals and economies that adhere to Islamic financial principles. Here are the key benefits of the Islamic capital market in detail:

1. Compliance with Shariah Principles: The most fundamental benefit of the Islamic capital market is that it operates in accordance with Islamic Shariah principles. This ensures that financial transactions are ethical and do not involve elements such as Riba (interest), Gharar (uncertainty), and Haram (forbidden) activities, making it suitable for Muslims seeking financial services in compliance with their faith.
2. Wealth Redistribution: Islamic finance principles encourage wealth redistribution and the fair sharing of profits and losses. In Islamic capital markets, the risk-sharing feature helps in wealth distribution by allowing both investors and entrepreneurs to share in the rewards and risks of investments.
3. Risk-Sharing: The Islamic capital marketplaces a strong emphasis on risk-sharing, where investors and entrepreneurs jointly share the risks and rewards of their investments (Alharbi, 2015). This promotes a more equitable distribution of risk and return compared to conventional financial systems.
4. Asset-Backed Financing: Islamic financial instruments are typically asset-backed, meaning that investments are tied to real assets. This provides a level of security for investors, as their investments are backed by tangible assets, reducing the risk of speculative and interest-driven activities.
5. Ethical Investments: Islamic capital markets focus on ethical and socially responsible investments. This means that investments must avoid industries or activities that are considered unethical or harmful, such as gambling, alcohol, and tobacco (Anggraini, 2019). This makes Islamic finance a more ethical and socially responsible choice.

6. Financial Stability: The risk-sharing nature of Islamic capital markets can contribute to financial stability by reducing the likelihood of asset bubbles and speculative behavior that can lead to financial crises.
7. Long-Term Perspective: Islamic finance encourages a long-term perspective on investments. This can lead to more prudent and sustainable investment decisions, as investors are encouraged to consider the long-term impact of their investments on society and the environment (Anggraini, 2019).
8. Innovation and Diversification: Islamic capital markets have evolved over time, leading to innovative financial instruments that meet the needs of both individuals and institutions (Ariss & Sarieddine, 2007). The industry has witnessed the development of various Sukuk (Islamic bonds) structures and Islamic investment funds, providing diversification opportunities for investors.
9. Financial Inclusion: Islamic finance aims to be more inclusive by providing financial services to those who may be excluded from conventional financial systems. It offers alternative financing options for individuals and businesses, particularly in regions where Islamic finance is prevalent (El Qorchi, 2005).
10. Economic Development: Islamic capital markets can contribute to economic development by facilitating investment in infrastructure projects, promoting entrepreneurship, and supporting economic growth. The risk-sharing approach can encourage entrepreneurship and innovation.
11. Global Reach: Islamic capital markets are not limited to Muslim-majority countries; they have gained recognition and popularity worldwide. Many non-Muslim countries have also established Islamic finance institutions and issued Sukuk to attract Islamic investments (El Qorchi, 2005).

CONCLUSION

In conclusion, the Islamic capital market offers a range of benefits, including ethical and socially responsible investment options, wealth redistribution, risk-sharing, and the promotion of economic development. These benefits make it an attractive option for individuals and institutions seeking financial services that align with Islamic principles and values.This research paper has delved into the profound potential of harnessing artificial intelligence and machine learning in the context of the Islamic Capital Market. The examination of these cutting-edge technologies, coupled with the principles of Islamic finance, has revealed a myriad of opportunities for optimizing investment strategies, risk management, and decision-making processes within the Islamic financial ecosystem.

In summary, the convergence of AI and ML with Islamic finance represents an exciting frontier for innovation and growth. While there are hurdles to overcome, the potential benefits in terms of efficiency, risk management, and ethical investment choices are immense. As the Islamic finance industry continues to evolve, embracing the power of artificial intelligence and machine learning can undoubtedly propel it towards a more prosperous and sustainable future. This research paper has shed light on the possibilities and challenges, paving the way for further exploration and implementation in this dynamic and evolving sector.

REFERENCES

Alam, N., Gupta, L., Zameni, A., Alam, N., & Gupta, L. (2019). *Digitalization and disruption in the financial sector.* Springer.

Alharbi, A. (2015). Development of the Islamic Banking System. *Journal of Islamic Banking and Finance*, *3*(1), 12–25. doi:10.15640/jibf.v3n1a2

Ali, S. S. (Ed.). (2008). *Islamic capital markets: Products, regulation and development*. Islamic Development Bank.

Anggraini, M. (2019). Islamic banking development and economic growth: A case of Indonesia. *Asian Journal of Islamic Management*, *1*(1), 51–65. doi:10.20885/ajim.vol1.iss1.art5

Antonio, M. S., Hafidhoh, & Fauzi, H. (2013). The Islamic capital market volatility: a comparative study between in Indonesia and Malaysia. *Buletin Ekonomi Moneter dan Perbankan.*

Ariss, R. T., & Sarieddine, Y. (2007). Challenges in implementing capital adequacy guidlines to Islamic banks. *Journal of Banking Regulation*, *9*(1), 46–59. doi:10.1057/palgrave.jbr.2350059

Bacha, O. I., & Mirakhor, A. (2019). *Islamic capital markets: A comparative approach*. Wiley.

Cox, S. (2005). Developing the Islamic Capital Market and Creating Liquidity. *Review of Islamic Economics*, *9*(1), 75–86.

Derigs, U., & Marzban, S. (2008). Review and analysis of current Shariah-compliant equity screening practices. *International Journal of Islamic and Middle Eastern Finance and Management*, *1*(4), 285–303. doi:10.1108/17538390810919600

DinarStandard. (2018). Islamic fintech report 2018: current landscape & path forward. *Dinar Standard.* https://www.dinarstandard.com/wp-content/uploads/2018/12/Islamic-Fintech-Report-2018.pdf

Dirican, C. (2015). The Impacts of Robotics, Artificial Intelligence on Business and Economics. *Procedia: Social and Behavioral Sciences*, *95*, 564–573. doi:10.1016/j.sbspro.2015.06.134

El Qorchi, M. (2005). Islamic Finance Gears Up: While gaining ground, the industry faces unique regulatory challenges. *Finance & Development, 42*(4).

Giancaspro, M. (2017). Is a „smart contract" really a smart idea? Insights from a legal perspective. *Computer Law & Security Report*, *33*(6), 825–835. doi:10.1016/j.clsr.2017.05.007

Islam FinTech. (2017). Global Islamic Finance Report. *Islamic Finance in the Digital Age*, 282–290.

Hassan, K., & Mahlknecht, M. (2011). *Islamic capital markets: products and strategies*. Wiley.

Hussain, M. S. (2015). *An overview of Islamic finance*. (IMF Working Paper). IMF.

Idelberger, F., Governatori, G., Riveret, R., & Sartor, G. (2016). Evaluation of Logic-Based Smart Contracts for Blockchain Systems. *Rule Technologies. Research, Tools, and Applications,10th International Symposium* (pp. 167-183). New York, United States: Springer, Cham. 10.1007/978-3-319-42019-6_11

ISRA. (2011). *Islamic Financial System*. International Shari'ah Research Academy for Islamic Finance.

Schmelzer, R. (2019). 5 benefits of AI in the banking industry. *TechTarget.* https://searchenterpriseai.techtarget.com/feature/AI-in-banking-industry-brings-operational-improvements

Tabash, M. I., & Dhankar, R. S. (2018). The relevance of Islamic finance principles in economic growth. *International Journal of Emerging Research in Management and Technology*, *3*(2), 49–54.

Chapter 7
A Study on the Role of Islamic Finance and Sustainable Development Goals:
A Bibliometric Analysis

S. Dhana Bagiyam
https://orcid.org/0000-0002-5268-178X
NSB Academy, India

Salih Mustafa Ahmed Mualley
University of Gezira, Sudan

Libeesh P. C.
https://orcid.org/0009-0006-0369-5460
NSB Academy, India

ABSTRACT

In core, Islamic finance and the sustainable development goals (SDGs) initiated by the United Nations have the same goal to educate and create good livelihood for the human life. For this chapter, the researchers collected few research articles in Scopus Database towards the intersection of Islamic finance and SDGs. The authors have selected few Islamic finance and Sustainable Developmental Goals articles as an inclusion criteria along with the year of publication from 2015 to October 2023. They selected papers that focused on Islamic finance as an inclusion criterion and excluded papers that from 1990 to 2015. They retrieved 32 papers and book chapters published from 2015 to 2022 from the Scopus database. By using Vos viewer, the researchers analyzed the keyword from the article, year wise prediction, and authors' contribution for Islamic finance for Sustainable Development Goals. The researchers used the data to predict the future growth of Islamic finance the researcher found that there is a wide gap for Islamic finance supports the SDGs.

DOI: 10.4018/979-8-3693-1038-0.ch007

1. INTRODUCTION

Islamic finance mention about the transactions between the contracting parties and exchange of goods and services in agreement with shariah. It involves partnership that is permitted under the law. Islamic finance means the corporations in the Islamic country includes lending banks, financial institution.

2. SDGs AND ISLAMIC FINANCE

SDGs provide an opportunity to redefine the role leading to people, empowerment, socio-economic development, and the environment. Islamic Finance roles have been defined about the Global Agenda and its enhancement towards Islamic finance. The SDGs Goals value have counterparts significance and its application towards Islamic finance.,

Islamic finance (Ahmed, 2017) the plan of UN estimation to deliver the SDGs, there is a need of 5 to 7 trillion per annum needs to be mobilised by 2030. Major developing countries face a great challenge for funding gap of USD 2.5 trillion to achieve SDGs. To fill this major gap low-income countries, require the largest public expenditure relative to GDP to fill this gap. (Ghlamallah, Alexakis, Dowling, & Piepenbrink, 2021) Islamic Finance mentions the financial practices governed by Islamic laws, for execution of business activities by eradicating the interest using profit- and loss-sharing mechanisms.

There is a proven potential growth and support for the implementation of the SDGs (Sustainable Development Goals) which was initiated by United Nations (UN. Islamic finance grown gradually with high significant in many challenges. Many of the developing countries have high poverty rates and low score in reaching the SDGs, which require empowerment in their infrastructure (Ahmed H.). Majorly the share of the resources for developmental purpose Islamic finance can be a novel option. The gradual has been rapidly increases from 10-20%.

(Refinitiv., 2021) Islamic finance has arisen as a device to help financial growth, in an annual symposium significant light has given to enlighten the Islamic finance and they have proven that the associated bank of (INCIF) supports for the growth of Sustainability.

(Azmat, Kabir Hassan, Ali, & Sohel Azad, 2021,) explained Islamic finance provides industry different ratios to the customers, especially inclination towards the religious requirement, products of this industry are highly satisfied by the Islamic customers due to reputed customers. simultaneously risk factors also involved in this sector due to spirituality and financial fragility. There is less scattered research. (Abduh, 2019).There is a still a dilemma exist in role of Islamic finance and sustainability, compared to conventional banks, few customers considered Islamic finance purely as a religious concept (Hummel & Hashmi, 2019). In that it can be viewed from all angles and can encompass all industries, sustainability has multiple aspects. Consequently, there is no accepted definition of sustainability in and of itself. The ability to live a long time and use few resources, however, is what gives it its essence. As a result, many industries, including manufacturing, agriculture, marketing, and construction, have incorporated this sustainability notion into their sector procedures (Ogunmakinde, Egbelakin, & Sher, 2021). The SDGs of the UN are described in detail in their sector process, 17 Sustainable Development Goals and targets (169) are the different goals, target, capacities and level of development and respecting national policies and priorities. The SDGs are built for peace, inclusive and well-governed with responsive communities and institution. Each goal is independent but integrated.

Figure 1. Sustainable developmental goals
(https://unosd.un.org/content/sustainable-development-goals-sdgs)

3. RESEARCH FRAMEWORK FOR ISLAMIC FINANCE AND SDGS

The agenda 2030 utilise the needs without compromising the needs for the future generation, for achieving this in loop with the Islamic finance deals with economic growth, inclusion of society and environmental protection. The theatres are crucial role in the first two aspects, making its analysis necessary.

3.1 Inclusive Finance

The accessibility of assistance in relation to the long-term development of low-income people's banking services. Research shows that more than 72% of Muslims worldwide do not use any formal financial assistance (NimrahKarim, 2008), and nearly all financial services provided are predominantly used by the wealthy (Mahmoud Mohieldin, 2011).

Furthermore, between 20 and 40 percent of people refrain from using financial services because of interest. Economic, the lack of financially secure individuals integrating in Muslim countries is due to social and religious factors. The most logical method of inclusive financing would be through Shari'ah compatible microfinance, taking into account these factors as well as the regional demographics. Risks and expenses should be taken into account. the establishment of Islamic microfinance institutions that could aid in achieving sustainable development and the eradication of poverty.

Taking into account these factors, as well as the regional demography, the most practical. Establishing viable channels for inclusive finance requires the establishment of Islamic microfinance organizations. (Mohammed Obaidullah, 2008) traditional financial institutions typically steer clear of this sort of financing (because to its higher risk and allocation of resources), it can assist IFIs in establishing the

Figure 2. Research framework: Islamic finance and sustainable developmental goals

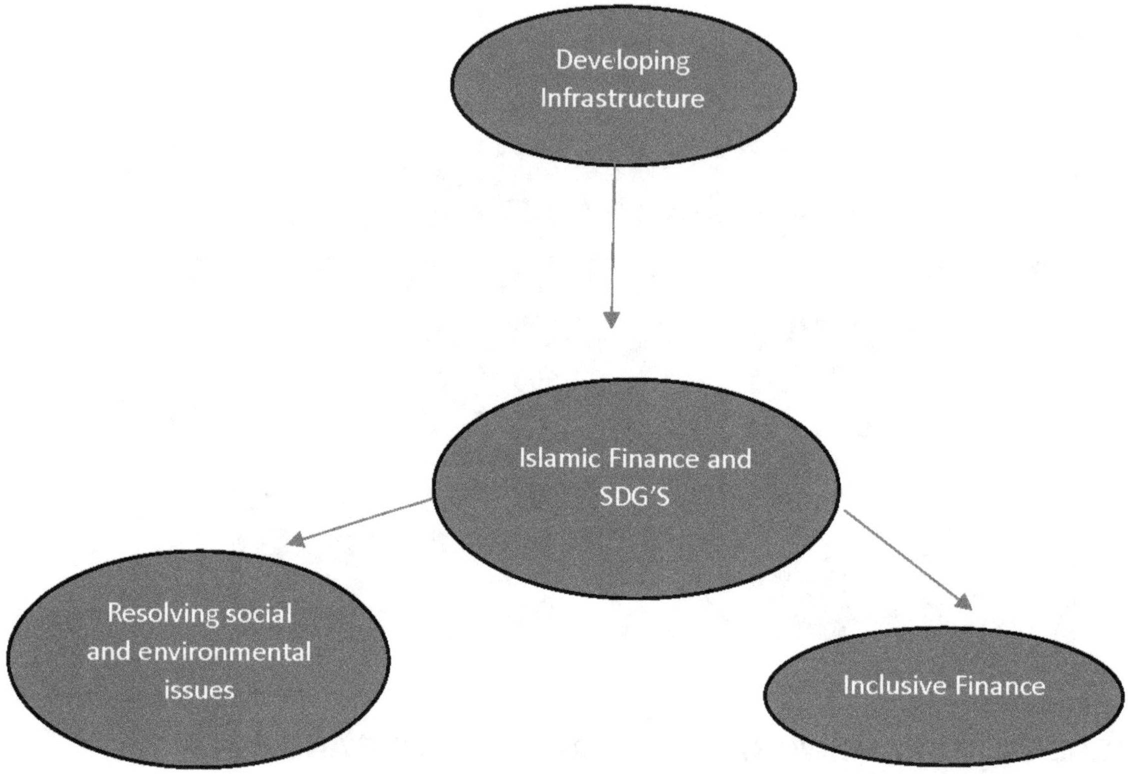

social role that Shari'ah principles support (NimrahKarim, "Islam Micro Finance: an Emerging", 2008). Additionally, research shows that effective financial the supply of microfinance at various levels is necessary for inclusion, best reach across different market sectors. existing market data demonstrates that IFIs have a higher prevalence of microfinance than their standard counterparts (Habib Ahmed, 2004). Due to the already-existing networks of bank locations that make it easy for customers to access them supported by current processes that permit effective transactions.

3.2 Resolving Social and Environmental Issues

In addition, the creation of public and private risk-sharing sukuk would open up new opportunities for investors and borrowers. From the standpoint of inclusive finance, financial institutions can create.

To expand the reach of Islamic banks, specialized units to serve microfinance diversify your organization through both individuals and groups. Retail and social sukuk While zakat and waqf-based securities are available on capital markets, sukuks. The social sector can benefit from the use of microfinance institutions. as of the from the financial, risk-management, and perspective of reducing vulnerability Institutions give low-income people a chance to save money and can build a platform to support the growth of micro-takaful. In the social sector.

According to a few studies, the Islamic financial sector plays either a very small or no role in promoting environmental and social goals. (Rania Kamla, 2013) examined the social reporting of 19 Islamic banks. did not find any evidence that Islamic banks were contributing to social having any "genuine plans focusing on neediness end or" improvement in improving equitable wealth redistribution in society. they justify that their inability to place social equity at the forefront of their priorities operations have increased the Islamic banks' frustration with their ability to satisfy their philosophical arguments. (RoszainiHaniffa, 2007) find out about high scores as an illustration of Islamic banks' accountability to partners, Borrowers and representatives' commitment to the community earned them the most lowered.

3.3 Infrastructural Development

The fundamental building blocks for trade and business, increase competition. Utilizing sustainable development techniques for infrastructure approaches that are friendly to both society and the environment. (MonzerKahf, 2000). (Young), 2008) Governments have traditionally been in charge of providing infrastructure facilities, but in the majority of nations, they are saddled with enormous deficits and debt and believe it is difficult to generate assets. the enormous Infrastructure investment interest necessitates collaborations between both the public and private sectors, with the latter playing a supporting role. The financing of infrastructure provided by the private sector, in any is still a small case. World Bank56 predicts that 70–75 percent of the total Public sector organizations provide funding for infrastructure in developing nations. 10 percentage came from assistance for authority development, and the remaining15% to 20% from industry. It is necessary to develop creative solutions.

4. METHODOLOGY

This research uses an Bibliometric approach to identify the relationship among Islamic finance and Sustainability. we identify the year wise prediction and growth of sustainability and Islamic finance. Then, we identify the authors contribution for SDGs, and we analysed the keywords highly contributing. The above research allows for a more complete details, includes the Islamic Finance contribution for SDGs.

From the above Figure 3, by percentage analysis the researcher has predicted in the year with the growth of Islamic finance 2015:2201, 2016:2345, 2017:500, 2018:2879,2019:3120, 2020:3345, 2021:3685,2023:3689 and the prediction for 2025:3875.

From the above analysis the researcher found the contribution by authors for Islamic finance Cluster 1 (alamad.s), Cluster 2 (amin.h), Cluster 3(billah m.m) likewise there are only few limited authors contributed for islamic finance and for sustainable development goals only one significant author highly contributed Ooi Kok Loang.

Keyword analysis has been done by using Vos viewer for the articles extracted from 2015 to 2023, through analysis around 7 Cluster with 83 items which are contributed for Islamic finance. Cluster 1 (24 items) shows challenge, economic, global crisis and so on, Cluster 2 (15 items) which supports comparative analysis, capital structure, etc.., Cluster 3 (14 items) consist of Sustainable Development, Islamic finance etc.., Cluster 4 (10 items) shows conceptual framework, corporate social responsibility Cluster 5(9 items) Islamic home financing, Islamic capital, etc., Cluster 6(6 items) bibliometric, Islamic finance, Islamic economics, etc., Cluster 7 (5 items) economics, literature review.

Table. 1 Year wise prediction

Growth (2015 -2030)	Islamic Finance Percentage
2015	2201
2016	2345
2017	2500
2018	2879
2019	3120
2020	3345
2023	3689
2025	3879

Figure 3. Year wise contribution

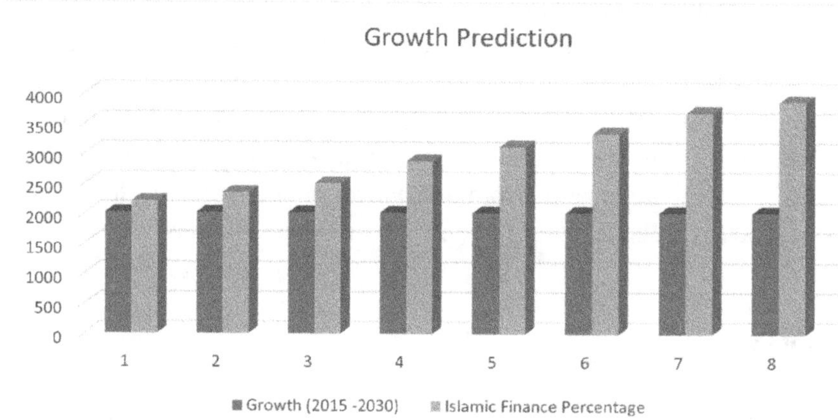

Figure 4. Authors' contribution

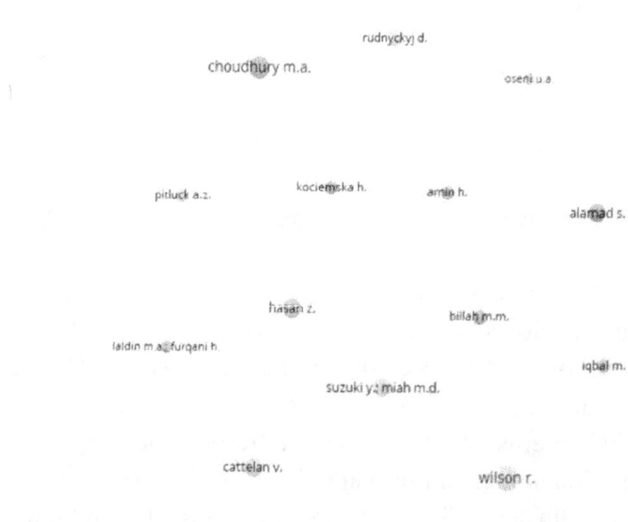

Figure 5. Keyword analysis using Vos viewer

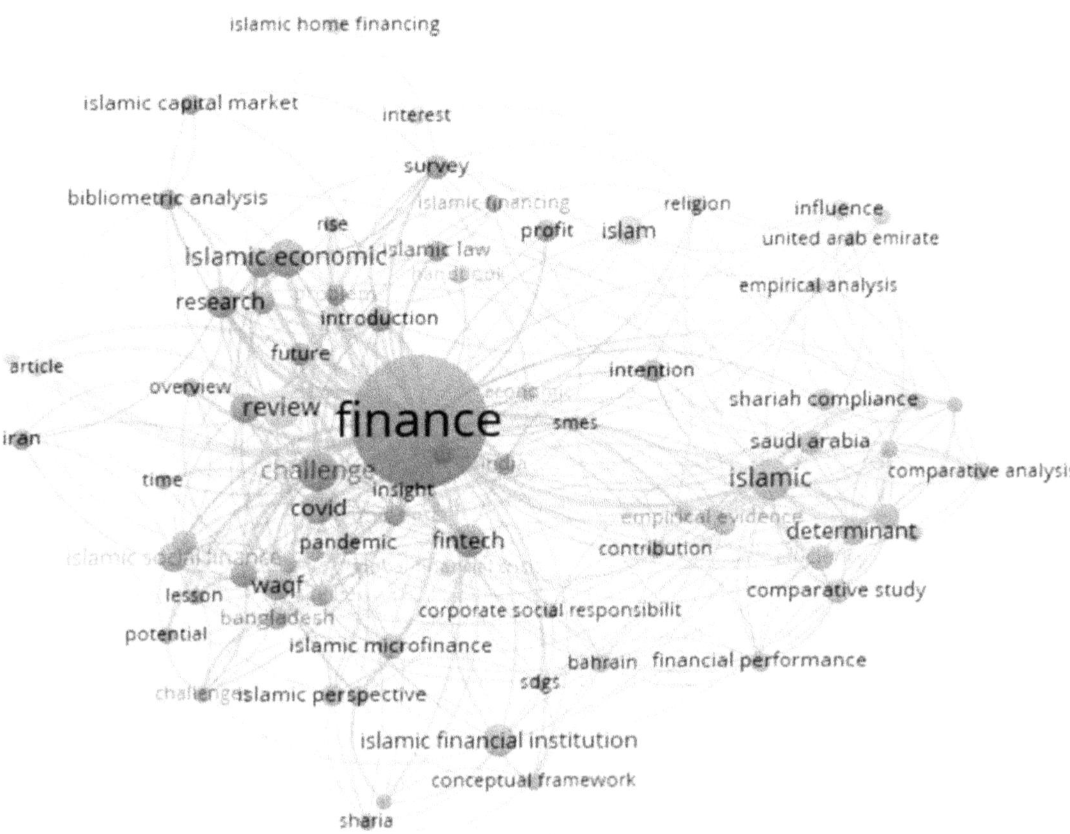

5. SUMMARY OF THE FINDINGS

This research work presents a detailed view of this study. The researcher aimed to address the relationship among the Islamic finance and SDGs. Accordingly, the researcher has done a search in Scopus database for the relevant publication from 2015-2030. After which the researcher has found 36 papers revealed the topic. To tell about the contribution of Islamic finance in various countries revealed its influence for (SDG 1) no poverty, no hunger (SDG 2), decent work and economic growth (SDG 8), industry innovation and infrastructure (SDG 9), Sustainable cities (SDG11), Public Private Partnership (SDG 17).

6. CONCLUSION

There is need of further research to prove how Islamic finance touches sustainable development in Islamic countries and other countries. Studies in individual countries will not be sufficient for generalization, specific country investigation may give a great insight about Islamic finance for SDGs. In contrast, cross-country empirical studies might lack data, and lot of difficulties. Through single-country empirical studies, researchers can conduct surveys and find out the role of Islamic banking on the aspects of SDGs Goal 1, 2,8,9, 11 and 17.

The main goal of this paper is to discuss the keyways that Islamic Finance accomplishment for sustainable development goals. In terms of the state of the economy. According to literature, researcher need to focus more in two variables Islamic Finance and Sustainable development goals rather than specific they can focus on increasing organizational diversity and switching to larger portfolios equity-based financing percentages.

REFERENCES

Abduh, M. (2019). Thought Civiliz. ISTAC 2019. *The Role of Islamic Social Finance in Achieving Sdg Number 2Achieve Food Security and Improved Nutrition and Promote Sustainable Agriculture*, 185–206.

Ahmed, H. (2017). *Contribution of Islamic Finance To the 2030 Agenda for Sustainable Development.* In *High-level Conference on Financing for Development and the Means of Implementation of the 2030 Agenda for Sustainable Development*, (pp. 8–19). Doha,Qatar.

Azmat, S., Kabir Hassan, M., Ali, H., & Sohel Azad, A. R. (2021). Neglected Risk and Asset Returns. *Journal of International Financial Markets, Institutions and Money, 74.*

Ghlamallah, E., Alexakis, C., Dowling, M., & Piepenbrink, A. (2021). *The Topics of Islamic Economics and Finance Research.* Science Direct.

Habib Ahmed, R. (2004). Jeddah: The Islamic Research and Teaching Institute (IRTI). Durham Technology.

Haniffa, R., & Hudaib, M. (2007). Exploring the Ethical Identity of Islamic Banks via Communication in Annual reports. *Journal of Business Ethics, 76*(1), 97–116. doi:10.100710551-006-9272-5

Hummel, D., & Hashmi, A. (2019). The Possibilities of Community Redevelopment with Islamic Finance. *J. Islam. Account. Bus. Res*, 259-273.

Mahmoud Mohieldin, Z. I. (2011). *The role of Islamic Finance in Enhancing Financial Inclusion in Organization of Islamic Cooperation (OIC).* Countries. doi:10.1596/1813-9450-5920

Mohammed Obaidullah, A. T. (2008). Islamic Microfinance Development. *Islamic Research & Training institute Policy Dialogue.* Islamic Research & Training institute.

Monzer Kahf, A. W. (2000). *Its Growth, Management and Development. Damascus: Dar al Fikr).* Monzer Kahf.

Nimrah Karim, M. T. (2008). *Islam Micro Finance: an Emerging.* Collective Group to Assist the Poor.

Ogunmakinde, O., Egbelakin, T., & Sher, W. (2021). Contributions of the Circular Economy to the UN Sustainable Development Goals. *Resources, Conservation and Recycling, 2021*(178), 106023.

Rania Kamla, H. (2013). Social Reporting by Islamic Banks: Does Social Justice Matter? *Accounting, Auditing & Accountability Journal*, (26), 911–945. doi:10.1108/AAAJ-03-2013-1268

Refinitiv. (2021). *Islamic Finance Development Report 2021.* Refinitiv: New York, NY, USA.

UN. (n.d.). *Transforming Our World: The 2030 Agenda for Sustainable Development*. United Nations,.

Young, E.Y. (2008). *Bridging the gap: Private Investment in Middle east Infrastructure*.

Chapter 8

Examining Customers' Intentions to Use Financial Technology in Islamic Banking:
Evidence From Indonesia

Nasrul Fahmi Zaki Fuadi
https://orcid.org/0000-0001-5176-632X
Universitas Islam Negeri Walisongo Semarang, Indonesia

Abdul Ghofur
Universitas Islam Negeri Walisongo Semarang, Indonesia

Mohammad Irfan
https://orcid.org/0000-0002-4956-1170
Business School, NSB Academy, India

Laily Nur Asyifa
Universitas Islam Negeri Walisongo Semarang, Indonesia

ABSTRACT

This study investigates the impact of Islamic Shariah compliance on customer satisfaction, focusing on the mediating effect of service quality within the context of Islamic banking services. Data obtained randomly from 124 Islamic bank customers in Indonesia were analyzed using multiple linear regression in SPSS. The results demonstrate that various factors, including attitude, subjective norms, and behavioral control, significantly influence the propensity of Islamic bank customers to adopt financial technology services offered by Islamic banks. It is important to note that this study is primarily centered on fintech-enabled Islamic banking services. This study underscores the need for Islamic Financial Institutions to enhance the success of fintech services and to promote these offerings to customers. Furthermore, it encourages Islamic financial institutions to harness technological advancements that streamline customer banking transactions. This study provides Islamic banks with valuable insights into the optimization of technology-driven financial services.

DOI: 10.4018/979-8-3693-1038-0.ch008

1. INTRODUCTION

Several studies identify diverse definitions of fintech. FinTech refers to the use of technology to provide financial solutions (Varma et al., 2022). FinTech is defined as the application of digital technology to financial intermediation issues (Griffin et al., 2023). The integration of financial technology (Fintech) plays a substantial role in enhancing the efficiency of the financial system through the reduction of operational costs, the provision of superior services, and the augmentation of consumer happiness (Hasan et al., 2023; Kou et al., 2021; Li et al., 2022; Qudah et al., 2023). In addition, fintech can play a relevant role in the SME transition towards a more sustainable business model, leading to better integration of circular economy practices (Pizzi et al., 2021). FinTech is an industry comprising companies that use technology to create a financial system and deliver financial services more efficiently (Griffin et al., 2023; Moro Visconti, 2020; Pentury, 2023).

The growth of internet use in Indonesia is already very high (Kharisma, 2022). More than 50 percent of Indonesian citizens are inseparable from the internet (Nopreza and Sumadi, 2022). The Indonesian Internet Service Providers Association (APJII) surveyed the Penetration and Behavior of Indonesian Internet Users in 2017". The results of a survey in collaboration with Technopreneurs stated that the penetration of internet users in Indonesia increased to 143.26 million people, or equivalent to 54.7 percent of the total population of the Republic of Indonesia (Annisya et al., 2023).

Government Regulations through Bank Indonesia and the Financial Services Authority (OJK) have made several regulations related to this fintech (Suryono et al., 2021). This is to provide security assurance to consumers, or in this case, to the broader public. The availability of rules makes rights and responsibilities a crucial aspect of financial businesses.

In the subsequent four years, only nine companies engaged in FinTech operations were added, resulting in 25 enterprises in 2011-2012. As a result, finTech companies expanded by approximately 177.78 percent that year, compared to a growth rate of approximately 300 percent in 2006-2007. In 2013-2014, the number of FinTech companies increased from 25 to 40, with a growth of around 60 percent. Finally, from 2014 to 2016, the number of FinTech companies increased from 124 to 165, a phenomenal expansion, indicating that the number of FinTech companies increased by approximately 312.5 percent compared with the previous year (Nizar, 2017).

The emergence of FinTech creates direct competition between Fintech and banks (Murinde et al., 2022). Fintech also pursues partnerships or sells its services to financial institutions (Dasilas and Karanović, 2023; Mogaji, 2023; Ozili, 2018). The first strategy involves the collaboration between banks and fintech companies (Golodova and Grechkin, 2022; Ruhland and Wiese, 2022). For example, fintech can access numerous growth sources including clients, distribution, data, finance, experience, licensing, and trust. Banks have access to new ideas, solutions, capabilities, information, and possible investment opportunities through fintech, which has a far lower cost structure (Lutfi, 2018; Zhou et al., 2022).

In contrast to other financial businesses, Islamic Banking in Indonesia has not increased its fintech use. According to the Chairman of the Board of Commissioners of the Financial Services Authority (OJK), Wimboh Santoso, the financing of Islamic commercial banks and Sharia business units amounted to Rp 282, 1 trillion in February 2018. This number declined by 1.3% compared to the end of the previous year (year to date)—/YTD), which equals 285,7 trillion IDR. As of March 2018, financial technology (fintech) had disbursed loans totaling Rp 4.47 trillion. In summary, Islamic financial financing is far greater than fintech financing. However, the rise in fintech loans is far quicker at 74.6 percent YTD (Sari, 2023).

The authors searched for literature pertinent to the theme and title of the study. Based on several investigations and prior research, the authors have described the following:

Kinanti and Baridwan (2012) investigated the determinants of e-ticketing information systems: an extended Theory approach. Using the Theory of Planned Behavior (TPB) model, this study investigates the elements influencing interest in an e-ticketing information system. The data collection method was a survey—a sample of 86 persons at Juanda International Airport, Surabaya–using e-ticketing. The analysis was conducted using the Smart PLS Software.

The findings of this study suggest that attitudes and perceived behavioral control influence the desire to use e-ticketing information systems. Subjective norms and beliefs had little influence on the desire to use e-ticketing information systems. The results of this study indicate that companies' management should pay greater attention to the aspects that influence the development of ticket-booking transactions using e-ticketing information systems.

Ayudya and Wibowo (2018) investigated the Intention to Use E-Money using the Theory of Planned Behavior and Locus of Control. Utilizing the Theory of Planned Behavior (TPB) and Locus of Control (LOC) as moderating variables, this study sought to identify the elements influencing the intention to utilize electronic money. The DIY community selected for this study's sample was dispersed across one municipality and four districts.

The results of this study indicate that the variables of attitude towards behavior and perceived behavioral control have a positive effect on the intention to use electronic money. At the same time, subjective norms have not been proven to significantly affect intention. However, specifically for respondents living in villages, the subjective norm variable affected the intention to use electronic money. In contrast, perceived behavioral control did not affect intentions. Locus of Control (LOC) was not proven to moderate the variables in the Theory of Planned Behavior (TPB) on the intention to use electronic money.

Nugroho, Najib, & Simanjuntak (2018) investigated the Factors Affecting Consumer Interest in Electronic Money Utilization Using the Theory of Planned Behavior (TPB). This study investigated the influence of consumer attitudes, subjective norms, and accepted behavioral constraints on consumers' interest in using electronic money. Respondents' responses to structured questionnaires were used to collect information. Several questions were formulated using a Likert scale, with five response options ranging from strongly disagree to strongly agree. Two hundred and ninety undergraduate students who had never utilized server-based electronic money were the respondents. The approach utilized for sampling was judgment sampling (non-probability sampling).

The results demonstrated that opinions about behavior had no significant effect on interest. Subjective standards and perceived behavioral control have a substantial impact on the desire to use electronic money.

An Empirical Study of the Effects of Perceived Security and Knowledge on the Continuous Intention to Use Mobile Fintech Payment Services (Lim et al., 2019) investigates the connection between perceived security, service knowledge, confirmation, utility, and satisfaction. In Fintech services, the researcher suggests a research model based on the Extended Post-Acceptance Model (EPAM) as a theoretical framework. The researcher then verified the model using data gathered from the service users.

According to the analysis, knowledge and perceived security of mobile fintech services substantially impact user confirmation and perceived usefulness. However, perceived security does not directly affect user happiness or the intent to continue using it. Researchers have also discovered a correlation between confirmation, perceived utility, satisfaction, and intention to continue using a service. Finally, the theoretical and practical contributions of the study are discussed.

Yaseen and El Qirem (2018) investigated Jordanian commercial banks' intentions to use e-banking services. This study seeks to identify the significant elements that influence Jordanian commercial bank customers' intentions to adopt e-banking services. This research adopts and modifies The Unified Theory of Acceptance and Use of Technology (UTAUT). Additionally, changes were made to clarify the aim of using banking services.

According to the findings of this study, the updated model explains 0.887% of the behavioral intention factors and 0.51% of the anticipated level of e-banking service utilization variables. Three factors were identified as predictors: corporate expectations, social influence, and perceived quality of e-banking services. The insignificant factors are performance expectations and hedonic motivation. Nonetheless, age alone significantly moderated all the three indicators.

The primary contribution is a better knowledge of the influential elements in adopting and using e-banking services. In addition, this study includes a new variable: perception of e-banking quality. Therefore, the suggested model has greater explanatory power than that of previous research.

2. LITERATURE REVIEW

2.1 Financial Technology Concepts

Bank Indonesia describes Financial Technology (FinTech) as a mix of financial services and technology that alters the business model from traditional to moderate, initially paying face-to-face and carrying some cash. This process can be completed within a few seconds (Departemen Komunikasi, 2018).

Financial Technology or financial technology (FinTech) spawned new capital that made consumer access to financial products and services more convenient. Financial Technology (FinTech) disrupted the status quo and transformed the operations of traditional financial institutions (Daud et al., 2022).

According to the World Bank, Financial Technology (FinTech) comprises companies that employ technology to make the financial system and delivery of financial services more efficient (Basdekis et al., 2022; Feyen et al., 2023). The Financial Stability Board defines FinTech as a technological innovation in financial services that can develop business models, apps, procedures, or products with tangible implications related to the delivery of financial services (Basdekis et al., 2022; Feyen et al., 2023).

Based on prior knowledge, we conclude that Financial Technology (FinTech) is a new development in the financial services industry in the form of a concept that combines technological advancements with the innovative financial sector to provide a more effective, efficient, secure, and modern financial transaction process.

2.2 Financial Technology's Background

The term financial technology (fintech) is derived from financial and financial technology. Fintech is defined as "innovation financial services" by the National Digital Research Center (NDRC) in Dublin, Ireland, which means "innovation in the fintech financial services" (Gold and Ali, 2019; Griffin et al., 2023; Hasan and Sunarti, 2019). This context explicitly refers to the financial innovations that incorporate current technologies. Fintech enables various financial transactions including payments, investments, transfers, financing, funding, financial plans, and product comparisons (Nagimova, 2022; Nicoletti, 2021; Reyes-Mercado, 2021).

Financial technology, also known as fintech, is the outcome of a collaborative effort between the financial services industry and technology sector. This partnership aims to transform the traditional business model into a more adaptive and modernized approach. Under this particular paradigm, it is possible to execute a payment in a remote manner and within a matter of seconds, even in cases when traditionally it would have required a physical presence and payment in cash (Bank Indonesia, 2018). Fintech is a disruptive innovation that has successfully transformed an existing system or market by adding pragmatism, ease of access, convenience, and affordable pricing (Joseph L. Bower and Clayton M. Christensen, 1995; Nagimova, 2022)

FinTech arose along with changes in people's lifestyles, which are presently dominated by information technology users, and the demands for fast-paced living (Sapulette et al., 2022). With the advent of FinTech, difficulties in purchasing and selling transactions and payments, such as a lack of time to search for goods at shopping locations, banks/ATMs transferring cash, and reluctance to visit locations because of poor service, can be mitigated. In other words, fintech facilitates more efficient and cost-effective purchasing and selling transactions and payment methods. In addition to altering the payment system in society, FinTech has assisted startups in reducing their initial capital expenditure and operational expenses (Bank Indonesia, 2018).

Fintech is a paradigm that emphasizes convenience and reduces the cost of creating money for credit cards and digital currency. Therefore, fintech inventions face severe competition to demonstrate their advantages over conventional fintech (Banna et al., 2022). In addition to competing with existing fintech goods, new fintech solutions that rely primarily on applications must contend with non-financial products such as email and text messaging. These conditions expose fintech companies to the risk of failure, notwithstanding their innovative and superior offerings (Hasan and Nita Putri, 2022).

Financial technology has a high level of efficacy in enhancing the quality of banking services (Asif et al., 2023), allowing banking management to implement it at all levels of Indonesian society, particularly for those who reside in 3T zones.

2.3 Regulation

Bank Indonesia has issued the following regulations concerning this fintech: (1) Bank Indonesia Regulation Number 18/40/PBI/2016 Regarding the Implementation of Payment Transaction Processing (Yunita and Munandar, 2023); (2) Bank Indonesia Regulation Number 19/12/PBI/2017 Regarding the Implementation of Financial Technology (Algamar and Ismail, 2023; Angkasa et al., 2023; Sukarmi et al., 2022); (3) Regulation of Members of the Board of Governors Number 19/14/PADG/2017 Regarding Financial Technology Regulatory Sandbox; (4) Regulation of Members of the Board of Governors Number 19/12/PBI/2017 Regarding the Implementation of Financial Technology; (5) Regulation in the meantime, the OJK has only released 1 (one) regulation for the supervision of fintech enterprises, namely the Financial Services Authority Regulation Number 77/POJK.01/2016 on Information Technology-Based Lending and Borrowing Services (Suryono et al., 2021).

2.4 Theory of Planned Behavior (TPB) Concepts

The initial name for this theory was the Theory of Reasoned Action (TRA), which was developed in 1967. Ajzen and Fishbein later made various improvements to this theory. Finally, this theory was developed in 1980 to research human behavior and produce more effective solutions. In 1988, numerous changes were made to TRA, which was eventually renamed Theory Planned of Behavior (TPB) to address the deficiencies and strengths identified by Ajzen and Fishbein in their TRA research (Fuadi et al., 2022). The TPB has three elements that explain the goal of attitude, subjective norms, and perceived behavior control, whereas the TRA has only two attitudes and subjective norms (Ajzen, 1991; Fuadi et al., 2022; Irimia-Diéguez et al., 2023).

According to Ajzen (1991) and Fishbein and Ajzen (1975), purpose is a dimension of the probability of a person's subjective location that links a person to a particular action. Intentions are also utilized to capture the motivating variables that drive action, and they indicate how strongly a person is willing to try and how much effort is needed to perform an activity. Essentially, the greater a person's purpose, the greater the likelihood that they will undertake an activity (Ajzen and Madden, 1986; Fuadi et al., 2022).

The Theory of Planned behavior describes a complete integration of the components of attitude (attitude), subjective norm (subjective norm), and perceived behavior control (perceived conduct control) to provide more accurate explanations and predictions regarding behavior. Thus, the most accurate predictor of behavior is the intention to purchase (Fuadi et al., 2022).

Saifuddin explained that the core of the Theory remains in the behavioral intention factor, but that the determinants of intention are not only two (attitudes towards the behavior in question and subjective norms) but also three, with the perceived behavioral control aspect being incorporated into this theory (Fuadi et al., 2022). The TRA has been successfully applied to behaviors under individual controls. However, if the conduct is not entirely under the individual's control or decision, they may not exhibit it, even if they are highly motivated by subjective attitudes and norms (Fuadi et al., 2022; Ratnaningrum, 2012).

3. METHOD

3.1 Types of Research

This study used a quantitative research design to examine whether there is a significant relationship between attitude, subjective norms, perceived behavior control, and the intent of Islamic bank clients to use FINTECH services. The quantitative study methodology was used to assess the extent to which the factors of attitude (attitude), Subjective Norm (Subjective Norm), and perceived behavioral control (perceived behavior control) influence customer intentions to use FINTECH services.

3.2 Research Instruments

This study employs a questionnaire to assess Islamic bank customers' attitudes, subjective norms, perceived behavioral control, and propensity to utilize FINTECH services. An ordinal scale, often known as the Likert scale, was used in the questionnaire development. The Likert scale allowed responders to articulate the intensity of their emotions. Responses to each question ranged from 1 to 4 in each category. Each question has four possible responses: strongly agree, agree, disagree, and strongly disagree.

The response options ranged from 1 to 4, assuming that the findings would be imprecise if too few responses were available. However, if there are too many response alternatives, it is anticipated that responders may be unable to differentiate between the options. How to respond to this survey question by placing checkmark (v) in the supplied column.

3.3 Data Analysis Method

The authors employed multi-regression analysis techniques. Using this strategy, the effect of the independent factors on the dependent variable in this study can be determined. In this study, attitude, subjective norms, and perceived behavioral control were the independent variables, whereas intention to use FINTECH services was the dependent variable. The following equation was derived:.

$$\text{Int} = \beta_0 + \beta_1 \text{ Att} + \beta_2 \text{ Sub} + \beta_3 \text{ Perc} + \mu_i$$

Int : Intention to Use FINTECH Services.
β_0 : Constant
β_1, β_2, β_3 : Regression coefficient
Att : Attitude
Sub : Subjective Norm
Perc : Perceiver Behavioral Control
μ_i : Residual variables

This analysis was performed using SPSS version 25.0 application. First, computation printout was used to interpret the results of the analysis, after which the following tests were conducted:

The application of a t-test was employed to assess the statistical significance of the regression coefficient in the context of hypothesis testing (Nasution and Usman, 2008).

H0: $\beta = 0$ (no influence)

H0: $\beta \neq 0$ (influenced)

If I t I is greater than t/2, then the null hypothesis that I = 0 is rejected at a confidence level of 100 & (1 –). In this case, I can be considered to be statistically significant.

3.4 Data Collection

The data collection method used in this study involved collection of secondary and primary data. This study gathered secondary data from related publications, articles, yearly reports, and other sources to support the research, which is considered library research.

According to the content of the questionnaire, primary data were gathered through a survey of questions. The questionnaire was administered to a sample of Semarang Islamic Bank clients.

3.5 Determination of Research Sample

The process of determining samples from customers is conducted with a non-probability sampling approach using the convenience sampling method, that is, the sampling method conducted for convenience concerning the provision of the necessary data. A sample size of 3,099,688 persons, which is indicative of the population's size and characteristics, was established using a Simple Cluster Sampling technique. The Slovin formula was employed, along with a ten percent allowance rate.

The overall population does not represent the number of customers of Islamic Banks in general but rather the number of third-party fund consumers at Islamic Banks. Therefore, in this study, we assumed that the number of clients represented the entire population.

4. RESULT

4.1 Overview of Research Objects

The subject of this study is customers of the Islamic Bank in Semarang, as it can be assumed that the features of Islamic Bank customers have highlighted the Sharia component of financial management. Therefore, it is reasonable to assume that awareness of the afterlife, which in this case is religion, is the top priority.

It is hoped that Islamic bank fintech services will increase due to knowledge of Islamic bank customers' aspirations. Therefore, socializing and promoting fintech will focus on pertinent Islamic financial institutions and For Islamic financial institutions to realize their goals and accomplishments.

4.2 Validity and Reliability Testing

Based on the results of the validity and reliability test of the questionnaire on a sample of 30 data points using SPSS 25 analysis, the results obtained in the Pearson Correlation and Corrected item-total correlation column of Table 1, the results of the validity test for each question item have a value greater than 0.3 and are therefore deemed valid. Moreover, this method can be used in additional studies.

The attitude, subjective norm, behavioral control, and intention variables in Table 2 have Cronbach's alpha values above the threshold value of 0.700, indicating that the questions in this variable are considered statistically trustworthy and can be utilized in future studies.

4.3 Understanding Descriptive FINTECH Statistics

Descriptive statistics were used to describe the distribution of respondents' answers in terms of frequency, percentage (percent), and cross-tabulations to determine the extent to which they were knowledgeable about financial technology (fintech).

Table 3 displays the results concerning the first research question, namely, how Islamic bank clients perceive fintech using the cross-tabulation method.

22.6 Of all respondents with high school education, 22.6% were aware of fintech, whereas 3.2% were unaware of it. Similarly, the percentage of respondents with D2/D3/D4 education between those who knew and did not equal the number of respondents, which was two for each category. Fifty-five percent of respondents with a bachelor's degree (S1) have a strong understanding of fintech, according to a survey of 57 respondents. Meanwhile, respondents with S2 and S3 education have an excellent comprehension of fintech; all of these respondents have an excellent understanding.

It may be concluded that a person's knowledge of technology finance increases with their level of education. Therefore, if parties associated with fintech wish to advance it, students are appropriate

Table 1. Validity test results

		Item-Total Statistics			
		Scale Mean if Item Deleted	**Scale Variance if Item Deleted**	**Corrected Item-Total Correlation**	**Cronbach's Alpha if Item Deleted**
Attitude	q1	13.2429	3.868	.565	.814
	q2	12.9571	3.317	.662	.786
	q3	13.0714	3.430	.676	.783
	q4	13.1857	3.255	.686	.779
	q5	13.1429	3.573	.562	.815
Subjective Norms	q6	11.3286	6.224	.651	.809
	q7	11.0000	5.768	.718	.790
	q8	11.1429	5.487	.776	.772
	q9	11.2000	5.786	.593	.827
	q10	10.9857	6.507	.514	.843
Behavioral Controls	q11	6.2429	1.491	.525	.621
	q12	6.0143	1.377	.529	.615
	q13	6.4286	1.379	.526	.618
Intention	q14	6.4429	1.178	.699	.817
	q15	6.3429	1.011	.772	.745
	q16	6.3857	1.110	.702	.813

Table 2. Reliability test result

Reliability Statistics		
Variable	**Cronbach's Alpha**	**N of Items**
Attitude	.830	5
Subjective Norms	.842	5
Behavioral Controls	.708	3
Intention	.852	3

Table 3. Is education familiar with FINTECH? Crosstabulation

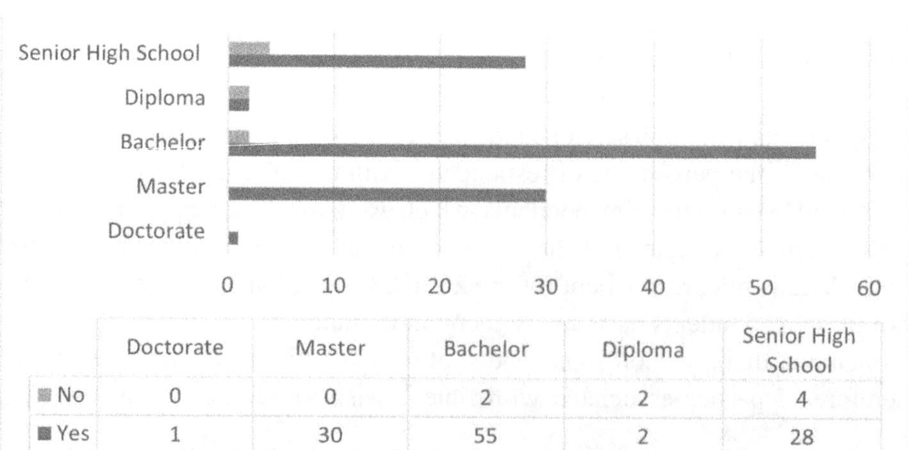

*Table 4. Income * Using FINTECH crosstabulation*

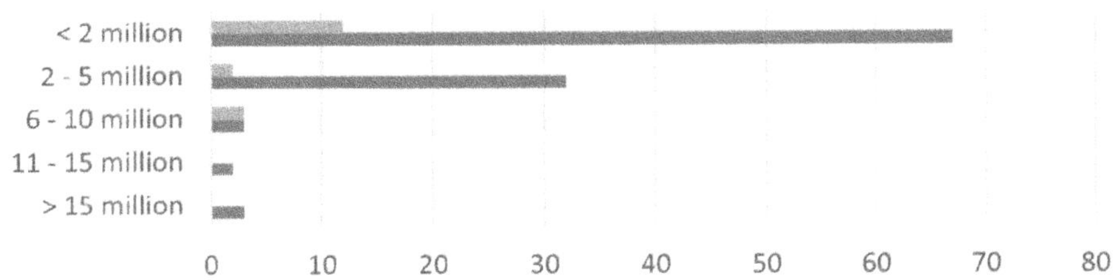

	> 15 million	11 - 15 million	6 - 10 million	2 - 5 million	< 2 million
No	0	0	3	2	12
Yes	3	2	3	32	67

*Table 5. Employment * source of FINTECH knowledge cross-tabulation*

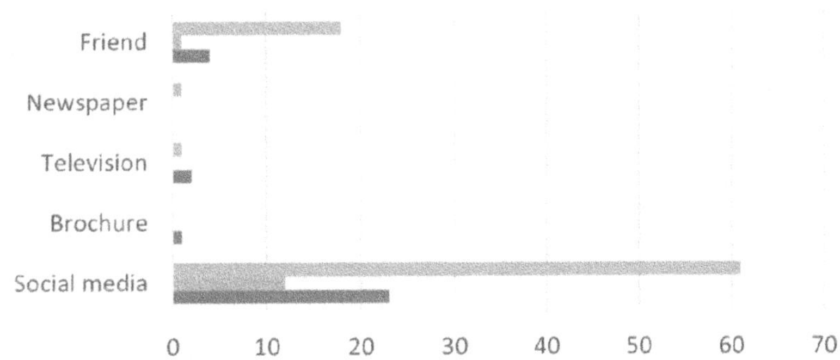

	Social media	Brochure	Television	Newspaper	Friend
Students	61	0	1	1	18
Private Sector Employees	12	0	0	0	1
Civil Servants	23	1	2	0	4

targets for socialization. In addition, customers with a high level of education can benefit from related parties' fintech services because they have a firm grasp of the technology and require less time to use it.

Table 4 shows that among the 79 respondents with incomes of less than $2 million, 84.8 percent have utilized fintech services. The number of respondents who have used fintech services is exceptionally high, as respondents from all income levels have done so.

Therefore, it can be inferred that affiliated parties and banks employ techniques in developing fintech services that encompass all aspects of clients with differing nominal incomes. Therefore, the service in question is consistent with the income classification.

Table 5 demonstrates that the respondents in the student/student group knew about fintech through social media. 75,3 percent of these categories know about fintech through social media, and friends informed the rest. The majority of respondents with private and government jobs were familiar with fintech through social media and personal connections.

It can be argued that social media networks are the best technique to promote fintech. This is consistent with Industry 4.0, in which technology plays a crucial role in an industry's success. Utilizing social media as a platform will reduce social strain in the industry and business. Utilize the remaining money for development and offer the best price to the clients.

4.4 Frequency Distribution of Respondents' Answers

Based on the data processing of the respondents' responses, the frequency distribution of respondents' responses can be interpreted as follows.

4.4.1 Attitude Variable

The following table depicts the frequency distribution of respondents' responses to the attitude factor regarding Islamic Bank customers' intentions to utilize FINTECH services.

According to the data in Table 6, the responses to the items indicate that, in general, respondents have a positive attitude towards their intent to utilize fintech services. Furthermore, regarding their awareness of the law and the benefits of fintech to people and society, respondents' attitudes towards fintech were fairly positive, as evidenced by the average rating of respondents' responses, which was 3 out of 4.

The most fantastic average value for the attitude variable is in Attitude Statement 2, which refers to the impression that utilizing FINTECH services will facilitate financial transactions. This demonstrates the positive attitude (support) of the responders. This conclusion is supported by the third attitude statement, which indicates that respondents believe that utilizing FINTECH services is more profitable. In addition,

Table 6. Frequency distribution of attitude factor responses

Statistics						
		S1	S2	S3	S4	S5
N	Valid	124	124	124	124	124
	Missing	0	0	0	0	0
Mean		3,0242	3,3952	3,2258	3,0887	2,9113
Median		3,0000	3,0000	3,0000	3,0000	3,0000
Mode		3,00	3,00	3,00	3,00	3,00
Skewness		-0,726	-0,641	-0,438	-0,268	-0,009
Std. Error of Skewness		0,217	0,217	0,217	0,217	0,217
Kurtosis		2,574	0,790	0,161	0,061	-0,660
Std. Error of Kurtosis		0,431	0,431	0,431	0,431	0,431
Sum		375,00	421,00	400,00	383,00	361,00
Percentiles	25	3,0000	3,0000	3,0000	3,0000	2,0000
	50	3,0000	3,0000	3,0000	3,0000	3,0000
	75	3,0000	4,0000	4,0000	3,7500	3,0000

the security of utilizing fintech services at the bank is a respondent preference, as seen in question four of the attitude survey, in which respondents believed that using fintech services at the bank would be safer.

To establish respondents' attitudes, they also considered the fundamental components of fintech regulation, beginning with their familiarity with fintech laws and regulations. This is evident from the statement regarding Attitude 1, which had a mean score of 3.0. However, owing to their lack of awareness of fintech-related laws and regulations, which are still relatively novel, this assertion is still minor compared to the other three.

4.4.2 Subjective Norm Variables

The following table displays respondents' responses to the subjective norm component of Islamic Bank customers' aspirations to use fintech services.

According to the data in Table 7, respondents' responses to the assertions revealed that, in general, their intentions were affected by Subjective Norms, including family, friends, and other influential persons. The influence of this subjective standard is demonstrated by the respondents' average rating of 2.8 on a maximum scale of 4.

For the subjective norm variable, the statement of norm 5 received the highest average score for the respondent's response; that is, other parties whose opinions I value advocate adopting FINTECH services at Islamic banks, indicating that the responder strongly desires to employ fintech services when a trusted entity or individual provides input and guidance.

Friends' confidence in utilizing fintech services also motivates respondents to use fintech services, as indicated by the average response of 2.80 or the second rank of the three statements associated with the subjective norm variable in this study. Before acquaintances or coworkers recommended financial

Table 7. Frequency distribution of subjective norm factor responses

Statistics						
		NS1	NS2	NS3	NS4	NS5
N	Valid	124	124	124	124	124
	Missing	0	0	0	0	0
Mean		2,5403	2,8871	2,7016	2,6290	2,9194
Median		3,0000	3,0000	3,0000	3,0000	3,0000
Mode		3,00	3,00	3,00	3,00	3,00
Skewness		0,113	-0,152	-0,052	-0,443	-0,401
Std. Error of Skewness		0,217	0,217	0,217	0,217	0,217
Kurtosis		-0,220	-0,169	-0,241	-0,087	0,535
Std. Error of Kurtosis		0,431	0,431	0,431	0,431	0,431
Sum		315,00	358,00	335,00	326,00	362,00
Percentiles	25	2,0000	2,0000	2,0000	2,0000	3,0000
	50	3,0000	3,0000	3,0000	3,0000	3,0000
	75	3,0000	3,0000	3,0000	3,0000	3,0000

services, distant relatives had more significant stake. It can be seen that utterances about friends or coworkers had the lowest average of 2.7%.

According to Ajzen's Theory of Planned Behavior, subjective norms reflect normative views, which include social pressure from parties deemed significant by an individual and the urge to comply with that demand. In other words, if an individual believes that influential individuals or organizations (referents) will encourage them to engage in the action, this will constitute social pressure on the individual.

4.4.3 Behavior Control Variables

Table 8 shows the frequency distribution of respondents' responses to behavioral control factors regarding Islamic Bank customers' plans to use fintech services.

Behavioral Control generally influences the respondents' propensity to utilize fintech services, as shown by their responses to the assertions. Using fintech services is an action under the control of the respondent's behavior; it is difficult for respondents with current income to use fintech services, and the respondents desire to continue using fintech services while they are in trials. The effect of this behavioral control is demonstrated by the average response score of 3.0 on a scale with a maximum of 4.

For the behavioral control variable, the statement with the highest average score is Control Statement 2, which states that the decision to utilize FINTECH services is entirely their own. This is supported by control statement 1, which claims that the respondent believes FINTECH services at Islamic banks are secure. This assertion ranks second, with an average value of 3.0.

The statement with the lowest value is Control Statement 3, which states that all Muslims should utilize FINTECH services in Islamic banks. As the decision to utilize fintech services is not directly tied to Sharia principles, respondents believe that Sharia and non-Sharia fintech concepts hold the same position in Sharia.

Table 8. Response frequency distribution for behavioral control factors

Statistics				
		KP1	**KP2**	**KP3**
N	Valid	124	124	124
	Missing	0	0	0
Mean		3,0726	3,2984	2,8548
Median		3,0000	3,0000	3,0000
Mode		3,00	3,00	3,00
Skewness		-0,253	-0,630	0,055
Std. Error of Skewness		0,217	0,217	0,217
Kurtosis		0,173	-0,166	-0,594
Std. Error of Kurtosis		0,431	0,431	0,431
Sum		381,00	409,00	354,00
Percentiles	25	3,0000	3,0000	2,0000
	50	3,0000	3,0000	3,0000
	75	3,0000	4,0000	3,0000

Table 9. Frequency distribution of answers for intensity variables

Statistics				
		I1	I2	I3
N	Valid	124	124	124
	Missing	0	0	0
Mean		2,9839	3,0726	3,1048
Median		3,0000	3,0000	3,0000
Mode		3,00	3,00	3,00
Skewness		-0,193	-0,518	-0,253
Std. Error of Skewness		0,217	0,217	0,217
Kurtosis		0,268	0,367	1,259
Std. Error of Kurtosis		0,431	0,431	0,431
Sum		370,00	381,00	385,00
Percentiles	25	3,0000	3,0000	3,0000
	50	3,0000	3,0000	3,0000
	75	3,0000	4,0000	3,0000

4.4.4 Variable Intention

The following table depicts respondents' responses to behavioral control factors regarding Islamic Bank customers' plans to use fintech services:

Based on the data in Table 9 and the responses to the provided statements, most respondents wanted to use fintech services through Islamic financial institutions, in this case, Islamic banking, in the following year or this year. This was demonstrated by the average score of the respondents' responses on a maximum scale of 4 was 3.0.

This variable contained only statements with a high value of 3.0. The respondents intended to utilize fintech services shortly thereafter. It is also associated with attitudes, subjective norms, and behavioral control.

4.5 Classic Assumption Test

In multiple linear regression models, classical assumption testing is necessary to determine whether the estimation results for regression are devoid of heteroscedasticity, multicollinearity, or autocorrelation. The conventional assumption test for the model created by the study was conducted using normality, multicollinearity, and heteroscedasticity tests. This study did not require an autocorrelation test because the data used were not time-series data. The following are the findings of the classical assumption test analysis using SPSS 25.0 for the proposed model:

4.6 Normality Test

The normality test was used to determine whether the data in this study had a normal distribution suitable for parametric statistics (inferential statistics). The Classical Assumption Test for data normality employs the following hypothesis.

Data were normally distributed.

The data did not follow normal distribution.

The results of the normality tests are shown in Figure 1.

The distribution of the data points in Figure 1 approaches and follows a diagonal or a normal line. Hence, the data in this study exhibited a normal distribution.

Based on the preceding histogram on Figure 2, the residuals are from a pattern-following curve and a bell-shaped normal distribution, indicating that the data follow a normal distribution.

Figure 1. Normality P-P graph

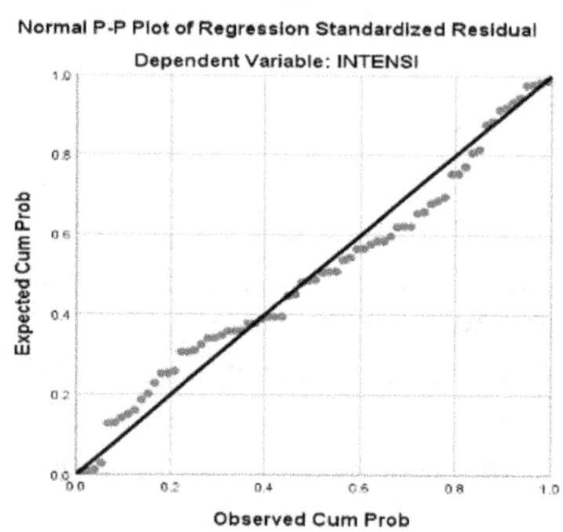

Figure 2. Data normality histogram

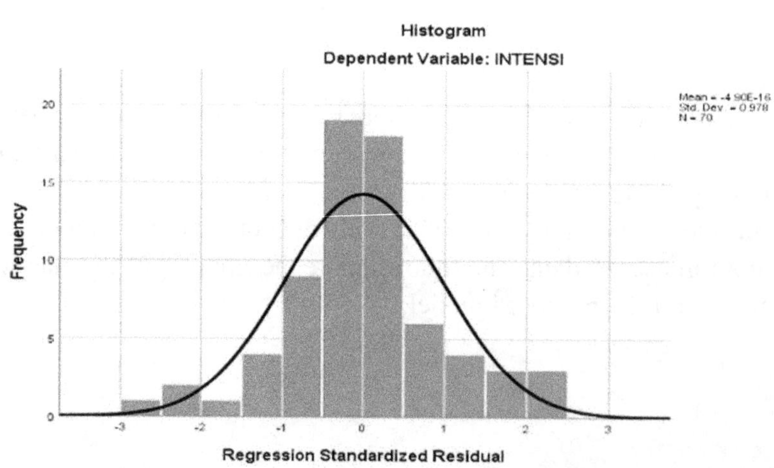

4.6.1 Multicollinearity Test

An excellent independent variable in a multiple regression model has a relationship with the dependent variable but no relationship with other independent variables. Calculating the Variation Inflation Factor (VIF) and TOL yielded this test (tolerance). If the TOL is close to 1, there is no collinearity, the VIF value is less than 10, and the independent variable is declared not to be multicollinear.

The VIF value for the attitude variable was 1.637, the VIF value for the subjective norm variable was 1.296, and the VIF value for behavioral control was 1.773, as shown in Table 10. Consequently, there was no multicollinearity between the independent variables, as all VIF values were less than 10. Similarly, the Tolerance values for the attitude, subjective norm, and behavioral control variables were 0.611, 0.772, and 0.564, respectively. Therefore, the Tolerance values of the three variables were close to one, indicating no multicollinearity among the independent variables.

4.6.2 Heteroskedasticity Test

The outcomes of testing for heteroscedasticity symptoms can be determined using the Glejser test. In addition to the Glejser test, a scatterplot can be used to detect heteroscedasticity, as shown in the Figure 3.

The test results depict a scatterplot between the error and the estimated moving variables dispersed and randomly scattered data points, demonstrating that the resulting research model lacks heteroscedastic characteristics.

Based on the traditional assumption test, it can be concluded that the suggested model lacks multicollinearity and heteroscedasticity issues, allowing for the simultaneous or partial testing of additional hypotheses.

After the variables have passed, the classical assumption test, data analysis, and the creation of the research model begin. Based on the outcomes of multiple regression analysis conducted using SPSS 25 software.

Table 10. Multicollinearity test results

Coefficients[a]									
Model		**Unstandardized Coefficients**		**Standardized Coefficients**	**t**	**Sig.**	**Collinearity Statistics**		
		B	**Std. Error**	**Beta**			**Tolerance**	**VIF**	
1	(Constant)	2,328	0,785		2,964	0,004			
	Attitude	0,182	0,059	0,279	3,085	0,003	0,611	1,637	
	Subjective Norm	0,160	0,044	0,292	3,629	0,000	0,772	1,296	
	Perceived behavioral control	0,196	0,086	0,214	2,278	0,024	0,564	1,773	
a. Dependent Variable: Intention									

Figure 3. Heteroscedasticity test results using scatterplot graph

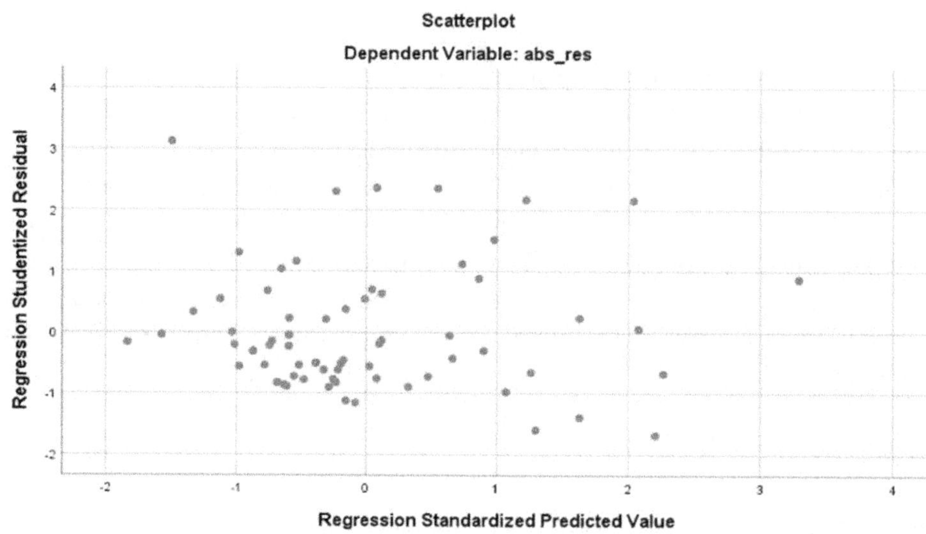

The second research question was answered after passing the multiple linear regression assumption test. How do attitudes, subjective norms, and behavioral controls affect Islamic Bank clients' intentions to use FINTECH? Therefore, the regression coefficients must be evaluated simultaneously and partially.

4.6.2.1 F Test

F simultaneously examines the regression coefficients of the multiple linear regression model. Subsequently, the following hypothesis was derived:

H0:1 = 2 = 3 = 0, indicating that the independent variable has no significant effect on the dependent variable.
H1:1 2 3 = 0, indicating a significant simultaneous effect between the independent variables.

If F Count > F table, H0 is rejected, indicating that the independent factors concurrently affect the dependent variable.

The following is the output of SPSS 25 processing:

Table 11 reveals that the computed value of F is 26,855, indicating that F count > F table, as demonstrated by the significance level of 5%. As a result, it can be concluded that the Attitude, Subjective Norm, and Behavioral Control variables all influence the intensity with which Sharia Bank customers utilize FINTECH services.

T Test

In addition to the simultaneous test, a partial test (t-test) was conducted to determine whether each independent variable partially affected the dependent variable. In this t-test, H0 is rejected if the t count is more than the t table, indicating a significant effect of each variable. The effects of each variable (factor) were partially evaluated, as shown in Table 10.

Table 11. Anova

ANOVA[a]						
Model		Sum of Squares	df	Mean Square	F	Sig.
1	Regression	102,340	3	34,113	26,855	.000[b]
	Residual	152,434	120	1,270		
	Total	254,774	123			
a. Dependent Variable: Intention						
b. Predictors: (Constant), Attitude, Subjective Norm, and Perceived behavioral control						

Therefore, for any variable, the t count > t table holds, which is also evident from the significance being below 5%. Except for the attitude variable, which has a significance level greater than 5%, this condition shows that the attitude variable does not affect the frequency with which FINTECH services are utilized.

4.6.3 Analysis and Interpretation of Model Results

The following regression model was derived based on the data presented.

INTENTION = 2,328 + 0,182 Attitude + 0,160 Subjective Norms + 0,196 Behavioral Controls

INTENTION = Intention to take advantage of FINTECH services

Att = Attitude/Attitudes of Islamic Bank customers to take advantage of FINTECH services.

Subjective norm/subjective norms of Islamic bank customers to take advantage of FINTECH services

Perc = Perceived behavioral control/perceived behavioral control of Islamic Bank clients in utilizing FINTECH services.

Table 12 shows that the R square (R2) value is 0.402, or 40.2%, based on an analysis conducted with SPSS 25, which indicates that attitude, subjective norms, and behavioral control can explain 40,2 percent of the variance in the Intention of Islamic Bank customers to use FINTECH services, with the remaining 59,8 percent explained by variables not considered in this research model.

Table 12. R square

Model Summary				
Model	R	R Square	Adjusted R Square	Std. Error of the Estimate
1	.634[a]	0,402	0,387	1,12707
a. Predictors: (Constant), Attitude, Subjective Norm, and Perceived behavioral control				

5. DISCUSSION AND CONCLUSION

This study investigates the factors that influence consumers' intention to adopt financial technology (FINTECH) in the context of Islamic banking. This study specifically concentrates on the clients of Islamic banks located in Semarang, Indonesia. This study highlights the importance of this inquiry in light of the distinctive characteristics of Islamic banking, which prioritizes adherence to Shariah principles and religious values. The proposition posits that an increased consciousness of religious doctrines, particularly adherence to Shariah rules, might have a favorable impact on the acceptance and utilization of FINTECH services provided by Islamic financial institutions. The report further emphasizes the significance of fostering social interactions and advocating the adoption of FINTECH services inside Islamic financial institutions to achieve their goals.

The questionnaire was validated and its reliability was tested using SPSS 25, which produced good results. These findings suggest that the survey questions were valid and suitable for future research. This study further emphasizes the statistical reliability of the attitude, subjective norm, and behavioral control variables, indicating their potential efficacy in future research.

The examination of descriptive statistics pertaining to FINTECH has yielded intriguing discoveries. The data demonstrated a positive correlation between an individual's educational attainment and familiarity with FINTECH, indicating that higher levels of education were associated with a higher level of awareness. Hence, directing socializing initiatives to students and offering services tailored to individuals with advanced educational backgrounds can yield advantageous outcomes.

The utilization of FINTECH services is not significantly influenced by income level, indicating that these services are available to customers in many income categories. The rise of social media has positioned it as a significant medium for disseminating information about FINTECH, highlighting its capacity as a viable channel for promotional activities.

The subsequent discourse explores the factors of attitude, subjective norms, and behavioral control in further detail. Overall, the findings indicate that participants exhibit a favorable disposition towards FINTECH services. This positive attitude is influenced by various factors including the facilitation of financial transactions, profitability, and security. Nevertheless, participants exhibited a comparatively limited understanding of the laws and regulations pertaining to FINTECH, indicating the need for enhanced efforts to educate clients on this matter.

Subjective norms encompassing familial, social, and influential acquaintances exert a substantial influence on customers' inclination to adopt FINTECH services. This study emphasizes the significance of trusted entities or individuals in incentivizing the adoption of financial technology (FINTECH).

Behavioral control characteristics indicate that clients exhibit a propensity to utilize FINTECH services and exercise significant control over this behavior. The perception of security among customers plays a significant role in the increased acceptance of FINTECH services offered by Islamic banks.

This study utilized traditional assumption tests, including tests for normality, multicollinearity, and heteroskedasticity, to establish the credibility of the multiple linear regression model. The findings suggest that the model does not exhibit any multicollinearity or heteroscedasticity.

The study's conclusions indicate that the utilization of FINTECH services in the context of Islamic banking is contingent on customer attitudes, subjective norms, and behavioral control. The combination of these factors accounts for 40.2 percent of the variability in consumers' intentions to utilize FINTECH services, whereas the remaining 59.8 percent are ascribed to unidentified variables. Customers who possess favorable attitudes are affected by trustworthy entities, and those who perceive a sense of behavioral control are more likely to exhibit a propensity towards utilizing FINTECH services. The utilization of FINTECH services does not appear to be greatly influenced by individuals' education level or income, indicating that these services are accessible to a wide range of client segments. The report proposes the implementation of focused socialization initiatives, ongoing educational programs on FINTECH laws and regulations, and the utilization of social media platforms for promotional purposes. The aforementioned findings offer significant insights that can be utilized by Islamic banks seeking to augment the adoption of FINTECH services among their clientele.

6. MANAGERIAL IMPLICATIONS, LIMITATION, AND FUTURE RESEARCH

The managerial implications of this study are significant and should be carefully considered by organizations. Several managerial implications arise for enhancing the utilization of fintech services in Islamic banking. First, it is imperative for Islamic banks to emphasize and consistently improve their commitment to Shariah principles, thereby guaranteeing that their offerings are in accordance with Islamic ethical standards. The dedication to adhering to Shariah principles not only cultivates customer contentment but also has a favorable impact on customer inclinations towards using fintech solutions. Furthermore, it is crucial to acknowledge the significant impact of service quality on client intentions. Managers within Islamic banks should prioritize investments aimed at improving service quality for both traditional and fintech services. This is because superior service quality has the potential to positively impact customer satisfaction levels and foster a higher inclination towards the use of technology-driven banking services. Furthermore, it is imperative to comprehend client attitudes, subjective norms, and behavioral controls. The use of surveys or evaluations can be beneficial in evaluating these aspects, as they enable customization of marketing and communication strategies to fit customers' tastes and expectations. In turn, this facilitates the promotion of fintech adoption. Ultimately, it is crucial to engage in proactive promotions and educational efforts to enhance the advantages and characteristics of fintech services. Islamic financial institutions could consider implementing strategic initiatives aimed at enhancing customer awareness and knowledge of the benefits of financial technology (fintech). This proactive approach contributes to the promotion and wider acceptance of fintech solutions within the customer base.

This study had several limitations that necessitated careful examination. This study's primary focus on fintech-enabled Islamic banking services in Indonesia restricts the applicability of its findings to other geographical regions and service industries. Subsequent investigations should examine analogous events in diverse contexts to authenticate and augment these findings. Furthermore, it should be noted that the sample size of 124 individuals who are customers of Islamic banks, although providing valuable insights, may not comprehensively encompass the wide range of opinions and behaviors that exist within a larger population. Increasing the sample size and diversity could potentially augment the overall strength of the study and broaden its potential for practical applications. Furthermore, it is important to acknowledge that this study's use of multiple linear regression analysis may have inherent limitations. Therefore, future research endeavors should explore alternative analytical methodologies to obtain a more comprehensive understanding of the intricate factors that impact customer intentions in the realms of Islamic banking and fintech adoption.

This study presents various areas for future research. First, conducting cross-cultural studies that compare countries or areas with distinct cultural backgrounds can yield useful insights into the role of cultural elements on customer intentions in the adoption of Islamic banking and fintech. In addition, it would be advantageous to conduct longitudinal studies that monitor the evolution of client intentions over time, taking into account the dynamic character of the fintech industry and the growing preferences of customers. Furthermore, the integration of qualitative research methodologies, such as in-depth interviews or focus groups, along with quantitative analysis can offer a more comprehensive understanding of the intricate elements that influence customer intentions and attitudes towards fintech in the context of Islamic banking. In conclusion, it is imperative to prioritize future research on the evaluation of the effects of developing technologies on consumer intentions and the adaptive measures implemented by Islamic banks, considering the swift rate at which technical breakthroughs occur.

7. ACKNOWLEDGMENT

Funded by the Operational Aid of Universitas Islam Negeri Walisongo Semarang

REFERENCES

Ajzen, I. (1991). The theory of planned behavior. *Organizational Behavior and Human Decision Processes*, *50*(2), 179–211. doi:10.1016/0749-5978(91)90020-T

Ajzen, I., & Madden, T. J. (1986). Prediction of goal-directed behavior: Attitudes, intentions, and perceived behavioral control. *Journal of Experimental Social Psychology*, *22*(5), 453–474. doi:10.1016/0022-1031(86)90045-4

Algamar, M. D., & Ismail, N. (2023). DATA SUBJECT ACCESS REQUEST: WHAT INDONESIA CAN LEARN AND OPERATIONALISE IN 2024? *Journal of Central Banking Law and Institutions*, *2*(3), 481–512. doi:10.21098/jcli.v2i3.171

Angkasa, A., Wamafma, F., Juanda, O., & Nunna, B. P. (2023). Illegal Online Loans in Indonesia: Between the Law Enforcement and Protection of Victim. *Lex Scientia Law Review*, *7*(1), 119–178. doi:10.15294/lesrev.v7i1.67558

Annisya, P.H. & Istiqomah, N. (2023). *Digital Era for Entrepreneurs: The Role of Social Media and Business Opportunities*. Atlantis Press. . doi:10.2991/978-2-38476-064-0_17

Asif, M., Khan, M. N., Tiwari, S., Wani, S. K., & Alam, F. (2023). The Impact of Fintech and Digital Financial Services on Financial Inclusion in India. *Journal of Risk and Financial Management*, *16*(2), 122. doi:10.3390/jrfm16020122

Ayudya, A. C., & Wibowo, A. (2018). The Intention to Use E-Money using Theory of Planned Behavior and Locus of Control. *Jurnal Keuangan Dan Perbankan*, *22*(2), 335–349. doi:10.26905/jkdp.v22i2.1691

Bank Indonesia. (2018). *Financial Technology*. Bank Sentral Republik Indonesia. https://www.bi.go.id/id/edukasi-perlindungan-konsumen/edukasi/produk-dan-jasa-sp/fintech/Pages/default.aspx

Banna, H., Hassan, M. K., Ahmad, R., & Alam, M. R. (2022). Islamic banking stability amidst the COVID-19 pandemic: The role of digital financial inclusion. *International Journal of Islamic and Middle Eastern Finance and Management*, *15*(2), 310–330. doi:10.1108/IMEFM-08-2020-0389

Basdekis, C., Christopoulos, A., Katsampoxakis, I., & Vlachou, A. (2022). FinTech's rapid growth and its effect on the banking sector. *Journal of Banking and Financial Technology*, *6*(2), 159–176. doi:10.100742786-022-00045-w

Dasilas, A., & Karanović, G. (2023). The impact of FinTech firms on bank performance: Evidence from the UK. *EuroMed Journal of Business*. doi:10.1108/EMJB-04-2023-0099

Daud, S. N. M., Ahmad, A. H., Khalid, A., & Azman-Saini, W. N. W. (2022). FinTech and financial stability: Threat or opportunity? *Finance Research Letters*, *47*, 102667. doi:10.1016/j.frl.2021.102667

Feyen, E. H. B., Natarajan, H., & Saal, M. (2023). Fintech and the Future of Finance : Market and Policy Implications. Washington, D.C. doi:10.1596/978-1-4648-1914-8

Fishbein, M., & Ajzen, I. (1975). *Belief Attitude Intention And Behavior*. Addison Wesley.

Fuadi, N. F. Z., Bukhari, B., & Firdiyanti, S. I. (2022). 'Halal Marketplace: The Influence of Attitude, Subjective Norms, and Perceived Behavior Control on Purchase Intention of Muslim Consumers', *Shirkah. Journal of Economics and Business*, *7*(1), 100–112. doi:10.22515hirkah.v7i1.451

Gold, M., & Ali, P. (2019). 'FinTech Challengers and Incumbents' Responses: A Window into Innovation Management Strategy Modes within Australia's Financial Services Sector.' SSRN *Electronic Journal*. doi:10.2139/ssrn.3467855

Golodova, Z. G., & Grechkin, N. V. (2022). Developing Financial Integration with the Introduction of Financial Technologies in the Eurasian Economic Union Countries. *International Relations*, *22*(1), 166–179. doi:10.22363/2313-0660-2022-22-1-166-179

Griffin, N., Uña, G., Bazarbash, M., & Verma, A. (2023). *Fintech Payments in Public Financial Management: Benefits and Risks*. (IMF Working Papers). doi:10.5089/9798400232213.001

Hasan, D. & Sunarti. (2019). *Analysis Of Banking Service Financial Technology (Fintech) Risk Management in Islamic Banks (Case Study at Bank Syariah X in Jakarta)*. KnE Social Sciences. . doi:10.18502/kss.v3i26.5396

Hasan, M., Hoque, A., & Le, T. (2023). Big Data-Driven Banking Operations: Opportunities, Challenges, and Data Security Perspectives. *FinTech*, *2*(3), 484–509. doi:10.3390/fintech2030028

Hasan, Z. & Nita Putri, M.R. (2022). Indonesian Sharia Banking in Facing the Industrial Revolution 4.0. *UMRAN - International Journal of Islamic and Civilizational Studies*, *9*(1), 37–47, . doi:10.11113/umran2022.9n1.546

Irimia-Diéguez, A., Velicia-Martín, F., & Aguayo-Camacho, M. (2023). Predicting Fintech Innovation Adoption: The Mediator Role of Social Norms and Attitudes. *Financial Innovation*, *9*(1), 36. doi:10.118640854-022-00434-6 PMID:36687792

Joseph, L. (1995). *Disruptive Technologies: Catching the Wave*. HBR. https://hbr.org/1995/01/disruptive-technologies-catching-the-wave

Kharisma, B. (2022). Surfing alone? The Internet and social capital: Evidence from Indonesia. *Journal of Economic Structures*, *11*(1), 8. doi:10.118640008-022-00267-7 PMID:35915843

Kinanti, F., & Baridwan, Z. (2012). ANALISIS DETERMINAN SISTEM INFORMASI E-TICKETING : PENDEKATAN EXTENDED THEORY OF PLANNED BEHAVIOUR. Jurnal Ilmiah Mahasiswa FEB, 1(1).

Komunikasi, D. (2018). *Mengenal Financial Teknologi.* BI. https://www.bi.go.id/id/edukasi/Pages/mengenal-Financial-Teknologi.aspx

Kou, G., Olgu Akdeniz, Ö., Dinçer, H., & Yüksel, S. (2021). Fintech investments in European banks: A hybrid IT2 fuzzy multidimensional decision-making approach. *Financial Innovation, 7*(1), 39. doi:10.118640854-021-00256-y PMID:35024283

Li, Y., Kou, G., Li, G., & Hefni, M. A. (2022). Fuzzy multi-attribute information fusion approach for finance investment selection with the expert reliability. *Applied Soft Computing, 126*, 109270. doi:10.1016/j.asoc.2022.109270

Lim, S. H., Kim, D. J., Hur, Y., & Park, K. (2019). An Empirical Study of the Impacts of Perceived Security and Knowledge on Continuous Intention to Use Mobile Fintech Payment Services. *International Journal of Human-Computer Interaction, 35*(10), 886–898. doi:10.1080/10447318.2018.1507132

Lutfi. (2018). FinTech dan Masa Depan Perbankan Indonesia - STIE Perbanas Surabaya. *Sekolah Tinggi Ilmu Ekonomi Perbanas.* https://www.perbanas.ac.id/id/component/k2/item/688-fintech-dan-masa-depan-perbankan-indonesia.

Mogaji, E. (2023). Redefining banks in the digital era: A typology of banks and their research, managerial and policy implications. *International Journal of Bank Marketing.* Advance online publication. doi:10.1108/IJBM-06-2023-0333

Moro Visconti, R. (2020). FinTech Valuation. SSRN *Electronic Journal.* doi:10.2139/ssrn.4132428

Murinde, V., Rizopoulos, E., & Zachariadis, M. (2022). The impact of the FinTech revolution on the future of banking: Opportunities and risks. *International Review of Financial Analysis, 81*, 102103. doi:10.1016/j.irfa.2022.102103

Nagimova, A. (2022). Islamic Fintech: Digitalization of Global Islamic Finance. *World Economy and International Relations, 66*(5), 50–58. doi:10.20542/0131-2227-2022-66-5-50-58

Nasution, M. E., & Usman, H. (2008). *Proses Penelitian Kuantitatif.* FEUI.

Nicoletti, B. (2021). *Proposition of Value and Fintech Organizations in Banking 5.0.* Springer. . doi:10.1007/978-3-030-75871-4_4

Nizar, M. (2017). Teknologi Keuangan (Fintech) : Konsep dan Implementasinya di Indonesia. Warta Fiskal, Jakarta.

Nopreza, M.A.A. (2022). Determinant factors of repurchase interest of buying fashion products online in e-commerce. *Asian Management and Business Review*, 162–175. . doi:10.20885/AMBR.vol2.iss2.art5

Nugroho, A., Najib, M., & Simanjuntak, M. (2018). Factors Affecting Consumer Interest In Electronic Money Usage With Theory Of Planned Behavior (TPB). *Journal of Consumer Sciences, 3*(1), 15. doi:10.29244/jcs.3.1.15-27

Ozili, P. K. (2018). Impact of digital finance on financial inclusion and stability. *Borsa Istanbul Review*, *18*(4), 329–340. doi:10.1016/j.bir.2017.12.003

Pentury, F. (2023). The Role of Knowledge and Penetration of Fintech Services in Improving MSMEs of Fishermen and Marine Farmers in Remote Small Islands Region. *Jurnal Manajemen Teori Dan Terapan| Journal of Theory and Applied Management*, *16*(1), 23–37. . doi:10.20473/jmtt.v16i1.43743

Pizzi, S., Corbo, L., & Caputo, A. (2021). Fintech and SMEs sustainable business models: Reflections and considerations for a circular economy. *Journal of Cleaner Production*, *281*, 125217. doi:10.1016/j.jclepro.2020.125217

Qudah, H., Malahim, S., Airout, R., Alomari, M., Hamour, A. A., & Alqudah, M. (2023). Islamic Finance in the Era of Financial Technology: A Bibliometric Review of Future Trends. *International Journal of Financial Studies*, *11*(2), 76. doi:10.3390/ijfs11020076

Ratnaningrum, D. P. (2012). *Intensi Mahasiswa Untuk Berwirausaha Dengan Pendekatan Theory of Planned Behaviour (Studi Terhadap Mahasiswa Pascasarjana Ekonomi Syariah Di Jakarta)*. Universitas Indonesia.

Reyes-Mercado, P. (2021). How Fintech Was Born? Springer. . doi:10.1007/978-3-030-53945-0_1

Ruhland, P., & Wiese, F. (2022). FinTechs and the financial industry: Partnerships for success. *The Journal of Business Strategy*. doi:10.1108/JBS-12-2021-0196

Sapulette, M. S., Effendi, N., & Santoso, T. (2022). FINTECH, BANKS, AND THE COVID-19 PANDEMIC: EVIDENCE FROM INDONESIA. *Buletin Ekonomi Moneter Dan Perbankan*, *24*(4), 559–588. doi:10.21098/bemp.v24i4.1470

Sari, Y. (2023). Sharia e-commerce in Indonesia: Sharia peer to peer lending. *Review of Islamic Social Finance and Entrepreneurship*, 90–102. . doi:10.20885/RISFE.vol2.iss1.art7

Sukarmi, S., Ganindha, R., & Dewantara, R. (2022). Cartel Indications on Determination of Loan Interest Rate in Fintech Lending. *Yustisia Jurnal Hukum*, *11*(3), 181. doi:10.20961/yustisia.v11i3.56339

Suryono, R. R., Budi, I., & Purwandari, B. (2021). Detection of fintech P2P lending issues in Indonesia. *Heliyon*, *7*(4), e06782. doi:10.1016/j.heliyon.2021.e06782 PMID:33981873

Varma, P., Nijjer, S., Sood, K., Grima, S., & Rupeika-Apoga, R. (2022). Thematic Analysis of Financial Technology (Fintech) Influence on the Banking Industry. *Risks*, *10*(10), 186. doi:10.3390/risks10100186

Yaseen, S. G., & El Qirem, I. A. (2018). Intention to use e-banking services in the Jordanian commercial banks. *International Journal of Bank Marketing*, *36*(3), 557–571. doi:10.1108/IJBM-05-2017-0082

Yunita, E., & Munandar, J. M. (2023). The Influence of Push-Pull-Mooring Effects on E-Wallet Customer Switching in Generation Z in DKI Jakarta. *The South East Asian Journal of Management*, *17*(1), 1–27. doi:10.21002eam.v17i1.1177

Zhou, G., Zhu, J., & Luo, S. (2022). The impact of fintech innovation on green growth in China: Mediating effect of green finance. *Ecological Economics*, *193*, 107308. doi:10.1016/j.ecolecon.2021.107308

Chapter 9
Future of Islamic Finance in India:
An Exploratory Study on Thematic Investment

Shipra Shukla
NSB Academy, India

Ezaz Ahmed
Columbia College, USA

Libeesh P. C.
https://orcid.org/0009-0006-0369-5460
Business School, NSB Academy, Bangalore, India

Sonali Dhimmar
Auro University, Surat, India

ABSTRACT

Thematic finance a study of financial investment approach on specific trends in society or economy with broader concept related to social, environmental, or economic changes that can include clean energy, technology innovation, healthcare advancements, or demographic shifts. It considers factors like asset class and geographical region. It covers investment details of companies or industry that are related to a specific trend. The area of Islamic finance with a thematic approach in India is growing, due to increase demand for ethical and Shariah-compliant investment option, the country's significant infrastructure needs, and the potential for socially responsible and sustainable investing. However, overcoming regulatory hurdles and increasing awareness remain essential for the growth of Islamic finance, including thematic finance, in the Indian financial landscape.

DOI: 10.4018/979-8-3693-1038-0.ch009

1. INTRODUCTION

Islamic finance is a financial system (Abedifar, Shahid M. Ebrahim, Et.al 2016) that operates in accordance with the principles of Islamic law, or Shariah. The key principles of Islamic finance (Alam, Intekhab, et al. 2020) are designed to promote ethical and socially responsible financial transactions while avoiding elements that are considered unethical or exploitative in Islamic jurisprudence. Here are some of the fundamental principles of Islamic finance (Alam, Intekhab, et al. 2020) . The most prominent principle in Islamic finance is the prohibition of riba (usury or interest). Islamic law strictly forbids earning or paying interest on loans. Money should not generate money by itself. Instead, profits and returns should be generated from real economic activities and risk-sharing arrangements. It also encourages risk-sharing between the financial institution and the customer. In Musharakah, both parties contribute capital and share profits and losses in proportion to their investments. In Mudarabah, one party provides the capital, and the other party provides the expertise and management, and they share the profits. All financial transactions in Islamic finance must be backed by tangible assets or services it is known as Asset backed financing. Financing should be linked to real economic activity and have an underlying physical asset, such as real estate or commodities.

Islamic finance avoids excessive uncertainty (gharar) and gambling (maisir). Contracts should be transparent, and parties involved should clearly understand the terms and conditions. Islamic finance encourages the redistribution of wealth through Zakat, which is a mandatory almsgiving requirement. A portion of an individual's wealth is given to those in need, helping to reduce economic disparities.

Islamic finance (Atif, Mohammad, M. Kabir Hassan,et.al 2021) promotes ethical and socially responsible investment and business practices. Investments in industries such as alcohol, gambling, pork, and any business considered harmful to society are prohibited. Ijara is a form of leasing where the financial institution purchases the asset and leases it to the customer for a specific period. At the end of the lease term, the customer may have the option to purchase the asset at an agreed-upon price. Sukuk are financial instruments that provide investors with a share in the ownership of an underlying asset. The returns to investors are based on the profit generated by the underlying asset. Sukuk are a Shariah-compliant alternative to conventional bonds.

Takaful is an Islamic insurance system where participants pool their resources to provide mutual financial assistance and support to those who suffer losses. It operates on the principle of shared responsibility and solidarity. To ensure compliance with Islamic principles, financial institutions in Islamic finance have Shariah boards or advisors that review and approve financial products and transactions to ensure they adhere to Shariah principles.

These principles are designed to create a financial system that is more equitable, fair, and just, promoting economic growth while adhering to ethical and moral values as prescribed by Islamic law. Islamic finance has gained prominence globally, and it continues to evolve and adapt to modern financial markets while maintaining its core principles.

1.1 Current State of Islamic Finance in India

Islamic finance (Atif, Mohammad, M. Kabir Hassan, et.al 2021). in India was in a developing phase. The Indian government had taken steps to promote and regulate Islamic finance to meet the financial needs of its Muslim population and attract investments from the Gulf countries and other regions where

Islamic finance is popular. However, it's important to note that the state of Islamic finance in India may have evolved since then. Here is an overview of the state of Islamic finance in India up to that point:

There was a growing interest in Islamic finance among various stakeholders, including financial institutions, investors, and regulators. This interest was driven by the desire to tap into a global market worth trillions of dollars and to cater to the financial needs of the Muslim population in India. In 2019, the Reserve Bank of India (RBI) had issued draft guidelines for the establishment of Islamic banks or Islamic windows within conventional banks. These guidelines aimed to allow Islamic banking products and services to be offered in India, subject to certain conditions and regulatory approval. The conventional banks in India had started offering Islamic banking (Abedifar, Pejman, Shahid M. Ebrahim, et.al 2016) windows to provide Shariah-compliant financial products.

Sukuk, which are Islamic bonds, had been discussed and considered as an alternative source of funding for various infrastructure and developmental projects in India. However, the regulatory framework for Sukuk issuance was still evolving. Takaful, or Islamic insurance, was being explored by insurance companies in India as a means of offering Shariah-compliant insurance products. The regulatory framework for Takaful was being developed. The development of Islamic finance in India faced challenges related to regulatory and legal hurdles, awareness and understanding of Islamic finance concepts, and a lack of standardized products and guidelines.

1.2 Scope of Research

- Explain the significance of Islamic finance in the context of the global financial system.
- Highlight the challenges and opportunities faced by the Islamic finance industry in India.
- Define thematic investment in the context of Islamic finance.
- Explore the specific thematic investment opportunities in India that cater to the Islamic finance sector.
- Examine the existing regulatory framework for Islamic finance in India and its compatibility with thematic investments.
- Identify the key financial institutions, banks, and investment firms involved in Islamic finance and thematic investments in India.

1.3 Objectives

1. To Understand the Current Landscape of Islamic Finance in India.
2. To Explore Thematic Investment Trends
3. To Analyze the regulatory challenges and opportunities for thematic investments.
4. To Identify and evaluate specific thematic investment opportunities that align with Islamic finance principles in the Indian market.
5. To Propose Recommendations for key stakeholders, including financial institutions, regulators, and investors, to foster the growth of thematic investments in Islamic finance in India.

1.4 Research Methodology

- Exploratory study should aim to provide a comprehensive overview.
- Primary and Secondary sources, conduct surveys or interviews with experts in the field, and review any recent reports or academic papers related to Islamic finance and thematic investments in India.

1.5 Historical Development of Islamic Finance

The historical development of Islamic finance (Atif, Mohammad, Mustafa Raza Rabbani, et.al 2021) in India can be traced back to several key milestones. While India has a substantial Muslim population, the formal establishment and growth of Islamic finance in the country have been relatively recent. Here is a brief overview of the historical development of Islamic finance in India:

1. Pre-Independence Era

Before India gained independence in 1947, various traditional Islamic financial instruments, such as the "Hundi" system, were in use. These were based on Islamic principles but did not conform to modern standards of financial regulation.

2. Post-Independence Period

After gaining independence, India adopted a secular legal system and did not provide specific recognition or regulation for Islamic finance. During this time, Islamic banking and finance were limited to informal arrangements and individual efforts, mainly practiced by Muslim communities and individuals.

3. 1980s - 1990s

The 1980s and 1990s saw some efforts to promote Islamic finance in India, primarily driven by the need to provide financial services that adhered to Islamic principles. The Islamic Investment and Finance Cooperative (IIFC) was established in the state of Maharashtra in 1986. IIFC aimed to provide Shariah-compliant financial products and services. However, during this period, the absence of a supportive regulatory framework and lack of awareness hindered the growth of Islamic finance.

4. 2000s Onward

The 2000s marked a more significant push towards Islamic finance in India. In 2008, the Kerala State Industrial Development Corporation (KSIDC) proposed the establishment of an Islamic investment company. This initiative aimed to cater to the financial needs of Kerala's Muslim population, which constitutes a significant portion of the state's population. The Reserve Bank of India (RBI) introduced guidelines for interest-free banking operations, allowing banks to offer Shariah-compliant banking products through designated windows.

The historical development of Islamic finance in India is a story of gradual progress. While there have been notable efforts to promote Islamic finance, regulatory challenges and the need for greater awareness and standardization have been significant hurdles. The state of Islamic finance in India continues to evolve, and regulatory changes and market developments will shape its future growth.

2. SIGNIFICANT MILESTONES OR REGULATORY CHANGES

1. RBI Guidelines for Islamic Banking Windows (2008)
2. Kerala State Industrial Development Corporation (KSIDC) Proposal (2008)
3. Reserve Bank of India (RBI) Draft Guidelines for Islamic Banking Operations (2016)
4. Sukuk Issuance Discussions
5. Discussion on Islamic Finance and Taxation (2019):
6. Continued Engagement with Islamic Countries:
7. Development of Islamic Banking and Finance Companies

It's important to note that while these milestones and regulatory changes represent significant steps toward the development of Islamic finance in India, the industry still faced challenges related to regulatory complexities, awareness, and standardization.

3. THEMATIC INVESTMENTS LINK TO ISLAMIC FINANCE

Thematic investments are a specific approach to investing that involves targeting companies, industries, or assets based on a particular theme or trend rather than traditional financial metrics. These themes are often driven by societal, environmental, or economic factors, and thematic investments aim to capitalize on these trends. The concept of thematic investments aligns with the principles of Islamic finance in several ways:

Figure 1. Islamic finance

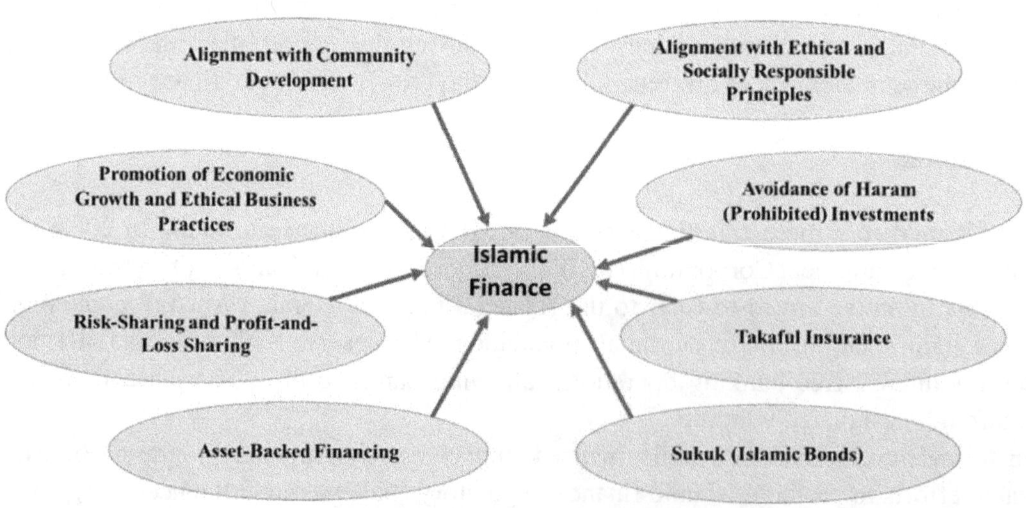

Thematic investments, when implemented within the framework of Islamic finance, can provide investors with opportunities to earn returns on their investments while adhering to Shariah-compliant principles. These investments focus on socially responsible and ethical themes, often emphasizing the betterment of society and the avoidance of prohibited activities, making them a suitable choice for those who wish to combine their financial goals with their ethical and moral values.

4. EXISTING REGULATORY FRAMEWORK FOR ISLAMIC FINANCE IN INDIA

The Reserve Bank of India (RBI) had taken several steps to accommodate Shariah-compliant financial activities. Here is an overview of the existing regulatory framework for Islamic finance in India up to that point:

1. The RBI had issued guidelines for the operation of Islamic banking (Ali, Hassnian, Rose Abdullah, et.al 2019) windows within conventional banks. These guidelines allowed banks to offer Shariah-compliant financial products and services. Under these guidelines, Islamic banking windows had to follow specific rules and ensure full compliance with Shariah principles.
2. The RBI had proposed draft guidelines for Islamic banking operations in 2016. These guidelines outlined the regulatory framework for banks that wished to offer full-fledged Islamic banking services. The guidelines covered various aspects of Islamic banking (Muhd Zaki Zaini. Et.al 2019) including risk management, governance, and accounting standards.
3. The Insurance Regulatory and Development Authority of India (IRDAI) had been working on regulations for Takaful, which is Islamic insurance. These regulations were intended to provide a framework for Takaful operators to offer Shariah-compliant insurance products.
4. The RBI had been exploring the possibility of introducing Sukuk in India. Sukuk is a form of Islamic bond, and discussions were ongoing to create a regulatory framework for the issuance and trading of Sukuk in the Indian market. This could provide an alternative source of funding for infrastructure and developmental projects.
5. India had been engaged with international Islamic finance bodies and organizations to better understand global best practices and regulatory standards in Islamic finance.
6. Some states in India, like Kerala, were actively exploring the potential for Islamic finance to meet the financial needs of their Muslim populations. The state governments had initiated discussions and proposals to promote Islamic finance initiatives.

It is important to note that while these developments indicated progress in the regulatory framework for Islamic finance in India, the industry was still in a nascent stage. The growth of Islamic finance in India also depended on various factors, including political will, awareness among the population, and the willingness of financial institutions to offer Shariah-compliant products and services.

CHALLENGES AND OPPORTUNITIES PRESENTED BY THESE REGULATIONS

The regulatory framework for Islamic finance in India presents both challenges and opportunities for the industry. These challenges and opportunities can significantly impact the growth and development of Islamic finance in the country. Here is an overview of some of the key challenges and opportunities:

4.1 Challenges

The regulatory framework for Islamic finance in India can be complex and may require financial institutions to navigate a set of regulations and guidelines specific to Shariah compliance. This complexity can make it challenging for both existing and new market participants to operate smoothly. There is a need for increased awareness and understanding of Islamic finance principles among the general population, investors, and financial institutions. The lack of awareness can hinder the growth of the industry as potential customers may be hesitant to engage with unfamiliar financial products. As of the last update in 2022, India did not have fully-fledged Islamic banks. The absence of dedicated Islamic banks limits the scope and scale of Islamic finance operations, as banks offering Islamic products do so through designated windows within their existing structures.

4.2 Opportunities

India has one of the world's largest Muslim populations. Islamic finance provides an opportunity to meet the financial needs and preferences of this substantial demographic. Establishing a robust Islamic finance industry in India can attract investments from international Islamic finance markets, including Gulf countries. India can benefit from foreign investments to support infrastructure and economic development. The growing interest in thematic investments, ethical finance, and socially responsible investing aligns with the principles of Islamic finance. India can leverage this trend to develop and promote ethical and sustainable investment products. Islamic finance offers an opportunity for financial institutions to diversify

Figure 2. Challenges

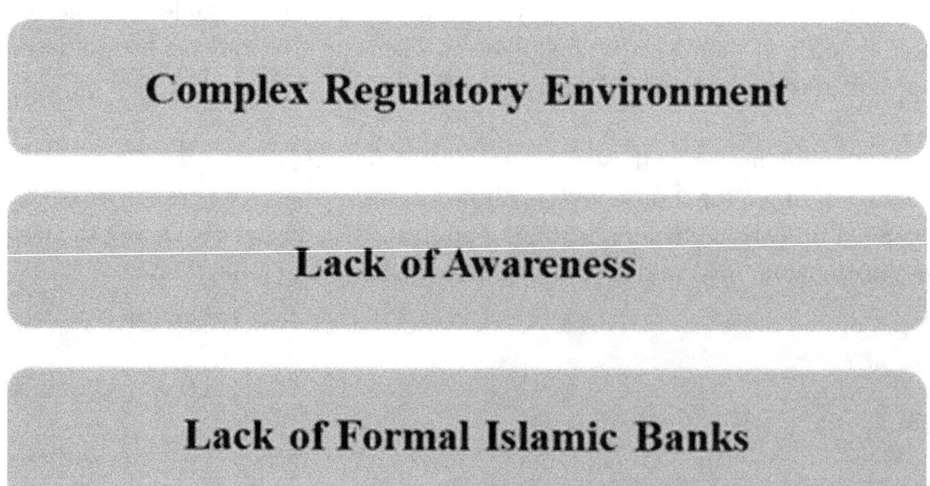

their services and cater to a broader range of customers, including those who prefer Shariah-compliant financial products. The issuance of Sukuk (Islamic bonds) can provide alternative funding sources for infrastructure projects and economic development, reducing the dependency on conventional financing.

The development of Islamic finance in India is a dynamic process, and the challenges can be addressed with proactive steps and cooperation among stakeholders. The opportunities presented by the regulations can help create a vibrant Islamic finance sector that aligns with the financial needs and values of India's diverse population.

5. ANALYZE THE KEY PLAYERS IN THE ISLAMIC FINANCE SECTOR IN INDIA, INCLUDING BANKS, FINANCIAL INSTITUTIONS, AND INVESTMENT FIRMS

The key players in the Islamic finance sector in India included both banks and financial institutions offering Shariah-compliant products and services. Here are some of the prominent players:

ICICI Bank, one of India's leading private sector banks, was among the first to introduce Islamic banking (Rose Abdullah, Muhd Zaki Zaini. Et.al 2019) windows. They offered products like Islamic savings accounts, home finance, and auto finance through these windows.

Axis Bank is another significant private sector bank in India that had introduced Islamic banking (Muhd Zaki Zaini. Et.al 2019) windows to provide Shariah-compliant financial services to its customers.

IDBI Mutual Fund launched a Shariah-compliant mutual fund named IDBIMF Equity Fund in collaboration with a Malaysia-based asset management company. This fund was designed to cater to investors seeking investments compliant with Islamic principles.

Taurus Mutual Fund launched the Taurus Ethical Fund, which followed ethical investment guidelines and was promoted as a Shariah-compliant investment option.

The KSIDC proposed the establishment of an Islamic investment company to meet the financial needs of Kerala's Muslim population. This initiative aimed to promote Islamic finance in the state.

The Kerala State Wakf Board had been exploring opportunities to develop Islamic finance and investment options to cater to the financial requirements of the state's Muslim population.

Some cooperative and regional banks in states with significant Muslim populations had started to explore Shariah-compliant banking services to serve their local communities.

It's important to note that the participation of conventional banks in offering Islamic finance products was a significant trend in India as of my last update. Full-fledged Islamic banks were not prevalent, and the sector was characterized by banks offering Islamic products through designated windows. The introduction of mutual funds with Shariah-compliant investment options was also a notable development.

6. ANALYZE THE CHALLENGES FACING ISLAMIC FINANCE IN INDIA

6.1 Lack of Comprehensive Regulatory Framework

One of the primary challenges is the absence of a comprehensive and dedicated regulatory framework for Islamic finance. While there have been guidelines for Islamic banking (Mohammad Kabir Hassan, et.al 2023) windows, the sector lacks clear and standardized regulations, which can lead to ambiguity and inconsistent practices.

6.2 Complex Regulatory Environment

The existing regulatory environment in India can be complex for Islamic finance. Banks and financial institutions offering Islamic products must navigate a regulatory framework designed primarily for conventional finance. This complexity can deter potential market participants.

6.3 Limited Product Range

Islamic finance in India has a limited product range compared to conventional finance. While some banks offer Islamic banking (Alshater, Muneer Maher, et.al 2023) windows, the variety of available Shariah-compliant financial products and services remains limited.

6.4 Lack of Awareness

There is a significant lack of awareness and understanding of Islamic finance concepts and principles among both the public and the financial industry. This lack of awareness can impede the sector's growth as potential customers may be hesitant to engage with unfamiliar financial products.

6.5 Standardization Issues

Achieving standardization in Islamic finance products can be challenging. Variability in product structures and contracts across different financial institutions can create confusion and impact the sector's credibility.

6.6 Shortage of Shariah-Compliant Experts

Finding and retaining qualified Shariah-compliant experts and scholars is a challenge. Financial institutions need access to individuals who can ensure their products and operations adhere to Islamic finance principles.

6.7 Lack of Dedicated Islamic Banks

India did not have dedicated full-fledged Islamic banks. The absence of such banks limits the scope and scale of Islamic finance operations, as banks offering Islamic products do so through designated windows within their existing structures.

6.8 Political and Regulatory Hurdles

The growth of Islamic finance can be affected by political considerations and regulatory challenges, making it subject to shifts in government policies and priorities.

6.9 Risk Management and Liquidity Challenges

Islamic finance principles emphasize risk-sharing and asset-backed financing. Implementing these principles can be complex, and managing risk while maintaining liquidity can be a challenge.

6.10 Perception and Prejudice

Some individuals may have misconceptions or prejudices against Islamic finance, believing it to be exclusive or misunderstood. These perceptions can affect the sector's acceptance and growth.

Despite these challenges, there is potential for Islamic finance to grow in India, especially given the significant Muslim population and the increasing awareness of ethical and sustainable finance. Government initiatives and the development of a more supportive regulatory framework can facilitate the growth of Islamic finance in the country. Addressing these challenges will be essential for realizing the full potential of Islamic finance in India.

7. POTENTIAL FUTURE OF ISLAMIC FINANCE IN INDIA.

The potential future of Islamic finance in India is promising, given the significant Muslim population, and increasing awareness of ethical and sustainable finance. While there are challenges to overcome, several factors suggest a positive outlook for the development of Islamic finance in the country:

7.1 Supportive Regulatory Framework

The development of a comprehensive and dedicated regulatory framework for Islamic finance can provide a clear path for the growth of the industry. Regulatory clarity and standardization will create a conducive environment for market participants and attract investments.

7.2 Government Initiatives

State governments, such as Kerala, have shown interest in promoting Islamic finance to cater to the financial needs of their Muslim populations. Government-led initiatives can provide significant momentum to the sector.

7.3 Foreign Investments

The appeal of India's large Muslim population and potential for Islamic finance growth can attract investments from international Islamic finance hubs, especially from Gulf countries and Malaysia.

7.4 Ethical and Sustainable Finance Trends

The global trend toward ethical, sustainable, and socially responsible investing aligns with the principles of Islamic finance. India can leverage this trend to develop ethical and sustainable investment products that cater to a wider audience.

7.5 Thematic Investments

The introduction of thematic investments that align with Islamic finance principles, such as renewable energy and healthcare innovation, can attract investors seeking Shariah-compliant options.

7.6 Financial Inclusion

Islamic finance can contribute to financial inclusion by providing services to underserved communities. Microfinance and Takaful (Islamic insurance) can address the financial needs of marginalized populations.

7.7 Social and Economic Development

Islamic finance can play a pivotal role in social and economic development by supporting projects related to affordable housing, education, and healthcare for underserved communities.

7.8 Standardization and Education

Efforts to standardize Islamic financial products and educate the public and industry professionals about Islamic finance can increase awareness and acceptance.

7.9 Corporate Governance and Ethical Finance

Emphasizing corporate governance and ethical business practices within the Islamic finance sector can enhance the industry's reputation and appeal to investors.

7.10 Community Development

Islamic finance has the potential to foster community development by supporting projects that align with the principles of social responsibility and ethical finance.

7.11 Technology and Fintech

Utilizing technology to develop user-friendly digital Islamic banking and fintech (Abdeljawad, Islam, Shatha et.al 2022) (solutions can enhance the accessibility and convenience of Islamic finance products.

7.12 Global Partnerships

Collaboration with international Islamic finance institutions and organizations can provide India with access to global best practices and expertise in the field.

While the future of Islamic finance in India holds promise, realizing this potential will require coordinated efforts from regulators, financial institutions, and the government. Addressing challenges, standardizing practices, and raising awareness are key steps toward harnessing the growth opportunities and serving the financial needs of India's diverse population. As the regulatory environment becomes more conducive and awareness continues to grow, Islamic finance in India is likely to gain a more significant foothold in the financial sector.

8. SUMMARY OF KEY FINDINGS OF THE RESEARCH

In this research, we explored the current state and potential future of Islamic finance in India, focusing on its principles, regulatory framework, key players, challenges, opportunities, and the role of thematic investments. Here are the key findings:

8.1 Current State of Islamic Finance in India

India's Islamic finance sector was emerging, with banks offering Islamic products through dedicated windows. Limited product diversity and the absence of a comprehensive regulatory framework were notable challenges.

8.2 Regulatory Framework

India had taken steps to establish guidelines for Islamic banking (Philip Molyneux, Amine Tarazi.et.al 2016) windows but lacked a comprehensive regulatory framework. Efforts were made to introduce Takaful (Islamic insurance) regulations and explore Sukuk (Islamic bonds) issuance.

8.3 Challenges

Challenges included a complex regulatory environment, limited awareness, lack of standardization, and a shortage of Shariah-compliant experts. The absence of dedicated Islamic banks and political/regulatory considerations also posed challenges.

8.4 Opportunities

Opportunities included serving India's significant Muslim population, attracting foreign investments, aligning with ethical and sustainable finance trends, and leveraging thematic investments. Government initiatives, thematic investments, and technology integration were highlighted opportunities.

8.5 Thematic Investments

Thematic investments, aligned with Islamic finance principles, offer a way to diversify portfolios and support ethical, sustainable, and socially responsible themes. They can promote ethical and socially responsible investing and enhance market awareness.

REFERENCES

Abdeljawad, I., Hashem, S. Q., & Rashid, M. (2022). Fintech and Islamic Financial Institutions: Applicationsand Challenges. In *FinTech in Islamic Financial Institutions: Scope, Challenges, and Implications in Islamic Finance* (pp. 193–222). PalgraveMacmillan. [CrossRef] doi:10.1007/978-3-031-14941-2_10

Abedifar, P., Ebrahim, S. M., Molyneux, P., & Tarazi, A. (2016). Islamic banking and finance: Recent empiricalliterature and directions for future research. In *A Collection of Reviews on Savings and Wealth Accumulation* (pp. 59–91). Wiley. [CrossRef] doi:10.1002/9781119158424.ch4

Abojeib, M., & Habib, F. (2021). Blockchain for Islamic social responsibility institutions. In *Research Anthology on BlockchainTechnology in Business, Healthcare, Education, and Government* (pp. 1114–1128). IGI Global. [CrossRef] doi:10.4018/978-1-7998-5351-0.ch061

Ahmad, S. M., & Al Mamun, A. (2020). Opportunities of Islamic FinTech: The Case of Bangladesh and Turkey. [CrossRef]. *CenRaPSJournal of Social Sciences*, *2*(3), 412–426. doi:10.46291/cenraps.v2i3.39

Ahmed, S., Alshater, M. M., El Ammari, A., & Hammami, H. (2022). Artificial intelligence and machine learning infinance: A bibliometric review. [CrossRef]. *Research in International Business and Finance*, *61*, 101646. doi:10.1016/j.ribaf.2022.101646

Alaeddin, O., Al Dakash, M., & Azrak, T. (2021). Implementing the blockchain technology in islamic financial industry:Opportunities and challenges. [CrossRef]. *Journal of Information Technology Management*, *13*, 99–115.

Ali, H., Abdullah, R., & Zaini, M. Z. (2019). Fintech and its potential impact on Islamic banking and finance industry: Acase study of Brunei Darussalam and Malaysia. [IJIEF]. *International Journal of Islamic Economics and Finance*, *2*(1), 73–108. doi:10.18196/ijief.2116

Alshater, M., Hassan, K., Khan, A., & Saba, I. (2021a). Influential and intellectual structure of Islamic finance: Abibliometric review. [CrossRef]. *International Journal of Islamic and Middle Eastern Finance and Management*, *14*(2), 339–365. doi:10.1108/IMEFM-08-2020-0419

Alshater, M. M., Khan, A., Hassan, M. K., & Paltrinieri, A. (2023). Islamic Banking: Past, Present andFuture. [CrossRef]. *Journal of College of Sharia and Islamic Studies*, *41*, 351.

Altarturi, B. H. M., Altarturi, H. H. M., & Anwar, H. A. O. (2021). Applications of financialtechnology in Islamic finance: A systematic bibliometric review. In *Artificial Intelligence and Islamic Finance* (p. 138161). Routledge. doi:10.4324/9781003171638-10

Atif, M., Hassan, M. K., Rabbani, M. R., & Khan, S. (2021). Islamic FinTech: The digital transformation bringing sustainability to Islamic finance. In *COVID-19 and Islamic Social Finance* (pp. 91–103). Routledge. doi:10.4324/9781003121718-9

Barbu, C. M., Florea, D. L., Dabija, D.-C., & Mihai, C. R. B. (2021). Customer experiencein fintech. [CrossRef]. *Journal of Theoretical and Applied Electronic Commerce Research*, *16*(5), 80. doi:10.3390/jtaer16050080

Belal, A. R., Mohammed, M. M. M., & Ali, M. (2019). Intellectual capital reporting practices in an Islamic bank: A case study. [CrossRef]. *Business Ethics (Oxford, England)*, *28*(2), 206–220. doi:10.1111/beer.12211

Belanche, D., Casaló, L. V., & Flavián, C. (2019). Artificial Intelligence in FinTech: Understanding robo-advisors adoption among customers. *Industrial Management & Data Systems*, *119*(7), 1411–1430. doi:10.1108/IMDS-08-2018-0368

Biancone, P. P., Saiti, B., Petricean, D., & Chmet, F. (2020). The bibliometric analysis of Islamic banking and finance. [CrossRef]. *Journal of Islamic Accounting and Business Research, 11*(9), 2069–2086. doi:10.1108/JIABR-08-2020-0235

Irfan, M., Elhoseny, M., Kassim, S., & Metawa, N. (2023). *Advanced Machine Learning Algorithms for Complex Financial Applications*., https://www.scopus.com/inward/record.uri?eid=2-s2.0-85147390132&doi=10.4018%2f978-1-6684-4483-2&partnerID=40&md5=, doi:10.4018/978-1-6684-4483-2

Irfan, M., Elmogy, M., Majid, M. S. A., & El-Sappagh, S. (2023). The impact of AI innovation on financial sectors in the era of industry 5.0. *The Impact of AI Innovation on Financial Sectors in the Era of Industry 5.0*, (pp. 1-320). IGI Global. 10.4018/9798369300824

Pal, T., Irfan, M., & Kassim, S. B. (2023). How do Machine Learning (ML) techniques benefit the insurance industry? An exploratory study. *The Impact of AI Innovation on Financial Sectors in the Era of Industry 5.0*, (pp. 108-130). IGI Global. https://www.scopus.com/inward/record.uri?eid=2-s2.0-85172988448&doi=10.4018%2f979-8-3693-0082-4.ch007&partnerID=40&, doi:10.4018/979-8-3693-0082-4.ch007

Ridho Kismawadi, E., Irfan, M., & Shah, S. M. A. R. (2023). Revolutionizing Islamic finance: Artificial intelligence's role in the future of industry. *The Impact of AI Innovation on Financial Sectors in the Era of Industry 5.0*, (pp. 184-207). IGI Global. https://www.scopus.com/inward/record.uri?eid=2-s2.0-85173027737&doi=10.4018%2f979-8-3693-0082-4.ch011&partnerID=40&, doi:10.4018/979-8-3693-0082-4.ch011

Chapter 10
Islamic Finance and Fintech: A Scoping Review

Nitish Kumar Minz
https://orcid.org/0009-0000-4770-0336
K.R. Mangalam University, India

Nikhat Mushir
https://orcid.org/0000-0002-0231-5642
K.R. Mangalam University, India

Sunita Tanwar
Central University of Haryana, India

Mustapha Chaffai
University of Sfax, Tunisia

ABSTRACT

The cohabitation of Financial Technology (FinTech) and Islamic Finance have far-reaching implications for the global financial market. This bibliographic review surveys pivotal research papers that elucidate diverse aspects of this amalgamation, encapsulating ethical considerations, regulatory complexities, technological vulnerabilities, and the ramifications of digital assets. Furthermore, it scrutinizes FinTech's role in advancing sustainability objectives, navigates the intricacies of peer-to-peer lending, and scrutinizes the manifold viewpoints regarding the digital metamorphosis of Islamic finance. Collectively, these scholarly works furnish a holistic comprehension of the evolving rapport between Islamic finance and FinTech, proffering invaluable insights for the future evolution of Islamic financial technology, all while upholding the tenets of Sharia principles.

DOI: 10.4018/979-8-3693-1038-0.ch010

1. INTRODUCTION

1.1 Background and Relevance

Islamic finance built upon Sharia principles prioritizes ethics, risk-sharing, and social responsibility (Suzuki, 2022). Financial Technology (FinTech) is a technological revolution reshaping traditional financial services, and leverages innovations like blockchain, artificial intelligence, and mobile banking, offering novel avenues for financial inclusion and efficiency (Bedoui, 2021). The adoption of Fin-tech by Shariah-based financial services brings remarkable advantages to Islamic finance industry since surprisingly, its fundamental values align seamlessly with FinTech (Hassan, 2022). Technology, blockchain enhances transparency and compliance, ensuring adherence to the Sharia principle of transparency forging trust among stakeholders. Furthermore, FinTech streamlines risk-sharing, promoting equitable distribution of financial risks and rewards through digital investment tools (Irfan M. E., 2023).

The integration of Islamic finance and FinTech represents a transformative landscape and far-reaching implications for the global financial market (Raza Rabbani, 2022). At the same time, the greatest challenge faced by digital technology concerns data security and privacy which stand in direct contractions with Shariah principle (Suzuki, 2022). Therefore, it is pertinent to explore and understand the current state of affairs through the academic lens, and how far this integration has been successfully implemented. As both fields are evolving research becomes pivotal guiding the future researches. To this end, this paper explores published literature in the domain of Islamic finance and Fintech to understand current state of work and to guide future researches by synthesising and summarising the published work. This paper is organised and divided into 4 sections: section 1 introduces the paper; section 2 discusses research methods and materials used. Section 3 synthesises the literature, section 4 elaborates the quantitative synthesis of the literature through bibliometric analysis and finally section concludes the paper.

1.2 Research Question

Is there a sufficient body of scholarly literature addressing the integration of Financial Technology (FinTech) and Islamic finance, and what key themes and trends can be identified within this literature through bibliometric analysis?

1.3 Advancing the Knowledge Frontier

This paper significantly contributes to the existing body of knowledge by pioneering an in-depth exploration of the confluence of Islamic finance and Financial Technology (FinTech). It offers novel insights into the evolving landscape of these two domains and their intricate interplay. This research not only enriches our understanding of the complex relationship between FinTech and Islamic finance but also provides valuable guidance for researchers, policymakers, and practitioners seeking to navigate this transformative intersection while upholding the principles of Sharia law. Through comprehensive literature synthesis and quantitative bibliometric analysis, this paper advances the knowledge frontier and sets the stage for informed and innovative future research in this critical field.

1.4 Pioneering Fresh Perspectives and Insights

This paper pioneers' fresh perspectives and offers unique insights into the amalgamation of Islamic finance and Financial Technology (FinTech). It unveils the non-neutrality of technological advancements within Islamic finance, underscoring how technology can both empower and challenge its core principles. It delves into the critical domain of risk management in Islamic FinTech, emphasizing the need for robust strategies to ensure sustainability. The paper explores the regulatory adaptations required to accommodate this convergence, navigating the delicate balance between innovation and adherence to Sharia principles. Additionally, it critically examines the compatibility of digital currencies with Islamic finance, addressing ethical and theological concerns. Through quantitative bibliometric analysis, this paper unveils key themes and trends in the existing literature, providing a comprehensive understanding of this dynamic field.

2. METHODS AND MATERIALS

The research commences with an extensive and meticulous search from Scopus ensuring a comprehensive and established approach to assessing research literature (Guz, 2009). This bibliographic review employs a systematic and rigorous research methodology to delve into the amalgamation of Islamic finance and Financial Technology (FinTech) and the profound implications it holds for the global financial landscape. The methodology comprises a series of well-defined steps, ensuring the thorough examination of relevant scholarly literature. By the comprehensive recommendations of Sarkis-Onofre et al. (2021), the research methodology rigorously adheres to the PRISMA Statement, ensuring a systematic and transparent approach throughout the review process. The PRISMA approach to performing systematic reviews and data collection is explained in Figure 1.

Figure 1. Flow chart of search strategy

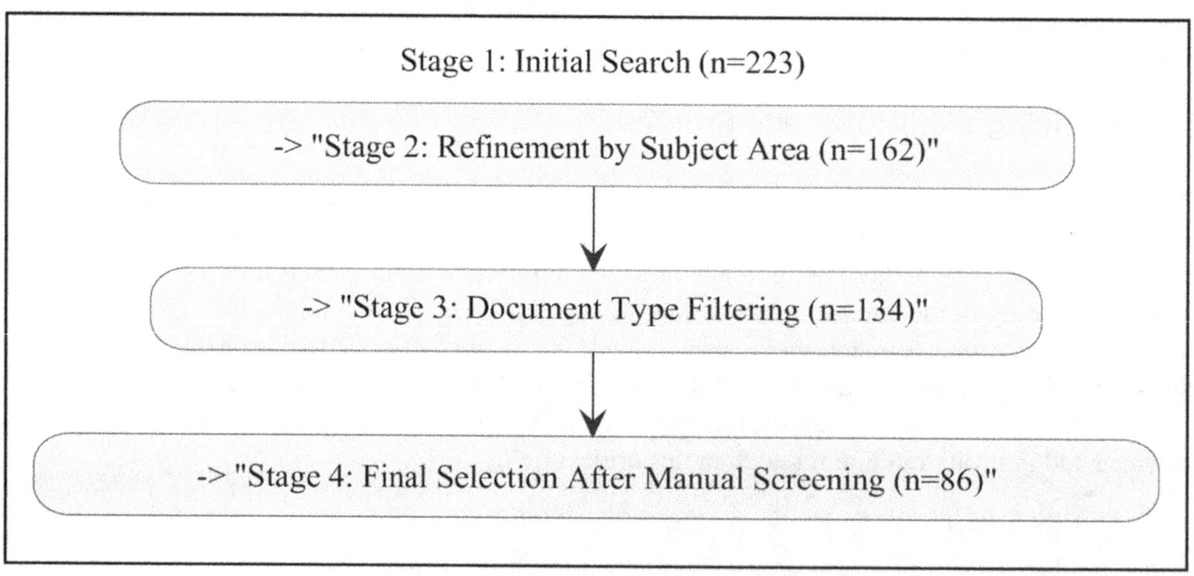

Box 1: Boolean String for Search

```
(TITLE-ABS-KEY (fintech*) OR TITLE-ABS-KEY (i-fintech) OR TITLE-ABS-KEY (fin-
tech) OR TITLE-ABS-KEY (financial AND technology) AND TITLE-ABS-KEY (shariah
AND finance) OR TITLE-ABS-KEY (shari'ah AND finance) OR TITLE-ABS-KEY (islamic
AND finance)) AND (LIMIT-TO (SUBJAREA, "BUSI") OR LIMIT-TO (SUBJAREA, "ECON"))
AND (LIMIT-TO (DOCTYPE, "ar") OR LIMIT-TO (DOCTYPE, "ch") OR LIMIT-TO (DOC-
TYPE, "cp"))
```

The systematic review process commenced with an exhaustive database search, initially yielding 125 documents. Subsequently, a meticulous screening process, in line with research paper standards, was implemented to enhance document quality and relevance. Following manual screening, 86 documents aligning with the research objectives were retained. The search strategy included keywords such as 'fintech,' 'i-fintech,' 'fin-tech,' 'financial technology,' 'shariah finance,' 'shari'ah finance,' and 'Islamic finance.' To ensure relevance to business and economics, filters were applied to select academic articles, conference papers, and book chapters (DOCTYPE: 'ar,' 'ch,' 'cp') within the 'BUSI' and 'ECON' subject areas. Lastly, we employed Biblioshiny (Aria, 2017) and VOS-viewer (Van Eck, 2017) tools to facilitate the development of our results and analysis.

3. LITERATURE REVIEW

The intersection of Islamic finance and Financial Technology (FinTech) represents a dynamic and evolving landscape within the global financial ecosystem. This literature review delves into key research contributions that shed light on various facets of this convergence. As FinTech continues to reshape the financial industry worldwide, it is essential to understand its impact on Islamic finance, which operates within the framework of Sharia principles. The reviewed papers encompass a wide array of topics, including the non-neutrality of technological advancements, risks associated with Islamic FinTech, regulatory transformations, cryptocurrency's compatibility with Islamic finance, legal complexities surrounding digital assets, and the potential of FinTech to align with Islamic principles and contribute to broader societal goals.

3.1 Impact of Technological Advancements on Islamic Finance and FinTech

The non-neutrality of technological advancements within the context of Islamic finance and FinTech has emerged as a pivotal research theme. (Belabes, 2021) explored this notion by arguing that technological advancements are not neutral and can influence how Islamic finance adheres to its core principles. This perspective challenges the assumption that technology merely serves as a tool and underscores the need for a nuanced understanding of the interplay between FinTech tools and Islamic finance principles. Technological advancements have the potential to both enhance and challenge the fundamental tenets of Islamic finance. For instance, the automation and digitization of financial transactions can improve efficiency and accessibility, aligning with the broader objectives of Islamic finance to promote financial inclusion and ethical financial practices. However, these advancements also introduce complexities, such as the need to ensure compliance with Sharia principles in automated processes and transactions. The non-neutrality of technology highlights the importance of considering the ethical and Sharia-compliant dimensions of FinTech tools and platforms.

3.2 Risk Management in Islamic FinTech

(Yusuf, 2021) delves into the risks associated with Islamic FinTech, emphasizing the importance of effective risk management strategies in this emerging field. The paper sheds light on potential pitfalls and challenges that Islamic FinTech encounters, offering valuable insights for practitioners and policymakers. This research underscores the need for a comprehensive risk assessment framework in Islamic FinTech to ensure its long-term sustainability. Risk management is a critical consideration in the convergence of Islamic finance and FinTech, as it involves navigating both conventional financial risks and those specific to Islamic finance. These risks encompass ethical and Sharia compliance, cybersecurity, operational challenges, and regulatory uncertainties. Ensuring effective risk management strategies is essential to foster trust among users and stakeholders and to sustain the growth of Islamic FinTech.

3.3 Risk Management in Islamic FinTech

(Hui, 2019) provides an in-depth analysis of the regulatory adaptations driven by FinTech, emphasizing the importance of regulatory agility and responsiveness to the digital ecosystem. The integration of FinTech into Islamic finance presents unique regulatory challenges and opportunities. Regulators are tasked with striking a balance between fostering innovation and safeguarding the integrity of Islamic finance (Ridho Kismawadi). The research highlights the need for regulatory frameworks that accommodate technological advancements while ensuring compliance with Sharia principles. Such frameworks are crucial to provide clarity and stability for businesses operating in the Islamic FinTech sector and to protect the interests of consumers.

3.4 Cryptocurrency and Islamic Finance

(Abubakar, 2019) critically examines whether cryptocurrency adoption raises ethical or theological concerns within Islamic finance. This research, conducted by scholars from institutions like the University of Lagos, Nigeria, scrutinizes the compatibility of digital currencies with Islamic finance principles and offers insights into the potential challenges and opportunities they present. The use of cryptocurrencies in Islamic finance has generated discussions on issues such as riba (usury), gharar (uncertainty), and speculative behaviour, which are prohibited in Islamic finance. However, proponents argue that digital currencies can facilitate financial inclusion, reduce transaction costs, and enhance transparency. As the digital currency landscape continues to evolve, further research and regulatory guidance are needed to address the compatibility of cryptocurrencies with Islamic finance.

(Raza Rabbani, 2022) provides an in-depth analysis of the compatibility and potential challenges associated with integrating digital currencies within the context of Islamic finance. The systematic review highlights the diverse viewpoints and debates surrounding cryptocurrency adoption in Islamic finance. It offers a comprehensive overview of the evolving landscape, addressing questions related to riba, gharar, and speculative behaviour. This research serves as a valuable resource for scholars, practitioners, and policymakers seeking to navigate the complex intersection of Islamic finance and cryptocurrency.

3.5 Legal Complexities in Shariah-Compliant FinTech

(Omoola, 2023) investigates these complexities. With affiliations at Ahmad Ibrahim Kulliyyah of Laws and Kaduna State University, the authors offer a critical perspective on the legal aspects of digital assets within Islamic FinTech. Their research highlights the need for robust legal frameworks and protections in this rapidly evolving domain. Digital assets encompass a wide range of assets, including cryptocurrencies, tokens, and digital contracts, all of which are integral to the functioning of FinTech platforms. These assets may raise legal questions related to ownership, custody, inheritance, and dispute resolution, which require careful consideration within the context of Sharia principles. Addressing these legal complexities is essential to provide a secure and transparent environment for Islamic FinTech users and investors.

3.6 FinTech Contribution to Sustainable Development Goals (SDGs)

(Bedoui, 2021) examines how FinTech can contribute to achieving the Sustainable Development Goals (SDGs) from an Islamic standpoint. Drawing on their affiliations with the Islamic Development Bank and various universities, the authors underline how FinTech can align with the ethical and societal objectives of Islamic finance, making a positive impact on broader developmental goals. This paper advocates for the potential of FinTech to catalyze social and economic progress in alignment with Islamic principles. Islamic finance places a strong emphasis on ethical and socially responsible financial practices. The research suggests that FinTech can play a pivotal role in promoting financial inclusion, supporting entrepreneurship, and addressing societal challenges, all while adhering to the principles of Islamic finance. This alignment between FinTech and Islamic finance offers opportunities to harness technology for social and economic development in a Sharia-compliant manner.

3.7 Challenges in Islamic Peer-to-Peer Lending

(Muhammad, 2021) investigates the factors contributing to the potential failure of Islamic peer-to-peer lending platforms in Indonesia. Employing a stakeholder-based approach, the paper offers valuable insights into the challenges and possible solutions within the context of Islamic peer-to-peer lending. It sheds light on the critical issues faced by this emerging sector. Islamic peer-to-peer lending platforms have gained popularity as alternatives to conventional financial intermediaries. However, they encounter challenges related to risk management, regulatory compliance, and building trust among stakeholders. Understanding these challenges is crucial for the sustainable growth of Islamic peer-to-peer lending and for addressing the financing needs of individuals and small businesses.

3.8 Digital Transformation in Islamic Finance

(Suzuki, 2022) critically examine the digital transformation within Islamic finance. Their research, conducted at Ritsumeikan Asia Pacific University and the University of Nizwa, Oman, respectively, provides a balanced view of the potential and challenges associated with digital transformation in Islamic finance. The paper contributes to a nuanced understanding of the ongoing evolution of Islamic FinTech and its alignment with core principles. Digital transformation in Islamic finance encompasses a wide range of innovations, including mobile banking, blockchain-based solutions, and digital payment platforms. While these innovations offer convenience and efficiency, they also require careful consideration of Sharia compliance, cybersecurity, and customer protection. The research underscores the importance of adopting a holistic approach to digital transformation in Islamic finance to reap the benefits of innovation while upholding Sharia principles.

3.9 Trends in FinTech and Industry 4.0

(Hassan, 2022) explore trends in FinTech, with a focus on Industry 4.0 and its impact on Islamic FinTech. The paper discusses the digital transformation of Islamic finance and its implications, offering valuable insights into the convergence of emerging technologies and Islamic finance. This research informs stakeholders about the evolving landscape of FinTech within Islamic financial institutions. The emergence of Industry 4.0, characterized by technologies like artificial intelligence, the Internet of Things, and big data analytics, presents both opportunities and challenges for Islamic finance. These technologies can enhance risk assessment, customer experience, and operational efficiency. However, they also require robust cybersecurity measures and regulatory adaptations to ensure that Islamic finance remains resilient and Sharia-compliant.

The convergence of Islamic finance and FinTech is a multifaceted and rapidly evolving phenomenon. The reviewed papers collectively contribute to a comprehensive understanding of this intersection by exploring topics ranging from the non-neutrality of technological advancements to regulatory transformations, risks, legal complexities, societal goals, challenges in peer-to-peer lending, digital transformation, and trends in FinTech and cryptocurrency integration. These research contributions underscore the importance of addressing both the opportunities and challenges presented by FinTech in the context of Islamic finance. As technology continues to shape the financial landscape, further research and regulatory guidance are essential to ensure that Islamic finance remains aligned with its core principles while harnessing the potential of FinTech for ethical and inclusive financial practices.

4. BIBLIOMETRIC ANALYSIS

4.1 Document Analysis

Table 1 provides a summary of data about research in the field of Islamic Finance and FinTech from 2018 to 2023 (Bowen, 2009) as document analysis. The data encompass 86 documents sourced from various journals and books, reflecting a robust annual growth rate of 61.54%. On average, these documents are relatively recent, with an average age of 1.95 years. They exhibit a commendable average citation rate of 6.442 and reference a total of 3,566 sources. The document contents include 66 Keywords Plus and 202 Author's Keywords. The research involves 185 unique authors, with 16 single-authored documents and a collaborative average of 2.72 co-authors per document. Furthermore, international co-authorships are prevalent, accounting for 39.53% of the research. The documents are diversified across types, with 35 articles, 43 book chapters, and 8 conference papers.

Table 1. Document analysis

Description	Results
Main information about the data	
Timespan	2018:2023
Sources (Journals, Books, etc.)	47
Documents	86
Annual growth rate %	61.54
Document average age	1.95
Average citations per doc	6.442
References	3566
Document contents	
Keywords plus (id)	66
Author's keywords (de)	202
Authors	
Authors	185
Authors of single-authored docs	16
Authors collaboration	
Single-authored docs	17
Co-Authors per Doc	2.72
International co-authorships %	39.53
Document types	
Article	35
Book chapter	43
Conference paper	8

Source: Author's compilation

4.2 Performance Analysis

4.2.1 Annual Scientific Production of Articles

Figure 2 depicts the Annual Scientific Production, showcasing the highest article count in 2021, reaching a peak of 21 articles. This visual representation underscores the research trend's robust growth over the years, mirroring the increasing significance of the amalgamation of Islamic finance and Financial Technology (FinTech) in the academic landscape. The rising number of articles suggests a growing interest in this dynamic convergence, highlighting its expanding influence on scholarly discussions and the broader financial arena.

4.2.2 Sources Production over Time

Figure 3 provides a dynamic visualization of the production trends of relevant sources over time. Notably, 'Finance in Islamic Financial Institutions: Scope, Challenges, and Implications in Islamic Finance'

Figure 2. Annual scientific production
(Author's Compilation)

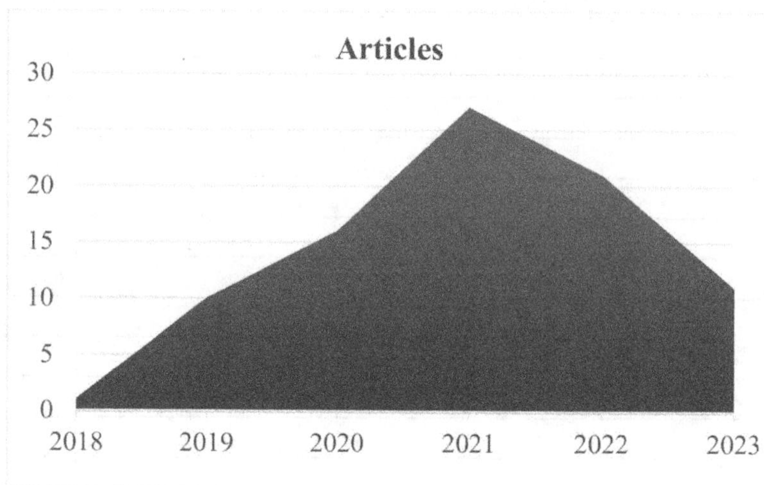

emerges as a prominent contributor, commencing in 2021 with no publications and steadily growing to 12 documents by 2022. This upward trajectory underscores the increasing scholarly attention and significance of this source in the context of Islamic finance research, reflecting its evolving influence and contributions to the field. Table 2 displays the production of sources over time, offering a comprehensive view of their publication trends and contributions to the field.

Figure 3. Sources production over time
(Author's Compilation)

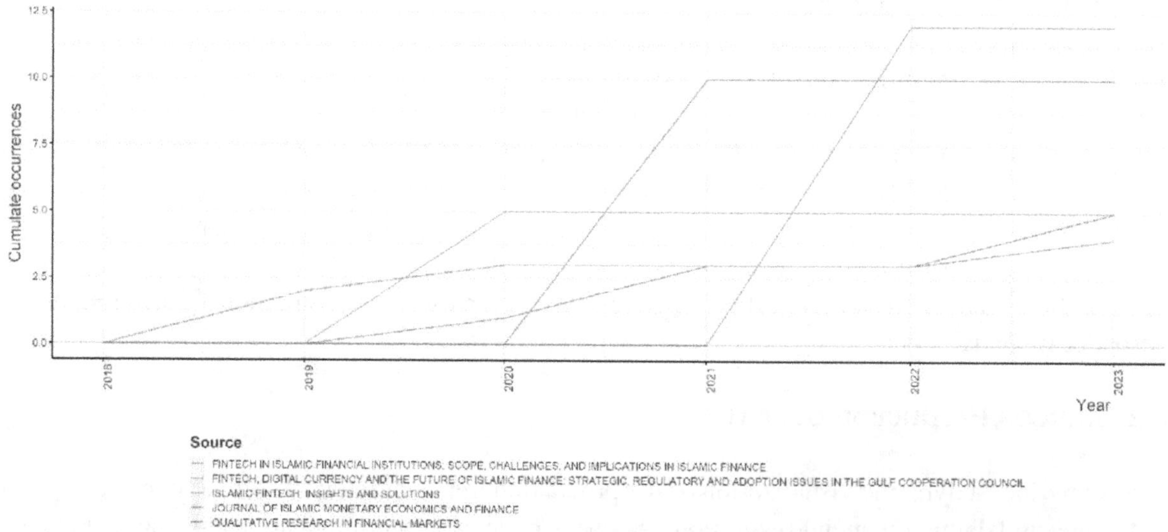

Table 2. Sources production over time

Year	Fintech in Islamic financial institutions: scope, challenges, and implications in Islamic finance	Islamic fintech: insights and solutions	Fintech, digital currency and the future of Islamic finance: strategic, regulatory and adoption issues in the Gulf Cooperation Council	Qualitative research in financial markets	Journal of Islamic monetary economics and finance
2018	0	0	0	0	0
2019	0	0	0	0	2
2020	0	0	5	1	3
2021	0	10	5	3	3
2022	12	10	5	3	3
2023	12	10	5	5	4

Source: Author's Compilation

4.2.3 Country's Production Over Time

Figure 4 charts the production of articles by country over time. Malaysia stands out with the highest output at 62 articles, followed by Bahrain with 34, Indonesia with 28, the USA with 19, and India with 12. This data showcases the varying research activity levels across these nations, underscoring Malaysia's prominent role in generating scholarly content within the specified domain, while also highlighting the global interest in the subject matter.

Figure 4.

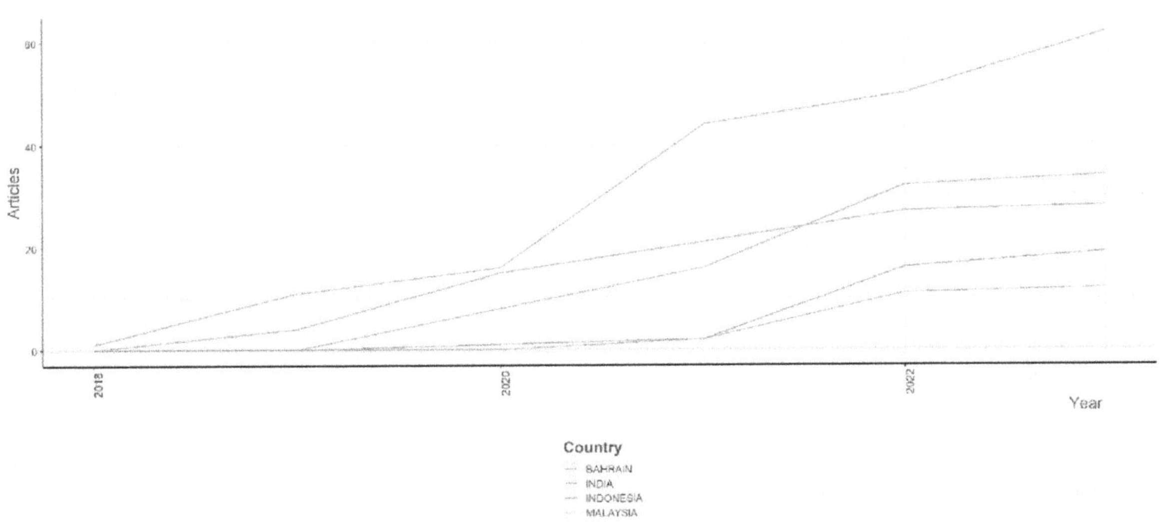

4.2.4 Most Relevant Source

Figure 5 presents a visual summary of the most pertinent sources in the realm of Islamic Fintech. 'Fintech in Islamic Institution Scope' leads with 12 documents, signifying its significant contribution to the field. Following closely is 'Islamic Fintech: Insights and Solutions,' which boasts 10 documents, further emphasizing its relevance and influence in the discourse. This snapshot underscores the importance of these sources in shaping the understanding and exploration of Islamic Fintech within the academic and research community.

Figure 5. Most relevant source
(Author's Compilation)

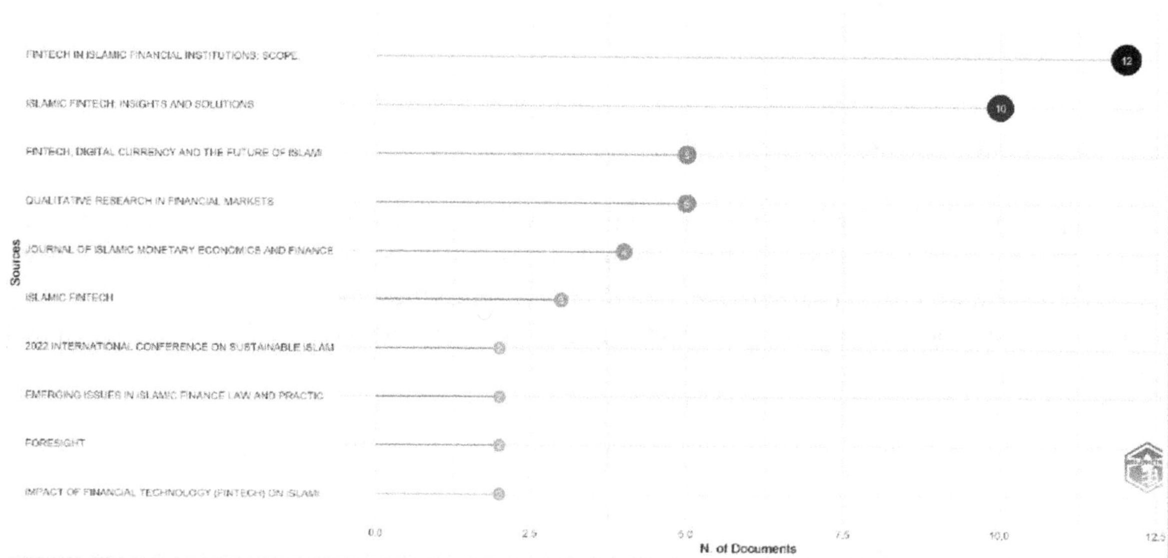

4.3 Co-Authorship Analysis

4.3.1 Citation Analysis of Articles

Figure 6 illustrates a diverse group of authors with collaborative tendencies. Notably, co-authorship is prominent among the listed authors, exemplified by Muhammad Khamis and Muhammad Abubakar co-authoring two papers with Muhammad Hassan. This collective authorship pattern suggests a collaborative and interdisciplinary approach, fostering cutting-edge research across various fields. While this figure provides valuable insights into author relationships, for a more comprehensive analysis, information regarding the specific articles these authors have authored and their corresponding citation metrics would be necessary. If such data is available, I would be delighted to offer a more detailed analysis.

Figure 6. Citation analysis of articles
(Author's Compilation)

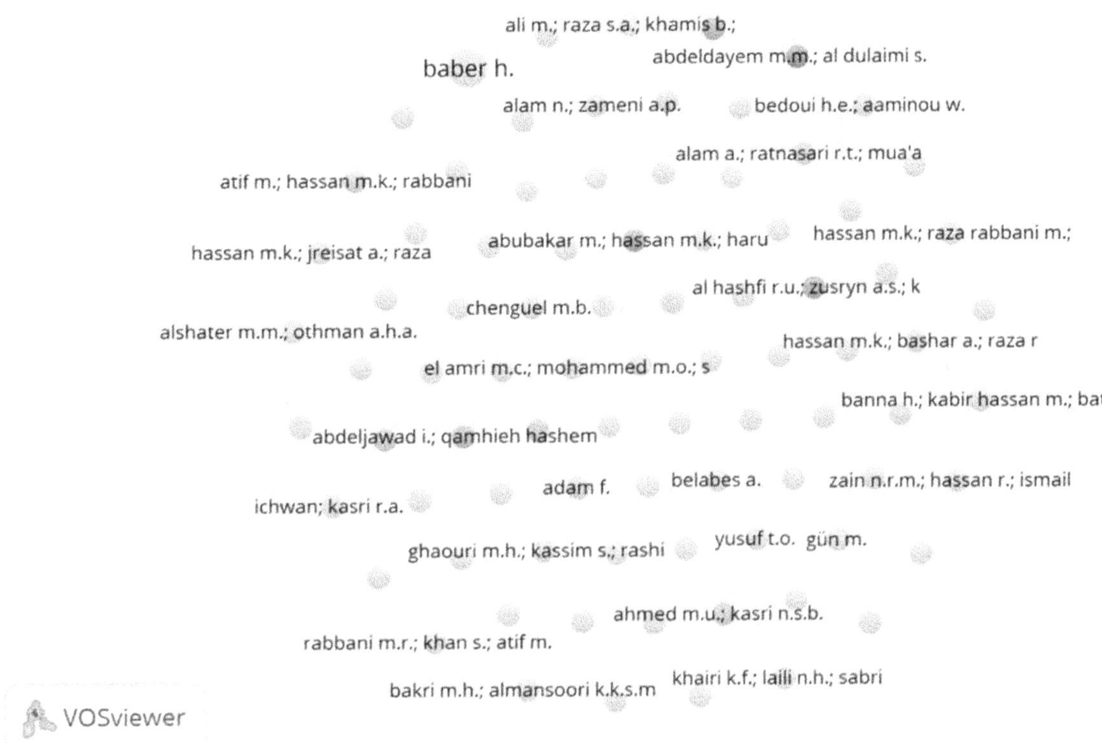

Figure 7. Most cited countries
(Author's Compilation)

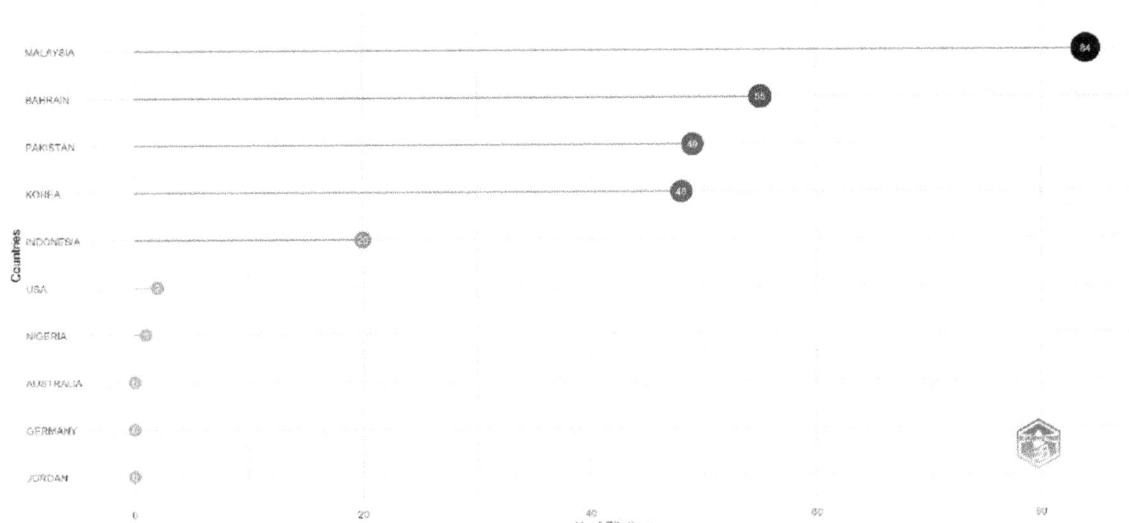

4.3.3 Most Cited Countries

Figure 7 presents a visualization of the most-cited countries, with Malaysia taking the lead with an impressive 84 citations. Table 3 complements this by offering an in-depth analysis of the most-cited countries, shedding light on their prominence and influence in the academic discourse. These representations collectively emphasize the global recognition and substantial scholarly contributions attributed to Malaysia, indicating its central role in shaping the cited literature. Additionally, they recognize other influential nations that have made significant contributions to the field, highlighting the collaborative and diverse nature of research in the domain of focus.

4.3.4 Most Cited Global Documents

Figure 8 offers a visual overview of the most-cited global documents, with 'HASSAN MK, 2020, JECON COOP DEV' standing out prominently with an impressive 77 global citations. This figure highlights the substantial influence and widespread recognition achieved by this specific document within the scholarly community, showcasing its pivotal role in shaping the discourse and research landscape of the subject matter. The high citation count signifies the document's enduring relevance and impact, affirming its status as a seminal work in the field and a valuable resource for researchers and academics seeking insights into the domain of focus.

Table 3. Most cited countries

Country		TC	Average Article Citations
MALAYSIA		84	4.9
BAHRAIN		55	27.5
PAKISTAN		49	16.3
KOREA		48	24
INDONESIA		20	4
USA		2	1
NIGERIA		1	1
AUSTRALIA		0	0
GERMANY		0	0
JORDAN		0	0
MOROCCO		0	0
SAUDI ARABIA		0	0
TUNISIA		0	0
TURKEY		0	0

Source: Author's Compilation

Figure 8. Most cited global documents
(Author's Compilation)

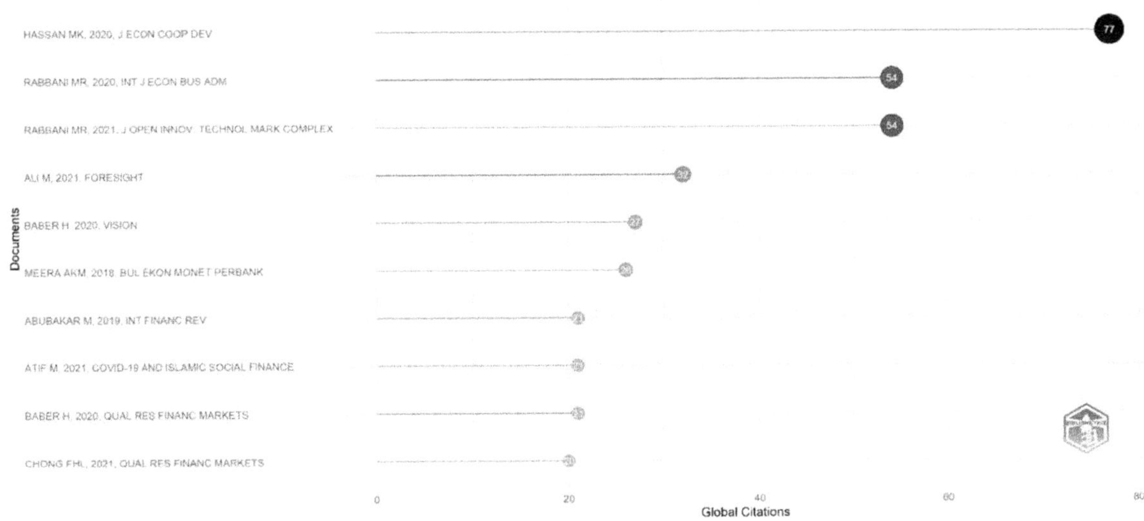

Figure 9. Countries collaboration world map
(Author's Compilation)

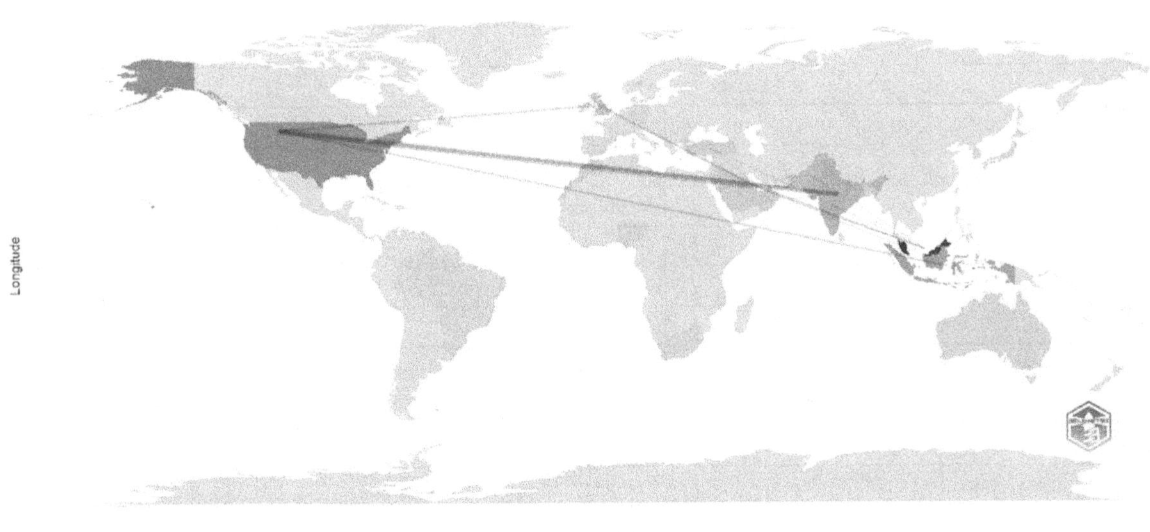

Table 4. Countries collaboration world map

From	To	Frequency
Bahrain	India	7
Bahrain	Indonesia	2
Bahrain	Kuwait	1
Bahrain	Malta	1
Bahrain	Oman	2
Bahrain	Pakistan	2
Bahrain	Qatar	1
Bahrain	Saudi Arabia	1
Bahrain	United Kingdom	3
Bahrain	USA	11
Bangladesh	Brazil	1
India	Oman	2
India	Pakistan	1
India	Saudi Arabia	1
Indonesia	Australia	1
Indonesia	United Kingdom	1
Indonesia	USA	3
Jordan	United Arab Emirates	1
Malaysia	Bahrain	3
Malaysia	Bangladesh	1
Malaysia	India	1
Malaysia	Nigeria	1
Malaysia	Oman	1
Malaysia	Pakistan	2
Malaysia	Qatar	1
Malaysia	Saudi Arabia	1
Malaysia	Singapore	1
Malaysia	Turkey	2
Malaysia	United Arab Emirates	2
Malaysia	United Kingdom	1
Malaysia	USA	1
Oman	Japan	1
Pakistan	Germany	1
Pakistan	South Africa	1
Pakistan	United Kingdom	1
Turkey	United Arab Emirates	2
United Kingdom	Saudi Arabia	1
USA	Bangladesh	1

continued on following page

Table 4. Continued

From	To	Frequency
USA	Brazil	1
USA	India	4
USA	Kuwait	1
USA	Oman	1
USA	Saudi Arabia	1
USA	United Kingdom	3

Source: Author's Compilation

4.4 Countries Collaboration Analysis

Figure 9 and Table 4 both represent the collaborative relationships between countries in the field of focus, offering insights into international cooperation in research and academic endeavours.

Figure 9, which is labelled as the "Countries collaboration world map," likely provides a visual depiction of these collaborations on a global map, visually illustrating the connections and partnerships between different nations. Unfortunately, the specific details of this map are not provided in the text, but it's essential for understanding the geographical distribution of research collaboration.

Meanwhile, Table 4 presents a tabulated summary of country-to-country collaborations, listing the pairs of countries along with the frequency of their collaborations. Here, we can observe the collaborative efforts between various countries, which contribute to the global exchange of knowledge and expertise in the field of interest.

Noteworthy collaborative relationships include Bahrain and the USA, with 11 collaborations, indicating a significant partnership in research efforts. Similarly, Bahrain collaborates extensively with India (7 collaborations), Oman (2 collaborations), and Pakistan (2 collaborations), suggesting a strong regional research network.

India, besides its collaborations with Bahrain, also partners with Saudi Arabia, Oman, and Pakistan, showcasing its diverse research engagements in the region. Indonesia collaborates with the United Kingdom and the USA, indicating international ties.

Malaysia, a prominent player in the region, collaborates with multiple countries, including Bahrain, the United Arab Emirates, Turkey, and the United Kingdom. These collaborations reflect Malaysia's active role in fostering international research relationships.

The table also highlights collaborations between countries from different continents, such as the USA and Brazil, signifying a global exchange of research ideas and efforts.

In summary, both Figure 8 and Table 3 provide valuable insights into the collaborative relationships between countries in the field of focus. These collaborations are instrumental in advancing research and knowledge dissemination on a global scale, facilitating the exchange of ideas, expertise, and resources among nations.

5. SCIENCE MAPPING

5.1 Co-Occurrence of Keywords

Figure 10 depicts the co-occurrence patterns of keywords related to Islamic finance, fintech, and blockchain. Notably, "fintech" and "Islamic finance" frequently appear together in sentences, indicating a strong association with 17 instances. Additionally, "blockchain" is less commonly associated with "Islamic finance" but is still present in 5 instances. Furthermore, keywords like "finance," "Islamic banks," "cryptocurrency," "Malaysia," "innovation," "shariah," and "financial inclusion" co-occur with "Islamic finance." These patterns signify a growing integration of Islamic finance with fintech and blockchain technologies, driven by their potential to enhance efficiency and accessibility in Islamic financial services. The total link strength, as shown in the image, highlights "Islamic finance" as the central keyword, closely followed by "fintech" and "finance." This suggests that "Islamic finance" plays a pivotal role and maintains strong connections with other keywords in the field. This co-occurrence analysis reveals the burgeoning integration of Islamic finance with fintech and blockchain, underlining their potential to revolutionize Islamic financial services by improving efficiency and accessibility.

Figure 10. Co-Occurrence of Keywords
(Author's Compilation)

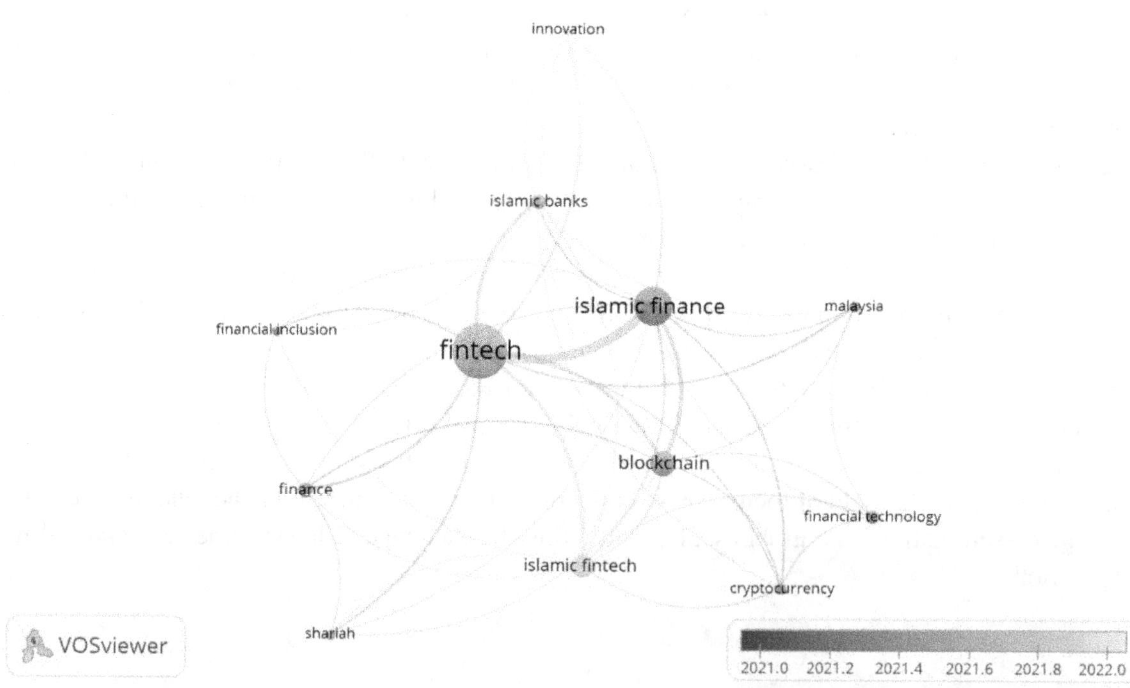

5.2 Bibliographic Coupling

Figure 10 highlights distinct clusters of articles within the field of Islamic fintech, indicating significant areas of research and innovation. One prominent cluster revolves around the utilization of blockchain technology in Islamic finance. This cluster encompasses articles exploring various aspects, such as the development of blockchain-based Islamic capital markets, enhanced efficiency in Islamic trade finance through blockchain, and the creation of innovative Islamic financial products via blockchain technology. Another closely connected cluster focuses on the creation of new fintech products and services tailored for Islamic banks. Articles in this cluster delve into subjects like the development of Islamic mobile banking applications, leveraging artificial intelligence to enhance the customer experience in Islamic banking, and utilizing big data to innovate new Islamic financial offerings. Several articles serve as bridges, connecting different clusters. For instance, some articles discuss using blockchain to enhance the efficiency of Islamic microfinance institutions, while others explore the development of fintech solutions for Islamic crowdfunding and peer-to-peer lending platforms.

The bibliographic coupling analysis underscores the rapid growth and innovation within the Islamic fintech field. This expansion is driven by increasing demand for Islamic financial products, the proliferation of blockchain technology, and the rising adoption of digital payment methods.

Figure 11. Bibliographic coupling
(Author's Compilation)

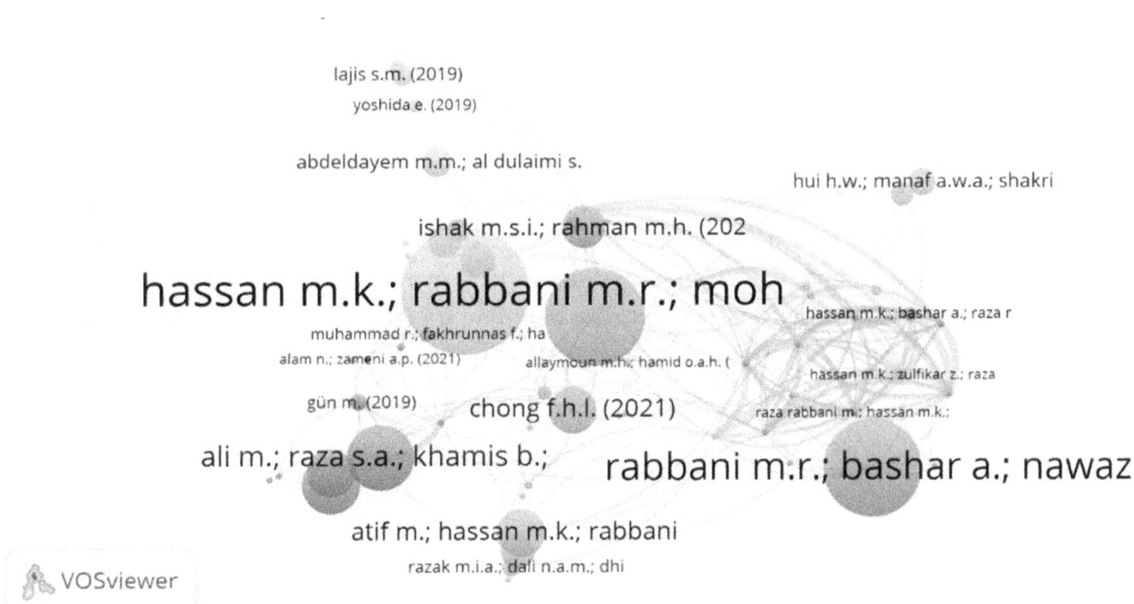

6. CONCLUSION AND IMPLICATIONS

The analysis of research at the intersection of Islamic finance and Financial Technology (FinTech) underscores the dynamic and burgeoning nature of this academic landscape. The significant surge in research activity, particularly in 2021, highlights the growing importance of Islamic FinTech in scholarly discourse. Key sources such as 'Fintech in Islamic Institution Scope' and 'Islamic Fintech: Insights and Solutions' have played pivotal roles in shaping this field, with 'Finance in Islamic Financial Institutions: Scope, Challenges, and Implications in Islamic Finance' also gaining recognition. Malaysia's leadership in research production reflects its pivotal role in generating scholarly content, though Bahrain, Indonesia, the USA, and India also exhibit significant interest. International collaborations, especially between Bahrain and the USA, emphasize the global nature of research in this domain. The implications of this analysis extend to research expansion, robust regulatory frameworks, specialized education, responsible market practices, and global cooperation. It highlights the convergence of Islamic finance and FinTech, offering opportunities for ethical and inclusive financial practices, grounded in Islamic principles. Stakeholders must harness these opportunities to ensure the enduring impact of Islamic FinTech on the global financial arena.

7. LIMITATIONS AND FURTHER SCOPE

This thematic evolution analysis, while shedding light on the intersection of Islamic finance and Financial Technology (FinTech), has notable limitations that must be considered. Firstly, the reliance on a specific dataset from Scopus might omit relevant publications from other sources, potentially limiting the comprehensiveness of the analysis. Additionally, the focus on English-language publications introduces a language bias, possibly overlooking valuable research in non-English languages. Citation counts, though informative, do not encompass a paper's full influence, warranting a more holistic evaluation. Furthermore, this analysis captures a moment in time, with data up to September 2021, potentially missing significant recent developments in the rapidly evolving Islamic FinTech landscape.

To address these limitations, future research should adopt a qualitative approach to delve deeper into influential papers' content. Expanding the geographical scope and considering research in various languages would offer a more inclusive view. Evaluating the real-world impact, conducting longitudinal studies, and exploring interdisciplinary intersections with law, economics, and technology can further enrich our understanding. Additionally, research should investigate policy, regulatory, ethical, and social implications, ensuring a comprehensive exploration of this dynamic field. By addressing these limitations and expanding research horizons, scholars can continue shaping the future of ethical and inclusive financial practices at the nexus of Islamic finance and FinTech.

REFERENCES

Abubakar, M. H., Hassan, M. K., & Haruna, M. A. (2019). Cryptocurrency tide and Islamic finance development: Any issue? *International Finance Review*, 189–200. doi:10.1108/S1569-376720190000020019

Aria, M., & Cuccurullo, C. (2017). bibliometrix: An R-tool for comprehensive science mapping analysis. *Journal of Informetrics, 11*(4), 959–975. doi:10.1016/j.joi.2017.08.007

Bedoui, H. E. (2021). Role of fintech to achieve the SDGS from an Islamic perspective. In Islamic Fintech. doi:10.4324/9781003014614-1

Belabes, A. (2021). Fintech and Maqāsid Dichotomy under the Prism of the Non-Neutrality of Techniques. In *Islamic FinTech*. Insights and Solutions. doi:10.1007/978-3-030-45827-0_3

Bowen, G. A. (2009). Document analysis as a qualitative research method. *Qualitative Research Journal, 9*(2), 27–40. doi:10.3316/QRJ0902027

Guz, A. N., & Rushchitsky, J. J. (2009). Scopus: A system for the evaluation of scientific journals. *International Applied Mechanics, 45*(4), 351–362. doi:10.100710778-009-0189-4

Hassan, M. K. (2022). Fintech Trends: Industry 4.0, Islamic Fintech, and Its Digital Transformation. In FinTech in Islamic Financial Institutions: Scope, Challenges, and Implications in Islamic Finance. Springer. doi:10.1007/978-3-031-14941-2_6

Hui, H. W. (2019). Fintech and the transformation of the Islamic finance regulatory framework in Malaysia. In Emerging Issues in Islamic Finance Law and Practice in Malaysia. Emerald Insight.

Irfan, M. E. (2023). *Advanced Machine Learning Algorithms for Complex Financial Applications.* IGI Global. doi:10.4018/978-1-6684-4483-2

Irfan, M. E.-S. (2023). *The Impact of AI Innovation on Financial Sectors in the Era of Industry 5.0.* 1-320. 10.4018/9798369300824

Muhammad, R. F. (2021). The Determinants of Potential Failure of Islamic Peer-to-Peer Lending: Perceptions of Stakeholders in Indonesia. *Journal of Asian Finance, Economics and Business.* doi:10.13106/jafeb.2021.vol8.no2.0981

Omoola, S., & Ibrahim, H. K. (2023). The Legal Implications of Abandoned Digital Assets in Sharīʿah-Compliant Fintech Platforms. *ISRA International Journal of Islamic Finance, 60*(2), 60–76. doi:10.55188/ijif.v15i2.542

Pal, T. I. (2023). How do Machine Learning (ML) techniques benefit the insurance industry? An exploratory study, In The Impact of AI Innovation on Financial Sectors in the Era of Industry 5.0. IGI Global. doi:10.4018/979-8-3693-0082-4.ch007

Raza Rabbani, M. H. (2022). Islamic Finance and Cryptocurrency: A Systematic Review. In FinTech in Islamic Financial Institutions: Scope, Challenges, and Implications in Islamic Finance. doi:10.1007/978-3-031-14941-2_14

Ridho Kismawadi, E. I. (n.d.). Revolutionizing Islamic finance: Artificial intelligence's role in the future of industry. In The Impact of AI Innovation on Financial Sectors in the Era of Industry 5.0 (pp. 184-207). IGI Global. doi:10.4018/979-8-3693-0082-4.ch011

Sarkis-Onofre, R. C.-L., Catalá-López, F., Aromataris, E., & Lockwood, C. (2021). How to properly use the PRISMA Statement. *Systematic Reviews*, *10*(1), 1–3. doi:10.118613643-021-01671-z PMID:33875004

Suzuki, Y. (2022). Digital transformation in Islamic finance: A critique of perfectionist's views on Islamic fintech. In Digital Transformation in Islamic Finance: A Critical and Analytical View. Taylor & Francis. doi:10.4324/9781003262169-3

Van Eck, N. J., & Waltman, L. (2017). Citation-based clustering of publications using CitNetExplorer and VOSviewer. *Scientometrics*, *111*(2), 1053–1070. doi:10.100711192-017-2300-7 PMID:28490825

Yusuf, T. O. (2021). The Risks of Islamic Fintech. In *Islamic FinTech*. Insights and Solutions. doi:10.1007/978-3-030-45827-0_20

Chapter 11
Legal Efficiency of Secure Transactions Framework in India:
A Multi-Dimensional Regulatory System

Nanda Pardhey
https://orcid.org/0000-0002-5348-7989
University of Petroleum and Energy Studies, India

Denis N. Yuni
National University of Lesotho, Lesotho

ABSTRACT

Virtual technological development has revolutionized banking, financial, and capital market transactions in the world. A majority of transactions are taking place through online banking, net banking, or Unified Payments Interface (UPI) transactions, with few other portals giving the ease and comfort to do transaction in one's comfort zone without going to banks or withdrawing money in offline modes to be paid. The rapid evolution of online and UPI transactions has transformed the way transactions are conducted, shifting a significant portion of commerce to the digital realm. In this context, the efficiency of legal frameworks for secure transactions is of paramount importance to ensure trust, reduce risks, and foster economic growth without sabotaging the customers transactions security concerns. The transactions taking place in past in offline mode and presently in online mode had delves into the nexus between secure transactions and electronic transactions, exploring the impact of emerging technologies such as blockchain, UPI, and net banking that have posed challenges.

1. INTRODUCTION

The digital revolution has fundamentally altered the landscape of secure transactions. Online transactions in banking sector, financial and capital markets have revolutionized completely post pandemic phase

DOI: 10.4018/979-8-3693-1038-0.ch011

as people now through online modes manages their all-financial tractions through multiple devices like phone, laptop and computer at their own convenience and hassle free from all formalities that were required by going to banks which gave them easy accessibility at their comfort zone. Indian had adapted like many other countries incorporated online transactions in virtual world through various devices with changes in the functioning of banking and financial sectors incorporating virtual mode of transactions swiftly but there are certain legal implications of such transactions that encompasses various aspects of concern on the persons security and privacy in virtual world and misuse risk of electronic transactions. Traditional legal frameworks are facing unprecedented challenges because of new technologies that have reshaped global online transactions and economic impact. Through analysing the implication of virtual transaction, we would investigate into the efficiency of the legal framework for stakeholders considering their intricate relationships between electronic transactions, blockchain technology, the dark web, and KYC protocols that overlaps and raises safety and security concerns of secure transactions.

1.1 Electronic Transactions and Legal Implications

The electronic transactions and their growing significance in modern transactional realm and e-commerce portals has transformed the transaction system under banking and financial market. Due to the exploring avenues of online transactions in the early 2010's had brought the modification and amendments into the legal foundation of electronic transactions by Reserve Bank of India (RBI) which regulates all financial transactions within India and due to security concerns emphasized upon modification the Information Technology Act in India to deals with safety and regulation of virtual transactions. Being the signatory to the United Nations Convention on the Use of Electronic Communications in International Contracts famously known as the UNCITRAL Model Law on Electronic Commerce has brought up changes in regulatory system as well as recognition and adaption of e-commerce through virtual mode. Analysing the efficiency of these legal provisions that exchange information during the transactions that should take place in banking or financial sector in a secure manner and importantly through reliable channels or recognised mechanisms under the system which should ensure and promote secure electronic transactions. Moreover, while doing so they regulatory body or channels should addresses challenges that the customer may face in form of data privacy, electronic signatures, and contract enforceability.

RBI which regulates all transactions through its master circulars and directives issues guidelines to all banks and financial institutes for safety measures to be taken while dealing with online/net banking in India. Though RBI had given through its circular guidelines for security transaction specifically in cases of cooperative banks that were directed to take suitable steps to ensure all security measures involving their Web Application and set in place reasonable security measures to mitigate issues of web security risk that they may face. As per guidelines all Web Application of such banks should take precautions to not to store any sensitive information in HTML hidden fields in their servers, cookies or any other client-side storage that could be compromised the clients/customer security integrity of their data. Further also emphasized on Re-establishment of any session after interruption should require normal user identification, authentication, and authorization and strong server-side validation should be enabled (Internet Banking - Security Features -RBI). All Cooperative banks in India needed to follow a defense-in-depth strategy so in case of any issues of security concern they could apply their robust security measures timely across their technology layers that they placed for their banks.

Incorporation of supportive regulatory mechanism adopted in India by all sector has created a secure environment for the customers that has emphasis Robustic focused safety measures, speedy in time and scalable been positioned from time to time in India as a leader in payment system innovation in banking and financial sector. Illustratively, UPI, India's instant payment system, launched in 2016, has witnessed remarkable growth in India with daily transactions averaging over 300 million in volume and 480 billion in value during May 2023 (Cyber Security for a safer Financial System RBI Bulletin. (n.d.)). Keeping in view of the proliferation of transaction in virtually that has also the increased risk of cyber-attacks for the customers for that could risk potential consequential risk for the customer and banks so to avoid such issues banks were directed wherein they should in their regulatory system implement two-factor authentication mechanism for all sort of fund transfers that takes place in net/internet banking. They should have appropriate implementation bodies who used authentication approaches should be assessed based on the risk that could be posed by banking or financial institution's own Internet or online banking systems, that risk must be evaluated keeping their type of customers into account like individual customer, business account customer, corporate or commercial customer based on their transactional capabilities in their individual capacity like daily transactions, various bill payments, different kinds of fund transactions etc depending on the sensitivity of transactions done by customers based on their volume of transactions history or information available. Not only this should be kept for secure transactions, but various technological factors should be incorporated depending on placing appropriate regulatory policies, procedural follow ups and controls on transactions depending on the kind of customer.

Whenever the banking and financial institutions use such effective authentication mechanisms that should keep all this consideration into account of the customer depending on kind of customer their Customer Acceptance Policy (CAP), their usage of transactions, reliability based on Know Your Customer (KYC) norms and performance of transactional history, scalability and growth taking place of such customer and interoperability that could be accessed where they are monitored under other systems too. Whenever there are any suspicious transactions for illegal purpose there is legal risk. Therefore, using asymmetric cryptosystem leads to risk involvement in secure transactions. For carrying out critical transactions like fund transfers, the banks, at the least, need to implement robust and dynamic two-factor authentication through user id/password combination and second factor like (a) a digital signature (through a token containing digital certificate and associated private key, preferably for corporate customers) or (b) One Time Password (OTP) / dynamic access code through various modes (like SMS over mobile phones or hardware token) (Internet Banking - Security Features -RBI). As per the RBI guidelines, there is enhance online and virtual processing mechanism to check security, confirmatory system for second channel procedures through various digital modes using phones, SMS delivery, email etc for maintaining security and safe transactions of customers wherein pre-set limits set for transactional values depending on kind of customer account. CAP helps to set this policies and rules with that of Customer Identification Procedure (CIP) in cases of new accounts linkages is followed by KYC. In case of registration of third-party transactions, the role of intermediaries specified how they are to follow registration norms and their payee details with laid down funds transfer limits.

Banking and financial institutions have to follow the authentication session process with that simultaneously encryption protocol sets for online/virtual transactions that should be intact whenever the transaction or interactions taking place with their customers and in any event of interference that may take place during such session in such situation, they should terminate such transactions. If any of such transactions that being affected should be resolved withing the said timely period set by RBI norms or reversed back to the person who had done it. In case where any money deducted from customers account after transaction failed, then they should promptly notify the same to banks as its being concluded or email, call on customer helpline or other means specified the banks or financial institutions. Now as per norms registering your phone or email Id is mandatory to notify the customer about all transactions, withdrawals and deductions through phone or email that they registered with bank or financial institution. In cases where there are changes in mobile number of customers, they have to make a request to the branch in which they have account for such change which is mandatory.

RBI has taken initiative through its various circulars wherein banks and financial institutions have to follow norms and policies for secure transactions not only this but customers are also advised to incorporate various security precautions while doing online or virtual transactions and how they should protect their personal details secure like account details, OTP, CVV, etc. not to share with anyone and keep it securely on their phones and personal computer that could be hacked and advised to avoid any financial transactions through public internet services freely available at cafes, malls, railway stations, etc that could be breached by hackers making them victim of financial fraud. All banks and financial institutions with their intermediaries are bound to follow risk-based approach to mitigate the risk by following monitoring of transactions or surveillance of process to avoid illegal transactions that should be placed well. However, whenever any online session of transaction gets automatically terminated due to some issues during transactions wherein after fixed period timeline that should be reversed to original one and unless the customer themselves re-authenticate their ongoing or existing session that they had maintained, this is followed so as to prevent the customer from the attacker who take advantage of such issues wherein internet banking if kept alive during session will affect customers monetarily impacting them indefinitely.

As per the rules and direction for authentication of customers during transaction for secure transaction multifactor authentication was required and followed by the banks and financial sector which are used from two or more categories like OTP through registered phone number and email or other authentication process chose. This kind of multiple solution authentication process has become the part of layered security and also provided compensating control approach for secure transaction. As an integral part of the two-factor authentication architecture, banks should also implement appropriate measures to minimise exposure to a middleman attack which is more commonly known as a man-in-the-middle attack (MITM), man-in-the browser (MITB) attack or man-in-the application attack (Internet Banking - Security Features -RBI). Therefore, keeping the authentication process banks had incorporated various control and security measures for secure transactions so as to minimize risk of customer victimization that may happen because of man-in-the middle attacks by following measures-

a. New payees are added through specific OTPs where every new payee has to be authorized by the account holder customer through OTP through second channel showing details of payee or customer's handwritten signature from manual procedure that is being verified by the banks/financial institutions.
b. For Value-transactions in case of payments and funds transfers provided individual OTPs in which there is approved list of specified value transactions laying down money transaction thresholds limit that is determined by customer himself that requires every time a new OTP.
c. Limited time OTP window which is challenged based, and time limited based OTP provide strong transaction security as this is completely controlled based on period of validity by banks and not specific through customer or user behavior. The time limit varies depending on banks and financial institutions which is limited OTP window timing not exceeding 100 seconds at a time keeping the server time into consideration to avoid and lower OTP misuse risk for customers.

d. Providing security during payment and fund transfer wherein digital signature is used based on account holder and Key-based Message Authentication Codes (KMAC) used for making payment or any fund transfer that could contemplated so as to detect certain unauthorized modifications or any kind of injection of transactions data which could be risk through middleman attack. This is given to provided security solution that work effectively for a customer who is using certain hardware token which they have to distinguish their process for generation of OTP from the process of digitally signing any transactions. In this process various crypto keys are being used for generating OTPs and signing transactions to provide secure transactions for customers and keeping their credentials safer through multilayering safety and data protections.
e. In the case of net or internet banking, banks have limited access, but they act on stop-payment based on instructions provided by the customer. Banks in case of net banking clearly notifies its customer about the timeline framework and the situation in which any stop-payment instructions how would be accepted.
f. Rights of the consumer has been covered under the Consumer Protection Act, 1986 that also covers banking services provided by banks wherein that specifies the rights and liabilities that could be availed by the bank's customer same is available in case of net/internet banking wherein before having exposed to internet they should be well explained about the services and educate them for internet banking. Keeping into account internet banking it's a mandate for banks to provided services that can protect the customer from hacking, unauthorized access and transfer of transactions through online banking or denial of service to the customer due to technological glitches and issues that had to be backed well as banks are covered under definition of service under consumer protection.
g. Secure transactions of customers has to be taken care by the banks and they have to provided protections and authentication of their hyperlinks which raises concerns on reputational involved risks that could mislead the customers making them believe that those hyperlinks may be sponsored by banks themselves or that may not relate to banking and the banks website links should be made kerbed only with those portal links for specific payment arrangements through them. Bank websites hyperlinks portals are utilized to pass the information about the customer's purchased done using banking portals. To make the secure transactions on various e-commerce or other portals banks are awareing the customers for using necessary security precautions and confidentiality the customer must use while purchasing through websites that relates to purchasing through online portals.
h. Banks and financial institutions now use second channel notification or confirmation for notifying their customers through SMS or emails about their fund transfer or payments done through the data provided by customer to banks.

Online transaction platforms used by capital markets for doing trading they are also regulated by RBI under the Reserve Bank authorises Electronic Trading Platforms (ETPs) under the Electronic Trading Platforms (Reserve Bank) Directions, 2018 (RBI - Financial Market. (2023, July 19)). ETPs are any electronic system, other than a recognised stock exchange, on which transactions in eligible instruments like securities, money market instruments, foreign exchange instruments, derivatives, etc. are contracted and no entity shall operate an ETP without obtaining prior authorisation of RBI (RBI - Financial Market. (2023, July 19)) so at to provide secure environment to its customers using this online trading platforms. To promote a robust, fair, liquid, open and appropriately transparent markets, underpinned by high ethical standards and to prevent abuse in markets regulated by the Reserve Bank, the Reserve Bank of India (Prevention of Market Abuse) Directions, 2019 have been put in place, in line with the best global practices (RBI - Financial Market. (2023, July 19). In case of Non-Banking Financial Companies (NBFC) information of their customers is their assets and Information Security (IS) of customer need to be protected as these is an asset for such financial companies and to achiever their organizational goals, they need to protect all such information as assets. IS whole purpose is to protect and control access in case of breach of access of sensitive information and they have to ensure that such information is used only by legitimate users who have access to them by authorization so that their data cannot be read or compromised by anyone without proper authorization given by the access holder or account holder. NBFCs must have a board approved IS Policy with the following basic tenets:

a. Confidentiality: Ensuring access to sensitive data to authorized users only;
b. Integrity: ensuring accuracy and reliability of information by ensuring that there is no modification without authorization;
c. Availability: ensuring that uninterrupted data is available to users when it is needed; and
d. Authenticity: For IS it is necessary to ensure that the data, transactions, communications or documents (electronic or physical) are genuine (RBI-Master directions- Information Technology Framework for the NBFC Sector. (n.d.)).

2. BLOCKCHAIN TECHNOLOGY AND ITS IMPACT ON SECURE TRANSACTIONS

Introduction of blockchain technology has revolutionized the transaction system as a disruptive force in secure transactions, offering transparency, immutability, and decentralization giving privacy and is restriction free technology for the user doing transaction through blockchain. Use of blockchain technology for secure transaction is not that safe because in this Virtual Currency (VC) is used which is not recognized by the law or regulator which is digital asset through which one can buy and sell goods or services, in this whole transaction cryptocurrency is in form of blockchain i.e., VC. In the blockchain system the transaction is at the risk of the doer of transaction as its done through the social network that is used by two people without the intervention of the regulators like banks or other institutions wherein files get hosted through peer-to-peer (P2P) networking between the host and receiver through online system of encryption and there is complete anonymity between them using anonymous proxy networks where they use Tor via which is done through anonymized series of connection that being created for blockchain transaction using cryptocurrencies.

The host and receiver directly do the transaction without any sort of intermediaries like banks or financial institutions intervention in their entire process of communication and transaction which is at risk of the receiver firstly. Blockchain is being integrated into various industries, such as finance, supply chain management, and intellectual property rights that raises concerns of security of transaction and risk of the users that could lead to victimisation as taking place decentralized mode and not regulated by the regulatory. In January 2017, the Institute for Development and Research in Banking Technology (IDRBT) established by RBI in 1996 as an institution to work at the intersection of banking and technology submitted a Whitepaper on "Applications of blockchain technology to banking and financial sector in India" (Internet & Mobile Association of India vs RBI). As blockchain function on four basic distinctiveness of a cryptocurrencies through bitcoin or other online currency i.e., firstly its digital in nature taking place online mode, secondly between private parties, thirdly globally recognized by individuals but not by regulators in many parts of the countries and lastly are run through autonomous and decentralized algorithm encryption. In India, cryptocurrency not legally recognized, but paradoxically blockchain technology is being accepted by RBI whereas cryptocurrency not by the apex regulator RBI in India. Government had taken initiative to explore the uses of blockchain technology in India proactively for guiding in digital economy which is growing rapidly. There are legal implications and regulatory challenges of blockchain technology in the context of secure transactions that are taking place P2P without intervention of any legally recognized regulatory which sometimes includes smart contracts pertaining to such transactions, legal recognition under India legislation, and potential legislative adaptations. In block blockchain system sometimes dark web or net is used which pose security risk for the transactions and can be risk for marketplaces like financial sector or capital markets for conducting illegal activities. These challenges the present regulation of dark net system which work anonymously for illegal transactions posing risk for cyber security and threats. Dark web is a big challenge which need to be answered through robust legal measures that are implemented by centralized manner to preserve the digital freedoms of the stakeholders.

3. KNOW YOUR CUSTOMER (KYC) AND TRANSACTION SECURITY

RBI through it Master circulars and directive from 2008 while making amendments in Prevention of Money Laundering Act (PMLA), 2002 specifying the importance of KYC protocols in preventing financial crimes, ensuring customer identity verification, and maintaining transaction security. KYC regulations in India and international standards laid down by Financial Action Task Force (FATF) through its recommendations was incorporated in India and necessary amendments were done in the banking laws and also to other financial institutions, which were to deal effectively curb money laundering and financing of terrorism in which KYC regulations in deterring money laundering, terrorism financing, and other illicit activities while balancing privacy concerns of customers by checking, monitoring and reporting of transactions under different categories of risks. Banks after coming into force of PMLA that was amended in 2015 wherein RBI issued their Master Circular directing the banks with regard to KYC norms for suspicious transactions and preventing money laundering and had incorporated risked based transactions under which all transactions that are suspicious in nature are monitored based on risk following the surveillance process laid down to study their customer's transaction behaviour pattern and avoiding the victimisation of customer through irregular transactions that are not initiated by the customer or in certain circumstances prior confirmation are taken from customer like in cases of EMI or loans were automatically money get deducted at specified dated decided between customer and bank.

UPI payment system has been used majorly following the KYC norms has provided the customer ease at their own space usage benefit, providing safety and security through verification and PIN system or OTP which is real-time feature that has transformed the secure transactions for customer transforming the payment mode through digital ecosystem in India. Now the banks and financial institutions are using more new features in addition that enables UPI that facilitate various payments needs through different portals and service providers like Paytm or Amazon pay etc. which has become need of the time of the economy. As Artificial Intelligence (AI) is becoming increasingly integrated into the digital economy, conversational instructions hold immense potential in enhancing ease of use, and consequently reach, of the UPI system and it is, therefore, proposed to launch an innovative payment mode viz., "Conversational Payments" on UPI, that will enable users to engage in a conversation with an AI-powered system to initiate and complete transactions in a safe and secure environment (RBI bulletin Statement on Developmental and Regulatory Policies. (n.d.)). As per RBI statement this would be made available in smartphones and feature phone that are UPI based platforms whereby, they will deepen the digital penetration in India through UPI secure transaction system which will be available in English and Hindi facility that can customer avail with more languages incorporated in future.

To provide secure transactions is the agenda to their customer is the mission taken up by the RBI not only online mode but also offline mode. With this agenda in mind and to increase speed of UPI, they had launched on-device wallet name as "UPI-Lite" that was launched last year in September 2022. This initiative was taken to optimise processing resources for banks specifically so s to reduce the failure that used to technical issues or glitches during transactions done by customer. The Indian Reserve Bank is constantly striving to improve is security system of online payment that provide customer with secure environment for online transactions by offering its all users safe, secure, fast, convenient, accessible, and affordable e-payment options (RBI- Building Blocks for a Sustainable Future: Some Reflections. (n.d.)). The Reserve Bank has been at the forefront to facilitate safe and inclusive growth in the digital financial sector and UPI has been recognised as the fastest growing retail payment system in the world and many countries have expressed interest in having a UPI-like platform (RBI- Building Blocks for a Sustainable Future: Some Reflections. (n.d.)). Together with the National Payments Corporation of India (NPCI), the Reserve Bank's initiatives in linking UPI with the fast payment systems in Singapore, Bhutan, Nepal, the UAE and several other countries demonstrate the huge potential of UPI in the years to come. The availability of RTGS on a 365x24x7 basis has helped in reducing the settlement and credit risks in the payment's ecosystem ((RBI- Building Blocks for a Sustainable Future: Some Reflections. (n.d.)). This kind of initiative and features has been introduced post pandemic to provide customer that will facilitate their experience and give them ease in digital environment for secure transactions not in India but collaborating with other countries for using single platform for payments online.

4. COMPARATIVE ANALYSIS: INDIAN AND INTERNATIONAL PERSPECTIVES

In modern times the globe had become interconnected due to liberalization and globalization and in era of technology where financial transactions traverse offline and online through various continents and function done transborder, there is a need felt for international cooperation when it comes to protection and preservation of customers that need to be protected and given a secure environment and prevent them from cyber-attacks and threats during online transactions in online mode. Combating such cyber threats during online transactions has become paramount consideration for the regulators. In virtual world cyber-attacker's targets websites of banks or their hyperlinks that not only jeopardize the safety and security of customers and bank but also effect the stability of the banks and disrupt the financial systems due to such issues that leads to victimization of customers and giving them safeguard while transaction taking place was essential and paramount which is taken cares post pandemic period. Government is taking efforts nationally and internationally to complement these efforts by having collaboration with international bodies while dealing with banking sector issues of cyber security and safety for transactions.

Technological innovation and adaptation have become a driving force that is being adopted by banking and financial sector that focuses on providing efficient, easily accessible and affordable transaction system at ease of customer. However, the current FinTech revolution is unique in many ways being defined by increased computing power and use of new technologies (RBI -Cyber Security for a safer Financial System. (n.d.)). The efficiency of Indian legal frameworks for secure transactions in light of electronic transactions, blockchain, the dark web, and KYC norms has been challenging at times that may affect the economically affecting due to jurisdictional issues in virtual online platform and therefore, India's approach with international counterparts, highlighting best practices and identifying areas for improvement in coming year to combat such cyber threats and attacks. Cyber-attacks can disrupt critical financial operations within banks, rendering them unable to process transactions, access customer accounts, or execute essential functions and this disruption can result in a loss of confidence in the banking system, as customers and businesses may face difficulties in accessing their funds or conducting normal financial activities (RBI -Cyber Security for a safer Financial System. (n.d.)). This kind of disruptions can restraint upon the financial instability by banks or financial institutions, especially when the attackers target multiple banks or are prolonged attacks. Indeed, the 2021 ransomware attack on Colonial Pipeline, though not a financial entity, highlighted the interconnectedness of critical infrastructure systems and the potential cascading effects on various sectors, including banking that illustrated how a cyberattack could spark a run, in this case, a run-on gas stations, amplifying the effects well beyond the original shock (RBI -Cyber Security for a safer Financial System. (n.d.)). The regulatory are extensively doing risk assessments and continuous ongoing supervision to deal them at their entity level to cap with cyber resilience and fill the gaps through reporting and risk assessment. Presently the banking, financial sector and capital markets need to have their security system at their entity level to consistent data security and cyber incidents to take necessary precautionary measure to avoid larger harm as online data prone to be attack as multiple users, service provider/ intermediaries using clouds data that could become risky based on reliability and interdependencies of these entities for internet, so the entities need to have backup system that could quickly enabled and protect the customers or entities data from cyber threats. In India, The Reserve Bank Innovation Hub (RBIH) has been set up for collaborating with financial sector institutions, the technology industry, and academic institutions for exchange of ideas and development of prototypes related to financial innovations (RBI -Cyber Security for a safer Financial System. (n.d.)).

Through international cooperation and collaboration recent legal developments in India are being put at place through government initiative to resolve issues of jurisdiction restraint and also deal with other jurisdictions concerns wherein government aims at enhancing secure transaction efficiency. Recently, India and Singapore tied up their UPI and Pay Now systems allowing for real time cross border money transfers between the two countries. Indeed, there is immense potential for use of UPI globally through partnership and collaboration with other countries (Cyber Security for a safer Financial System RBI Bulletin. (n.d.)). International organisations are stressing on the need for enhanced safeguards and global cooperation in this context. As cyber threats are of global nature and whatever efforts taken by the government, financial institutions at different levels, capital markets and various technological companies in this digital work becomes insufficient to protect against certain cyber threats and attacks as they are surpass geographical boundaries and involves multiple transborder in virtual digital world having proxy appearance showing multiple jurisdictions making it difficult for them to address them instantly due to complexity. At global level cyber security for online secure transaction should be taken up to build up a robust environment for not only customers but the entities themselves. Internationally the financial and banking sectors need to have better regulation removing jurisdictions barriers and understanding the operational and technological inter-connections when it comes to infrastructure and robust expert team to deal such matters. The countries need a better understanding and incorporation of cyber risk into their system to see the stability and need for improvement to mitigate the technological risk and being updated on technological front from time-to-time.

Cybersecurity is important for having secure transactions and due to multiple law of each country that leads to application of laws that leads to conflict of laws at times, so internationally should have minimum common framework to deal with risk of cyber security that could be devised in coordination and having a uniformity that could be outlined out of best practices and standards that could be laid to be followed by banks, financial institutions and capital markets that could ensure protection and mitigate risk of cyber threats. Apart from this at international level initiative, the domestic laws should be in consistent with international standards and such information of cyber threats and attacks could be shared to identify any emerging threats or probable attacks which could make identified to avoid and prevent such attacks by proactive steps. Setting up a system that could be developed to implement these plans and ensure coordination and cooperation in event of cyber threats in these sectors in investigation, preventing and risk management by those bodies which work in coordination nationally and internationally. Cyber threats are majorly taking place in virtual digital system that become platform for perpetrating cyber-attacks for the perpetrators for easy money and damaging the economy, such crimes should become more riskier for the attacker wherein they could be effectively punished, and their assets gain through proceed of crime should be confiscated and prosecuted under uniform laws nationally and internationally that would disrupt and become deterrent for the attackers to commit further such crimes. Countries those are prone to such attacks due to not having robust legal system to deal with cyber security that should collaborate and work on capacity building and adapting to a legal system that could be implemented through necessary experts and resources and infrastructure implement to manage cyber risks effectively. Technology do change fast and in case of cyber security from time-to-time best practices should be implemented at all levels, regulators should be updated with technological changes and training, creating a risk assessment and risk management system through planning based on the incidences of response and lastly using advanced technologies to detect such threats to prevent them before the incidence take place of cyber-attack.

5. REFERENCES FOR ENHANCING LEGAL FRAMEWORKS FOR SECURE TRANSACTIONS

Collaborative actionable regulatory system is required to improve the efficiency of secure transaction laws, considering the challenges posed by electronic transactions, blockchain, the dark web, and the evolving role of KYC. Advocate for a holistic approach to legal reforms that fosters innovation, safeguards security, and promotes economic growth. A proactive and informed approach for navigating risks needs to prioritise: (a) customer expectations; (b) cybersecurity threats; (c) data privacy; (d) sensitivity to ethical concerns related to bias, transparency and accountability; (e) collaboration among financial institutions and industry stakeholders for integration of processes; (f) regulatory compliance; and (g) minimising skill gap to keep pace with rapid technological changes (Reserve bank of India - Macrofinancial Risks Reports. (n.d.)). Legal complexities should be resolve when trans-border transactions taking place considering the individuals/customers, entities, and organisation involvement of parties and if they fall outside jurisdictions of India. Necessary regulatory compliances should be placed by banks those are operating cross-border complying with all regulations, rules and enactments applying domestically as well as the hosting country involved processing all legal requirements specified. Cross-border transactions has to comply with lots of legal requirements which led to jurisdictional issues due to application of different laws, governing laws for those banks, financial institutions etc. determining possible mechanism that could resolve dispute and has legal remedies those are enforceable in nature in trans-border transactions giving them secure environment.

Data privacy of customer during secure transactions when transferred across different border within and outside India must be securely protected maintaining the privacy laws of domestic law and international law while considering the host and recipient. In such cases, bank have to ensure that data privacy of customers should be securely making adequate technology safety, regulatory bodies, transborder transfer security and placing secure data transfer mechanism in cross-border. India has been signatories to many bilateral and multilateral agreements with specific countries which facilitate cooperation and also exchange financial information when engaged in cross-border in case of online-banking but sometimes implication of such agreements face bite compliance issues and ensuring any obligations could be made more workable arising from such agreements.

6. CONCLUSION

The convergence of electronic transactions, blockchain, the dark web, and KYC poses complex challenges for secure transaction laws. This research paper underscores the need for dynamic, adaptable legal frameworks that can harness the benefits of emerging technologies while effectively mitigating risks. Technological advancement in globalized world brought the world together that had also led to complexity in legal implementation of rules and due to growing interconnections across the world through virtual world had brought major changes in the society it also brought some risk like in case of online or net banking the cyber security risk for secure transaction and these risks of cyber threats needs to be curbed through national and international efforts. Collaborative efforts are required at various levels at national and internationally bodies to place a capacity building initiative on priority basis that threats economies at both levels that affects customer, entities and countries economy.

REFERENCES

Reserve Bank of India. (n.d.). *Annex-II Internet Banking: Security Features*. Reserve Bank of India. https://www.rbi.org.in/hindi1/Upload/content/PDFs/C229260416_2.pdf

Reserve Bank of India. (n.d.). *Cyber Security for a safer Financial System Reserve*. Bank of India. https://rbi.org.in/scripts/BS_ViewBulletin.aspx?Id=21858

Reserve Bank of India. (n.d.). *Internet And Mobile Association of India vs Reserve Bank of India*. Reserve Bank of India.

Irfan, M. (2018). The Impact of AI Innovation on Financial Sectors in the Era of Industry 5.0 (pp. 96-107). IGI Global. doi:10.4018/979-8-3693-0082-4.ch006

Irfan, M., Elhoseny, M., Kassim, S., & Metawa, N. (2023). *Advanced Machine Learning Algorithms for Complex Financial Applications*. https://www.scopus.com/inward/record.uri?eid=2-s2.0-85147390132&doi=10.4018%2f978-1-6684-4483-2&partnerID=40&md5=, doi:10.4018/978-1-6684-4483-2

Pardhey, N., & Issa, Y. H. (2023). *P. C., L.* Regulatory Mechanism of Cryptocurrency Blockchain in Banking, Financial, and Capital Markets in the Indian Panorama.

Reserve bank of India - Building Blocks for a Sustainable Future: Some Reflections. (n.d.). https://rbi.org.in/scripts/BS_SpeechesView.aspx?Id=1379

Reserve bank of India. (n.d.). *Cyber Security for a safer Financial System*. RBI. https://rbi.org.in/scripts/BS_SpeechesView.aspx?Id=1367

Reserve bank of India - Macrofinancial Risks Reports. (n.d.). https://rbi.org.in/scripts/PublicationReportDetails.aspx?ID=1237

Reserve bank of India. (n.d.). Master directions - Information Technology Framework for the NBFC Sector. RBI. https://www.rbi.org.in/scripts/BS_ViewMasDirections.aspx?id=10999

Reserve bank of India (n.d.). RBI bulletin Statement on Developmental and Regulatory Policies. RBI. https://rbi.org.in/scripts/BS_ViewBulletin.aspx?Id=21988

Chapter 12
Islamic Finance:
A Mechanism to Consummate Sustainable Development

Manali Agrawal
NSB Academy, India

Prateek Kumar Bansal
GLA University, India

Ankit Saxena
GLA University, India

Haidar Abbas
University of Technology and Applied Sciences, Salalah, Oman

ABSTRACT

Islamic Finance is one of the legitimate fields of investment these days. A mechanism which adopts ethical practices and sustainable growth altogether is what Islamic Finance is. The last several years have seen a notable rise in the Islamic finance sector due to growing consumer interest in ethical banking and financial services. Experts in this field claim that as the market grows, the industry is making an effort to incorporate ESG factors into future planning and projections. In an attempt to create a more equitable and sustainable future, non-financial principles known as environmental, social, and governance, or ESG, are being progressively integrated into financial operations.

1. INTRODUCTION

The fundamental idea of the Islamic financial system is equilibrium. This idea emphasizes that this system's main goal ought to be to contribute to society. Moreover, the concept suggests that humans are merely trustees and that Allah is the true owner of all riches. In order to promote justice and take care of this wealth, humans must follow Allah's instructions. Furthermore, Muslims are said to be free to enjoy

DOI: 10.4018/979-8-3693-1038-0.ch012

their money according to Islamic economics. They must use it in accordance with Sharia law. Islamic economics is based on the idea of a free market, in which the market is driven by supply and demand rather than by the government. It does, however, influence how the market operates by enforcing certain guidelines and morals. Social justice or balance is ensured in part by these laws and ethics. To remain committed to its objectives Islamic Finance, follow certain principles:

Islam considers that interest payments are unfair to borrowers and instead benefit lenders. It so forbids interest from being charged and paid by lenders and borrowers. Alcohol and pork are forbidden in Islam. Islam forbids investment in these kinds of ventures. Additionally, Islamic financial institutions abstain from any forms of gambling and speculation that rely on unpredictable future events. Islam forbids engaging in certain practices, such as short selling and derivative contracts, that involve excessive risk and uncertainty. One party cannot profit from a deal more than the other under Islamic economics. It denotes a shared profit, loss, or risk between the participants to a transaction. The main tools for the investments in case of Islam are Equities, Fixed Income instruments and Insurance as these involves less risks.

Undoubtedly it is interesting to know that if the banks are not charging any interest from their clients than how is the survival possible. It is done through purchase of different class of assets by making use of deposits money. After that, these assets are frequently given for lease or resold for more than the original market value. Moreover, the fundamental idea is that these banks purchase the assets with the money of their clients rather than making money on interest. Banks than purchase various types of investment assets on behalf of their clients as opposed to making loans. The same client is then leased it by them. However, the bank is the rightful owner and the consumer becomes the owner of the property when the lease expires. Over the past ten years, the Islamic finance sector has grown remarkably, and many optimistic projections have been made about its huge potential for future expansion. Financial institutions must make complicated judgments about investments, macroeconomic analysis, and credit evaluation as Industry 5.0 develops(Irfan, Elmogy, et al., 1 C.E.). AI technology's integration into Islamic banking offers important potential as well as challenges that must be overcome. These challenges include following Islamic law, moral considerations, risk reduction, and the potential for decision-making bias(Kismawadi et al., 2023).

2. LITERATURE REVIEW

A large number of studies have been conducted in the field of Islamic finance. There are few studies which have been conducted in alignment with sustainable investment opportunities.

As per a study Islamic finance is by definition required to endogenize ESG concerns in its supply of Islamic financial services, guided by the ethical principles of Islam. In contrast to the SRI industry, whose values are primarily socially determined and drawn from ideas like humanism, socialism, secularism, or environmentalism, ESG concerns under the Islamic finance paradigm are derived from Islamic principles that are rooted in Sharīfah (Islamic law)(Sairally, 2015).

Depending on how much stakeholders can shape the Islamic finance sector's future, it will play a part in advancing the SDGs. The household sector has dominated the industry's demand, with other sectors expressing varied degrees of interest, including companies, governments, and institutional investors. However, supply-side forces and concerns have pushed the market(Ahmed et al., 2015).

One such study on "Islamic finance development and banking ESG scores: Evidence from a cross-country analysis" concludes that there is social relativity between IFDI and ESG. Despite the fact that sustainability gains are not linear, this research supports the widely accepted relationship between Islamic finance and social responsibility(Paltrinieri et al., 2020).

Another author concludes that although ESG is a novel idea, there are a number of obstacles and difficulties in integrating it into financial institutions. In terms of ESG, several Islamic banks are ahead of the curve because they started promoting sustainability through financing and programs years ago. Though there are still a lot of obstacles to overcome before Islamic finance and ESG can work together to their full potential, this combination has the potential to have positive effects in the future(Al Ansari & Alanzarouti, 2020).

As per a study Islamic banking system is based on notions of social virtue, good governance, care for the environment and ethical behavior of individuals and organizations by Islamic ontological and epistemological principles. The rules of Islamic finance guide the Islamic banking and financial system and are known as Shariah principles, or Masjid al-Shariah(Brescia et al., 2021).

Using Islamic finance tools is one workable sustainable financing option for the global eradication of social and environmental problems such social inequality, poverty, corruption, biodiversity loss, environmental degradation, and climate change(Ma'ruf et al., 2021).

Results of a study indicate that Islamic businesses perform better in terms of the environment and society. To perform robustness tests, the sample is divided according to the size of the firm and the duration of the study. The findings indicate that, when it comes to social and environmental performance, Islamic businesses outperform their non-Islamic counterparts, but not when it comes to governance(Qoyum et al., 2022).

After separating IB behavior using more or less MS in earlier theoretical investigations, this study produced an advanced empirical model. This study used Instrumental Variable (IV) analysis and causal inference to separate this impact. The findings verify that implementing IB in various MS with comparable rising levels of competition results in varying financing growth. Compared to IBs without MS, those with MS have more funding. These findings support the idea that financing expansion and enhancing competition require consideration of sustainability(*Sustainability | Free Full-Text | The Effect of Applying Sustainability (Maqasid Shariah) and Competition on Islamic Bank Financing*, n.d.).

A study is conducted to argue the fact that Islamic banks do not invest enough in ESG-friendly projects. To comprehend the regulatory framework governing ESG activities, a brief discussion of the classification of ESG components and an examination of important frameworks and recommendations are presented. In order to ensure that Islamic banks stay relevant and competitive with conventional banks, the essay ends with a recommendation for the necessary steps that may be taken to improve ESG standards in Islamic banks(Abdullah & Haron, 2022).

One such analysis indicates a recent increase in scholarly papers in the field, but it also shows that there aren't many financial sustainability initiatives taking place globally. Three major themes were investigated, including—sustainable financial products, sustainable financial services delivery, and sustainable financial services marketing strategies(Tuyon et al., 2022). The main barrier to FinTech development in Islamic finance is the absence of regulatory frameworks and poor levels of financial knowledge(Alshater et al., 2022).

One of the study findings suggests because the ESG framework is complex and tailored to various industries, making it challenging to identify ESG risks and impacts, the adoption of ESG in the Islamic banking sector is still low. It is anticipated that the relationship between ESG and Shari'ah screening will enhance risk-adjusted performance in Islamic banks' financing and investing activities(Muhamad et al., 2022). Research findings of a study offers fresh perspectives on diversification and hedging tactics using Islamic finance to global investors and regulators in the midst of a catastrophic global economic crisis. We offer some policy suggestions for building a stronger financial system after COVID-19(Hasan et al., 2022).

ISF instruments at national and international level have the ability to spur national and international initiatives to create more cohesive and convergent strategies for allocating these resources to meet the needs of refugees(Tok et al., 2022).

Progressive companies have long-standing notions of environmental and business sustainability in their business language. Nevertheless, businesses have not yet investigated how environmental management practices (EMPs) affect financial performance (FP) and environmental performance (EP) by establishing the necessary connection between environmental, social, and governance disclosure (ESGD) (Ali et al., 2022).

According to findings of a research, businesses' performance and sustainability can be enhanced by ESG disclosures of their environmental, economic, and social sustainability performance. Businesses with a religious focus performed better in the socio environment, but not in governance. While dual-gender boards have a detrimental effect on ESG disclosure, autonomous governing boards have a beneficial effect. During the COVID-19 pandemic, significant diversification potential in ESG investments was noted(Ahmad et al., 2023).

Globally, ESG usage is growing, demonstrating its usefulness in evaluating corporate performance. There is proof that ESG disclosure in the business sector—environment, social sustainability, and economic performance—can improve a company's performance and sustainability(Ahmad et al., 2023). The author employs Al-Ghazali's Framework of Maqashid Al-Shariah and the SDGs from the UN to group findings into their relationship to Islamic law, then applies thematic analysis to synthesize the data. The research findings are then explained using a narrative method. Based on research findings, Islamic finance is the most significant contributor to the SDGs that benefit humanity. Furthermore, it is critical to understand that improving Islamic finance is crucial for achieving the SDGs and that the backing of the government, regulators, and associated organizations is required(Harahap et al., 2023). Today's scenario makes financial services more approachable for a retail investor by making use of artificial intelligence and machine learning(Irfan, Elhoseny, et al., 1 C.E.). AI gives insurers new resources to boost output, save expenses, and improve client satisfaction(Pal et al., 2023).

3. RESEARCH METHODOLOGY

The paper is based on a systematic review of the Islamic Finance. The keywords such as ESG and sustainable finance were used, and papers from the Scopus database have been analyzed concerning the current context. The review enhances the conceptual understanding of the researchers in the field. It makes a seminal contribution based on the ethical approach explaining how financial attitude can be well-formed on ethical attitude. Islamic finance in convergence with Environmental, Social and Governance concepts leads to sustainable growth.

3.1 Islamic Finance and ESG

The phrase "ESG" describes a company's entire effect on the environment, society, and the robustness and transparency of its corporate governance, incorporating issues like shareholder rights, audits, in-

Figure 1. Islamic finance
(Author's estimated)

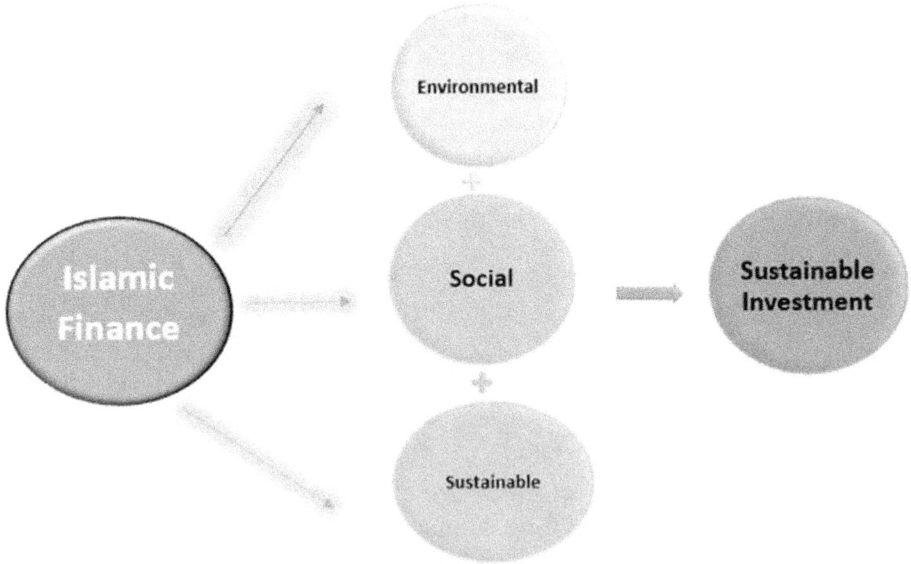

ternal controls, executive compensation, and company leadership. The company's efforts to reduce its environmental impact—such as resource depletion, greenhouse gas emissions, and deforestation—are the focus of its environmental considerations. Moreover, the social component of a business is how it impacts the workplace culture as well as the broader society. It focuses majorly on working circumstances, which include child labor and slavery, as well as health and safety of the employees working. However, the processes for decision-making, reporting, overseeing an organization's daily operations including matters pertaining to donations, political lobbying, corruption, and bribery are collectively referred to as governance. In an analogous way, Islamic finance, which is driven by the tenets of Shariah, is expanding quickly. The term "Islamic finance" describes financial services, like banking and investing, where capital is raised and allocated in accordance with Shari'ah. Interests (riba), gambling (maysir), uncertainty (gharar), and industries that are forbidden (such as alcohol and pornography) are all forbidden. Henceforth, it provides insights that closely correspond with the goals of ESG. ESG principles and objectives of Islamic finance align with each other. One area where Islamic finance and ESG coincide is that they both support financial stability and economic growth in addition to environmental preservation and the eradication of poverty. Islamic finance prioritizes financial investments in practical initiatives with significant social impacts. This emphasis is in sync with the ESG concept, which advocates for funding companies and projects that address social issues, create long-term value, and enhance community well-being overall.

Similar to ESG, Islamic Finance has prerequisites for banning specific industries, reflecting the values of customers and beneficiaries in portfolios, and aiming to prevent damages to the environment or to people in addition to fostering a society that is equitable and sustainable.

The screenings might be stringent; for example, they could forbid the use of firearms, porn, and cluster bombs. In cases where the screening is relative, the regulations may, for example, prohibit companies whose tobacco sales make up at least 10% of their overall income or companies which are against human

Figure 2. Screening of industries for Islamic finance

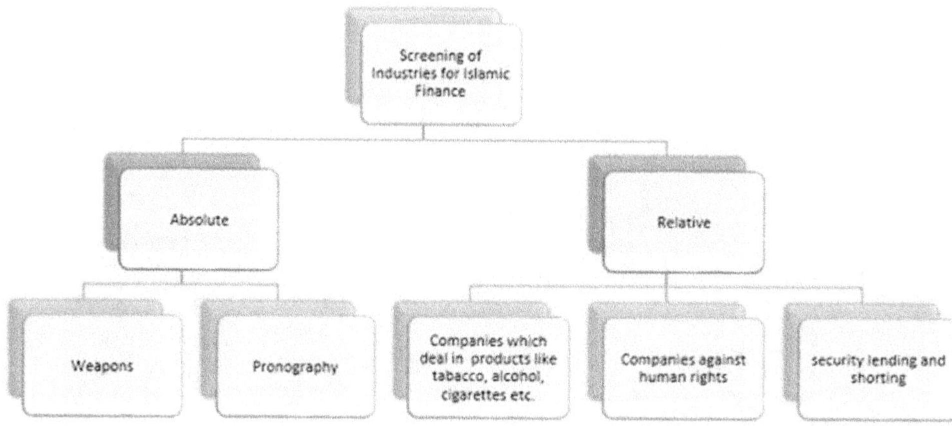

rights. Furthermore, under Islamic finance, investments in conventional financial services, cigarettes, alcohol, pork, pornography, firearms, gambling, human smuggling, and other commodities and activities that are deemed illegal are prohibited. Hence such companies or corporate houses can be debarred. Social responsibility is important to this economic framework and is a prerequisite that must be present in all of the operations that the financial institutions engage in(Franzoni & Ait Allali, 2018). Islamic finance prioritizes investments in practical initiatives with significant social impacts and actual assets. This focus is in line with the ESG concept, which advocates for funding companies and projects that address social issues, create long-term value, and enhance community well-being overall.

4. CONCLUSION

Overall, the convergence of Islamic finance with ESG presents an opportunity to strengthen the impact of ethical and responsible investing. It permits Islamic investors and financial organizations to adhere to their basic principles and beliefs while incorporating ESG considerations and promoting sustainable development. This convergence contributes to the creation of a more just and sustainable global financial system, promotes the growth of ethical finance, and expands the application of sustainable investment strategies. Islamic loans and syndications are being used for more environmental and socially conscious initiatives. Furthermore, with the rapid adoption of ESG and green Sukuk, it is clear that players in the Islamic finance industry, both from the public and private sectors, are becoming increasingly interested in sustainability. This is evident in the activities that range from regulatory developments to the introduction of additional ESG funds.

REFERENCES

Abdullah, N. A. I. N., & Haron, R. (2022). ESG REPORTING PRACTICES AMONG ISLAMIC BANKS: A GLOBAL PERSPECTIVE. *IIUM Law Journal*, *30*(S2), S2. doi:10.31436/iiumlj.v30iS2.755

Ahmad, H., Yaqub, M., & Lee, S. H. (2023). Environmental-, social-, and governance-related factors for business investment and sustainability: A scientometric review of global trends. *Environment, Development and Sustainability*. doi:10.100710668-023-02921-x PMID:36714213

Ahmed, H., Mohieldin, M., Verbeek, J., & Aboulmagd, F. (2015). *On the Sustainable Development Goals and the Role of Islamic Finance*. The World Bank. doi:10.1596/1813-9450-7266

Al Ansari, R. , & Alanzarouti, F. (2020). ESG and Islamic Finance: An Ethical Bridge Built on Shared Values. *Journal of Islamic Financial Studies*, *06*(1), 05–11. doi:10.12785/jifs/060101

Ali, Q., Salman, A., & Parveen, S. (2022). Evaluating the effects of environmental management practices on environmental and financial performance of firms in Malaysia: The mediating role of ESG disclosure. *Heliyon*, *8*(12), e12486. doi:10.1016/j.heliyon.2022.e12486 PMID:36590548

Alshater, M. M., Saba, I., Supriani, I., & Rabbani, M. R. (2022). Fintech in islamic finance literature: A review. *Heliyon*, *8*(9), e10385. doi:10.1016/j.heliyon.2022.e10385 PMID:36060472

BresciaV.Sa'adA.HassanR.AlhabshiS.LanzalongaF. (2021). *Exploring sustainability from the Islamic finance perspective*. https://doi.org/ doi:10.13135/2421-2172/6107-Published

Franzoni, S., & Ait Allali, A. (2018). Principles of Islamic Finance and Principles of Corporate Social Responsibility: What Convergence? *Sustainability (Basel)*, *10*(3), 3. doi:10.3390u10030637

Harahap, B., Risfandy, T., & Futri, I. N. (2023). Islamic Law, Islamic Finance, and Sustainable Development Goals: A Systematic Literature Review. *Sustainability (Basel)*, *15*(8), 8. doi:10.3390u15086626

Hasan, M., Rashid, M. M., Shafiullah, M., & Sarker, T. (2022). How resilient are Islamic financial markets during the COVID-19 pandemic? *Pacific-Basin Finance Journal*, *74*, 101817. doi:10.1016/j.pacfin.2022.101817

Irfan, M., Elhoseny, M., Kassim, S., & Metawa, N. (2022). *Advanced Machine Learning Algorithms for Complex Financial Applications*. IGI Global. https://www.igi-global.com/book/advanced-machine-learning-algorithms-complex/www.igi-global.com/book/advanced-machine-learning-algorithms-complex/290048

Irfan, M., & Elmogy, M. (2023). *The Impact of AI Innovation on Financial Sectors in the Era of Industry 5.0*. IGI Global. Https://services.igi-global.com/resolvedoi/resolve.aspx?doi=10.4018/979-8-3693-0082-4

Kismawadi, E. R., Irfan, M., & Shah, S. M. A. R. (2023). Revolutionizing Islamic Finance: Artificial Intelligence's Role in the Future of Industry. In The Impact of AI Innovation on Financial Sectors in the Era of Industry 5.0 (pp. 184–207). IGI Global. doi:10.4018/979-8-3693-0082-4.ch011

Ma'ruf, A., Mahomed, Z., & Mohamad, S. (2021). Sustainable Finance and a Sharī' Analysis of Environmental, Social and Governance (ESG) Criteria. In M. K. Hassan, M. Saraç, & A. Khan (Eds.), *Islamic Finance and Sustainable Development: A Sustainable Economic Framework for Muslim and Non-Muslim Countries* (pp. 193–217). Springer International Publishing. doi:10.1007/978-3-030-76016-8_9

Muhamad, S. F., Zain, F. A. M., Samad, N. S. A., Ab. Rahman, A. H., & Yasoa', M. R. (2022). Measuring Sustainable Performance of Islamic Banks: Integrating the principles of Environmental, Social and Governance (ESG) and Maqasid Shari'ah. *IOP Conference Series. Earth and Environmental Science, 1102*(1), 012080. doi:10.1088/1755-1315/1102/1/012080

Pal, T., Irfan, M., & Kassim, S. B. (2023). How Do Machine Learning (ML) Techniques Benefit the Insurance Industry?: An Exploratory Study. In The Impact of AI Innovation on Financial Sectors in the Era of Industry 5.0 (pp. 108–130). IGI Global. doi:10.4018/979-8-3693-0082-4.ch007

Paltrinieri, A., Dreassi, A., Migliavacca, M., & Piserà, S. (2020). Islamic finance development and banking ESG scores: Evidence from a cross-country analysis. *Research in International Business and Finance, 51*, 101100. doi:10.1016/j.ribaf.2019.101100

Qoyum, A., Sakti, M. R. P., Thaker, H. M. T., & AlHashfi, R. U. (2022). Does the islamic label indicate good environmental, social, and governance (ESG) performance? Evidence from sharia-compliant firms in Indonesia and Malaysia. *Borsa Istanbul Review, 22*(2), 306–320. doi:10.1016/j.bir.2021.06.001

Sairally, B. S. (2015). Integrating Environmental, Social and Governance (ESG) Factors in Islamic Finance: Towards the Realisation of Maqāṣid al-Sharīʿah. *ISRA International Journal of Islamic Finance, 7*(2), 145–154.

Tok, E., Yesuf, A. J., & Mohamed, A. (2022). Sustainable Development Goals and Islamic Social Finance: From Policy Divide to Policy Coherence and Convergence. *Sustainability (Basel), 14*(11), 11. doi:10.3390u14116875

Tuyon, J., Onyia, O. P., Ahmi, A., & Huang, C.-H. (2022). Sustainable financial services: Reflection and future perspectives. *Journal of Financial Services Marketing*, 1–27. doi:10.105741264-022-00187-4

Chapter 13
Monitoring of Islamic Finance Activity to Economic Growth:
An Indonesia Experience (2009-2023)

Sylva Alif Rusmita
University of Airlangga, Indonesia

Muhamad Said Fathurrohman
University of Airlangga, Indonesia

Eko Fajar Cahyono
University of Airlangga, Indonesia

Khairunnisa Abd Samad
Universiti Teknologi MARA, Malaysia

ABSTRACT

Increasing users of Sharia financial products can provide a stimulus for economic growth contribution in Indonesia. Considering that fact, this study aims to monitoring Islamic Finance activities on Economic Growth in the long and short term. Granger causality and VECM tests are appropriate analytical tools to determine the purpose study. The data from this research was taken from Indonesia financial service authority and Indonesia central bureau of statistics from 2009Q1 to 2023Q1. The results obtained show that the Islamic capital market influences economic growth, because investment can develop countries and at the end increase people's income. The implication research is that the government is expected to increase the stability of capital market conditions so that investors will generate capital gains from investment activities which in turn will increase economic growth. In addition, innovation and regulation are needed to increase the contributions of the Islamic banking and Islamic insurance sector to the Indonesian economic growth.

DOI: 10.4018/979-8-3693-1038-0.ch013

1. INTRODUCTION

Generally, a financial system is made up of two components: the bank-based component and the market-based component. If an economy is driven by financial intermediaries – such as banks and bank-like financial institutions – more than it is driven by financial markets – such as stock and bond markets – that economy's financial system is generally referred to as a bank based financial system. If securities markets share center stage with banks in driving economic growth via savings mobilization and allocation, corporate control, and risk management, that economy's financial system is generally referred to as a market-based financial system (Nyasha & Odhiambo, 2015). Furthermore, according to Ul Din et al. (2017), financial sector not only bank but also insurance (Islamic financial non-bank), based on his research non-life insurance has relationship with economic growth for developing countries whereas, in case of developed countries, the results are only significant when insurance density is used as a proxy for insurance. Moreover, the role of non-life insurance is more significant for developing countries as compared to developed countries. Islamic insurance is also a financial institution that plays a role in channeling funds to the public. The main activity carried out by Islamic insurance is to protect and help between a number of people from the risks to be faced. In addition, Islamic insurance also invests a collection of *Tabarru* 'funds and investment funds in non-usury instruments or in accordance with sharia (Lone, 2016:13).

According to the FSA in 2017 the market share of Islamic insurance is 4.94% with the growth in the number of assets each year. Data from the FSA shows if in 2018 Islamic insurance assets reached Rp41.96 trillions, with sharia life insurance as the biggest contributor. According to *oke finance* the sharia financial industry increased by 25% in February 2018 which increased Indonesia's position for a country with the potential for the development of the sharia industry in the world (Laucereno, 2017).

The Indonesian Islamic Banking SnapShoot in 2019 issued by the FSA (Financial Services Authority, 2019), Islamic banking has a positive growth based on asset development, disbursed funds and third party funds which are also in line with the positive main ratios. On the other hand, Activities undertaken by Islamic banking in general are raising funds from the community, channeling funds to the public and services. Islamic banking channel funds to the public in the form of financing and placement of other funds. This was done to prevent idle fund. From the distribution of funds, Islamic banking will get profits in accordance with the form of distribution of funds made (Lone, 2016:3).

Some previous research states that the activities of financial institutions have a role in supporting economic growth. As in research by Abduh (2012) which examines the relationship between Islamic banking and growth in Indonesia. In this study, Islamic banking are the whole of Islamic commercial banks, Islamic business units and Islamic people's finance banks, proxy for economic growth using GDP. The result of ARDL is found a significant positive relationship and correlation between Islamic bank financing with economic growth, this result also in line with Imam & Kpodar (2016). On the other side Nyasha and Odhiambo (2015) examines the impact of both bank- and market-based financial development on economic growth in South Africa during the period from 1980 to 2012. The empirical results of this study show that there is a positive relationship between bank-based financial development and economic growth but fail to find any relationship between market-based financial development and economic growth in South Africa

Separately, Ul Din (2017) examines the relationship between insurance and economic growth with *proxy* insurance activities are life insurance premiums and general insurance. The proxy of economic growth is GDP. This research also classifies Indonesia as a developing country, where the majority of people tend to choose general insurance. Similar research was conducted by Haiss (2008) which examines the relationship of insurance and economic growth. The variables used in this study are GDP, investment insurance, premiums from life and non-life insurance using panel data. This study in line with Chau et al. (2013), Oyodetun & Adesina (2015) and Webb et al. (2005) that states the positive impact of life insurance on economic growth in several countries.

Similar to previous research, Pradhan (2017) uses GDP as a proxy for economic growth, density and insurance penetration as a proxy for insurance activity. The Granger and VAR Causality Test results in that in the long run, developments in the banking and insurance industries have had a significant impact on the economic growth of the G-20 countries. In the short term, the interrelationships between the three factors prove more complex because they differ in each country at various stages of development.

Several previous studies have raised the relationship between financial institutions and economic growth. First, some research as conducted by Abduh (2012), Abduh and Chowdhury (2012), Kassim (2016) and Furqani (2009) discuss the relationship between Islamic banking and economic growth with financing proxies. The research focuses on finding out the relationship between Islamic banking and economic growth only.

Second, other research only focuses on the relationship between insurance and economic growth, as was done by Ward and Zurbruegg (2000) and Ul Din (2017). Both studies involve several countries to be studied, but only use conventional insurance companies. Third, research Yıldırım et al. (2020) and Smaoui and Nechi (2017) mention Sukuk had a positive effect on growth in the long run and short-term relationships, it was seen that sukuk variables did not have an effect on growth

Forth, G. Liu (2014), Pradhan (2017) and Adams (2009) combining the three, which is looking for a relationship between banking, insurance and economic growth. The study uses conventional insurance companies and does not make Indonesia as a researched country.

Although a number of studies have been conducted on the causal relationship between financial development and economic growth in many developing countries, the majority of these studies have used only bank development as a proxy for financial development or bank with insurance, or capital market. Some of them using insurance only. Specific studies addressing the dynamic causal relationship between banks based financial development, stock market development, insurance and economic growth are very scant. This study adopts some important parts of previous research by changing and adjusting some things. Unlike previous research, this study focuses on Islamic banks, Islamic insurance companies and also Islamic capital market in Indonesia. This study combines two Islamic financial institutions in Indonesia and two product Islamic capital market (share and sukuk) to prove whether the two Islamic financial intermediaries play a role in supporting economic growth or vice versa.

Islamic financial institutions are thought to have an important role in economic growth in Indonesia, looking at the positive growth. The increased market share of Islamic financial institutions (banks and insurance) and Islamic capital market indicates that Islamic financial play a role in economic growth in Indonesia. Based on this statement and several previous studies, this study chooses Islamic bank financing variables (financing and deposit, both Islamic Commercial Bank and Islamic Business Unit) as a proxy for Islamic banking activities, Contributions and density as Islamic insurance proxy, Sukuk outstanding and trading volume activity of share as Islamic capital market and GDP as proxy for economic growth.

This research contributes to empirical testing of existing theories relating to the existence of an influential relationship between bank and Islamic capital market and economic growth in Indonesia with updates data from 2009Q1 until 2023Q1. This research will provide insight to the public on the role of financial institutions in economic growth and vice versa in Indonesia; describe how financial institutions and Islamic capital market institution influence to economic growth or influence each other. This research meaningful and important for Indonesia because Islamic financial institutions in Indonesia have been in establish for more than ten years. With this basis, this research is titled Islamic Finance instrument and Economic Growth: Evidence from Indonesia.

This paper consists of six sections. Section I discusses the introduction, in which the background and rationale of the study is outlined. Section II covers the review of literature, of the relationship between financial development and economic growth. Section III covers the detail of the data and research methodology employed in this study. Section IV reports the findings and discussion. Section V outlines the conclusion and last but not least, Section VI suggests directions for future research.

2. LITERATURE REVIEW

2.1 Nexus of Banking, Insurance, and Capital Market on Economics Growth

The main activities of Islamic banking in general are raising funds from the public, channeling funds into society and services. Islamic banking raise funds from the community by offering several funding products such as *wadiah* current account, savings with a *wadiah* and *mudharabah* contract, *mudharabah* deposits, and other products that are in accordance with sharia (Lone, 2016:10-12).

Basically, the main activities of Islamic banking are those things. There is a difference between Islamic commercial banks, Islamic business units and Islamic people's finance banks. Just like Islamic commercial banks, Islamic business units also have the exact same activities. It is just that the Islamic business unit is a sharia-based conventional bank business unit. So IBU usually does not have its own deed of establishment. Whereas Islamic people's finance banks do not participate in payment or transaction traffic in demand deposits (Lone, 2016:4-6).

The concept of Islamic insurance is different from the concept of conventional insurance. With these different concepts, of course there are differences in operational activities carried out by both. The difference between Islamic and conventional insurance is how risks are managed and borne and also how insurance funds are managed. The next difference is the relationship between operators and participants. There are two types of Islamic insurance, namely Islamic life insurance and Islamic general insurance. The difference lies in the object that is borne. In Islamic life insurance, the object is human, while in Islamic general insurance the object is property.

Kassim (2016) Islamic finance has started to make important contributions to the real economy by effectively carrying out the financial intermediation role of pooling and channeling funds to the investment activities. Other study is G. Liu (2014). This research examines bank financing, life insurance premiums and non life insurance premiums on economic growth in developing and developed countries. Using the VAR method, the test results show that life insurance has an effect on economic growth in Japan and France. In addition, the study found a causal relationship between non-life insurance and bank credit in certain countries.

Adams (2009) finds out the relationship between financial institutions, banks and insurance on economic growth by using the GDP variable as a proxy for economic growth, bank credit as a proxy for banking activity and total annual premium (life and non-life) as a proxy for insurance activities. Integration, Granger and VAR stated that insurance granger-caused economic growth and bank loans in

Sweden, this research also in line with Hassan et al. (2011), Tabash, (2014), and Adu et al. (2013) whose explained financial development can affect economic growth in several counties.

Economic growth is an increase in GDP, regardless of whether the increase is greater or less than population growth and also changes in economic structure (Todaro & Smith, 2012:110). GDP measures the market value of the final product or service produced in a country in a certain period (Dornbusch et al., 2004). GDP is the total national income and total expenditure on goods and services for a certain period (Todaro & Smith, 2012:44). According to Mankiw (2006) a gross domestic product (GDP) shows the overall value of expenditure in the economic production of goods and services. There are several methods that can be used to calculate GDP, end-to-end methods and simple regression (Greenlaw & Shapiro, 2011: 135-143). According to Lone (2016:7-8) Islamic insurance is a risk management system that complies with Islamic regulations and practices of providing mutual support to participants and operators. Islamic insurance implements Sharia principles, provisions originating from the Qur'an and Sunnah.

According to Adjasi & Biekpe (2006), Enisan & Olufisayo (2009), Nurudeen (2009), and Zhu et al. (2004) stock markets may affect economic activity through the creation of liquidity. Levine (1996) mention liquid equity markets make investment less risky and more attractive because the investor (both corporate and individual) allow savers to acquire an asset. Equity asset more tradable, easily, quickly and cheaply if the investor inadequate liquidity or want to alter their portfolios. At the same time, companies enjoy permanent access to capital raised through equity issues. By facilitating longer-term, more profitable investments, liquid markets improve the allocation of capital and enhance prospects for long-term economic growth. Further, by making investment less risky and more profitable, stock market liquidity can also lead to more investment. According to this view, enhanced stock market liquidity may actually hurt economic growth.

There other tools in capital market is sukuk, or Islamic bond. The nexus of bond and economic growth was no doubt. Smaoui and Nechi (2017) mention that sukuk market development is conducive to economic growth, with a strong and robust evidence. They also mention the development of sukuk markets have promoted financial inclusion which colud stimulated investment and economic growth. Echchabi et al. (2016) mention sukuk issuance had an influence on the GDP and GCF only when all the countries were pulled together.

Previous research has focused on the effect of bank financing on economic growth, or sukuk di economic growth. Furthermore, some research focuses on the relationship between economic growth and insurance. All of previous study never analysis the spur effect of Islamic financial isntitution and islamic capital market to GDP together. So, with the new idea with combine all of financial instrument this paper become unique and important to represent the effect of Islamic to Economic Growth for several 12 years from 2009Q1 to 2023Q1.

3. HYPOTHESIS DEVELOPMENT

3.1 Islamic Insurance Activities and Economic Growth

Islamic insurance activity is predicted to affect economic growth using a GDP proxy. This is in accordance with research by Ul Din (2017) and Ward and Zurbruegg (2000) which states that insurance activities affect economic growth. Ul Din (2017) also states that GDP and insurance premiums, respectively, have a correlation and insurance leads to economic growth. The other studies conclude that economic growth and insurance premiums have bi-directional causalities in both the short and long run Lee et al. (2013), for the case of 41 countries in the period 1979–2007 and Nizar (2016) for the case of Indonesia in the period 1984–2014. Based on these studies the hypotheses obtained are as follows:

$H0_1$: Islamic insurance density and economic growth does not influence each other.
$H0_2$: Islamic insurance contribution and economic growth does not influence each other

3.2 Islamic Banking Activities and Economic Growth

Islamic Banking activity is predicted to affect economic growth. This is in accordance with research of Abduh (2012), Abduh and Chowdhury (2012), Kassim (2016), and Furqani (2009) which states that Islamic finance has a significant positive effect and correlates with economic growth, both in the long term and short term. Adams, Mike (2009), in the results of his research stated that bank loans encourage economic growth. Based on these studies the hypotheses obtained are as follows:

$H0_3$: Islamic Banking Deposit and economic growth does not influence each other.
$H0_4$: Islamic Banking Financing and economic growth does not influence each other.

3.3 Islamic Capital Market Activities and Economic Growth

According to Sari et al. (2018) Islamic capital market in the long-term there is a significant positive influence on economic growth. Contribution of sukuk, Islamic share proxies of Islamic capital market. Muharam et al. (2019) mention there is a bi-directional causality between the development of the Islamic stock market and sukuk market with economic growth in Indonesia. So, based on this research, the hypothesis obtained is as follows:

$H0_5$: Trading volume activity and economic growth does not influence each other
$H0_6$: Sukuk Governance outstanding and economic growth does not influence each other

4. RESEARCH METHODOLOGY

This research is a descriptive quantitative research. According to Gujarati and Porter (2009:1) the quantitative approach emphasizes the existence of variables as research objects and these variables must be defined in their respective operational form. It also requires a hypothesis and also testing before proceeding to the next step.

The population used in this study is Islamic banking (Islamic Commercial Bank, Islamic Business Unit and Islamic People's Finance Bank), Islamic Insurance (life and general) and Gross Domestic Product (GDP) in Indonesia. The sample used in this study is a saturated sample, where all data from Islamic insurance companies and Islamic Banking in 2009 to the first quarter of 2023 recorded in the FSA and GDP data in 2009 to the first quarter of 2023, were used as samples.

Sources of data used are Islamic Banking Statistics and Sharia Non-Bank Financial Industry Statistics which have been provided on the FSA official website, www.ojk.go.id. GDP data is obtained from the official website www.bps.go.id. The data taken is quarterly data from 2009-first quarter 2023.

4.1 Analysis Techniques

4.1.1 Stationarity Test

Most time series data are non-stationary or have unit roots, so the data is fluctuating or inconsistent. Data that fluctuate in value will not be around the average so it will be more difficult to estimate a model (Gujarati & Porter, 2009:737). This study uses the Phillips Perron method in unit root testing.

The Phillips Perron (PP) method is the development of the Augmented Dickey-Fuller (ADF) method. PP suggests a nonparametric method to control higher order serial correlations in a series, while also explaining the existence of autocorrelation between residuals without entering the independent variable in the lag of differentiation (Gujarati & Porter, 2009:758).

$$Yt = \rho Yt{-}1 + ut \quad -1 \leq \rho \leq 1 \tag{1}$$

Where:

Yt = series which is stationary at time t
ρ = constant
Yt-1 = proportion of the value of the series at the specified time
ut = residual value at time t

4.1.2 Optimum Lag Selection

VECM estimation is very dependent on the choice of lag length. If the lag used in the regression is too low, no white noise process will be generated so the model cannot estimate the actual error correctly (Harris, 1995: 65). As a result, γ and the standard error cannot be estimated properly. However, if you enter too much lag, it will reduce the ability to reject H_0 because too many additional parameters will reduce the degree of free.

Determination of the number of lags or orders can be determined by using the Akaike Information Criterion (AIC), Schwarz Information Criterion (SIC), and Hannan Quinnon (HQ) criteria. The asterisk contained in the results shows the optimal lag. The lag that has the lowest AIC, SIC and HQ values is the lag used.

$$\text{Akaike Information Criterion} = -2\frac{1}{T} + 2(k+T) \tag{2}$$

$$\text{Schwarz Information Criterion} = -2\frac{1}{T}k\log\left(\frac{\log(T)}{T}\right) \tag{3}$$

$$\text{Hannan-Quinn(HQ)}= -2\frac{1}{T}+2k\log\left(\frac{\log(T)}{T}\right) \quad (4)$$

Where:

1 = number of observations
K = estimated amount

4.1.3 Johanson Cointegration

As stated by Engle-Granger, the existence of non-stationary variables causes the possibility of a long-term relationship between variables in the system. Cointegration test is conducted to determine the existence of relationships between variables, especially in the long run. If there is cointegration of the variables used in the model, it can be ensured that there is a long-term relationship between the variables. The method that can be used in testing the existence of this cointegration is the Johansen Cointegration method.

4.1.4 Granger Causality Test

Granger Causality Test is used to determine whether endogenous variables can be used as exogenous variables. Granger causality test will illustrate whether the variable x affects the variable y and vice versa, the variable y can affect the variable x. According to Gujarati (2006: 214) in general the Granger Causality equation can be interpreted as follows:

1. *Unindirectional causality* from the dependent variable to the independent variable. This happens when the lag coefficient of the dependent variable deviates statistically from zero while the lag coefficient of all independent variables is equal to zero.
2. *Feedback/ bilateral causality* when the delay coefficient of all variables, both dependent and independent variables, statistically deviates significantly from zero.
3. *Independence* if the lag coefficient all the dependent and independent variables do not deviate statistically from zero.

In this study the Granger Causality Test was used to find the relationship between IBF, GDP, and IIC variables.

4.1.5 VECM

VECM is an econometric analysis model that can be used to determine the short-term behavior of a variable against the long-term due to permanent shock (Kostov, 2000). Hill et al. (2011:501) explained that VECM analysis can also be used to find solutions for non-stationary time series and non-stationary regression or spurious correlation in econometric analysis. The relationship between variables x and y can be known by comparing t-statistics with t-tables.

$$\Delta Y_t = \sum_{j-1}^{k-1} \Gamma_j \Delta Y_{t-j} + \alpha\beta Y_{t-k} + \eta + \varepsilon_t \quad (5)$$

4.2 Result

Based on the industrial sector, Islamic banking has channeled 56.46% of the total financing in the business sector. The second largest portion of funding was channeled to the non-business sector (households), amounting to 41.73%. Distribution of financing to the business sector is dominated by the construction sector, manufacturing industry and financial intermediaries. Meanwhile, the distribution of financing to the household sector is dominated by residential ownership and ownership of household appliances (including multipurpose).

Until the end of 2018, the overall assets of the Sharia IKNB will reach Rp97.12 trillion. 43.21% of Sharia IKNB assets or Rp.41.96 trillion are Islamic Insurance company assets (contributed by 35.50% of Islamic Life Insurance company assets, 5.79% of Islamic General Insurance company assets, and 1.92% of Islamic Reinsurance company assets). Islamic insurance began to develop rapidly since it was first established in Indonesia. Judging from these data, it can be said that Islamic insurance is the most prominent Islamic non-bank financial institution in Indonesia.

Indonesia's GDP per capita is increasing. In 2018, CBS recorded Indonesia's GDP per capita reaching Rp56 million, an increase of 7.93% from 2017. GDP is an indicator of a country's economic growth, because GDP includes the production of goods and services in that country. Rising GDP values indicate if the economy of a country is in good condition.

The results above illustrate that, when compared to Islamic banking, Islamic insurance is still less attractive to people in Indonesia. The lack of interest from the community due to lack of information and the public's not openness on the importance of insurance. Judging from the high amount of financing, Indonesians tend to prefer to use their money for consumption. On the other hand economic growth is also not very good, when viewed from the average amount of economic growth which is only half of its highest value.

5. RESULTS OF ESTIMATION AND PROOF OF HYPOTHESES

5.1 Stationarity Test

The first step taken was the stationarity test conducted on each variable. A data can be said to be stationary if the average value and its variance in sharing different lag values are constant (Gujarati, 2006). In this study to be able to determine the stationary variable is done by the Phillips Perron test.

The first step in stationary testing is testing data at the level. The data is declared stationary if the probability value is> 0.05. There are two variable that declared stationary at level that is, GDP which is a proxy for economic variable and VOL as a proxy for stock market trading activity, while the other variables are not stationary. There are variables that are not stationary at level, then all variables are tested again at the degree of first difference. Stationary data at the first difference degree is an important condition so that the data can be tested with VECM.

At first difference all stationary variables are with an indication of a probability value of less than 0.05. From the above data it can be concluded that all stationary variables at the first difference level of the Phillips Perron test with an indication of the PP test probability values of all variables are less than 0.05.

5.2 Determination of Lag Length

In the VECM estimation, the determination of the exact optimal amount of Lag is needed. The Lag length is used to determine the time taken for a variable to be affected by the past of each variable. This study determines the lag length by seeing the value of the Likehood Ratio (LR), Final Prediction Error (FPE), Akaike Information Crition (AIC), Schwarz Information Crition (SC) and Hann-Quin Crition (HQ).

It can be seen if the optimal lag is on lag 3 . Determination of lag 1 as the optimal lag based on the highest number of stars in the lag 3 . Optimal lag determination is needed to conduct further tests, both Johanson Cointegration test, Granger Causality Test and VECM.

5.3 Johanson Cointegration

Cointegration test is conducted to determine the existence of relationships between variables, especially in the long run. If there is a cointegration of the variables used in the model, it can be ensured that there is a long-term relationship between the variables. To be able to describe cointegration, we can look at the trace statistic and compared to the its critical value.

From the Johanson Cointegration test above it can be concluded if there is a cointegration relationship by looking at trace statistic values that are greater than the critical value of 5%. Cointegration between variables indicates if the data can be tested using VECM. Johanson's Cointegration Test shows if there is a cointegration relationship to the variable used.

5.4 Granger Causality Test

Granger causality test is used to test the causality relationship between variables namely IBF, IBD, IIC, DII, VOL, SGOV, and GDP variables. In this study the Granger causality test is intended to find out whether these variables influence each other or become the cause of each other. The test level used is 5% or 0.05 with a lag length of 3, according to the optimum lag length test results.

In the Granger Causality test that needs to be considered is the probability value. If the probability value is greater than 0.05 then H_0 is accepted or the X variable does not affect the Y variable. Conversely, if the probability value is less than 0.05 then H_0 is rejected and H_1 is accepted, that is, the significant X variable granger-causes variable Y. Table 6 is the result of the Granger Causality Test on IBF, IIC, and GDP variables.

From table 5 surprisingly, the deposit does not affect the GDP at all neither GDP to IBD. The financing variable IBF have granger-cause relationship with GDP, but the GDP does not affect IBF. Furthermore, based on the results of data processing in table 5 for the insurance sector, it is known that the insurance density variable has no Granger causality with GDP, and vice versa. While GDP has a Granger causality relationship with insurance contributions, the opposite does not apply. Interestingly, in the capital market sector, the Government Sukuk variable has a strong two-way Granger causality relationship with GDP. Meanwhile, the trade volume variable has absolutely no Granger causality relationship to GDP.

5.5 VECM Estimation

VECM estimation is obtained based on the optimum lag that has been calculated at the beginning. In this study the optimum lag used is 3. Estimation of VECM will show the presence or absence of a relationship between two variables. To be able analysis whether the variable X affects the Y variable, one must compare the t statistics obtained from the estimation results from reviews with t tables, the t table used is 2.02439. The variables significant applied on long and short term if the values of t-statistic > t-table. Table 6 is the estimated VECM result.

There was no significant variable for GDP in short term. Based on result on table 6, all variables have value under the t table. On the long term, most of variables were significant except IBD and IBF. DII, IBF, IIC and VOL have negative impact on GDP whereas SGOV and IBD have positive impact.

6. DISCUSSION

6.1 Islamic Insurance and Economic Growth

The Granger Causality Test also states that there is a causal relationship between economic growth and Islamic insurance contribution (table 5) with a probability value of 0.0028. Economic growth affects Islamic insurance because economic growth is related to people's welfare in income and consumption. When economic growth decreases, the amount of income received by the community will decrease, so that the community will also reduce consumption and reduce the amount of insurance demand. In line with the results of the study Ali et al. (2020), economic status such as income or GDP per capita has a significant effect on the demand for Islamic insurance in Indonesia.

In the long run, VECM shows negative relationship between economic growth and Islamic insurance contribution (table 6). Economic growth is a very sensitive factor for Islamic insurance because it is related to the people's purchasing power. When the purchasing power of the people increases, then the community will reduce their interest in insurance due to they have cash buffer to cover the risk without have plan in insurance. Moreover, Indonesian insurance is not a priority.

Meanwhile, in short term economic growth was not affected by Islamic insurance activities. That is because the scale of Islamic insurance is much smaller than conventional insurance, so Islamic insurance does not have too much impact on economic growth. Penetration of Islamic insurance in November 2019 is only 0.106% when compared to conventional insurance penetration which is 1.3% in 2018. It can be said if Islamic insurance in Indonesia is not optimal enough in performing its role as an financial intermediate.

6.2 Islamic Banking and Economic Growth

Both tests carried out, both Granger Causality and VECM did not show a relationship between economic growth and Islamic banking. Economic growth does not affect Islamic Banking activities and vice versa, Islamic Banking activities do not affect economic growth due to the lack of public interest in using Islamic banking. It can be seen from the share mockup level of Islamic banking which is only 5.95% while the rest is controlled by conventional banking (Financial Services Authority, 2019). This result is also in line with Al Fathan and Arundina (2019) which stated that the low market share of Sharia banking in

Indonesia when compared to conventional banking, this is what impacts on the lack of public interest in Islamic Banking has caused Islamic banks to not be optimal in carrying out their role as financial institutions. Previous research by Sumarti et al. (2018) also stated that Islamic financial institutions take a long time to be able to contribute significantly to the Indonesian economy.

In the long term, financing and deposit has a no significant and have negative effect on GDP. The insignificant describe the market share of Islamic banking that is limited. Although not significant, these results indicate that when financing is high, it can be indicated that the community cannot meet their needs independently without applying for financing from the banking sector. The low income stimulates people to get financing more intense. Moreover, based on industrial side the high financing could reduce the income of the company, because the obligation to pay the financing. So, the high finance could make the low income, in aggregate will reduce income and decrease the GDP. Other results show that GDP provides a positive stimulus to the increase in Sharia banking deposits, meaning that when prosperous people will allocate funds to deposits, this is in line with research Gani and Bahari (2021) and M. Anwar et al. (2020) which explains that when Deposit on bank increases, the bank have more sources to finance the deficit site. Banking financing activities will encourage the real sector to improve their business and revenue, which further increased the GDP.

6.3 Islamic Capital Market and Economic Growth

Based on the results of the granger causality test, shows that trading volume did not affect GDP. This result is in line with the research of Muharam et al. (2019), while the results of VOL granger causality did not affect GDP, which means stock exchange activity transactions did not have an impact on economic growth. The short term VECM shows that trading volume did not have significant impact on GDP and long term VECM results show negative results between the increased in GDP that can affect the increase in VOL. It is implied in short and long-term trading activity increase people's income, then allocated to sharia stock investment instruments may generate income to investor.

Granger causality tests show SGOV can significantly affect economic growth, which means that the use of SGOV funds is successfully allocated for infrastructure development or financing state spending deficit. This condition has an impact on improving the Indonesian economy, which supports the research of Yıldırım et al. (2020) and Smaoui and Nechi (2017). The short-term VECM result shows GDP does not affect on sukuk government while in the long-run GDP has a positive impact on sukuk government which indicates that Indonesia's economic growth is good. The government does not need assistance or in this case investment from the public, because the government has sufficient funds for the sustainability of infrastructure development and state spending needs and caused the number of sukuk government to decrease (Al Fathan and Arundina, 2019; Muharam et al., 2019). On the other side if the sukuk government increase it is indicated that the GDP was low, so the government need more investor to generate capital to increase sector rill in the end will increase income and GDP

7. CONCLUSION

This study aims to find out the relationship between Islamic banking activities, Islamic insurance activities, Islamic capital market and economic growth in Indonesia. Vector Error Correction Model (VECM) is used to find the relationship between the Islamic banking, Islamic Insurance and Islamic Capital Market.

The Granger Causality Test show that Islamic Banking Financing, and Sukuk Government cause GDP. Whereas GDP itself cause Sukuk Government and Islamic Insurance Contribution. In the short run, all of them did not have significant effect on GDP but long term does.

Insurance sector have significant negative impact on GDP. Otherwise, banking sector did not have any significant effect on GDP. Interestingly, we can see contrary effect by capital market sector. The result show that sukuk government have positive effect on GDP while trading volume is the otherwise.

From that result, we conclude GDP is growing in the long run where people's incomes are increasing, they tend to reduce the proportion of debt, this also applies to governments that reduce their outstanding sukuk issuance. In addition, the community also reduces the purchase of insurance products, it may be because there are enough public savings funds for the needs of just in case and prefer to allocate excess funds that they have in investment instruments such as deposits and stocks.

The results of this study indicate that the Islamic capital market contributes well to Indonesia's economy, so the government need to increase the Islamic capital market due to it can generate income that may increase the GDP. Islamic banking and Islamic insurance still cannot perform its role as a financial intermediate optimally. Islamic banking and insurance are expected to make the latest innovations to be able to develop, so that they can compete with conventional banking and insurance encourage economic growth in Indonesia. Islamic banking and insurance can also provide information to Indonesian people if customers of Islamic banking and insurance are not only limited to one religion, but all people can also use the facilities provided by Islamic banking and insurance.

REFERENCES

Abduh, M., & Azmi Omar, M. (2012). Islamic banking and economic growth: The Indonesian experience. *International Journal of Islamic and Middle Eastern Finance and Management*, *5*(1), 35–47. doi:10.1108/17538391211216811

Abduh, M., & Chowdhury, N. (2012). Does Islamic Banking Matter for Economic Growth in Bangladesh. *Journal of Islamic Economics, Banking and Finance, 8*, 104–113. https://ibtra.com/pdf/journal/v8_n3_article6.pdf

Adams, M., Andersson, J., Andersson, L.-F., & Lindmark, M. (2009). Commercial banking, insurance and economic growth in Sweden between 1830 and 1998. *Accounting Business & Financial History*, *19*(1), 21–38. doi:10.1080/09585200802667139

Adjasi, C. K. D., & Biekpe, N. B. (2006). Stock market development and economic growth: The case of selected African countries. *African Development Review*, *18*(1), 144–161. doi:10.1111/j.1467-8268.2006.00136.x

Adu, G., Marbuah, G., & Mensah, J. T. (2013). Financial development and economic growth in Ghana: Does the measure of financial development matter? *Review of Development Finance*, *3*(4), 192–203. doi:10.1016/j.rdf.2013.11.001

Al Fathan, R., & Arundina, T. (2019). Finance-growth nexus: Islamic finance development in Indonesia. *International Journal of Islamic and Middle Eastern Finance and Management*, *12*(5), 698–711. doi:10.1108/IMEFM-09-2018-0285

Ali, M. M., Devi, A., Furqani, H., & Hamzah, H. (2020). Islamic financial inclusion determinants in Indonesia: An ANP approach. *International Journal of Islamic and Middle Eastern Finance and Management, 13*(4), 727–747. doi:10.1108/IMEFM-01-2019-0007

Anwar, S., Junaidi, J., Salju, S., Wicaksono, R., & Mispiyanti, M. (. (2020). Islamic bank contribution to Indonesian economic growth. *International Journal of Islamic and Middle Eastern Finance and Management, 13*(3), 519–532. doi:10.1108/IMEFM-02-2018-0071

Chau, W. H., Khin, A. A., & Teng, K. L. L. (2013). Economic Development Cointegration and Malaysian Life and General Insurance Consumption. *Australian Journal of Basic and Applied Sciences, 7*(10), 538–546.

Chen, P. F., Lee, C. C., & Lee, C. F. (2011). How does the development of the life insurance market affect economic growth? Some international evidence. *Journal of International Development, 7*(24), 865–893.

Dornbusch, R. & Fischer, S. (2004). *Macroeconomics 8th Edition*. McGraw-Hill.

Echchabi, A., Aziz, H. A., & Idriss, U. (2016). Does Sukuk Financing Promote Economic Growth an Emphasis on the Major Issuing Countries. *Turkish Journal of Islamic Economics, 3*(2), 63–63. doi:10.15238/tujise.2016.3.2.63-73

Enisan, A. A., & Olufisayo, A. O. (2009). Stock market development and economic growth: Evidence from seven sub-Sahara African countries. *Journal of Economics and Business, 61*(2), 162–171. doi:10.1016/j.jeconbus.2008.05.001

Furqani, H. (2009). Islamic banking and economic growth: Empirical evidence from Malaysia. *Journal of Economic Cooperation & Development, 30*(2).

Gani, I. M., & Bahari, Z. (2021). Islamic banking's contribution to the Malaysian real economy. *ISRA International Journal of Islamic Finance*. doi:10.1108/IJIF-01-2019-0004

Greenlaw, S. A., & Shapiro, D. (2011). Principles of Macroeconomics 2e. Rice University.

Gujarati, D. N. (2006). Econometria Básica. In Basic Econometrics. Cooch Behar Panchanan Barma University.

Gujarati, D. N., & Porter, D. C. (2009). *Basic Econometrics* (5th ed.). McGraw-Hill.

Haiss, P., & Sümegi, K. (2008). The relationship between insurance and economic growth in Europe: A theoretical and empirical analysis. *Empirica, 35*(4), 405–431. doi:10.100710663-008-9075-2

Harris, R. (1995). *Using cointegration analysis in econometric modelling*. Pretice Hall.

Hassan, M. K., Sanchez, B., & Yu, J. S. (2011). Financial development and economic growth: New evidence from panel data. *The Quarterly Review of Economics and Finance, 51*(1), 88–104. doi:10.1016/j.qref.2010.09.001

Hill, R. C., Griffiths, W. E., & Lim, G. C. (2011). *Principles of Econometrics* (4th ed.). John Wiley & Sons.

Imam, P., & Kpodar, K. (2016). Islamic banking: Good for growth? *Economic Modelling, 59*, 387–401. doi:10.1016/j.econmod.2016.08.004

Indonesia Financial Service Authority. (2018). Snapshoot Perbankan Syariah Indonesia. Indonesia Islamic Banking.

Indonesia Financial Service Authority. (2019). Snapshoot Perbankan Syariah Indonesia. Indonesia Islamic Banking.

Indonesia Religion Department. (2008). *Al-Quran dan Terjemahannya*. Diponegoro.

Kassim, S. (2016). Islamic finance and economic growth: The Malaysian experience. *Global Finance Journal*, *30*, 66–76. doi:10.1016/j.gfj.2015.11.007

Kostov, Philip, and J. L. (2000). Regime-Switching Vector Error Correction Model (VECM). *Analysis Of UK Meat*.

Kumar, S., Sahu, N. C., & Kumar, P. (2020). Insurance consumption and economic growth in the post-liberalized India: An empirical analysis. *Asian Economic and Financial Review*, *10*(2), 218–228. doi:10.18488/journal.aefr.2020.102.218.228

Laucereno, S. F. (2017). *Berapa Pangsa Pasar Asuransi Syariah di RI? Ini Kata OJK [How much is the sharia insurance market share in Indonesia? This is what OJK says]*. Detik. https://finance.detik.com/moneter/d-3487655/berapa-pangsa-pasar-asuransi-syariah-di-ri-ini-kata-ojk

Lee, C. C., Lee, C. C., & Chiu, Y. (2013). The link between life insurance activities and economic growth: Some new evidence. *Journal of International Money and Finance*, *32*(1), 405–427. doi:10.1016/j.jimonfin.2012.05.001

Levine, R. (1996). Stock Markets: A Sput to Economic Growth. *Finance & Development*, *2*(4), 8–10. doi:10.20525/ijfbs.v2i4.160

Liu, G., He, L., Yue, Y., & Wang, J. (2014). The linkage between insurance activity and banking credit: Some evidence from dynamic analysis. *The North American Journal of Economics and Finance*, *29*, 239–265. doi:10.1016/j.najef.2014.06.014

Lone, F. A. (2016). Islamic banks and financial institutions: A Study of Their Objectives and Achievements. In Palagrave Macmillan: London. doi:10.1080/13602009708716362

Mankiw, N. Gregory, Euston Quah, and P. W. (2006). Macroeconomics 7th Edition. New York: Worth Publisher.

Muharam, H., Anwar, R. J., & Robiyanto, R. (2019). Islamic stock market and sukuk market development, economic growth, and trade openness (The case of Indonesia and Malaysia). *Business: Theory and Practice, 20*(2014), 196–207. . doi:10.3846/btp.2019.19

Nizar, M. A. (2016). Acceleration and Inclusiveness of the Financial Sector: Pathway to People's Welfare. In MPRA Paper (Vol. 97928).

Nurudeen, A. B. U. (2009). Does Stock Market Development Raise Economic Growth? Evidence from Nigeria. *Review of Finance and Banking*, *1*(1), 15–26.

Nyasha, S., & Odhiambo, N. M. (2015). The impact of banks and stock market development on economic growth in South Africa: An ARDL-bounds testing approach. *Contemporary Economics*, *9*(1), 93–108. doi:10.5709/ce.1897-9254.161

Oyodetun, T. M., & Adesina, B. D. (2015). Nexus between economic growth and insurance business in Nigeria. *Research Journal of Finance and Accounting*, *6*(9), 142–150.

Pradhan, R. P., Arvin, M. B., Nair, M., Hall, J. H., & Gupta, A. (2017). Is there a link between economic growth and insurance and banking sector activities in the G-20 countries? *Review of Financial Economics*, *33*(1), 12–28. doi:10.1016/j.rfe.2017.02.002

Pradhan, R. P., Dash, S., Maradana, R. P., Jayakumar, M., & Gaurav, K. (2017). Insurance market density and economic growth in Eurozone countries: the granger causality approach. *Financial Innovation, 3*(1), 0–24. . doi:10.1186/s40854-017-0065-x

Pradhana, R. P., Arvinb, M. B., & Norman, N. R. (2015). Insurance development and the finance-growth nexus: Evidence from 34 OECD countries. *Journal of Multinational Financial Management*, *31*, 1–22. doi:10.1016/j.mulfin.2015.02.001

Safitri, K. A. (2019). The contribution of life and non-life insurances on asean economic growth. *Management Science Letters*, *9*(7), 957–966. doi:10.5267/j.msl.2019.4.009

Sari, N., Syamsurijal, & Widiyanti, M. (2018). the Impact of Islamic Capital Market Development on Economic Growth: the Case of Indonesia. *Journal of Smart Economic Growth, 3*(2), 21–30.

Smaoui, H., & Nechi, S. (2017). Does sukuk market development spur economic growth? *Research in International Business and Finance*, *41*(April), 136–147. doi:10.1016/j.ribaf.2017.04.018

Sumarti, N., Hayati, M. M., Cahyani, N. L. P. A., Wahyudi, R. R., Tristanti, D. P., & Meylani, R. (2018). Has the growth of Islamic banking had impact to economic growth in Indonesia? *4th IEEE International Conference on Engineering Technologies and Applied Sciences, ICETAS 2017, 2018*. IEEE. 10.1109/ICETAS.2017.8277873

Tabash, M. I. (2014). The Flow of Islamic Finance and Economic Growth: An Empirical Evidence of Middle East. *Journal of Finance and Accounting*, *2*(1), 11. doi:10.11648/j.jfa.20140201.12

Todaro, M. P., & Smith, S. C. (2012). *Economic Developement* (11th ed.). Pearson.

Ul Din, S. M., Abu-Bakar, A., & Regupathi, A. (2017). Does insurance promote economic growth: A comparative study of developed and emerging/ developing economies. *Cogent Economics & Finance*, *5*(1), 1390029. Advance online publication. doi:10.1080/23322039.2017.1390029

Undang-Undang, No. 40 Tahun 2014 (2014), *Undang-Undang Republik Indonesia Nomor 40 Tahun 2014 Tentang Perasuransian* [Indonesia Insurance Constitution], § (2014). https://www.ojk.go.id/Files/201506/1UU402014Perasuransian_1433758676.pdf

Ward, D., & Zurbruegg, R. (2000). Does Insurance Promote Economic Growth? Evidence from OECD Countries. *The Journal of Risk and Insurance*, *67*(4), 489. doi:10.2307/253847

Webb, I., Grace, M. F., & Skipper, H. D. (2005). The effect of banking and insurance on the growth of capital and output. *SBS Revista de Temas Financieros, 2*, 1–32. http://dspace.fudutsinma.edu.ng/xmlui/bitstream/handle/123456789/885/The_Effect_Of_Banking_And_Insurance_On_The_Growth.pdf?sequence=1

Yıldırım, S., Yıldırım, D. C., & Diboglu, P. (2020). Does Sukuk market development promote economic growth? *PSU Research Review*, *4*(3), 209–218. doi:10.1108/PRR-03-2020-0011

Zhu, A., Ash, M., & Pollin, R. (2004). Stock market liquidity and economic growth: A critical appraisal of the Levine/Zervos model. *International Review of Applied Economics*, *18*(1), 63–71. doi:10.1080/0269217032000148645

APPENDIX

Table 1. Description of operational variables

Variable	Information
Islamic Bank Financing (IBF)	Sharia financing is the distribution of financing based on sharia principles. Islamic bank financing used is the total of Islamic commercial bank financing, Islamic business units and Islamic people's financing banks (Abduh, Muhamad, 2012).
Islamic Bank Deposit (IBD)	A total depositors fund with Mudharabah and Musyarakah akad
Islamic Insurance Contribution (IIC)	Contribution is the amount of money determined by the Islamic insurance company and approved by the policy holder, which is paid based on Islamic insurance arrangements to receive benefits from Tabarru 'funds and / or investment funds from participant investments and management fees or one of the legal fees and rules set forth in mandatory insurance programs to receive benefits (Law No. 40 of 2014, 2014).
Density Islamic Insurance (DII)	The value of insurance premiums (contributions) gross per capita (Chen et al., 2011)
Volume Activity (VA)	Total value of share traded on stock exchange market (Levine, 1996)
Sukuk Gov	
GDP	GDP measures the market value of the final product or service produced in a country in a certain period (Dornbusch et al. 2004). Gross domestic product (GDP) shows the total value of expenditure in the economic production of goods and services (Mankiw, 2006).

Table 2. Test results of Phillips Perron first difference

Variable	prob PP	Information
D(DII)	0.0000	Stationary
D(IIC)	0.0030	Stationary
D(IBD)	0.0000	Stationary
D(IBF)	0.0000	Stationary
D(VOL)	0.0000	Stationary
D(SGOV)	0.0000	Stationary
Source: own calculations based on www.ojk.go.id and www.bps.go.id from 2009-2023		

Table 3. Lag length testing

Lag	LogL	LR	FPE	AIC	SC
0	158.0127	NA	7.90e-12	-5.698594	-5.438367*
1	201.0509	73.08371	1.01e-11	-5.473620	-3.391802
2	266.0348	93.18447	6.05e-12	-6.076786	-2.173377
3	346.0067	93.55195*	2.44e-12*	-7.245534*	-1.520535

Source: own calculations based on www.ojk.go.id and www.bps.go.id from 2009-2023

Table 4. Johanson cointegration test results

Hypothesized No. of CE(s)	Eigenvalue	Max-Eigen Statistic	0.05 Critical Value	Prob.**
None *	0.746028	225.0294	125.6154	0.0000
At most 1 *	0.663552	153.7617	95.75366	0.0000
At most 2 *	0.465046	97.11741	69.81889	0.0001
At most 3 *	0.401782	64.58751	47.85613	0.0006
At most 4 *	0.334182	37.86993	29.79707	0.0048
At most 5 *	0.188343	16.71953	15.49471	0.0326
At most 6 *	0.106717	5.868317	3.841466	0.0154

Source: own calculations based on www.ojk.go.id and www.bps.go.id from 2009-2023

Table 5. Pairwise Granger causality test results

Null Hypothesis:	Obs	F-Statistic	Prob.
GDP does not Granger Cause DII	54	2.22878	0.0972
DII does not Granger Cause GDP		2.03548	0.1217
IBD does not Granger Cause GDP	54	0.97809	0.4111
GDP does not Granger Cause IBD		1.56529	0.2103
IBF does not Granger Cause GDP	54	5.52259	0.0025
GDP does not Granger Cause IBF		1.38583	0.2587
IIC does not Granger Cause GDP	54	1.31003	0.2823
GDP does not Granger Cause IIC		5.41616	0.0028
SGOV does not Granger Cause GDP	54	2.87184	0.0462
GDP does not Granger Cause SGOV		3.99519	0.0129
VOL does not Granger Cause GDP	54	0.29903	0.8259
GDP does not Granger Cause VOL		0.73051	0.5390
Source: own calculations based on www.ojk.go.id and www.bps.go.id from 2009-2023			

Table 6. VECM estimation

Estimation	Variables	Coefficient	t-statistic	Significantly
	CointEq1	-0.494612	-1.76198	Not significant
	D(GDP(-3))	-0.730278	-5.83173	Not significant
	D(IIC(-3))	-0.004318	-1.44825	Not significant
	D(DII(-3))	0.001405	0.12587	Not significant
	D(IBF(-3))	0.029381	1.07234	Not significant
Short Term	D(IBD(-3))	-0.032944	-1.15599	Not significant
	D(VOL(-3))	0.011030 -	-1.40351	Not significant
	D(SGOV(-3))	0.003899	0.14345	Not significant
	C	-0.001406	-0.22880	
	D(GDP(-1))	1.000000		
	D(IIC(-1))	-0.018516	-7.48967	Significant
	D(DII(-1))	-0.12174	-3.88334	Significant
Long Term	D(IBF(-1))	-0.001031	-0.10556	Not significant
	D(IBD(-1))	0.007331	1.52787	Not Significant
	D(VOL(-1))	-0.031536	-7.85862	Significant
	D(SGOV(-1))	-0.022812	2.66796	Significant

Source: own calculations based on www.ojk.go.id and www.bps.go.id from 2009-2023

Chapter 14
Theoretical Insights of Environmental, Social, and Governance (ESG) Disclosures and Investment Decision

Shweta
Central University of Haryana, India

Ashish Mathur
Central University of Haryana, India

Divya
Central University of Haryana, India

Raj Bahadur Sharma
College of Business Administration, University of Bahrain, Bahrain

ABSTRACT

Investors employ a variety of techniques to gain high-quality information while making investment decisions. Traditionally, they made decisions based solely on financial success, but these days they have more expectations than just financial gain. They make investing decisions based on ESG data. People want their investments to expand in tandem with their growing desire to be more sustainable. Moreover, ESG integration has lately evolved from a specialized concept to a standard practice in investment. The study aims to provide light on the intricate growth of environmental, social, and governance (ESG) integration into investment decisions by drawing on theoretical and methodical insights from pertinent literature. The chapter indicates that ESG integration has transformed society. The investment landscape has undergone significant transformation as individuals strive to align their financial objectives with their social and ethical convictions. The shifting in the role of ESG from a niche component to a mainstream consideration implies a fundamental change in the investment process itself.

DOI: 10.4018/979-8-3693-1038-0.ch014

1. INTRODUCTION

The industry is currently coping with a number of serious concerns, such as growing costs, more competition, and changing consumer expectations (Pal et al., 2023) and it is becoming more difficult for the sector to stand out from the competition and address these concerns. As a result, corporate communication practices have changed recently to become more inclusive and take emerging issues like environmental, social, and governance (ESG) into account. These parameters extend beyond traditional financial measurements and surround a wide range of characteristics. They give potential investors a thorough grasp of how a company operates and how well it can adjust to a dynamic environment. Here's a closer examination of each component:

- Environmental (E): Investigating a company's impact on the environment is what the "E" in ESG stands for. It examines how an organization uses energy, manages its environmental resources, and takes stances on issues like pollution and climate change. Companies that prioritize environmental sustainability tend to be more creative, efficient, and more prepared to handle the challenges presented by a changing climate.
- Social (S): The "S" in ESG evaluates an organization's relationships with its clients, employees, and the communities in which it works. It covers topics like labor practices, diversity and inclusion, human rights, and community involvement. Good social settings in the workplace are linked to higher output, less risk, and enhanced brand recognition.
- Governance (G): Governance is the study of internal business policies and practices, including executive compensation, board composition, and ethics. Robust governance ensures accountability, moral behavior, and transparency. It fosters stakeholder trust and lowers the risks associated with bad management.

Communication of ESG information is the clearest means by which a company may show its dedication to corporate social responsibility (CSR). A change to the internal control system could improve information compliance and reliability in the long run by promoting transparency about the social and environmental effects of corporate operations and governance frameworks (Cheng et al., 2014). The world's most astute and influential investors are paying close attention to environmental, social, and governance (ESG) investing practises.

1.1 ESG: Beyond Profits and Sustainable Development

Human culture is always seeking to improve itself. There are many opportunities and challenges in today's globe as the business and society expand. AI application increases the risk of irrational decision-making and may lead to employment losses (Kismawadi et al., 2023). In 2020, there were many "Black Swan" incidents. The spread of COVID-19, the delisting of Luckin Coffee due to fraud, the four US stock market meltdowns in a two-week period, the locust infestation in Africa, and other events have caused concern around the world. The challenges being addressed are social (S), governance (G), and environmental (E). The concept of comprehensive and sustainable development is currently trending heavily in global discourse. International organisations and nations all over the world have presented sustainable development action plans, like ESG, in response to the escalating serious sustainable development issues in the environment, society, and financial market. The goal of these plans is to create a comprehensive and sustainable framework for human society's development. (Li et. al, 2021)

The notion of sustainable development is worldwide (Ortas et.al, 2015), that emerged some decades ago (Nevado-Peña et al., 2015), and it is essential to be evaluated by all stakeholders (Waas et. al, 2014). In the current dynamic global financial environment, the essential criteria regulating investment choices have changed. The financial sector is becoming more and more interested in sustainable development (Kopnina,2016). People want their investments to grow in line with their increasing desire to be more sustainable, since sustainability is increasingly seen as the way of the future (Xiao, et.al, 2013). Even though financial performance is still a crucial component of investment analysis, modern investors are increasingly looking for a more comprehensive picture. This change is supported by a growing recognition that investments need to support social responsibility, sustainability, and good governance in addition to generating financial benefits. Corporate ESG disclosures provide information about a company's environmental, social, and governance practises and are in line with the Paris Agreement and SDGs. The Paris Agreement and the SDGs are therefore taken into consideration while creating several ESG frameworks (Park & Jang, 2021). The incorporation of Environmental, Social, and Governance (ESG) considerations into investment decisions is crucial in this particular setting.

The investment decisions of an individual are affected by demographic factors (Nagy & Obenberger, 1994), economic and behavioural factors (Aregbeyen & Mbadiugha, 2011; De Bondt & Thaler, 1995; Kourtidis et al., 2011). The investing landscape is changing dramatically in a time of environmental difficulties, social inequality, and corporate governance concerns. The integration of ESG factors represents a paradigm change that goes beyond traditional financial measures, encouraging investors to consider the wider impact of their investments on the globe. Based on an organization's ESG score, investments are made (Duuren et. al, 2016). Analysts view environmental, social, and governance (ESG) data as market signals and thus may compare and filter data based on ESG performance or ratings (Leins, 2020). ESG reports are frequently requested by international investors for their investment decisions. (Park & Jang, 2021)

However, Climate change, resource management, and ecological responsibility are all included in the category of environmental factors. Social elements include things like community involvement, diversity, labour practises, and human rights. All of a company's governing structures and policies, including those pertaining to ethics and transparency, are referred to as governance. When taken as a whole, these ESG components are essential indicators of a company's sustainability, long-term growth, and ability to contribute to society.

The largest legislative force behind business ESG adoption and ESG disclosure is the UN. As per UN PRI announcement in 2019, PRI signatories are required to share the PRI climate indicators on four categories: governance, strategy, risk management, and metrics. The first significant organisation to make the inclusion of ESG data in reports a requirement was the UN PRI. By putting into effect the EU Directive on Non-Financial and Diversity Information, the EU became the first economic community to impose ESG regulations (Park & Jang, 2021).

1.2 Development of ESG Into Investment Decision Making

The incorporation of Environmental, Social, and Governance (ESG) considerations into investment decision-making has undergone a significant transformation, maturing over multiple decades to become a fundamental aspect of contemporary financial markets. the key stages in the development of ESG into investment decision-making are:

a. *Ethical Investing*: ESG integration has its origins in ethical investing, which goes back to this era. Investors avoided companies in morally dubious industries throughout this time in an effort to match their investments with their personal ideals. Businesses involved in gambling, guns, alcohol, and tobacco were not included in the portfolios of ethical investors.
b. *Emergence of Socially Responsible Investing (SRI)):* In the 1960s, socially responsible investment (SRI) were formally established. Investors started actively choosing companies according to social and ethical standards. With an emphasis on businesses that are dedicated to social and environmental responsibility, SRI funds and strategies have been developed.
c. *Environmental Awareness:* As environmental movements and environmental challenges were more widely recognised, the environmental aspect of ESG started to take the stage. Businesses began to come under more scrutiny for their ecological footprint, which prompted investment decisions to take the environment into account.
d. *Governance Concerns:* Corporate scandals such as Enron and WorldCom characterised the late 20th and early 21st centuries, highlighting the significance of sound governance. The attention shifted to governance issues, including those pertaining to openness and ethical behaviour.
e. *Growth of ESG Reporting:* A number of ESG reporting frameworks and standards, including the Sustainability Accounting Standards Board (SASB) and the Global Reporting Initiative (GRI), were developed in the 2000s. These frameworks gave businesses an organised means of disclosing their ESG performance, which made it simpler for investors to evaluate and contrast.
f. *Institutionalization of ESG:* This method to investing has moved from being a specialised practise to a popular one. When institutional investors realised that ESG variables had a significant impact on risk management and financial performance, they started using ESG strategies, including asset managers and pension funds.
g. *Regulatory Support:* ESG-related laws and rules were introduced by governments and regulatory organisations globally, mandating businesses to report non-financial information. The Non-Financial Reporting Directive, for instance, was put into effect by the European Union and requires big businesses to report on ESG matters.
h. *Demonstrated Positive Correlation: An* increasing amount of studies started to show a link between long-term financial outperformance and robust ESG performance. Businesses that successfully manage the opportunities and risks associated with ESG are typically more flexible and resilient, which may translate into higher risk-adjusted returns.
i. *Emphasis on Impact and Sustainability (present and future):* It is anticipated that the use of ESG in financial decision-making would focus on matching investments to more general sustainability objectives. A growing subcategory of ESG, impact investing seeks to produce both positive social and environmental results and financial returns.

Table 1 indicates that the integration of ESG into investment decision-making has been a gradual process due to changing societal expectations, evolving global economic dynamics, and an increasing understanding of the significance of environmental, social, and governance factors in investment decisions. The integration of ESG into investment practises has become a crucial aspect of responsible and

Table 1. ESG's integration into investing decision-making

ESG's integration into investing decision-making	
Ethical Investing	Investors avoided companies in morally dubious industries throughout this time in an effort to match their investments with their personal ideals. Businesses involved in gambling, guns, alcohol, and tobacco were not included in the portfolios of ethical investors.
Emergence of Socially Responsible Investing (SRI)	Investors started actively choosing companies according to social and ethical standards. With an emphasis on businesses that are dedicated to social and environmental responsibility, SRI (Socially Responsible Investing) funds and strategies have been developed.
Environmental Awareness	The environmental aspect of ESG started to take the stage. Businesses began to come under more scrutiny for their ecological footprint, which prompted investment decisions to take the environment into account.
Governance Concerns	The attention shifted to governance issues, including those pertaining to openness and ethical behaviour.
Growth of ESG Reporting	A number of ESG reporting frameworks and standards, including the Sustainability Accounting Standards Board (SASB) and the Global Reporting Initiative (GRI), were developed in the 2000s
Institutionalization of ESG	This method to investing has moved from being a specialised practise to a popular one.
Regulatory Support	ESG-related laws and rules were introduced by governments and regulatory organisations globally, mandating businesses to report non-financial information
Demonstrated Positive Correlation	An increasing amount of studies started to show a link between long-term financial outperformance and robust ESG performance.
Emphasis on Impact and Sustainability	A growing subcategory of ESG, impact investing seeks to produce both positive social and environmental results and financial returns.

sustainable investing, impacting both corporate conduct and the financial sector's development. It has evolved from an ethical niche.

1.3 ESG's Significance in Investment Decision-Making

- *Risk management*: An organization's exposure to risks that may affect its long-term performance can be better understood thanks to ESG considerations. Risks related to the environment, such as resource shortages and climate change, can result in higher expenses and operational interruptions. Social risks can impact a company's profitability and reputation. Examples of these risks include labour disputes and supply chain concerns. Fraud and unethical behaviour are examples of governance concerns that can result in fines and legal consequences. Investors can detect and reduce these risks by taking ESG into account.
- *Long-Term Performance*: Strong ESG performance has been positively correlated with long-term financial outperformance, as per numerous studies. Businesses that handle ESG concerns well are typically more resilient and better suited to face the difficulties of a world that is changing quickly. Over time, investors who include environmental, social, and governance (ESG) factors into their decision-making process may reap the benefits of higher risk-adjusted returns.
- *Alignment with Values*: A growing number of investors are trying to match their financial decisions to their own values and perspectives. ESG gives people and organizations a way to invest in

businesses that are changing the world for the better. A sense of purpose and accomplishment that goes beyond material gain might result from this connection.

- *Regulatory Trends*: As governments and regulatory agencies come to understand the value of ESG, they have begun to mandate ESG disclosure and reporting. The importance of ESG in the investing landscape is further highlighted by this governmental backing, which also pushes businesses to disclose their non-financial performance more explicitly.

2. OBJECTIVE OF THE STUDY

The aim of this research is to attempt theoretical insights of the influence of environmental, social, and governance (ESG) on investment decisions made by investors. Additionally, the study aims to uncover the intricate growth of ESG integration into investment decisions by analysing existing literature.

3. LITERATURE REVIEW

Investment selection is an important procedure that entails picking a stock from a diversity of options offered on different stock markets. Efficient data processing and analysis are necessary due to the continuously increasing volume of financial activities (Irfan et. al, 2023). According to traditional economic theory, individuals are rational agents who can take advantage of opportunities and make objective decisions based on their expectations, knowledge, and experience. However the behavioural paradigm of financial decision-making, which takes into account psychological biases, ingrained thought patterns, and emotional inclination, characterizes how investors view the world and choose investments (Mutswenje,2009 ; Bikas et. al, 2013 ; Cohen & Kudryavtsev,2013). Previously, an ordinary triangle that included risk, liquidity, and return guided investment decisions. However, an increasing number of investors now employ the phenomenal square, which includes risk, liquidity, return, and sustainability (Von Wallis & Klein,2015).

Environmental, social, and governance (ESG) investment practises are gaining substantial attention from the world's most intelligent and large investors. ESG communication has already been examined from a variety of theoretical angles, including economic, interpretive, and information related to decision-usefulness (Grey et al., 1995).

Amel-Zadeh and Serafeim (2018) assert that investors' selection of ESG criteria determines the profitability of ESG portfolios, not whether the investor is interacting with ESG products or not. When it comes to making individual investing decisions, behavioural aspects are crucial, according to De Bondt and Thaler (1995) (USA). Aregbeyen and Mbadiugha (2011) discovered that decisions about investments are influenced by social, psychological, and economic aspects. According to the findings of several other research, investors' decisions about investments are influenced by accounting information, neutral information, and advocate recommendations (Ahmed, 2017; Gunathilaka, 2014; Merikas and Merika, 2006; Obamuyi, 2013; Shafi, 2014).

Investor decisions are influenced by the ESG score, which is important in revealing details about a company's fundamentals (Pedersen et. al, 2021). Cheng et al. (2015) examined what impact do the assurance and strategic relevance of reported sustainability information have on the investing decisions of non-professional investors, and it was found that Investors are more likely to put money into businesses that exhibit strong strategic relevance ESG metrics. De Franco (2020) examined how ESG-related disputes affected stock and portfolio performance and discovered that portfolios with severe ESG disputes or downgraded .ESGs performed relatively poorly. Better economic performance and sustainability are the factors expected by shareholders from corporations.

According to Matos et al. (2020), there is a higher probability of consistent dividend payments for sustainable firms. Long-term connections with stakeholders other than shareholders are also preferable for sustainable companies. Numerous studies in the body of literature indicate that investments in businesses with sound ESG policies yield higher returns, and that organisations with excellent ESG management can proactively avert unexpected shocks to their cash flows (Lee et al. 2013). After reviewing ESG/SRI research, Friede et al. (2015) discovered a strong positive correlation between financial performance and ESG performance.

According to Sharma et all (2022), that the firm value the market value of a company is positively impacted by ESG and governance pillar scores, but social and environmental pillar scores were not statistically significant. Furthermore, a substantial correlation has been observed between all ESG disclosures and ECG ratings.

Previous research shows that investors don't put equal importance to ESG dimensions. As discussed by Khemir et. al, 2019, Novethic (2008), conducted the survey among UK investors and French investors and found out that French investors prefers social indicators while UK investors put forward corporate governance indicators and Environmental aspect ranked last. Saghroun and Eglem (2008) discovered that financial analysts prioritise corporate governance over social and environmental factors. According to Pérez-Gladish et al. (2012), social issues are more important to socially conscious investors than environmental issues. According to Cohen et al. (2011), economic performance information ranks highest among retail investors, followed by corporate governance information and the company's socially responsible approach information.

The findings of the study conducted by Sultana et. al, 2018 revels that there is an insignificant effect of education level of investors on the investment decision which contradicts the previous literature by Dorfleitner & Utz, 2014; Viviers et.al,2012. His study showed the same result as shown by (Hood et.al, 2014 ; Escrig-Olmedo et. al, 2013) regarding the income level of investor and ESG inclination into investment that is greater inclination towards ESG issues by the investors with a higher income . Also, results showed the greater preference of the ESG issues by the investors with high investment amount invested in stock markets.

4. DISCUSSION AND CONCLUSION

Within the discipline of finance, key financial decisions including credit evaluation, macroeconomic analysis, and investment decision making are getting more complicated and In the realm of finance, artificial intelligence and machine learning have grown in significance due to their remarkable success and previously unheard-of accuracy (Irfan et. al, 2023). Along with artificial intelligence and machine learning, ESG is a topic of growing interest for many researchers in their work. They examine ESG from several perspectives. Some researchers examine issues from the perspective of the business; others examine from the perspective of investors; still others examine from the perspective of society and the government. This study considered ESG from investor's point of view.

There are many factors which affect the investment decision of any investor. Traditionally it was basically risk, liquidity and return on the basis of which investor make his investment decision but now a days investors want more comprehensive information to decide whether to invest or not i.e., along with risk, liquidity, return they want ESG information (environmental, social, governance) to make their investment decisions.

ESG is a vital lens that both investors and companies use to view business operations and investment decisions. From a company's point of view, ESG helps with reputation building, risk management, and long-term sustainability. For investors, ESG is crucial for risk assessment, long-term performance, alignment with values, and regulatory compliance.

ESG has emerged as a key component of investment decision-making in a time characterised by the goal of sustainability, ethical investing, and a growing understanding of global interdependence. It functions as a compass, pointing investors in the direction of possibilities that are consistent with their beliefs while also taking their portfolios' resilience and long-term sustainability into account. ESG is now a necessary and revolutionary force reshaping finance and fostering a more ethical and sustainable global community. Its position in investment decision-making is no longer optional. ESG integration is well-positioned to keep developing and promoting good change in the investment industry as more and more investors realise that profit shouldn't be made at the expense of the environment or society.

The extraordinary journey of integrating Environmental, Social, and Governance (ESG) concerns into investment decision-making has been driven by changing global dynamics and an increasing understanding of the complex effects of these aspects. The incorporation of ESG elements into investment decisions has become a fundamental component of modern investing, surpassing traditional financial measures and ethical considerations, as this study has systematically examined.

The world of investments has changed dramatically as people look to match their financial goals with their values and larger social agendas. The shift from ESG as a specialised niche to a mainstream factor in investing decisions suggests a fundamental shift in the process of making investments.

Thus, the world will be led towards a future in which achieving financial success and sustainability are goals that are mutually reinforcing as ESG continues to develop and have a greater influence on investment strategies and company behaviour. A more responsible and fair financial landscape may be shaped by investors, firms, and policymakers navigating this revolutionary journey together. One major limitation of this research is that, while it examined the growing influence of environmental, social, and governance (ESG) aspects in investment decisions based on existing literature, it did not collect field data from investors.

5. FUTURE STUDY DIRECTION

The current study examined the body of literature to focus on how environmental, social, and governance (ESG) factors are integrated into investment decisions. Further investigation into thorough case studies of companies and investors that have successfully integrated ESG principles into their strategies, however, may provide a deeper understanding of the practical implications and outcomes of these integrations.

The study of the behavioural finance components of ESG investing is an exciting area of research. The influence of psychological factors and cognitive biases on investment decisions in the field of ESG remains poorly studied. Analysing the ways in which these biases affect ESG investing choices can provide governments and investors with useful information. There are many prospects for additional research in the dynamic and always evolving subject of ESG integration into investment decisions, which could lead to more sustainable corporate practices, more moral and responsible financial practices, and more knowledgeable investors.

6. REFERENCES

Ahmad, S. (2017). Factors influencing individual investors' behaviour: An empirical study of Pakistan financial markets. *Journal of business & financial affairs, 4*(6), 1-8.

Aich, S., Thakur, A., Nanda, D., Tripathy, S., & Kim, H. C. (2021). Factors affecting ESG towards impact on investment: A structural approach. *Sustainability (Basel), 13*(19), 10868. doi:10.3390u131910868

Amel-Zadeh, A., & Serafeim, G. (2018). Why and how investors use ESG information: Evidence from a global survey. *Financial Analysts Journal, 74*(3), 87–103. doi:10.2469/faj.v74.n3.2

Aregbeyen, O., & Mbadiugha, S. O. (2011). Factors influencing investors decisions in shares of quoted companies in Nigeria. *Social Sciences, 6*(3), 205–212. doi:10.3923science.2011.205.212

Aregbeyen, O., & Mbadiugha, S. O. (2011). Factors influencing investors decisions in shares of quoted companies in Nigeria. *Social Sciences, 6*(3), 205–212. doi:10.3923science.2011.205.212

Bikas, E., Jurevičienė, D., Dubinskas, P., & Novickytė, L. (2013). Behavioural finance: The emergence and development trends. *Procedia: Social and Behavioral Sciences, 82*, 870–876. doi:10.1016/j.sbspro.2013.06.363

Cheng, B., Ioannou, I., & Serafeim, G. (2014). Corporate social responsibility and access to finance. *Strategic Management Journal, 35*(1), 1–23. doi:10.1002mj.2131

Cheng, M. M., Green, W. J., & Ko, J. C. W. (2015). The impact of strategic relevance and assurance of sustainability indicators on investors' decisions. *Auditing, 34*(1), 131–162. doi:10.2308/ajpt-50738

Cohen, G., & Kudryavtsev, A. (2012). Investor rationality and financial decisions. *Journal of Behavioral Finance, 13*(1), 11–16. doi:10.1080/15427560.2012.653020

Cohen, J., Holder-Webb, L., Nath, L., & Wood, D. (2011). Retail investors' perceptions of the decision-usefulness of economic performance, governance, and corporate social responsibility disclosures. *Behavioral Research in Accounting, 23*(1), 109–129. doi:10.2308/bria.2011.23.1.109

De Bondt, W. F., & Thaler, R. H. (1995). Financial decision-making in markets and firms: A behavioral perspective. *Handbooks in Operations Research and Management Science, 9*, 385–410. doi:10.1016/S0927-0507(05)80057-X

De Bondt, W. F., & Thaler, R. H. (1995). Financial decision-making in markets and firms: A behavioral perspective. *Handbooks in Operations Research and Management Science, 9*, 385–410. doi:10.1016/S0927-0507(05)80057-X

De Franco, C. (2020). Esg controversies and their impact on performance. *Journal of Investing, 29*(2), 33–45. doi:10.3905/joi.2019.1.106

Dorfleitner, G., & Utz, S. (2014). Profiling German-speaking socially responsible investors. *Qualitative Research in Financial Markets*, *6*(2), 118–156. doi:10.1108/QRFM-07-2012-0024

Escrig-Olmedo, E., Muñoz-Torres, M. J., & Fernández-Izquierdo, M. Á. (2013). Sustainable development and the financial system: Society's perceptions about socially responsible investing. *Business Strategy and the Environment*, *22*(6), 410–428. doi:10.1002/bse.1755

Friede, G., Busch, T., & Bassen, A. (2015). ESG and financial performance: Aggregated evidence from more than 2000 empirical studies. *Journal of Sustainable Finance & Investment*, *5*(4), 210–233. doi:10.1080/20430795.2015.1118917

Gray, R., Kouhy, R., & Lavers, S. (1995). Corporate social and environmental reporting: A review of the literature and a longitudinal study of UK disclosure. *Accounting, Auditing & Accountability Journal*, *8*(2), 47–77. doi:10.1108/09513579510146996

Gunathilaka, C. (2014). Financial Distress Prediction: A Comparative Study of Solvency Test and Z-Score Models with Reference to Sri Lanka. *IUP Journal of Financial Risk Management, 11*(3).

Hood, M., Nofsinger, J. R., & Varma, A. (2014). Conservation, discrimination, and salvation: Investors' social concerns in the stock market. *Journal of Financial Services Research*, *45*(1), 5–37. doi:10.100710693-013-0162-6

Irfan, M., Elhoseny, M., Kassim, S., Metawa, N. (2023). Advanced Machine Learning Algorithms for Complex Financial Applications. IGI Global. . doi:10.4018/978-1-6684-4483-2

Irfan, M., Elmogy, M., Majid, M. S. A., & El-Sappagh, S. (2023). The impact of AI innovation on financial sectors in the era of industry 5.0. *The Impact of AI Innovation on Financial Sectors in the Era of Industry*, *5*(0), 1–320.

Khemir, S., Baccouche, C., & Ayadi, S. D. (2019). The influence of ESG information on investment allocation decisions: An experimental study in an emerging country. *Journal of Applied Accounting Research*, *20*(4), 458–480. doi:10.1108/JAAR-12-2017-0141

Kopnina, H. (2016). The victims of unsustainability: A challenge to sustainable development goals. *International Journal of Sustainable Development and World Ecology*, *23*(2), 113–121. doi:10.1080/13504509.2015.1111269

Kourtidis, D., Šević, Ž., & Chatzoglou, P. (2011). Investors' trading activity: A behavioural perspective and empirical results. *Journal of Socio-Economics*, *40*(5), 548–557. doi:10.1016/j.socec.2011.04.008

Lee, D. D., Faff, R. W., & Rekker, S. A. (2013). Do high and low-ranked sustainability stocks perform differently? *International Journal of Accounting & Information Management*, *21*(2), 116–132. doi:10.1108/18347641311312267

Leins, S. (2020). 'Responsible investment': ESG and the post-crisis ethical order. *Economy and Society*, *49*(1), 71–91. doi:10.1080/03085147.2020.1702414

Li, T. T., Wang, K., Sueyoshi, T., & Wang, D. D. (2021). ESG: Research progress and future prospects. *Sustainability (Basel)*, *13*(21), 11663. doi:10.3390u132111663

Matos, P. V., Barros, V., & Sarmento, J. M. (2020). Does ESG affect the stability of dividend policies in Europe. *Sustainability (Basel)*, *12*(21), 8804. doi:10.3390u12218804

Merikas, A. G., & Merika, A. A. (2006). Stock prices response to real economic variables: The case of Germany. *Managerial Finance*, *32*(5), 446–450. doi:10.1108/03074350610657454

Mutswenje, V. S. (2009). *A survey of the factors influencing investment decisions: the case of individual investors at the NSE* [Doctoral dissertation, University of Nairobi].

Nagy, R. A., & Obenberger, R. W. (1994). Factors influencing individual investor behavior. *Financial Analysts Journal*, *50*(4), 63–68. doi:10.2469/faj.v50.n4.63

Nevado-Peña, D., López-Ruiz, V. R., & Alfaro-Navarro, J. L. (2015). The effects of environmental and social dimensions of sustainability in response to the economic crisis of European cities. *Sustainability (Basel)*, *7*(7), 8255–8269. doi:10.3390u7078255

Novethic. (2008). *Les investisseurs institutionnels se sentent-ils responsables des politiques ESG des entreprises dont ils sont actionnaires?* Novethic.

Obamuyi, T. M. (2013). Factors influencing investment decisions in capital market: A study of individual investors in Nigeria. *Organizations and Markets in Emerging Economies*, *4*(07), 141–161. doi:10.15388/omee.2013.4.1.14263

Ortas, E., Álvarez, I., & Garayar, A. (2015). The environmental, social, governance, and financial performance effects on companies that adopt the United Nations Global Compact. *Sustainability (Basel)*, *7*(2), 1932–1956. doi:10.3390u7021932

Pal, T., Irfan, M., & Kassim, S.B. (2023). How do Machine Learning (ML) techniques benefit the insurance industry? An exploratory study. *The Impact of AI Innovation on Financial Sectors in the Era of Industry 5.0,* (pp. 108-130). IGI Globa. doi:10.4018/979-8-3693-0082-4.ch007

Park, S. R., & Jang, J. Y. (2021). The impact of ESG management on investment decision: Institutional investors' perceptions of country-specific ESG criteria. *International Journal of Financial Studies*, *9*(3), 48. doi:10.3390/ijfs9030048

Patil, S., & Bagodi, V. (2021). A study of factors affecting investment decisions in India: The KANO way. *Asia Pacific Management Review*, *26*(4), 197–214. doi:10.1016/j.apmrv.2021.02.004

Pedersen, L. H., Fitzgibbons, S., & Pomorski, L. (2021). Responsible investing: The ESG-efficient frontier. *Journal of Financial Economics*, *142*(2), 572–597. doi:10.1016/j.jfineco.2020.11.001

Pérez-Gladish, B., Benson, K., & Faff, R. (2012). Profiling socially responsible investors: Australian evidence. *Australian Journal of Management*, *37*(2), 189–209. doi:10.1177/0312896211429158

Ridho Kismawadi, E., Irfan, M., & Shah, S. M. A. R. (2023). Revolutionizing Islamic finance: Artificial intelligence's role in the future of industry. The Impact of AI Innovation on Financial Sectors in the Era of Industry 5.0, (pp. 184-207). IGI Global. doi:10.4018/979-8-3693-0082-4.ch011

Saghroun, J., & Eglem, J. Y. (2008). A la recherche de la performance globale de l'entreprise: La perception des analystes financiers. *Comptabilité-Contrôle-Audit*, *14*(1), 93–118. doi:10.3917/cca.141.0093

Shafi, M. (2014). Determinants influencing individual investor behavior in stock market: A cross country research survey. *Nigerian Chapter of Arabian Journal of Business and Management Review*, *62*(1100), 1–12. doi:10.12816/0003720

Sharma, R. B., Lodha, S., Sharma, A., Ali, S., & Elmezughi, A. M. (2022). Environment, social and governance reporting and firm performance: Evidence from GCC countries. *International Journal of Innovative Research and Scientific Studies*, *5*(4), 419–427. doi:10.53894/ijirss.v5i4.1006

Sultana, S., Zulkifli, N., & Zainal, D. (2018). Environmental, social and governance (ESG) and investment decision in Bangladesh. *Sustainability (Basel)*, *10*(6), 1831. doi:10.3390u10061831

Van Duuren, E., Plantinga, A., & Scholtens, B. (2016). ESG integration and the investment management process: Fundamental investing reinvented. *Journal of Business Ethics*, *138*(3), 525–533. doi:10.100710551-015-2610-8

Viviers, S., Venter, D. J. L., & Krüger, J. (2012). The relative importance of ethics, environmental, social and governance criteria. *African Journal of Business Ethics*, *6*(2), 120. doi:10.4103/1817-7417.111021

Von Wallis, M., & Klein, C. (2015). Ethical requirement and financial interest: A literature review on socially responsible investing. *Business Research*, *8*(1), 61–98. doi:10.100740685-014-0015-7

Waas, T., Hugé, J., Block, T., Wright, T., Benitez-Capistros, F., & Verbruggen, A. (2014). Sustainability assessment and indicators: Tools in a decision-making strategy for sustainable development. *Sustainability (Basel)*, *6*(9), 5512–5534. doi:10.3390u6095512

Xiao, Y., Faff, R., Gharghori, P., & Lee, D. (2013). An empirical study of the world price of sustainability. *Journal of Business Ethics*, *114*(2), 297–310. doi:10.100710551-012-1342-2

Chapter 15
Shariah-Compliant Robo-Advisors:
Exploring the Development and Implementation of Islamic Finance's Automated Investment Solutions

Jayant Hooda
https://orcid.org/0000-0002-3491-9272
SRM University Delhi-NCR Sonepat, India

Vinita Singh
SRM University Delhi-NCR Sonepat, India

Mansur Ahmed Kazaure
https://orcid.org/0000-0002-0563-2619
Universiti Putra Malaysia, Malaysia

Rohit Singh
Royal Global University, India

ABSTRACT

This chapter discusses the role of financial technology in Islamic finance. The chapter explores the Islamic finance principles and the key components of the robo-advisory systems, including portfolio management, client profiling, socially responsible investing, and key players in the Shariah-compliant investment horizon. The present chapter also explores the opportunities and challenges associated with Shariah-compliant robo advisory, like cost-effectiveness, accessibility, regulatory considerations, and the human-machine interaction paradigm. The conclusion of this study highlights the significance of Shariah-compliant robo-advisory services and their potential impact on investors and various stakeholders within the financial industry.

DOI: 10.4018/979-8-3693-1038-0.ch015

1. INTRODUCTION

Robo-advisors, automated investment platforms driven by sophisticated algorithms and digital interfaces, have become an integral part of modern portfolio management. They offer diversified investment strategies and accessible and cost-effective financial advice, making investment more accessible to a broader range of individuals. The increase in robo-advisors is evidence of the effectiveness and efficiency of automation in the financial sector, as well as the growing demand for tailored investment solutions.

Islamic finance is based on Shariah principles that support its ethical and religious framework. This principle prohibits usury (riba), excessive uncertainty (gharar) and participation in activities considered incompatible with Islamic beliefs. Islamic finance focuses on ethical investment, risk-sharing and responsible financial practices, strengthening the commitment to social justice and financial inclusion. Adherence to Shariah-compliant investment practices is essential for the integrity and ethical foundations of Islamic finance.

The combination of the robo-advisors and Islamic finance has created a new area in the field of Islamic finance. This combination has led to creation of robo advisors that adhere to Shariah principles. These robo advisors provide the solutions to the investors, who are interested/ believe in the Shariah Law. These automated investment solutions offer affordable and ethical wealth management services to the investors which makes the Islamic finance accessible to a wide range of investors.

This paper explores the different aspects of Shariah-compliant robo-advisors. It focuses on their development, and the challenges and advantages that are consistent with Islamic finance principles.

2. LITERATURE REVIEW

For better understanding of the subject matter review of literature is divided in to three different sections. First section is related to the studies on Islamic finance principles and the need for Shariah-compliant investment solutions. Second section focuses on the rise of robo-advisors and their role in modern portfolio management. The third section is dedicated to examining studies pertaining to the development of Shariah-compliant robo-advisors.

2.1 Islamic Finance Principles and the Need for Shariah-Compliant Investment Solutions

Islamic finance aims to offer financial services and products that comply with Shariah, based on the religious beliefs of Muslims. The principles of Islamic finance include the prohibition of interest or usury (riba), the avoidance of excessive risk (gharar), and the prohibition of gambling (maysir) (Cortelezzi, 2022). Islamic finance emphasizes social justice, fair commercial relations, and the promotion of human well-being (Hailu & Tekdoğan, 2023). To ensure compliance with Shariah principles, a Shariah governance framework is necessary, which can be centralized or decentralized (Vismara, 2022). The availability of a centralized Shariah governance framework is crucial for overseeing and controlling the application of Islamic finance (Hasan et al., 2019). The development of Islamic finance has been significant in recent years, with its expansion in Muslim and non-Muslim countries (Hassan & Noor, 2021). However, there are differences between Islamic finance principles and the laws of other legal systems, highlighting the need for careful consideration and adaptation when applying Islamic finance principles in different contexts.

2.2 The Rise of Robo-Advisors and Their Role in Modern Portfolio Management

Robo-advisors have emerged as a disruptive trend in modern portfolio management, offering innovative asset management services through automated investment platforms that use quantitative algorithms to provide advice to investors. They have become widely used in mean-variance analyses, allowing investors to create efficiently diversified investment portfolios (Holtfort et al., 2022). Robo-advisors primarily rely on modern portfolio theory (MPT) as the framework for asset allocation, although some employ new approaches. The average performance of robo-advisors appears to outperform the market benchmark, but not significantly during the Corona crisis. Factors influencing their performance include the number of allocation methods applied and the technique of rebalancing (Yeh et al., 2022). Robo-advisors aim to offer personalized financial advice by adapting the risk-return tradeoff to the client's risk profile, incorporating idiosyncratic characteristics, market returns, and economic conditions. The optimal portfolio personalization involves balancing timely information from the client and mitigating behavioral biases in the communicated risk profile (Capponi et al., 2022). Additionally, robo-advisors assess client risk tolerance, build and recommend portfolios, manage risk, optimize taxes, and implement goal-based investing, socially responsible investing, and smart beta strategies (Grealish & Kolm, 2021). Classical financial theories and techniques, such as Constant Rebalancing and Modern Portfolio Theory, can still be relevant when combined with social media sentiments, as demonstrated by the Sentimental All-Weather and Sentimental MPT models (Leow et al., 2021).

2.3 Previous Research on the Development of Shariah-Compliant Robo-Advisors

Previous research on the development of Shariah-compliant robo-advisors is limited. There is a lack of literature addressing the long-term physical asset investment behavior of Shariah-compliant firms (Akguc & Rahahleh, 2020). However, there have been studies on the implementation and functionality of robo-advisors in the financial industry (Snihovyi et al., 2018). These studies have examined the use of machine learning and neural networks in building investment plans for cryptocurrencies investors (Ivanov et al., 2018). Additionally, research has explored the acceptance of robo-advisory services, considering factors such as technology characteristics, human-like characteristics, and consumer characteristics (Aw et al., 2023). While there is some understanding of the potential role of robo-advisors in cost saving and transparency in the financial service industry, further research is needed to determine if they will become a disruptive technology (Lee et al., 2018).

Therefore the present study explore the challenges and opportunities for Shariah-compliant robo-advisors.

2.4 Background and Motivation

Islamic finance, guided by Shariah law, has experienced notable growth, with a focus on ethical and transparent practices that avoid interest and speculative transactions. A significant aspect is Shariah-compliant investments, aligning with Islamic principles.

The rise of robo-advisory services, offering automated investment solutions, provides an opportunity to integrate Islamic values into modern finance. These digital platforms are known for cost-efficiency and accessibility. Shariah-compliant robo-advisors, tailored to Islamic ethical standards, can bridge contemporary financial technology and meet the specific needs of Islamic investors.

2.5 Objectives of the chapter

The present chapter aims to:

Study the benefits of Shariah-compliant robo-advisor to an investor
Examine the benefits of Shariah-compliant robo-advisor to financial service provider
Analyse the challenges faced by investors, investing through Shariah compliant robo advisory service
Investigate the challenges faced by the Shariah compliant robo advisory service provider

3. METHODOLOGY

3.1 Res

This conceptual paper employed a review of existing literature on Islamic finance principles and the Sahriah compliant by robo advisor. By exploring and analyzing existing literature, this paper develops the inclusive understanding of Islamic finance principles and the Sahriah compliant by robo advisor. It is pertinent to mention that this paper does not involve the collection of primary data; instead, it relies on the foundation of pre-existing research and established knowledge within the field.

4. BENEFITS OF SHARIAH-COMPLIANT ROBO-ADVISOR TO INVESTOR

4.1 Cost-Effectiveness

One of the key advantages of robo-advisory is its cost-effectiveness. Human-based financial advisory services generally involve high fees and minimum investment requirements, making them inaccessible to individuals with lower investable assets. Robo advisory platforms, on the other hand, typically offer lower fees and reduced minimum investment thresholds. By leveraging automation and scalable technology, robo-advisors can provide cost-effective solutions, making quality financial advice more accessible to a broader range of investors. This cost advantage enables individuals with limited resources to benefit from professional investment management and portfolio diversification in the field of Islamic finance.

4.2 Unbiased Advice

Being social and emotional human advisors have some element of biasness while robo advisors are automated processes that are based on mathematical algorithms. Therefore they are free from human behaviour and influence.

Human advisors are generally considered more biased than robo-advisors as the former may have their personal judgments based on a number of factors like their relationship with the employer etc. but advice of the robo-advisor will be based on the data provided by the investor. Therefore the robo-advisor reduces the chance of bias in the advisory service.

4.3 Alignment With Ethical and Religious Values

Shariah-compliant robo-advisors are designed to comply with the principles of Islamic finance and ensure that investment strategies conform to Shariah law. Investments are checked in order to avoid activities considered unethical or prohibited in Islam, such as interest-based transactions or investments in alcohol, gambling, or pork.

Shariah-compliant robo-advisors are designed to comply with the principles of Islamic finance and ensure that investment plans suggested by robo-advisors comply with the required standards. This knowledge creates additional reliability and religious belief for investors. Therefore Shariah-compliant robo-advisors present opportunities for individuals and institutions to access the stock market and make investments that align with their ethical and religious values (Hatta et al., 2022).

4.4 Socially Responsible Investing

Socially Responsible Investing (SRI) is a compelling advantage of Shariah-compliant advisors, offering investors the opportunity to align their financial goals with their ethical and religious values. Shariah-compliant advisors adhere to Islamic finance principles, ensuring that investments are free from industries and practices deemed unethical under Shariah law, such as alcohol, gambling, and tobacco. This alignment extends beyond Islamic values, since the SRI principles also support investments focusing on environmental and social responsibility. As a result, investors are able to invest ethically and responsibly, avoiding businesses involved in harmful activities, while supporting those that contribute positively to society and the environment. A combination of Shariah compliance and SRI criteria strengthens investor confidence, promotes ethical investment and responds to the growing global demand for investment strategies that promote financial well-being and social responsibility.

These robo-advisors can provide individualized investment services that are both Shariah-compliant and environmentally sustainable, catering to the growing demand for socially responsible investments (Katterbauer & Moschetta, 2022).

4.5 Individualized Investment Services

In the modern era of financial technology and investment management, Shariah-compliant robo-advisors play a pivotal role by delivering a high degree of personalization. They achieve this by fine-tuning investment strategies to align with the specific idiosyncrasies of investors (Hooda et al., 2024). This includes accommodating individual preferences, assessing and accommodating varying levels of risk tolerance, and diligently considering distinct financial objectives. The end result is an investment landscape that effortlessly conforms to the unique demands and requisites of each investor, thus facilitating the construction of portfolios that are meticulously tailored to cater to these distinctive financial profiles.

4.6 Data-Driven and Unsupervised Learning

The integration of data-driven and unsupervised learning techniques in Shariah-compliant robo advisors strengthens their appeal and effectiveness by enabling these platforms to carefully tailor investment portfolios and ensure strict compliance with Islamic financial principles. This advanced technology makes it possible to create optimised portfolios balancing risk and return and allows continuous monitoring and real-time adjustments. In addition, the absence of human bias in decision-making ensures transparent and consistent investment strategies. In addition, the scalability of these robo advisors caters to both individual investors and institutions, expanding the scope of Shariah-compliant investment strategies. As a result, these data-driven and unsupervised learning approaches not only enhance the value proposition of Shariah-compliant robo advisors but also simplify the process for retail investors to establish their own Shariah-compliant portfolios, thereby making ethical investments more accessible and objective (Masri, 2017).

4.7 Potential for Attractive Risk-Adjusted Returns

Shariah-compliant robo advisors offer attractive risk-adjusted returns by emphasising diversified, ethically screened and stable portfolios. These investment strategies can reduce risk exposures, promote long-term perspectives and comply with investor ethical principles, ultimately contributing to better risk-adjusted returns compared to traditional investment approaches.

Additionally, the performance of market-weighted Shariah-compliant portfolios has been found to be generally less risky than conventional benchmark portfolios, indicating the potential for attractive risk-adjusted returns (Ashraf & Khawaja, 2016).

4.8 Convenience and Accessibility

The advantage of "Convenience and Accessibility" in the context of Shariah-compliant robo-advisors is that they make ethical and Shariah-compliant investing accessible to a wider audience while offering user-friendly, cost-effective, and convenient solutions. This makes it possible for individuals to easily incorporate ethical and religious considerations into their investment strategies, irrespective of the level of financial expertise or geographical location. Overall, Shariah-compliant robo-advisors offer a convenient and accessible way for investors to engage in ethical and socially responsible investing while also achieving their financial goals.

5. ADVANTAGES THAT SHARIAH-COMPLIANT ROBO-ADVISOR OFFER TO FINANCIAL SERVICE PROVIDERS

5.1 Widening the Client Base

Using Shariah-compliant robo advisor, financial service providers can provide services to a large number of clients as compared to human advisors. This will generate more revenue for the service providers.

5.2 Costs and Efficiency

Shariah-compliant robo-advisors save money for both financial service providers and their clients. They significantly reduce the overhead costs of hiring human advisors as they don't require salaries, benefits, or office space, making them a cost-effective option. The analysis speed of robo-advisors is high compared to a human advisor which makes them more efficient.

5.3 Effective Risk Management

Robo-advisors use algorithms and data analysis to optimize portfolios and effectively manage risk. This can lead to improved risk-adjusted returns, ultimately increasing the reputation and goodwill of the financial service provider.

6. Challenges Faced by Investors in Availing the Shariah Compliant Robo Advisory Service

6.1 Limited Availability and Awareness

Shariah-compliant robo-advisory services may not be as widely available as traditional robo-advisors. The level of awareness about Shariah-compliant robo-advisory services is very low among the investor community. Investors in certain regions or markets may have limited access to these services, which can restrict their options.

6.2 Complex Screening Process

Ensuring that investment portfolios remain compliant with Shariah principles requires a complex screening process. This can make Shariah-compliant robo-advisors more time-consuming and challenging to set up compared to conventional robo-advisory platforms.

6.3 Initial Investment Requirements

Some Shariah-compliant robo-advisory services may have relatively higher minimum investment requirements. This can pose a challenge for investors with limited capital, especially those who are just starting their investment journey.

6.4 Educational Barriers

Investors who are not well-versed in Shariah principles may face challenges in understanding the criteria used for compliance. Education and awareness about Shariah-compliant investing can be a hurdle for some.

6.5 Monitoring and Compliance Challenges

Investors need to stay informed about any changes in the Shariah compliance criteria and ensure that their portfolios remain in alignment with these principles. This may require ongoing vigilance and understanding of evolving guidelines.

6.6 Lack of Personalization

While robo-advisors offer automated and algorithm-driven services, some investors may prefer a more personalized approach to their investments. Achieving a balance between personalization and Shariah compliance can be challenging.

6.7 Market Liquidity

Finding Shariah-compliant investment opportunities with sufficient liquidity can be challenging, particularly in certain sectors or asset classes. This may limit the choices available to investors.

6.8 Regulatory Differences

The regulatory environment for Shariah-compliant investments can vary from one country to another. Investors operating in multiple regions may need to navigate different sets of regulations and guidelines.

6.9 Regulatory Challenges

Shariah-compliant robo advisors face a number of regulatory challenges due to the need to ensure compliance with Islamic finance principles. These challenges include the complexities of interpretation of Shariah law, as different scholars may have different views. In addition, there is a lack of a standardized global regulatory framework for Islamic finance, resulting in different compliance requirements across regions. Transparency and disclosure standards are also a challenge, since investors need to be well informed of ethical screening criteria and investment strategies used by robo advisors. These challenges require cooperation between financial authorities and Shariah scholars in order to establish consistent and internationally accepted standards for Shariah-compliant robo advisors. Besides these there is a need for regulators to develop capacities to assess the honesty, competence, and suitability of these automated advisors, as they cannot simply be assumed (Ashraf & Khawaja, 2016).

6.10 Data Privacy and Security

Data privacy is a significant challenge in the context of robo-advisory services. Robo advisors use sensitive personal and financial information to provide personalized financial services. Maintaining robust data privacy and security measures is vital to protect investors' information from unauthorized access, breaches, or misuse. Robo advisory platforms must adhere to stringent data protection regulations, implement secure encryption protocols, and maintain strong cybersecurity defenses. Addressing data privacy concerns and building trust with investors regarding the handling and storage of their data is paramount for the long-term success and adoption of robo-advisory.

6.11 Challenges in Sourcing Qualified Professionals

Qualified professionals are a key but limited resource for Shariah-compliant robo-advisors who often require a unique blend of financial expertise and Islamic knowledge. There is a shortage of professionals in this sector, which makes it difficult for firms to recruit and retain. The shortage of qualified Shariah practitioners, poses a risk to Shariah compliance assurance in the Islamic finance industry (Baker & Dellaert, 2018).

6.12 Challenges in Enhancing Consistency in Shariah Screening Standards

Additionally, there is a need for greater consistency in applying Shariah screening standards for Shariah-compliant portfolios, as the negligible difference in performance based on different criteria indicates a lack of uniformity (Erragragui & Revelli, 2016).

6.13 Social Responsibility in Shariah-Compliant Investments: A Performance Dilemma

Furthermore, the integration of social performance measures in Islamic portfolios presents a challenge, as disengagement from shariah-compliant stocks with community and human rights controversies can lead to negative performance (Farook & Farooq, 2011).

Overall, these challenges highlight the importance of addressing regulatory, practitioner qualification, consistency, and social performance issues in the development of Shariah-compliant robo-advisors.

6.14 Investor Preference for Human Financial Advisors

Some investors consider robo-advisors to be a tool mainly suitable for quantitative analysis and do not consider them to be a complete replacement for human advisors. These investors believe that human involvement is essential to understanding and interpreting the emotional aspects of investment decisions (Bhatia et al., 2021).

7. SHARIAH-COMPLIANT ROBO ADVISORS

This section provides the illustrative list of some Shariah-compliant robo-advisors.

7.1 Wahed Invest

Wahed Invest was founded by Junaid Wahedna, a former investment banker, who recognized this gap in the market and the potential for using technology to address it. The company's mission was clear: to provide Muslim investors with a convenient and transparent way to invest in accordance with their values. Wahed Invest started as a small startup and quickly gained attention and popularity among Muslim investors, particularly millennials, who were looking for a modern approach to halal investing. Based in the United States, Wahed Invest offers Shariah-compliant robo-advisory services to retail investors (Investing, n.d.).

7.2 Sarwa

Sarwa is a financial technology company based in Dubai, United Arab Emirates, and is known for revolutionizing the investment landscape in the Middle East. Sarwa was founded by three friends and financial industry professionals—Mark Chahwan, Jad Sayegh, and Nadine Mezher. Recognizing the need for a change, they set out to democratize investing and make it accessible to the masses in the Middle East. Sarwa aimed to simplify the investment process, lower costs, and provide a user-friendly platform that could empower individuals to achieve their financial goals. Operating in the United Arab Emirates, Sarwa provides both conventional and Shariah-compliant robo-advisory services (Sarwa | Hands-off Investing, n.d.).

7.3 Simply Ethical

Simply Ethical, established in 2009, has emerged as a prominent provider of Sharia-Compliant and Socially Responsible investment solutions and pension options for individuals in the United Kingdom. The company operates under the direct authorization and regulation of the Financial Conduct Authority (FCA). Simply Ethical is dedicated to promoting ethical investments as a primary means of savings, allowing individuals to make positive contributions to society while working toward their financial objectives. Simply ethical is a UK-based platform that provides Shariah-compliant investment solutions, including robo-advisory services (Who We Are, n.d.).

8. SUMMARY OF FINDINGS

The emergence and growth of both financial technology and Islamic finance has given rise to Shariah-compliant robo-advisors. This chapter has explored the key components and principles of Islamic finance and the role of robo-advisory systems. It has also examined the opportunities and challenges presented by Shariah-compliant robo-advisory services. The significance of these services for investors and stakeholders in the financial industry cannot be overstated. They bridge the gap between modern finance and Islamic ethics, providing accessibility, ethical investment options, and cost-effective wealth management. However, several challenges, including regulatory hurdles, a shortage of qualified professionals, and the need for consistency in Shariah screening standards, must be addressed to maximize the potential of Shariah-compliant robo-advisors.

8.1 Implications

The implications of this study are significant, as they highlight the transformative potential of Shariah-compliant robo-advisory services in the Islamic finance landscape. The alignment of ethical and religious values through these platforms opens new avenues for investors to participate in financial markets while adhering to their principles. Socially responsible investing, individualized services, and data-driven compliance checks offer a comprehensive approach to wealth management. Furthermore, the pursuit of attractive risk-adjusted returns and the convenience and accessibility of these services make them an attractive option for both retail and institutional investors.

8.2 Scope of Future Research

The exploration of Shariah-compliant robo-advisors is still in its infancy, and numerous areas deserve further investigation. Future research can focus on the development of standardized regulatory frameworks specific to these automated advisors, taking into account their unique characteristics and compliance requirements. Additionally, studies can explore the development of educational programs that equip professionals with the necessary financial and Islamic knowledge for effective Shariah-compliant robo-advisory services.

REFERENCES

Akguc, S., & Rahahleh, N. A. (2020, January 4). Shariah Compliance and Investment Behavior: Evidence from GCC Countries. *Emerging Markets Finance and Trade*. Taylor & Francis. doi:10.1080/1540496X.2019.1706164

Ashraf, D., & Khawaja, M. (2016, December 1). Does the Shariah screening process matter? Evidence from Shariah compliant portfolios. *Journal of Economic Behavior and Organization. Elsevier BV.* doi:10.1016/j.jebo.2016.10.003

Aw, E. C. X., Zha, T., & Chuah, S. H. W. (2023, January 18). *My new financial companion! non-linear understanding of Robo-advisory service acceptance*. Service Industries Journal; Taylor & Francis. https://doi.org/ doi:10.1080/02642069.2022.2161528

Baker, T., & Dellaert, B. G. C. (2018, January 1). *Regulating Robo Advice across the Financial Services Industry*. SciSpace - Paper. https://typeset.io/papers/regulating-robo-advice-across-the-financial-services-144738fryr

Bhatia, A., Chandani, A., Atiq, R., Mehta, M., & Divekar, R. (2021, September 5). Artificial intelligence in financial services: a qualitative research to discover robo-advisory services. *Qualitative Research in Financial Markets*. Emerald Publishing Limited. doi:10.1108/QRFM-10-2020-0199

Capponi, A., Ólafsson, S., & Zariphopoulou, T. (2022, April 1). *Personalized Robo-Advising: Enhancing Investment Through Client Interaction*. Management Science; Institute for Operations Research and the Management Sciences. doi:10.1287/mnsc.2021.4014

Cortelezzi, F. (2022, July 6). *Global Islamic Finance: Principles and Products*. Routledge eBooks. doi:10.4324/9781003155218-10

Erragragui, E., & Revelli, C. (2016, November 1). Is it costly to be both shariah compliant and socially responsible? *Review of Financial Economics*. Elsevier BV. doi:10.1016/j.rfe.2016.08.003

FarookS.FarooqM. O. (2011, January 1). *Shariah Governance for Islamic Finance: Challenges and Pragmatic Solutions*. Social Science Research Network; RELX Group (Netherlands). doi:10.2139/ssrn.1813483

Grealish, A., & Kolm, P. N. (2021, September 15). Robo-Advisors Today and Tomorrow: Investment Advice Is Just an App Away. *The Journal of Wealth Management; Euromoney Institutional Investor*. doi:10.3905/jwm.2021.1.149

Hailu, S. M., & Tekdoğan, M. F. (2023, June 30). *Ensuring The Compliance of Islamic Finance Applications with Shariah Principles in Ethiopia: The Way Forward*. Hitit Ilahiyat Dergisi. doi:10.14395/hid.1247875

Hasan, H., Maamor, S., & Abdullah, H. (2019, January 1). Evaluating The Effect Of Islamic Financing To Financial Development: Evidence From OIC Countries. *International Journal of Management Studies*. doi:10.32890/ijms.25.2.2018.10501

Hassan, R., & Noor, F. A. M. (2021, January 1). *Promoting peace and equality through the practice of good Islamic governance: the case of Islamic finance*. SciSpace. https://typeset.io/papers/promoting-peace-and-equality-through-the-practice-of-good-4r2qwhtbtr

Hatta, M., Zainorin, N. D. E., Jalaludin, S., Nor, N. M., & Ramli, S. (2022, December 1). Financial Robo-Advisor Savings2u For Shariah-Compliant Savings And Investment Application. *Journal of Information System and Technology Management*. doi:10.35631/JISTM.729006

Holtfort, T., Horsch, A., & Schwarz, J. (2022, January 1). Robo-advisors as part of industry 4.0 in financial markets: Evolutionary development, methods, and first performance insights. *Risk Governance and Control: Financial Markets & Institutions*. Virtus Interpress. doi:10.22495/rgcv12i2p3

Hooda, J., Singh, V., Irfan, M., & Hawaldar, I. T. (2024). Unleashing the Power of AI. In *The Impact of AI Innovation on Financial Sectors in the Era of Industry 5.0* (pp. 58–76). IGI Global. doi:10.4018/979-8-3693-0082-4.ch004

Investing. (n.d.). https://www.wahed.com/global/investing

Katterbauer, K., & Moschetta, P. (2022, June 1). *A robo-advisory framework for Islamic and Environmental, Social and Governance (ESG) compliance – A benchmark study on the S&P 500 stock index*. JMIFR. doi:10.33102/jmifr.v19i1.408

Lee, S., Choi, J., Ngo-Ye, T. L., & Cummings, M. (2018, January 1). *Modeling Trust in the Adoption Decision Process of Robo-Advisors: An Agent-Based Simulation Approach*. SciSpace. https://typeset.io/papers/modeling-trust-in-the-adoption-decision-process-of-robo-217oxlfw5k

Leow, E. K. W., Nguyen, B. P., & Chua, M. C. H. (2021, October 1). Robo-advisor using genetic algorithm and BERT sentiments from tweets for hybrid portfolio optimisation. *Expert Systems With Applications*. Elsevier BV. doi:10.1016/j.eswa.2021.115060

Masri, H. (2017, December 1). A Shariah-compliant portfolio selection model. *Journal of the Operational Research Society*. Palgrave Macmillan. doi:10.1057/s41274-017-0223-6

Seyyed, F. J., Shehzad, C. T., & Ashfaq, H. (2019, December 17). *Millat Tractors Limited: A Shariah-compliant Investment Opportunity*. Asian Journal of Management Cases; SAGE Publishing. doi:10.1177/0972820119884399

Snihovyi, O., Ivanov, O., & Kobets, V. (2018, September 1). *Implementation of Robo-Advisors Using Neural Networks for Different Risk Attitude Investment Decisions*. IEEE. doi:10.1109/IS.2018.8710559

Vismara, F. (2022, July 6). *Application of the Legal Principles of Islamic Finance to Our Legal System*. Routledge eBooks. doi:10.4324/9781003155218-15

Who we are. (n.d.). Simply Ethical. https://simplyethical.com/who-we-are/#our-services-compared

Yeh, H. C., Yu, M. C., Liu, C. H., & Huang, C. I. (2022, June 14). Robo-advisor based on unified theory of acceptance and use of technology. *Asia Pacific Journal of Marketing and Logistics*. Emerald Publishing Limited. doi:10.1108/APJML-07-2021-0493

Chapter 16
The Effect of Strategic Partnership on Innovation and Business:
Performance of the Fintech Industry in Bahrain

Zakir Hossen Shaikh
https://orcid.org/0000-0003-4733-4166
Kingdom University, Bahrain

Mohammad Irfan
https://orcid.org/0000-0002-4956-1170
NSB Academy, India

Naji Mansour Nomran
Kingdom University, Bahrain

Moïse Laïfoya Lawin
Ministry of Economy and Finance of Benin, Benin

ABSTRACT

Nothing could have prepared any of us for the recent outbreak of COVID 19. It has impacted individuals, communities, economies, and countries around the world. It has acted as a catalyst for growth because its impact has gone beyond a physical, financial, and economic level. The purpose of this study was to discuss the impact of strategic partnerships on driving innovation, accelerating digital transformation across financial services in the Kingdom of Bahrain, and economic growth. The Central Bank of Bahrain (CBB) Digital Lab, a collaborative effort, between the CBB and several strategic Partners of FinHub973 including the Bahrain Economic Development Board, Bank ABC, Benefit, BisB, ila Bank, and the National Bank of Bahrain, enables local and global FinTechs to connect seamlessly to explore, test, and prototype new and innovative solutions on a centralized digital sandbox. These new solutions are commonly referred to as fintech. Collaborative partnerships are essential to catalyse innovation in finance, for the benefit of the industry, economy, and society at large.

DOI: 10.4018/979-8-3693-1038-0.ch016

1. INTRODUCTION

A collaborative effort, between the Bahrain Central Bank (CBB) Digital Lab, and several "strategic partners of FinHub973 including the Bahrain Economic Development Board (EDB), Bank ABC, Benefit, BisB, ila Bank, and the National Bank of Bahrain" empowers local and global fintech's to link flawlessly with Bahrain's financial organizations to explore, test, and prototype new and advanced solutions on a centralized digital sandbox. "Financial services (such as payments, remittances, and credit) that may be accessed and supplied through digital channels, including mobile devices, are referred to as digital financial services (DFS)". These include dependable tools (like debit and credit cards) generally provided by banks, as well as cutting-edge cloud computing, digital platforms, distributed ledger technology (DLT) solutions, crypto-assets, and peer-to-peer (P2P) applications. These new solutions are commonly referred to as fintech.

In Bahrain, 87% of professionals are either interested in partnering with fintech companies or have already done so. Such collaborations will be facilitated and accelerated by the MENA region's largest fintech hub, Bahrain Fintech Bay. The development of fintech is being aided by Bahrain's well-established financial services sector, its position as a key center for Islamic finance, and the country's push for financial inclusion. Around 400 domestic, regional, and international financial institutions are now located in Bahrain. The financial industry is eager to investigate working with fintech's and implement cutting-edge new solutions. Rowad and Bahrain Development Bank have joined forces strategically, according to Bahrain Fintech Bay (BFB). The Bahrain Development Bank will collaborate closely with the BFB and be one of its founding partners to develop the Rowad Program, Seed Fuel-Rowad, and the Invested Platform and support fintech entrepreneurship programs, which offers qualifying fintech businesses access to the 'BFB's Seed Fuel program, which offers equity investments of up to BHD 25,000 and entrepreneur support programs, as well as the investor platform. (Bahrain Fintech Ecosystem Report 2022).

It is crucial to emphasize that Islamic fintech differs from traditional fintech since it must adhere to Shariah regulations. However, the development of Islamic financial institutions (IFIs) now has wider accessibility thanks to fintech solutions. opportunity to enhance their product offering and infrastructure (Jamil & Seman, 2019). As a result, studies on the use of fintech in the field of Islamic finance have been more prevalent recently (Abojeib & Habib, 2019; Jamil & Seman, 2019). In 2022, Shaikh, Z.H., Sarea, A., and Irfan, M. fintech may make Islamic banking more competitive with traditional finance without compromising on advantages, allowing the business to draw in more customers, increase efficiency, save costs, and provide a larger choice of products.

The structure of this chapter contains: An introduction is given in part one, and a survey of the literature on fintech that complies with Shariah is the main topic of section two. The impact of strategic partnerships on innovation and commercial success of Bahrain's fintech industry is discussed in Section 3. The last section concludes the study analysis and discusses the project's future direction. Section four discusses current fintech innovation and economic progress.

1.1 Background of the Study

Islamic finance's foundation is built on socioeconomic disparity and sustainable growth because it is founded on the teachings and examples of the Holy Quran [6]. It is predicated on the idea that we should strive for sustainable growth to prevent resource shortage issues for future generations. It is founded on Islamic morals, which apply to all aspects of human life, including the economy, policies, culture, religion, and other spheres of life [7]. The Islamic faith now unites more than one-fourth of the world's population [8]. Islamic finance is gaining popularity and supporting the economic growth of both Muslim and non-Muslim communities [9]. It differs greatly from traditional finance in terms of both its principles and features [10]. The foundation of an Islamic economy is the idea of shared accountability and cooperation. In the Islamic economy, it is crucial that both parties benefit from the economic trade. It supports earning money through economic activity that is productive and restricts (haram) a few sectors of the economy that might be detrimental to society.

Bahrain, which ranks second in the MENA and fourth globally for the growth of Islamic finance, is recognized as the world's preeminent expert on the subject. (ICD 2021). Bahrain is one of the top five Islamic finance economies in the world (Islamic Finance Development Indicator (IFDI-2022), The Kingdom's high position reflects its avant-garde thinking and inventive methods, as well as the cutting-edge financial environment it provides for both old and new financial institutions. Islamic fintech's are expected to reach a value of $128 billion by 2025, according to the Global Islamic Fintech Report 2021. The worldwide fintech market for conventional financing accounts for barely 0.8 percent of the rapidly expanding Islamic fintech market, which Moody's reported rose by 61% in 2021 despite starting from a low foundation. The rating agency anticipates that the sector will expand mostly going forward. Islamic banking systems in the Middle East and some regions of Asia are moving more and more in the direction of "open" banking regulations that support advancements in digital finance. Given the regulatory trend towards the digitalization of financial services and the developing open banking rules, Moody's anticipates that competition will increase in accordance with our estimate of growth in the Islamic fintech sector.

Islamic financial technology advancements could hasten the movement of capital to a more resilient digital economy. Additionally, it can aid in attaining global policy goals, particularly those related to reducing the effects of climate change and advancing the sustainable development agenda for the benefit of society. To do this, Islamic fintech's must focus on fostering sustainability innovation to draw not only conventional Islamic investors but also the expanding impact investor base. As the fintech industry matures, it is now up to nations like Bahrain, which have powerful sovereign wealth funds and sizable Islamic banking institutions, to take the initiative and establish venture capital funds and funds that can facilitate later-stage investments globally in Islamic fintech or the larger Islamic digital economy.

2. LITERATURE REVIEW

Financial technology (Fintech) is a dynamic and continually evolving sector, but defining it precisely has been a challenge, with no unanimous agreement on a single definition. The current focus is primarily on tech-reliant companies aiming to enhance their financial services provision through innovative technologies [11]. Fintech is generally defined as technology-driven financial solutions that include all the services that banks typically offer while integrating cybersecurity and IT control. [12 -14]. It integrates IT with financial services including asset management, payments, and remittances, so establishing a new paradigm for the provision of financial services. [13, 15]. What sets fintech apart from traditional finance is the extent of involvement in financing, asset management, and payment facilitation, marking a notable departure in approach [16].

Fintech can be divided into four categories: financing, asset management, payment processing, and other financial technologies. Crowdfunding, credit factoring, group investing, and lending are examples of financing practices. [17]. Asset management includes both personal and social trading, which are seen

Figure 1. The Islamic Fintech services landscape

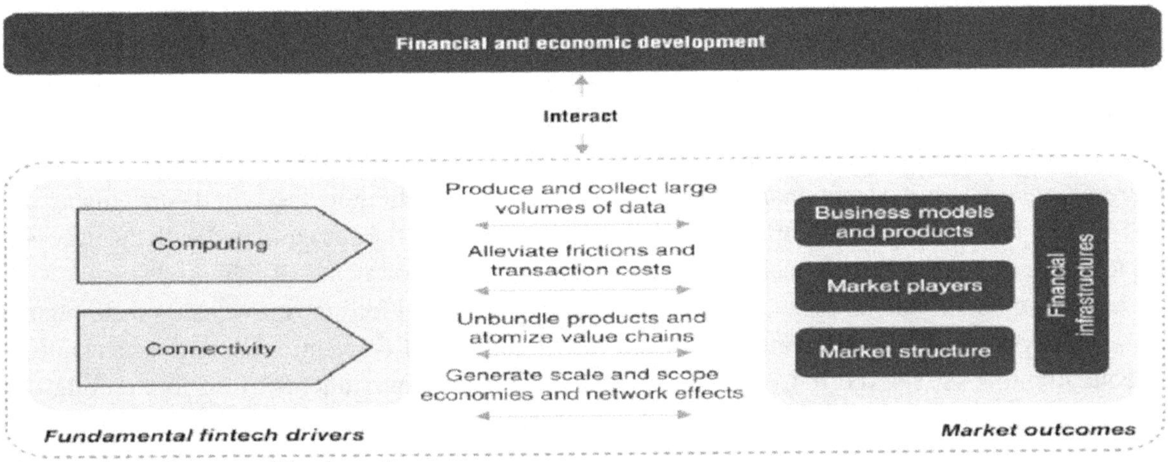

Source: https://www.worldbank.org/

as essential elements of intellectual capital. [12, 18, 19]. Enabling payment streamlines administrative procedures and allows clients to receive services to which they are legally entitled in a timely manner. [20-23]. Finally, search engine platforms, insurance applications, and IT infrastructure for financing are examples of more financial technology. [24-27].

Estimating the size, growth rate, and impact of fintech on conventional banking parameters has proven challenging due to its rapid evolution. However, the financial inflow into the fintech industry has been substantial, underlining its potential as an investment opportunity. In 2016, investments in this industry exceeded $25 billion across more than 1000 agreements, signaling a burgeoning investment prospect in financial technology firms [26, 28,29]. According to another source, the industry was worth $14 billion because of around 850 transactions, and by the end of the year, about 9,000 businesses had collected at least $100 billion. [20,42]. The industry witnessed a remarkable year-on-year growth of 75% between 2014 and 2015, and this upward trajectory has persisted in subsequent years, reinforcing fintech's significance and growth prospects within the financial landscape [30-33].

Financial technology (Fintech) has ushered in a fundamental shift in the operational standards of financial institutions and their service delivery to clients within the banking industry [42]. To align with global growth, enhance customer service delivery, and reduce transaction costs, banks have made significant investments in technology. Financial institutions have widely embraced Fintech networks to provide an extensive array of value-added services, acting as a facilitator for enhanced productivity and economic advancement at the organizational level [34-37]. Fintech achieves this by making financial commodities more accessible and cost-effective, ultimately reducing trading transaction costs for banks [38, 42].

Bahrain is one of the leading nations in the Middle East, has made substantial investments in technology within the financial sector. The Bahrain Central Bank's committed innovative fintech units have been established to promote a conducive regulatory framework that fosters fintech innovation and adoption [39-41]. Several initiatives have been introduced to enable startups and fintech firms to offer innovative banking and financial solutions to their clients while ensuring compliance with Sharia-compliant and contemporary services [42]. The development and implementation of fintech solutions, along with their associated benefits, significantly influence regulatory advancements at both regional and international levels. These regulatory advancements are crucial in guiding fintech initiatives and stakeholders within Bahrain's financial sector [43-45].

Moreover, integrating fintech financial processes enhances information disclosure, promoting equality in sharing and utilizing information among decision-makers through platforms like the Internet and social media [16, 18, 46]. However, the adoption of such technology amplifies the demand for skilled employees, necessitating educational institutions to adapt their teaching methods and curricula accordingly [47-49]. The evolving landscape underscores the need for a workforce equipped with the necessary skills to thrive in an increasingly technology-driven financial environment [49-50].

Due to the global financial crises, the world embarked on a quest for innovative methods to regulate its financial systems. This pursuit stemmed from the limitations of conventional control mechanisms. Consequently, this shift paved the way for both individuals and governments to explore cutting-edge technologies, aimed at bolstering the oversight and assessment of compliance with established rules and regulations. This endeavour holds the promise of elevating overall performance [27,33]. Over the past 15 years, this transformative journey has continued.

Fintech has become an indispensable tool for financial institutions, transforming the way they operate and interact with clients. Bahrain's proactive approach to embracing fintech and driving regulatory frameworks demonstrates the vital role technology plays in advancing the financial sector [[15,50]. The simultaneous challenges and opportunities posed by fintech emphasize the importance of education and skill development to navigate this rapidly evolving industry.

3. RESEARCH METHODOLOGY

This paper is considered using qualitative techniques and secondary data as a foundation. Various official & and annual reports, articles, research, websites, and other sources were used to gather the data. The Global Islamic Fintech Report (2019), the Islamic Fintech Report 2018, the Islamic Finance Development Indicator (IFDI-2022), and the Islamic Finance Development (ICD) 2021 reports were all used to gather the data.

4. FINTECH IN BAHRAIN: A GLIMPSE OF ITS REGULATORY INITIATIVES AND STRATEGIC PARTNERSHIP

According to United Nations (UN) estimates for 2020, the Kingdom of Bahrain, which is situated in the Arabian Gulf, has a total population of more than 1.7 million people living within its small 765.3 square kilometer territory. The country has been creative and has given the industry priority, particularly since the emergence of fintech. It is considered to be the historical hub of the Middle East, especially in terms of finance. As part of its continuous steps towards the Kingdom's financial digital transformation and advancements in digital financial services, the Bahrain Central Bank (CBB) established a fintech and innovation Unit. The goal of this unit is to guarantee that corporate and individual clients in the financial services industry receive the best possible care by promoting an adaptable regulatory environment that supports fintech and innovation. One of the ways it will do this is by establishing a Regulatory Sandbox, which will facilitate regulatory testing. Irfan, M., Elhoseny, M., Kassim, S., Metawa, N., Ad-

Figure 2. Conceptual framework for Fintech: Interactions between markets, policy, and development

Source: Global Islamic Fintech Report 2021

vanced Machine Learning Algorithms for Complex Financial Applications, (2023), pp. 1-292, discusses sophisticated financial applications, like big data environments financial risk management. This book provides state-of-the-art research on the applications of machine learning and artificial intelligence in the financial sectors.

4.1 FinHub973: Bahrain Central Bank (CBB)'s Digital Lab

The Bahrain Central Bank (CBB)'s FinHub 973 is the first international digital innovation platform in the field that connects and encourages cooperation between fintech's that come under its jurisdiction and financial institutions. FinHub 973, is supported by Fintech Galaxy and makes it simple for local and foreign fintech businesses to get in touch with Bahrain's financial institutions to conduct research, test ideas, and develop prototypes on an integrated digital sandbox. FinHub973 integrates technical digital technology testing and validation with the CBB's regulatory framework. an effort by Bahrain's central bank to foster innovation in the financial sector by guaranteeing the existence of a strong regulatory environment, a top-notch innovation lab, and a platform for collaboration, investment, buying, and stra-

Figure 3. Strategic partners of Bahrain Central Bank

Source-CBB, Bahrain

tegic partnerships within a state-of-the-art financial ecosystem. "The Effect of AI Innovation in the Age of Industry 5.0 on the Financial Sectors emerges as a crucial instrument, propelling advancements that will shape the future of the financial environment. "Elmogy, M. El-Sappagh, Irfan, 2023."

4.2 Post Pandemic Strategies

- **FINX**: Fintech solutions can be developed, tested, and deployed using the open API platform known as FINX. With matchmaking and crowdsourcing tools that address client pain points and quicken the financial innovation journey, it provides a marketplace that links Institutions to thousands of fintech's from across the world.
- **The Regulatory Sandbox** is a virtual environment for fintech's, startups, and established companies with fintech initiatives interested in testing their technology-based innovative banking and financial solutions such as foster fair competition, push for financial inclusion, enhance the customer experience, and accept new technologies.
- **Startup Acceleration** inspires business owners and aids emerging fintech firms in developing prototypes, forming business alliances, accelerating growth, and navigating the regulatory environment.
- **Powering Corporate Innovation** access to competent, strategically positioned early- and growth-stage firms, as well as assistance in resolving their innovation-related problems.
- **Investment opportunities** a special stream of screened, high-potential fintechs, as well as practical operational, governmental, and business support for portfolio businesses
- **Crowdsourcing Global Brainpower** the largest fintech, insurtech, and regtech ecosystem in the world, with access to exceptional talent and strong resources to support and realize transformational ambitions.

The Bahrain Central Bank is launching the 'Bahrain Supernova Fintech Challenges 2022 on FinHub 973' to support exposed inventions in the economic facilities and to encourage collaboration and integration between emerging companies using open APIs and incumbent financial institutions. The emergence of technical innovations and advancements in every part of our existence has been expedited by the Co-

Figure 4. Regulatory initiatives of Bahrain

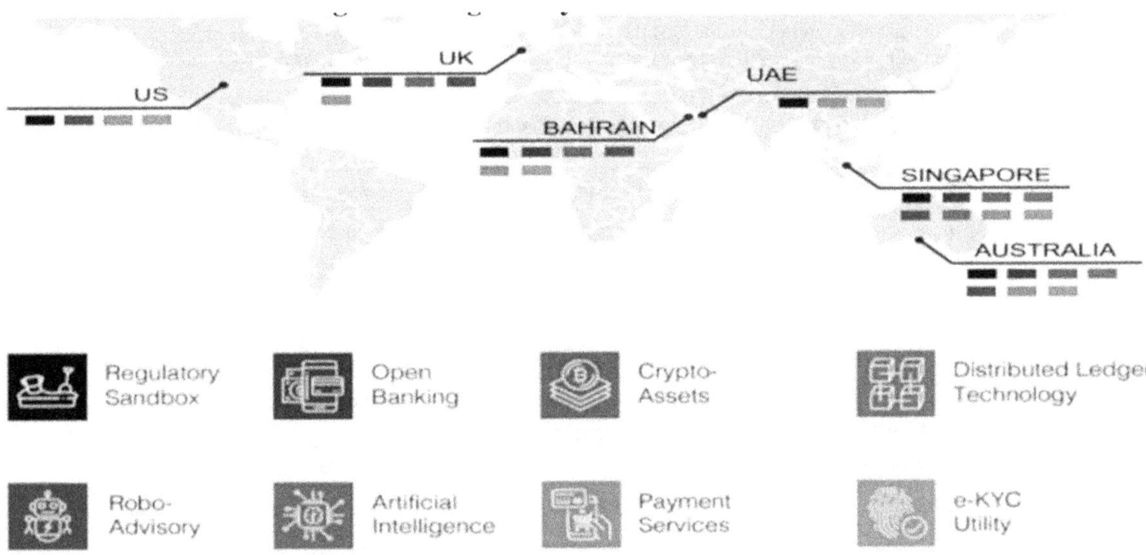

Source: Bahrain Fintech Regulatory Report 2019

vid-19 epidemic. The launch of this challenge comes at a critical juncture when financial institutions and governments worldwide are focusing on the transition from open banking to open finance. Innovative startups and tech firms from the Kingdom of Bahrain and the surrounding region can submit proposals via the FinHub 973 digital platform by addressing issue statements under the following themes with the help of strategic partners. The automation process for restricting and unblocking accounts is the Bahrain Central Bank's use of regtech.

- Bank ABC - Finance with Autonomy.
- The BENEFIT Company - Enhancing Nearby/Wearable Device Payment Services.
- Ila Bank - AI, Banking, and User Experience,
- National Bank of Bahrain - Combining Customer Accounting System with NBB for Banking Requirements.

Bahrain continues to lag behind countries such as Singapore and Australia with respect to several significant, regulated fintech norms. Bahrain's laws do cover open banking, robo-advisory, crypto assets, payment services, and regulatory sandboxes, but they may be more stringent when it comes to blockchain and AI. Ridho Kismawadi, E., Irfan, M., and Shah, S.M.A.R. (2023), illuminated, Revolutionizing Islamic finance: The role of artificial intelligence in the industrial future, is significant because it closes a gap in the information about the integration of AI skill in Islamic system investigating the probable rewards and contests of using AI to the business.

Table 1. Fintech-strategic partnership

November 2016	A delegation from Bahrain attended the 2016 China High Tech Fair. MoUs were signed, one of which included a commitment by the "EDB and Shenzhen Capital Group" to increase business prospects for Chinese and Bahraini firms.
December 2016	Aiming to serve the whole GCC area, the Bahrain Central Bank introduced fintech laws and pushed forward-thinking businesses to establish a base of operations in Bahrain.
May 2017	The Mastercard office has opened in the Kingdom, according to the Bahrain EDB.
August 2017	In association with Amazon Web Services, the Information & eGovernment Authority of Bahrain hosted a session titled "Strategic Direction for Cloud Computing."
September 2017	Amazon announced that it will build an "AWS territory in the Middle East, positioned in the Kingdom, starting in the beginning of 2019".
January 2018	Robust Wealth and Bahrain Fintech (BFB) Bay together to develop robo-advisory technology.
February 2018	BFB collaborated with Sigma Ratings, a fintech company creating non-credit risk rating services that are powered by artificial intelligence.
May 2018	Travelex and Murabaha Club have established strategic alliances with Bahrain Fintech Bay.
September 2018	Bahrain Fintech Bay established collaborations with Careem, the region's top ride-sharing app, and Google Developer Group Manama.
October 2018	An agreement was made between Bahrain Polytechnic and BFB to assist students in honing their talents and enhancing their chances of finding jobs in the field.
November 2018	The Monetary Authority of Singapore and the Bahrain Central Bank have signed a Memorandum of Understanding (MoU) to advance their mutual financial services collaboration.
January 2019	Fintech Bay and Labiba formed a joint venture (Artificial Intelligence) with the goal of extending fintech solutions specific to informal Interface and Voice-User Interface (VUI) in the local and regional markets.
April 2019	The Bahrain EDB and the Istanbul Development Agency signed a Memorandum of Understanding to collaborate on developing startup ecosystems in their respective countries.
July 2019	Together, the "Bahraini Economic Development Board and the government of UK are testing new instructions for the application of AI to public procurement.
2020	The first complete digital fintech lab in Bahrain and the first cross-border effort to establish a network of people working together to research, test, and prototype on a centralized digital sandbox is FinHub 973 of CBB.
2021	FinHub 973's Bahrain Supernova Fintech Challenges encourage open innovation in the financial industry and the development of fintech.
2022	The Bahrain Central Bank (CBB) introduced the e-KYC framework, crowdfunding, open banking, and other new regulations and policies.
Vision 2030	Digital transformation is one of the pillars of Bahrain's Economic Vision 2030, which aims to promote "sustainability, competitiveness, and fairness".

Source: Bahrain Fintech Ecosystem Report 2018

4.3 Fintech-Strategic Partnership and Outreach

"By promoting increased market collaboration between all relevant parties and encouraging the sharing of information, commercial prospects, and experiences. Bahrain may prove to be a model trial market for nascent fintech enterprises exploring to prove or debut in the country".

Figure 5. Bahrain Fintech partners map

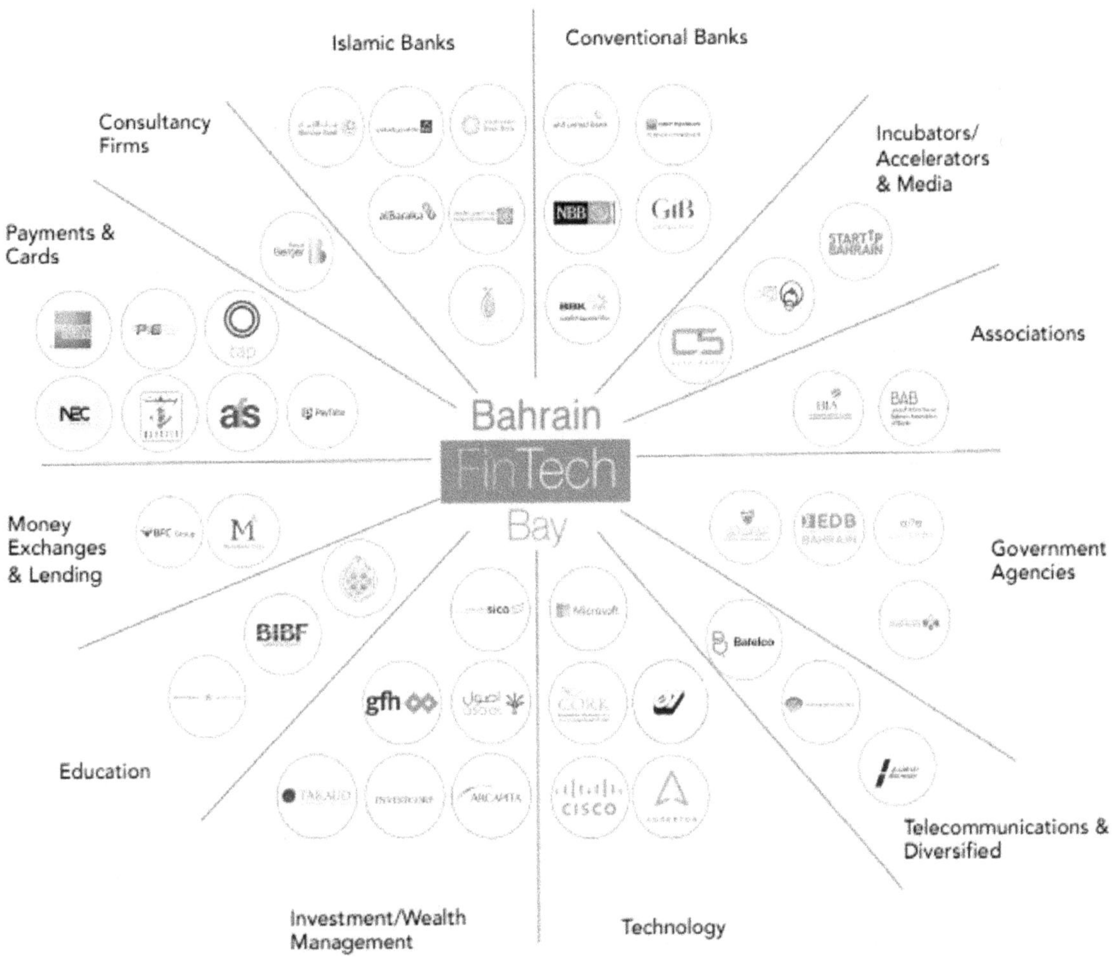

Source: Bahrain Fintech Ecosystem Report 2018

5. DIGITAL TRANSFORMATION AND ECONOMIC GROWTH

Islamic fintech's place a strong emphasis on innovation. The facilitation of Sadaqah (voluntary contribution) and Zakat (obligatory donation), which can amass $200 billion to $1 trillion globally, is a significant potential and might play a significant role in reducing global poverty (World Bank, 2020). The official charitable organization of Saudi Arabia, "Ehsan," received 24 million voluntary donations during the month of Ramadan, generating over $493 million. All of Ehsan's donations came from online sources only (Arab News, 2022). Pal, T., Kassim, S.B., Irfan, M., What are the advantages of machine learning (ML) approaches for the insurance sector? The finance industry has witnessed a rise in the significance of artificial intelligence and machine learning, as demonstrated by an exploratory study conducted in 2023 that investigated remarkable success and unprecedented accuracy.

Over 350 financial institutions with licenses to operate in Bahrain, representing a diverse range of national, international, and regional brands, are listed by the Bahrain Central Bank. With the financial industry contributing around seventeen percent comprise the Economy of the entire kingdom, it is one of the most significant non-oil sectors of the economy. With specializations and concentrations in wholesale banking, insurance, and fund and asset management, the regulated organizations offer a comprehensive variety of financial services. With over 85% of the total financial assets, Bahrain's banking sector, which is made up of both conventional and Islamic banks, is the biggest part of the country's financial system. Over 66% of the workforce in the financial sector is Bahraini, making it one of the country's top employers. Some noteworthy information is that the Bahrain Central Bank has been the only authority on financial sector governance and regulation since 2002. It also holds the top spot in the Middle East and Africa (MENA) region for Finance Freedom. Data and Electronic Government Bahrain is making strides in the direction of a digital economic transformation considering the observed advancements in technology. The implementation of the SDGs and the Government Action Plan, which encourages innovation and creativity in service delivery, will be greatly aided by economic digitization.

The King of Bahrain introduced the Economic Vision 2030 in October 2008. It is a comprehensive economic plan that offers guidance for the Kingdom's economy's future growth and, at its core, a common objective of improving the quality of life for all Bahrainis. To put it briefly, it appears that the economy by 2030 will be diverse, entrepreneurial, and heavily invested in by the private sector, to mention a few. Financial services are far more crucial to Bahrain's economy than is indicated by Vision 2030.

6. RESULTS, FINDINGS, AND FUTURE SCOPE

Some of the key topics are now changing the fintech industry such as assets, payments, investments, capital raising, and neo-banking progressing digitally. Digital modes of payment are becoming more and more common because consumers utilize mobile payment options for everyday purchases. The demand for affordable and easily navigable investing options is propelling the expansion of digital investment platforms. Additionally, digital capital raising has become a more popular choice for startups and SMEs' because it grants a speedy track to get finance. The emergence of digital mode of assets such as NFTs plus cryptocurrencies has established further prospects for traders and investors. Via innovative, customer-focused results that satisfy the needs of present tech-savvy clients, neo-banks have completely transformed traditional banking.

Digital transfers, mobile point-of-sale payments, and digital commerce transactions all fall under the category of digital payments. Neo brokers and robo-advisors are examples of digital investing. "Crowdfunding, crowd investing, crowd lending, and marketplace lending" are all forms of digital capital raising. Cryptocurrencies, NFTs, and DeFi are all included in the market for digital assets, and the neo-banking sector primarily concentrates on digital banks.

The market includes standard assets under management (AUM) per user, user penetration rates of regular income per user, and normal transaction value per user, The operation standards for the digital outflow industry comprise customer dealings made online or using mobile wallets. The earnings displayed come from the profits made by neo-banks, cryptocurrency exchanges, and virtual operating stages.

Figure 6. Fintech market structure

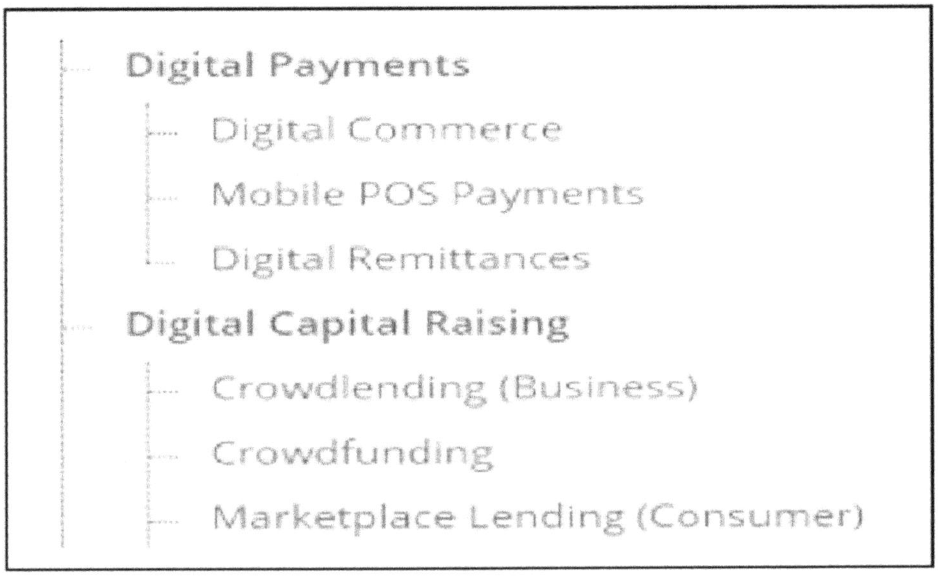

Source: Statista Market Insights

Figure 7. Transaction value by segment

Source: Statista Market Insights

Figure 8. Average transaction value per user

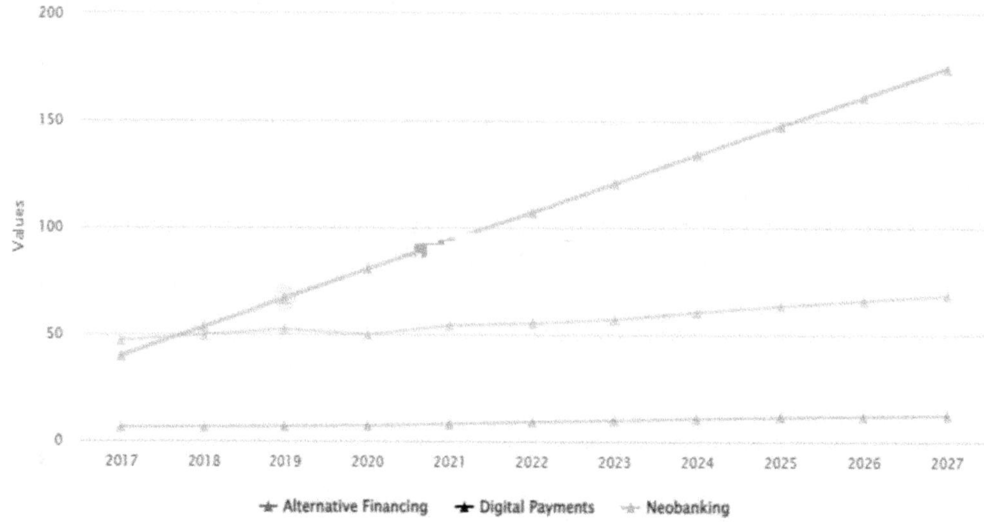

Source: Statista Market Insights

Figure 9. Assets under management

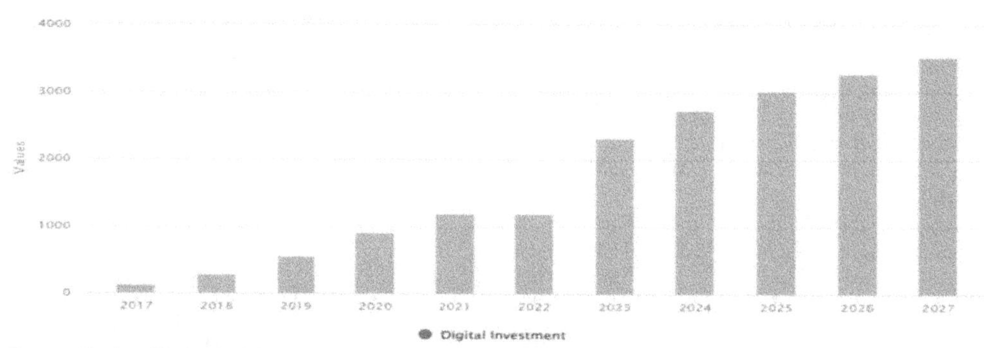

Source: Statista Market Insights

Figure 10. Revenue change

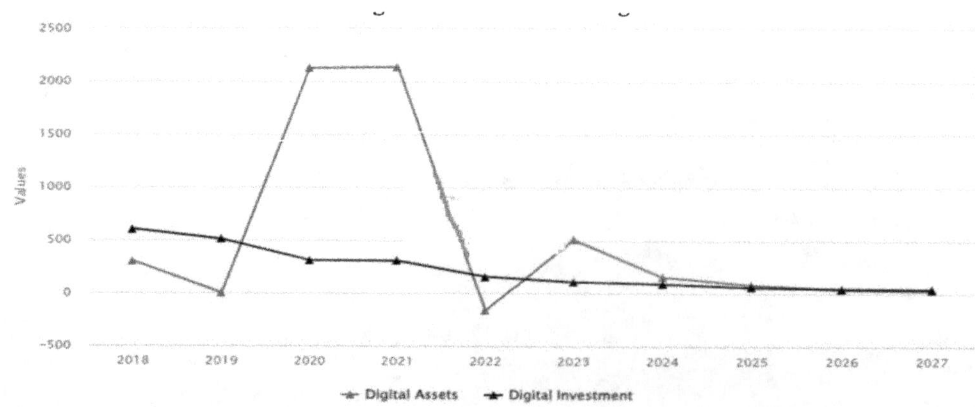

Source: Statista Market Insights

Figure 11. Number of campaigns

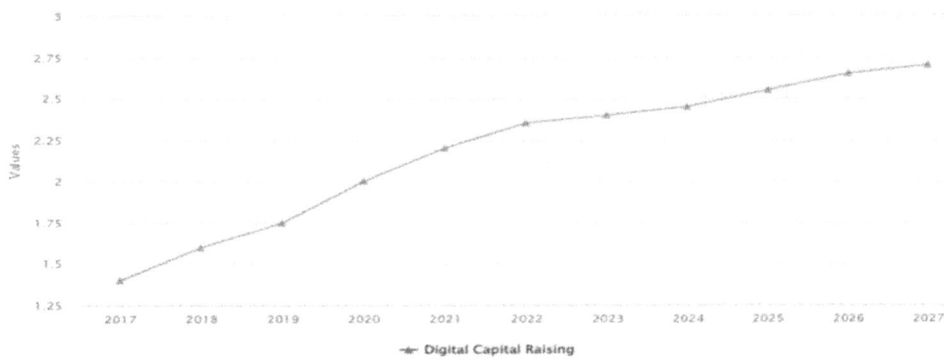

Source: Statista Market Insights

6.1 Findings

- In 2023, Digital Investment will be the largest market, with an AUM of US$11.99m.
- In the digital investment market, the average AUM per user is anticipated to reach US$294.40 in 2023.
- It is projected that the revenue generated by the digital asset industry will increase by 30.9% by 2024.
- In the market for digital payments, there are anticipated to be 1,243.00k users by 2027.
- In 2023, the market for digital investments is expected to have a total AUM of US$11.99m.
- The unique traits of KPIs within the fintech industry make it impossible to combine and show them as a single number that represents the whole fintech sector.

6.2 Future Scope

As Bahrain moves toward a cashless and digital economy, the government unveils its Economic Recovery Plan, aiming to attract $2.5 billion, create 20,000 high-quality jobs, and quicken economic growth in direct foreign investment by 2023. (Report on the Bahrain fintech Ecosystem, 2022). Particularly, important ideas emphasized in the plan for fostering the growth of fintech and financial services in Bahrain include:

- Digital Dinar using a round-the-clock accessible payment platform.
- Strengthening the BENEFIT Company's network and infrastructure.
- GCCNET payment network, which will connect and support all points of sale.
- Expanding the services provided by the BENEFIT Company by upgrading the Electronic Funds Transfer infrastructure.
- Retail banks ought to be included in the Arabian Gulf System for Financial Automated Quick Payment Transfer (AFAQ).
- Creating an always-available platform for fast payments.
- Including retail banks in "Buna," an Arab Region platform for multicurrency international payments.
- Adopting Sup-Tech to improve supervision techniques.

- Enhancing the FINHUB973 platform's offerings by adding a virtual marketplace.
- Automated communication of information between the CBB and approved financial institutions.

At the opening of the 3rd Arab Savings & Financial Literacy Conference in 2023, Fintech Robos, a Bahrain-based provider of digital solutions for savings and investments as well as an organizer of financial events for the Arab markets, announced a partnership with Aflatoun International, a Dutch non-profit organization, for the purpose of promoting financial literacy globally. Through the agreement, the two parties will collaborate closely on a variety of projects, including research and surveying, curriculum and training material promotion, financial education advocacy and communications, and the planning of specialist workshops and conferences.

It is anticipated that the fintech sector will maintain its strong growth trajectory because of current high-tech innovations, varying customer behaviour, and supervisory cooperation. Digital modes of transactions and mobile payment choices are anticipated to continue a prominent curve, as customers value speed along with convenience. It is expected that the number of people looking to manage their finances online will increase, which will benefit digital investing platforms. Furthermore, the rise of digital modes and neo-banking is probable to persist due to modifications that redefine the business model. All things considered, it is expected that the fintech industry will remain creative and dynamic, with innovative strategies acting to converge developing customer challenges.

7. CONCLUSION

Fintech adoption in the Islamic financial space is still in its infancy. Even with the advent of Islamic robo-advisors, most players are in the crowdsourcing sector. Bahraini initiatives devoted to Islamic finance fintech include the Islamic fintech Alliance and the Global Islamic fintech Hub. It looks like a promising future. The positive outlook is primarily indicated by rising stakeholder awareness, encouragement from monetary authorities, supportive regulatory environments in significant Islamic financial markets, other supportive elements of the larger fintech ecosystem, customer demands, and a largely unexplored potential market.

Bahrain is gradually growing in fintech. A favourable regulatory environment and the financial services industry's need for innovation are the key forces behind this. The best way to hasten local fintech adoption is to make use of academic support to develop fintech-focused curricula and to encourage funding by fostering stronger ties. Going forward, Bahrain should anticipate an increase in the number of major foreign investors willing to fund local firms that localize the idea of a successful worldwide financial solution. Given that PropTech is growing thanks to tools like tokenization, the real estate industry will see substantial investment potential from the future adoption of fintech. conventional work roles shifting increasingly in the direction of fintech and larger-scale innovation. The focus will be on the responsibilities that play in growing previously established businesses, particularly in regulatory compliance. Furthermore, firms looking to launch new fintech subsidiaries or digital platforms will be looking for personnel with experience in the fintech space. There are still a few gaps, despite Bahrain's image as a MENA talent hub being continuously improved.

The creation of technical programs, awareness campaigns, and the provision of fintech diplomas and programs are listed as Bahrain's top priority for enhancing its reputation as a talent hub. Bahrain offers a small choice of certifications for fintech programs such as the Georgetown, Harvard, and Oxford fintech

Programs. Nevertheless, the Kingdom has progressed past the recognition phase of recognizing the core ideas of the program. Understanding technologies is essential, but there is yet more to learn about them since a lack of technological skills is thought to be the largest deficit in the local talent pool.

REFERENCES

Abdulrasool, F. E., & Turnbull, S. I. (2020). Exploring security, risk, and compliance driven IT governance model for universities: Applied research based on the COBIT framework. *Int J Electron Bank, 2*(3), 237–265. doi:10.1504/IJEBANK.2020.111438

Abojeib, M., & Habib, F. (2021). Blockchain for Islamic Social Responsibility Institutions. In I. Management Association (Ed.), Research Anthology on Blockchain Technology in Business, Healthcare, Education, and Government (pp. 1114-1128). IGI Global. doi:10.4018/978-1-7998-5351-0.ch061

Al-Sartawi, A. (2015). The effect of corporate governance on the performance of the listed companies in the gulf cooperation council countries. *Jordan J Bus Adm 11*(3), 705–725.

Al-Sartawi, A. (2018). Corporate governance and intellectual capital: evidence from gulf cooperation council countries. *Acad Acc Financ Stud J 22*(1), 1–12 23.

Al-Sartawi, A. (2018). Institutional ownership, social responsibility, corporate governance and online financial disclosure. *Int J Critical Acc 10*(3/4), 241–255 22.

Al-Sartawi, A. (2018). Ownership structure and intellectual capital: evidence from the GCC countries. *Int J Learn Intellect Capital, 15*(3), 277–291 21.

Al-Sartawi A (2019) Assessing the relationship between information transparency through social media disclosure and firm value. *Manag Acc Rev 18*(2), 1–20.

Al-Sartawi A (2020) Information technology governance and cybersecurity at the board level. *Int J Crit Infrastruct 16*(2), 150–161.

Al-Sartawi, A. (2020). Social media disclosure of intellectual capital and firm value. *Int J Learn Intellect Capital 17*(4), 312–323.

Al-Sartawi A, Sanad Z (2019) Institutional ownership and corporate governance: evidence from Bahrain. *Afro-Asian J Finan Acc 9*(1), 101–115 20.

Alam, N., Gupta, L., & Zameni, A. (2019). *Fintech and Islamic Finance: Digitalization, Development and Disruption*. Palgrave Macmillan., doi:10.1007/978-3-030-24666-2

Alam, N., Gupta, L., & Zameni, A. (2019). *Fintech and Islamic Finance*. Springer International Publishing., doi:10.1007/978-3-030-24666-2

Alhakimi, W., & Esmail, J. (2019). The factors influencing the adoption of internet banking in Yemen. *Int J Electron Bank, 2*(2), 97–117. doi:10.1504/IJEBANK.2020.109655

Ali, M. (2021). Understanding the Impact of FinTechs on Service Innovation on the Future Sustainability of Global Business. In Remote Work and Sustainable Changes for the Future of Global Business (pp. 45–59). IGI Global. doi:10.4018/978-1-7998-7513-0.ch004

Bahrain fintech bay. (2018). *Bahrain FinTech Ecosystem Report 2018*. Bahrain Fintech Bay. https://www.bahrainfintechbay.com/, .

Banker, T. A. (2017). Central Bank of Bahrain announces landmark regulatory sandbox for fintech startups. *The Asian Banker*. https://www.theasianbanker.com/press-releases/central-bank-of-bahrain-announces-landmark-regulatory-sandbox-for-fintech-startups

Bartlett, R., Morse, A., Stanton, R., & Wallace, N. (2018). *Consumer-lending discrimination in the era of FinTech. Unpublished working paper*. University of California. https://lendingtimes.com/wp-content/uploads/2018/11/discrim.pdf

Boukhatem, J., & Ben Moussa, F. (2018). The effect of Islamic banks on GDP growth: Some evidence from selected MENA countries. *Borsa Istanbul Review*, *18*(3), 231–247. doi:10.1016/j.bir.2017.11.004

Central Bank Of Bahrain. (2020). *About FinTech & Innovation*. CBB's FinTech & Innovation Unit. https://www.cbb.gov.bh/fintech/

Chong, F. H. L. (2021). Enhancing trust through digital Islamic finance and blockchain technology. *Qualitative Research in Financial Markets*, *13*(3), 328–341. doi:10.1108/QRFM-05-2020-0076

Dogarawa, A. (2012). Global financial crisis and the search for new financial architecture: can Islamic finance provide alternative. *Journal of Islamic Economics, Banking and Finance*.

EDB. (2016). *Innovation in payment services focus of panel discussion in Bahrain - Invest in Bahrain*. EDB BAHRAIN. https://www.bahrainedb.com/latest-news/innovation-in-payment-services-focus-of-panel-discussion-in-bahrain

Feyen, E. Natarajan, H., & Matthew, S. (2023). *Fintech and the Future of Finance: Market and Policy Implications (English)*. Washington, D.C.: World Bank Group.

Xi'an University. (2020). Fin Tech instrument and islamic finance: The GCC perspective. *Journal of Xi'an University of Architecture & Technology*, *XII*(II), 2736–2747. https://www.xajzkjdx.cn/gallery/226-feb2020.pdf

Gupta, M., & Sikarwar, T. S. (2020). Modelling credit risk management and bank's profitability. *Int J Electron Bank*, *2*(2), 170–183. doi:10.1504/IJEBANK.2020.109663

Gupta, N. (2019). Influence of demographic variables on synchronization between customer satisfaction and retail banking channels for customers' of public sector banks of India. *Int J Electron Bank 1*(3), 206–219 344

Irfan, H., & Ahmed, D. (2018). Fintech: The opportunity for Islamic finance. In Fintech in Islamic Finance: Theory and Practice (pp. 19–32). Taylor and Francis. doi:10.4324/9781351025584-2

Irfan, M., Elhoseny, M., Kassim, S., & Metawa, N. (2023). Advanced Machine Learning Algorithms for Complex Financial Applications. IGI Global. doi:10.4018/978-1-6684-4483-2

Irfan, M., Elmogy, M., Majid, M. S. A., & El-Sappagh, S. (2023). *The impact of AI innovation on financial sectors in the era of industry 5.0.* IGI Global. https://www.scopus.com/inward/record.uri?eid=2-s2.085172984281&doi=10.4018%2f9798369300824&partnerID=40&md5=60218f4b384b49deb3ac378b0f4414ea, DOI: doi:10.4018/9798369300824

Jamil, N. N., & Seman, J. A. (2019). The Impact of Fintech On The Sustainability Of Islamic Accounting And Finance Education In Malaysia. Journal of Islamic, Social [JISED]. *Economics and Development*, *4*(17), 74–88.

Kassim, S. (2016). Islamic finance and economic growth: The Malaysian experience. *Global Finance Journal*, *30*, 66–76. doi:10.1016/j.gfj.2015.11.007

Khan, H. (2018). Islamic economics and a third fundamental theorem of welfare economics. *World Economy*, *41*(3), 723–737. Advance online publication. doi:10.1111/twec.12508

Komijani, A., & Taghizadeh-Hesary, F. (2019). An overview of Islamic banking and finance in Asia. In Routledge Handbook of Banking and Finance in Asia. Routledge.

Mansoor, S., & Ahmed, Z. U. (2021). Responsible Artificial Intelligence in Islamic Finance: A Framework. *Pacific-Basin Finance Journal.*

Micu, I., & Micu, A. (2016). Financial technology (Fintech) and its implementation on the Romanian non-banking capital market. *Practical Appl Sci*, *IV*(2(11)), 379–384.

Musleh Al-Sartawi, A. M. A. (2020). E-learning improves accounting education: case of the higher education sector of bahrain. In M. Themistocleous, M. Papadaki, & M. M. Kamal (Eds.), *Information systems. EMCIS 2020. Lecture notes in business information processing* (Vol. 402, p. 26). Springer. doi:10.1007/978-3-030-63396-7_20

Pal, T., Irfan, M., & Kassim, S. B. (2023). How do Machine Learning (ML) techniques benefit the insurance industry? An exploratory study. The Impact of AI Innovation on Financial Sectors in the Era of Industry 5.0, (pp. 108-130). IGI Global. https://www.scopus.com/inward/record.uri?eid=2-s2.0-85172988448&doi=10.4018%2f979-8-3693-0082-4.ch007&partnerID=40&, doi:10.4018/979-8-3693-0082-4.ch007

Panigrahi, R.R. (2023). Review of Machine Learning Techniques in the Supply Chain Management of Indian Industry. *Advanced Machine Learning Algorithms for Complex Financial Applications.* IGI Global. . doi:10.4018/978-1-6684-4483-2.ch013

Rabbani, M. R. (2022). Islamic Finance and Cryptocurrency: A Systematic Review. In *FinTech in Islamic Financial Institutions* (pp. 279–306). Springer International Publishing. doi:10.1007/978-3-031-14941-2_14

Rammal, H. G., & Zurbruegg, R. (2020). Fintech and Islamic Finance: A Review and Research Agenda. *Pacific-Basin Finance Journal*, *66*, 101488.

Ridho Kismawadi, E., Irfan, M., & Shah, S. M. A. R. (2023). Revolutionizing Islamic finance: Artificial intelligence's role in the future of industry. *The Impact of AI Innovation on Financial Sectors in the Era of Industry 5.0.* IGI Global. https://www.scopus.com/inward/record.uri?eid=2-s2.0-85173027737&doi=10.4018%2f979-8-3693-0082-4.ch011&partnerID=40&, DOI: doi:10.4018/979-8-3693-0082-4.ch011

Sanad Z. & Al-Sartawi, A. (2016). Investigating the relationship between corporate governance and internet financial reporting (IFR). *Jordan J Bus Adm 12*(1), 239– 269 24.

Sarea, A. M. (2019). Establishment of The First WAQF Bank in Bahrain: Exploratory Study. *Journal of Developing Areas, 53*(2), 221–228. doi:10.1353/jda.2019.0032

Schweitzer, M. E., & Barkley, B. (2017) Is 'Fintech' Good for Small Business Borrowers? *Impacts on Firm Growth and Customer Satisfaction.* Ideas. https://ideas.repec.org/p/fip/fedcwp/1701.html

Shahzad, A., & Rahman, Z. (2021). Fintech and Islamic Banking: A Framework for Financial Inclusion. *Thunderbird International Business Review, 63*(2), 175–188.

Shaikh, Z. H., Sarea, A., & Irfan, M. (2022). Islamic Banking Strategies in the World of Fintech: Success Story of Bahrain. In *Artificial Intelligence for Sustainable Finance and Sustainable Technology. ICGER 2021. Lecture Notes in Networks and Systems* (pp. 97–104). Springer. doi:10.1007/978-3-030-93464-4_10

Tabachnick, D. (2019). Regtech for fintech: A framework for regulatory and supervisory responses. *Georgetown Journal of International Law, 50*(2), 451–504.

Tarazi, A., & Fechtali, O. (2020). Fintech and Islamic Finance: A New Dawn for Financial Inclusion? *The World Bank Research Observer, 36*(1), 29–54.

Tarazi, A., & Trinugroho, I. W. (2021). Fintech in Islamic Banking: A Review and Future Research Directions. *Research in International Business and Finance, 58*, 10139.

Warde, I. (2012). Islamic Finance in Theory and Practice. Islamic Finance in the Global Economy.

Wilson, R., & El-Desouky, A. (2019). Fintech, Islamic Finance, and Financial Inclusion. In Routledge Handbook of Social and Sustainable Finance (pp. 433-447). Routledge.

Yusuf, M., & Rahman, M. (2019). Emerging Trends of Islamic Fintech Startups in the Middle East. *Journal of Islamic Marketing.*

Zavolokina, L., Dolata, M., & Schwabe, G. (2017). FinTech Transformation: How IT-Enabled Innovations Shape the Financial Sector. In Enterprise Applications, Markets and Services in the Finance Industry (pp. 75–88). Springer. doi:10.1007/978-3-319-52764-2_6

Zulkhibri, M. (2020). Fintech and Islamic Finance: The Convergence of Two Worlds. *ISRA International Journal of Islamic Finance, 12*(1), 75–82.

Chapter 17
Transforming Finance:
Exploring the Role of Blockchain and Smart Contracts

G. Sowmya
https://orcid.org/0000-0002-9275-7726
Jawaharlal Nehru Technological University, Hyderabad, India

R. Sridevi
Jawaharlal Nehru Technological University, Hyderabad, India

Sri Ganesh Shiramshetty
State University of New York, USA

ABSTRACT

This chapter examines the transformative power of blockchain technology and smart contracts in the financial industry. It explores the advantages of blockchain, such as enhanced security, transparency, and traceability, along with the automation capabilities offered by smart contracts. The research investigates their potential impact on traditional financial systems, focusing on areas like cross-border payments, trade finance, supply chain finance, and asset tokenization. It discusses the benefits of increased efficiency and cost reduction that can be achieved through blockchain implementation. The study also addresses the challenges associated with scalability, energy consumption, privacy, and smart contract vulnerabilities. Regulatory considerations and the importance of collaboration between industry stakeholders, regulators, and policymakers are emphasized. The chapter concludes by highlighting the transformative role of blockchain and smart contracts in creating a more inclusive, secure, and efficient future for finance.

1. INTRODUCTION

The financial industry is going through big changes thanks to new technologies like Artificial Intelligence, Machine Learning, Blockchain and one technology that has caught a lot of attention is blockchain. Blockchain is like a digital ledger that keeps records of transactions, and it's known for being secure and

DOI: 10.4018/979-8-3693-1038-0.ch017

transparent. Along with blockchain, there's another technology called smart contracts that can automatically execute agreements (Irfan, Elmogy, Majid et al, 2023).

In the dynamic realm of modern finance, the relentless march of technology compels an urgent exploration of blockchain, smart contracts, and machine learning. At the forefront of this evolution, the financial industry stands poised to fundamentally transform transactional frameworks, security, digital asset management, and decision-making processes. Blockchain, as a decentralized and immutable ledger, represents a revolutionary technology in finance. It ensures transparency, trust, and tamper-resistant records of transactions, revolutionizing how financial data is stored and shared (Ridho Kismawadi et al., 2023).

In this chapter, we'll explore how blockchain and smart contracts can transform finance. We'll look at how blockchain's features, like decentralization and immutability, can make financial transactions safer and more transparent. By using blockchain and smart contracts, we can reduce the need for middlemen and make transactions faster and cheaper.

Furthermore, we will examine practical instances illustrating the utilization of blockchain and smart contracts in the realm of finance. This exploration will cover their enhancements in cross-border payments, trade finance, supply chain finance, and the innovative tokenization of assets. These technologies have the potential to make these processes more efficient and accessible to everyone.

However, we'll also discuss the challenges that come with using blockchain and smart contracts in finance. We'll look at issues like scalability, energy usage, privacy concerns, and the risks of smart contracts. It's important to address these challenges and work with regulators and policymakers to ensure responsible adoption and development.

By the end of this chapter, it will be clear that blockchain and smart contracts can bring about significant changes in finance. We'll see that by embracing these technologies and finding solutions to the challenges, we can create a financial system that is more efficient, inclusive, and secure. This chapter sets the stage for further research and innovation as we shape the future of finance.

2. BLOCKCHAIN AND SMART CONTRACTS

2.1 Blockchain

Blockchain technology has emerged as a decentralized and immutable digital ledger with the potential to transform industries such as finance. It functions across a decentralized network of computers, guaranteeing transparency, security, and accountability. The fundamental principles of blockchain encompass decentralization, immutability, transparency, and consensus. It offers applications beyond cryptocurrencies, enabling streamlined cross-border payments, trade finance automation, asset tokenization, and identity verification (Nakamoto, 2008).

The figure Figure 1 shows the working of a blockchain. A block is generated and incorporated into the blockchain through a seven-step process, as illustrated in Figure 2.

i. **Data Creation**: Transactions or data are created by participants within the blockchain network. These transactions can represent various types of digital assets, such as cryptocurrency transfers, supply chain data, or ownership records.

Figure 1. Working of blockchain

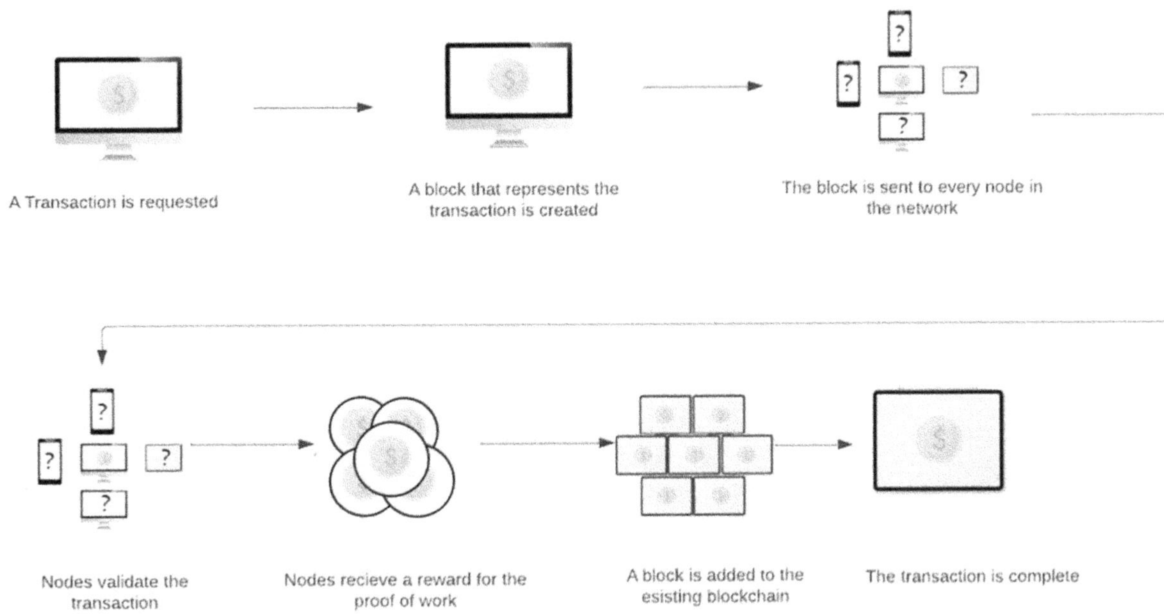

ii. **Block Formation:** Newly generated transactions are assembled into a block. This block includes a distinct identifier known as a cryptographic hash, created through a hashing algorithm based on the data within the block.

iii. **Block Validation:** The block is distributed to the network participants, who then authenticate its contents and integrity. This validation procedure entails confirming the legitimacy and accuracy of the transactions, ensuring adherence to predefined rules and protocols.

iv. **Consensus Mechanism:** Blockchain networks employ a consensus mechanism to determine the block's validity and its addition to the chain. This mechanism varies based on the blockchain protocol used, with commonly known consensus mechanisms such as proof of work (PoW), proof of stake (PoS), or delegated proof of stake (DPoS).

v. **Block Reward:** Blockchain network gives incentive to miners for successfully adding a new block which termed as block reward.

vi. **Block Addition:** Upon validation and approval by the network, the block becomes part of the existing blockchain. Its hash is connected to the previous block's hash, creating a sequential chain of blocks. This linking mechanism secures the immutability and integrity of the entire blockchain, as any modification to a prior block would render subsequent blocks invalid.

vii. **Block Replication**: The newly added block is distributed to all nodes within the network, each of which retains a copy of the complete blockchain. This replication procedure guarantees that each participant possesses an updated version of the blockchain, fostering transparency and decentralization.

Figure 2. Flowchart representation of blockchain working

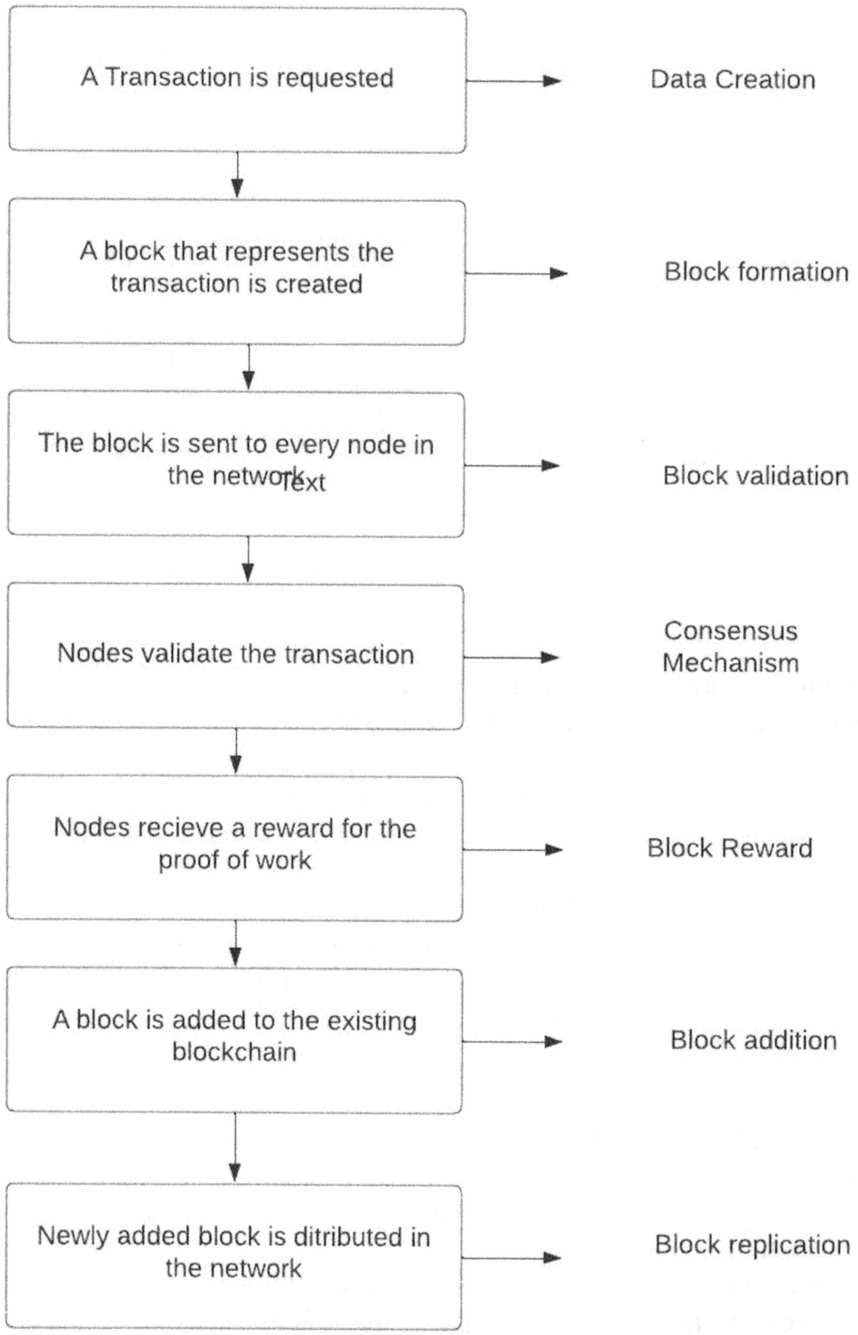

2.1.1 Features of Blockchain

Blockchain technology encompasses several key features that contribute to its unique characteristics and potential applications. Here are some important features of blockchain:

Decentralization: Functioning as a decentralized network, blockchain eliminates the necessity for a central authority or intermediary. Transactions and data are dispersed across numerous nodes or computers, ensuring that no single entity holds control over the entire network (Tapscott & Tapscott, 2016).

Immutable Ledger: Upon recording a transaction in the blockchain, it becomes highly challenging to alter or tamper with the information. Each block holds a distinctive cryptographic hash that connects it to the preceding block, establishing an unbroken sequence of records.

Transparency: Blockchain facilitates transparency by enabling anyone to access the transaction history and stored data on the network. This fosters trust and accountability, as participants have the ability to independently verify and validate transactions.

Security: Blockchain utilizes sophisticated cryptographic techniques to safeguard transactions and data. The decentralized structure of the network, combined with cryptographic algorithms, significantly fortifies its resistance to hacking and fraudulent attempts.

Consensus Mechanisms: To establish consensus among network participants regarding the validity of transactions, consensus mechanisms such as Proof of Work (PoW), Proof of Stake (PoS), and Practical Byzantine Fault Tolerance (PBFT) are commonly employed. These mechanisms guarantee agreement among all participants without necessitating a central authority (Werbach, 2018).

Traceability: Each transaction within the blockchain is logged and timestamped, establishing an auditable and traceable sequence of events. This attribute is particularly beneficial in supply chain management, enabling transparent tracking of the origin and movement of goods.

Smart Contracts: Smart contracts are self-executing contracts encoded within the blockchain. They autonomously carry out predetermined actions when specific conditions are fulfilled. These contracts facilitate automation, efficiency, and trust in a broad spectrum of applications, ranging from financial agreements to supply chain management.

Privacy: Even though blockchain transactions are transparent, privacy can be upheld using methods such as encryption and zero-knowledge proofs. Private or permissioned blockchains control access, limiting it to authorized participants, thereby ensuring confidentiality when required.

Together, these characteristics render blockchain a powerful technology applicable in finance, supply chain management, healthcare, voting systems, and various other fields. Its potential to transform industries lies in bolstering security, transparency, and efficiency while diminishing reliance on intermediaries.

2.1.1 Blockchain Adoption in Financial Sector

a. **Increased Institutional Interest:** Notably, institutions and corporations continued to display a growing interest in blockchain technology. Companies such as Visa, Mastercard, and PayPal had announced plans to integrate blockchain or were already involved in blockchain-based projects.
b. **Growing Investments**: Investment in blockchain technology and related startups had surged. Venture capitalists and major financial institutions had injected substantial capital into blockchain initiatives, signifying confidence and potential for future growth.

c. **Evolving Regulatory Landscape:** Governments and regulatory bodies worldwide had begun acknowledging and, in some cases, developing frameworks to govern blockchain and cryptocurrencies, thereby legitimizing their use in the financial sector.

2.2 Smart Contracts

Smart contracts are self-executing contracts encoded as computer code on a blockchain network. They automate agreement execution, removing intermediaries. They operate on a transparent and immutable blockchain, executing based on predefined triggers. Smart contracts are decentralized, execute without human intervention, and can manage assets (Delmolino, 2018).

2.2.1 Features of Smart Contracts

Smart contracts possess several key features that make them unique and versatile. Here are some important features of smart contracts:

Self-executing: Smart contracts are specifically crafted to autonomously carry out actions and enforce pre-set terms and conditions without requiring intermediaries or manual intervention. Once the conditions outlined in the contract are satisfied, the contract automatically executes the agreed-upon actions (Buterin, 2014).

Autonomy: Smart contracts operate autonomously and independently, executing as programmed. They eliminate the reliance on third parties to enforce contract terms, reducing the potential for errors, delays, or manipulation.

Transparency: Smart contracts exhibit transparency, given that their code and execution logic are observable and accessible to all participants within the blockchain network. This transparency fosters trust and enables independent verification of contract execution.

Immutable: Once integrated into a blockchain, smart contracts become immutable and resistant to tampering. The contract's code and execution history are stored within the blockchain, rendering it exceedingly difficult to retroactively alter or manipulate the contract's behavior.

Trust and Security: Smart contracts rely on blockchain technology, harnessing the innate security elements of distributed ledger systems. They employ cryptographic algorithms and consensus mechanisms to safeguard the integrity and security of contract execution.

Efficiency: Smart contracts streamline processes by automating contract execution, eliminating the necessity for intermediaries. This automation leads to increased efficiency and cost savings by reducing manual tasks, paperwork, and potential errors in the execution of contractual agreements.

Auditability: Smart contracts provide a high degree of auditability since all transactions and contract executions are recorded on the blockchain. This feature enables transparent and traceable verification of the contract's performance and adherence to the agreed-upon terms.

The functionalities of smart contracts form the cornerstone for automating and improving various applications such as financial transactions, supply chain management, decentralized finance (DeFi), digital identity, and beyond. They facilitate secure, efficient, and trustless execution of agreements, thereby revolutionizing traditional contract-based interactions.

2.1.2 Smart Contracts Adoption in Financial Sector

a. **Integration in Diverse Sectors:** Smart contracts were gaining traction not only in financial services but also in various other industries like real estate, supply chain management, and healthcare, among others. This expansion indicated the versatility and applicability of smart contract technology beyond finance.
b. **Efficiency and Cost Reduction**: Companies that implemented smart contracts reported improved efficiency, cost reduction, and minimized human error in their operations. This progress acted as a catalyst for further adoption in the financial domain.
c. **Ecosystem Development:** The development of smart contract platforms and the expansion of decentralized finance (DeFi) projects illustrated an evolving ecosystem aimed at diversifying and refining smart contract applications.

3. CHALLENGES IN FINANCE SECTOR

In the finance industry, several challenges exist. Some of the challenges are listed below:

Data Integrity: Safeguarding the integrity of financial data is paramount to ensure accuracy and trustworthiness. Challenges emerge from the potential risk of data breaches, cyberattacks, and fraudulent activities. Financial institutions must implement robust security measures, encryption techniques, and authentication protocols to shield sensitive data from unauthorized access or tampering (Lall & Sharma, 2016).

Efficiency: Many financial processes still rely on manual and paper-based systems, leading to inefficiencies, delays, and errors. Legacy systems and complex workflows hinder operational efficiency. Embracing digital transformation and adopting technologies like blockchain and automation can streamline processes, eliminate redundancies, and enhance overall efficiency.

Customer Experience: Traditional financial institutions often struggle to provide seamless and personalized customer experiences. Lengthy onboarding processes, complex documentation requirements, and limited accessibility can frustrate customers. Embracing digital channels, implementing intuitive user interfaces, and leveraging data analytics can enhance customer experience, offering convenience, personalized services, and real-time interactions.

Cost of Business: The expense of conducting financial operations presents a substantial challenge. Legacy infrastructure, manual processes, and the costs associated with regulatory compliance contribute to high operational expenses. Embracing emerging technologies like cloud computing, blockchain, and artificial intelligence can significantly enhance cost efficiencies by reducing paperwork and automating compliance processes, thereby leading to cost savings for financial institutions.

These challenges can be addresses using blockchain and smart contracts.

4. BLOCKCHAIN AND SMART CONTRACTS IN FINANCE

The financial sector encompasses banks, investment funds, insurance companies, and real estate entities. Typically, credit and financial institutions operate with the aid of mediators or intermediaries. In the traditional business system, these intermediaries introduce the essential element of trust, resulting in the services provided by institutions being costly. Blockchain has the potential to eliminate the necessity for intermediaries, allowing banks to offer more cost-effective services directly to customers (Cocco et al., 2017).

Blockchain technology can introduce a new operational model for finance, as depicted in Figure 3. Its features including immutability, transparency, high security, low operational costs, and the distributed ledger structure have positioned it as an emerging and sought-after solution, even within the highly conservative and regulated banking industry. Smart contracts, adding an additional layer of documentation, can fulfill contractual obligations, reducing reliance on intermediaries for resolving disputes.

The significant challenges associated with cross-border payments and trade finance could be effectively addressed through blockchain. By reducing the need for intermediaries, blockchain's geographical independence can lead to cost savings in capital markets, particularly in post-trade settlement and regulatory reporting.

Figure 3. Blockchain in finance

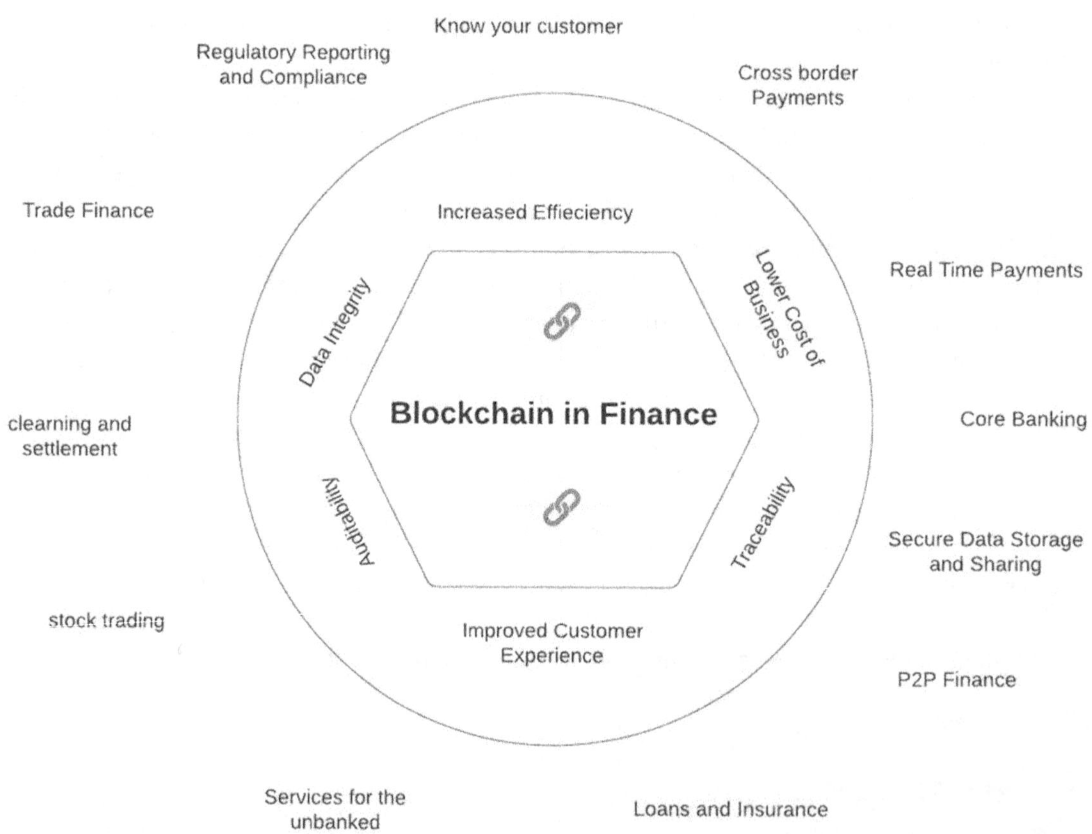

4.1 Literature Survey

Numerous significant research studies and scientific publications have thoroughly investigated the impact of blockchain and smart contracts on the financial industry, offering a fundamental basis for comprehending their effects. Some of these influential works encompass:

"Bitcoin: A Peer-to-Peer Electronic Cash System" by Satoshi Nakamoto: This groundbreaking white paper introduced the concept of blockchain technology via Bitcoin, establishing the foundation for decentralized digital currencies. Although not exclusively centered on the financial industry, it sparked discussions on the potential of blockchain for financial applications.

"Smart Contracts: The Blockchain Technology That Will Replace Lawyers" by Nick Szabo: Szabo's work coined the term "smart contracts" and explored their potential to automate contractual agreements, significantly impacting various sectors, particularly finance (Patidar, 2020).

"**Blockchain and Financial Market Innovation"** by Rebecca Lewis: This academic paper thoroughly examines how blockchain technology, particularly in the form of distributed ledgers, could transform financial market infrastructure by improving transparency, reducing costs, and enhancing security (, R et al., 2017).

"**Global insight: Blockchain in banking: Disruptive threat or tool?":** This article outlines a roadmap for the implementation of distributed ledger technology within the financial sector (Stanley, 2016).

"**Distributed ledger technology in payment, clearing and settlement: An analytical framework,":** This report tells how distributed technology used in payments, clearing settlements (Bank for International Settlements, 2017).

4.2 How Blockchain's Features Can Make the Financial Transactions Safer and Secure

Blockchain technology provides several features that contribute to the safety and security of financial transactions. Here are ways in which blockchain enhances the security of financial transactions:

Distributed Ledger: Blockchain employs a distributed ledger, where transaction records are stored across a network of computers (nodes) instead of a centralized authority. This decentralization poses challenges for hackers aiming to manipulate or alter transaction data, as they would need to compromise a majority of the network's nodes simultaneously (Zavolokina et al., 2019).

Immutable Records: Upon recording a transaction on the blockchain, altering or deleting it becomes exceedingly difficult. Each new transaction is linked to prior ones through cryptographic hashes, creating a chain of interconnected blocks. Any effort to tamper with a previous transaction would necessitate changing subsequent blocks, becoming progressively more challenging as more blocks are added. This immutability feature ensures the integrity of transaction history and mitigates the risk of fraudulent activities.

Consensus Mechanism: Blockchain networks depend on consensus mechanisms, such as Proof-of-Work (PoW) or Proof-of-Stake (PoS), to authenticate and collectively agree on the legitimacy of transactions. This consensus mechanism guarantees that all participants in the network come to a unified agreement regarding the sequence and authenticity of transactions, making it challenging for malicious actors to introduce false transactions or manipulate the system.

Transparency: Blockchain facilitates transparency by making transaction data accessible to all network participants. Each transaction is meticulously recorded on the blockchain, creating an audit trail that is open for verification by any participant. This transparency significantly mitigates the risk of fraud, allowing participants to autonomously verify the authenticity of transactions and detect any discrepancies (Xu & Gupta, 2018).

Cryptographic Security: Blockchain relies on advanced cryptographic techniques to secure transactions. Digital signatures are used to authenticate the identities of participants, ensuring that only authorized individuals can initiate and validate transactions. Encryption methods safeguard sensitive data, like personal information or account details, making it highly complex for unauthorized parties to access or decode the information.

Smart Contracts: As previously explained, smart contracts are self-executing agreements with terms directly inscribed into code. These contracts facilitate the automated and tamper-resistant execution of financial transactions. By enforcing predetermined rules and conditions, smart contracts ensure that transactions are only executed when all specified conditions are met, thereby decreasing the risk of fraud or non-compliance.

Auditing and Accountability: The transparency and immutability inherent in blockchain technology support auditing and accountability. With all transactions recorded on the blockchain, tracking and verifying the flow of funds becomes more accessible. This characteristic proves especially beneficial for regulatory compliance, enabling regulators or auditors to access transaction data and verify adherence to legal requirements.

Enhanced Security Measures: Blockchain networks employ robust security measures, such as public-key cryptography, consensus algorithms, and data encryption, to protect against unauthorized access, data tampering, and hacking attempts. These security measures strengthen the overall security of financial transactions conducted on the blockchain.

By leveraging these features, blockchain technology creates a more secure and trustworthy environment for financial transactions.

4.2.1 Know Your Customer (KYC)

Laws and regulations impose obligations on banks and other financial organisations to identify and verify their clients. Credit institutions must finish KYC when processing applications.

The KYC process is time-consuming, expensive, and tedious. For the verification, a lot of paperwork and data were needed. There is a risk of inaccuracy, slow delivery, and duplication of effort because the information is not gathered, all of which have a negative impact on customer satisfaction. A potential solution could involve a distributed ledger-based customer identity system. With this approach, user identity information could be securely added, stored, and made accessible to other participating banks, leveraging the capabilities of blockchain technology. As soon as a client or customer is located in the blockchain, information about them is securely stored, with other banks or FI only being allowed access by the proper authority.

Consequently, the Know Your Customer (KYC) process for the customer wouldn't need to be reiterated for new services or applications (Casaburi & Girardone, 2018).

4.2.2 Cross-Border Payments

Over the last two centuries, global business and trade have shown consistent growth, leading to significant transformations in the global economy and fostering overall expansion. foreign payments that be difficult. There are several issues with the current cross-border payment mechanism, though. Three to five working days are normally needed for an international transaction. Beneficiary visitors are not informed about foreign payments. Because the conversion rate isn't determined until the funds are received, it's necessary to estimate the payment's delivery window. The involvement of multiple financial institutions creates a complex web of procedures, often accompanied by transactional fees and charges at various stages. As a result, the process is pricy, time-consuming, and less suited to the requirements of today's global ecommerce. To tackle existing operational inefficiencies, financial institutions and banks are increasingly adopting blockchain technology to facilitate almost instant cross-border payments. This adoption promises heightened security, transparency, reliability, and reduced costs. Moreover, the tamper-proof nature of transactions on the blockchain leads to a decrease in the expenses associated with case investigations and litigation.

4.2.3 Trade Finance

Several different parties are involved in a normal business transaction, including banks, shippers, importers, exporters, regulatory agencies, and customs officials.

There is a verification point at each node in the supply chain, and any problem there would cause a delay (Fan, 2018).

The process of obtaining clearances from various governmental organizations, such as customs, port authorities, and documentation for transportation via trucks or rail, as well as other essential formalities for transferring goods across borders, needs to be simplified. The complex process of trade finance can be expedited using blockchain when all stakeholders have the required access to the Ledger, encouraging more accountability and trust among firms, regulators, and customers. Blockchain technology holds the potential to decrease the expenses associated with record-keeping. It can curtail the reliance on paper-based systems, which not only waste time and money but also necessitate intermediaries in the process. The blockchain is useless. employed by legal organisations for approvals as well as by anyone curious in the status of the approvals. The blockchain ledger can serve as the sole source of truth to record the payment transfer between importer and exporter banks, documenting the receipt of goods.

4.1.4 Insurance

Brokers and insurers today have a massive amount of paper work to manage in addition to electronic documents created by experts like lawyers, claims adjusters, and other lawyers.(Zheng, 2018)

The process of exchanging data would be sped up and made more effective with a claim system built on blockchain technology. There will be substantial operational savings for all stakeholders.

People can get payments instantly and insurance payments are automated thanks to the programming of smart contracts. The insurance policy is instantly triggered when an insured occurrence is reported by a trustworthy source, processing the claim in accordance with the smart contract's set policy term and paying the client on schedule (Pal et al., 2023).

Blockchain technology can benefit the insurance industry by decreasing the cost of processing insurance claims, lowering instances of insurance fraud, and enhancing customer satisfaction.

4.2 How Smart Contract's Features Can Make the Financial Transactions Safer and Secure

Smart contracts present multiple functionalities that can significantly improve the safety and security of financial transactions. Here are several ways in which smart contracts can establish a more secure and protected environment:

Trustless Execution: Smart contracts function within blockchain technology, allowing for trustless execution. They automatically execute transactions according to predetermined rules and conditions, bypassing the need for intermediaries. This eradicates the risk of fraud or manipulation by third parties (Tama, 2019).

Immutable and Transparent: Once implemented on a blockchain, smart contracts remain immutable, impervious to alteration or tampering. All transactional data is registered on the blockchain, establishing a transparent and auditable history. This transparency mitigates potential disputes and offers a clear, traceable trail of transactions.

Elimination of Middlemen: Conventional financial transactions commonly involve intermediaries like banks or brokers, introducing vulnerabilities and increasing costs. Smart contracts eliminate the necessity for intermediaries, thereby diminishing the risks associated with human error, manipulation, or biased actions.

Automated Compliance: Smart contracts can be coded to automatically enforce regulatory and compliance requisites. By integrating compliance rules within the contract's code, transactions will only execute if all essential conditions are satisfied. This approach reduces the likelihood of non-compliance and ensures adherence to legal frameworks.

Conditional Payments: Smart contracts facilitate conditional payments, ensuring that funds are disbursed solely upon the fulfillment of specific predefined conditions. For instance, in a real estate transaction, the buyer's funds can be held in escrow until the title is transferred. This attribute significantly diminishes the risk of non-payment or the misuse of funds.

Enhanced Security Measures: Smart contracts have the capacity to integrate advanced cryptographic techniques, such as digital signatures, to authenticate the identity of participants and uphold the integrity of transactions. These robust security measures act as a safeguard against unauthorized access, forgery, and data manipulation (Rehman et al., 2020).

Decentralization and Distributed Consensus: Smart contracts function within decentralized blockchain networks where transactions are validated and agreed upon by a distributed network of nodes. This decentralized consensus mechanism enhances security by eliminating single points of failure and making it challenging for malicious actors to manipulate the system.

Multi-Signature Functionality: Smart contracts have the capability to incorporate multi-signature functionality, necessitating digital signatures from multiple parties to authorize a transaction. This feature augments security by demanding the consensus of multiple participants, thereby reducing the risk of unauthorized transactions.

By leveraging these features, smart contracts create a more secure and trustworthy environment for financial transactions.

4.2.1 Syndicated Loans

Smart contracts can streamline the syndicated loan process by automating various stages. This includes the creation of loan agreements, defining repayment terms, interest rates, and repayment schedules. The contract can ensure that loan funds are automatically distributed to the borrower based on predetermined conditions. Additionally, smart contracts can facilitate the syndication process by automatically distributing repayments and interest among multiple lenders according to their respective shares. This automation eliminates manual processing, reduces administrative overhead, enhances transparency, and ensures accurate and efficient loan servicing (Ramachandran & Watts, 2020).

4.2.2 Securities

Smart contracts can revolutionize the issuance, trading, and management of securities. By tokenizing traditional securities and representing them as digital assets on a blockchain, ownership and transfer of securities can be facilitated securely and with reduced intermediaries. Smart contracts can automate dividend payments, interest distributions, and other financial obligations directly to token holders based on predefined conditions. Tokenized securities on a blockchain provide increased liquidity, accessibility, and transparency while minimizing settlement times and the need for intermediaries.

Integrating machine learning with blockchain technology represents a pivotal advancement in fortifying security measures within financial systems. By combining the predictive and analytical capabilities of machine learning with the inherent security features of blockchain, the network gains a powerful shield against potential threats. Machine learning algorithms, adept at detecting anomalies, predicting security risks, and identifying fraudulent activities, provide an adaptive and proactive security layer. This amalgamation not only ensures robust protection against evolving threats but also instills confidence by reinforcing the resilience and integrity of the entire blockchain network, transforming the landscape of financial security (Irfan, Elhoseny, Kassim et al, 2023).

4.2.3 Trade and Finance

Smart contracts can streamline trade finance operations, such as letters of credit, by automating verification processes and ensuring secure and timely payments. By incorporating the necessary documentation, such as shipping records and invoices, into the smart contract, the verification process can be automated, reducing the time and cost associated with manual checks. Upon meeting the conditions outlined in the smart contract, like the successful delivery of goods, payment can be automatically triggered. This streamlined process reduces delays and fosters enhanced trust between involved parties (Kumari et al., 2021).

4.2.4 Derivatives

Smart contracts can bring efficiency and accuracy to derivative contracts by automating their execution and settlement. By encoding the terms and conditions of derivative contracts into smart contract code, transactions can be automatically executed based on predefined triggers or market conditions. Settlements can be made instantly, reducing counterparty risk and increasing liquidity. Smart contracts can also enable complex derivatives, such as options or swaps, to be executed without relying on intermediaries or manual processes, resulting in faster and more transparent transactions.

4.2.5 Clearing and Settlement

Smart contracts can revolutionize clearing and settlement processes by automating the matching, validation, and reconciliation of transactions. By using blockchain technology, smart contracts provide a single, shared source of truth that all parties can access and trust. This reduces the risk of errors, disputes, and fraudulent activities. The transparency and real-time visibility of transactions on a blockchain contribute to faster settlement times, eliminating the requirement for intermediaries and reducing associated costs.

4.2.6 Regulatory Compliance

Smart contracts can assist in regulatory compliance by embedding compliance rules directly into the contract code. These rules can ensure that transactions and financial activities adhere to regulatory requirements automatically. By integrating compliance rules into smart contracts, the risk of non-compliance can be significantly reduced. Moreover, the transparency inherent in blockchain technology enables regulators to monitor transactions in real-time, bolstering their capacity to enforce regulations and conduct audits effectively (Kshetri, 2018).

5. REAL-WORLD EXAMPLES OF HOW BLOCKCHAIN AND SMART CONTRACTS CAN BE USED IN FINANCE

There are several real-world examples of how blockchain and smart contracts are already being utilized in the financial industry. Here are a few prominent ones:

Cross-Border Payments: Blockchain-based solutions are being employed to streamline and hasten cross-border payments. For example, Ripple utilizes blockchain technology and its native cryptocurrency, XRP, to facilitate rapid, cost-effective international money transfers. This is achieved by removing the necessity for numerous intermediaries and decreasing settlement times (Ali et al., 2014).

Trade Finance: Blockchain and smart contracts offer significant potential for optimizing trade finance processes, such as letter of credit (LC) issuance and supply chain financing. By digitizing and automating the exchange of documents, verifying the authenticity of goods, and automating payment settlements, blockchain-based platforms like Marco Polo and we. Trade enhance transparency, reduce fraud risks, and expedite trade financing.

Asset Tokenization: Blockchain technology facilitates the tokenization of assets, converting real-world assets such as real estate, artwork, or investment funds into digital tokens on the blockchain. This process of fractional ownership enhances liquidity, diminishes barriers to entry, and facilitates simpler transfer of ownership. Platforms like Polymath and Harbor are notable examples that offer such capabilities.

Peer-to-Peer Lending: Blockchain-based peer-to-peer lending platforms leverage smart contracts to enable direct lending and borrowing without the need for traditional financial intermediaries.

These platforms, such as ETHLend and SALT Lending, facilitate secure and transparent lending transactions, automating loan agreements, collateral management, and repayment processes.

Identity Verification: Blockchain technology can be utilized for secure and decentralized identity verification, improving Know Your Customer (KYC) processes in the financial sector. Platforms like uPort and Civic allow individuals to control and share their identity data securely, reducing the risk of data breaches and identity theft.

Insurance Claims Processing: Smart contracts can automate insurance claims processing, reducing administrative costs, enhancing transparency, and expediting claim settlements. Companies like Aigang and Etherisc are exploring blockchain-based solutions for decentralized insurance applications, enabling self-executing claim processes based on predefined conditions.

Digital Asset Exchanges: Cryptocurrency exchanges and decentralized exchanges (DEXs) rely on blockchain and smart contracts to facilitate secure, transparent, and efficient trading of digital assets. Platforms like Binance, Coinbase, and Uniswap utilize smart contracts to automate trade executions, settlement, and asset custody.

These examples highlight the potential of blockchain and smart contracts in transforming various aspects of the financial industry, offering increased efficiency, transparency, and security while reducing costs and reliance on intermediaries.

6. FUTURE RESEARCH AND INNOVATION

The future possibilities for exploring the transformative role of blockchain and smart contracts in finance are extensive. There are several areas of interest that can be further investigated to enrich the understanding of this topic. These include emerging use cases, technological advancements, industry adoption experiences, regulatory developments, interdisciplinary perspectives, ethical considerations, and future challenges and opportunities. By delving into these areas, readers can gain valuable insights into the evolving landscape of blockchain and smart contracts in the financial industry.

REFERENCES

Ali, R., Barrdear, J., Clews, R., & Southgate, J. (2014). Innovations in Payment Technologies and the Emergence of Digital Currencies. *Bank of England Quarterly Bulletin*, *54*(3), 262–275.

Bank for International Settlements. (2017). *Distributed ledger technology in payment, clearing and settlement: An analytical framework.* Committee on Payments and Market Infrastructures.

Buterin, V. (2014). *Ethereum: A Next-Generation Smart Contract and Decentralized Application Platform.* (White Paper).

Casaburi, L., & Girardone, C. (2018). Blockchain Technology in Finance: Benefits, Challenges, and Emerging Applications. *International Journal of Financial Studies*, *6*(2), 38. doi:10.3390/ijfs6020038

Cocco, L., Concas, G., Marchesi, M., & Pinna, A. (2017). Banking on Blockchain: Costs Savings Thanks to the Blockchain Technology. In *International Workshop on Open Problems in Network Security* (pp. 281-293). Springer. 10.3390/fi9030025

Delmolino, K. (2018). Towards Safer Ethereum Smart Contracts: A Survey of Languages, Tools, and Verification Methods. *ACM Computing Surveys*, *51*(6), 118. 10.1145/3230762

Fan, K. (2018). Blockchain-based Cryptocurrency Payment Systems: A Decentralized Sustainable Financial Solution. *Sustainable Cities and Society*, *39*, 82–88. doi:10.1016/j.scs.2018.02.011

Irfan, M., Elhoseny, M., Kassim, S., & Metawa, N. (2023). *Advanced Machine Learning Algorithms for Complex Financial Applications*. doi:10.4018/978-1-6684-4483-2

Irfan, M., Elmogy, M., Majid, M. S. A., & El-Sappagh, S. (2023*). The impact of AI innovation on financial sectors in the era of industry 5.0.* IGI Global. 10.4018/9798369300824

Kshetri, N. (2018). Blockchain's Roles in Strengthening Cybersecurity and Protecting Privacy. *Telecommunications Policy*, *42*(7), 567–578. doi:10.1016/j.telpol.2018.05.003

Kumari, A., Sharma, P., & Chhabra, J. (2021). Improving Security in Financial Transactions Using Smart Contracts. In *Proceedings of the 2021 International Conference on Information Science and Communications Technologies* (pp. 1-6). IEEE.

Lall, A. R., & Sharma, R. (2016). *Impact of Financial Innovations and Technology on the Banking Industry*. NIH.

Lewis, R., McPartland, J., & Ranjan, R. (2017). *Blockchain and Financial Market Innovation*. (Policy Discussion Paper Series 93559). Federal Reserve Bank of Chicago.

Nakamoto, S. (2008). *Bitcoin: A Peer-to-Peer Electronic Cash System*. Bitcoin. https://bitcoin.org/bitcoin.pdf

Pal, T., Irfan, M., & Kassim, S. B. (2023). How do Machine Learning (ML) techniques benefit the insurance industry? An exploratory study. *The Impact of AI Innovation on Financial Sectors in the Era of Industry 5.0,* (pp. 108-130). IGI Global. doi:10.4018/979-8-3693-0082-4.ch007

Patidar, S. (2020). The Blockchain technology that will substitute Lawyers and Middlemen. *Medium*.

Ramachandran, M., & Watts, S. (2020). Enhancing Financial Transaction Security with Smart Contracts. *International Journal of Advanced Computer Science and Applications*, *11*(2), 42–47. doi:10.14569/IJACSA.2020.0110206

Rehman, M. U., Khan, S. U., & Iqbal, W. (2020). A Systematic Review of Smart Contracts: Challenges and Future Directions in Finance. *Journal of Ambient Intelligence and Humanized Computing*, *11*(2), 1029–1043. doi:10.100712652-018-0984-9

Ridho Kismawadi, E., Irfan, M., & Shah, S. M. A. R. (2023). Revolutionizing Islamic finance: Artificial intelligence's role in the future of industry. *The Impact of AI Innovation on Financial Sectors in the Era of Industry 5.0,* (pp. 184-207). doi:10.4018/979-8-3693-0082-4.ch011

Stanley, M. (2016). Global insight: Blockchain in banking: Disruptive threat or tool? *Global Financials/ FinTech, Morgan Stanley Global Insight.*

Tama, B. A. (2019). Smart Contracts in the Financial Industry: Applications, Challenges, and Benefits. *International Journal of Engineering Research & Technology (Ahmedabad), 12*(6), 1329–1332. https://www.ijert.org/research/smart-contracts-in-the-financial-industry-applications-challenges-and-benefits-IJERTV12IS060173.pdf

Tapscott, D., & Tapscott, A. (2016). *Blockchain Revolution: How the Technology Behind Bitcoin is Changing Money, Business, and the World.* Penguin.

Werbach, K. (2018). *Blockchain and the New Architecture of Trust.* MIT Press. doi:10.7551/mitpress/11449.001.0001

Xu, M., & Gupta, H. (2018). Blockchain's Role in Facilitating Accounting and Audit Processes: Current Applications and Future Directions. *Journal of Emerging Technologies in Accounting*, *15*(2), 107–126. doi:10.2308/jeta-52094

Zavolokina, L., Dolata, M., & Schwabe, G. (2019). Transforming business models with blockchain: A framework and typology. *Journal of Management Information Systems*, *36*(3), 868–904.

Zheng, Y. (2018). Blockchain Challenges and Opportunities: A Survey and a Case Study. *International Journal of Financial Research, 9*(2), 283-295. doi:. v9n2p283 doi:10.5430/ijfr

Chapter 18
Using Machine Learning and Deep Learning Methods in Predicting the Islamic Index Price

Ahmed Ihsan Simsek
https://orcid.org/0000-0002-2900-3032
Firat University, Turkey

ABSTRACT

In recent years, there has been a noticeable surge in the popularity of Islamic financing. The utilization of Fin-Tech tools assumes significance for investors adhering to Islamic principles in order to effectively navigate investing choices. The utilization of these technologies enables the generation of more precise price forecasts for investors. This will facilitate investors adhering to Islamic principles in making more precise investing choices. This study utilized a dataset consisting of 3453 daily observations of the MSCI ACWI Islamic Index. The acquired data was subjected to processing utilizing various machine learning algorithms, including LSTM, CNN, GRU, RF, and XGBoost. Subsequently, an evaluation was conducted to ascertain the predictive performance of each method and establish the superior approach. Based on the results, it was found that the GRU approach exhibited the highest level of prediction performance.

1. INTRODUCTION

The emergence of Islamic finance in the 1970s was a significant development in the global financial landscape, with the founding of the the initial Islamic commercial bank, Dubai Islamic Bank, in 1975. Subsequent to that, the Islamic finance sector has consistently achieved notable advancements (Kassim, 2016). Based on the most recent findings presented by Mordor Intelligence, it has been seen that the Islamic finance sector had a notable expansion in 2021, with its total value nearing USD 4 trillion. This growth is indicative of a 17% increase, surpassing the 14% growth rate recorded in the preceding year of 2020. According to a research from Mordor Intelligence (A.D. 21.09.2023), the overall net revenue

DOI: 10.4018/979-8-3693-1038-0.ch018

of Islamic financial institutions worldwide increased significantly in 2021. From 2020 to 2021, the net profits increased to USD 32 billion. Islamic finance is a specialized field within the realm of finance that adheres to the principles and guidelines set forth by Islamic law, also known as Shariah. One of the key principles of Islamic finance is the restriction of interest-based transactions, both in terms of charging and earning interest. According to Abbahaddou and Chiadmi (2022), the application of ML algorithms has demonstrated potential in forecasting the performance of Islamic stock market indexes (Abbahaddou & Chiadmi, 2022).

One of the primary obstacles encountered by financial participants pertains to the task of forecasting forthcoming movements within the stock market. Indeed, the task of making appropriate investing decisions is challenging due to the inherent volatility of the market. The examination of financial stock indexes' performance can be approached through various methods, including sentiment analysis, technical analysis, and fundamental analysis. The methodology entails generating predictions on the performance of a stock index by capitalizing on the concept that stock prices demonstrate trends, often in a cyclical fashion, hence facilitating the identification of stock price fluctuations. These methodologies frequently depend on a range of data points, encompassing the lowest and greatest prices as well as volume. These entities have been widely utilized, however they have also encountered substantial scrutiny. In the context of the weak version of efficient markets, it is widely held that the share price is considered to directly assimilate historical price information. Currently, a diverse range of techniques are utilized in an effort to predict stock prices in the present era. These systems utilize historical price data and trading volume, with Machine Learning (ML) being a prominent example. The field of machine learning (ML) has witnessed a substantial surge in growth in its usage and implementation for the purpose of automating various processes in a wide range of domains. In the domain of market finance, it is noteworthy that there exists a body of research focused on the examination of stock price behavior and the forecasting of index fluctuations, which incorporates the utilization of Machine Learning algorithms (Abbahaddou & Chiadmi, 2022). In recent years, the advancement of Islamic finance has broadened the scope of financial interactions among global participants, extending beyond the confines of the Islamic world. The expeditious advancement of technological advances in the financial sector has prompted the adoption of novel tools in Islamic countries (Demyanova, 2017).

The use of Fintech technologies in the financial world is quite old. However, the application of these technologies in the Islamic finance sector has been quite limited compared to other examples. It is noteworthy that the studies conducted in this field are mostly in the form of literature review rather than application (Bioncone et al., 2020; Rabbani et al., 2020; Hassan et al., 2021; Tijjani et al., 2021; Alshater et al., 2022; Pal et al., 2023; Kismawadi et al., 2023; Irfan et al., 2023). It is also possible to come across studies on the effects of blockchain technologies (Alam et al., 2019; Kirchner, 2020; Chong, 2021, Irfan et al., 2023). Considering the applied studies on Islamic finance, there is a research examining the extent to which Islamic Stock Markets might be considered as safe havens (Chkili, 2017), comparing Islamic markets with conventional markets (Rahmadhani et al., 2015; Nasr et al., 2016; Jawadi et al., al., 2020), measuring the efficiency of Islamic stock markets (Setianto & Manap, 2015), investigating the volatility of Islamic markets (Chkili & Hamdi, 2021; Bahloul, Khemakhem, 2021), portfolio diversification (Ashraf et al., 2023). However, in the literature research, it is observed that the studies using ML and DL approaches in the Islamic finance market are quite limited. Abu Bakar&Rosbi (2017) applied the ARIMA method to evaluate the stock market trend of Islamic Bank Malaysia. Abbahaddou&Chiadmi (2021) tried to determine the predictive ability of the ANN model to predict the MSCII and JKII index price. In another study, Abbahaddou&Chiadmi (2022) predicted MSCII and JKII stock market prices using SVM, CART, RF and ANN methods and stated that the best result among these approaches was obtained by SVM. Katterbauer&Moschetta (2021) estimated the stock price of companies in the Saudi Tadawul Stock Exchange using the LSTM-NLP method. Abbahaddou&Chiadmi (2022) compared the performances of Islamic Stock Markets using ARIMA-GARCH, ANN and SVM methods. The findings obtained in the study were evaluated using MAPE and RMSE statistical coefficients. The study concluded that the artificial neural network (ANN) approach provided superior outcomes compared to the alternative two techniques. When we look at the literature above, it is observed that studies using machine and deep learning methods in the field of Islamic Finance are quite limited. This study will try to close this gap in the literature.

Machine learning and deep learning techniques are commonly employed in financial forecasting models. The aim of this research is to forecast the price of The MSCI ACWI Islamic Index by employing a range of machine learning and deep learning techniques. The MSCI ACWI Islamic Index is constructed to adhere to Sharia investment standards and serves as a metric for evaluating the performance of the big and medium capitalization sectors in 23 Developed and 24 Emerging Markets, which hold significance for Islamic investors. The index comprises a total of 699 members and employs rigorous screening measures the exclusion of stocks based on two separate categories of criteria, namely firm activities and financial ratios that are generated from the total assets. The proposed LSTM, Random Forest, XGBoost, CNN and GRU models will be applied to the data set to be obtained. In the models to be proposed, 80% of the data will be allocated for training the models and 20% for testing the models. The proposed model will be used in Python programming language and model performances will be compared using MSE, RMSE, MAE, MAPE and R^2 statistical coefficients. In this way, it will reveal the model that best predicts the price of MSCI ACWI Islamic Index, one of the largest Islamic Finance indices in the world. In this way, it is thought that it will be a reference source for individual and institutional investors who want to invest in Islamic financial indices around the world in choosing the best model to be used for index price prediction.

2. LONG SHORT-TERM MEMORY (LSTM) MODEL

The initial proposal of LSTM was put forth by Hochreiter and Schmidhuber in 1997. This innovative approach involved the meticulous incorporation of memory attributes into RNN architecture, aiming to mitigate the issue of prolonged dependencies. The RNN exhibits a vanishing gradient problem due to the unconstrained information updates within its network layer, resulting in chaotic dynamics and the potential loss of information. The LSTM network incorporates a forgetting unit and a memory unit within the hidden layer, enabling the network to selectively discard less significant information upon receiving fresh input, while retaining crucial information in its long-term memory. The units in LSTM networks are commonly referred to as gates. The primary components of these gating mechanisms consist of a single cell and three distinct gates: the input gate, the output gate, and the forget gate (Zhou et al., 2022).

The several steps of the LSTM technique are outlined in Equation 1-7 as follows:

$$x_{scaled} = \frac{x - x_{\min}}{x_{\max} - x_{\min}} \qquad (1)$$

$$f_t = \sigma_g(W_f x_t + U_f h_{t-1} + b_f) \tag{2}$$

$$i_t = \sigma_g(W_i x_t + U_i h_{t-1} + b_i) \tag{3}$$

$$C'_t = \sigma_c(W_c x_t + U_c h_{t-1} + b_c) \tag{4}$$

$$C_t = f_t x C_{t-1} + i_t x C'_t \tag{5}$$

$$o_t = \sigma_g(W_o x_t + U_o h_{t-1} + b_o) \tag{6}$$

$$h_t = o_t \times \tanh(C_t) \tag{7}$$

The data has been subjected to normalization using Equation 1. Equation 2 encompasses the inclusion of several variables, namely x_t, h_{t-1}, f_t, and σg. These variables represent the input of the time series, the prior hidden state, output vector, and the activation function, respectively. Furthermore, the bias coefficient is commonly symbolized as bf whereas the forget gates are typically designated by Wf and Uf. The forget gate is linked to the output vector. The relationship is denoted by Equation 2. Equations 3 and 4 delineate the correlation between the current point within the time series input, represented as xt, and the hidden state, indicated as ht_{-1} originating from the preceding time frame. The values of the coefficients it and C'_t within this gate are determined by these variables. The determination of these coefficients entails the application of the activation function. The weight coefficients are denoted by variables W_i, U_i, W_c, and U_c, whereas the activation function is denoted by the symbols σg and σc. In Equation 5, the cell state, denoted as Ct, undergoes an update process by combining the product of the output of the input gate, it, and the cell candidate data, C'_t, with the result of multiplying the previous cell state, Ct_{-1}, by the output of the forget gate, ft. The calculation offers a description of the altered cellular state, referred to as Ct_{-1}. Equation 6 illustrates the generation of the output vector ot by the application of the activation function σg to the input vectors ht_{-1} and xt. The bias coefficient, commonly designated as bo, together with the weighted values of the cell state, typically expressed as Wo and Uo, are associated with the input gate. The value obtained from the output gate, which is represented as ot, is multiplied by the current sequential cell state, written as Ct after it has been generated. The output of the hidden layer is computed by applying the hyperbolic tangent activation function to the resulting value, as illustrated in Equation 7.

3. RANDOM FOREST (RF) MODEL

The random-subspace technique was initially proposed by Ho (1995) and later expanded upon by Breiman (2001) to create the random forest algorithm. A RF can be described as a collection of decision trees that exhibit a hierarchical, tree-like arrangement. In this context, it can be observed that every leaf node inside the given structure symbolizes a classification or choice. On the other hand, each non-leaf node that is internal in nature signifies an attribute test (Ali et al., 2012; Hu et al., 2022). The random forest algorithm offers a distinctive amalgamation of predictive precision and model interpretability when compared to other widely used machine learning techniques. The utilization of random sampling and ensemble procedures in RF allows for the attainment of accurate predictions and improved generalization capabilities. The primary emphasis is placed on three key attributes of random forest. The model offers precise forecasts for a wide range of applications. Additionally, the model training process allows for the assessment of the significance of each feature. Lastly, the trained model may be utilized to quantify the pairwise closeness between samples (Breiman, 2001; Qi, 2012). Let us consider a hypothetical scenario in which we have a training dataset, denoted as T, specifically designed for the MSCI ACWI Islamic Index. To further enhance the learning process, we draw k distinct training sample sets from T, which we will refer to as S. Consequently, the training process yields k distinct learners, designated as f(S). Subsequently, the calculation for the projected price of the MSCI ACWI Islamic Index can be determined as Equation 8.

$$\hat{\theta} = \frac{1}{k}\sum_{k=1}^{k} f\left(S\right) \tag{8}$$

The RF algorithm assesses the significance of variables by calculating their potential impact on the prediction error when subjected to permutation, while keeping all other variables constant. The significance of this factor can offer valuable insights into the extent to which the factors included are essential for elucidating and forecasting housing prices (Archer & Kimes, 2008).

According to (Archer & Kimes, 2008) The RF algorithm can be described as follows:

To obtain a random sample of n observations with replacement from the population *L*, repeat the sampling process B times, where b is the iteration number ranging from 1 to B. The term “bootstrap sample” is commonly known as L_b in academic literature.

Utilize the element L_b in constructing a computational model known as a CT, incorporating the subsequent alterations:

1. Step: At time point t, a random selection is made from the set of p independent variables, resulting in a sample size of m.
2. Step: For each of the sampled variables, denoted as k = 1,...,m, the objective is to identify the optimal split, s_k, from all feasible splits for the k_{th} variable.
3. Step: Select the optimal split s* from the set of k = 1,...,m most favorable splits s_k in order to divide the node t. The variable indexed by j, denoted as c_{s*}, is utilized to partition node t at its designated cut point.

4. The data at this node is split by assigning the observations with $x_{ij} < c_{s*}$, where i ranges from 1 to n, to the left descendant node, and assigning the observations with $x_{ij} \geq c_{s*}$ to the right descendant node.
5. Step: Proceed to iterate steps 1–4 on all descendant nodes in order to expand the tree, T_b, to its maximum size.

4. CONVOLUTIONAL NEURAL NETWORKS (CNN) MODEL

CNN is a mathematical model that typically has three essential layers: convolution, pooling, and fully connected layers. The first two layers, specifically the convolutional and pooling layers, are tasked with extracting distinctive characteristics. Conversely, the third layer, known as the fully connected layer, is tasked with the mapping of the extracted characteristics in order to provide the ultimate output, which may encompass categorization (Yamashita et al., 2018). One notable advantage of CNNs in comparison to their predecessors is their ability to autonomously identify and extract salient characteristics without the need for human intervention. This characteristic has contributed to the widespread adoption and utilization of CNNs in various domains. Thus, a comprehensive analysis of CNN has been conducted, wherein the principal elements of the network have been elucidated. In addition, we have included comprehensive explanations of the prevailing CNN structures, commencing with the AlexNet model and concluding with the High-Resolution network (Alzubaidi et al., 2021). The structure of the CNN model is given below as Equation 9-11.

Equation 9 defines the variable x_j^d as the jth feature map of the convolution layer. The feature map is a key component. The activation function, denoted by ∅, is applied to the input M_j, where d represents the dimensionality of the input minus one. The input feature set of the layer refers to the set of features that are provided as input to the layer. The variable w_{ij}^d represents the attribute map of the jth attribute in the dth convolutional layer. The attribute of the (d-1)^th^ element. Attribute j of the convolution layer and attribute i of layer (d-1) are considered in Layer i. The variable b_i^d represents the bias term associated with the respective layer.

$$x_j^d = \phi\left(\sum\nolimits_{i \in M_j} x_i^{d-1} * w_{ij}^d + b_i^d\right) \tag{9}$$

The subtraction functioning down(.) and the value of the weight matrix β are denoted in Equation 10. In Equation 11, following the application of the convolution and pooling layer, the process of classification is carried out utilizing the complete link layer. Equation 14 represents a mathematical expression wherein many variables are defined. The variable "k" denotes the layer index, "y^k" represents the output of the full link layer, "x^{k-1}" signifies the input of the full link layer, "w^k" denotes the weighting value, and "b^k" represents the difference between the two results.

$$x_j^d = \phi\left(\beta_j^d down\left(x_j^{d-1}\right) + b_i^d\right) \tag{10}$$

$$y^k = \phi\left(w^k x^{k-1} + b^k\right) \tag{11}$$

5. GATED RECURRENT UNIT (GRU) MODEL

The GRU, which is a variant of the RNN, was initially introduced by Cho et al. (2014). In contrast to the LSTM network, the GRU network possesses a reduced number of gates by one. The GRU network consists of two gates, specifically the reset gate and the update gate. The reset gate is responsible for integrating the current input with the existing memory and regulating the degree to which the prior memory is disregarded. A decrease in the reset gate value corresponds to an increase in the amount of memory that is disregarded. The update gate is utilized to ascertain the extent of memory allocation prior to an event. The magnitude of the update gate directly correlates with the amount of information it will produce. By assigning a value of 1 to all reset gates and a value of 0 to all update gates, the resulting model can be described as a general neural network (Liu et al., 2019).

The operational principles of the GRU are established by Equation 12 and 13. The candidate status value of the GRU unit, written as $\tilde{h}_t$, is obtained according to Equation 14 during the procedures of resetting and updating the gate. Additionally, the final output status value, expressed as h_t, is generated as illustrated in Equation 15.

$$z_t = \sigma(W_z * \left[h_{t-1}, x_t)\right] \tag{12}$$

$$r_t = \sigma(W_r * \left[h_{t-1}, x_t)\right] \tag{13}$$

$$\tilde{h}_t = \tanh(W_{\tilde{h}_t} * (\left[r_t * h_{t-1}, x_t\right]) \tag{14}$$

$$h_t = (1-z_t) * h_{t-1} + z_t * \tilde{h}_t \tag{15}$$

6. EXTREME GRADIENT BOOSTING (XGBOOST) MODEL

The XGBoost model, also known as Extreme Gradient Boosting, was initially introduced by Chen et al. (2011). The conventional Boosting Tree models solely rely on the utilization of first derivative information. Implementing distributed training for the nth tree poses challenges due to the utilization of the residual from the preceding n-1 trees. XGBoost employs a second-order Taylor expansion technique on the loss function, enabling it to effectively leverage the multiple threads capabilities of the CPU for parallel processing. In addition, XGBoost employs a range of techniques to mitigate the issue of overfitting (Li et al., 2019). Equations 16-22 provide a visual representation of the sequential procedures involved in the XGBoost algorithm.

$$\hat{y}_i = \phi(x_i) = \sum_{k=1}^{K} f_k(y_i), f_k \in \mathcal{F} \tag{16}$$

$$\min L^{(t)}(y_i, \hat{y}_i^{(t)}) = \min\left[\sum_{i=1}^{n} l\left(y_i, \hat{y}_i^{(t)}\right) + \sum_{k=1}^{t} \Omega(f_k)\right] \tag{17}$$

$$\Omega(f) = \gamma T + \frac{1}{2}\lambda w^2 \tag{18}$$

$$\min L^{(t)} = min\left(\sum_{i=1}^{n}\left[g_i f_t(x_i) + \frac{1}{2} h_i f_t(x_i)\right] + ©(f_t)\right) \tag{19}$$

$$g_i = \partial_{\hat{y}_i^{(t-1)}} l\left(y_i, y_i^{t-1}\right) \tag{20}$$

$$h_i = \partial^2_{y_i^{t-1}} l\left(y_i, y_i^{t-1}\right) \tag{21}$$

$$w_j^* = -\frac{\Sigma g_i}{\Sigma h_i + \lambda} \tag{22}$$

$$obj^* = -\frac{1}{2}\sum_{j=1}^{T}\frac{(\Sigma g_i)^2}{\Sigma h_i + \lambda} + \gamma.T \tag{23}$$

In order to predict the outcome of a dataset consisting of n samples and m features, a tree ensemble model utilizes K additive functions represented as $D = \{(x_i, y_i)\}(|D| = n, x_i \in \mathcal{R}^m, y_i \in \mathcal{R}$. Equation 16 represents the set of regression trees, denoted as F, within the context of this study. The variable f_k denotes the quantity of weak learners, while K indicates the total number of weak learners. The formal definition of the objective function of the algorithm at time t, denoted as $L^{(t)}$, is given by Equation 17.

The parameter $l\left(y_i, \hat{y}_i^{(t)}\right)$ contains a range of loss functions that are employed to address specific problems. Equation 17 introduces a commonly utilized approach for measuring the discrepancy between the observed value (y_i) and the predicted value ($\hat{y}_i^{(t)}$), as well as the overall intricacy of the model, denoted by $\sum_{k=1}^{t}\Omega\left(f_k\right)$. The assessment of the objective function entails substituting the expected value ($\hat{y}_i^{(t)}$) for the ith sample in the tth iteration. The calculation is performed using the second-order approximation of the Taylor expansion at the predicted amount of y from the previous iteration, indicated as $\hat{y}_i^{(t-1)}$), as described in Equation 16. The variables g_i and h_i in Equation 19 represent the first and second derivatives of the loss function $l\left(y_i, \hat{y}_i^{(t)}\right)$, respectively. By substituting the formulas represented as Equation 19, Equation 20, and Equation 21 into the previously described Equation 17, we may thereafter proceed to calculate the derivative. Solutions can be derived by employing Equations 22 and 23. Equations 19 and 20 denote the variable obj^*, which represents the quantitative value of the loss function's score. A lower score indicates a tree structure that is more closely aligned with the ideal. The symbol w_j^* denotes the ideal solution for the weights in the particular scenario being examined.

7. RESULTS

The primary objective of the MSCI ACWI Islamic Index is to assess the financial performance of the big and mid-cap sectors within 23 established and emerging economies, while simultaneously adhering to the requirements of Sharia investment. This study was undertaken to forecast the performance of this index by employing many machine learning and deep learning methodologies, such as LSTM, RF, CNN, GRU, and XGBoost. 3453 daily data of MSCI ACWI Islamic Index between 04.01.2010 and 20.09.2023 were used for the analysis. These data were obtained from www.investing.com. The dataset was first separated into an 80% training subset and a 20% testing subset and coded using the necessary libraries in Python. Performance metrics of the approaches used in the study were evaluated using RMSE, MSE, MAE, MAPE and R^2 coefficients. The calculation formulas of these statistical coefficients are given below in Equation 24-28.

$$MSE = \frac{1}{N}\sum_{i=1}^{N}\left(y_i - \hat{y}_i\right)^2 \tag{24}$$

$$RMSE = \sqrt{\frac{\sum_{i=1}^{N}\left(y_i - \hat{y}_i\right)}{N}} \tag{25}$$

$$MAE = \frac{\sum_{i=1}^{n}\left|y_i - x_i\right|}{n} \tag{26}$$

Table 1. Statistical results of proposed models

Model/Coeff.	RMSE	MSE	MAE	R^2
LSTM	0.032887	0.001082	0.029879	0.893764
CNN	0.018348	0.000337	0.014834	0.966932
GRU	0.017039	0.00029	0.013964	0.971482
RF	0.914888	0.83702	0.599347	0.997452
XGBoost	0.861021	0.741357	0.560062	0.997743

$$MAPE = \frac{\sum_{t=1}^{n} \frac{u_t}{Y_t}}{n} * 100 \tag{27}$$

$$R^2 = 1 - \frac{\sum_i \left(y_i - \hat{y}_i\right)^2}{\sum_i \left(y_i - \mu\right)^2} \tag{28}$$

Statistical coefficients of the models applied in the study are given in Table 1.

When Table 1 is examined, it is seen that the RMSE, MSE, MAE, R^2values for the LSTM model are 0.032887, 0.001082, 0.029879 and 0.893764, respectively. The LSTM model has lower RMSE and MSE values compared to other methods. But at the same time, the R^2 value is much lower than other methods. This shows that the LSTM model fits the data less well and the predictions explain less variance. It can be said that the CNN model performs well for all statistical metrics. The GRU model showed almost similar performance to other models and the R^2 value was around 0.97. This shows that the estimated values explain the variance well. In the RF model, RMSE, MSE and MAE values are slightly higher than other methods. However, the R^2 value is 0.9974, indicating that the model fits the data very well. RMSE, MSE and MAE values for the XGBoost model are higher than other methods. However, similar to the RF model, the R^2 value is 0.9977. As a result, it can be said that CNN and GRU models generally have the best performance. The LSTM model also has a good performance, but its R^2 value is lower than the CNN and GRU models. Although the R^2 value of the RF and XGBoost models is quite high, they performed very poorly compared to other methods in other error metrics. This points to an overfitting problem.

8. CONCLUSION

Islamic finance has been gaining increasing popularity in recent years. This situation can be associated with the increasing Muslim population in the world. Therefore, investors who pay attention to Islamic rules have turned to Islamic finance and directed their investments. This situation causes the Islamic finance sector to grow over the years. At this point, the use of Fin-Tech technologies becomes important for investors with Islamic sensitivities to make the right investment decisions. With the use of these technologies, more accurate price predictions of investment instruments traded in Islamic markets can be made. For example, the prediction performances of studies using machine learning or deep learning methods are much higher compared to predictions made with classical methods. This will enable investors with Islamic sensitivities to make more accurate investment decisions.

In this study, 3453 daily data of the MSCI ACWI Islamic Index, one of the largest Islamic Finance Indices in the world, between 04.01.2010 and 20.09.2023 were used. The obtained data was processed using LSTM, CNN, GRU, RF and XGBoost methods and it was determined which method gave better prediction performance. According to the results obtained, it was determined that the method with the best prediction performance was the GRU method. The CNN method showed a very good prediction performance, just like the GRU method, but it performed slightly worse than the GRU method in both RMSE, MSE and MAE values and R^2 value. Although the RF and XGBoost methods have an R^2 value of around 99.7%, they have much higher error coefficients in RMSE, MSE and MAE values compared to other methods. At this point, investors who will invest in MSCI ACWI Islamic Index will obtain better results by using CNN and GRU methods in price prediction.

The estimation of a financial index might be influenced by several variables. Future research could examine different variables that influence the MSCI ACWI Islamic Index.Furthermore, it is possible to compare the outcomes derived from alternative methodologies to those employed in this investigation, such as machine learning and deep learning techniques. Furthermore, there exist hybrid techniques such as CNN-BiLSTM that integrate machine learning and deep learning methodologies. This study can be repeated using hybrid methods in future studies.

REFERENCES

Abbahaddou, K., & Chiadmi, M. S. (2021). Study of the Use of Artificial Neural Networks in Islamic Finance. *World Conference on Management and Economics*, 45–53.

Abbahaddou, K., & Chiadmi, M. S. (2022). *Study Of The Performance Of Machine Learning Algorithms in the Case Of Islamic Stock Market.* Mohammed V University in Rabat.

Abu Bakar, N., & Rosbi, S. (2017). Data modeling diagnostics for share price performance of Islamic Bank in Malaysia using Computational Islamic Finance approach. *International Journal of Advanced Engineering Research and Science*, *4*(7), 174–179. doi:10.22161/ijaers.4.7.27

Alam, N., Gupta, L., Zameni, A., Alam, N., Gupta, L., & Zameni, A. (2019). Application of blockchain in Islamic finance landscape. *Fintech and Islamic Finance: Digitalization, Development and Disruption*, (pp. 81-98). Springer.

Ali, J., Khan, R., Ahmad, N., & Maqsood, I. (2012). Random forests and decision trees. *IJCSI International Journal of Computer Science Issues*, *9*(5), 272–278.

Alshater, M. M., Saba, I., Supriani, I., & Rabbani, M. R. (2022). Fintech in islamic finance literature: A review. *Heliyon*, *8*(9), e10385. doi:10.1016/j.heliyon.2022.e10385 PMID:36060472

Alzubaidi, L., Zhang, J., Humaidi, A. J., Al-Dujaili, A., Duan, Y., Al-Shamma, O., Santamaría, J., Fadhel, M. A., Al-Amidie, M., & Farhan, L. (2021). Review of deep learning: concepts, CNN architectures, challenges, applications, future directions. In Journal of Big Data, 8(1). Springer International Publishing. doi:10.118640537-021-00444-8

Archer, K. J., & Kimes, R. V. (2008). Empirical characterization of random forest variable importance measures. *Computational Statistics & Data Analysis*, *52*(4), 2249–2260. doi:10.1016/j.csda.2007.08.015

Ashraf, S., de Almeida, A. M. M., Naz, I., & Latief, R. (2023). Diversification of the Islamic stock market, Bitcoin, and Bullions in response to the Russia-Ukraine conflict and the COVID-19 outbreak. *Heliyon*, *9*(8), e19023. doi:10.1016/j.heliyon.2023.e19023 PMID:37636415

Bahloul, S., & Khemakhem, I. (2021). Dynamic return and volatility connectedness between commodities and Islamic stock market indices. *Resources Policy*, *71*, 101993. doi:10.1016/j.resourpol.2021.101993

Biancone, P. P., Saiti, B., Petricean, D., & Chmet, F. (2020). The bibliometric analysis of Islamic banking and finance. *Journal of Islamic Accounting and Business Research*, *11*(9), 2069–2086. doi:10.1108/JIABR-08-2020-0235

Breiman, L. (2001). Random forests. *Machine Learning*, *45*(1), 5–32. doi:10.1023/A:1010933404324

Chkili, W. (2017). Is gold a hedge or safe haven for Islamic stock market movements? A Markov switching approach. *Journal of Multinational Financial Management*, *42*, 152–163. doi:10.1016/j.mulfin.2017.10.001

Chkili, W., & Hamdi, M. (2021). An artificial neural network augmented GARCH model for Islamic stock market volatility: Do asymmetry and long memory matter? *International Journal of Islamic and Middle Eastern Finance and Management*, *14*(5), 853–873. doi:10.1108/IMEFM-05-2019-0204

Cho, K., Van Merrienboer, B., & Gulcehre, C. (2014). *Learning ¨ phrase representations using RNN encoder-decoder for statistical machine translation.* arXiv preprint arXiv:1406.1078. doi:10.3115/v1/D14-1179

Chong, F. H. L. (2021). Enhancing trust through digital Islamic finance and blockchain technology. *Qualitative Research in Financial Markets*, *13*(3), 328–341. doi:10.1108/QRFM-05-2020-0076

Demyanova, E. A. (2017). Development of companies in modern conditions of introduction of financial technologies. *Property relations in the Russian Federation, 7*(190), 104-113.

Hassan, M. K., Alshater, M. M., Hasan, R., & Bhuiyan, A. B. (2021). Islamic microfinance: A bibliometric review. *Global Finance Journal*, *49*, 1–14. doi:10.1016/j.gfj.2021.100651

Ho, T. K. 1995. Random decision forests. In *Proceedings of 3rd International Conference on Document Analysis and Recognition*, (pp. 278–282). Piscataway, NJ: IEEE.

Hochreiter, S., & Schmidhuber, J. (1997). Long short-term memory. *Neural Computation*, *9*(8), 1735–1780. doi:10.1162/neco.1997.9.8.1735 PMID:9377276

Hu, L., Chun, Y., & Griffith, D. A. (2022). Incorporating spatial autocorrelation into house sale price prediction using random forest model. *Transactions in GIS*, *26*(5), 2123–2144. doi:10.1111/tgis.12931

Irfan, M., Elhoseny, M., Kassim, S., & Metawa, N. (2023). *Advanced Machine Learning Algorithms for Complex Financial Applications.*

Irfan, M., Elmogy, M., & El-Sappagh, S. (Eds.). (2023). *The Impact of AI Innovation on Financial Sectors in the Era of Industry 5.0*. IGI Global.

Jawadi, F., Jawadi, N., & Idi Cheffou, A. (2020). Wavelet analysis of the conventional and Islamic stock market relationship ten years after the global financial crisis. *Applied Economics Letters*, *27*(6), 466–472. doi:10.1080/13504851.2019.1631438

Kassim, S. (2016). Islamic finance and economic growth: The Malaysian experience. *Global Finance Journal*, *30*, 66–76. doi:10.1016/j.gfj.2015.11.007

Katterbauer, K., & Moschetta, P. (2021). An innovative artificial intelligence and natural language processing framework for asset price forecasting based on islamic finance: A case study of the saudi stock market. *Econometric Research in Finance*, *6*(2), 183–196. doi:10.2478/erfin-2021-0009

Kirchner, I. K. (2020). Are Cryptocurrencies ḥalāl? On the Sharia-Compliancy of Blockchain-Based Fintech. *Islamic law and society, 28*(1-2), 76-112.

Kismawadi, E. R., Irfan, M., & Shah, S. M. A. R. (2023). Revolutionizing Islamic Finance: Artificial Intelligence's Role in the Future of Industry. In The Impact of AI Innovation on Financial Sectors in the Era of Industry 5.0 (pp. 184-207). IGI Global.

Li, W., Yin, Y., Quan, X., & Zhang, H. (2019). Gene Expression Value Prediction Based on XGBoost Algorithm. *Frontiers in Genetics*, *10*(November), 1–7. doi:10.3389/fgene.2019.01077 PMID:31781160

Liu, Y., Wang, Z., & Zheng, B. (2019). Application of Regularized GRU-LSTM Model in Stock Price Prediction. *2019 IEEE 5th International Conference on Computer and Communications*, (pp. 1886–1890). IEEE. 10.1109/ICCC47050.2019.9064035

Nasr, A. B., Lux, T., Ajmi, A. N., & Gupta, R. (2016). Forecasting the volatility of the Dow Jones Islamic Stock Market Index: Long memory vs. regime switching. *International Review of Economics & Finance*, *45*, 559–571. doi:10.1016/j.iref.2016.07.014

Pal, T., Irfan, M., & Kassim, S. B. (2023). How Do Machine Learning (ML) Techniques Benefit the Insurance Industry?: An Exploratory Study. In The Impact of AI Innovation on Financial Sectors in the Era of Industry 5.0 (pp. 108-130). IGI Global.

Qi, Y. (2012). Random forest for bioinformatics. *Ensemble Machine Learning: Methods and ApplicatiOns,* (pp. 307–323). Research Gate. https://doi.org/ doi:10.1007/9781441993267_10

Rabbani, M. R., Khan, S., & Thalassinos, E. I. (2020). *FinTech, blockchain and Islamic finance: An extensive literature review.* Research Gate.

Rahmadhani, A., Purqon, A., Kim, S., & Kim, S. Y. (2015, September). Complex network analysis of conventional and Islamic stock market in Indonesia. In AIP Conference Proceedings. AIP Publishing. doi:10.1063/1.4930741

Setianto, R. H., & Abdul Manap, T. A. (2015). *Examining the Islamic stock market efficiency: Evidence from nonlinear ESTAR unit root tests*. Indonesian Capital Market Review.

Tijjani, B., Ashiq, M., Siddique, N., Ajmal, K., & Rasul, A. (2021). A bibliometric analysis of quality research papers in Islamic finance: Evidence from web of science. *ISRA International Journal of Islamic Finance*, *13*(1), 84–101. doi:10.1108/IJIF-03-2020-0056

Yamashita, R., Nishio, M., Do, R. K. G., & Togashi, K. (2018). Convolutional neural networks: An overview and application in radiology. *Insights Into Imaging*, *9*(4), 611–629. doi:10.100713244-018-0639-9 PMID:29934920

Zhou, F., Huang, Z., & Zhang, C. (2022). Carbon price forecasting based on CEEMDAN and LSTM. *Applied Energy*, *311*(January), 118601. doi:10.1016/j.apenergy.2022.118601

Compilation of References

Abbahaddou, K., & Chiadmi, M. S. (2022). *Study Of The Performance Of Machine Learning Algorithms in the Case Of Islamic Stock Market.* Mohammed V University in Rabat.

Abbahaddou, K., & Chiadmi, M. S. (2021). Study of the Use of Artificial Neural Networks in Islamic Finance. *World Conference on Management and Economics*, 45–53.

Abdeljawad, I., Hashem, S. Q., & Rashid, M. (2022). Fintech and Islamic Financial Institutions: Applicationsand Challenges. In *FinTech in Islamic Financial Institutions: Scope, Challenges, and Implications in Islamic Finance* (pp. 193–222). PalgraveMacmillan. [CrossRef] doi:10.1007/978-3-031-14941-2_10

Abduh, M. (2019). Thought Civiliz. ISTAC 2019. *The Role of Islamic Social Finance in Achieving Sdg Number 2Achieve Food Security and Improved Nutrition and Promote Sustainable Agriculture*, 185–206.

Abduh, M., & Chowdhury, N. (2012). Does Islamic Banking Matter for Economic Growth in Bangladesh. *Journal of Islamic Economics, Banking and Finance, 8*, 104–113. https://ibtra.com/pdf/journal/v8_n3_article6.pdf

Abduh, M., & Azmi Omar, M. (2012). Islamic banking and economic growth: The Indonesian experience. *International Journal of Islamic and Middle Eastern Finance and Management*, *5*(1), 35–47. doi:10.1108/17538391211216811

Abdul Razak, D., & Noordin, B. A. (2020). Fintech and IF: A Perfect Symbiosis. *ISRA International Journal of IF*, *12*(1), 83–98.

Abdullah, N. (2021). AML/KYC Compliance in Islamic Fintech: A Blockchain-Based Approach. *Journal of Financial Crime*, *28*(2).

Abdullah, N. A. I. N., & Haron, R. (2022). ESG REPORTING PRACTICES AMONG ISLAMIC BANKS: A GLOBAL PERSPECTIVE. *IIUM Law Journal*, *30*(S2), S2. doi:10.31436/iiumlj.v30iS2.755

Abdulrasool, F. E., & Turnbull, S. I. (2020). Exploring security, risk, and compliance driven IT governance model for universities: Applied research based on the COBIT framework. *Int J Electron Bank*, *2*(3), 237–265. doi:10.1504/IJEBANK.2020.111438

Abdulrazzaq, A. (2019). Developing an AI-Based Personalized Investment Recommender System in Islamic Banking. *International Journal of Financial Research*, *10*(2).

Abedifar, P., Ebrahim, S. M., Molyneux, P., & Tarazi, A. (2016). Islamic banking and finance: Recent empiricalliterature and directions for future research. In *A Collection of Reviews on Savings and Wealth Accumulation* (pp. 59–91). Wiley. [CrossRef] doi:10.1002/9781119158424.ch4

Abojeib, M., & Habib, F. (2021). Blockchain for Islamic social responsibility institutions. In *Research Anthology on BlockchainTechnology in Business, Healthcare, Education, and Government* (pp. 1114–1128). IGI Global. [CrossRef] doi:10.4018/978-1-7998-5351-0.ch061

Abu Bakar, N., & Rosbi, S. (2017). Data modeling diagnostics for share price performance of Islamic Bank in Malaysia using Computational Islamic Finance approach. *International Journal of Advanced Engineering Research and Science, 4*(7), 174–179. doi:10.22161/ijaers.4.7.27

Abubakar, M. H., Hassan, M. K., & Haruna, M. A. (2019). Cryptocurrency tide and Islamic finance development: Any issue? *International Finance Review*, 189–200. doi:10.1108/S1569-376720190000020019

Abuzov, A. (2023). The role of technological innovations in institutional regulation of the financial capital market. *E3S Web of Conferences, 376*. doi:10.1051/e3sconf/202337605047

Adams, M., Andersson, J., Andersson, L.-F., & Lindmark, M. (2009). Commercial banking, insurance and economic growth in Sweden between 1830 and 1998. *Accounting Business & Financial History, 19*(1), 21–38. doi:10.1080/09585200802667139

Adjasi, C. K. D., & Biekpe, N. B. (2006). Stock market development and economic growth: The case of selected African countries. *African Development Review, 18*(1), 144–161. doi:10.1111/j.1467-8268.2006.00136.x

Adu, G., Marbuah, G., & Mensah, J. T. (2013). Financial development and economic growth in Ghana: Does the measure of financial development matter? *Review of Development Finance, 3*(4), 192–203. doi:10.1016/j.rdf.2013.11.001

Ahmad, A. U. F. (2001). *Problems of Islamic Banking in Bangladesh*. Islamic Economics Research Bureau, Dhaka, Bangladesh.

Ahmad, S. (2017). Factors influencing individual investors' behaviour: An empirical study of Pakistan financial markets. *Journal of business & financial affairs, 4*(6), 1-8.

Ahmad, A., & Bashir, R. (2014). An investigation of customer's awareness level and customer's service utilization decision in Islamic banking. *Pakistan Economic and Social Review, 52*(1), 59–74.

Ahmad, H., Yaqub, M., & Lee, S. H. (2023). Environmental-, social-, and governance-related factors for business investment and sustainability: A scientometric review of global trends. *Environment, Development and Sustainability*. doi:10.100710668-023-02921-x PMID:36714213

Ahmad, S. M., & Al Mamun, A. (2020). Opportunities of Islamic FinTech: The Case of Bangladesh and Turkey. [CrossRef]. *CenRaPSJournal of Social Sciences, 2*(3), 412–426. doi:10.46291/cenraps.v2i3.39

Ahmed, A, Rehman, K., & Saif, I. (2023). Islamic Banking Experience of Pakistan: comparison between Islamic and Conventional Banks. *International Journal of Business and Management, 5*(2), 137-143.

Ahmed, H., Mohieldin, M., Verbeek, J., & Aboulmagd, F. (2015). *On the Sustainable Development Goals and the Role of Islamic Finance*. The World Bank. doi:10.1596/1813-9450-7266

Ahmed, H. (2017). *Contribution of Islamic Finance To the 2030 Agenda for Sustainable Development*. In *High-level Conference on Financing for Development and the Means of Implementation of the 2030 Agenda for Sustainable Development*, (pp. 8–19). Doha,Qatar.

Ahmed, S., Alshater, M. M., El Ammari, A., & Hammami, H. (2022). Artificial intelligence and machine learning infinance: A bibliometric review. [CrossRef]. *Research in International Business and Finance, 61*, 101646. doi:10.1016/j.ribaf.2022.101646

Ahsanul, H. (2010). Islamic Banking in Malaysia: A study of attitudinal difference of Malaysian customers. *European Journal of Economics Finance and Administrative Sciences, 18*(1), 7–18.

Aich, S., Thakur, A., Nanda, D., Tripathy, S., & Kim, H. C. (2021). Factors affecting ESG towards impact on investment: A structural approach. *Sustainability (Basel), 13*(19), 10868. doi:10.3390u131910868

Ajzen, I. (1991). The theory of planned behavior. *Organizational Behavior and Human Decision Processes, 50*(2), 179–211. doi:10.1016/0749-5978(91)90020-T

Ajzen, I., & Madden, T. J. (1986). Prediction of goal-directed behavior: Attitudes, intentions, and perceived behavioral control. *Journal of Experimental Social Psychology, 22*(5), 453–474. doi:10.1016/0022-1031(86)90045-4

Akguc, S., & Rahahleh, N. A. (2020, January 4). Shariah Compliance and Investment Behavior: Evidence from GCC Countries. *Emerging Markets Finance and Trade*. Taylor & Francis. doi:10.1080/1540496X.2019.1706164

Akhtar, M. F., & Ali, F. (2021). Exploring the Nexus between Fintech and IF: Challenges and Opportunities. *Journal of Financial Regulation and Compliance, 29*(3), 489–508.

Akhtar, N. (2020). A review of the applications of artificial intelligence in IF. *Journal of Islamic Marketing, 11*(6).

Akhtar, S. A., & Akhtar, M. F. (2020). Fintech and IF: A Synergy to Foster Financial Inclusion. *ISRA International Journal of IF, 12*(1), 35–47.

Akram, W., & Aboukhamseen, S. M. (2021). A Framework for Sukuk Issuance Using Blockchain. In: *2021 IEEE International Conference on Blockchain*. IEEE.

Al Ansari, R. , & Alanzarouti, F. (2020). ESG and Islamic Finance: An Ethical Bridge Built on Shared Values. *Journal of Islamic Financial Studies, 06*(1), 05–11. doi:10.12785/jifs/060101

Al Balushi, Y., Locke, S., & Boulanouar, Z. (2019). Determinants of the decision to adopt Islamic finance: Evidence from Oman. *ISRA International Journal of Islamic Finance, 11*(1), 6–26. doi:10.1108/IJIF-02-2018-0020

Al Fathan, R., & Arundina, T. (2019). Finance-growth nexus: Islamic finance development in Indonesia. *International Journal of Islamic and Middle Eastern Finance and Management, 12*(5), 698–711. doi:10.1108/IMEFM-09-2018-0285

Al Janabi, M. A. M. (2022). Optimization algorithms and investment portfolio analytics with machine learning techniques under time-varying liquidity constraints. *Journal of Modelling in Management, 17*(3), 864–895. doi:10.1108/JM2-10-2020-0259

Alaeddin, O., Al Dakash, M., & Azrak, T. (2021). Implementing the blockchain technology in islamic financial industry:Opportunities and challenges. [CrossRef]. *Journal of Information Technology Management, 13*, 99–115.

Alam, N., Gupta, L., Zameni, A., Alam, N., & Gupta, L. (2019). *Digitalization and disruption in the financial sector.* Springer.

Alam, N., Gupta, L., Zameni, A., Alam, N., Gupta, L., & Zameni, A. (2019). Application of blockchain in Islamic finance landscape. *Fintech and Islamic Finance: Digitalization, Development and Disruption*, (pp. 81-98). Springer.

Alam, N., Gupta, L., & Zameni, A. (2019). *Fintech and Islamic Finance: Digitalization, Development and Disruption.* Palgrave Macmillan., doi:10.1007/978-3-030-24666-2

Albastaki, Y. A. (2020). When technology meets finance: A review approach to fintech. In Innovative Strategies for Implementing FinTech in Banking (pp. 1–21). IGI Global. doi:10.4018/978-1-7998-3257-7.ch001

Alexander, K., & Karametaxas, X. (2021). Digital transformation and financial inclusion. In Routledge Handbook of Financial Technology and Law (pp. 273–290). Routledge. doi:10.4324/9780429325670-15

Algamar, M. D., & Ismail, N. (2023). DATA SUBJECT ACCESS REQUEST: WHAT INDONESIA CAN LEARN AND OPERATIONALISE IN 2024? *Journal of Central Banking Law and Institutions*, *2*(3), 481–512. doi:10.21098/jcli.v2i3.171

Algharaballi, W., & Elamir, E. A. H. (2019). Digital Islamic Banks: A Framework for Ensuring Compliance with Shariah Principles. *Journal of Islamic Marketing*, *10*(1).

Alhakimi, W., & Esmail, J. (2019). The factors influencing the adoption of internet banking in Yemen. *Int J Electron Bank*, *2*(2), 97–117. doi:10.1504/IJEBANK.2020.109655

Alharbi, A. (2015). Development of the Islamic Banking System. *Journal of Islamic Banking and Finance*, *3*(1), 12–25. doi:10.15640/jibf.v3n1a2

Ali, M. (2021). Understanding the Impact of FinTechs on Service Innovation on the Future Sustainability of Global Business. In Remote Work and Sustainable Changes for the Future of Global Business (pp. 45–59). IGI Global. doi:10.4018/978-1-7998-7513-0.ch004

Ali, M. M. S., & Haneef, M. A. (2018). Blockchain in Islamic Finance: Smart Sukuk as a Case Study. In 2018 *7th International Conference on Computer and Communication Engineering (ICCCE)* (pp. 197-201). IEEE.

Ali, M. M. S., & Haneef, M. A. (2019). Blockchain for Islamic Finance: Current Pitfalls and Future Directions. In *2019 8th International Conference on Computer and Communication Engineering (ICCCE)* (pp. 74-79). IEEE.

Ali, H. (2018). Ethical Considerations in the Blockchain Ecosystem: A Case of IF. *IEEE Access : Practical Innovations, Open Solutions*.

Ali, H. F. (2021). Islamic Finance and Decentralized Finance (DeFi): A Conceptual Overview and Potential Synergies. *International Journal of Islamic and Middle Eastern Finance and Management*, *14*(5), 639–655.

Ali, H., Abdullah, R., & Zaini, M. Z. (2019). Fintech and its potential impact on Islamic banking and finance industry: Acase study of Brunei Darussalam and Malaysia. [IJIEF]. *International Journal of Islamic Economics and Finance*, *2*(1), 73–108. doi:10.18196/ijief.2116

Ali, J., Khan, R., Ahmad, N., & Maqsood, I. (2012). Random forests and decision trees. *IJCSI International Journal of Computer Science Issues*, *9*(5), 272–278.

Ali, M. (2021). Artificial Intelligence for Ethical Finance in Islamic Banking: Issues and Challenges. *Sustainability*, *13*(8).

Ali, M. M., Devi, A., Furqani, H., & Hamzah, H. (2020). Islamic financial inclusion determinants in Indonesia: An ANP approach. *International Journal of Islamic and Middle Eastern Finance and Management*, *13*(4), 727–747. doi:10.1108/IMEFM-01-2019-0007

Ali, Q., Salman, A., & Parveen, S. (2022). Evaluating the effects of environmental management practices on environmental and financial performance of firms in Malaysia: The mediating role of ESG disclosure. *Heliyon*, *8*(12), e12486. doi:10.1016/j.heliyon.2022.e12486 PMID:36590548

Ali, R., Barrdear, J., Clews, R., & Southgate, J. (2014). Innovations in Payment Technologies and the Emergence of Digital Currencies. *Bank of England Quarterly Bulletin*, *54*(3), 262–275.

Ali, S. S. (Ed.). (2008). *Islamic capital markets: Products, regulation and development*. Islamic Development Bank.

Alqahtani, F., Mayes, D. G., & Brown, K. (2020). Fintech in Islamic banking and finance: A review and research agenda. *Research in International Business and Finance*, *54*, 101281.

Alsalman, R., Salah, K., & Jayaraman, R. (2020). Secure and transparent user authentication system for Islamic finance based on blockchain. *IEEE Transactions on Industrial Informatics, 16*(9), 5769–5776.

Al-Sartawi A (2019) Assessing the relationship between information transparency through social media disclosure and firm value. *Manag Acc Rev 18*(2), 1–20.

Al-Sartawi A (2020) Information technology governance and cybersecurity at the board level. *Int J Crit Infrastruct 16*(2), 150–161.

Al-Sartawi A, Sanad Z (2019) Institutional ownership and corporate governance: evidence from Bahrain. *Afro-Asian J Finan Acc 9*(1), 101–115 20.

Al-Sartawi, A. (2015). The effect of corporate governance on the performance of the listed companies in the gulf cooperation council countries. *Jordan J Bus Adm 11*(3), 705–725.

Al-Sartawi, A. (2018). Corporate governance and intellectual capital: evidence from gulf cooperation council countries. *Acad Acc Financ Stud J 22*(1), 1–12 23.

Al-Sartawi, A. (2018). Institutional ownership, social responsibility, corporate governance and online financial disclosure. *Int J Critical Acc 10*(3/4), 241–255 22.

Al-Sartawi, A. (2018). Ownership structure and intellectual capital: evidence from the GCC countries. *Int J Learn Intellect Capital, 15*(3), 277–291 21.

Al-Sartawi, A. (2020). Social media disclosure of intellectual capital and firm value. *Int J Learn Intellect Capital 17*(4), 312–323.

Al-Shari, H. A., & Lokhande, M. A. (2023). The relationship between the risks of adopting FinTech in banks and their impact on the performance. *Cogent Business & Management, 10*(1), 2174242. doi:10.1080/23311975.2023.2174242

Alshater, M. M., Khan, A., Hassan, M. K., & Paltrinieri, A. (2023). Islamic Banking: Past, Present andFuture. [CrossRef]. *Journal of College of Sharia and Islamic Studies, 41*, 351.

Alshater, M. M., Saba, I., Supriani, I., & Rabbani, M. R. (2022). Fintech in islamic finance literature: A review. *Heliyon, 8*(9), e10385. doi:10.1016/j.heliyon.2022.e10385 PMID:36060472

Alshater, M., Hassan, K., Khan, A., & Saba, I. (2021a). Influential and intellectual structure of Islamic finance: Abibliometric review. [CrossRef]. *International Journal of Islamic and Middle Eastern Finance and Management, 14*(2), 339–365. doi:10.1108/IMEFM-08-2020-0419

Al-Tamimi, A. M., & Yasin, N. M. (2020). An Analysis of Islamic Banking in the Age of Blockchain Technology: A Theoretical Framework. *Journal of Theoretical and Applied Information Technology, 98*(1), 108–118.

Altarturi, B. H. M., Altarturi, H. H. M., & Anwar, H. A. O. (2021). Applications of financialtechnology in Islamic finance: A systematic bibliometric review. In *Artificial Intelligence and Islamic Finance* (p. 138161). Routledge. doi:10.4324/9781003171638-10

Al-Turjman, F. M., & Bibi, I. (2019). Blockchain for trade finance in the context of Islamic finance. In *Blockchain for Sustainable Business Models* (pp. 73–87). Springer.

Al-Turjman, F. M., & Elbarrawy, A. M. (2018). Enabling blockchain technology in industry 4.0: A survey, challenges, and future trends. *IEEE Access : Practical Innovations, Open Solutions, 6*, 32110–32127.

Al-Twaijry, A. A. (2020). Smart Contracts in IF: A Use Case of Musharakah Mutanaqisah Smart Contracts. *Journal of King Abdulaziz University: Islamic Economics, 33*(1).

Alvarado Quito, K., & Campodónico Durango, G. (2023). ANALYSIS OF FINTECH AND THEIR CONTRIBUTION TO THE DEVELOPMENT OF SMES IN GUAYAQUIL-ECUADOR. *Universidad y Sociedad, 15*(2), 475–483. https://www.scopus.com/inward/record.uri?eid=2-s2.0-85160102411&partnerID=40&md5=006d093931084e38c1dcc5e1e87eae66

Alvi, U. H., & Butt, S. A. (2020). Digital Transformation in Islamic Banking and Finance: A Comprehensive Review. *Journal of Islamic Marketing, 11*(2), 517–530.

Alzubaidi, L., Zhang, J., Humaidi, A. J., Al-Dujaili, A., Duan, Y., Al-Shamma, O., Santamaría, J., Fadhel, M. A., Al-Amidie, M., & Farhan, L. (2021). Review of deep learning: concepts, CNN architectures, challenges, applications, future directions. In Journal of Big Data, 8(1). Springer International Publishing. doi:10.118640537-021-00444-8

Amel-Zadeh, A., & Serafeim, G. (2018). Why and how investors use ESG information: Evidence from a global survey. *Financial Analysts Journal, 74*(3), 87–103. doi:10.2469/faj.v74.n3.2

Amin, H., & Hanifa, A. (2018). A blockchain-based model for Sukuk securities: A study of feasibility and viability. *Journal of Corporate Real Estate, 20*(3), 160–180.

Ammar, A. (2021). RegTech Adoption in IF: An Empirical Investigation. *Journal of Financial Services Marketing*.

Anggraini, M. (2019). Islamic banking development and economic growth: A case of Indonesia. *Asian Journal of Islamic Management, 1*(1), 51–65. doi:10.20885/ajim.vol1.iss1.art5

Angkasa, A., Wamafma, F., Juanda, O., & Nunna, B. P. (2023). Illegal Online Loans in Indonesia: Between the Law Enforcement and Protection of Victim. *Lex Scientia Law Review, 7*(1), 119–178. doi:10.15294/lesrev.v7i1.67558

Annisya, P.H. & Istiqomah, N. (2023). *Digital Era for Entrepreneurs: The Role of Social Media and Business Opportunities*. Atlantis Press. . doi:10.2991/978-2-38476-064-0_17

Anshari, M., Almunawar, M. N., Masri, M., & Hrdy, M. (2021). Financial technology with ai-enabled and ethical challenges. *Society, 58*(3), 189–195. doi:10.100712115-021-00592-w

Antonio, M. S., Hafidhoh, & Fauzi, H. (2013). The Islamic capital market volatility: a comparative study between in Indonesia and Malaysia. *Buletin Ekonomi Moneter dan Perbankan.*

Anwar, S., Junaidi, J., Salju, S., Wicaksono, R., & Mispiyanti, M. (. (2020). Islamic bank contribution to Indonesian economic growth. *International Journal of Islamic and Middle Eastern Finance and Management, 13*(3), 519–532. doi:10.1108/IMEFM-02-2018-0071

Archer, K. J., & Kimes, R. V. (2008). Empirical characterization of random forest variable importance measures. *Computational Statistics & Data Analysis, 52*(4), 2249–2260. doi:10.1016/j.csda.2007.08.015

Aregbeyen, O., & Mbadiugha, S. O. (2011). Factors influencing investors decisions in shares of quoted companies in Nigeria. *Social Sciences, 6*(3), 205–212. doi:10.3923science.2011.205.212

Aria, M., & Cuccurullo, C. (2017). bibliometrix: An R-tool for comprehensive science mapping analysis. *Journal of Informetrics, 11*(4), 959–975. doi:10.1016/j.joi.2017.08.007

Arif, A. I. M. (2019). Social Responsibility Practices of Islamic Fintech Companies: A Comparative Analysis. *Journal of Islamic Marketing, 10*(4).

Arif, M., & Majid, M. S. A. (2021). Machine Learning for Sukuk Selection: An Empirical Analysis. *Pacific-Basin Finance Journal.*

Ariss, R. T., & Sarieddine, Y. (2007). Challenges in implementing capital adequacy guidlines to Islamic banks. *Journal of Banking Regulation, 9*(1), 46–59. doi:10.1057/palgrave.jbr.2350059

Ashraf, D., & Khawaja, M. (2016, December 1). Does the Shariah screening process matter? Evidence from Shariah compliant portfolios. *Journal of Economic Behavior and Organization. Elsevier BV.* doi:10.1016/j.jebo.2016.10.003

Ashraf, S., de Almeida, A. M. M., Naz, I., & Latief, R. (2023). Diversification of the Islamic stock market, Bitcoin, and Bullions in response to the Russia-Ukraine conflict and the COVID-19 outbreak. *Heliyon, 9*(8), e19023. doi:10.1016/j.heliyon.2023.e19023 PMID:37636415

Asif, M., Khan, M. N., Tiwari, S., Wani, S. K., & Alam, F. (2023). The Impact of Fintech and Digital Financial Services on Financial Inclusion in India. *Journal of Risk and Financial Management, 16*(2), 122. doi:10.3390/jrfm16020122

Atif, M., Hassan, M. K., Rabbani, M. R., & Khan, S. (2021). Islamic FinTech: The digital transformation bringing sustainability to Islamic finance. In *COVID-19 and Islamic Social Finance* (pp. 91–103). Routledge. doi:10.4324/9781003121718-9

Aw, E. C. X., Zha, T., & Chuah, S. H. W. (2023, January 18). *My new financial companion! non-linear understanding of Robo-advisory service acceptance.* Service Industries Journal; Taylor & Francis. https://doi.org/ doi:10.1080/02642069.2022.2161528

Ayudya, A. C., & Wibowo, A. (2018). The Intention to Use E-Money using Theory of Planned Behavior and Locus of Control. *Jurnal Keuangan Dan Perbankan, 22*(2), 335–349. doi:10.26905/jkdp.v22i2.1691

Azmat, S., Kabir Hassan, M., Ali, H., & Sohel Azad, A. R. (2021). Neglected Risk and Asset Returns. *Journal of International Financial Markets, Institutions and Money, 74.*

Azzi, M., & Alobaidy, M. (2018). Blockchain and Waqf: An Opportunity for Transparency and Efficiency. In: *IEEE/ACS 15th International Conference on Computer Systems and Applications (AICCSA).* IEEE.

Bacha, O. I., & Mirakhor, A. (2019). *Islamic capital markets: A comparative approach.* Wiley.

Bahloul, S., & Khemakhem, I. (2021). Dynamic return and volatility connectedness between commodities and Islamic stock market indices. *Resources Policy, 71*, 101993. doi:10.1016/j.resourpol.2021.101993

Bahrain fintech bay. (2018). *Bahrain FinTech Ecosystem Report 2018.* Bahrain Fintech Bay. https://www.bahrainfintechbay.com/, .

Baker, T., & Dellaert, B. G. C. (2018, January 1). *Regulating Robo Advice across the Financial Services Industry.* SciSpace - Paper. https://typeset.io/papers/regulating-robo-advice-across-the-financial-services-144738fryr

Bank for International Settlements. (2017). *Distributed ledger technology in payment, clearing and settlement: An analytical framework.* Committee on Payments and Market Infrastructures.

Bank Indonesia. (2018). *Financial Technology.* Bank Sentral Republik Indonesia. https://www.bi.go.id/id/edukasi-perlindungan-konsumen/edukasi/produk-dan-jasa-sp/fintech/Pages/default.aspx

Banker, T. A. (2017). Central Bank of Bahrain announces landmark regulatory sandbox for fintech startups. *The Asian Banker.* https://www.theasianbanker.com/press-releases/central-bank-of-bahrain-announces-landmark-regulatory-sandbox-for-fintech-startups

Banna, H., Hassan, M. K., Ahmad, R., & Alam, M. R. (2022). Islamic banking stability amidst the COVID-19 pandemic: The role of digital financial inclusion. *International Journal of Islamic and Middle Eastern Finance and Management, 15*(2), 310–330. doi:10.1108/IMEFM-08-2020-0389

Barbu, C. M., Florea, D. L¸., Dabija, D.-C., & Mihai, C. R. B. (2021). Customer experiencein fintech. [CrossRef]. *Journal of Theoretical and Applied Electronic Commerce Research, 16*(5), 80. doi:10.3390/jtaer16050080

Barredo Arrieta, A., Díaz-Rodríguez, N., Del Ser, J., Bennetot, A., Tabik, S., Barbado, A., Garcia, S., Gil-Lopez, S., Molina, D., Benjamins, R., Chatila, R., & Herrera, F. (2020). Explainable Artificial Intelligence (XAI): Concepts, taxonomies, opportunities and challenges toward responsible AI. *Information Fusion*, *58*, 82–115. doi:10.1016/j.inffus.2019.12.012

Bartlett, R., Morse, A., Stanton, R., & Wallace, N. (2018). *Consumer-lending discrimination in the era of FinTech. Unpublished working paper*. University of California. https://lendingtimes.com/wp-content/uploads/2018/11/discrim.pdf

Basdekis, C., Christopoulos, A., Katsampoxakis, I., & Vlachou, A. (2022). FinTech's rapid growth and its effect on the banking sector. *Journal of Banking and Financial Technology*, *6*(2), 159–176. doi:10.100742786-022-00045-w

Bashir, N. (2020). Design and Development of Shariah-Compliant Digital Wallet: A Proposed Framework. *Journal of Islamic Marketing*, *11*(2).

Bassen, A., & Mählmann, T. (2019). The impact of ESG information on market performance: Evidence from the European real estate market. *Sustainability*, *11*(18).

Beck, T., Demirgüç-Kunt, A., & Merrouche, O. (2013). Islamic vs. conventional banking: Business model, efficiency, and stability. *Journal of Banking & Finance*, *37*(2), 433–447. doi:10.1016/j.jbankfin.2012.09.016

Bedoui, H. E. (2021). Role of fintech to achieve the SDGS from an Islamic perspective. In Islamic Fintech. doi:10.4324/9781003014614-1

Beik, I. S., & Nursyamsiah, T. (2021). SWOT ANALYSIS ON RESEARCH METHODOLOGIES AND TECHNIQUES ADOPTED IN ISLAMIC ECONOMICS AND FINANCE. In Teaching and Research Methods for Islamic Economics and Finance (pp. 29–41). Taylor & Francis. doi:10.4324/9781003252764-5

Belabes, A. (2021). Fintech and Maqāsid Dichotomy under the Prism of the Non-Neutrality of Techniques. In *Islamic FinTech*. Insights and Solutions. doi:10.1007/978-3-030-45827-0_3

Belal, A. R., Mohammed, M. M. M., & Ali, M. (2019). Intellectual capital reporting practices in an Islamic bank: A case study. [CrossRef]. *Business Ethics (Oxford, England)*, *28*(2), 206–220. doi:10.1111/beer.12211

Belanche, D., Casaló, L. V., & Flavián, C. (2019). Artificial Intelligence in FinTech: Understanding robo-advisors adoption among customers. *Industrial Management & Data Systems*, *119*(7), 1411–1430. doi:10.1108/IMDS-08-2018-0368

Belleflamme, P., Lambert, T., & Schwienbacher, A. (2014). Crowdfunding: Tapping the right crowd. *Journal of Business Venturing*, *29*(5), 585–609. doi:10.1016/j.jbusvent.2013.07.003

Benedetti, H., Nikbakht, E., Sarkar, S., & Spieler, A. C. (2020). Blockchain and corporate fraud. *Journal of Financial Crime*, *28*(3), 702–721. doi:10.1108/JFC-09-2020-0187

Bhatia, A., Chandani, A., Atiq, R., Mehta, M., & Divekar, R. (2021, September 5). Artificial intelligence in financial services: a qualitative research to discover robo-advisory services. *Qualitative Research in Financial Markets*. Emerald Publishing Limited. doi:10.1108/QRFM-10-2020-0199

Bhatia, M. S., Chaudhuri, A., Kayikci, Y., & Treiblmaier, H. (2023). Implementation of blockchain-enabled supply chain finance solutions in the agricultural commodity supply chain: A transaction cost economics perspective. *Production Planning and Control*, 1–15. doi:10.1080/09537287.2023.2180685

Bhattacharya, U. (2020). Assessing sustainability reporting from the perspective of financial analysts. *European Accounting Review*, *29*(1).

Bhatti, I. (2020). Microfinance in the Era of Islamic Fintech: An Exploratory Study. *Journal of Islamic Marketing*.

Biancone, P. P., Saiti, B., Petricean, D., & Chmet, F. (2020). The bibliometric analysis of Islamic banking and finance. [CrossRef]. *Journal of Islamic Accounting and Business Research*, *11*(9), 2069–2086. doi:10.1108/JIABR-08-2020-0235

Bian, W., Wang, S., & Xie, X. (2023). How valuable is FinTech adoption for traditional banks? *European Financial Management*, eufm.12424. doi:10.1111/eufm.12424

Bikas, E., Jurevičienė, D., Dubinskas, P., & Novickytė, L. (2013). Behavioural finance: The emergence and development trends. *Procedia: Social and Behavioral Sciences*, *82*, 870–876. doi:10.1016/j.sbspro.2013.06.363

Bonetti, F., Montecchi, M., Plangger, K., & Schau, H. J. (2023). Practice co-evolution: Collaboratively embedding artificial intelligence in retail practices. *Journal of the Academy of Marketing Science*, *51*(4), 867–888. doi:10.100711747-022-00896-1 PMID:36035334

Boto Ferreira, M., Costa Pinto, D., Maurer Herter, M., Soro, J., Vanneschi, L., Castelli, M., & Peres, F. (2021). Using artificial intelligence to overcome over-indebtedness and fight poverty. *Journal of Business Research*, *131*, 411–425. doi:10.1016/j.jbusres.2020.10.035 PMID:33100428

Boukhatem, J., & Ben Moussa, F. (2018). The effect of Islamic banks on GDP growth: Some evidence from selected MENA countries. *Borsa Istanbul Review*, *18*(3), 231–247. doi:10.1016/j.bir.2017.11.004

Bowen, G. A. (2009). Document analysis as a qualitative research method. *Qualitative Research Journal*, *9*(2), 27–40. doi:10.3316/QRJ0902027

Breiman, L. (2001). Random forests. *Machine Learning*, *45*(1), 5–32. doi:10.1023/A:1010933404324

Brendel, A. B., Mirbabaie, M., Lembcke, T. B., & Hofeditz, L. (2021). Ethical management of artificial intelligence. *Sustainability (Basel)*, *13*(4), 1974. doi:10.3390u13041974

BresciaV.Sa'adA.HassanR.AlhabshiS.LanzalongaF. (2021). *Exploring sustainability from the Islamic finance perspective*. https://doi.org/ doi:10.13135/2421-2172/6107-Published

Brusseau, J. (2023). AI human impact: Toward a model for ethical investing in AI-intensive companies. *Journal of Sustainable Finance & Investment*, *13*(2), 1030–1057. doi:10.1080/20430795.2021.1874212

Burger, C., & Weinmann, J. (2022). Blockchain Platforms in Energy Markets—A Critical Assessment. *Journal of Risk and Financial Management*, *15*(11), 516. doi:10.3390/jrfm15110516

Buterin, V. (2014). *Ethereum: A Next-Generation Smart Contract and Decentralized Application Platform.* (White Paper).

Cakir, M., & Raei, R. (2021). Fintech in IF: A Catalyst for Inclusion and Innovation. IMF Working Paper, WP/21/78.

Capponi, A., Ólafsson, S., & Zariphopoulou, T. (2022, April 1). *Personalized Robo-Advising: Enhancing Investment Through Client Interaction*. Management Science; Institute for Operations Research and the Management Sciences. doi:10.1287/mnsc.2021.4014

Casaburi, L., & Girardone, C. (2018). Blockchain Technology in Finance: Benefits, Challenges, and Emerging Applications. *International Journal of Financial Studies*, *6*(2), 38. doi:10.3390/ijfs6020038

Castillo, D., Canhoto, A. I., & Said, E. (2021). The dark side of AI-powered service interactions: Exploring the process of co-destruction from the customer perspective. *Service Industries Journal*, *41*(13–14), 900–925. doi:10.1080/02642069.2020.1787993

Catalini, C., & Gans, J. S. (2016). Some Simple Economics of the Blockchain. *NBER Working Paper No. 22952.*

Central Bank Of Bahrain. (2020). *About FinTech & Innovation*. CBB's FinTech & Innovation Unit. https://www.cbb.gov.bh/fintech/

Chapra, M. U. (2019). IF and the Global Economy. *Islamic Economic Studies*, *27*(1), 1–18.

Chau, W. H., Khin, A. A., & Teng, K. L. L. (2013). Economic Development Cointegration and Malaysian Life and General Insurance Consumption. *Australian Journal of Basic and Applied Sciences*, *7*(10), 538–546.

Chen, J., Storchan, V., & Kurshan, E. (2021). Beyond fairness metrics: Roadblocks and challenges for ethical ai in practice. *arXiv preprint arXiv:2108.06217*.

Chen, C., Xiao, B., Wang, J., & Ye, H. (2023). The effects of fintech development on financing constraints of small and medium-sized enterprises—Evidence from China. *MDE. Managerial and Decision Economics*, *44*(7), 4161–4172. doi:10.1002/mde.3920

Cheng, A. (2023). Evaluating Fintech industry's risks: A preliminary analysis based on CRISP-DM framework. *Finance Research Letters*, *55*, 103966. doi:10.1016/j.frl.2023.103966

Cheng, B., Ioannou, I., & Serafeim, G. (2014). Corporate social responsibility and access to finance. *Strategic Management Journal*, *35*(1), 1–23. doi:10.1002mj.2131

Cheng, M. M., Green, W. J., & Ko, J. C. W. (2015). The impact of strategic relevance and assurance of sustainability indicators on investors' decisions. *Auditing*, *34*(1), 131–162. doi:10.2308/ajpt-50738

Chen, J., Tong, Q. Q., Verma, H., Sharma, A., Dahbura, A., & Liew, J. K.-S. (2023). The Complexity of Blockchain Risks Simplified and Displayed: Introduction of the Johns Hopkins Blockchain Risk Map. *Journal of Financial Data Science*, *5*(1), 96–109. doi:10.3905/jfds.2022.1.117

Chen, P. F., Lee, C. C., & Lee, C. F. (2011). How does the development of the life insurance market affect economic growth? Some international evidence. *Journal of International Development*, *7*(24), 865–893.

Chen, S., Li, X., Liu, K., & Wang, X. (2023). Chatbot or human? The impact of online customer service on consumers' purchase intentions. *Psychology and Marketing*, *40*(11), 2186–2200. doi:10.1002/mar.21862

Chen, T. H., & Chang, R. C. (2021). Using machine learning to evaluate the influence of FinTech patents: The case of Taiwan's financial industry. *Journal of Computational and Applied Mathematics*, *390*, 113215. doi:10.1016/j.cam.2020.113215

Chen, Z., Da, Z., & Zhao, H. (2020). The fintech advantage: Robo-advisors and their potential impact on individual investors. *Journal of Financial Services Research*, *57*(2), 149–176.

Cheteni, P. (2014). Awareness of Islamic Banking Products and Services among Consumers in South Africa. *Mediterranean Journal of Social Sciences*, *5*(9), 96–103.

Chkili, W. (2017). Is gold a hedge or safe haven for Islamic stock market movements? A Markov switching approach. *Journal of Multinational Financial Management*, *42*, 152–163. doi:10.1016/j.mulfin.2017.10.001

Chkili, W., & Hamdi, M. (2021). An artificial neural network augmented GARCH model for Islamic stock market volatility: Do asymmetry and long memory matter? *International Journal of Islamic and Middle Eastern Finance and Management*, *14*(5), 853–873. doi:10.1108/IMEFM-05-2019-0204

Cho, K., Van Merrienboer, B., & Gulcehre, C. (2014). *Learning ¨phrase representations using RNN encoder-decoder for statistical machine translation.* arXiv preprint arXiv:1406.1078. doi:10.3115/v1/D14-1179

Chong, F. H. L. (2021). Enhancing trust through digital Islamic finance and blockchain technology. *Qualitative Research in Financial Markets*, *13*(3), 328–341. doi:10.1108/QRFM-05-2020-0076

Cocco, L., Concas, G., Marchesi, M., & Pinna, A. (2017). Banking on Blockchain: Costs Savings Thanks to the Blockchain Technology. In *International Workshop on Open Problems in Network Security* (pp. 281-293). Springer. 10.3390/fi9030025

Cocco, L., & Marchesi, M. (2016). Modelling and Simulation of the Economics of Mining in the Bitcoin Market. *PLoS One*, *11*(10), e0164603. doi:10.1371/journal.pone.0164603 PMID:27768691

Cocco, L., Marchesi, M., & Setzu, A. (2017). Payment Systems: A Blockchain Approach. *Journal of Economic Behavior & Organization*, *141*, 233–246.

Cohen, G., & Kudryavtsev, A. (2012). Investor rationality and financial decisions. *Journal of Behavioral Finance*, *13*(1), 11–16. doi:10.1080/15427560.2012.653020

Cohen, J., Holder-Webb, L., Nath, L., & Wood, D. (2011). Retail investors' perceptions of the decision-usefulness of economic performance, governance, and corporate social responsibility disclosures. *Behavioral Research in Accounting*, *23*(1), 109–129. doi:10.2308/bria.2011.23.1.109

Cortelezzi, F. (2022, July 6). *Global Islamic Finance: Principles and Products*. Routledge eBooks. doi:10.4324/9781003155218-10

Cowton, C. (1999). Accounting and financial ethics: From margin to mainstream? *Business Ethics (Oxford, England)*, *8*(2), 99–107. doi:10.1111/1467-8608.00134

Cox, S. (2005). Developing the Islamic Capital Market and Creating Liquidity. *Review of Islamic Economics*, *9*(1), 75–86.

Darus, F., Mad, S., & Nejati, M. (2015). Ethical and social responsibility of financial institutions: Influence of internal and external pressure. *Procedia Economics and Finance*, *28*, 183–189. doi:10.1016/S2212-5671(15)01099-0

Dasilas, A., & Karanović, G. (2023). The impact of FinTech firms on bank performance: Evidence from the UK. *EuroMed Journal of Business*. doi:10.1108/EMJB-04-2023-0099

Daud, S. N. M., Ahmad, A. H., Khalid, A., & Azman-Saini, W. N. W. (2022). FinTech and financial stability: Threat or opportunity? *Finance Research Letters*, *47*, 102667. doi:10.1016/j.frl.2021.102667

De Bondt, W. F., & Thaler, R. H. (1995). Financial decision-making in markets and firms: A behavioral perspective. *Handbooks in Operations Research and Management Science*, *9*, 385–410. doi:10.1016/S0927-0507(05)80057-X

De Franco, C. (2020). Esg controversies and their impact on performance. *Journal of Investing*, *29*(2), 33–45. doi:10.3905/joi.2019.1.106

de Manuel, A., Delgado, J., Parra Jounou, I., Ausín, T., Casacuberta, D., Cruz, M., Guersenzvaig, A., Moyano, C., Rodríguez-Arias, D., Rueda, J., & Puyol, A. (2023). Ethical assessments and mitigation strategies for biases in AI-systems used during the COVID-19 pandemic. *Big Data & Society*, *10*(1), 20539517231179199. doi:10.1177/20539517231179199

Delmolino, K. (2018). Towards Safer Ethereum Smart Contracts: A Survey of Languages, Tools, and Verification Methods. *ACM Computing Surveys*, *51*(6), 118. 10.1145/3230762

Demyanova, E. A. (2017). Development of companies in modern conditions of introduction of financial technologies. *Property relations in the Russian Federation, 7*(190), 104-113.

Derigs, U., & Marzban, S. (2008). Review and analysis of current Shariah-compliant equity screening practices. *International Journal of Islamic and Middle Eastern Finance and Management*, *1*(4), 285–303. doi:10.1108/17538390810919600

Dhillon, G., & Madi, A. (2019). Zakat distribution and the potential role of blockchain. In *Financial Cryptography and Data Security* (pp. 416–428). Springer.

DinarStandard. (2018). Islamic fintech report 2018: current landscape & path forward. *Dinar Standard.* https://www.dinarstandard.com/wp-content/uploads/2018/12/Islamic-Fintech-Report-2018.pdf

Dirican, C. (2015). The Impacts of Robotics, Artificial Intelligence on Business and Economics. *Procedia: Social and Behavioral Sciences, 95*, 564–573. doi:10.1016/j.sbspro.2015.06.134

Dogarawa, A. (2012). Global financial crisis and the search for new financial architecture: can Islamic finance provide alternative. *Journal of Islamic Economics, Banking and Finance.*

Dong, L., Jiang, P., & Xu, F. (2023). Impact of Traceability Technology Adoption in Food Supply Chain Networks. *Management Science, 69*(3), 1518–1535. doi:10.1287/mnsc.2022.4440

Dorfleitner, G., & Utz, S. (2014). Profiling German-speaking socially responsible investors. *Qualitative Research in Financial Markets, 6*(2), 118–156. doi:10.1108/QRFM-07-2012-0024

Dornbusch, R. & Fischer, S. (2004). *Macroeconomics 8th Edition.* McGraw-Hill.

Dua, S., Sharma, M. G., Mishra, V., & Kulkarni, S. D. (2023). Modelling perceived risk in blockchain enabled supply chain utilizing fuzzy-AHP. *Journal of Global Operations and Strategic Sourcing, 16*(1), 161–177. doi:10.1108/JGOSS-06-2021-0046

Du, G., & Elston, F. (2022). Financial risk assessment to improve the accuracy of financial prediction in the internet financial industry using data analytics models. *Operations Management Research : Advancing Practice Through Research, 15*(3–4), 925–940. doi:10.100712063-022-00293-5

Du, X. (2020). Evaluating the financial market effects of the global ESG disclosure standards: A multi-country study. *Journal of Corporate Finance,* •••, 62.

Echchabi, A., Aziz, H. A., & Idriss, U. (2016). Does Sukuk Financing Promote Economic Growth an Emphasis on the Major Issuing Countries. *Turkish Journal of Islamic Economics, 3*(2), 63–63. doi:10.15238/tujise.2016.3.2.63-73

EDB. (2016). *Innovation in payment services focus of panel discussion in Bahrain - Invest in Bahrain.* EDB BAHRAIN. https://www.bahrainedb.com/latest-news/innovation-in-payment-services-focus-of-panel-discussion-in-bahrain

Eitel-Porter, R. (2021). Beyond the promise: Implementing ethical AI. *AI and Ethics, 1*(1), 73–80. doi:10.100743681-020-00011-6

El Basri, M., & Mirakhor, A. (2019). Fintech and IF: A Convergence towards Financial Inclusion. *Islamic Economic Studies, 27*(1), 51–70.

El Qorchi, M. (2005). Islamic Finance Gears Up: While gaining ground, the industry faces unique regulatory challenges. *Finance & Development, 42*(4).

El Tiby, M. (2016). Innovation in Islamic Finance: A Framework for Shari'ah Compliance. *Journal of Islamic Accounting and Business Research, 7*(1), 36–50.

El Tiby, M., & Hassouna, A. (2017). Integrating blockchain technology with Islamic finance: A framework. In: *2017 International Conference on Islamic Applications in Computer Science and Technologies (IMAN).* IEEE.

Elamir, E. A. H. (2019). Artificial Intelligence and Credit Risk Assessment: A Case of Islamic Banks in the UAE. *Journal of Enterprise Information Management.*

Elamir, E. A. H., & Algharaballi, W. (2020). Financial Inclusion and Fintech Adoption in Muslim-Majority Countries. *Journal of Islamic Marketing, 11*(3).

El-Galfy, A. S. (2021). Fintech and the Transformation of IF. In Handbook of Blockchain, Digital Finance, and Inclusion (pp. 363-374). Springer.

Elkamhi, R., Ghandar, A., & Waring, A. (2017). Blockchain technology: Principles and applications. In Handbook of Blockchain, Digital Finance, and Inclusion, 1 (pp. 29-41). Academic Press.

El-Qorchi, M. (2018). *IF and Blockchain: The Potential of Distributed Ledger Technology*. (IMF Working Paper). IMF.

Elzarka, A. (2020). Blockchain-Based Sukuk: A Comprehensive Case Study. *Journal of Corporate Finance*.

Elzarka, A. (2021). Tokenization of Sukuk on Blockchain: A Comprehensive Case Study. *Journal of Islamic Marketing*.

Enisan, A. A., & Olufisayo, A. O. (2009). Stock market development and economic growth: Evidence from seven sub-Sahara African countries. *Journal of Economics and Business, 61*(2), 162–171. doi:10.1016/j.jeconbus.2008.05.001

Erragragui, E., & Revelli, C. (2016, November 1). Is it costly to be both shariah compliant and socially responsible? *Review of Financial Economics*. Elsevier BV. doi:10.1016/j.rfe.2016.08.003

Escrig-Olmedo, E., Muñoz-Torres, M. J., & Fernández-Izquierdo, M. Á. (2013). Sustainable development and the financial system: Society's perceptions about socially responsible investing. *Business Strategy and the Environment, 22*(6), 410–428. doi:10.1002/bse.1755

Esmaeilpour Moghadam, H., & Karami, A. (2023). Financial inclusion through FinTech and women's financial empowerment. *International Journal of Social Economics, 50*(8), 1038–1059. Advance online publication. doi:10.1108/IJSE-04-2022-0246

Fahmi, I., & Rosly, S. A. (2020). The Impact of Fintech on Islamic Crowdfunding in Malaysia: A Conceptual Framework. *Journal of Islamic Marketing, 11*(1).

Fallahi, S., Mellquist, A.-C., Mogren, O., Listo Zec, E., Algurén, P., & Hallquist, L. (2022). Financing solutions for circular business models: Exploring the role of business ecosystems and artificial intelligence. *Business Strategy and the Environment*. doi:10.1002/bse.3297

Fan, K. (2018). Blockchain-based Cryptocurrency Payment Systems: A Decentralized Sustainable Financial Solution. *Sustainable Cities and Society, 39*, 82–88. doi:10.1016/j.scs.2018.02.011

FarookS.FarooqM. O. (2011, January 1). *Shariah Governance for Islamic Finance: Challenges and Pragmatic Solutions*. Social Science Research Network; RELX Group (Netherlands). doi:10.2139/ssrn.1813483

Fersi, M., Boujelbéne, M., & Arous, F. (2023). Microfinance's digital transformation for sustainable inclusion. *European Journal of Management and Business Economics*. doi:10.1108/EJMBE-10-2022-0332

Feyen, E. H. B., Natarajan, H., & Saal, M. (2023). Fintech and the Future of Finance : Market and Policy Implications. Washington, D.C. doi:10.1596/978-1-4648-1914-8

Feyen, E. Natarajan, H., & Matthew, S. (2023). *Fintech and the Future of Finance: Market and Policy Implications (English)*. Washington, D.C.: World Bank Group.

Fieberg, C., Metko, D., Poddig, T., & Loy, T. (2023). Machine learning techniques for cross-sectional equity returns' prediction. *OR-Spektrum, 45*(1), 289–323. doi:10.100700291-022-00693-w

Fishbein, M., & Ajzen, I. (1975). *Belief Attitude Intention And Behavior*. Addison Wesley.

Floridi, L., Cowls, J., Beltrametti, M., Chatila, R., Chazerand, P., Dignum, V., & Vayena, E. (2021). An ethical framework for a good AI society: Opportunities, risks, principles, and recommendations. *Ethics, governance, and policies in artificial intelligence*, 19-39.

Fotheringham, D., & Wiles, M. A. (2023). The effect of implementing chatbot customer service on stock returns: An event study analysis. *Journal of the Academy of Marketing Science*, *51*(4), 802–822. doi:10.100711747-022-00841-2

Franzoni, S., & Ait Allali, A. (2018). Principles of Islamic Finance and Principles of Corporate Social Responsibility: What Convergence? *Sustainability (Basel)*, *10*(3), 3. doi:10.3390u10030637

Friede, G., Busch, T., & Bassen, A. (2015). ESG and financial performance: Aggregated evidence from more than 2000 empirical studies. *Journal of Sustainable Finance & Investment*, *5*(4), 210–233. doi:10.1080/20430795.2015.1118917

Fuadi, N. F. Z., Bukhari, B., & Firdiyanti, S. I. (2022). 'Halal Marketplace: The Influence of Attitude, Subjective Norms, and Perceived Behavior Control on Purchase Intention of Muslim Consumers', *Shirkah. Journal of Economics and Business*, *7*(1), 100–112. doi:10.22515hirkah.v7i1.451

Furqani, H. (2009). Islamic banking and economic growth: Empirical evidence from Malaysia. *Journal of Economic Cooperation & Development*, *30*(2).

Gampfer, S., & Hock, S. (2020). Machine learning for ESG investment. *Frontiers in Artificial Intelligence*, 3.

Gani, I. M., & Bahari, Z. (2021). Islamic banking's contribution to the Malaysian real economy. *ISRA International Journal of Islamic Finance.* doi:10.1108/IJIF-01-2019-0004

Gao, B. (2022). The Use of Machine Learning Combined with Data Mining Technology in Financial Risk Prevention. *Computational Economics*, *59*(4), 1385–1405. doi:10.100710614-021-10101-0

Gardner, A., Smith, A. L., Steventon, A., Coughlan, E., & Oldfield, M. (2022). Ethical funding for trustworthy AI: Proposals to address the responsibilities of funders to ensure that projects adhere to trustworthy AI practice. *AI and Ethics*, *2*(2), 1–15. doi:10.100743681-021-00069-w PMID:34790951

Ghlamallah, E., Alexakis, C., Dowling, M., & Piepenbrink, A. (2021). *The Topics of Islamic Economics and Finance Research.* Science Direct.

Giancaspro, M. (2017). Is a „smart contract" really a smart idea? Insights from a legal perspective. *Computer Law & Security Report*, *33*(6), 825–835. doi:10.1016/j.clsr.2017.05.007

Giri, P. K., De, S. S., Dehuri, S., & Cho, S.-B. (2021). Biogeography based optimization for mining rules to assess credit risk. *International Journal of Intelligent Systems in Accounting Finance & Management*, *28*(1), 35–51. doi:10.1002/isaf.1486

Gold, M., & Ali, P. (2019). 'FinTech Challengers and Incumbents' Responses: A Window into Innovation Management Strategy Modes within Australia's Financial Services Sector.' SSRN *Electronic Journal.* doi:10.2139/ssrn.3467855

Golodova, Z. G., & Grechkin, N. V. (2022). Developing Financial Integration with the Introduction of Financial Technologies in the Eurasian Economic Union Countries. *International Relations*, *22*(1), 166–179. doi:10.22363/2313-0660-2022-22-1-166-179

Gomber, P., Koch, J. A., & Siering, M. (2017). Digital finance and fintech: Current research and future research directions. *Journal of Business Economics*, *87*(5), 537–580. doi:10.100711573-017-0852-x

Goodell, J. W., Kumar, S., Lim, W. M., & Pattnaik, D. (2021). Artificial intelligence and machine learning in finance: Identifying foundations, themes, and research clusters from bibliometric analysis. *Journal of Behavioral and Experimental Finance, 32*, 100577. doi:10.1016/j.jbef.2021.100577

Goodfellow, I., Pouget-Abadie, J., Mirza, M., Xu, B., Warde-Farley, D., Ozair, S., Courville, A., & Bengio, Y. (2020). Generative adversarial networks. *Communications of the ACM, 63*(11), 139–144. doi:10.1145/3422622

Gray, R., Kouhy, R., & Lavers, S. (1995). Corporate social and environmental reporting: A review of the literature and a longitudinal study of UK disclosure. *Accounting, Auditing & Accountability Journal, 8*(2), 47–77. doi:10.1108/09513579510146996

Grealish, A., & Kolm, P. N. (2021, September 15). Robo-Advisors Today and Tomorrow: Investment Advice Is Just an App Away. *The Journal of Wealth Management; Euromoney Institutional Investor.* doi:10.3905/jwm.2021.1.149

Greenlaw, S. A., & Shapiro, D. (2011). Principles of Macroeconomics 2e. Rice University.

Griffin, N., Uña, G., Bazarbash, M., & Verma, A. (2023). *Fintech Payments in Public Financial Management: Benefits and Risks.* (IMF Working Papers). doi:10.5089/9798400232213.001

Guidotti, R. (2018). A Survey of Methods for Explaining Black Box Models. *ACM Computing Surveys.*

Gujarati, D. N. (2006). Econometria Básica. In Basic Econometrics. Cooch Behar Panchanan Barma University.

Gujarati, D. N., & Porter, D. C. (2009). *Basic Econometrics* (5th ed.). McGraw-Hill.

Gunathilaka, C. (2014). Financial Distress Prediction: A Comparative Study of Solvency Test and Z-Score Models with Reference to Sri Lanka. *IUP Journal of Financial Risk Management, 11*(3).

Günaydın, Y., Correia, A., & Kozak, M. (2022). Comparing efficiency in all-inclusive and bed and breakfast hotel businesses: A multi-period data envelopment analysis in Turkey. *European Journal of Management and Business Economics, 31*(4), 439–452. doi:10.1108/EJMBE-11-2021-0308

Gupta, N. (2019). Influence of demographic variables on synchronization between customer satisfaction and retail banking channels for customers' of public sector banks of India. *Int J Electron Bank 1*(3), 206–219 344

Gupta, M., & Sikarwar, T. S. (2020). Modelling credit risk management and bank's profitability. *Int J Electron Bank, 2*(2), 170–183. doi:10.1504/IJEBANK.2020.109663

Guz, A. N., & Rushchitsky, J. J. (2009). Scopus: A system for the evaluation of scientific journals. *International Applied Mechanics, 45*(4), 351–362. doi:10.100710778-009-0189-4

Habib Ahmed, R. (2004). Jeddah: The Islamic Research and Teaching Institute (IRTI). Durham Technology.

Hafiz, M. R. (2020). Smart Contracts in IF: Concept and Operational Framework. *International Journal of Islamic and Middle Eastern Finance and Management, 13*(3).

Hagendorff, T. (2020). The ethics of AI ethics: An evaluation of guidelines. *Minds and Machines, 30*(1), 99–120. doi:10.100711023-020-09517-8

Hailu, S. M., & Tekdoğan, M. F. (2023, June 30). *Ensuring The Compliance of Islamic Finance Applications with Shariah Principles in Ethiopia: The Way Forward.* Hitit Ilahiyat Dergisi. doi:10.14395/hid.1247875

Haiss, P., & Sümegi, K. (2008). The relationship between insurance and economic growth in Europe: A theoretical and empirical analysis. *Empirica, 35*(4), 405–431. doi:10.100710663-008-9075-2

Hakim, D., & Meressa, A. (2019). The Potential of Blockchain Technology in Islamic Finance. In: *2019 International Conference on Information Management and Technology (ICIMTech)*. IEEE.

Hamid, S., & Omar, S. S. (2019). Blockchain Technology in Islamic Finance: A Comprehensive Review. *International Journal of Engineering & Technology, 8*(1.8), 234-238.

Hamid, A., & Nordin, N. (2001). A study on Islamic banking education and strategy for the new millennium Malaysian experience. *International Journal of Islamic Financial Services, 2*(4), 3–11.

Hamoudi, H. A. (2007). You Say You Want a Revolution: Interpretive Communities and the Origins of Islamic Finance, 48 [Hereinafter Hamoudi]. *Virginia Journal of International Law*, 249.

Haneef, M. A. (2019). Blockchain Technology, Fintech, and Islamic Social Finance: Building Ethical Finance for Unbanked and Underprivileged Communities. *Frontiers in Blockchain, 2*.

Haneef, M. A. (2020). Ethical Considerations in Islamic Fintech: Issues and Challenges. *Journal of Islamic Marketing, 11*(6).

Haneef, M. A. (2021). Artificial Intelligence in Islamic Microfinance for Financial Inclusion: A Conceptual Framework. *Frontiers in Artificial Intelligence*.

Haniffa, R., & Hudaib, M. (2007). Exploring the Ethical Identity of Islamic Banks via Communication in Annual reports. *Journal of Business Ethics, 76*(1), 97–116. doi:10.100710551-006-9272-5

Harahap, B., Risfandy, T., & Futri, I. N. (2023). Islamic Law, Islamic Finance, and Sustainable Development Goals: A Systematic Literature Review. *Sustainability (Basel), 15*(8), 6626. doi:10.3390u15086626

Harris, R. (1995). *Using cointegration analysis in econometric modelling*. Pretice Hall.

Hasan, D. & Sunarti. (2019). *Analysis Of Banking Service Financial Technology (Fintech) Risk Management in Islamic Banks (Case Study at Bank Syariah X in Jakarta)*. KnE Social Sciences. . doi:10.18502/kss.v3i26.5396

Hasan, H., Maamor, S., & Abdullah, H. (2019, January 1). Evaluating The Effect Of Islamic Financing To Financial Development: Evidence From OIC Countries. *International Journal of Management Studies*. doi:10.32890/ijms.25.2.2018.10501

Hasan, M., & Dridi, J. (2019). *IF: Opportunities, Challenges, and Policy Options*. IMF Staff Discussion Note, SDN/19/08.

Hasan, Z. & Nita Putri, M.R. (2022). Indonesian Sharia Banking in Facing the Industrial Revolution 4.0. *UMRAN - International Journal of Islamic and Civilizational Studies, 9*(1), 37–47, . doi:10.11113/umran2022.9n1.546

Hasan, M. M., Hossain, M. S., & Zikria, Y. B. (2018). Legal and regulatory challenges of blockchain technology in Islamic finance. In *2018 IEEE International Conference on Engineering, Technology and Innovation (ICE/ITMC)* (pp. 1-6). IEEE.

Hasan, M., Hoque, A., & Le, T. (2023). Big Data-Driven Banking Operations: Opportunities, Challenges, and Data Security Perspectives. *FinTech, 2*(3), 484–509. doi:10.3390/fintech2030028

Hasan, M., Rashid, M. M., Shafiullah, M., & Sarker, T. (2022). How resilient are Islamic financial markets during the COVID-19 pandemic? *Pacific-Basin Finance Journal, 74*, 101817. doi:10.1016/j.pacfin.2022.101817

Hasan, Z. (2019). Islamic finance: An ethical alternative to conventional finance. *Journal of Business Ethics, 157*(4), 995–1017.

Hassan, K., & Mahlknecht, M. (2011). *Islamic capital markets: products and strategies*. Wiley.

Hassan, M. K. (2022). Fintech Trends: Industry 4.0, Islamic Fintech, and Its Digital Transformation. In FinTech in Islamic Financial Institutions: Scope, Challenges, and Implications in Islamic Finance. Springer. doi:10.1007/978-3-031-14941-2_6

Hassan, M. K., & Abubakar, B. (2018). Islamic Finance and Blockchain Technology: A New Opportunity. In Handbook of Blockchain, Digital Finance, and Inclusion, 1(pp. 115-130). Academic Press.

Hassan, R., & Noor, F. A. M. (2021, January 1). *Promoting peace and equality through the practice of good Islamic governance: the case of Islamic finance*. SciSpace. https://typeset.io/papers/promoting-peace-and-equality-through-the-practice-of-good-4r2qwhtbtr

Hassan, M. K., Aliyu, S. U. R., & Chiappetta Jabbour, C. J. (2020). Fintech and IF: A Review and Research Agenda. *Journal of Islamic Accounting and Business Research*, *11*(6), 1135–1156.

Hassan, M. K., Alshater, M. M., Hasan, R., & Bhuiyan, A. B. (2021). Islamic microfinance: A bibliometric review. *Global Finance Journal*, *49*, 1–14. doi:10.1016/j.gfj.2021.100651

Hassan, M. K., & Mahlknecht, M. (2019). IF: Debt versus Equity-based Financing in the Light of Basel III. *Pacific-Basin Finance Journal*, *53*, 482–498.

Hassan, M. K., Sanchez, B., & Yu, J. S. (2011). Financial development and economic growth: New evidence from panel data. *The Quarterly Review of Economics and Finance*, *51*(1), 88–104. doi:10.1016/j.qref.2010.09.001

Hassan, R. (2019). Exploring the Role of AI Transparency in Shariah Compliance. *Pacific-Basin Finance Journal.*

Hassan, R. (2021). Role of FinTech in Islamic Banks' Risk Assessment and Mitigation: A Conceptual Model. *Journal of Financial Crime*, *28*(4).

Hassan, R., & Ali, M. (2021). Enhancing AML/KYC Compliance in IF Using Blockchain Technology. *Journal of Money Laundering Control*, *24*(3).

Hassan, R., & Rashid, B. (2020). An Empirical Analysis of Anti-Money Laundering (AML) Risk Assessment using Machine Learning Techniques in Islamic Banking. *Journal of Financial Crime.*

Hassan, R., & Safi, S. (2020). The Role of Mobile Banking in Financial Inclusion: A Study in Islamic Countries. *Journal of Islamic Marketing.*

Hatta, M., Zainorin, N. D. E., Jalaludin, S., Nor, N. M., & Ramli, S. (2022, December 1). Financial Robo-Advisor Savings2u For Shariah-Compliant Savings And Investment Application. *Journal of Information System and Technology Management.* doi:10.35631/JISTM.729006

Hendershott, T., Zhang, X., Leon Zhao, J., & Zheng, Z. (2021). Fintech as a game changer: Overview of research frontiers. *Information Systems Research*, *32*(1), 1–17. doi:10.1287/isre.2021.0997

Hill, R. C., Griffiths, W. E., & Lim, G. C. (2011). *Principles of Econometrics* (4th ed.). John Wiley & Sons.

Hochreiter, S., & Schmidhuber, J. (1997). Long short-term memory. *Neural Computation*, *9*(8), 1735–1780. doi:10.1162/neco.1997.9.8.1735 PMID:9377276

Holtfort, T., Horsch, A., & Schwarz, J. (2022, January 1). Robo-advisors as part of industry 4.0 in financial markets: Evolutionary development, methods, and first performance insights. *Risk Governance and Control: Financial Markets & Institutions.* Virtus Interpress. doi:10.22495/rgcv12i2p3

Hooda, J., Singh, V., Irfan, M., & Hawaldar, I. T. (2024). Unleashing the Power of AI. In *The Impact of AI Innovation on Financial Sectors in the Era of Industry 5.0* (pp. 58–76). IGI Global. doi:10.4018/979-8-3693-0082-4.ch004

Hood, M., Nofsinger, J. R., & Varma, A. (2014). Conservation, discrimination, and salvation: Investors' social concerns in the stock market. *Journal of Financial Services Research*, *45*(1), 5–37. doi:10.100710693-013-0162-6

Hoque, A. (2023). Fintech's game-changing opportunities for SMEs: A study on selected SMEs in Bangladesh. *Asian Economic and Financial Review*, *13*(5), 308–319. doi:10.55493/5002.v13i5.4780

Ho, T. K. 1995. Random decision forests. In *Proceedings of 3rd International Conference on Document Analysis and Recognition*, (pp. 278–282). Piscataway, NJ: IEEE.

Hu, W., & Chen, Y. (2022). Application of Artificial Intelligence in Financial Risk Management. In Lecture Notes in Computer Science (including subseries Lecture Notes in Artificial Intelligence and Lecture Notes in Bioinformatics): Vol. 13338 LNCS (pp. 180–188). Springer. doi:10.1007/978-3-031-06794-5_15

Huang, J. Y., Gupta, A., & Youn, M. (2021). Survey of EU ethical guidelines for commercial AI: Case studies in financial services. *AI and Ethics*, *1*(4), 569–577. doi:10.100743681-021-00048-1

Hui, H. W. (2019). Fintech and the transformation of the Islamic finance regulatory framework in Malaysia. In Emerging Issues in Islamic Finance Law and Practice in Malaysia. Emerald Insight.

Hu, L., Chun, Y., & Griffith, D. A. (2022). Incorporating spatial autocorrelation into house sale price prediction using random forest model. *Transactions in GIS*, *26*(5), 2123–2144. doi:10.1111/tgis.12931

Hummel, D., & Hashmi, A. (2019). The Possibilities of Community Redevelopment with Islamic Finance. *J. Islam. Account. Bus. Res*, 259-273.

Hussain, M. S. (2015). *An overview of Islamic finance*. (IMF Working Paper). IMF.

Hussain, I., & Sultan, S. (2010). Analysis of Procrastination among University Students. *Procedia: Social and Behavioral Sciences*, *5*, 1897–1904. doi:10.1016/j.sbspro.2010.07.385

Hussein, R., Deng, H., & Luthra, S. (2018). Blockchain technology applications in Islamic finance: A comprehensive review. *Journal of King Saud University. Computer and Information Sciences*.

Iansiti, M., & Lakhani, K. R. (2017). The Truth About Blockchain. *Harvard Business Review*, *95*(1), 118–127.

Idelberger, F., Governatori, G., Riveret, R., & Sartor, G. (2016). Evaluation of Logic-Based Smart Contracts for Blockchain Systems. *Rule Technologies. Research, Tools, and Applications,10th International Symposium* (pp. 167-183). New York, United States: Springer, Cham. 10.1007/978-3-319-42019-6_11

Idrees, M., & Mahmood, A. N. (2019). A Survey on the Application of Blockchain Technology in Islamic Finance. In: *2019 IEEE International Conference on Blockchain (Blockchain)*. IEEE.

Idrees, S., & Gani, A. (2018). A survey of blockchain technologies for open innovation. *Journal of Network and Computer Applications*, *107*, 62–84.

Imam, P., & Kpodar, K. (2016). Islamic banking: Good for growth? *Economic Modelling*, *59*, 387–401. doi:10.1016/j.econmod.2016.08.004

Indonesia Financial Service Authority. (2018). Snapshoot Perbankan Syariah Indonesia. Indonesia Islamic Banking.

Indonesia Religion Department. (2008). *Al-Quran dan Terjemahannya*. Diponegoro.

Investing. (n.d.). https://www.wahed.com/global/investing

Iqbal, M. (2022). Machine learning applications in e-commerce. In *The Future of E-Commerce* (pp. 65–89). SCOPUS. https://www.scopus.com/inward/record.uri?eid=2-s2.0-85144997084&partnerID=40&md5=475f705c5259c1a7c9ab9a72756ebb8d

Iqbal, Z., & Mirakhor, A. (2020). Fintech and IF: A New Era of Convergence. In Handbook of Blockchain, Digital Finance, and Inclusion (pp. 347-361). Springer.

Iqbal, M., & Abbas, S. (2020). Shariah-Compliant Cryptocurrencies: An Analysis of Digital Currencies under Islamic Law. *Journal of Islamic Marketing*.

Iqbal, M., & Ahmad, A. (2019). Regulation of Cryptocurrencies and Fintech in IF. *Journal of Financial Regulation and Compliance*, *27*(1).

Iqbal, M., & Molyneux, P. (2005). *Thirty years of Islamic Banking:History,Performance and Prospects.* PalgraveMacmiltan. doi:10.1007/978-0-230-50322-9

Iqbal, S., Asad, S., & Ayub, U. (2018). Blockchain Technology for Supply Chain Financing in Islamic Banking and Finance. In: *International Conference on Frontiers of Information Technology (FIT)*. IEEE.

Irfan, H., & Ahmed, D. (2018). Fintech: The opportunity for Islamic finance. In Fintech in Islamic Finance: Theory and Practice (pp. 19–32). Taylor and Francis. doi:10.4324/9781351025584-2

Irfan, M. (2018). The Impact of AI Innovation on Financial Sectors in the Era of Industry 5.0 (pp. 96-107). IGI Global. doi:10.4018/979-8-3693-0082-4.ch006

Irfan, M., Elhoseny, M., Kassim, S., & Metawa, N. (2022). *Advanced Machine Learning Algorithms for Complex Financial Applications.* IGI Global. https://www.igi-global.com/book/advanced-machine-learning-algorithms-complex/www.igi-global.com/book/advanced-machine-learning-algorithms-complex/290048

Irfan, M., Elhoseny, M., Kassim, S., & Metawa, N. (2023). *Advanced Machine Learning Algorithms for Complex Financial Applications.*

Irfan, M., Elmogy, M., Majid, M. S. A., & El-Sappagh, S. (2023). The impact of AI innovation on financial sectors in the era of industry 5.0. *The Impact of AI Innovation on Financial Sectors in the Era of Industry 5.0,* (pp. 1-320). Research Gate. 10.4018/9798369300824

Irfan, M., Elmogy, M., Majid, M.S.A., & El-Sappagh, S. (2023). *The impact of AI innovation on financial sectors in the era of industry 5.0.* Research Gate.

Irfan, M., Elhoseny, M., Kassim, S., & Metawa, N. (2023). *Advanced Machine Learning Algorithms for Complex Financial Applications*. doi:10.4018/978-1-6684-4483-2

Irfan, M., & Elmogy, M. (2023). *The Impact of AI Innovation on Financial Sectors in the Era of Industry 5.0.* IGI Global. Https://services.igi-global.com/resolvedoi/resolve.aspx?doi=10.4018/979-8-3693-0082-4

Irfan, M., Elmogy, M., Majid, M. S. A., & El-Sappagh, S. (2023). The impact of AI innovation on financial sectors in the era of industry 5.0. *The Impact of AI Innovation on Financial Sectors in the Era of Industry*, *5*(0), 1–320.

Irimia-Diéguez, A., Velicia-Martín, F., & Aguayo-Camacho, M. (2023). Predicting Fintech Innovation Adoption: The Mediator Role of Social Norms and Attitudes. *Financial Innovation*, *9*(1), 36. doi:10.118640854-022-00434-6 PMID:36687792

Islam FinTech. (2017). Global Islamic Finance Report. *Islamic Finance in the Digital Age*, 282–290.

Islamic Research and Training Institute. (2015). *Principles of IF.* IRTI. https://www.irti.org/English/Research/Documents/ISF1.pdf

Islam, J. U., & Rahman, Z. (2017). Awareness and willingness towards Islamic banking among Muslims: An Indian perspective. *International Journal of Islamic and Middle Eastern Finance and Management*, *10*(1), 92–101. doi:10.1108/IMEFM-01-2016-0017

ISRA. (2011). *Islamic Financial System.* International Shari'ah Research Academy for Islamic Finance.

Ivanchenkova, L., Shevtsiv, L., Beisenova, L., Shakharova, A., & Berdiyorov, T. (2023). Analysis of the Risks of Using the Blockchain Technology in the Accounting and Audit of a Fuel and Energy Complex Enterprise. *International Journal of Energy Economics and Policy, 13*(2), 316–321. doi:10.32479/ijeep.14047

Jamil, N. N., & Seman, J. A. (2019). The Impact of Fintech On The Sustainability Of Islamic Accounting And Finance Education In Malaysia. Journal of Islamic, Social [JISED]. *Economics and Development, 4*(17), 74–88.

Jan, I. U., Ji, S., & Kim, C. (2023). What (de) motivates customers to use AI-powered conversational agents for shopping? The extended behavioral reasoning perspective. *Journal of Retailing and Consumer Services, 75*, 103440. doi:10.1016/j.jretconser.2023.103440

Jawadi, F., Jawadi, N., & Idi Cheffou, A. (2020). Wavelet analysis of the conventional and Islamic stock market relationship ten years after the global financial crisis. *Applied Economics Letters, 27*(6), 466–472. doi:10.1080/13504851.2019.1631438

Jena, J. R., Biswal, S. K., Shrivastava, A. K., & Panigrahi, R. R. (2023). A bibliographic overview of financial engineering in the emerging financial market. *International Journal of System Assurance Engineering and Management*, 1-18.

Jena, R. K. (2022). Examining the Factors Affecting the Adoption of Blockchain Technology in the Banking Sector: An Extended UTAUT Model. *International Journal of Financial Studies, 10*(4), 90. doi:10.3390/ijfs10040090

Jobin, A., Ienca, M., & Vayena, E. (2019). The global landscape of AI ethics guidelines. *Nature Machine Intelligence, 1*(9), 389–399. doi:10.103842256-019-0088-2

Joseph, L. (1995). *Disruptive Technologies: Catching the Wave.* HBR. https://hbr.org/1995/01/disruptive-technologies-catching-the-wave

Kamilaris, A., et al. (2021). RegTech and SupTech: A survey of enabling technologies for regulatory and supervisory challenges. *Frontiers in Blockchain, 4.*

Kari, F. (2020). FinTech Innovation in IF: A Conceptual Framework and Research Agenda. *Pacific-Basin Finance Journal*, 61.

Karim, A., & Tarazi, A. (2020). Fintech in Islamic Microfinance: A Review. *IF Development Report, IFDI 2020.*

Karimi, A. (2005). Bank ka Sood Halal Hai-Subhat Azala, (3rd ed). Al-Halal Educational Society, Katihar.

Kassim, S. (2016). Islamic finance and economic growth: The Malaysian experience. *Global Finance Journal, 30*, 66–76. doi:10.1016/j.gfj.2015.11.007

Katterbauer, K., & Moschetta, P. (2022, June 1). *A robo-advisory framework for Islamic and Environmental, Social and Governance (ESG) compliance – A benchmark study on the S&P 500 stock index.* JMIFR. doi:10.33102/jmifr.v19i1.408

Katterbauer, K., & Moschetta, P. (2021). An innovative artificial intelligence and natural language processing framework for asset price forecasting based on islamic finance: A case study of the saudi stock market. *Econometric Research in Finance, 6*(2), 183–196. doi:10.2478/erfin-2021-0009

Kavita, C., & Krishan, R. (2011). Challenges and opportunities of Islamic Banking in India. *Asian Journal of Research in Social Sciences and Humanities, 1*(3), 34–40.

Kazancoglu, Y., Ozbiltekin-Pala, M., Sezer, M. D., Luthra, S., & Kumar, A. (2023). Resilient reverse logistics with blockchain technology in sustainable food supply chain management during COVID-19. *Business Strategy and the Environment, 32*(4), 2327–2340. doi:10.1002/bse.3251

Kempf, A. (2019). Does financial education impact financial knowledge and financial behavior, and if so, when? *Journal of Banking & Finance*, 98.

Khafafa, A. J., & Shafii, Z. (2013). Customer satisfaction and islamic banking awareness in the islamic banking window system in Libya. *Middle East Journal of Scientific Research.*

Khalid, S., & Abbas, S. (2019). Regulatory Challenges and Opportunities in Islamic Fintech. *Journal of Financial Regulation and Compliance*, *27*(4).

Khan, H. (2018). Islamic economics and a third fundamental theorem of welfare economics. *World Economy*, *41*(3), 723–737. Advance online publication. doi:10.1111/twec.12508

Khan, M., Salah, K., Alazab, M., & Hitchens, M. (2018). Blockchain and Internet of Things: A Survey. *IEEE Access : Practical Innovations, Open Solutions*, *6*, 32979–33001. doi:10.1109/ACCESS.2018.2842685

Khanna, P., & Haldar, A. (2023). Will adoption of blockchain technology be challenging: Evidence from Indian banking industry. *Qualitative Research in Financial Markets*, *15*(2), 361–384. doi:10.1108/QRFM-01-2022-0003

Khan, T. (2020). Fintech meets IF: The Digital Transformation of Islamic Financial Services. *ISRA International Journal of IF*, *12*(1), 1–16.

Khan, Z., Anwar, Z., & Soomro, K. A. (2020). Blockchain for halal food traceability: A comprehensive review. *Journal of Cleaner Production*, *256*, 120626.

Kharisma, B. (2022). Surfing alone? The Internet and social capital: Evidence from Indonesia. *Journal of Economic Structures*, *11*(1), 8. doi:10.118640008-022-00267-7 PMID:35915843

Khattak, N., & Rehman, K. (2010). Customer satisfaction and awareness of Islamic banking system in Pakistan. *African Journal of Business Management*, *4*(5), 662–671.

Khemir, S., Baccouche, C., & Ayadi, S. D. (2019). The influence of ESG information on investment allocation decisions: An experimental study in an emerging country. *Journal of Applied Accounting Research*, *20*(4), 458–480. doi:10.1108/JAAR-12-2017-0141

Kinanti, F., & Baridwan, Z. (2012). ANALISIS DETERMINAN SISTEM INFORMASI E-TICKETING : PENDEKATAN EXTENDED THEORY OF PLANNED BEHAVIOUR. Jurnal Ilmiah Mahasiswa FEB, 1(1).

Kismawadi, E. R., Irfan, M., & Shah, S. M. A. R. (2023). Revolutionizing Islamic Finance: Artificial Intelligence's Role in the Future of Industry. In The Impact of AI Innovation on Financial Sectors in the Era of Industry 5.0 (pp. 184-207). IGI Global.

Kolisnyk, O., Hurina, N., Druzhynska, N., Holovchak, H., & Fomina, T. (2023). INNOVATIVE TECHNOLOGIES IN ACCOUNTING AND AUDITING: THE USE OF BLOCKCHAIN TECHNOLOGY. *Financial and Credit Activity: Problems of Theory and Practice*, *3*(50), 24–41. doi:10.55643/fcaptp.3.50.2023.4082

Komijani, A., & Taghizadeh-Hesary, F. (2019). An overview of Islamic banking and finance in Asia. In Routledge Handbook of Banking and Finance in Asia. Routledge.

Komunikasi, D. (2018). *Mengenal Financial Teknologi*. BI. https://www.bi.go.id/id/edukasi/Pages/mengenal-Financial-Teknologi.aspx

Kopnina, H. (2016). The victims of unsustainability: A challenge to sustainable development goals. *International Journal of Sustainable Development and World Ecology*, *23*(2), 113–121. doi:10.1080/13504509.2015.1111269

Kostov, Philip, and J. L. (2000). Regime-Switching Vector Error Correction Model (VECM). *Analysis Of UK Meat.*

Kou, G., Olgu Akdeniz, Ö., Dinçer, H., & Yüksel, S. (2021). Fintech investments in European banks: A hybrid IT2 fuzzy multidimensional decision-making approach. *Financial Innovation*, *7*(1), 39. doi:10.118640854-021-00256-y PMID:35024283

Kourtidis, D., Šević, Ž., & Chatzoglou, P. (2011). Investors' trading activity: A behavioural perspective and empirical results. *Journal of Socio-Economics*, *40*(5), 548–557. doi:10.1016/j.socec.2011.04.008

Kshetri, N. (2018). Blockchain's Roles in Strengthening Cybersecurity and Protecting Privacy. *Telecommunications Policy*, *42*(7), 567–578. doi:10.1016/j.telpol.2018.05.003

Kumar, A. S., Katta Lakshmi Narayan Setty, V., & Ravi, G. (2022). How blockchain enables financial transactions in the banking sector. *International Journal of Business and Globalisation*, *31*(1), 1–6. doi:10.1504/IJBG.2022.124545

Kumari, A., Sharma, P., & Chhabra, J. (2021). Improving Security in Financial Transactions Using Smart Contracts. In *Proceedings of the 2021 International Conference on Information Science and Communications Technologies* (pp. 1-6). IEEE.

Kumar, S., Sahu, N. C., & Kumar, P. (2020). Insurance consumption and economic growth in the post-liberalized India: An empirical analysis. *Asian Economic and Financial Review*, *10*(2), 218–228. doi:10.18488/journal.aefr.2020.102.218.228

Lacity, M., & Hirschheim, R. (2018). The Blockchain Folk Theorem. *MIS Quarterly Executive*, *17*(3), 139–153.

Lahmiri, S., & Bekiros, S. (2019). Can machine learning approaches predict corporate bankruptcy? Evidence from a qualitative experimental design. *Quantitative Finance*, *19*(9), 1569–1577. doi:10.1080/14697688.2019.1588468

Lai, K., et al. (2019). Social impact investing with blockchain: A systematic review. *Frontiers in Blockchain, 2*.

Lall, A. R., & Sharma, R. (2016). *Impact of Financial Innovations and Technology on the Banking Industry*. NIH.

Lateh, N., Ismail, S., & Ariffin, N. M. (2009). Customers' Perceptions on the Objectives, Characteristics and Selection Criteria of Islamic Bank in Thailand. *Gadjah Mada International Journal of Business*, *11*(2), 167–189. doi:10.22146/gamaijb.5525

Laucereno, S. F. (2017). *Berapa Pangsa Pasar Asuransi Syariah di RI? Ini Kata OJK [How much is the sharia insurance market share in Indonesia? This is what OJK says]*. Detik. https://finance.detik.com/moneter/d-3487655/berapa-pangsa-pasar-asuransi-syariah-di-ri-ini-kata-ojk

Lee, S., Choi, J., Ngo-Ye, T. L., & Cummings, M. (2018, January 1). *Modeling Trust in the Adoption Decision Process of Robo-Advisors: An Agent-Based Simulation Approach*. SciSpace. https://typeset.io/papers/modeling-trust-in-the-adoption-decision-process-of-robo-217oxlfw5k

Lee, C. C., Lee, C. C., & Chiu, Y. (2013). The link between life insurance activities and economic growth: Some new evidence. *Journal of International Money and Finance*, *32*(1), 405–427. doi:10.1016/j.jimonfin.2012.05.001

Lee, D. D., Faff, R. W., & Rekker, S. A. (2013). Do high and low-ranked sustainability stocks perform differently? *International Journal of Accounting & Information Management*, *21*(2), 116–132. doi:10.1108/18347641311312267

Lee, S. M., & Lee, S. (2018). Smart contract-based Islamic crowdfunding: A comprehensive analysis. *Sustainability*, *10*(9), 3034.

Lee, S.-M., & Kim, H.-K. (2022). The Effect of System and User Characteristics on Intention to Use: An Empirical Study of Face Recognition Payment. *Journal of System and Management Sciences*, *12*(3), 318–344. 10.33168/JSMS.2022.0316

Leimeister, J. M., Huber, M., Bretschneider, U., & Krcmar, H. (2009). Leveraging crowdsourcing: Activation-supporting components for IT-based ideas competition. *Journal of Management Information Systems*, *26*(1), 197–224. doi:10.2753/MIS0742-1222260108

Leins, S. (2020). 'Responsible investment': ESG and the post-crisis ethical order. *Economy and Society*, *49*(1), 71–91. doi:10.1080/03085147.2020.1702414

Leow, E. K. W., Nguyen, B. P., & Chua, M. C. H. (2021, October 1). Robo-advisor using genetic algorithm and BERT sentiments from tweets for hybrid portfolio optimisation. *Expert Systems With Applications*. Elsevier BV. doi:10.1016/j.eswa.2021.115060

Lestari, N. I., Hussain, W., Merigo, J. M., & Bekhit, M. (2023). A Survey of Trendy Financial Sector Applications of Machine and Deep Learning. In Lecture Notes of the Institute for Computer Sciences, Social-Informatics and Telecommunications Engineering, LNICST: Vol. 467 LNICST (pp. 619–633). doi:10.1007/978-3-031-23944-1_68

Levine, R. (1996). Stock Markets: A Sput to Economic Growth. *Finance & Development*, *2*(4), 8–10. doi:10.20525/ijfbs.v2i4.160

Lewis, M. K., & Algaoud, L. M. (2019). Fintech, Financial Inclusion, and IF. In Fintech, IF and Financial Inclusion (pp. 3-24). Springer.

Lewis, R., McPartland, J., & Ranjan, R. (2017). *Blockchain and Financial Market Innovation*. (Policy Discussion Paper Series 93559). Federal Reserve Bank of Chicago.

Li, C., Xu, Y., Zheng, H., Wang, Z., Han, H., & Zeng, L. (2023). Artificial intelligence, resource reallocation, and corporate innovation efficiency: Evidence from China's listed companies. *Resources Policy*, *81*, 103324. doi:10.1016/j.resourpol.2023.103324

Li, J., Liu, Z., & Zhou, J. (2020). How to become the chosen one in the artificial intelligence market: The evidence from China. *International Journal of Technology Management*, *84*(1–2), 8–24. doi:10.1504/IJTM.2020.112122

Lim, S. H., Kim, D. J., Hur, Y., & Park, K. (2019). An Empirical Study of the Impacts of Perceived Security and Knowledge on Continuous Intention to Use Mobile Fintech Payment Services. *International Journal of Human-Computer Interaction*, *35*(10), 886–898. doi:10.1080/10447318.2018.1507132

Li, T. T., Wang, K., Sueyoshi, T., & Wang, D. D. (2021). ESG: Research progress and future prospects. *Sustainability (Basel)*, *13*(21), 11663. doi:10.3390u132111663

Liu, Y., Wang, Z., & Zheng, B. (2019). Application of Regularized GRU-LSTM Model in Stock Price Prediction. *2019 IEEE 5th International Conference on Computer and Communications*, (pp. 1886–1890). IEEE. 10.1109/ICCC47050.2019.9064035

Liu, G., He, L., Yue, Y., & Wang, J. (2014). The linkage between insurance activity and banking credit: Some evidence from dynamic analysis. *The North American Journal of Economics and Finance*, *29*, 239–265. doi:10.1016/j.najef.2014.06.014

Li, W., Yin, Y., Quan, X., & Zhang, H. (2019). Gene Expression Value Prediction Based on XGBoost Algorithm. *Frontiers in Genetics*, *10*(November), 1–7. doi:10.3389/fgene.2019.01077 PMID:31781160

Li, X., Jiang, P., Chen, T., Luo, X., & Wen, Q. (2017). A survey on the security of blockchain systems. *Future Generation Computer Systems*, *82*, 1–14.

Li, Y., Kou, G., Li, G., & Hefni, M. A. (2022). Fuzzy multi-attribute information fusion approach for finance investment selection with the expert reliability. *Applied Soft Computing*, *126*, 109270. doi:10.1016/j.asoc.2022.109270

Lone, F. A. (2016). Islamic banks and financial institutions: A Study of Their Objectives and Achievements. In Palagrave Macmillan: London. doi:10.1080/13602009708716362

Loonam, J., & McDermott, J. (2019). AI and financial services: Understanding the rise of chatbots, robo-advisors and beyond. *Business Horizons*, *62*(6), 645–657.

Lutfi. (2018). FinTech dan Masa Depan Perbankan Indonesia - STIE Perbanas Surabaya. *Sekolah Tinggi Ilmu Ekonomi Perbanas*. https://www.perbanas.ac.id/id/component/k2/item/688-fintech-dan-masa-depan-perbankan-indonesia.

Ma'ruf, A., Mahomed, Z., & Mohamad, S. (2021). Sustainable Finance and a Sharī' Analysis of Environmental, Social and Governance (ESG) Criteria. In M. K. Hassan, M. Saraç, & A. Khan (Eds.), *Islamic Finance and Sustainable Development: A Sustainable Economic Framework for Muslim and Non-Muslim Countries* (pp. 193–217). Springer International Publishing. doi:10.1007/978-3-030-76016-8_9

Mahmood, F., Shahzad, U., Nazakat, A. L. I., Ahmed, Z., Rjoub, H., & Wong, W.-K. (2022). THE NEXUS between CASH CONVERSION CYCLE, WORKING CAPITAL FINANCE, and FIRM PERFORMANCE: EVIDENCE from NOVEL MACHINE LEARNING APPROACHES. *Annals of Financial Economics*, *17*(2), 2250014. doi:10.1142/S2010495222500142

Mahmoud Mohieldin, Z. I. (2011). *The role of Islamic Finance in Enhancing Financial Inclusion in Organization of Islamic Cooperation (OIC)*. Countries. doi:10.1596/1813-9450-5920

Majumadar, N. (2002). *Financial Sector Reforms & India's Economic Development*. Academic Foundation.

Malhotra, A., O'Neill, H., & Stowell, P. (2022). Thinking strategically about blockchain adoption and risk mitigation. *Business Horizons*, *65*(2), 159–171. doi:10.1016/j.bushor.2021.02.033

Malik, S., Kamal, M., & Qureshi, K. (2019). Towards Shari'ah Compliance in Blockchain Technology: A Comprehensive Analysis and Future Perspective. In: *Proceedings of the 2nd International Conference on Blockchain Computing and Applications*. Research Gate.

Mallikarjuna, M., & Rao, R. P. (2019). Evaluation of forecasting methods from selected stock market returns. *Financial Innovation*, *5*(1), 40. doi:10.118640854-019-0157-x

Mankiw, N. Gregory, Euston Quah, and P. W. (2006). Macroeconomics 7th Edition. New York: Worth Publisher.

Mansoor, A., Hassan, M. K., & Rehman, M. A. (2019). Fintech and IF: A Review and Research Agenda. *Pacific-Basin Finance Journal*, *55*, 306–324.

Mansoor, S., & Ahmed, Z. U. (2021). Responsible Artificial Intelligence in IF: A Framework. *Pacific-Basin Finance Journal*.

Mansoor, S., & Ahmed, Z. U. (2021). Responsible Artificial Intelligence in Islamic Finance: A Framework. *Pacific-Basin Finance Journal*.

Mapanje, O., Karuaihe, S., Machethe, C., & Amis, M. (2023). Financing Sustainable Agriculture in Sub-Saharan Africa: A Review of the Role of Financial Technologies. *Sustainability (Basel)*, *15*(5), 4587. doi:10.3390u15054587

Martín-Martín, A., Orduna-Malea, E., Thelwall, M., & Delgado López-Cózar, E. (2018). Google Scholar, Web of Science, and Scopus: A Systematic Comparison of Citations in 252 Subject Categories. [CrossRef]. *Journal of Informetrics*, *12*(4), 1160–1177. doi:10.1016/j.joi.2018.09.002

Masri, H. (2017, December 1). A Shariah-compliant portfolio selection model. *Journal of the Operational Research Society*. Palgrave Macmillan. doi:10.1057/s41274-017-0223-6

Matos, P. V., Barros, V., & Sarmento, J. M. (2020). Does ESG affect the stability of dividend policies in Europe. *Sustainability (Basel), 12*(21), 8804. doi:10.3390u12218804

Max, R., Kriebitz, A., & Von Websky, C. (2021). Ethical considerations about the implications of artificial intelligence in finance. *Handbook on Ethics in Finance*, 577-592. Research Gate.

McKinsey & Company. (2016). *The Fintech Sector in Germany: An Analysis of the Status Quo and the Opportunities for German FinTech Companies*. McKinsey. https://www.mckinsey.com/~/media/mckinsey/industries/financial%20services/our%20insights/the%20fintech%20sector%20in%20germany%20opportunities%20and%20challenges/the-fintech-sector-in-germany-opportunities-and-challenges-vf.ashx

Mehrotra, A. (2023). FinTech driven financial inclusion – the hype and the reality of missed targets. *International Journal of Public Sector Performance Management, 11*(2), 165–176. doi:10.1504/IJPSPM.2023.129690

Meng, L. (2020). Blockchain applications in global supply chains. In Sustainable Supply Chain Management (pp. 71-84). MDPI.

Merikas, A. G., & Merika, A. A. (2006). Stock prices response to real economic variables: The case of Germany. *Managerial Finance, 32*(5), 446–450. doi:10.1108/03074350610657454

Merkaš, Z., Perkov, D., & Bonin, V. (2020). The significance of blockchain technology in digital transformation of logistics and transportation. *International Journal of E-Services and Mobile Applications, 12*(1), 1–20. doi:10.4018/IJESMA.2020010101

Mettler, T. (2020). Detecting Fraud in Islamic Banks Using Machine Learning: A Systematic Review. *Journal of Financial Services Marketing, 25*(3).

Michael, B., Koroleska, N., Tai, A., & Wong, D. W. H. (2022). A critical look at using financial technology policy to promote the sustainable development goals. *Sustainable Development (Bradford), 30*(6), 1911–1920. doi:10.1002d.2358

Micu, I., & Micu, A. (2016). Financial technology (Fintech) and its implementation on the Romanian non-banking capital market. *Practical Appl Sci, IV*(2(11)), 379–384.

Miller, T. (2019). Explanation in artificial intelligence: Insights from the social sciences. *Artificial Intelligence, 267*, 1–38. doi:10.1016/j.artint.2018.07.007

Mishra, S., Ewing, M. T., & Cooper, H. B. (2022). Artificial intelligence focus and firm performance. *Journal of the Academy of Marketing Science, 50*(6), 1176–1197. doi:10.100711747-022-00876-5

Mogaji, E. (2023). Redefining banks in the digital era: A typology of banks and their research, managerial and policy implications. *International Journal of Bank Marketing*. Advance online publication. doi:10.1108/IJBM-06-2023-0333

Mohammed Obaidullah, A. T. (2008). Islamic Microfinance Development. *Islamic Research & Training institute Policy Dialogue*. Islamic Research & Training institute.

Mohd Haridan, N., Sheikh Hassan, A. F., Mohammed Shah, S., & Mustafa, H. (2023). Financial innovation in Islamic banks: Evidence on the interaction between Shariah board and FinTech. *Journal of Islamic Accounting and Business Research, 14*(6), 911–930. doi:10.1108/JIABR-11-2022-0305

Moher, D., Stewart, L., & Shekelle, P. (2016). Implementing PRISMA-P: Recommendations for prospective authors. *Systematic Reviews, 5*(1), 1–6. doi:10.118613643-016-0191-y PMID:26822481

Mohieldin, M. (2020). *Fintech and IF: Technology and Ecosystem Evolution*. World Bank Group.

Mohieldin, M., & Metwally, M. (2019). The Role of Fintech in Enhancing Financial Inclusion in the Arab World. *Islamic Economic Studies*, *27*(1), 189–204.

Monzer Kahf, A. W. (2000). *Its Growth, Management and Development. Damascus: Dar al Fikr).* Monzer Kahf.

Moon, K.-S., & Kim, H. (2023). EFFICIENT ASSET ALLOCATION BASED ON PREDICTION WITH ADAPTIVE DATA SELECTION. *Economic Computation and Economic Cybernetics Studies and Research*, *57*(1), 57–72. doi:10.24818/18423264/57.1.23.04

Moro Visconti, R. (2020). FinTech Valuation. SSRN *Electronic Journal*. doi:10.2139/ssrn.4132428

Mougayar, W. (2016). *The Business Blockchain: Promise, Practice, and Application of the Next Internet Technology*. John Wiley & Sons.

Muhamad, S. F., Zain, F. A. M., Samad, N. S. A., Ab. Rahman, A. H., & Yasoa', M. R. (2022). Measuring Sustainable Performance of Islamic Banks: Integrating the principles of Environmental, Social and Governance (ESG) and Maqasid Shari'ah. *IOP Conference Series. Earth and Environmental Science*, *1102*(1), 012080. doi:10.1088/1755-1315/1102/1/012080

Muhammad, R. F. (2021). The Determinants of Potential Failure of Islamic Peer-to-Peer Lending: Perceptions of Stakeholders in Indonesia. *Journal of Asian Finance, Economics and Business*. doi:10.13106/jafeb.2021.vol8.no2.0981

Muharam, H., Anwar, R. J., & Robiyanto, R. (2019). Islamic stock market and sukuk market development, economic growth, and trade openness (The case of Indonesia and Malaysia). *Business: Theory and Practice, 20*(2014), 196–207. . doi:10.3846/btp.2019.19

Murinde, V., Rizopoulos, E., & Zachariadis, M. (2022). The impact of the FinTech revolution on the future of banking: Opportunities and risks. *International Review of Financial Analysis*, *81*, 102103. doi:10.1016/j.irfa.2022.102103

Musleh Al-Sartawi, A. M. A. (2020). E-learning improves accounting education: case of the higher education sector of bahrain. In M. Themistocleous, M. Papadaki, & M. M. Kamal (Eds.), *Information systems. EMCIS 2020. Lecture notes in business information processing* (Vol. 402, p. 26). Springer. doi:10.1007/978-3-030-63396-7_20

Mutswenje, V. S. (2009). *A survey of the factors influencing investment decisions: the case of individual investors at the NSE* [Doctoral dissertation, University of Nairobi].

Nagimova, A. (2022). Islamic Fintech: Digitalization of Global Islamic Finance. *World Economy and International Relations*, *66*(5), 50–58. doi:10.20542/0131-2227-2022-66-5-50-58

Nagy, R. A., & Obenberger, R. W. (1994). Factors influencing individual investor behavior. *Financial Analysts Journal*, *50*(4), 63–68. doi:10.2469/faj.v50.n4.63

Najem, R., Amr, M. F., Bahnasse, A., & Talea, M. (2022). Artificial Intelligence for Digital Finance (Vol. 203). Axes and Techniques,Procedia Computer Science., https://www.sciencedirect.com/science/article/pii/S1877050922006974, , ISSN 1877-0509. doi:10.1016/j.procs.2022.07.092

Nakamoto, S. (2008). *Bitcoin: A Peer-to-Peer Electronic Cash System*. Bitcoin. https://bitcoin.org/bitcoin.pdf

Narayanan, A., Bonneau, J., Felten, E., Miller, A., & Goldfeder, S. (2016). *Bitcoin and Cryptocurrency Technologies: A Comprehensive Introduction*. Princeton University Press.

Nasr, A. B., Lux, T., Ajmi, A. N., & Gupta, R. (2016). Forecasting the volatility of the Dow Jones Islamic Stock Market Index: Long memory vs. regime switching. *International Review of Economics & Finance*, *45*, 559–571. doi:10.1016/j.iref.2016.07.014

Nasution, M. E., & Usman, H. (2008). *Proses Penelitian Kuantitatif.* FEUI.

Nevado-Peña, D., López-Ruiz, V. R., & Alfaro-Navarro, J. L. (2015). The effects of environmental and social dimensions of sustainability in response to the economic crisis of European cities. *Sustainability (Basel)*, *7*(7), 8255–8269. doi:10.3390u7078255

Nicoletti, B. (2021). *Proposition of Value and Fintech Organizations in Banking 5.0.* Springer. . doi:10.1007/978-3-030-75871-4_4

Nimrah Karim, M. T. (2008). *Islam Micro Finance: an Emerging.* Collective Group to Assist the Poor.

Nizar, M. (2017). Teknologi Keuangan (Fintech) : Konsep dan Implementasinya di Indonesia. Warta Fiskal, Jakarta.

Nizar, M. A. (2016). Acceleration and Inclusiveness of the Financial Sector: Pathway to People's Welfare. In MPRA Paper (Vol. 97928).

Nopreza, M.A.A. (2022). Determinant factors of repurchase interest of buying fashion products online in e-commerce. *Asian Management and Business Review*, 162–175. . doi:10.20885/AMBR.vol2.iss2.art5

Novethic. (2008). *Les investisseurs institutionnels se sentent-ils responsables des politiques ESG des entreprises dont ils sont actionnaires?* Novethic.

Nugraha, D. P., Setiawan, B., Nathan, R. J., & Fekete-Farkas, M. (2022). Fintech Adoption Drivers for Innovation for SMEs in Indonesia. *Journal of Open Innovation*, *8*(4), 208. doi:10.3390/joitmc8040208

Nugroho, A., Najib, M., & Simanjuntak, M. (2018). Factors Affecting Consumer Interest In Electronic Money Usage With Theory Of Planned Behavior (TPB). *Journal of Consumer Sciences*, *3*(1), 15. doi:10.29244/jcs.3.1.15-27

Nurudeen, A. B. U. (2009). Does Stock Market Development Raise Economic Growth? Evidence from Nigeria. *Review of Finance and Banking*, *1*(1), 15–26.

Nyasha, S., & Odhiambo, N. M. (2015). The impact of banks and stock market development on economic growth in South Africa: An ARDL-bounds testing approach. *Contemporary Economics*, *9*(1), 93–108. doi:10.5709/ce.1897-9254.161

O'Dair, M., & Hobson, A. (2019). The Politics and Performativities of Blockchain Communities: A Cross Case Analysis. *Journal of Information Technology*, *34*(2), 162–177.

Obamuyi, T. M. (2013). Factors influencing investment decisions in capital market: A study of individual investors in Nigeria. *Organizations and Markets in Emerging Economies*, *4*(07), 141–161. doi:10.15388/omee.2013.4.1.14263

Ogbeibu, S., Chiappetta Jabbour, C. J., Burgess, J., Gaskin, J., & Renwick, D. W. S. (2022). Green talent management and turnover intention: The roles of leader STARA competence and digital task interdependence. *Journal of Intellectual Capital*, *23*(1), 27–55. doi:10.1108/JIC-01-2021-0016

Ogunmakinde, O., Egbelakin, T., & Sher, W. (2021). Contributions of the Circular Economy to the UN Sustainable Development Goals. *Resources, Conservation and Recycling*, *2021*(178), 106023.

Omoola, S., & Ibrahim, H. K. (2023). The Legal Implications of Abandoned Digital Assets in Sharīʿah-Compliant Fintech Platforms. *ISRA International Journal of Islamic Finance*, *60*(2), 60–76. doi:10.55188/ijif.v15i2.542

Ortas, E., Álvarez, I., & Garayar, A. (2015). The environmental, social, governance, and financial performance effects on companies that adopt the United Nations Global Compact. *Sustainability (Basel)*, *7*(2), 1932–1956. doi:10.3390u7021932

Osei-Assibey Bonsu, M., Wang, Y., & Guo, Y. (2023). Does fintech lead to better accounting practices? Empirical evidence. *Accounting Research Journal*, *36*(2–3), 129–147. doi:10.1108/ARJ-07-2022-0178

Ouda, H., & Salah, K. (2018). Scalability challenges in blockchain systems: A comprehensive review. *IEEE Access : Practical Innovations, Open Solutions*, *6*, 55108–55133.

Oyodetun, T. M., & Adesina, B. D. (2015). Nexus between economic growth and insurance business in Nigeria. *Research Journal of Finance and Accounting*, *6*(9), 142–150.

Ozili, P. K. (2018). Impact of digital finance on financial inclusion and stability. *Borsa Istanbul Review*, *18*(4), 329–340. doi:10.1016/j.bir.2017.12.003

Page, M. J., McKenzie, J. E., Bossuyt, P. M., Boutron, I., Hoffmann, T. C., Mulrow, C. D., Shamseer, L., Tetzlaff, J. M., Akl, E. A., & Brennan, S. E. (2021). The PRISMA 2020 Statement: An Updated Guideline for Reporting Systematic Reviews. [CrossRef]. *BMJ (Clinical Research Ed.)*, *88*, 105906. PMID:33782057

Pal, T., Irfan, M., & Kassim, S. B. (2023). How do Machine Learning (ML) techniques benefit the insurance industry? An exploratory study. *The Impact of AI Innovation on Financial Sectors in the Era of Industry 5.0*, (pp. 108-130). IGI Global. doi:10.4018/979-8-3693-0082-4.ch007

Pal, T., Irfan, M., & Kassim, S. B. (2023). How Do Machine Learning (ML) Techniques Benefit the Insurance Industry?: An Exploratory Study. In The Impact of AI Innovation on Financial Sectors in the Era of Industry 5.0 (pp. 108-130). IGI Global.

Pal, T., Irfan, M., & Kassim, S.B. (2023). *How do Machine Learning (ML) techniques benefit the insurance industry? An exploratory study*. OUCI.

Pal, T., Irfan, M., Kassim, S.B. (2023). *How do Machine Learning (ML) techniques benefit the insurance industry? An exploratory study*. OUCI.

Paltrinieri, A., Dreassi, A., Migliavacca, M., & Piserà, S. (2020). Islamic finance development and banking ESG scores: Evidence from a cross-country analysis. *Research in International Business and Finance*, *51*, 101100. doi:10.1016/j.ribaf.2019.101100

Panigrahi, R.R. (2023). Review of Machine Learning Techniques in the Supply Chain Management of Indian Industry. *Advanced Machine Learning Algorithms for Complex Financial Applications.* IGI Global. . doi:10.4018/978-1-6684-4483-2.ch013

Pardhey, N., & Issa, Y. H. (2023). *P. C., L.* Regulatory Mechanism of Cryptocurrency Blockchain in Banking, Financial, and Capital Markets in the Indian Panorama.

Park, S. R., & Jang, J. Y. (2021). The impact of ESG management on investment decision: Institutional investors' perceptions of country-specific ESG criteria. *International Journal of Financial Studies*, *9*(3), 48. doi:10.3390/ijfs9030048

Patidar, S. (2020). The Blockchain technology that will substitute Lawyers and Middlemen. *Medium.*

Patil, S., & Bagodi, V. (2021). A study of factors affecting investment decisions in India: The KANO way. *Asia Pacific Management Review*, *26*(4), 197–214. doi:10.1016/j.apmrv.2021.02.004

Pedersen, L. H., Fitzgibbons, S., & Pomorski, L. (2021). Responsible investing: The ESG-efficient frontier. *Journal of Financial Economics*, *142*(2), 572–597. doi:10.1016/j.jfineco.2020.11.001

Pentury, F. (2023). The Role of Knowledge and Penetration of Fintech Services in Improving MSMEs of Fishermen and Marine Farmers in Remote Small Islands Region. *Jurnal Manajemen Teori Dan Terapan| Journal of Theory and Applied Management*, *16*(1), 23–37. . doi:10.20473/jmtt.v16i1.43743

Pérez-Gladish, B., Benson, K., & Faff, R. (2012). Profiling socially responsible investors: Australian evidence. *Australian Journal of Management*, *37*(2), 189–209. doi:10.1177/0312896211429158

Pizzi, S., Corbo, L., & Caputo, A. (2021). Fintech and SMEs sustainable business models: Reflections and considerations for a circular economy. *Journal of Cleaner Production*, *281*, 125217. doi:10.1016/j.jclepro.2020.125217

Pnevmatikakis, A., Kanavos, S., Matikas, G., Kostopoulou, K., Cesario, A., & Kyriazakos, S. (2021). Risk assessment for personalized health insurance based on real-world data. *Risks*, *9*(3), 1–15. doi:10.3390/risks9030046

Pradhan, R. P., Dash, S., Maradana, R. P., Jayakumar, M., & Gaurav, K. (2017). Insurance market density and economic growth in Eurozone countries: the granger causality approach. *Financial Innovation*, *3*(1), 0–24. . doi:10.1186/s40854-017-0065-x

Pradhana, R. P., Arvinb, M. B., & Norman, N. R. (2015). Insurance development and the finance-growth nexus: Evidence from 34 OECD countries. *Journal of Multinational Financial Management*, *31*, 1–22. doi:10.1016/j.mulfin.2015.02.001

Pradhan, R. P., Arvin, M. B., Nair, M., Hall, J. H., & Gupta, A. (2017). Is there a link between economic growth and insurance and banking sector activities in the G-20 countries? *Review of Financial Economics*, *33*(1), 12–28. doi:10.1016/j.rfe.2017.02.002

Qi, Y. (2012). Random forest for bioinformatics. *Ensemble Machine Learning: Methods and ApplicatiOns,* (pp. 307–323). Research Gate. https://doi.org/ doi:10.1007/9781441993267_10

Qoyum, A., Sakti, M. R. P., Thaker, H. M. T., & AlHashfi, R. U. (2022). Does the islamic label indicate good environmental, social, and governance (ESG) performance? Evidence from sharia-compliant firms in Indonesia and Malaysia. *Borsa Istanbul Review*, *22*(2), 306–320. doi:10.1016/j.bir.2021.06.001

Qudah, H., Malahim, S., Airout, R., Alomari, M., Hamour, A. A., & Alqudah, M. (2023). Islamic Finance in the Era of Financial Technology: A Bibliometric Review of Future Trends. *International Journal of Financial Studies*, *11*(2), 76. doi:10.3390/ijfs11020076

Rabbani, M. R., Khan, S., & Thalassinos, E. I. (2020). *FinTech, blockchain and Islamic finance: An extensive literature review.* Research Gate.

Rabbani, M. R., Sarea, A., Khan, S., & Abdullah, Y. (2022). Ethical concerns in artificial intelligence (AI): The role of RegTech and Islamic finance. In *Artificial Intelligence for Sustainable Finance and Sustainable Technology: Proceedings of ICGER,* (pp. 381-390). Springer International Publishing

Rabbani., M., Khan, S., & Thalassinos, E. (2020). FinTech, Blockchain, and Islamic Finance: An Extensive Literature Review. *International Journal of Economics and Business Administration, VIII*(2), 65–86.

Rabbani, M. R. (2022). IF and Cryptocurrency: A Systematic Review. In *FinTech in Islamic Financial Institutions* (pp. 279–306). Springer International Publishing. doi:10.1007/978-3-031-14941-2_14

Rabbani, M. R., Khan, S., & Atif, M. (2023). Machine learning-based P2P lending Islamic Fintech model for small and medium enterprises in Bahrain. *International Journal of Business Innovation and Research*, *30*(4), 565–579. doi:10.1504/IJBIR.2023.130079

Raffinetti, E. (2023). A Rank Graduation Accuracy measure to mitigate Artificial Intelligence risks. *Quality & Quantity*, *57*(S2), 131–150. doi:10.100711135-023-01613-y

Rahadian, A., & Thamrin, H. (2023). Analysis of Factors Affecting MSME in Using Fintech Lending as Alternative Financing: Technology Acceptance Model Approach. *Brazilian Business Review*, *20*(3), 301–322. doi:10.15728/bbr.2023.20.3.4.en

Rahmadhani, A., Purqon, A., Kim, S., & Kim, S. Y. (2015, September). Complex network analysis of conventional and Islamic stock market in Indonesia. In AIP Conference Proceedings. AIP Publishing. doi:10.1063/1.4930741

Rahman, M. (2021). Islamic Fintech and Financial Inclusion: A Conceptual Discussion. *Frontiers in Blockchain, 4*.

Rahman, M. S., Bag, S., Hossain, M. A., Abdel Fattah, F. A. M., Gani, M. O., & Rana, N. P. (2023). The new wave of AI-powered luxury brands online shopping experience: The role of digital multisensory cues and customers' engagement. *Journal of Retailing and Consumer Services*, *72*, 103273. doi:10.1016/j.jretconser.2023.103273

Ramachandran, M., & Watts, S. (2020). Enhancing Financial Transaction Security with Smart Contracts. *International Journal of Advanced Computer Science and Applications*, *11*(2), 42–47. doi:10.14569/IJACSA.2020.0110206

Rammal, H. G., & Zurbruegg, R. (2007). Awareness of Islamic banking products among Muslims: The case of Australia. *Journal of Financial Services Marketing*, *12*(1), 65–74. doi:10.1057/palgrave.fsm.4760060

Rammal, H. G., & Zurbruegg, R. (2020). Fintech and Islamic Finance: A Review and Research Agenda. *Pacific-Basin Finance Journal*, *66*, 101488.

Rania Kamla, H. (2013). Social Reporting by Islamic Banks: Does Social Justice Matter? *Accounting, Auditing & Accountability Journal*, (26), 911–945. doi:10.1108/AAAJ-03-2013-1268

Rashid, S. (2019). Blockchain Technology Adoption in IF: Regulatory Challenges and the Way Forward. [IJEAT]. *International Journal of Engineering and Advanced Technology*, *9*(2).

Ratnaningrum, D. P. (2012). *Intensi Mahasiswa Untuk Berwirausaha Dengan Pendekatan Theory of Planned Behaviour (Studi Terhadap Mahasiswa Pascasarjana Ekonomi Syariah Di Jakarta)*. Universitas Indonesia.

Raza Rabbani, M., Hassan, M. K., Khan, S., & Muneeza, A. (2022). A Fintech-Based Zakat Model Using Artificial Intelligence. In *FinTech in Islamic Financial Institutions* (pp. 49–63). Scope, Challenges, and Implications in Islamic Finance. doi:10.1007/978-3-031-14941-2_3

Razak, D. A. (2019). Enhancing Regulatory Compliance in IF through Blockchain Technology. *Journal of Financial Regulation and Compliance*, *27*(4).

Razak, D. A., & Aziz, M. R. A. (2020). Bitcoin and IF: What are the Opportunities and Challenges? *Journal of Islamic Accounting and Business Research*, *11*(5).

Refinitiv. (2021). *Islamic Finance Development Report 2021.* Refinitiv: New York, NY, USA.

Regona, M., Yigitcanlar, T., Xia, B., & Li, R. Y. M. (2022). Opportunities and Adoption Challenges of AI in the Construction Industry: A PRISMA Review. *Journal of Open Innovation*, *8*(1), 45. doi:10.3390/joitmc8010045

Rehman, M. U., Khan, S. U., & Iqbal, W. (2020). A Systematic Review of Smart Contracts: Challenges and Future Directions in Finance. *Journal of Ambient Intelligence and Humanized Computing*, *11*(2), 1029–1043. doi:10.100712652-018-0984-9

Reserve bank of India - Building Blocks for a Sustainable Future: Some Reflections. (n.d.). https://rbi.org.in/scripts/BS_SpeechesView.aspx?Id=1379

Reserve bank of India - Macrofinancial Risks Reports. (n.d.). https://rbi.org.in/scripts/PublicationReportDetails.aspx?ID=1237

Reserve bank of India (n.d.). RBI bulletin Statement on Developmental and Regulatory Policies. RBI. https://rbi.org.in/scripts/BS_ViewBulletin.aspx?Id=21988

Reserve bank of India. (n.d.). Master directions - Information Technology Framework for the NBFC Sector. RBI. https://www.rbi.org.in/scripts/BS_ViewMasDirections.aspx?id=10999

Reserve Bank of India. (n.d.). *Annex-II Internet Banking: Security Features.* Reserve Bank of India. https://www.rbi.org.in/hindi1/Upload/content/PDFs/C229260416_2.pdf

Reserve Bank of India. (n.d.). *Cyber Security for a safer Financial System Reserve.* Bank of India. https://rbi.org.in/scripts/BS_ViewBulletin.aspx?Id=21858

Reserve bank of India. (n.d.). *Cyber Security for a safer Financial System.* RBI. https://rbi.org.in/scripts/BS_SpeechesView.aspx?Id=1367

Reserve Bank of India. (n.d.). *Internet And Mobile Association of India vs Reserve Bank of India.* Reserve Bank of India.

Reyes-Mercado, P. (2021). How Fintech Was Born? Springer. . doi:10.1007/978-3-030-53945-0_1

Ridho Kismawadi, E., Irfan, M., & Shah, S. M. A. R. (2023). Revolutionizing Islamic finance: Artificial intelligence's role in the future of industry. *The Impact of AI Innovation on Financial Sectors in the Era of Industry 5.0,* (pp. 184-207). IGI Global. https://www.scopus.com/inward/record.uri?eid=2-s2.0-85173027737&doi=10.4018%2f979-8-3693-0082-4.ch011&partnerID=40&, 10.4018/979-8-3693-0082-4.ch011

Ridho Kismawadi, E., Irfan, M., Shah, S.M.A.R. (2023). Artificial intelligence's role in the future of industry. *The Impact of AI Innovation on Financial Sectors in the Era of Industry, 5.0,* 184-207

Ridho Kismawadi, E., Irfan, M., Shah, S.M.A.R. (2023). Revolutionizing Islamic finance: Artificial intelligence's role in the future of industry. The *Impact of AI Innovation on Financial Sectors in the Era of Industry 5.0,* (pp. 184-207). IGI Global.

Ruhland, P., & Wiese, F. (2022). FinTechs and the financial industry: Partnerships for success. *The Journal of Business Strategy.* doi:10.1108/JBS-12-2021-0196

S&P Global. (2020). *How can AI help ESG investing?* S&P Global. https://www.spglobal.com/en/research-insights/articles/how-can-ai-help-esg-investing

Saeed, Z., & Al-Busaidi, A. (2018). An Islamic Perspective on Smart Contracts: An Overview and Comparative Analysis. In: *15th International Conference on Smart Cities: Improving Quality of Life Using ICT & IoT.* Springer.

Safitri, K. A. (2019). The contribution of life and non-life insurances on asean economic growth. *Management Science Letters, 9*(7), 957–966. doi:10.5267/j.msl.2019.4.009

Saghroun, J., & Eglem, J. Y. (2008). A la recherche de la performance globale de l'entreprise: La perception des analystes financiers. *Comptabilité-Contrôle-Audit, 14*(1), 93–118. doi:10.3917/cca.141.0093

Saiti, B. (2018). Blockchain and Islamic Banking: A Comprehensive Literature Review. *Journal of King Abdulaziz University: Islamic Economics, 31*(2).

Saiti, B. (2020). InsurTech Innovations in Islamic Insurance: A Review and Potential Research Directions. *Journal of Financial Services Marketing, 25*(3).

Sampat, B., Mogaji, E., & Nguyen, N. P. (2023). The dark side of FinTech in financial services: A qualitative enquiry into FinTech developers' perspective. *International Journal of Bank Marketing.* doi:10.1108/IJBM-07-2022-0328

Sanad Z. & Al-Sartawi, A. (2016). Investigating the relationship between corporate governance and internet financial reporting (IFR). *Jordan J Bus Adm 12*(1), 239– 269 24.

Sandhu, H. S., & Ramayah, T. (2019). Fintech in IF: A Comprehensive Literature Review and Research Agenda. *Journal of Islamic Marketing, 11*(2), 494–516.

Sapulette, M. S., Effendi, N., & Santoso, T. (2022). FINTECH, BANKS, AND THE COVID-19 PANDEMIC: EVIDENCE FROM INDONESIA. *Buletin Ekonomi Moneter Dan Perbankan, 24*(4), 559–588. doi:10.21098/bemp.v24i4.1470

Sarea, A. M. (2019). Establishment of The First WAQF Bank in Bahrain: Exploratory Study. *Journal of Developing Areas, 53*(2), 221–228. doi:10.1353/jda.2019.0032

Sari, N., Syamsurijal, & Widiyanti, M. (2018). the Impact of Islamic Capital Market Development on Economic Growth: the Case of Indonesia. *Journal of Smart Economic Growth, 3*(2), 21–30.

Sari, Y. (2023). Sharia e-commerce in Indonesia: Sharia peer to peer lending. *Review of Islamic Social Finance and Entrepreneurship*, 90–102. . doi:10.20885/RISFE.vol2.iss1.art7

Sarkis, J. (2021). A systematic review of blockchain applications in supply chains, transportation, and logistics. *Sustainability, 13*(6).

Sarkis-Onofre, R. C.-L., Catalá-López, F., Aromataris, E., & Lockwood, C. (2021). How to properly use the PRISMA Statement. *Systematic Reviews, 10*(1), 1–3. doi:10.118613643-021-01671-z PMID:33875004

Schmelzer, R. (2019). 5 benefits of AI in the banking industry. *TechTarget.* https://searchenterpriseai.techtarget.com/feature/AI-in-banking-industry-brings-operational-improvements

Scholtens, B., & Tiba, S. (2021). Green fintech's: The new insurgents in sustainable and responsible finance. *Sustainability, 13*(8).

Schueffel, P. (2016). Taming the beast: A scientific definition of fintech. *Journal of Innovation Management, 4*(4), 32–54. doi:10.24840/2183-0606_004.004_0004

Schweitzer, M. E., & Barkley, B. (2017) Is 'Fintech' Good for Small Business Borrowers? *Impacts on Firm Growth and Customer Satisfaction.* Ideas. https://ideas.repec.org/p/fip/fedcwp/1701.html

Seo, K. H., & Lee, J. H. (2021). The emergence of service robots at restaurants: Integrating trust, perceived risk, and satisfaction. *Sustainability (Basel), 13*(8), 4431. doi:10.3390u13084431

Seppälä, A., Birkstedt, T., & Mäntymäki, M. (2021, December). From ethical AI principles to governed AI. In *Proceedings of the 42nd International Conference on Information Systems (ICIS2021).* Research Gate.

Setianto, R. H., & Abdul Manap, T. A. (2015). *Examining the Islamic stock market efficiency: Evidence from nonlinear ESTAR unit root tests.* Indonesian Capital Market Review.

Seyyed, F. J., Shehzad, C. T., & Ashfaq, H. (2019, December 17). *Millat Tractors Limited: A Shariah-compliant Investment Opportunity.* Asian Journal of Management Cases; SAGE Publishing. doi:10.1177/0972820119884399

Shafi, M. (2014). Determinants influencing individual investor behavior in stock market: A cross country research survey. *Nigerian Chapter of Arabian Journal of Business and Management Review, 62*(1100), 1–12. doi:10.12816/0003720

Shah, S. Z. A., & Safi, S. (2020). Blockchain-Based Waqf Management: A Case Study. *Journal of Islamic Marketing.*

Shahzad, A., & Rahman, Z. (2021). Fintech and Islamic Banking: A Framework for Financial Inclusion. *Thunderbird International Business Review, 63*(2), 175–188.

Shaikh, Z. H., Sarea, A., & Irfan, M. (2021, September). Islamic banking strategies in the world of Fintech: success story of Bahrain. In *The International Conference On Global Economic Revolutions* (pp. 97-104). Cham: Springer International Publishing.

Shaikh, Z. H., Sarea, A., & Irfan, M. (2022). Islamic Banking Strategies in the World of Fintech: Success Story of Bahrain. In *Artificial Intelligence for Sustainable Finance and Sustainable Technology. ICGER 2021. Lecture Notes in Networks and Systems* (pp. 97–104). Springer. doi:10.1007/978-3-030-93464-4_10

Sharma, A., Kumar, D., & Arora, N. (2022). Supply chain risk factor assessment of Indian pharmaceutical industry for performance improvement. *International Journal of Productivity and Performance Management.* Advance online publication. doi:10.1108/IJPPM-01-2022-0035

Sharma, R. B., Lodha, S., Sharma, A., Ali, S., & Elmezughi, A. M. (2022). Environment, social and governance reporting and firm performance: Evidence from GCC countries. *International Journal of Innovative Research and Scientific Studies*, *5*(4), 419–427. doi:10.53894/ijirss.v5i4.1006

Siau, K., & Wang, W. (2020). Artificial intelligence (AI) ethics: Ethics of AI and ethical AI. [JDM]. *Journal of Database Management*, *31*(2), 74–87. doi:10.4018/JDM.2020040105

Silva, T. F., & Santos, R. (2017). Insurtech: Overview and future prospects. *The Geneva Papers on Risk and Insurance. Issues and Practice*, *42*(4), 647–667.

Simpson, L. (2021). Fintech for financial inclusion: A study of government-supported savings groups in Papua New Guinea. *Frontiers in Blockchain, 4.*

Smaoui, H., & Nechi, S. (2017). Does sukuk market development spur economic growth? *Research in International Business and Finance*, *41*(April), 136–147. doi:10.1016/j.ribaf.2017.04.018

Snihovyi, O., Ivanov, O., & Kobets, V. (2018, September 1). *Implementation of Robo-Advisors Using Neural Networks for Different Risk Attitude Investment Decisions.* IEEE. doi:10.1109/IS.2018.8710559

Söderlund, M. (2023). What is it like to be idle versus busy for a service machine? *Psychology and Marketing*, *40*(6), 1237–1248. doi:10.1002/mar.21806

Soumik, M. (2008). *Islamic Banking in India-What is the future potential.* Crisil Young Thought Leader.

Stanley, M. (2016). Global insight: Blockchain in banking: Disruptive threat or tool? *Global Financials/FinTech, Morgan Stanley Global Insight.*

Sukarmi, S., Ganindha, R., & Dewantara, R. (2022). Cartel Indications on Determination of Loan Interest Rate in Fintech Lending. *Yustisia Jurnal Hukum*, *11*(3), 181. doi:10.20961/yustisia.v11i3.56339

Sulaiman, S. (2020). Ethical and Social Responsibility of Islamic Fintech Companies: A Comparative Analysis. *Journal of Islamic Marketing*, *11*(6).

Sultana, S., Zulkifli, N., & Zainal, D. (2018). Environmental, social and governance (ESG) and investment decision in Bangladesh. *Sustainability (Basel)*, *10*(6), 1831. doi:10.3390u10061831

Sumarti, N., Hayati, M. M., Cahyani, N. L. P. A., Wahyudi, R. R., Tristanti, D. P., & Meylani, R. (2018). Has the growth of Islamic banking had impact to economic growth in Indonesia? *4th IEEE International Conference on Engineering Technologies and Applied Sciences, ICETAS 2017, 2018.* IEEE. 10.1109/ICETAS.2017.8277873

Suratgar, D. A. (1984). Forward: The Impact of Islamic Banking on World Financial and Commercial Relations, 16 [Hereinafter Suratgar]. *Law and Policy in International Business*, 1089.

Suryono, R. R., Budi, I., & Purwandari, B. (2021). Detection of fintech P2P lending issues in Indonesia. *Heliyon*, *7*(4), e06782. doi:10.1016/j.heliyon.2021.e06782 PMID:33981873

Suzuki, Y. (2022). Digital transformation in Islamic finance: A critique of perfectionist's views on Islamic fintech. In Digital Transformation in Islamic Finance: A Critical and Analytical View. Taylor & Francis. doi:10.4324/9781003262169-3

Svetlova, E. (2022). AI ethics and systemic risks in finance. *AI and Ethics*, *2*(4), 713–725. doi:10.100743681-021-00129-1 PMID:35043105

Tabachnick, D. (2019). Regtech for fintech: A framework for regulatory and supervisory responses. *Georgetown Journal of International Law*, *50*(2), 451–504.

Tabash, M. I. (2014). The Flow of Islamic Finance and Economic Growth: An Empirical Evidence of Middle East. *Journal of Finance and Accounting*, *2*(1), 11. doi:10.11648/j.jfa.20140201.12

Tabash, M. I., & Dhankar, R. S. (2018). The relevance of Islamic finance principles in economic growth. *International Journal of Emerging Research in Management and Technology*, *3*(2), 49–54.

Takaful, M. A. (2019). Blockchain-Based Takaful: An Empirical Study on Its Feasibility. *Journal of Islamic Marketing*, *10*(4).

Tama, B. A. (2019). Smart Contracts in the Financial Industry: Applications, Challenges, and Benefits. *International Journal of Engineering Research & Technology (Ahmedabad)*, *12*(6), 1329–1332. https://www.ijert.org/research/smart-contracts-in-the-financial-industry-applications-challenges-and-benefits-IJERTV12IS060173.pdf

Tapscott, D., & Tapscott, A. (2016). *Blockchain Revolution: How the Technology Behind Bitcoin is Changing Money, Business, and the World.* Penguin.

Tapscott, D., & Tapscott, A. (2016). *Blockchain Revolution: How the Technology Behind Bitcoin Is Changing Money, Business, and the World.* Penguin.

Tarazi, A., & Fechtali, O. (2020). Fintech and IF: A New Dawn for Financial Inclusion? *The World Bank Research Observer*, *36*(1), 29–54.

Tarazi, A., & Fechtali, O. (2020). Fintech and Islamic Finance: A New Dawn for Financial Inclusion? *The World Bank Research Observer*, *36*(1), 29–54.

Tarazi, A., & Trinugroho, I. W. (2021). Fintech in Islamic Banking: A Review and Future Research Directions. *Research in International Business and Finance*, *58*, 101391.

Tariq, U., & Malik, I. H. (2021). Development of Shariah-Compliant Cryptocurrency: Challenges and Prospects. *Journal of Islamic Marketing*.

Thomas, N. M. (2023). Modeling key enablers influencing FinTechs offering SME credit services: A multi-stakeholder perspective. *Electronic Markets*, *33*(1), 18. doi:10.100712525-023-00627-6 PMID:37220555

Thompson, B. S., & Rust, S. (2023). Blocking blockchain: Examining the social, cultural, and institutional factors causing innovation resistance to digital technology in seafood supply chains. *Technology in Society*, *73*, 102235. doi:10.1016/j.techsoc.2023.102235

Tian, H., Siddik, A. B., Pertheban, T. R., & Rahman, M. N. (2023). Does fintech innovation and green transformational leadership improve green innovation and corporate environmental performance? A hybrid SEM–ANN approach. *Journal of Innovation and Knowledge*, *8*(3), 100396. doi:10.1016/j.jik.2023.100396

Tijjani, B., Ashiq, M., Siddique, N., Ajmal, K., & Rasul, A. (2021). A bibliometric analysis of quality research papers in Islamic finance: Evidence from web of science. *ISRA International Journal of Islamic Finance, 13*(1), 84–101. doi:10.1108/IJIF-03-2020-0056

Todaro, M. P., & Smith, S. C. (2012). *Economic Developement* (11th ed.). Pearson.

Tok, E., Yesuf, A. J., & Mohamed, A. (2022). Sustainable Development Goals and Islamic Social Finance: From Policy Divide to Policy Coherence and Convergence. *Sustainability (Basel), 14*(11), 11. doi:10.3390u14116875

Truby, J., Dahdal, A., & Ibrahim, I. A. (2022). Sandboxes in the desert: Is a cross-border 'gulf box' feasible? *Law, Innovation and Technology, 14*(2), 447–473. doi:10.1080/17579961.2022.2113674

Turetsky, M. (2017). Smart Contracts in Islamic Finance. In: *2017 19th International Conference on Advanced Communication Technology (ICACT).* Research Gate.

Tuyon, J., Onyia, O. P., Ahmi, A., & Huang, C.-H. (2022). Sustainable financial services: Reflection and future perspectives. *Journal of Financial Services Marketing*, 1–27. doi:10.105741264-022-00187-4

Ul Din, S. M., Abu-Bakar, A., & Regupathi, A. (2017). Does insurance promote economic growth: A comparative study of developed and emerging/ developing economies. *Cogent Economics & Finance, 5*(1), 1390029. Advance online publication. doi:10.1080/23322039.2017.1390029

Umer, C. (2009). The Global Financial Crisis: Can Islamic Finance Help. *International financial crisis from an Islamic perspective.* Islamic Economic Research Centre.

UN. (n.d.). *Transforming Our World: The 2030 Agenda for Sustainable Development.* United Nations,.

Undang-Undang, No. 40 Tahun 2014 (2014), *Undang-Undang Republik Indonesia Nomor 40 Tahun 2014 Tentang Perasuransian* [Indonesia Insurance Constitution], § (2014). https://www.ojk.go.id/Files/201506/1UU402014Perasuransian_1433758676.pdf

Van Duuren, E., Plantinga, A., & Scholtens, B. (2016). ESG integration and the investment management process: Fundamental investing reinvented. *Journal of Business Ethics, 138*(3), 525–533. doi:10.100710551-015-2610-8

Van Eck, N. J., & Waltman, L. (2017). Citation-based clustering of publications using CitNetExplorer and VOSviewer. *Scientometrics, 111*(2), 1053–1070. doi:10.100711192-017-2300-7 PMID:28490825

Vannucci, E., Pagano, A. J., & Romagnoli, F. (2021). *Climate change management: a resilience strategy for flood risk using Blockchain tools.* Decisions in Economics and Finance., doi:10.100710203-020-00315-6

Varma, P., Nijjer, S., Sood, K., Grima, S., & Rupeika-Apoga, R. (2022). Thematic Analysis of Financial Technology (Fintech) Influence on the Banking Industry. *Risks, 10*(10), 186. doi:10.3390/risks10100186

Vismara, F. (2022, July 6). *Application of the Legal Principles of Islamic Finance to Our Legal System.* Routledge eBooks. doi:10.4324/9781003155218-15

Viviers, S., Venter, D. J. L., & Krüger, J. (2012). The relative importance of ethics, environmental, social and governance criteria. *African Journal of Business Ethics, 6*(2), 120. doi:10.4103/1817-7417.111021

Von Wallis, M., & Klein, C. (2015). Ethical requirement and financial interest: A literature review on socially responsible investing. *Business Research, 8*(1), 61–98. doi:10.100740685-014-0015-7

Waas, T., Hugé, J., Block, T., Wright, T., Benitez-Capistros, F., & Verbruggen, A. (2014). Sustainability assessment and indicators: Tools in a decision-making strategy for sustainable development. *Sustainability (Basel), 6*(9), 5512–5534. doi:10.3390u6095512

Wall, L. D. (2018). Some financial regulatory implications of artificial intelligence. *Journal of Economics and Business, 100*, 55–63. doi:10.1016/j.jeconbus.2018.05.003

Wang, L., Huang, N., Hong, Y., Liu, L., Guo, X., & Chen, G. (2023). Voice-based AI in call center customer service: A natural field experiment. *Production and Operations Management, 32*(4), 1002–1018. doi:10.1111/poms.13953

Wang, X., Lin, X., & Shao, B. (2022). How does artificial intelligence create business agility? Evidence from chatbots. *International Journal of Information Management, 66*, 102535. doi:10.1016/j.ijinfomgt.2022.102535

Wani, S. M., & Noordin, M. F. (2020). Blockchain technology in Islamic finance: Regulatory and compliance issues. In: *International Conference on Applied Internet and Information Technologies*. Research Gate.

Ward, D., & Zurbruegg, R. (2000). Does Insurance Promote Economic Growth? Evidence from OECD Countries. *The Journal of Risk and Insurance, 67*(4), 489. doi:10.2307/253847

Warde, I. (2012). Islamic Finance in Theory and Practice. Islamic Finance in the Global Economy.

Webb, I., Grace, M. F., & Skipper, H. D. (2005). The effect of banking and insurance on the growth of capital and output. *SBS Revista de Temas Financieros, 2*, 1–32. http://dspace.fudutsinma.edu.ng/xmlui/bitstream/handle/123456789/885/The_Effect_Of_Banking_And_Insurance_On_The_Growth.pdf?sequence=1

Werbach, K. (2018). *Blockchain and the New Architecture of Trust*. MIT Press. doi:10.7551/mitpress/11449.001.0001

Who we are. (n.d.). Simply Ethical. https://simplyethical.com/who-we-are/#our-services-compared

Wilson, R., & El-Desouky, A. (2019). Fintech, IF, and Financial Inclusion. In Routledge Handbook of Social and Sustainable Finance (pp. 433-447). Routledge.

Wilson, R., & El-Desouky, A. (2019). Fintech, Islamic Finance, and Financial Inclusion. In Routledge Handbook of Social and Sustainable Finance (pp. 433-447). Routledge.

Wilson, R. (2020). The Global IF Ecosystem: Mapping the Territory. *ISRA International Journal of IF, 12*(1), 17–34.

Wong, R. Y. (2020). An ethical framework for blockchain-enabled sustainable supply chains. *Frontiers in Blockchain, 3*.

Xi'an University. (2020). Fin Tech instrument and islamic finance: The GCC perspective. *Journal of Xi'an University of Architecture & Technology, XII*(II), 2736–2747. https://www.xajzkjdx.cn/gallery/226-feb2020.pdf

Xiao, Y., Faff, R., Gharghori, P., & Lee, D. (2013). An empirical study of the world price of sustainability. *Journal of Business Ethics, 114*(2), 297–310. doi:10.100710551-012-1342-2

Xu, M., & Gupta, H. (2018). Blockchain's Role in Facilitating Accounting and Audit Processes: Current Applications and Future Directions. *Journal of Emerging Technologies in Accounting, 15*(2), 107–126. doi:10.2308/jeta-52094

Xu, Y., Shieh, C.-H., van Esch, P., & Ling, I.-L. (2020). AI customer service: Task complexity, problem-solving ability, and usage intention. *Australasian Marketing Journal, 28*(4), 189–199. doi:10.1016/j.ausmj.2020.03.005

Yahaya, N. Z., & Alias, N. (2020). The Potential of Blockchain Technology in Islamic Finance: A Review. *International Journal of Advanced Science and Technology, 29*(7), 3091–3103.

Yamashita, R., Nishio, M., Do, R. K. G., & Togashi, K. (2018). Convolutional neural networks: An overview and application in radiology. *Insights Into Imaging, 9*(4), 611–629. doi:10.100713244-018-0639-9 PMID:29934920

Yang, Q., Liu, Y., Chen, T., & Tong, Y. (2019). Federated machine learning: Concept and applications. *ACM Transactions on Intelligent Systems and Technology, 10*(2), 1–19. doi:10.1145/3298981

Yang, X. (2023). The effects of AI service quality and AI function-customer ability fit on customer's overall co-creation experience. *Industrial Management & Data Systems*, *123*(6), 1717–1735. doi:10.1108/IMDS-08-2022-0500

Yaseen, S. G., & El Qirem, I. A. (2018). Intention to use e-banking services in the Jordanian commercial banks. *International Journal of Bank Marketing*, *36*(3), 557–571. doi:10.1108/IJBM-05-2017-0082

Yeh, H. C., Yu, M. C., Liu, C. H., & Huang, C. I. (2022, June 14). Robo-advisor based on unified theory of acceptance and use of technology. *Asia Pacific Journal of Marketing and Logistics*. Emerald Publishing Limited. doi:10.1108/APJML-07-2021-0493

Yigitcanlar, T., Kamruzzaman, M., Foth, M., Sabatini-Marques, J., da Costa, E., & Ioppolo, G. (2019). Can Cities Become Smart without Being Sustainable? A Systematic Review of the Literature. *Sustainable Cities and Society*, *45*, 348–365. doi:10.1016/j.scs.2018.11.033

Yıldırım, S., Yıldırım, D. C., & Diboglu, P. (2020). Does Sukuk market development promote economic growth? *PSU Research Review*, *4*(3), 209–218. doi:10.1108/PRR-03-2020-0011

Yli-Huumo, J., Ko, D., Choi, S., Park, S., & Smolander, K. (2016). Where is current research on blockchain technology? A systematic review. *PLoS One*, *11*(10), e0163477. doi:10.1371/journal.pone.0163477 PMID:27695049

Young, E.Y. (2008). *Bridging the gap: Private Investment in Middle east Infrastructure.*

Young, K. E. (2018). Prioritizing renewable energy in a time of fiscal austerity. In The Economics of Renewable Energy in the Gulf (pp. 77–99). Routledge. doi:10.4324/9780429434976-5

Youssef, T., & Allam, M. (2020). AI Chatbots in IF: Adoption Barriers and Ethical Considerations. *Journal of Islamic Marketing*.

Yunita, E., & Munandar, J. M. (2023). The Influence of Push-Pull-Mooring Effects on E-Wallet Customer Switching in Generation Z in DKI Jakarta. *The South East Asian Journal of Management*, *17*(1), 1–27. doi:10.21002eam.v17i1.1177

Yusof, N. M. (2019). Crowdfunding for Islamic Social Finance: A Blockchain-Based Framework. *International Journal of Islamic and Middle Eastern Finance and Management*, *12*(4).

Yusuf, M., & Rahman, M. (2019). Emerging Trends of Islamic Fintech Startups in the Middle East. *Journal of Islamic Marketing*.

Yusuf, T. O. (2021). The Risks of Islamic Fintech. In *Islamic FinTech*. Insights and Solutions. doi:10.1007/978-3-030-45827-0_20

Zakariya, H. (2021). Sukuk Tokenization on Blockchain: A New Era of IF. *Journal of Islamic Marketing*.

Zaman, M., & Khairudin, N. H. (2021). Fintech and IF: A Review. *Journal of IF, 10*(Special Issue), 086-097.

Zavolokina, L., Dolata, M., & Schwabe, G. (2017). FinTech Transformation: How IT-Enabled Innovations Shape the Financial Sector. In Enterprise Applications, Markets and Services in the Finance Industry (pp. 75–88). Springer. doi:10.1007/978-3-319-52764-2_6

Zavolokina, L., Dolata, M., & Schwabe, G. (2019). Transforming business models with blockchain: A framework and typology. *Journal of Management Information Systems*, *36*(3), 868–904.

Zavvar Sabegh, M., & Tarofder, A. K. (2022). Fintech Innovations in IF: A Systematic Literature Review. *Journal of IF and Business Research*, *11*(1), 18–34.

Zhang, X., & Mahadevan, S. (2019). Ensemble machine learning models for aviation incident risk prediction. *Decision Support Systems*, *116*, 48–63. doi:10.1016/j.dss.2018.10.009

Zhang, Y., Ramanathan, L., & Maheswari, M. (2021). A hybrid approach for risk analysis in e-business integrating big data analytics and artificial intelligence. *Annals of Operations Research*. doi:10.100710479-021-04412-6

Zhang, Y., & Xiao, X. (2020). Machine learning and financial market anomalies. *Journal of Accounting and Economics*, *69*(1), 101295.

Zhang, Y., Xing, C., & Guo, X. (2023). The Shielding Effect of Access to Finance on Small and Medium-Sized Enterprises during the COVID-19 Crisis: Comparing Fintech and Traditional Finance. *Emerging Markets Finance & Trade*, *59*(8), 2383–2397. doi:10.1080/1540496X.2022.2072201

Zheng, Y. (2018). Blockchain Challenges and Opportunities: A Survey and a Case Study. *International Journal of Financial Research, 9*(2), 283-295. doi:. v9n2p283 doi:10.5430/ijfr

Zheng, G., Kong, L., & Brintrup, A. (2023). Federated machine learning for privacy preserving, collective supply chain risk prediction. *International Journal of Production Research*, *61*(23), 8115–8132. doi:10.1080/00207543.2022.2164628

Zhong, J., & Wang, Z. (2022). Artificial intelligence techniques for financial distress prediction. *AIMS Mathematics*, *7*(12), 20891–20908. doi:10.3934/math.20221145

Zhou, F., Huang, Z., & Zhang, C. (2022). Carbon price forecasting based on CEEMDAN and LSTM. *Applied Energy*, *311*(January), 118601. doi:10.1016/j.apenergy.2022.118601

Zhou, G., Zhu, J., & Luo, S. (2022). The impact of fintech innovation on green growth in China: Mediating effect of green finance. *Ecological Economics*, *193*, 107308. doi:10.1016/j.ecolecon.2021.107308

Zhu, A., Ash, M., & Pollin, R. (2004). Stock market liquidity and economic growth: A critical appraisal of the Levine/Zervos model. *International Review of Applied Economics*, *18*(1), 63–71. doi:10.1080/0269217032000148645

Zhu, Y., & Tarazi, A. (2021). Fintech and IF: A Comprehensive Review and Future Research Agenda. *Pacific-Basin Finance Journal*, *66*, 101477.

Zohar, A. (2015). Bitcoin: Under the Hood. *Communications of the ACM*, *58*(9), 104–113. doi:10.1145/2701411

Zohar, A., & Leloup, L. (2015). Bitcoin, Islamic finance, and the compliance of non-interest banking and finance. In *Business Transformation through Blockchain* (Vol. 1, pp. 287–298). Springer.

Zou, Z., Liu, X., Wang, M., & Yang, X. (2023). Insight into digital finance and fintech: A bibliometric and content analysis. *Technology in Society*, *73*, 102221. doi:10.1016/j.techsoc.2023.102221

Zulkhibri, M. (2020). Fintech and IF: The Convergence of Two Worlds. *ISRA International Journal of IF*, *12*(1), 75–82.

Zulkhibri, M. (2020). Fintech and Islamic Finance: The Convergence of Two Worlds. *ISRA International Journal of Islamic Finance*, *12*(1), 75–82.

About the Contributors

Mohammad Irfan is presently working as an Associate Professor at NSB Academy Business School, Bangalore. He was associated with the School of Business, AURO University, Surat, Gujarat for five years. He is MBA (Finance and Marketing) and M.Com (Account and Law). Dr. Irfan has done this Ph.D. from the Central University of Haryana. He has qualified UGC-SRF/NET in Management and UGC-NET in Commerce. Dr. Irfan has also qualified NSEs (NCFM) and BSEs Certification. He has experience of thirteen years in the area of Financial Management, Security Analysis and Portfolio Management, FAD, Data Analysis for Business, Financial Engineering, Financial Analytics, Fintech, Financial modeling in Excel, Green Finance, and Alternative Finance. He has to his credit various research papers published in Scopus Indexed Journals including International of Business International Journal of Business Excellence (IJBEX), Indian Journal of Finance (IJF). He is an editorial board member/reviewer in several national and international journals. Dr. Irfan presented papers in IIM-A, IIM-C, IIM-Indore, IIM-Shillong, IIT-Roorkee, Indonesia, Malaysia, Switzerland.

Seifedine Kadry (Senior Member, IEEE) received the bachelor's degree from Lebanese University, in 1999, the dual M.S. degree from Reims University, France, in 2002, and EPFL, Lausanne, the Ph.D. degree from Blaise Pascal University, France, in 2007, and the H.D.R. degree from Rouen University, in 2017. His current research interests include data science, education using technology, system prognostics, stochastic systems, and probability and reliability analysis.

Muhammad Sharif, PhD (IEEE Senior Member) is an Associate Professor at COMSATS University Islamabad, Wah Cantt Pakistan. He has completed his PhD in Image Processing from COMSATS Institute of IT, Islamabad in 2013. He got his MS (CS) degree from the same institute in 2007 and MCS degree from Quaid-e-Azam University, Islamabad Pakistan in 1995. He has worked one year in Alpha Soft UK based software house as a developer/team leader in 1995. He is an Oracle Certified Professional in Developer Track. He has adopted teaching profession since 1996 to date. He has more than 150 research publications in IF, SCI and ISI journals as well as in national and international conferences and obtained 100+ Impact Factor. He has been supervised 40 MS (CS) thesis till date. Currently, he is supervising 05 PhD (CS) students and co-supervising 10 PhD (CS) students. Recently, one of his student successfully defended PhD (CS) thesis. In addition, more than 350 undergraduate students have successfully completed their degree project work under his supervision. His research interests include Medical Imaging, Biometrics, Computer Vision, Machine Learning and Agriculture/Plants imaging. He is being awarded with COMSATS Research Productivity Awards continuously since 2010 till now. He has been served in the TPC for the IEEE FIT 2013-17. He is also currently serving as an Associate

Editor for IEEE Access Journal and Guest Editor in four Journal special issues as well as reviewer for many well reputed journals. He has headed the Department of Computer Sciences COMSATS Institute of IT, Wah Cantt from 2008 to 2011 and successfully achieved the targeted outputs. He also attended a number of prestigious national and international conferences throughout his career.

Habib Ullah Khan received the Ph.D. degree in management information system area from Leeds Beckett University, U.K. He is currently working as a Professor of information systems with the Department of Accounting and Information Systems, College of Business and Economics, Qatar University. Academic experience-wise, he was associated with many leading universities of Gulf, USA, and Europe. Overall he has more than 21 years of working and research experience in different multinational companies (on different managerial positions), and reputed educational institutions in U.K., USA, Oman, United Arab Emirates, Saudi Arabia, and Qatar. During his past experience, he was an excellent team player and leader; his diversified experience helped him to manage multicultural students and the workforce in educational institutions. He has a strong skill set in managing undergraduate and graduate-level teaching of MIS and general management courses at the university level. The ability to analyze complex management procedures and extensive knowledge in information systems helped him to meet the challenge of remaining current with new and developing technology, and its applications in the management functions. He successfully demonstrated his skills in information management, client relations, training, and communication in a high-pressure environment with a successful management experience in the Gulf Region.

***

S. Dhanabagiyam, Associate Professor, NSB Academy, Bangalore is specialized in Human Resources, Marketing, Tourism, and Hospitality. She is vibrant, enthusiastic with 17 years of Academic experience, authoring a book titled "Multi rater Feedback for Succession Planning". She has published articles in reputed Journals with few listed in UGC Care, WoS, and Scopus.

Mustapha Chaffai is working in the high business school of sfax, Dr. Chaffai is an experienced finance Teacher in the University of Sfax, he have a teaching experience in many fields mainly portfolio management, Behavioral finance and investment decision. He is specialized in Portfolio selection and Decision-making in a risky universe and Islamic finance. Chaffai Mustapha have many contributions in research, he has presented paper in Turkey, Morocco et he participates in conferences organized by the ERF. research contribution includes publications in many indexed journals: MDPI (International Journal of Financial Studies), Emerald (Revue of Behavioral Finance, International journal of Islamic and middle eastern finance and management). Revue of behavioral Finance and China Finance Revue International.

Rui Dias is a professor and researcher in the areas of accounting and finance at Lusófona University and at the School of Business Sciences of the Polytechnic Institute of Setúbal. He is currently an integrated member of the Centre for Advanced Training Studies in Management and Economics (CEFAGE) of the University of Évora.

G. Sowmya is pursuing her PhD in JNTUH Hyderabad, in Computer Science and Engineering. She has around 10 years of teaching experience from reputed Engineering Institutions. She is working as

Assistant Professor in the CSE Department, MLR Institute of Technology, Hyderabad, India. She has published more than 10 papers in refereed journals and conference proceedings. Her research interests include blockchain technology, Artificial Intelligence, Machine Learning, Internet of Things.

Swati Gupta, Associate Professor at Karnavati University, Gujarat. She has 16 years of teaching experience in the field of finance and accounts. Her expertise lies in managerial accounting, fintech, rural finance, and entrepreneurship. Her impactful contributions extend beyond the classroom; she has published and presented extensively at national and international forums.

K. Kusuma works as an Assistant professor at GITAM University, Rushikonda, Visakhapatnam. She has 26 years of teaching experience in the field of accounting and Finance. She has expertise in Financial Accounting, Management and cost Accounting, Financial Services, Stock Market operations, Security Analysis and Portfolio Management, and Derivatives. I finished my M.Phil. and Ph.D. in Mutual Funds and was given an opportunity to write one chapter by NCERT in Risk Management. Successfully completed one minor project in Mutual Funds. Guided around 200 students in project work.

Salina Kassim has a great passion in writing scholarly articles in various areas of Islamic banking and finance. She has published extensively in academic journals with nearly 200 scholarly articles in the areas of her research interests. She has also published several books mainly in the areas of Islamic finance. In recognition to her dynamic role as a subject matter expert, she has been appointed as member of the editorial boards of several reputable international and local journals. At present, she is supervising (and has supervised) nearly 80 post-graduate candidates at the PhD and Masters levels. She has also served as internal and external examiners for Masters and PhD theses in several universities, apart from being appointed as Adjunct Professor, Visiting Research Fellow and trainer at several universities and institutes, locally and abroad.

H. Early Ridho Kismawadi, S.E.I, MA is a lecturer at the Department of Islamic Banking, Faculty of Islamic Economics and Business IAIN Langsa, Aceh, Indonesia, he has been a lecturer since 2013, he has completed a doctoral program in 2018 majoring in Sharia economics at the State Islamic University of North Sumatra, he was appointed as Head of the Sharia Banking Study Program (2020) and Sharia Financial Management (2019) at the Langsa State Islamic Institute (IAIN Langsa), Aceh, Indonesia. In addition, he is also the general secretary of the Islamic Economic Society of Langsa city, besides that he is also a member of several other organizations His research interests include financial economics, applied econometrics, Islamic economics, banking, and finance. He has published articles in national and international journals. In addition, he is also a reviewer of several reputable international journals such as Finance Research Letters, Financial Innovation, Cogent Business &; Management, Journal of Islamic Accounting and Business Research. He has also presented his papers at various local and international seminars.

Lawin Laïfoya Moïse is engineer-statistician-economist, with a degree from the Ecole Nationale Supérieure de Statistiques et d'Economie Appliquée (ENSEA) in Abidjan (Côte d'Ivoire). His research focuses on sustainable development issues (tax revenue mobilization, governance, peace and security, gender promotion, economics, international trade, child nutrition). Since 2020, he has been working as a consultant for the Direction Générale de l'Economie, Ministry of Economy and Finance of Benin. In

2023, he became a professional membership of the International Society for Development and Sustainability (ISDS, Japan), and he received in October 2023 the Award for Best Research Paper in Taxation Category under The Institute of Chartered Accountants of India (ICAI) International Research Awards 2023.

Naji Mansour Nomran is an Assistant Professor at the College of Business Administration, Department of Finance and banking, Kingdom University, Bahrain.

Nitish Kumar Minz is an exceptional Bachelor of Commerce student specializing in Business Administration and Management at K.R. Mangalam University. With an unwavering commitment to excellence and a remarkable work ethic, Mr. Minz has consistently demonstrated his dedication to academic and professional pursuits. His academic achievements extend beyond the classroom, as he has made significant contributions to several research papers and book chapters that are currently in the final stages of publication. His insightful contributions and research expertise have earned him recognition within his field of study. Nitish Kumar Minz, as the President of the Student Council at K.R. Mangalam University, holds a prestigious position. In this leadership role, he has demonstrated exceptional skills in managing various projects and strategic initiatives. His internship at KEIC (KRMU Entrepreneurship & Incubation Center) has allowed him to further refine his project management and strategic planning abilities, providing valuable hands-on experience in the field. Furthermore, he has been selected as NEP SAARTHI- Student Ambassador for Academic Reforms in Transforming Higher Education at K.R. Mangalam University. This esteemed role demonstrates his passion for educational reforms and his commitment to improving the quality of higher education. As a Student Ambassador, Mr. Minz actively engages with fellow students, faculty, and staff, promoting a culture of academic excellence and facilitating positive changes within the university. Recognizing his outstanding accomplishments and exceptional contributions, he has recently been honored with the prestigious CHANCELLOR'S EXCELLENCE AWARD. This esteemed award serves as a testament to his dedication, hard work, and exemplary performance throughout his academic journey. Mr. Nitish Kumar Minz's academic prowess, research contributions, leadership roles, and recognition through awards highlight his exceptional abilities and potential for future success. He continues to inspire and make a significant impact within the academic community, demonstrating his commitment to excellence in all his endeavors.

Nikhat Mushir is an Assistant Professor in the School of Management and Commerce, K.R. Mangalam University, Gurugram. She has 5 years of teaching experience. Dr. Nikhat Mushir has holds Ph.D (Islamic Finance), M.Com (Business Administration) and B. Com (Hons.). She has earned her degrees from Jamia Millia Islamia University, New Delhi. She has several research papers published in national and international journals. She has presented papers in national and international conferences.

Paluri Sheela has 28 years of experience in teaching, research, and administration. She has published research articles in Finance, Insurance, Business Ethics, Entrepreneurship, and Social Entrepreneurship.

Libeesh P. C. is a passionate professor of management and commerce subjects. He has cleared UGC-NET and Kerala SET. He holds a bachelor's degree in commerce and education. He has around Thirteen years of teaching experience, which includes 4.5 years of experience as a HOD of the Department of Commerce in TTGI Coimbatore. He is doing his Ph.D. in finance from Dr. NGP Arts and Science College

Coimbatore. His teaching interests include Accounting, Taxation, Financial Management, and Business Economics. He has more than Eight years of experience in training and motivation, and he worked as a trainer and training coordinator of WWTA (World Wide Teacher Academy) for more than Three years and trained so many teachers.

Rashmi Ranjan Panigrahi (PhD), MBA, (ORCID ID- 0000-0002-2199-293X) is working as an Assistant Professor at GITAM School of Business, GITAM, deemed to be University, Visakhapatnam, Andhra Pradesh, India. Before joining GITAM, he was working as Research Associate, at IBCS, SOA-DU, he had also served in the position of Asst. Professor cum Principal-in-charge of RCST&M college under (Rajdhani Group of Institution) Mancheswar Railway Colony, Bhubaneswar, affiliated to Utkal University, Bhubaneswar, Odisha. He is well known as a Researcher/Educator cum Administrator in Odisha, India. He has 12 years of teaching, research and administrative experience. He teaches finance, inventory management, SCM, RM and core papers for master's degree students, such as financial management and statistics for managers,. As of now, I have published 24 articles in Scopus, WOS Index, UGC Care listed Journals, ABDC Category Journal, and 4 book chapters in Springer Nature publication house, CRS Press, IGI Global, and Routledge of Taylor & Francis publication house. I had received a short-term project approval titled as "Adoption of Digitalization among Indian MSMEs Impacting the Firm Performance – An Empirical Study of select areas of Bihar, Jharkhand, West Bengal, and Odisha" from Indian Council of Social Science Research (hereinafter referred to as Council), Aruna Asaf Ali Marg, New Delhi-110067 vide letter No. ICSSR-CRP-2023-1415 dated-29/08/2023.

Ankit Saxena is currently working as associate professor at Institute of Business Management, GLA University, Mathura. He is a Director Medalist from Dayalbagh Educational Institute, Agra. He qualified NET-JRF (UGC). He has excellent academic background and a rich experience of 17 years in research and academics. He has published number of research papers and contemporary business case studies. His area of interest comprises Strategic Financial Management and behavior of market participants.

Zakir Shaikh is an Assistant Professor, Department of Accounting and Finance, School of Business Administration, Kingdom University, Bahrain. Prior to this, he worked more than 28 years in commercial and academic industry. He has published numerous articles in referred journals and presented many papers in various conferences, both local and abroad in the different area of Accounting, management and Islamic Banking and Finance. He has also participated in a variety of seminars, forums, workshops and international conferences. He obtained his Ph.D. (Islamic Banking and Finance) from India in 2018. His doctoral thesis explored the entrepreneurial phenomenon from an Islamic perspective and argued for profit and loss sharing (PLS) contracts as viable alternatives to conventional interest-based financing instruments. He holds Master degree in Commerce, Business Administration & Finance and Control. He is a member of AAA, Chartered Institute of Islamic Finance Professionals (CIIF), Malaysia; Indian Accounting Association; Orissa Commerce Association, India and associated with Accounting & Auditing Organization for Islamic Financial Institution (AAOIFI), Bahrain.

Raj Bahadur Sharma is an intellectual academician of high caliber with extensive experience of over seventeen years in the higher education industry in India and abroad. Presently, Dr. Raj is providing his services as an 'Assistant Professor' at the Department of Accounting, College Business Administration, University of Bahrain, Kingdom of Bahrain. Before this, he worked at Prince Sattam Bin Abdulaziz

University (PSAU), Kingdom of Saudi Arabia. Along with his master and doctoral academic degrees in accounting, he has patents of two books in the area of accounting. He has nearly forty research papers published in the Scopus, Web of Sciences, peer-reviewed, and UGC-listed journals. Besides, he has presented several research papers at national and international conferences and has also attended workshops, reference courses, Faculty Development Program (FDP).

Ahmed Ihsan Simsek graduated from Marmara University Faculty of Business and Administrative Sciences in 2012. He completed his master degree in First University Social Sciences Institute Business & Administration program in 2016. In 2022, he completed his PhD in Inonu University Social Sciences Institute Operations Management & Marketing program with a thesis titled "A mathematical model for selection of emergency facility locations with earthquake risk analysis in Elazig province". Between 2013 and 2015, he worked as an specialist in Turkish Airlines. Between 2015-2023, he worked as an research assistant in the Department of Business & Administration at Faculty of Economics and Administrative Sciences in Fırat University. He is currently working as an assistant professor at the same university. He has many articles, books and book chapters in the field of finance and operations management, as well as papers presented at national and international congresses. His research interests are: decision support systems, time series analysis, multi-criteria decision making and linear programming.

Rohit Singh has joined The Assam Royal Global University as Pro Vice Chancellor. Prior to joining this University Prof Singh worked as Professor and Dean Academics at AURO University, Surat Gujarat as a founding faculty member and has a teaching experience spanning over twenty-two years. He served as Associate Professor at GD Goenka World Institute Lancaster University, Gurgaon, and at the School of Management Sciences, Varanasi as Reader. He started his teaching career from a Constituent College of the University of Allahabad. He has to his credit a Ph.D. in Advertising Management from the Department of Commerce and Business Administration (MONIRBA), University of Allahabad, and a Master Diploma in Business Administration and Post Graduate Degree in Commerce with specialization in Marketing from Banaras Hindu University, Varanasi. He has the distinction of clearing both UGC NET and UP SLET in Commerce. He is an Associate Fellow of the UK Higher Education Academy. His area of interest is Marketing, with special emphasis on Advertising and Branding, he loves grooming and training students in the areas of financial accounting and analysis. Dr Singh engage classes in Strategic Marketing, Rural Marketing, Research Methodology, Service Marketing, Sales & Distribution Management for PG, UG, PG Diploma and research students. A researcher at heart, Dr Singh has published nearly thirty-nine papers and articles in leading international and national journals. He has contributed ten chapters in edited books, attended six dozen seminars and conferences for active deliberations and paper presentations, conducted and participated in more than twenty-three Quality Improvements Programs and Management Development Programs at IITs, IIM, IIFT, VNSGU, AIMA and leading management institutes in the areas of Marketing, Strategy, Research Methodology & Finance for professional developments. Dr. Singh has conducted few Management Development Programs and training programs for the Ministry of Micro, Small and Medium Enterprises, Agri Business and Agri Clinic Centres for the Government of India. He has been invited as a Keynote Speaker in the International Conference on Precarious Lives Uncertain Future, University of Rome Tor Vergata, Rome, Italy in 2020. He is an avid reader and is keenly aware of new and emerging issues in Marketing, Branding, Rural Marketing and Consumer Experience. He has the expertise of playing a key role as founding member in Planning, Designing, Executing New Academic & Institutional Building Projects & Plans. He has discharged his responsibility as Head-International Relations Office at AURO University, Principal Coordinator - Unnat Bharat Abhiyaan for Ministry of HRD, Govt of India. He was a member of CII Gujarat Panel on Skill Development 2020-21. He is also a member of AIMA Delhi, Executive Committee and Life Member of Indian Economic Association, Strategic Management Forum of India (SMFI) & IRSSM, India. At AURO University, Surat he has designed and successfully worked on AURO Rural Immersion Program (ARIP) at the University, Surat for integrating classroom learning of students with society and stakeholders of the rural landscape and space through active, meaningful teaching and learning process. His commitment and hard work have brought him many laurels in his journey of academic excellence.

R. Sridevi received her B.Tech from Madras University, Chennai in Computer Science and Engineering and M.Tech in Computer Science and Engineering from Andhra University, Andhra Pradesh and PhD in CSE from JNTUH College of Engineering Hyderabad. She has around 16 years of teaching experience from JNTUHCEH. She works as Professor in CSE & Coordinator, Centre of Excellence in Cyber Security, JNTUH College of Engineering Hyderabad, India. She has published more than 20 papers in refereed journals and conference proceedings. Her research interests include Computer Networks, Information Security, and Network Security.

Denis Yuni is a professor in department of Economics in South Africa.

Index

A

B

C

D

E

F

G

I

L

M

O

R

S

T

Recommended Reference Books

IGI Global's reference books are available in three unique pricing formats: Print Only, E-Book Only, or Print + E-Book.

Order direct through IGI Global's Online Bookstore at **www.igi-global.com** or through your preferred provider.

ISBN: 9781799887096
EISBN: 9781799887119
© 2022; 413 pp.
List Price: US$ **250**

ISBN: 9781799874157
EISBN: 9781799874164
© 2022; 334 pp.
List Price: US$ **240**

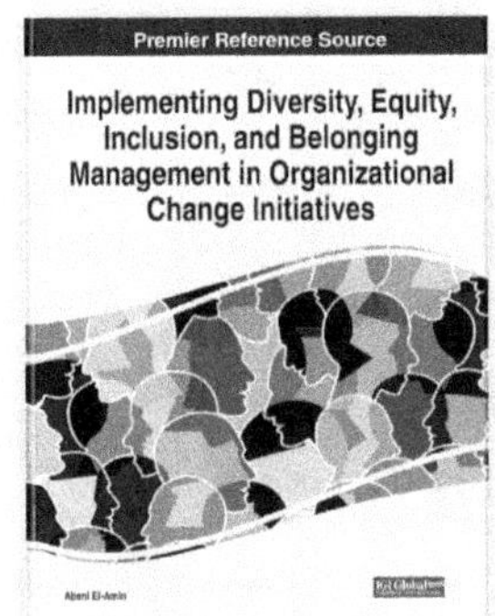

ISBN: 9781668440230
EISBN: 9781668440254
© 2022; 320 pp.
List Price: US$ **215**

ISBN: 9781799889502
EISBN: 9781799889526
© 2022; 263 pp.
List Price: US$ **240**

ISBN: 9781799885283
EISBN: 9781799885306
© 2022; 587 pp.
List Price: US$ **360**

ISBN: 9781668455906
EISBN: 9781668455913
© 2022; 2,235 pp.
List Price: US$ **1,865**

Do you want to stay current on the latest research trends, product announcements, news, and special offers?
Join IGI Global's mailing list to receive customized recommendations, exclusive discounts, and more.
Sign up at: **www.igi-global.com/newsletters.**

Publisher of Timely, Peer-Reviewed Inclusive Research Since 1988

IGI Global
PUBLISHER of TIMELY KNOWLEDGE

www.ingramcontent.com/pod-product-compliance
Lightning Source LLC
LaVergne TN
LVHW062138300926
849161LV00010B/2565